Social Security Law in Britain and Ireland

A Bibliography

Social Security Law in Britain and Ireland

A Bibliography

Paul O'Higgins and Martin Partington
with the assistance of Sally Hughes

Mansell Publishing Limited
London and New York

First published 1986 by Mansell Publishing Limited
(A subsidiary of The H.W. Wilson Company)
6 All Saints Street, London N1 9RL, England
950 University Avenue, Bronx, New York 10452, U.S.A.

British Library Cataloguing in Publication Data

O'Higgins, Paul
  Social security law in Britain and Ireland:
  a bibliography.
  1. Social security—Law and legislation
  —Great Britain—Bibliography
  I. Title   II. Partington, Martin
  III. Hughes, Sally
  016.344104 '2   KD3241

  ISBN 0–7201–1794–1

Library of Congress Cataloging in Publication Data

O'Higgins, Paul.
  Social security law in Britain and Ireland.

  Includes index.
  1. Social security—Law and legislation—Great
Britain—Bibliography. 2. Social security—Law and
legislation—Ireland—Bibliography. I. Partington,
Martin.   II. Hughes, Sally.   III. Title.
KD3191.035 1986   016.34441 '02   86–2701
ISBN 0–7201–1794–1   016.3441042

Printed in Great Britain by
Whitstable Litho Ltd., Whitstable, Kent

Contents

Introduction

Until recently, social security law was a subject that was largely ignored by lawyers, whether academic or practising. Analysis of matters relating to social security was left largely to experts in economics, social policy or social administration. However this situation has been changing rapidly. Social security law is now taught, practised and written about by legal experts much more widely than ever before, and social policy analysts have themselves become more interested in many of the legal issues that arise out of the social security system.

Because of these developments, we wanted to create a working research tool that would encourage the growth of this area of study by both lawyers and non-lawyers, by making access to the literature on social security law easier than it had been hitherto. To this end we applied to and successfully obtained from the Economic and Social Research Council (formerly the Social Science Research Council) a grant in order to enable us to employ a research assistant, Sally Hughes, who could undertake the basic data collection. In making their grant to us, the Economic and Social Research Council imposed three broad conditions.

First, we were asked to ensure that the bibliography would be kept in 'machine-readable' form. In the event, the complete bibliography has been word processed on the computing facilities at the London School of Economics (where one of the authors was working at the time the grant was made). Arrangements are now being made for the data as collected and sorted to be stored; it is also intended that the bibliography will be kept up to date by the publication of regular supplements. Precise arrangements have not yet been finalized, but details will be available from Martin Partington at Brunel University in due course.

Secondly, we were asked to ensure that the bibliography incorporated reference to official publications relating to social security. These are cited extensively in their appropriate locations in the bibliography.

Thirdly, since the grant came from the Economic and Social Research Council, it was stressed that we should endeavour to make the bibliography useful to 'socio-legal' scholars. This was more problematic since we find it hard to define precisely where the 'legal' ends and the 'socio' begins; for us, law merely sets the boundaries within which social policy operates. In complying with this condition, therefore, we have sought to include reference to all other material which seems to us to throw some light on or offer some explanation of how particular areas of social security law have developed or currently operate in practice.

Methodology

Those who compile bibliographies have two basic methods which they can adopt. One is for the compiler to examine the contents of particular libraries, taking the details of each book or article from the book or journal itself. This method has the obvious advantage of accuracy and of avoiding mistakes made by earlier bibliographers. It also enables the compiler to identify books which are relevant, but whose title may be misleading; and conversely, books that might appear relevant from their titles may be excluded on being found to be irrelevant. Finally, the compiler is enabled to make an accurate record of the location of each of the titles cited as at the date of compilation. The obvious disadvantage of this method is that it is extremely expensive both in terms of cash resources and time, particularly with a new subject such as social security law. This may be described as the 'primary source method'.

The alternative method, which may be described as the 'secondary source method' involves the compiler sorting out from other bibliographies, catalogues, booksellers lists and the texts of related subject matter those entries that appear to be relevant to the subject matter in hand. Despite the problems of accuracy that may result from the adoption of this method, it may nonetheless be a more cost effective method, particularly in relation to a bibliography that is seeking to cover new ground.

In the event, we have used both methods in the compilation of this bibliography. Our basic collection of references was made using the 'secondary' method outlined above; details of the sources used are set out further below. But this has been supplemented by drawing on primary source material wherever possible, and insofar as our resources permitted, in order to add to the material initially obtained and to cross check as far as possible the information that we had derived from the secondary sources.

Even so, the total period of time over which this bibliography has been prepared has been a long one.

Primary responsibility for the initial collection of materials rested with Sally Hughes who, for eighteen months, culled all relevant material from the catalogues of the following libraries:

(i) The British Library of Political and Economic Science at the London School of Economics, using their published annual volumes of *A London Bibliography of the Social Sciences* (Mansell).

(ii) The Social Security Library of the Department of Health and Social Security, London.

(iii) The University Library at Cambridge University.

In addition an extensive range of references was culled from the following bibliographical sources:

G.S. Bain and G.B. Woolven. *A Bibliography of British Industrial Relations*. Cambridge, 1978.

Margaret Canney & David Knott. *University of London Library: Catalogue of the Goldsmith's Library of Economic Literature. Vol.1: Printed Books to 1800*. Cambridge 1970. [with Joan Gibbs]. *Vol.II: Printed Books 1801–1850*. Cambridge, 1975.

R.D. Collison Black. *A Catalogue of Pamphlets on Economic Subjects published between 1750 and 1900 and now housed in Irish Libraries*. Belfast, 1969.

L.W. Hanson. *Contemporary Printed Sources for British and Irish Economic History*. Cambridge, 1963.

Henry Higgs. *Bibliography of Economics 1751–1775*. Cambridge, 1935.

B.A. Hepple, J.M. Neeson & Paul O'Higgins. *A Bibliography of the Literature on British and Irish Labour Law*. London, 1975.

B.A. Hepple, J. Hepple, Paul O'Higgins and Paula Stirling. *Labour Law in Great Britain and Ireland to 1978*. London, 1981.

Paul O'Higgins. *A Bibliography of Periodical Literature relating to Irish Law*. Belfast, 1966. *First Supplement*. Belfast, 1973. *Second Supplement*. Belfast, 1983.

Paul O'Higgins. *A Bibliography of Irish Trials and other Legal Proceedings*. Abingdon, Oxon, 1986.

Paul O'Higgins. *Labour Law in Great Britain and Ireland 1979–1984*. London, 1986.

Martin Partington, John Hull and Susan Knight. *Welfare Rights: a bibliography on law and the poor, 1970–75*. London, 1976.

D. Raistrick and J. Rees. *Lawyers' Law Books*. Abingdon, Oxon, 1977. *First Supplement*. Abingdon, Oxon, 1979. *Second Supplement*. Abingdon, Oxon, 1982. (2nd Edition in preparation).

This initial work was supplemented by an extensive additional compilation of references by the two principal authors.

Additional bibliographical aids likely to be of use to scholars are listed in Part I of the bibliography (General Works and Bibliographies) at the start of the main text. Not all the references collected have been used in this volume; additional references will be kept in the custody of Professor Paul O'Higgins.

Subject Matter

Setting precise boundaries to the concept of 'social security' has proved extremely difficult. There is a tendency on many people's part to regard social security as those areas of social policy which provide cash benefits to disadvantaged groups in the community, which are administered by the State. But any understanding of the framework of twentieth century social security law and policy has to be founded in the earlier operation of, in particular, the Poor Law, and also the work of charitable and other organizations such as friendly societies which during the nineteenth century performed many of the tasks now undertaken by agencies of the State. In addition, in the present day, the boundaries between the 'public' (or state) and 'private' sectors involved in the delivery of welfare policies have become and are continuing increasingly to become extremely blurred (e.g. in the context of retirement provisions, and sick pay).

We have thus included in our bibliography topics which we regard as so intimately related to social security policy, as traditionally understood, that they cannot properly be ignored. In this category, we would draw attention to the following heads: charities and friendly societies (Part II, Section 3): statutory sick pay (Part III, Section 5 (b)); occupational pensions (Part III, Section 9 (b)); and low pay (Part III, Section 12 (i)).

In terms of our coverage of the subject matter, two particular difficulties had to be faced:

(i) Material on the Poor Law

The literature on the poor law is massive, and could justify an extensive bibliography in its own right. We decided that, in relation to material on the poor law, we *had* to be selective. What we have attempted to do, therefore, is to include all those items which have come to our attention which seem to make some *general* point about the operation of the poor law; but to exclude material which relates only to the operation of the poor law in *specific* areas of the country — counties, towns, or villages. It is appreciated that in so doing, reference to some important work may have been omitted; but this seemed to be the only practical compromise available to us.

(ii) The Historical Division in 1946

The other main problem relates to the decision we have taken to distinguish in Parts II and III of the bibliography between material relating to social security before 1946, and that relating to material after 1946. The fact is that some literature, particularly the more general historical works (see Part II) bridge this date. Furthermore, we could have taken the development of particular issues (e.g. workmen's compensation leading to the industrial injuries scheme) from their earliest manifestations in the literature up to the present. However, if we combined subjects in this way, wc felt that each individual section might have become rather unwieldy and difficult to handle. Furthermore, 1946 is such an important date in the creation of the modern Welfare State in Britain that we felt that, whatever difficulties and anomalies might arise, on balance the advantages outweighed the disadvantages.

Further details of the scope of the subject-matter of this volume can, of course, be obtained by looking at the contents pages, to which reference should now be made.

Geographical Scope

This bibliography contains, in the main, material in English (with occasional reference to material in other languages) relating to social security law and policy in England, Wales, Scotland, Northern Ireland and the Republic of Ireland. (Where appropriate, as may be seen from the contents pages, special sub-headings have been created relating, in particular, to Scotland and Ireland). Part V, 'Miscellaneous Works', contains some references to social security law in other parts of the United Kingdom, for example, Isle of Man and the Channel Islands. In addition, there is reference (though not comprehensive) to important literature from other jurisdictions (e.g. U.S.A., Commonwealth countries and European countries) which is available for consultation in British libraries. Finally, the importance of international movements in regard to the development of social security, particularly through the International Labour Organization, and more recently through the European Economic Community, is reflected in Part IV of the Bibliography.

Chronological Scope

The chronological scope of the bibliography is extensive. Our basic starting point was the Elizabethan Poor Law of 1601, though there is occasional reference to material earlier than that date. We have attempted to bring our coverage up-to-date to the end of 1983, though certain important works published in 1984 have been included. As noted above, it is intended to keep the data base we have created up to date by the issuing of further supplements.

Information Provided

The references in the pages which follow refer to books, pamphlets, articles in periodicals and, where discovered and relevant, particular chapters in books (e.g. collections of essays). The following information is provided:

(a) Books and Pamphlets

1.   Author. If there is no known author the item has been listed under 'Anon' and appears at the beginning of each section. These items are arranged chronologically by date of publication. Official publications are listed either under the name of the country producing them (e.g. United Kingdom) or, where identifiable or appropriate, by the particular Ministry or Department responsible for preparing the document (e.g. Ministry of Labour; Department of Health and Social Security).
2.   Title.
3.   Place of publication. If this is uncertain, the place name is set in square brackets. If no place is indicated, this is shown by 'n.p.'

4.   Year of publication. Where there is uncertainty the date is set in square brackets; if there is no date, this is shown by 'n.d.'
5.   Number of pages (whenever possible).
6.   Location. In most cases, at least one library location is given as a place where the work referred to may be consulted. This does *not* imply that the location given is the only possible location. If no location has been traced at all, this is indicated by 'n.l.'. A full list of the locations given, and appropriate abbreviations are set out below.

We have attempted to record all editions of books and pamphlets. But the information is sometimes incomplete and some editions are not included as they did not appear in the library catalogues or bibliographies which we consulted.

(b) Periodicals and chapters in books

The following information is provided:

1.   Author. If unsigned, entered under 'Anon'.
2.   Title, in quotation marks.
3.   Title of periodical (underlined and abbreviated as per the list of periodical abbreviations below); or the name of the book in which the chapter appears.
4.   Volume number (if any).
5.   Year.
6.   Beginning and (usually) terminal pages.

(c) Author index

This does not include items entered under 'Anon'.

Arrangement of material

Basically this can be discerned by looking at the contents pages. But since some works cited clearly fit into more than one category we have also included a number of cross-references.

Entries in each section or sub-section are arranged in alphabetical order, save that where needed 'Anon' begins each section. Where there is more than one item attributed to a particular author (or, of course,

'Anon'), the works are listed chronologically by date of publication.

Development of the work

Since the material will be stored in a computerized data base, we very much hope that the scope of the work (and thus its usefulness as a tool for scholarship) will expand. Suggestions from readers as to what improvements could be found helpful would thus be most welcome, as would notes about any errors or omissions.

Please address such comments to Professor M. Partington, c/o Law Department, Brunel University, Uxbridge, Middlesex, UB8 3PH, England.

Acknowledgements

We wish to express our appreciation to the Economic and Social Research Council, first for funding the grant which made the research and compilation of this volume possible and secondly for their indulgence in waiting so patiently for the final version of the work which was the subject of the grant. We would like to thank all the librarians and staff at the various libraries we have used for their help and assistance.

Special thanks must go to Susan Hunt of the Law Department at the London School of Economics, who, with her usual skill and efficiency, has undertaken the lengthy and complex task of moulding the text of the bibliography into a shape which is suitable for publication. In so doing, she has worked willingly, way beyond the call of duty. We should also thank the staff of the Computer Services Unit at the London School of Economics for their forbearance with the technical and practical problems caused by the word-processing of the text.

List of Periodicals and Abbreviations

A.-A.L.R.   *Anglo-American Law Review*. (1971–   ). *Chichester*.

Admin.   *Administration*. Institute of Public Administration. (1953–   ). Dublin.

Age Concern Today. London.

A.L.J.   *Australian Law Journal*. (1927–   ). Sydney.

Amat.Hist.   *Amateur Historian*. (Superseded by *Local Historian*). London.

Am.Econ.Rev.   *American Economic Review*. Nashville, Tennessee.

American Historical Review. Washington, D.C.

American Journal of Sociology. Chicago.

Am.J.Comp.L.   *American Journal of Comparative Law*. Berkeley, California.

Am.Pol.Sc.Rev.   *American Political Science Review*. Baltimore.

Arch.Hib   *Archivium Hibernicum*. Maynooth, Ireland.

A.S.C.L.   *Annual Survey of Commonwealth Law*. (1965–1978). London.

A.S.E.L.   *Annual Survey of English Law*. London.

Australian Journal of Social Issues. Sydney, N.S.W.

Benefits Int.   *Benefits International*. London.

B.J.I.R.   *British Journal of Industrial Relations*. (1963–   ). London.

B.J.L.S.   *British Journal of Law and Society*. (1974–1982). (Continued as *Journal of Law and Society*: J.Law.Soc.). London.

B.M.J.   *British Medical Journal*. London.

Bell, The. Dublin.

British Journal of Psychiatry. Ashford, Kent.

Brit.Jo.Admin.Law   *British Journal of Administrative Law* (1954–1957). (Incorporated in *Public Law*). London

Brit.Jo.Pol.Sci.   *British Journal of Political Science*. Cambridge.

Brit.Jo.Prev.Soc.Med.   *British Journal of Preventative and Social Medicine*. London.

Brit.Jo.Soc.   *British Journal of Sociology*. Henley-on-Thames, Oxon.

Brit.J.Soc.Wk.   *British Journal of Social Work*. (1971–   ). London.

Br.Q.Rev.   *British Quarterly Review*. London.

Br.Tax.Rev   *British Tax Review*. London.

Bull.I.S.S.A.   *Bulletin of the International Social Security*

Association. (1948–1966). (Superseded by *International Social
Security Review*). Montreal, then Geneva.
Bulletin of the Oxford University Institute of Economics and Statistics.
Oxford.
Bull.Soc.for Study of Lab.Hist.   *Bulletin of the Society for the Study
of Labour History*. (1960–   ). Sheffield.
Cah.dr.europ.   *Cahiers de Droit Europeen*. Brussels.
Cal.L.R.   *California Law Review*. Berkeley, California.
Cambrian L.R.   *Cambrian Law Review*. (1970–   ). Aberystwyth.
Can.J.Econ.Polit.Sci.   *Canadian Journal of Economic and Political
Science*. (Superseded by *Canadian Journal of Economics*). Toronto.
Case Con.   *Case Conference*. (Irregular. 1970–   ). London.
Cath.Bull.*Catholic Bulletin*. Dublin.
C.B.R.   *Canadian Bar Review*. (1923–   ). Toronto.
Child Care, Health and Development. Oxford.
Char.Org.Rep.   *Charity Organization Reporter*. (Became *Charity
Organization Review*). London.
Char.Org.Rev.   *Charity Organization Review*. (Formerly *Charity
Organization Reporter*; became *Charity Organization Quarterly*).
London.
Chr.R.   *Christus Rex*. (Incorporated in *Social Studies*, October 1971).
Maynooth, Ireland.
C.L.J.   *Cambridge Law Journal*. (1921/23–   ). Cambridge.
Clearinghouse Review. Chicago, I11.
Clogh.Rec.   *Clogher Record*. Monaghan, Ireland.
C.L.P.   *Current Legal Problems*. (1948–   ). London.
C.M.L.Rev.   *Common Market Law Review*. The Hague,
Netherlands.
Community Care. Sutton, Surrey.
Contemp.Rev.   *Contemporary Review*. London.
Conv.   *Conveyancer, The*. London.
Court. Henley-on-Thames.
Crim.L.R.   *Criminal Law Review*. London.
Critical Social Policy. London.
Crossbow. London.
D. & L. Mag.   *Dublin & London Magazine*. London.
D.E.G.   *Department of Employment Gazette*. (1968–   ).
    (Continuation of *Ministry of Labour Gazette*: see Lab.G.). London.
Disability Rights Bulletin. London.
Droit Social. Paris
Dub.Hist.Rec.   *Dublin Historical Record*. Dublin.

Dub.Rev. *Dublin Review.* (1839–1862–3; (n.s.) 1863–1960). London.

D.U.M. *Dublin University Magazine.* Dublin.

Economic Bulletin for Europe. Oxford.

Ec. & Soc. Review *Economic and Social Review.* (1969–). Dublin.

Ec.H.R. *Economic History Review.* (1st series, 1927–1948; 2nd series, 1948/50 to date). London.

Economica. London.

Economic Digest. London.

Econ.Rev. *The Economic Review.* London.

Econ. Trends *Economic Trends.* London.

Edin.Rev. *Edinburgh Review.* Edinburgh.

Eire *Eire-Ireland: Journal of Irish Studies.* St. Paul, Minn.

E.H.R. *English Historical Review.* London.

E.J. *Economic Journal.* (1890–). London.

Engl.Rev. *English Review, The.* (1908–1935). London.

Epidemiology and Community Health. London.

Eur.L.R. *European Law Review.* London.

Fam.L. *Family Law.* Bristol.

F.B.I. Review *Federation of British Industries Review.* London.

Fem.Rev. *Feminist Review.* London.

Finanzarchiv. Tuebingen, W. Germany

Fisc.Stud. *Journal of the Institute of Fiscal Studies.* London.

Flklfe. *Folklife: A Journal of Ethnographical Studies.* Cardiff.

F.N. *Federation News.* (1950–). London.

Fortnight. Belfast.

Fort.Rev. *Fortnightly Review.* (1865–1934). London.

Funeral Service Journal. Uxbridge, Middx.

Galway Reader. Galway.

General Practitioner. London.

G.I.L.S.I. *Gazette of the Incorporated Law Society of Ireland.* Dublin.

Harv.L.R. *Harvard Law Review.* Cambridge, Mass.

Health and Society Service Journal. London.

Health Trends. London.

Hist.J. *Historical Journal.* (1958–). (Continuation of the *Cambridge Historical Journal*). Cambridge.

Hist.Stud. *Historical Studies.* London.

Howard J. *Howard Journal of Penology and Crime Prevention.* (Superseded by *Howard Journal of Criminal Justice*). Oxford.

I.C.L.Q. *International and Comparative Law Quarterly.* (1952–). London.

I.H.S.   *Irish Historical Studies*. (1938–   ). Dublin.

I.Lab.R.   *International Labour Review*. (1921–   ). Geneva.

I.L.J.   *Industrial Law Journal*. (1972–   ). London.

I.L.O.Bull.   *International Labour Office Bulletin*. (1902–   ). (3rd series). Geneva.

I.L.T.S.J.   *Irish Law Times and Solicitors' Journal*. Dublin.

India Q.   *India Quarterly*. New Delhi.

Ind.L.R.   *Industrial Law Review*. (1947–1960). Henley, Suffolk.

Ind.Relations   *Industrial Relations*. Berkeley, California.

Ind.Soc.   *Industrial Society*. (1967–   ). (Formerly *Industrial Welfare*). London.

Ind.Welfare   *Industrial Welfare*. (1929–1960). (Superseded by *Industrial Society*). London.

Industry Week. Cleveland, Ohio.

Information Design Journal. Milton Keynes.

Inst.Hist.Res.Bull.   *Bulletin of the Institute of Historical Research*. (1923–   ). London.

Int.J.Soc.Econ.   *International Journal of Social Economics*. Bradford, Yorks.

Int.Migration   *International Migration*. Geneva.

Int.Rev.Ad.Sc.   *International Review of Administrative Sciences*. Brussels.

Int.Rev.Soc.Hist.   *International Review of Social History*. (1956–   ). (Formerly, *Bulletin of the International Institute of Social History*). Assen, Netherlands.

Int.Soc.Sec.Rev.   *International Society Security Review*. (1967–   ). (Formerly *Bull.I.S.S.A.*). Geneva.

Ir.Archiv.Bull.   *Irish Archives Bulletin*. Dublin.

I.R.J.   *Industrial Relations Journal*. (1970–   ). London.

Ir.Jur.   *Irish Jurist*. (1935–   ). Dublin.

Ir.Rev.   *Irish Review*. Dublin.

I.R.R.R.   *Industrial Relations Review and Report*. (1971–   ). London.

J.B.L.   *Journal of Business Law*. (1957–   ). London.

J.Brit.Stud.   *Journal of British Studies*. Chicago, I11.

J.Comp.Leg.   *Journal of Comparative Legislation*. (1896–1951). London.

J.Cr.L.   *Journal of Criminal Law and Criminology*. (Formerly *Journal of Criminal Law, Criminology and Police Science*). Chicago, I11.

Jo.Econ.Affairs   *Journal of Economic Affairs*. Harlow, Essex.

Jo.Econ.Hist.   *Journal of Economic History.* (1941–   ). New York.

J.Law Soc.   *Journal of Law and Society.* (1982–   ). (Formerly B.J.L.S.). Oxford.

Journal of the Chartered Insurance Institute. London.

Journal of Common Market Studies. Oxford.

J.P.   *Justice of the Peace.* Chichester.

J.Polit.Econ.   *Journal of Political Economy.* Chicago, Ill.

J.Pub.Econ.   *Journal of Public Economics.* Lausanne.

J.Soc.Pol.   *Journal of Social Policy.* (1972–   ). Cambridge.

J.S.S.I.S.I.   *Journal of the Statistical and Social Inquiry Society of Ireland.* Dublin.

J.S.W.L.   *Journal of Social Welfare Law.* (1979–   ). London.

Jur.Rev.   *Juridical Review.* (1889–1955; (n.s.) 1956–   ). Edinburgh.

K.C.   *King's Counsel.* London.

Lab.G.   *Ministry of Labour Gazette.* (1893–1967). (Continued as *Department of Employment Gazette*: see D.E.G.). London.

L.A.G.Bull.   *Legal Action Group Bulletin.* (1971–   ). London.

Leg.Iss.   *Legal Issues of European Integration.* Deventer, Netherlands.

L.J.   *Law Journal.* (1866–1964). (Continued as N.L.J.). London.

Lloyds B.R.   *Lloyds Bank Review.* London.

L.M.   *Law Magazine and Quarterly Review of Jurisprudence.* (1828–1871). (Continued as *Law Magazine and Review*: see L.M.R.). London.

L.M.R.   *Law Magazine and Review.* (1872–1915). London.

Low Pay Review. (1977–   ). London.

L.R.   *Labour Research.* (1917–   ). London

L.Q.R.   *Law Quarterly Review.* (1885–   ). London.

L.S.G.   *Law Society's Gazette.* London.

L.T.   *Law Teacher.* (1973–   ). (Formerly *Journal of the Association of Law Teachers*). London.

Manch.Sch.   *Manchester School of Economic and Social Studies.* Manchester

Manch.Statist.Soc.Trans.   *Transactions of the Manchester Statistical Society.* Manchester.

M.C.L.R.D.   *Monthly Circular of the Labour Research Department.* (1919–1930). London.

Medico-Legal Jo.   *Medical-Legal Journal.* London.

M.L.R.   *Modern Law Review.* (1937–   ). London.

Mon.Rev.   *Monthly Review.* New York, N.Y.

National Review. New York, N.Y.

Nat.West.Bk.Q.Rev.   *National Westminster Bank Quarterly Review. London.*

New Community. London.

New Statesman. London.

N.I.J.   *New Irish Jurist.* Dublin.

New Ire.Rev.   *New Ireland Review.* Dublin.

N.I.L.Q.   *Northern Ireland Legal Quarterly.* (1936/7–   ). Belfast.

Nineteenth Century   *Nineteenth Century and After.* (1877–1950). (Continued as *Twentieth Century.*) London.

N.I.R.   *New Ireland Review.* Dublin.

N.L.J.   *New Law Journal.* (1965–   ). London.

N.Month.Mag.   *New Monthly Magazine.* London.

N.S.   *New Society.* (1962–   ). London

Nth.Hist.   *Northern History.* Leeds.

O. & M.Bull.   *O. & M. Bulletin.* H.M. Treasury. London.

Occupational Health. London.

Occupational Safety and Health. London.

Omega. Emsford, N.Y.

O. & C.Rev.   *Oxford and Cambridge Review.* London.

O.Krankenk.   *Die Ortskrankenkasse.* Bad Godesburg, West Germany.

P. & P.   *Past and Present.* Oxford.

P.H.   *Policy Holder Insurance Journal.* (Superseded by *Policy Holder Insurance News*). Brentford, Middx.

P.L.   *Public Law.* (1956–   ). London

Planning.   (Political and Economic Planning). London.

Plebs. (Journal of the National Council of Labour Colleges). London.

Policy & Politics. (1972–   ). London.

Pol.Q.   *Political Quarterly.* (1930–   ). London.

Polit.Sci.Q.   *Political Science Quarterly.* Boston.

Pol.Stu.   *Political Studies.* Guildford, Surrey.

Population Trends. London.

Poverty. (1966–   ). London.

Previdenza Soc.   *Previdenza Sociale.* Rome.

Pub.Admin.   *Public Administration.* (1923–   ). London.

Quest. Newtonards, Co. Antrim.

Questions de Securite Sociale. Paris.

Q.J.Econ.   *Quarterly Journal of Economics.* New York, N.Y.

Recht der Arbeit. Munich.

Reformer. London.

Rev.Belge de Sec.Soc.   *Revue Belge de Sécurité Sociale.* Brussels.

Review of Economics and Statistics. Amsterdam, Netherlands.
Rights. (National Council for Civil Liberties). London.
R.Inst.Corn.J.   *Royal Institution of Cornwall Journal.*
R.Statist.Soc.J.   *Journal of the Royal Statistical Society.* London.
Safety and Rescue. London.
S.B.C. Notes and News. (1973–1980). London.
Scolag.   *Scottish Legal Action Group Bulletin.* (1975–   ). Dundee.
Scot.Jo. of Polit.Econ. *Scottish Journal of Political Economy.*
    Edinburgh.
S.H.R.   *Scottish Historical Review.* Glasgow and Edinburgh.
S.L.T.   *Scots Law Times.* (1893–   ). (Incorporating *Scottish Law
    Reporter*). Edinburgh
S.J.   *Solicitors' Journal.* (1857–   ). London.
Soc. & Econ.Ad.   *Social and Economic Administration.* (Superseded
    by *Social Policy and Administration*). Oxford.
Social Security. Canberra, Australia.
Social Security Bulletin. Washington, D.C.
Social Services Quarterly. London.
Social Trends. (1970–   ). London.
Social Work Service. London.
Soc.Pol. and Admin.   *Social Policy and Administration.* (Formerly
    Social and Economic Administration). Oxford.
Soc.Reg.   *Socialist Register.* London.
Soc.Stud.   *Social Studies.* (Formerly *Christus Rex*). Maynooth,
    Ireland.
Socio.Rev.   *Sociological Review.* Keele, Staffs.
Spare Rib. London.
Statistical News. London.
Stud.   *Studies.* Dublin.
Studies for Trade Unionists. London.
Survey.Instn.Trans.   *Surveyors Institution Transactions.* London.
S.W.T.   *Social Work Today.* (1970–   ). Birmingham.
Three Banks Review, The. London.
Tomorrow. London.
Topical Law. London.
Transactions of the Devonshire Association. Exeter.
T.U.Info.   *Trade Union Information.* Dublin.
Ulster J.Arch.   *Ulster Journal of Archaeology.* Belfast.
Unemployment Unit Bulletin. London.
University of Birmingham Historical Journal. Birmingham.
Univ.Rev.   *University Review.* Dublin.

Victorian Studies. (1957–   ). Bloomington, Indiana.
Welfare Rights Bulletin. (1974–   ). London.
Welsh Hist.Rev.   *Welsh History Review*. Cardiff.
Westm.Rev.   *Westminster Review*. London.
Which. London.
Women's Studies International Quarterly. (Now *Women's Studies International Forum*; formerly, *Women's Studies*). Oxford.
Yale L.J.   *Yale Law Journal*. New Haven, Connecticut.
Yorkshire Bull.of Econ. & Soc.Res.   *Yorkshire Bulletin of Economic and Social Research*. (Now *Bulletin of Economic Research*). Oxford.

Key to Library Locations

BCL	Belfast Central Library
BL	British Library (formerly British Museum), London
Bod.	Bodleian Library, Oxford
C	University College, London
DHSS	Social Security Library, Department of Health and Social Security, London
CUL	Cambridge University Library
G	Goldsmith's Library of Economic Literature, University of London
I	Royal Institute of International Affairs, London
IALS	Institute of Advanced Legal Studies, University of London
KI	King's Inns, Dublin.
LI	Lincoln's Inn, Library, London
LSE	British Library of Political and Economic Science, London School of Economics
MT	Middle Temple, Library, London
NLI	National Library of Ireland, Dublin
NLS	National Library of Scotland, Edinburgh
P	National Institute of Industrial Psychology, London
QUB	Queen's University, Belfast
R	The Reform Club, London (political and historical pamphlets)
RDS	Royal Dublin Society, Dublin
RIA	Royal Irish Academy, Dublin
S	Royal Statistical Society, London
Sq	Squire Law Library, Cambridge
TCD	Trinity College, Dublin
U	University Library, London
UCD	University College, Dublin
Z	Material in personal library of Professor P. O'Higgins

Abbreviations

Anon.	Anonymous
B.P.P.	British Parliamentary Papers
C./Cd./Cmd./ Cmnd.	Command Papers
c.	circa
CAB	Citizen's Advice Bureau
coll.	collection
comp.	compiler
CPAG	Child Poverty Action Group
ed.	edition/editor/edited
EEC	European Economic Community
et al	and others
H.C.	House of Commons (Paper)
FES	Family Expenditure Survey
ff	and following
fo.	folio
gen.	general
HMSO	Her Majesty's Stationery Office
IEA	Institute of Economic Affairs
ILO	International Labour Organization
ISSA	International Social Security Association
LRD	Labour Research Department
n.d.	no date
n.l.	not located
n.p.	no publisher
n.s.	new series
no./nos.	number/s
o.s.	official series
pp.	pages
pseud.	pseudonym
pt./s	part/s
RCAP Coll.	Royal Commission on the Aged Poor Collection
rev.	revised
ser.	series
S.I.	Statutory Instruments

SM2, 3, 4 or 5	Sweet & Maxwell (*see* Bibliographies)
unpag.	pages not numbered
unpub.	not formally published
var.pag.	various paginations
vol./s	volume/s
w.	with

PART I   General Works and Bibliographies

A description of the methodology used in compiling this bibliography is set out in the Introduction. Many of the works cited will, of course, contain their own bibliographies. Here we list a number of other bibliographies or bibliographical aids that are likely to be of additional use to scholars working in the area of social security.

1. ANON.   "Reports and papers respecting out-relief". Char.Org.Rep. 7. (1878). pp.87-88.

2. ABRAMSKY, C.   "Check-list of labour periodicals, 1794-1920". Bull.Soc. for Study of Lab.Hist. (1972). XXV.

3. ALDERSON, M. & WHITEHEAD, F.   "Central government routine health statistics", by Michael Alderson.   "Social security statistics", by Frank Whitehead. London: Heinemann Education for the Royal Statistical Society and Social Science Research Council. 1974. pp.xiv + 145 + 112. DHSS.

4. ALMAN, M. Aslib directory: a guide to sources of information in Great Britain and Ireland. London: 1957. 2 vols. DHSS.

5. ATKINSON, A.B.   A bibliography of published research on the measurement of inequality and poverty 1970-1982. [Redhill]: 1982. pp.13. DHSS.

6. BEALE, J.H.   A bibliography of early English law books. Cambridge, Mass: 1926. pp.vii + 304. LSE.

7. BLACKSTONE, T.   Social policy and administration in Britain - a bibliography. London: 1975. pp.130. DHSS.

8. BRITISH INSTITUTE OF MANAGEMENT.   Social security in the European Community: a guide to sources of information. London: 1975. pp.8. (European Management Information Sheet No.1). DHSS.

9. CHILD POVERTY ACTION GROUP. Welfare Rights Bulletin. passim. 1974-date.

10. COMFORT, A.F. & LOVELESS, C. et al. Guide to government data: a survey of unpublished social science material in libraries of government departments in London; compiled for British Library of Political and Economic Science by A.F. Comfort and C. Loveless. London: 1974. pp.xi + 404. DHSS.

11. DEPARTMENT OF EMPLOYMENT.   Library.   Unemployment insurance 1921 to 1930. London: 1979. DHSS.

12. DEPARTMENT OF HEALTH AND SOCIAL SECURITY. Annual report on departmental research and development. London: 1973 to date. LSE.

13. DEPARTMENT OF HEALTH AND SOCIAL SECURITY. A guide to health and social services statistics. London: 1974. pp.64. DHSS.

14. DEPARTMENT OF HEALTH AND SOCIAL SECURITY. Handbook of research and development. A list of projects supported by the Department in the financial year 1975/76. London: 1976. unpag. series; 1976/77, 1978. DHSS.

15. DEPARTMENT OF HEALTH AND SOCIAL SECURITY. Beveridge and beyond. Selected official publications on social security developments in the United Kingdom from the Beveridge Report 1942 to 1981. London: 1982. DHSS.

16. DEPARTMENT OF HEALTH AND SOCIAL SECURITY. Non take-up of benefits. Selected references on the non take-up of benefits. London: 1982. DHSS.

17. DEPARTMENT OF HEALTH AND SOCIAL SECURITY. INTERNATIONAL RELATIONS BRANCH LIBRARY. Glossary of social security terms. English-French. London: 1977. var.pag. DHSS.

18. FORD, P. & FORD, G. A breviate of Parliamentary papers 1917-1939. Oxford: 1951. pp.xlviii + 571. CUL.

19. FORD, P. & FORD, G. Hansards catalogue and breviate of Parliamentary papers 1969-1834. Oxford: 1953. pp.xv + viii + 220. DHSS.

20. FORD, P. & FORD, G. Select list of British Parliamentary papers 1833-1899. Oxford: 1953. pp.xxii + 165. DHSS.

21. FORD, P. & FORD, G. A breviate of Parliamentary papers 1900-1916. The foundation of the welfare state. Oxford: 1957. pp.ix + 470. DHSS; LSE.

22. FORD, P. & FORD, G. Breviate of parliamentary papers, 1940-1954. War and reconstruction. Oxford: 1961. pp.515. DHSS; LSE.

23. FORD, P. & FORD, G. Select list of Parliamentary papers, 1955-1964. Shannon: 1970. pp.vii + 117. LSE.

24. FORD, P. & FORD, G. A guide to Parliamentary papers: what they are, how to find them, how to use them. 3rd ed. Shannon: 1972. pp.xiv + 87. DHSS.

25. GOVERNMENT SOCIAL SURVEY. List of published Social Survey Reports. London: 1966. pp.40. DHSS.

26. H.M.S.O. Statistics: publications of United Kingdom government departments and international organisations. London: 1975. pp.iv + 56. (HMSO Subject Catalogue No.1). DHSS.

27. HARRISON, R.J. et al. The Warwick guide to British labour periodicals, 1790-1970: a check list. Hassocks: 1977. pp.685. LSE.

28. HOUSE OF COMMONS LIBRARY. Bibliography No.50. National Health Insurance.

29. HOUSE OF COMMONS LIBRARY. Bibliography No.37 & 52. National Insurance.

30. I.L.O. Bibliography of unemployment. Geneva: 1926. pp.155. LSE.

31. I.L.O. Bibliography of unemployment. 2nd ed. covering the period 1920-1929. Geneva: 1930. pp.viii + 217. LSE; I.

32. I.L.O. Catalogue of publications of the I.L.O. [1919-1953]. Geneva: 1953. pp.84. LSE.

33. I.L.O. Publications of the I.L.O., 1944-1957. Geneva: 1958. pp.53. LSE.

34. I.L.O. Publications of the I.L.O., 1944-1962. Geneva: 1962. pp.69. LSE.

35. I.L.O. Bibliography on social security. Geneva: 1963. pp.v + 167. (Bibliographical Contributions No.20). LSE.

36. I.L.O. Bibliography of research sources on labour questions (compiled by Marie-Henriette Pacaud). Geneva: 1965. pp.vi + 129. (Bibliographical Contributions No.24). LSE.

37. I.L.O. Publications of the I.L.O., 1954-1965. Geneva: 1966. pp.vi + 64. LSE.

38. I.L.O. LIBRARY. Bibliographical reference lists, No.64. Publications periodique courantes des ministeres du travail et de la securite sociale. Geneva: 1953. pp.6. LSE.

39. I.L.O. LIBRARY. Bibliographical reference lists, No.65. Administration of labour and social legislation. Geneva: 1953. pp.11. LSE.

40. I.L.O. LIBRARY. Bibliographical contributions No.22. Catalogue of publications of the International Association for Labour Legislation, International Association on Unemployment and International Association for Social Progress and their national sections; etc. Geneva: 1962. pp.134. LSE.

41. I.S.S.A. Social security abstracts. 1965. LSE. (Contains many valuable references).

42. I.S.S.A. Economic aspects of social security, research on social security: bibliography. Geneva: 1971. pp.x + 36. (Documentation Series No.4). DHSS.

43. INSTITUTE OF ADVANCED LEGAL STUDIES. Union lists of legal periodicals. 3rd ed. London: 1968. IALS.

44. INTERDEPARTMENTAL COMMITTEE ON SOCIAL AND ECONOMIC RESEARCH. Guides to official sources: No.5, social security statistics. London: 1961. pp.viii + 171. DHSS; LSE.

45. INTERNATIONAL LABOUR OFFICE. Bibliography of unemployment. Geneva: 1926. pp.155. LSE.

46. JOHNSON, S. (compiler). Poverty and inequality in Northern Ireland: a preliminary bibliography; prepared for the United Kingdom study on the nature, causes and extent of poverty and on policies implemented to combat poverty. London: 1980. pp.[ii] + 22. DHSS.

47. LAW SOCIETY GAZETTE. Regular features (since 1978) on social security law.

48. MAUNDER, W.R. (ed.). Review of United Kingdom statistical sources. Vols.1-5. London: 1974-1976. LSE.

49. MICKLEWRIGHT, J. A selective bibliography of recent research on unemployment in Britain. [London] : 1981. pp.26. (Unemployment project working note No.7). DHSS.

50. MINISTRY OF PENSIONS AND NATIONAL INSURANCE. Catalogue of books, pamphlets. London: 1957. LSE.

51. MINISTRY OF PENSIONS AND NATIONAL INSURANCE AND NATIONAL ASSISTANCE BAORD. Social security statistics. London: 1961. (Guides to Official Sources No.5). pp.viii + 171. LSE.

52. MORGA, M.A. & STEPHEN, L.R. British government publications: an index to chairmen, 1967-1971. London: [1976]. pp.40. LSE.

53. MORLEY, L.H. Unemployment compensation: a chronological bibliography of books, reports and periodical articles in English, 1891-1927. New York: 1928. pp.vi + 117. LSE.

54. MYATT, A.G. Keyword index of guides to the serial literature. Boston Spa: British Library Lending Division. 1974. pp.35. DHSS.

55. ORGANISATION OF ECONOMIC COOPERATION AND DEVELOPMENT. International migration of manpower - bibliography. Paris: 1969. pp.137. DHSS.

56. PALIC, V.M. (compiler). Government publications: a guide to bibliographic tools;... Oxford: [1977]. pp.553. LSE.

57. PHADRAIG, M.N.G. "Bibliography of social aspects of our legal system". Soc.Stud. 1. (1972). pp.480-98.

58. PRINCETON UNIVERSITY, DEPARTMENT OF ECONOMICS AND SOCIOLOGY, INDUSTRIAL RELATIONS SECTION. Selected bibliography: unemployment prevention, compensation and relief. Princeton: 1933. pp.23. LSE.

59. PUBLIC RECORDS OFFICE. Guide to public records. London: 1949. pp.70. DHSS.

60. PUBLIC RECORDS OFFICE. The records of the Cabinet Office to 1922. London: 1966. pp.52. DHSS.

61. PUBLIC RECORD OFFICE. Classes of departmental papers for 1906-1939. London: 1966. pp.viii + 39. DHSS.

62. PUBLIC RECORD OFFICE. Records of interest to social scientists: unemployment insurance 1911 to 1939. London: 1975. pp.261. BL.

63. ROLSTON, B. et. al. A social science bibliography of Northern Ireland, 1945-1983. Belfast: 1983. LSE.

64. SOCIAL SCIENCE RESEARCH COUNCIL.. Reviews of Current Research. 5. Research on poverty. London: Heinemann. 1968. pp.ix + 57. LSE.

65. SWEET AND MAXWELL. A legal bibliography of the British Commonwealth of Nations. 2nd ed. 1955-. Vol.1. English law to 1800, including Wales, the Channel Islands and the Isle of Man... compiled by W.H. and L.F. Maxwell. London: 1955. pp.xvi + 687; Vol.2. English law 1801-1954, compiled by J.S. James and L.F. Maxwell. London: 1957. pp.vii + 519; Vol.4. Irish law to 1956, compiled by L.F. and W.H. Maxwell. London: 1957. pp.vii + 127. Vol.5. Scottish Law to 1956. London: 1957. pp.vii + 187. CUL; BL.

66. TAYLOR, F.I. A bibliography of unemployment. London: 1909. pp.76. LSE; DHSS.

67. UNITED STATES. DEPARTMENT OF HEALTH EDUCATION AND WELFARE. Poverty studies in the sixties - a selected annotated bibliography. DHSS.

68. UNITED STATES. SOCIAL SECURITY ADMINISTRATION. LIBRARY STAFF. An index to the legislative history of public law 96-265. Social Security Disability Amendments of 1980. [Washington, DC]: 1981. pp.[i] + 33. DHSS.

69. UNITED STATES. SOCIAL SECURITY ADMINISTRATION. OFFICE OF RESEARCH AND STATISTICS. Four decades of international social security research: a bibliography of studies by the Social Security Administration 1937-80. Washington, D.C.: 1981. pp.vi + 68. (SSA Publication No.13-11733). DHSS.

70. WARD, J. Directory of voluntary organisations concerned with action against poverty in the United Kingdom. London: UK Advisory Committee on European Economic Community's Action Against Poverty Programme. 1975. pp.19. DHSS.

71. WILLIAMS, G.H., comp.). Poverty and policy in the United Kingdom: a classified bibliography. London: 1980. pp.[ii] + 84. DHSS.

PART II   History of Social Security to 1946

In this part, we present first, general works on the history of the development of social security in the United Kingdom and Ireland. Inevitably some of these accounts do not stop at 1945, but on balance we have found it more helpful to gather together all general historical works on the development of social security into one place. This general section is followed by a lengthy section on the poor law, including special sections on the poor law in Ireland and Scotland. Then comes a section on the role of charities and friendly societies as welfare agencies. This is followed by a more detailed section on other specific developments in social security provision. Finally there is a section on the Beveridge Report and responses thereto.

Section 1   General History

For historical studies of the development of particular benefits, see also the relevant benefit headings.

72. ANON. Foreign poor law. London: 1835. pp.15. LSE.

73. ANON. "Legislation on social economy". L.M. 36. (1846). 290-7.

74. ANON. "Compulsory insurance in Germany". Lab.G. 2. (1894). pp.49-50.

75. ANON. "Accident and old age insurance in Germany, 1895". Lab.G. 5. (1897). pp.36-37.

76. ANON. "German insurance laws and pauperism". Lab.G. 5. (1897). pp.325-326.

77. ANON. "The social services - 1601-1875: I". L.R. XXV. (1936). pp.108ff.

78. ANON. "Social security: is Britain ahead?". L.R. XLVII. (1958). pp.160ff.

79. ABEL-SMITH, B. "The welfare state: breaking the post-war consensus". Pol.Q. 51. (1980). pp.17-23.

80. AGGARWALA, K.C. "The development of the social security system in the U.K.". India Q. VIII. (1952). pp.42-62.

81. AMERICAN ACADEMY OF POLITICAL AND SOCIAL SCIENCE. Social insurance. Philadelphia: 1933. pp.ix + 204. LSE.

82. APPLEBY, P.H. Public administration for a welfare state. London: [1961]. pp.ix + 105. LSE.

83. ARMSTRONG, B.N. Insuring the essentials: minimum wage plus social insurance: a living wage program. New York: 1932. pp.xvii + 717. LSE.

84. ASHLEY, A. The social policy of Bismarck: a critical study, with a comparison of German and English insurance legislation. London: 1912. pp.xi + 95. (Birmingham Studies in Social Economics and Adjacent Fields 3).

85. ATKINSON, A. The national insurance and pension scheme as formulated by A. Atkinson. Bradford: 1894. pp.16. BL.

86. ATKINSON, A.B. Poverty in Britain and the reform of social security. London: Cambridge University Press, 1969. pp.224. (University of Cambridge, Department of Applied Economics, Occasional Paper 18). DHSS. LSE. CUL.

87. AYDELOTTE, W.O. "The conservative and radical interpretations of early Victorian social legislation". Victorian Studies. 11. (1967-8). pp.225-36.

88. BARRETT, R.M. Foreign legislation on behalf of destitute and neglected children. Dublin: 1896. pp.76. LSE.

89. BAUMOL, W.J. The theory of welfare and control. London: 1949. Fo. pp.iii + 260. LSE.

90. BAYLY, W.D. The state of the poor and the working classes considered, with practical plans for improving their condition in society, and superseding the present system of compulsory assessment. London: 1820. TCD.

91. BEVERIDGE, SIR W.H. "Social security: some trans-Atlantic comparisons". R.Statist.Soc.J. CVI. (1943). pp.305-21. Discussion. pp.322-32.

92. BEVERIDGE, W.H. Full employment in a free society. London: 1944. pp.429. Sq.

93. BLACKLEY, M.J.J. Thrift and national insurance as a security against pauperism. London: 1906. pp.151. DHSS; CUL.

94. BLACKLEY, REV. W.L. "National insurance. A cheap, practical and popular means of abolishing poor rates". Nineteenth Century. 1878. November. pp.834-857.

95. BLACKLEY, REV. W.L. "The House of Lords and national insurance". Nineteenth Century. VIII. (41). 1880. pp.107-118.

96. BLACKLEY, W.L. "National insurance considered economically and practically". Manch.Statist.Soc.Trans. (1879-80). pp.23-42.

97. BOOKER, H.S. "Lady Rhys Williams' proposals for the amalgamation of direct taxation with social insurance". E.J. LVI. (1946). pp.230.

98. BOOTH, C. (ed.). [Labour and life of the people, 1889-91; Life and labour of the people in London, 1892-97 and 1902-03]. London: 1886-1903. 450 vols. [manuscript, pr. and typescript, w. typescript index]. LSE.

99. BOOTH, C. Life and labour of the people in London. London: 1902. 17 vols. DHSS.

100. BOOTH, C. & OTHERS. Family budgets: being the income and expenses of twenty-eight British householders, 1891-1894. London: 1896. pp.76. LSE; G.

101. BOWLEY, A.L. & HOGG, M.H. Has poverty diminished? London: 1925. pp.viii + 236. CUL.

102. BRABROOK, SIR E. "Social insurance". R.Statist.Soc.J. LXXI. (1908). pp.601-618.

103. BROAD, T.T. An "all-in" national insurance scheme. London: 1924. pp.38. DHSS.

104. BRUCE, M. The coming of the welfare state. London: 1961. pp.ix + 307. CUL. 2nd ed. 1965. pp.xi + 308. CUL. 4th ed. 1968. pp.374. DHSS; CUL.

105. BULL, D. (ed.). Family poverty: programme for the seventies. London: 1971. pp.vi + 208. DHSS; LSE; CUL; Sq. 2nd ed. 1972. pp.216. DHSS; LSE; CUL.

106. BULLOCK, E. Compulsory insurance. New York: 1918. pp.266. DHSS.

107. BURNS, E.M. Social security and public policy. New York: 1956. pp.xvi + 291. LSE; CUL.

108. CARNARVON, EARL OF. "A few more words on national insurance". Nineteenth Century. VIII. (1880). pp.384-93.

109. CARR-SAUNDERS, A.M. "The state and the social problem: some lessons from a quarter of a century of social insurance". Pub.Admin. XIV. (1936). p.240.

110. CHADWICK, W.E. The church, the state and the poor: a series of historical sketches. London: 1914. pp.viii + 223.

111. CHECKLAND, S.G. The rise of industrial society in England, 1815-1885. London: 1964. pp.xiv + 471. DHSS.

112. CHILD POVERTY ACTION GROUP. Poverty and the Labour government. London: 1970. pp.32. (Poverty Pamphlet 3). (Originally published under the title: An incomes policy for families. 1970. pp.30). DHSS; LSE; CUL.

113. CLARKE, C.E. Social insurance in Britain. London: 1950. pp.x + 136. DHSS; LSE.

114. CLARKE, J.S. Social security. London: [1943]. pp.23. LSE.

115. CLARKE, J.S. Social security guide. London: Social Security League. 1944. pp.16. DHSS.

116. CLARKE, J.S. "Social insecurity". Pol.Q. XVI. (1945). p.30.

117. COHEN, J.L. Insurance by industry examined. London: 1923. pp.120. LSE; S.

118. COHEN, J.L. Social insurance unified, and other essays. London: 1924. pp.157. DHSS; CUL.

119. COHEN, P. The British system of social insurance. London: 1932. pp.278. DHSS; LSE; CUL.

120. COLE, M.I. Social services and the Webb tradition. London: 1946. pp.12.

121. CONSTABLE, A.H.B. National insurance. Edinburgh: 1892. pp.41-60. G.

122. COOTES, R.J. The making of the welfare state. London: 1966. pp.viii + 136. DHSS.

123. DAWSON, W.H. "Insurance legislation: the larger view". Fort.Rev. 89. (1911). pp.534-47.

124. DAWSON, W.H. Social insurance in Germany 1883-1911, its history, operation, results. And a comparison with the National Insurance Act, 1911. London: 1912. pp.283. CUL.

125. DAWSON, W.H. "Social insurance in England and Germany: a comparison". Fort.Rev. 92. (1912). pp.304-20.

126. DEACON, A. "An end to the means test? Social security and the Attlee government". J.Soc.Pol. (1982). pp.289-306.

127. DEACON, A. & BRADSHAW, J. Reserved for the poor. The means test in British social policy. Oxford: 1983. pp.228. DHSS.

128. DEARNLEY, I.H. Public assistance administration and accounts. London: 1931. pp.348. CUL.

129. DRAGE, G. The state and the poor. London: [1914?]. pp.264. LSE.

130. EDE, W.M. State relief and other artificial obstacles to thrift. [c.1890]. pp.15.

131. FAMILY WELFARE ASSOCIATION. Report of a committee on all-in insurance. London: 1925. pp.6. LSE.

132. FAWCETT, H. Pauperism: its causes and remedies. London: 1871. pp.viii + 270. LSE.

133. FERAUD, L. "Introduction to the financial problems of social insurance". I.Lab.R. XXXVIII. (1938). pp.1ff.

134. FIEGEHEN, G.C., LANSLEY, P.S. & SMITH, A.D. Poverty and progress in Britain 1953-73: a statistical study of low income households: their numbers, types and expenditure patterns. London: 1977. pp.xiv + 173. (National Institute of Economic and Social Research Occasional Paper XXIX). DHSS; LSE; CUL.

135. FIELD, F. Poverty and politics: the inside story of the CPAG campaigns in the 1970s. London: 1982. pp.x + 205. LSE; DHSS.

136. FIELDING, H. A proposal for making an effectual provision for the poor, for amending their morals, and for rendering them useful members of society... London: 1753. pp.iv + 93. G; LSE.

137. FORD, B.J.T. Steps towards industrial peace: a pensions and assurance scheme in operation. [Birmingham]: 1927. pp.135. LSE.

138. FRANK, W.F. "Law in the welfare state". Ind.L.R. 5. (1950-51). pp.166-185.

139. FRASER, D. The evolution of the British welfare state: a history of social policy since the industrial revolution. London: 1973. pp.xviii + 299. DHSS; LSE; CUL. 2nd ed. 1984. DHSS.

140. FRIEDMANN, W. "Social security and some recent developments in the common law". C.B.R. XXI. (1943). pp.369-393.

141. FRIEDMANN, W.G. "Social insurance and the principles of tort liability". Harv.L.R. 63. (1949-50). pp.241-265.

142. FURNISS, N. & TILTON, T.A. The case for the welfare state: from social security to social equality. Bloomington: [1977]. pp.249. LSE.

143. GARLAND, D. "The birth of the welfare sanction". B.J.L.S. 8. (1981). pp.29-46.

144. GIBBS, E.R. National insurance and social service for everyman. Oxford: 1948. pp.70. DHSS.

145. GILBERT, B.B. Evolution of national insurance in Britain. London: 1966. pp.497. DHSS; LSE; CUL.

146. GILBERT, B.B. British social policy 1914-39. London: 1970. pp.viii + 343. Sq; DHSS; LSE; CUL.

147. GLEIZE, H. Les assurances sociales. London: 1924. pp.143. LSE; S.

148. GORDON, A. Social insurance: what it is and what it might be. London: Fabian Society. 1924. pp.x + 150. DHSS; CUL.

149. GRANDJACQUES, H. Les tendances internationales de l'assurance sociale. Paris: 1930. pp.158. LSE.

150. GREGG, P. The welfare state: an economic and social history of Great Britain from 1945 to the present day. London: 1967. pp.xii + 388. DHSS; CUL.

151. GRIGGS, C.H. National insurance. [Birmingham] : 1944. pp.12. LSE.

152. HABER, W. & COHEN, W.J. Social security: programs, problems and policies. Home, Ill.: 1967. pp.xv + 610. DHSS.

153. HADLEY, R. & HATCH, S. Social welfare and the failure of the state. London: 1981. pp.vi + 186. LSE.

154.   HAGENBUCH, W.   "The rationale of the social services".   Lloyds
       B.R.   29.   (July 1953).   pp.1-16.

155.   HAGENBUCH, W.   "The Welfare State and its finances".   Lloyds
       B.R.   49 (July 1958).   pp.1-17.

156.   HAMPSON, E.M.   The treatment of poverty in Cambridgeshire,
       1597-1834. Cambridge: 1934. pp.xx + 308. DHSS.

157.   HANDLER, J.F. (ed.).   Family law and the poor.   Essays by
       Jacobus Tenbroek. Wesport, Conn.: 1971. pp.xix + 220. CUL.

158.   HANSON, C.G.   "Craft unions, welfare benefits, and the case
       for trade union law reform, 1867-75".   Ec.H.R.   (2nd ser.).
       28. (1975). pp.243-259.

159.   HANSON, C.G.   "Craft unions, welfare benefits, and the case
       for trade union law reform, 1867-75: a reply".   Ec.H.R.   (2nd
       ser.). 29. (1976). pp.631-635.

160.   HANSON, E.   The politics of social security: the 1938 Act and
       some later developments. [Auckland]: 1980. pp.181. DHSS.

161.   HARRIS, R.W.   How do I stand in regard to social insurance?
       London: 1942. pp.158. DHSS.

162.   HARTWELL, R.M. & OTHERS.   The long debate on poverty: eight
       essays on industrialisation and "the condition of England".
       London: 1972.   pp.xvi + 243.   LSE; CUL.   2nd ed.   1974.
       pp.xxxii + 243. (IEA Readings No.9). DHSS; CUL.

163.   HAY, J.R.   The origins of the Liberal welfare reforms
       1906-1914. London: 1975. pp.78. (Studies in Economic and
       Social History). DHSS; LSE.

164.   HAYNES, A.T. & KIRTON, R.J.   Income tax in relation to social
       security. London: [1943]. pp.30. LSE.

165.   HECLO, H.   Modern social politics in Britain and Sweden: from
       relief to income maintenance.   New Haven, London: 1974.
       pp.xii + 349. DHSS; LSE.

166.   HENNOCK, E.P.   "Social security: a system emerges".   N.S.
       XI.   284.   (7 March 1968).   pp.336-8.   (The Origins of the
       Social Services 6). DHSS.

167.   HILLIER, A.P.   "National insurance and the commonweal".
       Nineteenth Century. LXX. (1911). pp.339-49.

168.   HIRSCHFELD, G.   Significance of social security.   Chicago:
       Research Council for Economic Security. 1943. pp.5. DHSS.

169.   HOBMAN, D.L.   The welfare state.   London: 1963.   pp.127.
       DHSS; LSE.

170.   HOBSON, J.A. Poverty. London: 1905. pp.16. LSE.

171.   HOHMAN, H.F.   The development of social insurance and minimum
       wage legislation in Great Britain.   Boston: 1933.   pp.xxi +
       441. LSE.

172. HOOD, K.   Room at the bottom: national insurance in the welfare state. London: 1960. pp.72. LSE; DHSS.

173. HURRY, J.B. Poverty and its vicious circles. London: 1917. pp.xiv + 180. CUL. 2nd ed. 1921. pp.xvi + 411. CUL.

174. INGLIS, B. Poverty and the industrial revolution. London: 1971. pp.437. DHSS.

175. INTERDEPARTMENTAL COMMITTEE ON MIGRATION AND SOCIAL INSURANCE. Report. London: 1926. pp.32. (Cmd.2608). LSE.

176. INTERNATIONAL CONGRESS OF ACTUARIES.   Papers on social insurance. London: 1927. pp.232. DHSS.

177. INTERNATIONAL CONGRESS OF SOCIAL INSURANCE EXPERTS, 2ND CONGRESS, 1936. Bericht uber die Arbeiten der Kongresses. Stuttgart: 1938. pp.218. LSE.

178. INTERNATIONAL COUNCIL ON SOCIAL WELFARE. Social welfare and human rights. New York: 1969. pp.xii + 393. DHSS.

179. INTERNATIONAL LABOUR OFFICE.   Actuarial technique and financial organisation of social insurance: compulsory pension insurance. Geneva: 1940. pp.568. DHSS.

180. JENKS, C.W. Law, freedom and welfare. London: 1963. pp.xi + 162. LSE.

181. KELSO, R.W. Poverty. New York: 1929. pp.viii + 374. LSE.

182. KING, SIR G.   "The development of the social security system"., Social Services Journal. 13. (1960). pp.4-8.

183. KOHLER, P.A. et al.   The evolution of social insurance 1881-1981. London: 1982. pp.500. LSE.

184. KRZECZKOWSKI, K.   "Social insurance and international legislation". I.Lab.R. VIII. (1923). pp.637ff.

185. KULP, C.A. Social insurance coordination: an analysis of German and British organization. Washington, D.C.: 1938. pp.xiv + 333.

186. LABOUR PARTY. The welfare state. Discussion Pamphlet No.4. London: 1952. p.30. DHSS; LSE.

187. LABOUR PARTY. Towards equality: Labour's policy for social justice. London: 1956. pp.32. LSE.

188. LAFITTE, F. Britain's way to social security. London: 1945. pp.110. DHSS; LSE.

189. LAFITTE, F. Social security - ways and means. Birmingham: 1969. pp.17. DHSS.

190. LAVERGNE, A.DE & HENRY, P.L.   Le chomage: causes, consequences, remedes. Paris: 1910. pp.420. LSE; S.

191. LEAGUE OF NATIONS. Social insurance [in its national and international aspects and in relation to the work of the International Labour Organization of the League of Nations]. London: 1925. pp.x + 248. DHSS; CUL.

192. LEWIS, F.W. State insurance: a social and industrial need. London: 1909. pp.233. LSE.

193. LIBERAL PARTY ORGANISATION. Reform of income tax and social security payments. London: 1950. pp.40. LSE; DHSS.

194. LUBENOW, W.C. The politics of government growth: early Victorian attitudes towards state intervention, 1833-1848. Newton Abbott: 1971. pp.237. LSE.

195. LUBOVE, R. (ed.). Social welfare in transition: selected English documents, 1834-1909. Pittsburgh, Penn.: 1966. pp.xiii + 334. BL.

196. MACKAY, T. Working class insurance. London: 1890. pp.vi + 78. TCD.

197. MADDICK, H. Problems of the welfare state in Great Britain. New Delhi: [1956]. pp.26. LSE.

198. MALLON, J.J. & LASCELLES, E.C.P. Poverty, yesterday and today. London: 1930. pp.100. LSE.

199. MANCHESTER CITY COUNCIL. SOCIAL SERVICES DEPARTMENT. Development of the welfare rights service in the City of Manchester 1972-1976. Manchester: 1976. pp.ii + 44. DHSS.

200. MARSHALL, T.H. The right to welfare and other essays. London: 1981. pp.192. CUL.

201. MARTIN, I. From workhouse to welfare: the founding of the welfare state. Harmondsworth: 1971. pp.96. DHSS.

202. MAYNARD, A. "A survey of social security in the U.K.". Soc. & Econ.Ad. 7. (1973). pp.39-57.

203. MEARNS, A. The bitter cry of outcast London: an inquiry into the condition of the abject poor". Originally published 1883. New impression in A. Humphreys (ed.), Homes of the London poor and the bitter cry of outcast London. 1970. pp.24. (Cass Library of Victorian Times No.6). CUL.

204. MENCHER, S. Poor law to poverty program: economic security policy in Britain and the United States. Pittsburgh: 1967. pp.xix + 476. LSE; DHSS.

205. MENDELSOHN, R.S. The evolution of social security: the record of four British countries. London: 1950. Fo. (4) + 614 + (27). LSE.

206. MENDELSOHN, R.S. Social security in the British Commonwealth. London: 1954. pp.xv + 391. LSE; DHSS; CUL.

207. METROPOLITAN LIFE INSURANCE COMPANY. Social insurance legislation: origin and present provision of the unemployment, health and pension systems in six European countries. New York: 1932. pp.70. LSE.

208. MIDWINTER, E.C. Victorian social reform. London: 1968. pp.vii + 112. DHSS.

209. MINISTRY OF LABOUR AND NATIONAL SERVICE. The cost of living index number. Method of compilation. London: 1944. pp.12. DHSS.

210. MINISTRY OF PENSIONS AND NATIONAL INSURANCE. STAFF TRAINING BRANCH. The long road; the story of British social security. London: 1964. pp.43. DHSS.

211. MONEY, SIR L.G.C. Insurance versus poverty. London: 1912. pp.xxiii + 396. DHSS; CUL.

212. MOWAT, C.L. "Social legislation in Britain and the United Kingdom in the early twentieth century: a problem in the history of ideas" Hist. Stud. 7. (1969).

213. MUSSON, A.E. "Craft unions, welfare benefits, and the case for trade union law reform, 1867-75: a comment". Ec.H.R. (2nd ser.). 29. (1976). pp.626-630.

214. NEW SOCIETY. The origins of the social services. London: [1968]. pp.34. Sq.

215. NICHOLSON, G.M. Profit sharing and national insurance as an aid to the solution of the labour question. London: [1907]. pp.20. LSE.

216. NICHOLSON, J.L. Variations in working class family expenditure. London: 1949. pp.60. DHSS.

217. OASTLER, R. The right of the poor to liberty and life. London: [1838]. pp.vi + 53. LSE.

218. OGUS, A.I. "Conditions in the formation and development of social insurance: legal development and legal history". Schriftenreihe fur Internationales und Vergeliechendes Sozialrecht. 3. (1979). pp.337-48.

219. OGUS, A.I. "Landesbericht Grossbritannien". in Peter A. Kohler & Hans F. Zacher, Ein Jahrhundert Sozialversicherung in der Bundesrepublik Deutschland, Grossbritannien, Osterreich and der Schweiz. Berlin: 1981. at pp.270-443.

220. ORMEROD, J.R. National insurance: its inherent defects. London: 1930. pp.46. S; DHSS.

221. ORR, J.B. Food, health and income. Report on a survey of adequacy of diet in relation to income. London: 1936. pp.72. CUL. 2nd ed. 1937. pp.83. CUL.

222. PARRY, E.A. The law and the poor. London: 1914. pp.xxi + 316. LSE.

223. PEPPERCORNE, J.W. The rights of necessity and the treatment of the necessitous by various nations. London: 1839. pp.92. G.

224. PERRIN, G. "Reflections on fifty years of social security". I.Lab.R. 99. (1969). pp.249-292.

225. PIGOU, A.C. Economics of welfare. 4th ed. rev. London: 1952. pp.xxxi + 876. DHSS.

226. PIPKIN, C.W. The idea of social justice: a study of legislation and administration and the labour movement in England and France between 1900 and 1926. New York: 1927. pp.xvii + 597. LSE.

227. PLUMMER, A. "Some aspects of the history and theory of social insurance". Economica. 20. (June 1927). pp.203-23.

228. POLITICAL AND ECONOMIC PLANNING. Family needs and the social services. London: 1961. pp.xi + 233. DHSS; CUL.

229. POWELL, E. The welfare state. London: 1961. pp.22. DHSS; LSE.

230. PRIBRAM, K. "Social insurance in Europe and social security in the United States: a comparative analysis". I.Lab.R. XXXVI. (1937). pp.743ff.

231. RAYNAUD, H. The fight for social security. London: 1952. pp.42. DHSS.

232. RAYNES, H.E. Social security in Britain: a history. London: 1957. pp.vii + 244. LSE; DHSS; CUL. 2nd ed. 1961. pp.viii + 264. DHSS; LSE; CUL.

233. RHODES, J.M. "Pauperism, past and present". Manch.Statist.Soc.Trans. (1890-91). pp.61-112.

234. RHYS-WILLIAMS, LADY J. Taxation and incentive. London: 1953. pp.188. DHSS.

235. RIMLINGER, G.V. "Welfare policy and economic development: a comparative historical perspective". J.Econ.Hist. XXVI. (1966). pp.556-76.

236. ROACH, J.L. & ROACH, J.K. (eds.). Poverty: selected readings. Harmondsworth: 1972. pp.350. DHSS; LSE; CUL.

237. ROBERTS, D. Victorian origins of the British Welfare State. New Haven: 1960. pp.xii + 369. DHSS; LSE.

238. RODGERS, B. The battle against poverty. Vol.1. From pauperism to human rights. London: 1969. pp.83. DHSS; LSE; CUL.

239. RODGERS, B. The battle against poverty. Vol.2. Towards a welfare state. London: 1969. pp. x + 84. DHSS; LSE; CUL.

240. ROOKE, P.J. The growth of social services. London: 1968. pp.144. n.l.

241. ROWNTREE, B.S. The human needs of labour. London: 1919. pp.168. CUL. New ed.rev. London, New York: 1937. pp.162. CUL; BL.

242. ROWNTREE, B.S. & LAVERS, G.R. Poverty and the welfare state: a third social survey of York dealing only with economic questions. London: 1951. pp.vii + 104. LSE; CUL.

243. ROWNTREE, B.S. Poverty: a study of town life. 3rd ed. London: 1902. pp.xxii + 452. DHSS; LSE; C; G; U. New ed. 1922. pp.xx + 496. CUL. Reprint of 1922 ed. New York: 1971. CUL.

244. RUBINOW, I.M. Social insurance. London: 1913. pp.525. CUL.

245. RUNCIMAN, W.G. Relative deprivation and social justice: a study of attitudes to social inequality in twentieth-century England. London: 1966. pp.344. DHSS. Rev.ed. Harmondsworth: 1972. pp.xv + 432. DHSS; LSE; CUL.

246. SAKMANN, M. Unemployment and health insurance in Great Britain, 1911-1937. Washington, D.C.: 1938. pp.v + 44. (U.S. Social Security Board. Bureau of Research and Statistics. Bureau Report 3). BL.

247. SCHULZ, T. "Human needs" and average food consumption. Oxford: 1962. pp.8. DHSS.

248. SCHULZ, T. The cost of a human needs diet. Spring 1963. Oxford: 1963. pp.13. DHSS.

249. SCHULZ, T. The cost of a human needs diet. Autumn 1964: the cost of nutrients. Oxford: 1964. pp.8. DHSS.

250. SCHWEINITZ, K. de. England's road to social security: from the Statute of Laborers in 1349 to the Beveridge report of 1942. Philadelphia: 1943. pp.x + 281. LSE; CUL; DHSS.

251. SEAMAN, R.D.H. The Liberals and the welfare state. London: 1968. pp.66. DHSS.

252. SIMS, G.R. How the poor live. London: 1883. pp.64. LSE.

253. SLATER, G. Poverty and the state. London: 1930. pp.viii + 480. LSE; DHSS; CUL.

254. SLEEMAN, J.F. The welfare state: its aims, benefits and costs. London: 1973. pp.viii + 199. DHSS; LSE; CUL.

255. SMITH, C.L. "National insurance". Char.Org.Rep. 7. (1878). pp.218-219.

256. SMITH, C.S. People in need: a study of contemporary social needs and of their relation to the welfare state. London: 1957. pp.156. DHSS; CUL.

257. SMITH, N.J. Poverty in England 1601-1936. Newton Abbott: 1972. pp.96. CUL.

258. SNOWDEN, P. The living wage. London: [1912]. pp.xvi + 189. LSE; CUL.

259. STACK, M. "The meaning of social security". J.Comp.Leg. 23. (1941). pp.113-129.

260. STEER, W.S. "The origins of social insurance". Transactions of the Devonshire Association. 96. (1964). pp.303-17.

261. STEER, W.S. "Eighteenth century social insurance". N.S. 2. (1963). (64). pp.12-13.

262. STEIN, B. Work and welfare in Britain and the U.S.A. London: 1976. pp.xvi + 112. DHSS; LSE.

263. STEVENS, R.B. Statutory history of the United States: income security. New York: 1970. pp.x + 919. CUL.

264. STOCKMAN, H.W. "History and development of social security in Great Britain". Bull. I.S.S.A. X. (1957). pp.3-71.

265. TAWNEY, R.H. "The theory of pauperism". Sociol.Rev. II. (1909). pp.361-74.

266. TAYLOR, G. The problem of poverty 1660-1834. London: 1969. pp.viii + 146. (Seminar Studies in History). CUL.

267. THANE, P. "The history of social welfare". N.S. 29. (1974). pp.540-542.

268. THANE, P. "Craft unions, welfare benefits, and the case for trade union law reform, 1867-75: a comment". Ec.H.R. (2nd ser.). 29. (1976). pp.617-625.

269. THEONES, D. The elite in the welfare state. London: 1966. pp.236. DHSS; LSE.

270. TITMUSS, R.M. Commitment to welfare. London: 1968. pp.272. DHSS; LSE; CUL. 2nd ed. 1976. pp.272. DHSS; CUL.

271. TOWNSEND, P. Poverty, socialism and the Labour government. London: 1966. pp.29. DHSS.

272. TREMENHEERE, H.S. "State aid and control in industrial assurance". Nineteenth Century. VIII. (1880). pp.175-93.

273. TUCKWELL, G. & SMITH, C. The worker's handbook. London: 1908. pp.xi + 251. CUL.

274. UNITED NATIONS. Methods of social welfare administration. New York: 1950. pp.v + 299. DHSS.

275. WALDHEIM, H. VAN. "War policy of the British and German social insurance schemes". Pub.Admin. XIX. (1941). p.36.

276. WEBB, B. Our partnership. (Ed. by Barbara Drake and Margaret I. Cole). London, New York, Toronto: 1948. pp.544. LSE.

277. WHITESIDE, N. "Welfare legislation and the unions during the First World War". Hist.J. 23. (1980). pp.857-74.

278. WICKWAR, W.H. The social services. A historical survey. 1. The genesis of the social services. 2. Poor relief. 3. Education. 4. Public health. 5. Natural contingencies - sickness and disablement, old age, premature death, blindness. 6. Economic contingencies: unemployment. 7. The social service state. 8. State and society. London: 1936. pp.268. CUL. Rev. ed. 1949. pp.302. CUL.

279. WILLIAMS, G. The coming of the welfare state. London: 1967. pp.119. DHSS; LSE.

280. WILLOUGHBY, G. "Social security in France and Britain". Pol.Q. XIX. (1948). pp.49-59.

281. WILSON, D.H. "The economic causes of pauperism". Westm.Rev. CLXV. (1906). pp.135-47.

282. WINKLER, H.R. (ed.). Twentieth century Britain: national power and social welfare. New York: 1976. pp.272. LSE.

283. WITTELS, F. An end to poverty. London: 1925. pp.224. DHSS; CUL.

284. WOOD, S. The British welfare state 1900-1950. Cambridge: 1982. pp.48. DHSS.

Section 2   The Poor Law

(a) Poor Law (General)

285.   ANON. Effect of the Act of Parliament for the reliefe of the poore. [43 Eliz. c.2]. Wolfe. 1599. n.l.

286.   ANON. Certeine articles concerning the statute [43 Eliz. c.2] lately made for the reliefe of the poore. Wolfe. 1599. n.l.

287.   ANON. An ease for overseers of the poore: abstracted from the statutes... with an easie... table for recording the number, names... of the poore, fit to be observed of the overseers in every parish... (1601). Cambridge: 1601. pp.38. G; BL; Columbia Univ. N.Y.

288.   ANON. Foure statutes... to be carefully put in execution. [Orders for health, punishment of rogues and vagabonds, etc.]   4to. 1609.

289.   ANON. Orders and directions, together with a commission for the better administration of justice, and more perfect information of his majesty; how and by whom the laws and statutes tending to the relief of the poor, the well ordering and training up of youth in trades, and the reformation of disorders and disordered pesons, are executed throughout the kingdom, which his royal majesty hath commanded to be published and inquired of, by the body of his privy council, whom he hath made principal commissioners for that purpose. 2 pts. 1630.

290.   ANON. Modest proposals for... provision for the poor and likewise for the better suppression of thieves... and other lewd livers, etc. London: 1696. pp.32. G.

291.   ANON. The Bill intituled, An Act for the Relief, Imployment and Settlement of the Poor, which came from the House of Commons; and also the Bill, intituled, An Act for the further and better Relief, Imployment and Maintenance of the Poor: and the Scheme of an Act for the Relief of the Poor Delivered into the House of Peers from the Commissioners of Trade and Plantations as Drawn by them. London: 1705. pp.46. CUL.

292.   ANON. Laws concerning the poor; wherein is treated of overseers and their office, of rates and contributions of settlements of families, vagrants, children, servants, etc.

1705. pp.(24) + 192 + (23). G.

293. ANON. The laws concerning the poor. 2nd ed. London: 1708. NLS.

294. ANON. The compleat parish-officer, containing, I. The authority and proceedings of high-constables...;   II. of churchwardens; how chosen...; II. of overseers of the poor, and their officers...; of surveyors of the highways and scavengers, how elected, etc. London: 1718. pp.iv + 133 + x. LSE.

295. ANON. Poor laws: or, the laws and statutes relating to the settling, maintenance, and employment of the poor... [London]: 1724. pp.122. G.

296. ANON. Account of several work-houses for employing... the poor,... rules... also of several charity-schools, etc. London: 1725. pp.vi + 112. G.

297. ANON. Laws and statutes relating to the settling, maintenance, etc., of the poor. 1727. n.l.

298. ANON. Some few letters. Selected, from an account of work-houses and charity schools for employment of the poor in England, with a preface to excite some such application of our charity in Ireland. Dublin: [1728?]. pp.(14) + 50. RIA; LU.

299. ANON The Compleat Parish Officer; containing, I The Authority and Proceedings of High Constables,... etc. II of Church Wardens,... III Of Overseers of the Poor, and their Office; their Power in Relieving, Employing and Settling, etc. of poor Persons; the Laws relating to the Poor, and Settlements, and the Statutes concerning Masters and Servants. IV Of Surveyors of Highways, and Scavengers,... 5th ed. In the Savoy: 1729. pp.168 + (11). CUL.

300. ANON. Cases and resolutions of cases, ajudg'd in the Court of King's Bench, concerning settlements and removals, from the first year of King George I to the present reign. 2nd ed. London: 1729. pp.160. G; All Souls, Oxford. 3rd ed. London: 1732. BL. 4th ed. London: 1742. BL.

301. ANON. The statutes at large concerning the provisions for the poor, being a compleat collection of all the Acts of Parliament relating thereto. To which is added a table... London: 1733. pp.94 + xviii. G.

302. ANON. A bill for the better relief and employment of the poor, and for the more effectual punishing rogues and vagabonds; and for reducing the laws relating to the poor, and to rogues and vagabonds into one law. n.p.: [1736]. pp. 27. BL; G.

303. ANON. A new scheme for reducing the laws relating to the poor into one act of Parliament, and for the better providing the impotent poor with necessaries, the industrious with work, and for the correction of the idle poor. London: 1936. pp.26. G. 2nd ed. London: 1737. BL.

304. ANON. Some regulations with regard to the begging poor, and a scheme for providing employment for labourers of all kinds, etc. [Edinburgh: 1741]. pp.16. G.

305. ANON. Observations upon the vagrant laws, proving that the statutes in Queen Elizabeth's time are the most proper foundation for a law of that nature, etc. London: 1742. pp.14. G.

306. ANON. Sessions cases adjudged in the Court of King's Bench, chiefly touching settlements, from the latter end of Queen Ann's reign, to the present time. London: 1750. BL.

307. ANON. The statutes at large concerning the provision for the poor, being a collection of all the Acts of Parliament relating thereto, now in force... London: 1755. pp.121. G.

308. ANON. Considerations on the fatal effects... of the present excess of public charities... plan for a new system of poor laws proper. London: 1763. pp.53. G.

309. ANON. A proposal for the support and regulation of the poor, by subjecting them to the care, and maintaining them at the charge of their respective parishes, with notes and explanations in support of this scheme. Belfast: 1763. pp.37. CUL; QUB.

310. ANON. Inquiry into the management of the poor, and our usual polity respecting the common people, etc. London: 1767. pp.100. G.

311. ANON. A digest of the poor laws in order to their being reduced into one act. With references to the statutes, and marginal observations. 1768. pp.xxvii + 74 + (6) [by O. Ruffhead?]. CUL; G.

312. ANON. The miseries of the poor are a national sin, shame and charge: by making them happy, all shall pay old debts with new taxes. In passing one effective law concerning the poor... London: 1768. pp.(4) + xxii. TCD.

313. ANON. Parliamentary reports (first and second) on the laws concerning the poor, vagrants and houses of correction. 1775. Fol. n.l.

314. ANON. Account of the work-houses in Great Britain in the year 1732. London: 1786. pp.xvi + 202. G.

315. ANON. A draught of a bill for the relief and employment of the poor. With introductory remarks. With a summary of the statutes now in being for the above purposes. London: 1787. pp.44. X. [Introductory remarks signed "W".]

316. ANON. Parochial plan for ameliorating the condition of the labouring poor. London. 1800. pp.40. G.

317. ANON. Remarks on the poor law and on the state of the poor. Brentford: 1802. pp.166. G.

318. ANON. Remarks upon a Bill (as amended by the committee) 'for promoting and encouraging of industry amongst the labouring classes of the community and for the relief and regulation of the necessitous and criminal poor'. London: 1807. pp.31. G.

319. ANON. An essay on the poor laws, as they regard the real interests both of rich and poor. London: 1810. pp.52. G.

320. ANON. An Act for the better relief of the poor. London: 1813. pp.144. G.

321. ANON. The law of parochial settlement; with references to the latest editions of Burn, Bott, and Nolan. By a magistrate of the county of Essex. 2nd ed. London: 1815. pp.xxii + 191. CUL.

322. ANON. A dissertation on the poor laws. By a well-wisher to mankind. 1786. London: 1817. pp.120. RIA. [By Joseph Townsend].

323. ANON. Rapports presentes en 1817 et 1818 a la Chambre des Communes d'Angleterre par le comite charge de l'examen des lois rel aux pauvres. Paris: 1818. pp.xl + 164. G.

324. ANON. Remarks on the Report of the Select Committee of the House of Commons on the Poor Laws; in which the proposed alteration of the laws of settlement, and Pauperism, its causes, consequences, and remedies, are distinctly considered. By a Monmouthshire Magistrate. Bristol: 1818. pp.64. G; LSE; TCD. [By John H. Moggridge].

325. ANON. The oppressed labourers: the means for their relief. London: 1819. pp.viii + 40. G.

326. ANON. Justice to the poor and justice to every other class of the people as respects the situation of the poor and the state of agriculture and commerce. Northampton: 1820. pp.96. G.

327. ANON. Poor laws: the injustice, inexpediency and inhumanity of the present system. 2nd ed. Barnet: 1822. pp.14. BL.

328. ANON. Administration of the poor law. London: 1823. pp.42. LSE.

329. ANON Observations on the lawfulness and expediency of establishing fixed scales for the relief of the poor. London: 1825. pp.48. LSE.

330. ANON. A letter to the magistrates of the south and west of England, on the expediency and facility of correcting certain abuses of the poor laws. London: 1828. pp.30. TCD. [By G.J.D. Poulett Scrope].

331. ANON. "On the custom of making allowances out of the poor rate to able-bodied labourers in increase of their wages". <u>L.M.</u> 1. (1828-9). pp.90-8.

332. ANON. Report of the committee appointed for considering the best means to afford relief to the "working manufacturers"

suffering distress through want of employment. London: 1829. pp.124. G.

333.   ANON.   An enquiry into the principles of population, exhibiting a system of regulations for the poor. London: 1832. pp.xvi, 336. LSE.

334.   ANON. Administration of the poor law. n.p.: 1832. pp.40. G.

335.   ANON.   An enquiry into the principles of population, exhibiting a system of regulations for the poor. London: 1832. pp.xvi + 336. LSE.

336.   ANON. "Position of independent labourers under the operation of poor laws in England". N.Month.Mag. 37. (1833). pp.277-84.

337.   ANON. The poor law question. London: 1833. pp.27. LSE.

338.   ANON. Act for the amendment of the law relating to the poor. London: 1834. pp.(60) + 104. LSE.

339.   ANON. Hints on the mal-administration of the poor laws with a plan for bringing the collection and appropriation of the poor rates under the immediate superintendance and control of His Majesty's Government. Edinburgh: 1834. pp.29. NLI.

340.   ANON. The poor laws: their present operation, and their proposed amendment. Chiefly drawn from the evidence and reports of the Poor Law Commissioners. Section I. London: 1834. pp.52. RIA.

341.   ANON.   The poor laws: their present operation and their proposed amendment. London: 1834. pp.100. G.

342.   ANON. The new poor law. London: 1834. pp.29. LSE.

343.   ANON. Principles of delegated, central, and special authority applied to the Poor Law Amendment Bill. London: 1834. pp.16. LSE.

344.   ANON. Legislative reports on the poor laws, from the years 1817 to 1833 inclusive, with remedial measures proposed. London: 1834. pp.58. LSE; TCD.

345.   ANON. Remarks on the report of the Poor Law Commisssioners. London: [1834?]. pp.16. TCD.

346.   ANON. Able-bodied pauperism. London: 1835. pp.37. [Bound in 'Pamphlets: Poor Laws']. LSE.

347.   ANON.   Abolition of pauperism: A discovery in internal national polity to cause the abrogation of the poor law. London: 1835. pp.24. C.

348.   ANON. Act for the amendment of the law relating to the poor. London: 1836. pp.xxiv + 104. G; LSE.

349.   ANON.   "Fallacies on poor laws". Westm.Rev. 28. (1836-7).

pp.357-81.

350. ANON. Parish and the union; or, the poor and the poor law under the old system and the new. London: 1837. pp.viii + 246. G.

351. ANON. Hints on the new Poor Law Bill. Hull: 1837. pp.43. LSE.

352. ANON. Letter addressed to the Earl of Cawdor, on the poor law with an address to the members of benefit societies; by a magistrate. London: 1837. pp.v + 66. G.

353. ANON. Remarks on the new poor law. London: 1837. pp.28. LSE.

354. ANON. Robbers detected; or, a consideration of the cause and probable consequences of the passing of the Poor Law Amendment Act; by one of the Cobbett Club. London: 1842. pp.76. G.

355. ANON. Remarks on the 'Prohibitory Order' of the Poor Law Commissioners; and on the discretionary power of guardians. London: 1842. pp.23. LSE.

356. ANON. The Poor Law Amendment Act, an act (7 & 8 Vict. Cap.101) for the amendment of the laws relating to the poor in England and Wales. Passed 9th August 1844. With a copious index, by a barrister. London: [1844]. pp.31. G.

357. ANON. The English Poor Law and Poor Law Commission in 1847. London: 1847. pp.56. NLS; TCD; G; UCL.

358. ANON. The poor law and its medical officers. London: 1853.

359. ANON. The poor laws unmasked: being a general exposition of our workhouse institutions. By a late relieving officer. London: 1859. BL.

360. ANON. "The conference [on cooperation between charity and the poor law...]". Char.Org.Rep. (1872). pp.58-62.

361. ANON. "Out-door parish relief". Westm.Rev. 101. (1874). pp.323-34.

362. ANON. "Outdoor relief". Char.Org.Rep. 4. (1875). pp.87-88.

363. ANON. "Proceedings of council. Poor law relief". Char.Org.Rep. 4. (1875). pp.101-102.

364. ANON. "Proceedings of council. The effect of existing legislation upon the charities for the blind, idiotic, and other afflicted and neglected classes of the poor". Char.Org.Rep. 5. (1876). pp.1-2, 11-12.

365. ANON. "Proceedings of council. Legislation for the afflicted classes". Char.Org.Rep. 5. (1876). pp.37-38.

366. ANON. "Summary of the existing provisions for the care and education on imbeciles and idiots, with suggested further

arrangements". <u>Char.Org.Rep.</u> 5. (1876). pp.46-47.

367. ANON.   "Poor law conferences.   Restrictions on outdoor
      relief". <u>Char.Org.Rep.</u> 5. (1876). pp.142, 147-148, 163.

368. ANON.   "Proceedings of council.   Restrictions on outdoor
      relief". <u>Char.Org.Rep.</u> 5. (1876). pp.149-151.

369. ANON.   "Out-relief lists".   <u>Char.Org.Rep.</u>   6.   (1877).
      pp.68-69.

370. ANON. "Proceedings of council. The supplementation of poor
      law out-relief". <u>Char.Org.Rep.</u> 8. (1879). pp.18-21, 24-25.

371. ANON. "Election of guardians".   <u>Char.Org.Rep.</u> 9. (1880).
      pp.55-57.

372. ANON. "Proceedings of council. Out-relief". <u>Char.Org.Rep.</u>
      9. (1880). pp.126-127, 132-134.

373. ANON. "The work of women as poor law guardians". <u>Westm.Rev.</u>
      123. (1885). pp.386-95.

374. ANON. "The relief of the destitute". <u>Edin.Rev.</u> CLXIX. 346.
      (1889). pp.398-415.

375. ANON. "The Poor Law as an obstascle to thrift and voluntary
      insurance". <u>Char.Orgn.Rev.</u> 7. (1891). pp.113-25.

376. ANON. "Agencies and methods for dealing with the unemployed".
      <u>Lab.G.</u> 1. (1893). pp.162-163.

377. ANON. "Poor law reform". <u>Q.Rev.</u> CXCI. (1900). pp.155-75.

378. ANON.   "Relief of the unemployed".   <u>Lab.G.</u>   XII.   (1904).
      p.358.

379. ANON.   Poor law unions, England and Wales: abstract of
      statistics, with remarks. London: [1906?]. pp.iv + 31 +
      lxix. LSE.

380. ANON. Memorandum analysing the different branches of work
      comprised in the present poor law system. n.p. 1908. pp.15.
      LSE.

381. ANON. "The poor law report of 1909". <u>Edin.Rev.</u> CCIX. 428.
      (1909). pp.439-73.

382. ANON. "Royal Commission on the Poor Laws". <u>Lab.G.</u> XVII.
      (1909). pp.77-79.

383. ANON. New poor law or no poor law. Being a description of
      the majority and minority reports of the Poor Law Commission.
      [With an introductory note by Canon Barnett]. London: 1909.
      pp.173. CUL.

384. ANON. The Poor Law Commission and the medical profession; by
      a medical practitioner. London: 1909. pp.16. LSE.

385. ANON. The minority report: a criticism. London: 1910.

pp.32.   LSE; CUL.

386. ANON.   Out-door relief orders: report of the Departmental
      Commission. n.p. [1911]. pp.123. LSE.

387. ANON.   Conference of Northern Poor-Law Unions and other local
      authorities, distress due to unemployment: deputation to the
      Minister of Labour Sir Arthur Steel-Maitland, 27th October,
      1927: Report of Proceedings. n.p. n.d. pp.29. LSE.

388. ANON.   Prospects and present condition of the labouring
      classes, considered with respect to the probable operation of
      the new poor law. London: n.d. pp.14. [In 'Pamphlets: Poor
      Laws']. LSE.

389. A BARRISTER.   An elementary ABC guide to the poor law.
      London: 1895. pp.vii + 32. BM.

390. ADAMS, A.M. Report of an inspection of English... workhouses,
      etc. London: 1848. pp.38. G. Report on an inspection of
      English and Irish workhouses; with observations on the
      operation of the poor laws. Glasgow: 1848. pp.38. G.

391. AITKEN, W.   An essay on remedies for the relief... of the
      labouring population etc. Ayr: 1847. pp.104. G.

392. ALCOCK, T. Observations on the defects of the poor laws, and
      on the causes and consequences of the great increase and
      burden of the poor, with a proposal for redressing these
      grievances, in a letter to a member of Parliament. London:
      1752. pp.76. CUL.

393. ALLEN, W.   A plan for diminishing the poor's rates in
      agricultural districts. London: 1833. pp.ii + 28. LSE.

394. AMOS, A. Lectures on the poor law, etc. London: 183-
      (irregular). fo.287. LSE.

395. ANSTRUTHER, I. The scandal of the Andover workhouse. London:
      1973. pp.xiv + 176. CUL.

396. ARCHBOLD, J.F. The Act for the amendment of the poor laws,
      1834... with introduction, notes and forms. London: 1834.
      pp.iv + 162. BL. 2nd ed. 1834. pp.vi + 162. CUL. 3rd ed.
      1835. pp.xii + 269. CUL. 4th ed. 1836. pp.xii + 290.
      CUL. 5th ed. 1839. pp.xii + 319. BL; CUL.

397. ARCHBOLD, J.F. The Act for the Amendment of the Poor Laws,
      with a practical introduction and forms. 3rd ed. (With many
      valuable additions... and an Appendix.) London: 1835.
      pp.267. G.

398. ARCHBOLD, J.F.   The poor law, comprising all the
      authorities... London: 1840. 3rd ed. 1844. pp.xlii + 656.
      [entitled The poor law, comprising all the authorities to
      October, 1843]. CUL. 4th ed. 1845. pp.1697. [... to October
      1844]. CUL. 6th ed. 1850. pp.lv + 807. [entitled: The poor
      law, comprising the whole of the law of settlement, and all
      the authorities upon the poor law generally brought down to
      April 1850...]. CUL. 7th ed. 1853. pp.lxiii + 902. [...

brough down to March, 1853]. CUL. 9th ed. 1858. pp.lx +
843. Index. [... brought down to Trinity term, 1857]. CUL.
10th ed. 1860. pp.liv + 838. Index. [... brought down to
Michaelmas term, 1859]. CUL. 12th ed. [by W. Cunningham Glen].
1873. pp.xliv + 1047. [entitled: The poor law, comprising
the whole of the law of relief, settlement, and removal of the
poor; together with the law relating to the poor rate]. CUL.
13th ed. 1878. pp.xlvii + 1106. LSE; CUL. 14th ed. 1885.
pp.xlviii + 1090. [entitled: The poor law, together with the
law relating to pauper lunatics and the poor rate]. CUL. 15th
ed. [by J.B. Little]. 1898. pp.lii + 1078 + 140. CUL. 16th
ed. [by E. Gilbert Woodward]. 1930. pp.xliii + 490 + 65.
[entitled: Archbold's poor law]. CUL.

399. ARCHBOLD, J.F. The law relative to pauper lunatics;... also
the law and practice in appeals against lunatic orders.
London: 1851. pp.xvi + 228. CUL.

400. ARCHBOLD, J.F. Abridgement of poor law cases, Vol.3.
1842-58. 1858. [Source: SM 2]. BL.

401. ARCHBOLD, J.F. The consolidated and other orders of the Poor
Law Commissioners and of the Poor Law Board... London: 1859.
pp.vi + 404. CUL.

402. ARCHBOLD, J.F. The poor law: comprising the whole of the law
of relief, settlement, and removal of the poor. London:
1878. pp.dlvii + 1106. LSE.

403. ARCHBOLD, J.F. The new Poor Law Amendment Act, and the recent
rules and orders of the Poor Law Commissioners. With a
practical introduction, notes and forms. London: 1842.
pp.170. TCD.

404. ARCHBOLD, J.F. Buller's Acts, 11 & 12 Victoria, cc.82, 91,
114; relating to the payment of parochial debts, the audit of
accounts, the chargeability of paupers upon unions, and the
education of the infant poor, with practical notes and index.
London: 1848. pp.58. TCD.

405. ARCHER, T. The pauper, the thief, and the convict: sketches
of some of their homes, haunts and habits. London: 1865.
pp.(4) + 239. CUL.

406. ASCHROTT, P.F. The English poor law system: past and
present. [Das Englische Armen-Wesen]. Trans. Herbert Preston-
Thomas. London: 1888. pp.xvii + 332. CUL; DHSS. 2nd ed.
1902. pp.xxx + 376. CUL; LSE.

407. ASCHROTT, P.F. Die Entwickelung des Armenwesens in England
seit dem Jahre 1885. Leipzig: 1898. pp.68. LSE.

408. ASHDOWNE, J. An essay on the existing poor-laws...; means of
bettering the condition of the poor, etc. London: 1817.
pp.30. G.

409. AUSTIN, R.C. The Metropolitan Poor Act, 1867. London: 1867.
pp.xxx + 50. G.

410. AVELING, H.F. & OTHERS. The history sheet or case-paper

system. London: 1909. pp.167. CUL.

411. BAGLEY, J.J. & BAGLEY, A.J. The English poor law. London: 1966. pp.72. DHSS.

412. BAILEY, W. A treatise on the better employment, and more comfortable support, of the poor in workhouses. Together with some observations on the growth and culture of flex. With divers new inventions, neatly engraved on copper, for the improvement of the linen manufacture, of which the importance and advantages are considered and evinced. London: 1758. pp.79. CUL.

413. BAILWARD, W.A. The reports of the Poor Law Commissions of 1834 and 1909. London: 1909. pp.16. LSE.

414. BAILWARD, W.A. "Recent developments of poor relief". E.J. XXII. (1912). pp.542ff.

415. BAILWARD, W.A. Some recent developments of poor relief. London: 1914. pp.46. LSE.

416. BAKER, B. "Poor law and charity". Char.Org.Rep. 9. (1880). pp.261-63.

417. BAKER, T.B.L. "Administration of poor law relief". Char.Org.Rep. 6. (1877). pp.112-113.

418. BANFILL, S. A letter to Sir T.D. Acland containing hints for improving the condition of the laboring classes and reducing parochial assessments, by adapting the poor law. Exeter: 1817. pp.17. G.

419. BARNES, W. The rights of the necessitous considered. London: 1841. pp.31. G.

420. BARNETT, A. The poor laws and their administration. London: 1833. pp.88. G.

421. BARNETT, DAME H.O.W. The ethics of the poor law. Derby: [1907]. pp.6. LSE.

422. BARNETT, S.A. "Poor law reform". Contemp.Rev. LXIII. (1893). pp.322-34.

423. BARROW, F.W. "Church and poor law reform". Westm.Rev. 165. (1906). pp.387-400.

424. BARTLEY, G.C.T. A handy-book for guardians of the poor. London: 1876. pp.vii + 234. LSE.

425. BATE, H. A few observations respecting the... state of the poor; and the defects of the poor laws: with some remarks upon parochial assessments, and expenditures. London: 1802. pp.36. G. 3rd ed. London: 1802. pp.36. G.

426. BAUKE, A.C. Poor law guardian, his powers and duties in the right execution of his office. London: 1862. pp.vi + 143. CUL.

427. BAUKE, A.C. The poor law guardian: his powers and duties. London: 1872. pp.viii + 37. LSE.

428. BAXTER, G.R.W. The book of the Bastiles; or, the history of the working of the new poor law. London: 1841. pp.xiii + 609. LSE.

429. BAXTER, S.S. Poor laws, stated and considered: the evils of the present system exposed, and a plan suggested, founded on the true principles of political economy, for placing such laws on a firm and equitable basis. London: 1831. pp.42. NLI; TCD; LSE.

430. BAYLDON, R. Hints on legislation for bettering the condition of the poor. [Leeds: 1844]. pp.16. C.

431. BAYLEE, J.T. "The minimum wage and the poor law". Westm.Rev. 152. (1899). p.628-40.

432. BEALES, H.L. "The passing of the poor law". Pol.Q. XIX. (1948). pp.312-22.

433. BELLERS, J. An essay for employing the poor to profit, humbly dedicated to the Lords and Commons of Great Britain. London: 1723. pp.8. BL.

434. BELLERS, J. An essay toward the improvement of physick [...] with an essay for imploying the able poor. London: 1714. pp.58. BL.

435. BELSHAM, W. Remarks on the Bill for the better support and maintenance of the poor, etc. London: 1797. pp.20. G.

436. BENTHAM, F.H. The position of the poor law in the problem of poverty. London: 1905. pp.25.

437. BENTHAM, J. Situation and relief of the poor. London: 1797. pp.34. LSE.

438. BENTHAM, J. Outline of a work entitled, Pauper management improved. London: [1798]. pp.288. G; U.

439. BENTHAM, J. Pauper management improved, particularly by means of an application of the panopticon principle of construction, etc. London: 1812. pp.322. G.

440. BENTHAM, J. Observations on the Poor Bill, introduced by the Right Honourable William Pitt. Written February, 1797. London: [1838]. pp.48. G. In his Works. London: 1843. Vol.8. pp.440-59. LSE.

441. BENTLEY, J. Exposition of the monstrous conspiracy against the interests and rights of the provident classes, by poor law officials, banks. London: [1870]. pp.158. LSE.

442. BERESFORD, P. "The relieving officer: poor law personified". N.S. 14. (1969). pp.721-723.

443. [BERNARD, SIR T.]. Case on the Act for the Relief of the Poor, submitted to the opinion of Mr. Serjeant Snigge. n.p.

[1803?]. pp.14. RIA. Another ed. London: 1837. pp.26.
TCD.

444. BERNARD, T. A letter to the Lord Bishop of Durham on the
principle and detail of the measures now under the
consideration of Parliament for promoting and encouraging
industry, and for the relief and regulation of ·the poor.
London: 1807. pp.66. G.

445. BICHENO, J.E. An inquiry into the nature of benevolence,
chiefly with a view to elucidate the principle of the poor
laws and to show their immoral tendency. London: 1817.
pp.iv + 145. LSE.

446. BICHENO, J.E. An inquiry into the poor laws as a scheme of
national benevolence. London: 1824. pp.xvi + 162. U.

447. BIRLEY, M. et al. New poor law or no poor law; being a
description of the majority and minority reports of the Poor
Law Commission, etc. London: 1909. pp.xiii + 176. LSE.

448. BLAUG, M. "The myth of the old poor law and the making of the
new". J.Econ.Hist. XXIII. (1963). pp.151-84.

449. BLAUG, M. "The poor law report re-examined". J.Econ.Hist.
XXIV. (1964). pp.229-45.

450. BLEAMIRE, W. Remarks on the poor law and the maintenance of
the poor. London: 1800. pp.36. LSE.

451. BLYTH, M.E. The poor law and the people. London: 1930.
pp.22.

452. BONE, J. Outline of a plan for reducing the poor's rate.
London: 1805. pp.61. G.

453. BONE, J. The wants of the people and the means of the
government; or, Objections to the interference... affairs of
the poor, etc. London: 1807. pp.105. C.

454. BONGARS, Y. Les regulations en detresse de la Grande
Bretagne. Brest: 1938. pp.120. LSE.

455. BOOTH, C. Reform of the poor law by the adaptation of the
existing poor law areas and their administration, etc. n.p.:
[1910]. pp.38. LSE.

456. BOOTH, C. Comments on proposals for the reform of the poor
law. n.p.: [1911]. pp.23. LSE.

457. BOOTH, C. Poor law reform. Being memoranda submitted in 1907
to the Royal Commission on the Poor Law and Relief of
Distress. London: 1910. pp.92. LSE; CUL. New issue with
additional remarks. 1911. pp.136. CUL.

458. BOOTH, C. "Poor law statistics". E.J. VI. (1896).
pp.70ff.

459. BOOTH, H. The question of the poor law considered, and the
causes of pauperism, in connection with the principle of

population. London: 1818. pp.48. G.

460. BOOTH, W. The Salvation Army and poor law reform. London: 1909. pp.xxxvi + 64. LSE.

461. BOSANQUET, B. "The limitations of the poor law". E.J. II. (1892). pp.369-71.

462. BOSANQUET, H. The poor law report of 1909: a summary explaining the defects of the present system and the principal recommendations of the Commission, so far as relates to England and Wales. London: 1909. pp.vi + 263. LSE; DHSS; CUL.

463. BOSANQUET, H. Reform of the poor law. London: 1909. pp.15. LSE.

464. BOSANQUET, H. "The historical basis of English poor-law policy". E.J. XX. 78. (1910). pp.182-94.

465. BOSWORTH, J. The necessity of the anti-pauper system. London: 1829. pp.xii + 52. G.

466. BOSWORTH, J. The practical means of reducing the poor's rate, encouraging virtue. London: 1824. pp.vii + 48. G; TCD.

467. BOSWORTH, J. Misery in the midst of plenty; or, The perversions of the poor law. London: 1833. pp.(38). G.

468. BOTT, E. A collection of decisions of the Court of King's Bench upon the poor's law, down to the present time...; to which are prefixed, extracts from the statutes concerning the poor. London: 1773. pp.(48) + lxxxii + 401. LSE.

469. BOTT, E. Collection of decisions of the Court of King's Bench upon the poor's laws. With extracts from the statutes concerning the poor. [First edition anonymous]. London: 1771. 8vo eds. pp.(35) + 291 + (73).. 2nd ed. 1773. pp.(48) + 398 + (73). 3rd ed. with a digest by Francis Const. 1793. 2 vols. G. 4th ed. by F. Const. 1800. 3 vols. LSE. 5th ed. by F. Const. 1807. 3 vols. supplements, Pt.1 to Hilary Term, 1814, 8vo, 1815; Pt.2 to 1820. G. 6th ed. by J.T. Pratt. 1827. 2 vols. supplement, including cases 1827-33. 8vo.

470. BOWEN, J. New poor law. The Bridgewater case. Is killing in an union workhouse criminal, if sanctioned by the Poor Law Commissioners? A question raised on certain facts deposed to on oath before a late Committee of the House of Lords and... submitted to the... consideration of both Lords and Commons. London: 1839. pp.iv + 92. G.

471. BOWEN, J. The union work-house and board of guardians system as worked under the control of Poor Law Commissioners; exemplified by official documents and plan: with an address to Sir Robert Peel. London: 1842. pp.63. G.

472. BRADDON, L. An abstract of the draught of a bill for relieving, reforming and employing the poor. London: 1714. pp.xxxvi + 24. G.

473. BRADDON, L.   An abstract of the draught of a bill for relieving, reforming, and employing the poor... Hereunto is prefix'd, a brief account of what was done by both Lords and Commons in 1704, for reducing all laws, relating to the poor, into one general bill - and also herein is set forth, the principal considerations, upon which this scheme is grounded, and the publick benefit from thence proceeding. n.p.: [1717?]. pp.24. G.

474. BRADDON, L. An humble proposal for relieving, reforming and employing the poor. And herein by vertue of one general law, instead of near forty statutues... London: 1720. pp.59. G. Another ed. London: 1721. pp.96. G. French translation entitled Plan pour assister, corriger & emploier tous les pauvres de la Grande Bretagne... London: 1721. Manchester Public Library.

475. BRADDON, L. The form of a petition submitted to... those noblemen and gentlemen who desire to subscribe... for relieving, reforming and employing the poor... Westminster, etc. London: 1722. pp.40. G.

476. BRADDON, L.   Particular answers to the most material objections made to the proposal humbly presented to His Majesty for relieving, reforming, and employing all the poor of Great Britain. n.p.: 1722. pp.104 + 19. BL; G.

477. BRADLAUGH, C. Parliament and the poor: what the legislature can do. London: 1889. pp.14. LSE.

478. BRAND, J. Observations on some of the probable effects of Mr. Gilbert's Bill [for the relief and employment of the poor], etc. London: 1776. pp.ii + 121. G.

479. BRERETON, C.D. Observations on the administration of the poor law in agricultural districts. Norwich: [1824?]. pp.i + 124. G.

480. BRERETON, C.D. An inquiry into the workhouse system and the law of maintenance in agricultural districts. Norwich:[1824?] . pp.124. CUL. 2nd ed. London; Norwich: 1826. pp.124. LSE.

481. BRERETON, C.D. The subordinate magistracy and parish system considered, in their connexion with the causes and remedies of modern pauperism, with some observations on the relief of the poor in England, Scotland, and Ireland, and on parochial emigration. London: [1827]. pp.222. NLI; TCD.

482. BRIGGS, E. "The myth of the pauper disqualification". Soc. Pol. & Admin. 13. (1979). pp.138-41.

483. BROOKER, C. Appeal to the British nation as to a petition for the repeal of the Poor Law Amendment Act. Brighton: 1840. pp.vii + 31. LSE.

484. BROOKES, S. Thoughts on the poor law; with a plan for reducing the poors' rates, preparatory to their abolition. London: 1822. pp.43. G.

485. BROUGHAM, H. Corrected report of the speech of [Brougham] on moving the second reading of the Bill to amend the Poor Law. London: 1834. pp.65. G.

486. BROWN, J. "The appointment of the 1905 Poor Law Commission". Inst.Hist.Res.Bull. XLII. (1969). pp.239-42.

487. BROWN, J. "The poor law commission and 1905 Unemployed Workmen Act". Inst.Hist.Res.Bull. 44. (1971). pp.318-23.

488. BRUNDAGE, A. "Landed interests and the new poor law: a reappraisal of the revolution in government". E.H.R. 87. (1972). pp.27-48; 90. (1975). pp.347-51.

489. BRYDGES, S.E. Letters on the poor law. London: 1813. pp.72. G.

490. BULL, G.S. The new poor law, shewn to be unconstitutional etc. London: 1838. pp.16. G.

491. BURN, R. The history of the Poor Laws: with observations. London: 1764. pp.295. CUL; Sq; LSE; G.

492. BURN, R. Observations on the Bill... for the better relief and employment of the poor, etc. London: 1776. pp.56. G.

493. BURNS, R. Historical dissertations on the law and practice of Great Britain, and particularly of Scotland, with regard to the poor, on the modes of charity, and on the means of promoting the improvement of the people. Edinburgh: 1819. pp.xviii + 503. LSE.

494. BUTTERWORTH, J. A compendium of the law respecting the poor. London: 1803. pp.vi + 324. LSE.

495. CALDWELL, J.S. A digest of the laws relating to the poor. London: 1821. pp.xv + 456. CUL; BL; LI; LSE. 2nd ed. 1825. n.l. [Source: SM 2].

496. CALVERT, F. Suggestions for a change in administration of the poor law. London: 1831. pp.53. G.

497. CAMERON, C.H. & OTHERS. Two reports addressed to His Majesty's Commissioners appointed to inquire into the administration and operation of the poor laws. London: 1834. pp.228. G; CUL; BL.

498. CAMPBELL, J.F. A letter on the poor law. London: 1837. pp.v + 66. U.

499. CANNAN, E. "The stigma of pauperism". Econ.Rev. V. (1895). pp.380-91.

500. CAPLAN, M. "The new poor law and the struggle for union chargeability". Int. Rev. Soc. Hist. 24. (1979). pp.267-300.

501. [CARMALT, W.] A letter to the Right Honourable George Canning on the principle and administration of the English poor law;

by a select vestryman of the parish of Putney. London: 1823. pp.v + 90. LSE.

502. CARPENTER, D. Reflections suggested by Mr. Whitbread's bill on the subject of the poor law with the outlines of a further plan. London: 1807. pp.xvi + 70. G.

503. [CARTER, S.] Legal provisions for the poor; or, treatise of the common and statute laws concerning the poor, either as to relief, settlement or punishment. By S.C. 16mo eds. pp.(12) + 494 + (42). 1710. 3rd ed. 1718. G. 4th ed. pp.(18) + 358 + 21. 1720. 5th ed. pp.(12) + 387 + (38). 16mo. 1725. G. (3rd and 4th eds., entitled "Laws concerning the poor, etc." Anon.)

504. CARY, J. A proposal offered to the committee of the House of Commons appointed to consider ways for the better providing for the poor and setting them on work. London: [1696?]. pp. 8. G.

505. CENTRAL (UNEMPLOYED) BODY FOR LONDON. A report upon the work and procedure of the distress committees in London... London: 1907. pp.15. LSE.

506. CHADWICK, Sir E. Article on the principle and progress of the Poor Law Amendment Act, etc. London: 1837. pp.75. (See "Pamphlets: Poor Laws"). LSE.

507. CHALMERS ASSOCIATION FOR DIFFUSING INFORMATION ON IMPORTANT SOCIAL QUESTIONS. Pauperism and the poor laws: the lectures delivered... under the auspices of the Chalmers Association, in 1869-70 with kindred papers; edited by Thomas Ivory. Edinburgh: 1870. pp.vi + (229). LSE.

508. CHALMERS, DR. "'A comparison of Scotch and English pauperism' being the substance of an article in the Edinburgh Review of February, 1818, entituled Report from the Select Committee on the Poor Laws... 1817". In: Dr. Chalmers and the Poor Laws. [Preface by Mrs. George Kerr and Introduction by Miss Grace Chalmers Wood]. Edinburgh: 1911. pp.1-62. CUL.

509. CHALMERS, T. On the parliamentary means for the abolition of pauperism in England, etc. Glasgow: 1824. pp.34. LSE.

510. CHAMBERS, G.F. A handy digest of cases relating to poor law matters, comprising all the recent and many of the old cases. London: 1896. pp.vii + 112. Sq; CUL.

511. CHANCE, SIR W. The better administration of the poor law. London: 1895. pp.xii + 260. (Charity organisation series). BL.

512. CHANCE, W. "The Elberfeld and English poor law systems". E.J. VII. (1897). pp.332ff.

513. CHANCE, W. Principle and practice of the English poor law. London: [1902?]. pp.19. LSE.

514. CHANCE, W. Poor law reform: via tertia: the case for the guardians. London: 1910. pp.95. LSE; CUL; S.

515. CHANCE, W. The Ministry of Health and the poor law. London: 1923. pp.12. S.

516. CHAPMAN, J. Three essays on the poor law, with introductions: the workhouse; the tramp question; and out-door relief. Macclesfield: 1881. pp.46. LSE.

517. CHAPMAN, S.J. & HALLSWORTH, H.M. Unemployment. The results of an investigation made in Lancashire and an examination of the report of the Poor Law Commission. Manchester: 1909. pp.164. CUL.

518. CHARITY ORGANISATION SOCIETY. The state and the unemployed, with notes regarding the action of vestries in different parts of London, 1892-3. London: 1893. pp.30. LSE.

519. CHARITY ORGANISATION SOCIETY. Poor law commissioners for London. London: 1926. pp.10. LSE.

520. CHECKLAND, S.G. & CHECKLAND, E.D.A. (eds.). Poor Law Report of 1834. Harmondsworth: 1974. pp.518. CUL.

521. CHESHIRE, E. Statistics of poor relief in England and Wales for the year 1851; compiled from the 4th annual report of the Poor Law Board. Dublin: 1853. pp.18. (Dublin Statistical Society. [Publications]. No.76). LSE.

522. CHEVALLIER, E. La loi des pauvres et la societe Anglaise. Paris: 1895. pp.412. LSE; G.

523. CHOLMLEY, G. A discussion on the poor law of England and Scotland, on the state of the poor of Ireland and on emigration. London: 1827. pp.vi + 128. G.

524. CLARK, W. Thoughts on the management and relief of the poor; on the cause of their increase; and on the measures that may be best calculated to amend the former, and check the latter. Bath: 1815. pp.68. KI; TCD.

525. CLARKE, J.J. Social administration including the poor laws. London: 1922. pp.viii + 364. DHSS; LSE; CUL. 2nd ed. 1935. pp.xi + 776. DHSS; CUL. 3rd ed. 1939. [entitled Social administration (including the poor laws)]. pp.x + 784. CUL. 4th ed. 1946. [entitled Social administration]. pp.x + 774. DHSS; CUL.

526. CLARKE, J.S. "The break-up of the poor law". In M.I. Cole (ed.). The Webbs and their work. London: 1949. pp.101-15.

527. CLARKSON, W. An inquiry into the cause of the increase of pauperism and poor rates; with a remedy for the same, and a proposition for equalising the rates throughout England and Wales. London: 1815. pp.78. KI; TCD.

528. CLAY, A. & OTHERS. The manufacture of paupers. London: 1907. pp.vi + 140. S.

529. CLAY, A. The principles of poor law reform. London: 1910. pp.38. CUL.

530. CLIFFORD, M. Poor-law work: suggestions and new departures. 2nd ed. London and Bristol: 1897. pp.51.

531. CLIVE, A. A few words to the poor and to overseers, on the new poor law. Birmingham: 1836. pp.8. [In "Pamphlets: Poor Laws"]. LSE. 1837. C.

532. COATS, A.W. "Economic thought and poor law policy in the eighteenth century". Ec.H.R. (2nd ser.). 13. (1960-61). pp.39-51.

533. COATS, A.W. "The relief of poverty, attitudes to labour, and economic change in England, 1660-1782". Int.Rev.Soc.Hist. XXI. (1976). pp.98-115.

534. COBBETT, J.P. Petition to the House of Commons against the poor law separation of man from wife. London: [1836]. pp.16. G.

535. COLQUHOUN, P. The state of indigence and the situation of the casual poor in the metropolis explained;... with suggestions shewing the necessity... of an establishment of pauper police, etc. London: 1799. pp.32. G.

536. COLQUHOUN, P. A treatise on indigence; exhibiting a general view of the national resources for productive labour, etc. London: 1806. pp.xii + 307. LSE; G.

537. COPLAND, W. A letter to the Rev. C.D. Brereton, in reply to his "Observations on the administration of the poor laws in agricultural districts", etc. Norwich: 1824. pp.126. TCD.

538. [COPLESTON, E.] A letter to the Right Honourable Robert Peel on the pernicious effects of a variable standard of value, especially as it regards the condition of the lower orders and the poor laws. Oxford: 1819. pp.102. LSE.

539. [COPLESTON, E.] A second letter to the Right Honourable Robert Peel on the causes of the increase of pauperism, and on the poor laws. Oxford: 1819. pp.111. LSE.

540. CORMACK, U. The welfare state: the Royal Commission on the Poor Laws, 1905-1909, and the welfare state. London: Family Welfare Association. 1953. pp.33. (Lock Memorial Lecture, 1953). DHSS.

541. COSTELLOE, B.F.C. The reform of the poor law. London: [1891]. pp.15. LSE.

542. COUNTY COUNCILS ASSOCIATION. Proposals for poor law administration, after consideration of majority and minority reports... London: 1911. pp.vii + 86.

543. COURTENAY, T.P. A treatise upon the poor law. London: 1818. pp.vi + 168. LSE; G; KI; TCD.

544. COWELL, J.W. A letter to the Rev. John T. Becher, of Southwell, in reply to certain charges... made in the introduction to a second edition of his anti-apuper system,

etc. London: 1834. pp.62. LSE.

545.   COX, H. "The value of the poor law". Fort.Rev. 85. (1909). pp.123-35.

546.   CRAIGIE, P.G. "The English poor rate: some recent statistics of its administration and pressure". R.Statist.Soc.J. LI. (1888). pp.450-93.

547.   CROS-MAYREVIEILLE, G. Le droit des pauvres... en Europe, etc. Paris: 1889. pp.xxii + 208. S.

548.   CROWDER, A.G. "The strict administration of the poor law". Char.Org.Rep. 6. (1877). pp.108-110.

549.   CROWDER, A.G. Statement for the information of the Royal Commission on the Poor Law and Relief of Distress. London: 1906. pp.16. LSE.

550.   CURTIS, SIR J. "The English poor law system". Pub.Admin. IV. (1926). p.52.

551.   CUTTLE, G. The legacy of the rural guardians. A study of conditions in mid-Essex. Cambridge: 1934. pp.viii + 384. CUL.

552.   DAKYNS, A.L. "Bentham's influence in municipal and poor law reform". Pub.Admin. XIII. (1935). pp.44-50.

553.   DALTON, J.H.C. Poor law reform. Cambridge: 1910. pp.23.

554.   DAVEY, H. The Poor Law Act, 1897, with notes and appendix. London: 1897. pp.51. BL.

555.   DAVEY, H. The Poor Law Acts, 1894-1908, revised and annotated, with notes of decisions of the courts, and of the orders of the local government board and other departments. London: 1909. pp.xxiv + 400. CUL.

556.   DAVEY, H. & SMITH, A.J. The Poor Law Statutes, annotated, being the consolidating Poor Law Act of 1927, as recently amended... with... explanatory notes. London: 1928. pp.xxxvi + 463. CUL. (Supplement). 1929. pp.96. CUL. 2nd ed. entitled Poor Law statutes and orders. Being the consolidating Poor Law Act of 1930 with the other enactments and orders of the Minister of Health relating to powers and duties of the poor law authorities... 1930. pp.xxxix + 507. Sq; CUL.

557.   DAVEY, S. Maintenance and desertion under the poor law and under the Summary Jurisdiction (Separation and Maintenance) Acts 1895 to 1925 with a chapter on affiliation orders. London: 1928. pp.xxxv + 231. DHSS.

558.   DAVISON, J. Considerations on the poor laws. Oxford: 1817. pp.126. KI.

559.   DAY, W. An inquiry into the poor laws and surplus labour, and their mutual reaction. London: 1832. n.l. with postscript. 1833. pp.114. BL. G.

560. DAY, W. Correspondence with the Poor Law Commissioners, with observations on the working of certain points of the poor law and on Sir James Graham's proposed alteration in the law of settlement. London: 1844. BL.

561. DEACON, E.E. Guide to magistrates out of session, including a digest of the poor laws, with practical forms of orders, commitments, and convictions. London: 1843. 2 vols. pp.xxxii + 1594. CUL.

562. DEARLE, N.B. "The poor law and the unemployed". E.J. XVI. (1906). pp.1241ff.

563. DEARMER, P. The reform of the poor law. London: 1908. pp.14. (Christian Social Union Pamphlet 16).

564. DEAS, A.O. (ed.). The poor law and local government magazine. Edinburgh: 1903-21. Vols.3-19. BL. Vols.13-31.

565. DENISON, W. Abstract of evidence taken before the committee appointed by the House of Commons, the 27th February, 1837 to inquire into the operation and effect of the Poor Law Amendment Act, with introductory remarks. London: 1837. pp.132. G; TCD.

566. DEPARTMENTAL COMMITTEE ON ADMINISTRATION OF OUTDOOR RELIEF. Report. London: 1911. pp.62. (Cd. 5525). LSE.

567. DEPARTMENTAL COMMITTEE ON THE RELIEF OF THE CASUAL POOR. Report. London: 1930. pp.99. (Cmd.3640). (B.P.P. 1929-30, XVII). LSE.

568. DEPARTMENTAL COMMITTEE ON POOR LAW ORDERS. Report. London: 1913. pp.89. (Cd. 6988). LSE.

569. DICKSON, T.A. "The report of the Royal Commission on the Poor Laws". Survey.Instn.Trans. XLII. (1909-10). pp.363-422.

570. DIGBY, A. The poor law in nineteenth-century England and Wales. London: 1982. pp.40. (Historical Association General Series No.104). CUL.

571. DILL, T.R.C. The Poor Law Guardians' and District Councillors' election manual... London: 1894. pp.xv + 306. CUL.

572. DODD, F.S. Poor law reform. Oxford: 1890. pp.19.

573. DODD, J.T. The unemployed and the powers of the guardians of the poor. London: 1903. pp.19.

574. DODD, J.T. Notes on the administration of relief to the poor and the infantile mortality in London unions. Oxford: 1906. pp.8. LSE. (Pamphlet Collection).

575. DODD, J.T. Administrative reform and the Local Government Board. London: 1906. pp.xxxiii + 105. LSE.

576. DODD, J.T. Mistakes of the Local Government Board and of

other 'authorities' in poor law administration, being a memorandum laid before the Poor Law Commission. Oxford, London: 1908. pp.12. BL.

577.   DODD, J.T.   The majority report of the Poor Law Commission, and why we should reject it. London: 1910. pp.19. LSE.

578.   DODD, J.T.   The poor and their rights: how to obtain them under existing legislation. London: 1910. pp.28. LSE.

579.   DRAGE, G.   "Poor law reform". Econ.Rev.   VIII.   (1889). pp.77-87).

580.   DRAGE, G.   Public assistance. London: 1930.   pp.xiv + 396. CUL; DHSS; LSE.

581.   DUDLEY, SIR H.B.   A few observations respecting the present state of the poor. London: 1802. pp.36. LSE.

582.   DUMSDAY, W.H.   The relieving officers' handbook, being a complete and practical guide to the law relating to the powers, duties and liabilities of relieving officers. London: 1902. pp.xxii + 211. CUL. 2nd ed. 1912. pp.xxx + 264. 3rd ed. 1923. pp.xxx + 285. CUL. 4th ed. 1929. pp.xxxii + 365. [By the author and (with) John Moss]. CUL. 5th ed. 1930. pp.xxxii + 362. 6th ed. 1935. pp.xxxiii + 416. BL. 7th ed. 1938. p.xxx + 447. [By John Moss]. DHSS; Sq.

583.   DUMSDAY, W.H.   Hadden's overseers' handbook: being a complete and practical guide to the law relating to the powers, duties and liabilities of overseers, etc. London: 1906. pp.xlii + 435. LSE.

584.   DUMSDAY, W.H.   The Poor Law Institutions Order, 1913... London: 1914. pp.235.

585.   DUNKLEY, P.   "The landed interest and the new poor law: a critical note". E.H.R.   88. (1973). pp.836-4.

586.   DUNKLEY, P.   "The 'hungry forties' and the poor law: a case study". Hist.J.   17. (1974). p.329.

587.   DUNKLEY, P.   "Paternalism, the magistracy and poor relief in England 1795-1834".   Int. Rev. Soc. Hist.   24.   (1979). pp.371-97.

588.   DUNKLEY, P.   "Whigs and paupers: the reform of the English poor laws, 1830-1834".   J.Brit.Stud.   20.   (1980-81). pp.124-49.

589.   DUNSTAN, J.   A treatise on the poor law of England, being a review of the origin, and various alterations that have been made in the law of settlements and removals. London: 1850. pp.xvi + 258. CUL.

590.   EDEN, SIR F.M.   State of the poore;   or an history of the labouring classes in England from the conquest to the present period;   with a chronological table of the prices of labour, provisions, etc. 1797. 3 vols. CUL; LSE. (Abridged edition edited by A.G.L. Rogers with an introduction.). 1928. pp.li

+ 383. CUL; LSE.

591. EDEN, SIR F.M. Etat des pauvres; ou histoire des classes travaillantes de la societe en Angleterre, etc. Paris:[1800]. pp.262. LSE.

592. EDINBURGH REVIEW. An article on the principle and progress of the Poor Law Amendment Act. London: 1837. pp.75. LSE.

593. EDMONDS, G. Edmonds's appeal to the labourers of England: an exposure of aristocratic spies and machinery of the Poor Law Murder Bill. London: 1836. pp.12. G.

594. EDSALL, N.C. The anti-poor law movement 1834-44. Manchester: 1971. pp.285. CUL.

595. ELTON, G.R. "An early Tudor poor law". Ec.H.R. (2nd ser.). VI. (1953-54). pp.55-67.

596. EMMINGHAUS, C.B.A. Poor relief in different parts of Europe. London: 1873. pp.xi + 314. LSE.

597. ENSOR, G. The poor and their relief. London: 1823. pp.384. G; NLI.

598. EVEREST, H.B. A practical treatise showing how the case paper system can be worked. London: [1912]. pp.96. LSE.

599. EXLEY, C.H. The guide to poor relief. Liverpool: 1932. pp.160. CUL. 2nd ed. 1932. pp.160. CUL. 3rd ed. 1932. pp.191. CUL; DHSS. 4th ed. 1935. pp.356. CUL; LSE.

600. FABIAN SOCIETY. Break up the poor law and abolish the workhouse, being Part I of the minority report of the Poor Law Commission. London: 1909. pp.601. (By Sidney and Beatrice Webb: issued without the authors' names).

601. FABIAN SOCIETY. The remedy for unemployment, being Part II of the minority report of the Poor Law Commission. London: 1909. pp.345. (By Sidney and Beatrice Webb: issued without the authors' names).

602. FABIAN SOCIETY. A plea for poor law reform. London: 1893. pp.3. (Fabian Tract 44). (By Frederick Whelan; issued without the author's name.) Revised. 1907. pp.3. CUL.

603. FABIAN SOCIETY. The reform of the poor law. Manchester: 1891. (Fabian Tracts No.17). LSE; CUL.

604. FABIAN SOCIETY. Questions for Poor Law Guardians. 2nd ed. London: 1893. pp.3. (Fabian Tract No.20). CUL.

605. FABIAN SOCIETY. The abolition of Poor Law Guardians. London: 1906. pp.23. (Fabian Tract No.126). CUL.

606. FAMILY WELFARE ASSOCIATION. Why is it wrong to supply outdoor relief? London: [1893]. pp.7. (Occasional Papers No.31). LSE.

607. FAMILY WELFARE ASSOCIATION. Outdoor relief. London: 1889.

pp.10. LSE.

608. FAY, C.R. "The old poor law and the new". In Life and labour
      in the nineteenth century. Cambridge: 1947. pp.89-108.
      Earlier eds. 1920, 1933, 1943.

609. FERGUSSON, W. Thoughts and observations upon pauperism, poor
      laws, emigration, medical relief, and the prevention of crime.
      London: 1839. pp.23. C.

610. [FIRMIN, T.] Some proposals for the employing of the poor,
      especiallky in and about the City of London. And for the
      prevention of begging... London: 1678. pp.24. G.

611. FLINN. M.W. "The Poor Employment Act of 1817". E.C.H.R. 2nd
      ser. XIV. (1961). pp.82-92.

612. FOLEY, R. Laws relating to the poor, from the forty-third of
      Queen Elizabeth to the third of Kind George II. With cases
      adjudged in the Court of King's Bench, upon the several
      clauses of them... [1556-1730]. pp.(30) + 284 + (20). BL;
      CUL.2nd ed. corrected. [London]: 1743. pp.284. G. 3rd ed.
      London: 1751. pp.328. BL. 4th ed. London: 1758. pp.438.
      DHSS.

613. FOOTE, W. Suggestions for reducing the poors' rate and
      abolishing poor law settlements, etc. London: 1845. pp.41.
      LSE.

614. FOWLE, T.W. The poor law. London: 1881. pp.163. New ed.
      London: 1893. pp.vii + 175. LSE.

615. FOWLE, T.W. "The poor law". In Henry Craik (ed.), The
      English citizen: his rights and responsibilities. London:
      1881-1914. 30 vols. Various eds. BM.

616. FOX, R.M. Poor laws in England and Ireland. Dublin: 1849.
      pp.84. NLI; RIA; TCD; LSE.

617. FRAZER, D. (ed.). The new poor law in the nineteenth century.
      London: 1976. pp.218. CUL; LSE.

618. FREEMAN, A. "The place of charge and recovery in the minority
      report of the Royal Commission on the poor laws". E.J. XXI.
      (1911). pp.294-301.

619. FRY, D.P. The Poor Law Acts of 1851:... London: 1851.
      pp.144. CUL.

620. FRY, D.P. Handbook for the election of Guardians of the Poor.
      3rd ed. (by J.G. Pease). London: 1892. pp.xvi + 205. CUL.

621. FRY, D.P. The Union Assessment Acts, 1860 to 1880, and the
      Rating Act, 1874. 6th ed. London: 1880, pp.viii + 268. 7th
      ed. by R.C. Glen and A.D. Laurie. 1887. pp.xxvii + 439. 8th
      ed. by R.C. Glen. 1897. pp.xxix + 431. (Previous editions.
      2nd. 1862. 4th. 1864. 5th. 1870).

622. FURNIVALL, F.J. & COWPER, J.M. (eds.). Four supplications,
      1529-1553. London: 1871. pp.xviii + 115. CUL.

623. FUST, SIR H.J. Poor law orders. London: 1907. pp.xxiii + 822. (Supplement). Poor law orders: the Relief Regulation Order, 1911 and the Boarding Out Order, 1912. 1912. pp.viii + 119. BL.

624. GALT, J. "On the principles of property and the poor laws". N.Month.Mag. 31. (1831). pp.50-8.

625. GARNIER, Rev. T. Plain remarks upon the New Poor Law Amendment Act, more particularly addressed to the labouring classes,... Winchester: 1835. pp.35. CUL.

626. GASKELL, P. Prospects of industry: with remarks on the operation of the Poor Law Bill. London: 1835. pp.44. LSE.

627. [GILBERT, T.] A scheme for the better relief and employment of the poor, etc. London: 1764. pp.(iv) + 23). LSE.

628. GILBERT, T. A Bill, intended to be offered to parliament for the better relief and employment of the poor, within that part of Great Britain called England. London: 1775. BL.

629. GILBERT, T. Observations upon the orders and resolutions of the House of Commons, with respect to the poor, vagrants and houses of correction. London: 1775. pp.(2) + 41. BL.

630. GILBERT, T. Considerations on the bills for the better relief and employment of the poor,... intended to be offered to Parliament this session. London: 1787. pp.47. BL.

631. GILBERT, T. A bill intended to be offered to Parliament for the better relief and employment of the poor, and for the improvement of the police of this country. Manchester: 1789. pp.30. BL.

632. GILBERT, W. On the present system of rating for the relief of the poor in the metropolis. London: 1857. pp.32. LSE (Pamphlet Collection).

633. GILLINGS, W.G. Knight's guide to the poor law institutions orders. London: 1913. unpag. DHSS.

634. GILLINGWATER, E. An essay on parish work-houses; containing observations on the present state of English work-houses. Bury St. Edmonds: 1786. pp.64. LSE.

635. GLASSE, G.H. Advice to masters and apprentices, in vol.5 of the Reports of the Society for Bettering the Condition and Increasing the Comforts of the Poor, with an Appendix. London: [1807]. LSE.

636. GLEN, R.A. Glen's Poor Law Act 1930. London: 1930. pp.xxx + 130. CUL.

637. GLEN, R.A. & ASHFORD, E.B. The law relating to public assistance. London: 1933. pp.xxx + 786. CUL; LSE.

638. GLEN, R.C. The Union Assessment Committee Acts with circulars of the Local Government Board and introduction and notes

thereon being the eighth edition of Fry's Union Assessment Committee Acts... London: 1897. pp.xxix + 421. CUL.

639. GLEN, W.C. The Poor Law Board Act, 12 & 13 Vict. c.103, for charging the costs of certain relief upon the common fund; and for amending the laws for the relief of the poor. London: 1849. pp.16. TCD.

640. GLEN, W.C. The general consolidated order issued by the poor law commissioners of the 24th July 1847, and the other general orders applicable to the unions to which the order is addressed; with a commentary and notes of the several articles. London: 1847. pp.xv + 279 CUL. 3rd ed. entitled The consolidated and other orders of the poor law commissioners, and of the poor law board, with explanatory notes elucidating the provisions of the several orders, and index. 1855. pp.lxxv + 316. 4th ed. 1859. pp.xvi + 496. CUL. 5th ed. entitled The general consolidated and other orders of the poor law commissioners and the poor law board; together with the general orders relating to the poor law accounts; the statutes relating to the amount of accounts, appeals, and the payment of debts. 1864. pp.xx + 547. 6th ed. 1868. pp.xxiii + 593. 7th ed. 1871. pp.xxiv + 661. CUL. 8th ed. entitled The poor law orders of the poor commissioners, the poor law board, and the local government board; with explanatory notes elucidating the orders, tables of statutes, cases and index. 1879. pp.xxiv + 870. 9th ed. 1883. pp.xxciii + 945. 10th ed. 1889. pp.xxxii + 1129. 11th ed. by R.C. Glen. 1898. pp.li + 1573. CUL.

641. GLEN, W.C. The consolidated and other orders of the poor law commissioners. London: 1855. pp.lxxv + 316. LSE.

642. GLEN, W.C. The Poor Law Guardian; his powers and duties in the right execution of his office. London: 1855. pp.viii + 137. CUL.

643. GLEN, W.C. The Poor Rate Assessment and Collection Act, 1869,... London: 1869. pp.xii + 32. CUL.

644. GLEN, W.C. The statutes in force relating to the Poor Laws. London: 1873-90. 4 vols. CUL; LSE.

645. GODFREY, W.H. The English almshouse. London: 1955. pp.95. DHSS.

646. GORST, SIR J.E. "The reports on the poor law". Sociol.Rev. 2. (1909). pp.217-27.

647. [GOURLAY, R.] Tyranny of poor laws exemplified. Bath: 1815. pp.15. LSE.

648. GOURLAY, W. History of the distress in Blackburn, 1861-5, and the means adopted for its relief. Blackburn: 1865. pp.180. LSE.

649. GRADY, S.G. The diminution of the poor rate by improved legislation and a more just distribution of the burden. 2nd ed. London: 1862.

650. GRAHAM, J.E.   The law relating to the poor and to parish councils. Edinburgh: 1905. pp.xii + 699. BL.   New ed. Edinburgh, London: 1922. pp.xxvi + 394. BL; Sq.

651. GREEN, G.   The history of the poor law.   London: 1893. pp.16. LSE.

652. GURNEY, J.H.   The new poor law explained and vindicated. London: 1841. pp.xxx + 102. BL.

653. HALCOMB, J.   A practical measure of relief from the present system of the poor laws; submitted to the consideration of Parliament and the country, etc. London: 1826. pp.32. LSE.

654. HALDANE, J.B.   The social workers' guide.   A handbook of information and counsel for all who are interested in public welfare. London: 1911. pp.484. CUL.

655. HALE, SIR M.   A discourse touching provision for the poor. London: 1716. LSE.

656. HALL, J.   A plan for the abolition of the present poor rates; and for effecting a grand moral improvement in the lower classes of soviety; with a view to the ultimate annihilation of poverty. London: 1824. pp.(2) + 1v + 33. TCD.

657. HAMILTON, C.J.   "The principles of the poor law: a contrast between 1834 and 1909". Char.Org.Rev. (n.s.). XXVI.   151. (1909). pp.23-46. Discussion, pp.47-55.

658. HAMILTON, C.J.   "The poor law controversy". E.J.   XX. (1910). pp.472ff.

659. HAMPSHIRE ARCHIVISTS GROUP. Poor law in Hampshire through the centuries. Hampshire: 1970. pp.78. DHSS; LSE.

660. [HANCOCK, G.] A conversation in political economy: being an attempt to explain familiarly to the understanding of every man the true causes of the evil operation of any general system of poor law. London: 1832. pp.72. G.

661. HANCOCK, W.N.   Should boards of guardians endeavour to make pauper labour self-supporting, or should they investigate the causes of pauperism?   A paper read before the statistical section of the British Association, at Ipswich, 1851. Dublin: 1851. pp.13. NLI; RIA; TCD.

662. HANNING, W.   A letter to the members of the select committees of the two Houses of Parliament appointed to examine and report on the poor law. Taunton: 1818. pp.46. LSE.

663. HART, SIR W.E.   "The reform of the poor law". Pub.Admin. IV. (1926). pp.223-231.

664. [HAY, W.] Remarks on the laws relating to the poor. With proposals for their better relief and employment. By a Member of Parliament. London: [1735] pp.55. BL.   Another ed. London: 1751. pp.xii + 74. G.   Reprinted in the author's Works, 1794. BL.

665.   HAYWARD, A. The secretaryship of the Poor Law Board. London:
       1854. pp.16. LSE.

666.   HENNOCK, E.P. "The poor law era". N.S. XI. 283. (1968).
       pp.301-3.

667.   HINDLE, G.B.   Provision for the relief of the poor in
       Manchester 1754-1826.   Manchester: The Chetham Society.
       1975. pp.viii + 192. CUL.

668.   HOARE, H.N.H.   On the development of the English poor law.
       London: 1893. pp.28.

669.   HOLROYD, J.B. (EARL OF SHEFFIELD).   Observations on the
       impolicy, abuses, and false interpretation of the poor laws,
       and on the reports of the two Houses of Parliament. London:
       1818. pp.62. NLI. 2nd ed. London: 1818. pp.78. G.

670.   HOLROYD, J.B. (EARL OF SHEFFIELD). Remarks on the Bill of the
       last Parliament for the amendment of the poor laws;   with
       observations   on   their   impolicy,   abuses,   and   ruinous
       consequences;   together with some suggestions for their
       amelioration, and the the better management of the poor.
       London: 1819. pp.106. G; NLI.

671.   HONEYMAN, J.   "Sir John Gorst and poor law reform".
       Westm.Rev. 161. (1904). pp.648-52.

672.   HORTON, R.J.W. The causes and remedies of pauperism in the
       United Kingdom considered: introductory series: being a
       defence of the principles and conduct of the Emigration
       Committee against the charges of Mr. Sadler. London: 1830.
       pp.viii + 150. LSE; G.

673.   HORTON, R.J.W. An inquiry into the causes and remedies of
       pauperism: first series containing correspondence with C.
       Poulett Thomson, Esq., M.P., upon the conditional under which
       colonization would be justifiable as a national measure. 2nd
       ed. London: 1831. pp.38. LSE; G.

674.   HORTON, R.J.W. An inquiry into the causes and remedies of
       pauperism: second series: containing correspondence with M.
       Duchatel...; with an explanatory preface. 2nd ed. London:
       1831. pp.46. LSE; G.

675.   HORTON, R.J.W. An inquiry into the causes and remedies of
       pauperism: third series: containing letters to Sir Francis
       Burdett, Bart, M.P. upon pauperism in Ireland.   2nd ed.
       London: 1831. pp.iv + 86. LSE; G

676.   HORTON, R.J.W. Causes and remedies of pauperism: fourth
       series: explanation of Mr. Wilmot Horton's Bill in a letter
       and queries addressed to N.W. Senior... with his answers, etc.
       London: 1830. pp.vi + 3-112 + xxiv. LSE; G.

677.   HOTSON, W.C.   An exemplified edition of the Poor Law
       Commissioners' general order relating to accounts. London:
       1847. pp.116. LSE.

678.   HOUSE OF COMMONS. Report, with appendix, from the committee

to whom the petition of the proprietors of the Charitable Corporation for relief of industrious poor by assisting them with small sums upon pledges, etc., was referred, and the proceedings. pp.134. Fol.1733.

679. HOUSE OF LORDS. Select committee on poor law relief. Report, with proceedings, minutes of evidence, appendix and index. London: 1888. (H.C. 363). Facsimile reprint published. Shannon: 1970. (B.P.P., poor law, 27).

680. HOWELL, G. "Pauperism: its nature and extent, its causes and remedies. A review of poor law administration" Co-operative Wholesale Societies: Annual for 1890. pp.187-208.

681. HUGHES, E. Compendium of the operations of the Poor Law Amendment Act, with some practical observations on its present results, and future apparent usefulness. London: 1836. pp.127. G.

682. HUNT, R. Provision for the poor by the union of houses of industry with country parishes, etc. London: 1797. pp.40. LSE.

683. HUTCHINS, B.L. Working women and the poor law. London: 1909. pp.12. LSE.

684. HUTCHINSON, G.L. A proposed plan for the equalization of the poor rates throughout the various parishes of the United Kingdom. London: 1846. pp.(3) + 186. BL. 3rd ed. London: 1849. BL.

685. HUTCHINSON, G.L. A plan for the equalization of the poor rates. London: 1849. pp.ix + 151. LSE.

686. HUTCHINSON, G.L. The equalization of the poor's rate of the United Kingdom proved to be both equitable and practical. London: 1858. pp.87. BL.

687. HUZEL, J.P. "Malthus, the poor law and population in early nineteenth century England". Ec.H.R. (2nd ser.). 22. (1969). pp.430-452.

688. JAMES, W. Thoughts upon the theory and practice of the poor law. London: 1847. pp.93. LSE.

689. JEE, T. Practical observations on the management of the poor, and the law relating to them. London: 1817. pp.563-81. LSE.

690. JENKIN, A.F. A manual for overseers being a practical treatise on the appointment, powers, and duties of overseers, etc. 2nd ed. London: 1901. pp.xii + 444. CUL. 3rd ed. London: 1906. pp.xiii + 512. CUL.

691. JENNER-FUST, H. Poor law orders arranged and annotated. London: 1907. pp.xxiii + 822. 2nd ed. with supplement. 1912. pp.viii + 119. CUL.

692. JENNINGS, W.I. The poor law code: being the Poor Law Act, 1930, and the poor law orders now in force, annotated... London: 1930. pp.lxxxviii + 302. DHSS, LSE. 2nd ed.

[entitled The poor law code and the law of unemployment assistance]. 1936. pp.xl + 488. BL. Sq.

693. JENNINGS. H.R. "Poor law administration in the 18th century". R.Instn.Corn.J. XXII. 3. (1928). pp.338-49.

694. JERRAM, C. .Considerations on the impolicy and pernicious tendency of the poor laws; with remarks on the Report of the Select Commitee of the House of Commons, upon them; and suggestions for improving the condition of the poor. London: 1818. pp.157. G.

695. JOHNSON, E.J. Supplementary memorandum submitted to the Executive Committee of the Necessitous Poor Law Areas Commission upon the Local Government Bill for reform in local government. London: [1928]. pp.9. LSE.

696. JOHNSON, E.J. Memorandum submitted to the executive committee of the Necessitous Poor Law Areas Committee... upon Ministry of Health proposals for reform in local government. London: 1928. pp.19. LSE.

697. JONES, E. The prevention of poverty by beneficial clubs, with preliminary observations upon houses of industry, and the poor laws. London: 1796. pp.48. LSE.

698. KEAY, J.H. Poor law reform in its medical aspects. London: 1910. pp.14. LSE.

699. KEITH-LUCAS, B. "A local act for social insurance". C.L.J. XI. (1952). pp.191-197.

700. KLEINSCHROD, C.T.V. Die neue Armengesetzgebung Englands und Irlands in ihrem zehnjahrigen Vollzuge, als Fortsezung des Pauperism in England, 1845 etc. Augsburg: 1849. pp.138. LSE.

701. KNIGHT, C. The suggested new poor-law: Knight's synopsis of the majority and minority reports of the Royal Commission on the poor law and relief of distress. London: 1909. pp.vii + 195. LSE.

702. KNIGHT, C. & CO. Knight's guide to the law and practice of poor relief: being an annotation of the Relief Regulation Order, 1911, etc. London: 1912. pp.156. LSE.

703. KNIGHT, C. & CO. A key to the Poor Law Act 1927. London: 1927. pp.144. CUL.

704. KNIGHT, F.W. The parochial system versus centralization; Part 1, Statistics of "close and open parishes"; Part 2, Effects of settlement and removal on the poor; remarks on union rating. London: 1854. 2 vols in 1. LSE; G.

705. KNIGHT, F.W. A statistical report to the Poor Law Board on the subject of close and open parishes. London: 1854. pp.148. LSE; G.

706. LANSBURY, E. "Reform of the poor law". L.R. XV. (1926). pp.37ff.

707. LANSBURY, G. The development of the humane administration of the poor law under the Poplar Board of Guardians. London: n.d. pp.15. LSE.

708. [LATEY, J.L.] Letters to working people on the new poor law. London: 1841. pp.108. LSE.

709. LEACH, R.A. The evolution of poor law administration. Great Malvern: 1924. pp.15.

710. LEIGH, P.B. A practical treatise on the poor laws, with an appendix of forms and statutes. London: 1836. pp.xxiv + 727. CUL. Supplement: 1838. pp.130. CUL.

711. LEIGH, P.B. A supplement to Leigh's Practical Treatise on the Poor Laws; containing all the statutes and deisions relating to the poor laws,... London: 1838. pp.131. CUL.

712. LEIGHTON, B. Depauperisation. London: 1875. pp.32. LSE.

713. LEONARD, E.M. The early history of English poor relief. Cambridge: 1900. pp.xix + 397. LSE. Reprinted. London: 1965.

714. LESLIE, J. A practical illustration of the principle upon which the Poor Law Amendment Act is founded, as exhibited in the administration of the poor rates in the parish of St. George, Hanover Square, for the year... 1835. 13th ed. London: 1835. pp.37. LSE.

715. LESLIE, J. A letter to the industrious classes on the operation of the poor law as affecting their independence and comfort. London: 1835. pp.12. LSE.

716. LESLIE, J. Remarks on the present state of the poor law question. 2nd ed. London: 1834. pp.30. LSE.

717. LEWIN, SIR G.A. Summary of the law relating to the government and maintenance of the poor. London: 1828. pp.xii + 746. LSE.

718. LEWIS, SIR G.C. The English poor law, etc. London: 1847. pp.56.

719. LEWIS, W.G. "Reconstruction" of the poor law: the devoted work of the guardians. London: 1918. pp.viii + 80. U.

720. LIFFORD, LORD. "The 'canker-worm' - out-door relief". Nineteenth Century. XIII. (1883). pp.453-457.

721. LITTLE, J.B. The Poor Law Statutes, comprising the statutes in force relating to the poor... from Elizabeth to the end of Victoria. London: 1901-1. 3 vols. pp.2355 + [282]. CUL; LSE.

722. LLOYD, C.M. The present state of the poor law. London: [1920]. pp.8. LSE.

723. LLOYD, C.M. The scandal of the poor law. London: 1920.

pp.19. (Fabian Tracts, No.195). LSE; CUL.

724. LLOYD, W.F. Four lectures on Poor Laws, delivered before the University of Oxford, in Michaelmas Term, 1834. London and Oxford: 1835. pp.128. G; KI; RIA; TCD; LSE.

725. LLOYD, W.F. Two lectures on Poor Laws, delivered before the University of Oxford, in Hilary Term, 1836. London and Oxford: 1836. pp.71. G; KI; LSE.

726. LOCAL GOVERNMENT BOARD, INTELLIGENCE BRANCH. Report on distress in England and Wales (excluding London). London: 1914-15. 37 pts. (in 1). LSE.

727. LOCAL GOVERNMENT BOARD. Return of paupers in the workhouses of England on 31 March 1881, who had been members of benefit societies. London: 1881. pp.23. DHSS [RCAP COLL].

728. LOCAL GOVERNMENT BOARD. Return of persons over 60 years of age... in receipt of relief from the guardians on 1st August 1890. London: 1890. pp.34. DHSS [RCAP COLL].

729. LOCAL GOVERNMENT BOARD. Return of paupers in the workhouses of England and Wales on 31 March 1891, who had been members of benefit societies. London: 1891. pp.20. DHSS [RCAP COLL].

730. LOCAL GOVERNMENT BOARD. Return relating to the poor law (indoor and outdoor relief) for the year ended at Lady Day 1892. London: 1892. pp.73. DHSS [RCAP COLL].

731. LOCAL GOVERNMENT COMMITTEE. Report on transfer of functions of poor law authorities.. London: 1918. pp.26. (Cd.8917). LSE.

732. LOCH, C.S. "Some controverted points in the administration of poor relief". E.J. III. (1893). pp.425, 584.

733. LOCH, C.S. The Reports of the Royal Commission on the poor law and relief of distress. London: 1909. pp.10. LSE.

734. LONDON AND WESTMINSTER REVIEW. Fallacies on poor law. London: 1837. pp.23. LSE. C; U.

735. LONDON COUNTY COUNCIL. LCC and poor law administration. n.p.: [1908]. pp.16. LSE.

736. LONDON COUNTY COUNCIL. The London relieving officer. London: 1939. pp.xii + 273. DHSS; LSE.

737. LONDON COUNTY COUNCIL. Annual Report of the Council. Part II on public assistance. London: 1930-1937. var. pag. DHSS.

738. LONDON COUNTY COUNCIL. PUBLIC ASSISTANCE COMMITTEE. Administration of relief (with an appendix on the determination of transitional payments). (P.A.4). London: 1933. pp.29. DHSS; LSE.

739. LONDON COUNTY COUNCIL. PUBLIC ASSISTANCE COMMITTEE. Administration of relief. (P.A.5). London: 1935. pp.42. DHSS; LSE.

740. LONDON   COUNTY   COUNCIL.   PUBLIC   ASSISTANCE   COMMITTEE.
      Administration of relief (P.A.6).   London: 1938.   pp.47.
      DHSS; LSE.

741. LONDON COUNTY COUNCIL.   Rules of the public assistance
      committee. London: 1938. pp.80. DHSS.

742. LONDON. COURT OF ALDERMEN. Order appointed to be executed in
      the cittie of London for setting roges and idle persons to
      worke and for releefe of the poore.   London: 1793.   pp.18.
      G.

743. LONG, G. Observations on a Bill to amend the laws relating to
      the relief of the poor in England, lately introduced into the
      House of Commons by James Scarlett, Esq.   London: 1821.
      pp.58. TCD.

744. LONGFIELD, M.   Four lectures on poor laws, delivered in
      Trinity Term, 1834. Dublin: 1834. pp.100. G; KI; NLI; TCD.

745. LONGMATE, N.   The workhouse: a social history.   London:
      1974. pp.320. DHSS; LSE; CUL.

746. LONSDALE, S.   The evils of a lax system of outdoor relief.
      1895. pp.8.

747. LONSDALE, S.   The English poor laws: their history,
      principles and administration.   London: 1897.   pp.85.   LI.
      2nd ed. 1902. pp.viii + 89. LSE.

748. LOVELASS, P. A proposed practicable plan for such a speedy
      easement of the poor rates throughout England;   assuming that
      in the course of a few years, the parishes may be eased of one
      fourth... of their present burdens etc.   London: 1804.
      pp.32. LSE.

749. LOW, J. Statement relating to the reduction in the poor rates
      resulting from the cessation of litigation.   Hammersmith:
      1837. pp.25. C.

750. LUBBOCK, G. Some poor relief questions. With arguments on
      both sides.   A manual for workers.   London: 1895.   pp.x +
      329. BL.

751. LUMLEY, W.G. An abridgment of the cases upon the subject of
      the poor law, decided since the passing of the 4 and 5 Will.
      IV. c.76.   And a collection of the subsequent enactment.
      London: 1840-64. 3 vols. [Continuation, 1842-1858, by J.F.
      Archbold and 1857-1863, by J. Paterson]. pp.xxvii + 434. BL;
      Sq.

752. LUMLEY, W.G.   The Poor Law Commission Continuance Act, and
      other Poor Law Acts of this Session. London: 1842. pp.71.
      CUL.

753. LUMLEY, W.G. Collection of statutes of general use relating
      to the relief of the poor. London: 1843-52. 2 vols. LSE;
      CUL.

754. LUMLEY, W.G. The act for the further amendment of the laws relating to the poor in England, with other statutes affecting the poor law passed in the Parliament of 1844. With notes, forms and index. London: 1844. pp.188. G.

755. LUMLEY, W.G. The Act for the further amendment of the laws relating to the poor in England (with the other statutes affecting the poor law passed in the Parliament of 1844). 2nd ed. London: 1844. pp.212. CUL.

756. LUMLEY, W.G. The Poor Law Acts introduced by Mr. Buller... passed in the session of 1848. London: [1848]. pp.107. LSE.

757. LUMLEY, W.G. Manuals of the duties of poor law officers. Master and Matron of the Workhouse. London: 1848. pp.143. CUL. 2nd ed. London: 1869. p.208. CUL.

758. LUMLEY, W.G. Manuals of the duties of poor law officers. The Relieving Officer. London: 1848. pp.viii + 104. CUL.

759. LUMLEY, W.G. Manuals of the duties of poor law officers. The Treasurer. London: 1849. pp.viii + 31. CUL.

760. LUMLEY, W.G. Emigration of the poor. Practical instructions to boards of guardians and parish officers as to proceedings to be taken in respect of the emigration of poor persons at the cost of the poor rate. London: 1849. pp.68. TCD.

761. LUMLEY, W.G. The General Consolidated Order of the Poor Law Commissioners to Unions dated July 24th, 1847;... London: 1852. pp.252. CUL.

762. LUMLEY, W.G. The General Orders of the Poor Law Commissioners now in force... London: 1852. pp.xxx + 486. CUL.

763. LUMLEY, W.G. The poor law election manual. London: 1855. pp.viii + 140. LSE. 5th ed. by W.C. Glen. London: 1886. LSE.

764. LUMLEY, W.G. The Union Assessment Committee Act, 1862; with introduction, notes, and an appendix containing the circular letters of the Poor Law Board upon the Act. 6th ed. London: 1864. pp.166. TCD. 9th ed. London: 1870. pp.xci + 130. CUL. Rev. ed. [entitled: Union Assessment Act to which we added the Parochial Assessment Act, 1836, the Poor Relief Act 1743 and the Poor Rate Act, 1801]. London: 1895. pp.xcii + 200. LSE.

765. LYSTER, R.A. Progress in public health or how to break up the poor law by means of the Local Government Act, 1929. Bolton: 1931. pp.16. LSE.

766. M'FARLAN, J. Inquiries concerning the poor. Edinburgh: 1782. pp.xix + 494. LSE.

767. M., T. "Note on the gradual introduction of the poor law of Elizabeth". Char.Org.Rev. (n.s.). VIII. 48. (1900). pp.369-79).

768. MABERLY, F.H. To the poor: substance of speeches exhibiting the oppressive nature of the new Poor Law Amendment Act. London: 1836. pp.48. G.

769. MACDONELL, G.P. "The state and the unemployed". Br.Q.Rev. LXXXIII. 166. (1866). pp.348-64.

770. MACKAY, T. The English poor: a sketch of their social and economic history. London: 1889. pp.xi + 303. G.

771. MACKAY, T. "The interest of the working class in the poor law". Char.Org.Rev. 7. (1891). pp.446-54.

772. MACKAY, T. "Politics and the poor law". Fort.Rev. 57. (1895). pp.408-22.

773. MACKAY, T. A history of the English poor law. Vol.III from 1834 to the present time. Being a supplementary volume to "A History of the English Poor Law" by Sir George Nicholls K.C.B. London: 1899. pp.xv + 617. DHSS; CUL.

774. MACKAY, T. Public relief of the poor. London: 1901. pp.vi + 214. LSE; BL.

775. MACKAY, T. "The poor law and the economic order". Econ.Rev. XII. (1902). pp.278-288.

776. MACKAY, T. "The reform of the poor law". Char.Org.Rev. (n.s.). XIV. (1903). pp.317-326.

777. MACKAY, T. "Poor law reform". In C. Loch (ed.), Methods of social advance. London: 1904. pp.158-168.

778. MACKENZIE, W.W. The Overseers' Handbook, being a statement of the duties and summary of the law relating to overseers, churchwardens, assistant overseers, collectors of the poor rate, vestry clerks, and other parish officers; together with a calendar of overseers' duties. London: 1889. pp.xv + 214. CUL; 2nd ed. 1893. pp.xv + 276. CUL; 3rd. ed. 1895. pp.xvii + 310. CUL; 4th ed. 1896. pp.xxiv + 360. CUL. MACKENZIE, W.W. & COMYNS, H.J. The Overseers' Handbook. 6th ed. 1906. pp.xxxi + 502 + 113. CUL; 7th ed. 1910. pp.xxxv + 528 + 147. CUL; 8th ed. 1915. pp.xxviii + 568 + 183. CUL; 9th ed. 1925. (by William C. Howe and F.J. Ogden). pp. lvi + 479 + 160. CUL.

779. MACKENZIE, W.W. The poor law guardian: his powers and duties. 3rd ed. London: 1892. pp.xii + 328. CUL. 4th ed. 1895. pp.xii + 360. LSE; CUL.

780. MACKINNON, J.M. The English poor law of 1834, with special reference to its working between 1834 and 1847. London: 1930. [Typescript]. U.

781. MACPHAIL, J. Observations on tendency of the poor laws, their policy vindicated, state of England compared with that of Scotland, Ireland, and France, where no poor rate is levied. London: 1819. pp.58. LSE.

782. MAGUIRE, J. "Poor law reform". J.S.S.I.S.I. XV. (1925).

pp.134-42.

783. MAHON, J.N. The Poor Laws, as they were, and as they are; or the recent alterations in the Poor Laws, by the Statute 4 and 5 William IV. Cap.76 with the reasons for those alterations plainly stated showing 1. the old law; 2. the present law; and 3. the grounds, and anticipated effect, of the new enactments. London: 1835. pp.187. CUL; G.

784. MAINTENANCE AND EMPLOYMENT SOCIETY, ADVISORY COMMITTEE. The draft of a bill to provide work and maintenance for the people of the U.K. of Great Britain and Ireland without any increase of taxation or rates. London: 1905. pp.45. LSE.

785. MANNING, CARDINAL. "A note on outdoor relief". Fort.Rev. 43. (1888). pp.151-6.

786. MANSION HOUSE COMMITTEE. Report of the Mansion House Committee appointed 1893, to investigate the existence of distress in London, caused by lack of employment, and to consider the best means of dealing with it. London: 1893. pp.147. G.

787. MARRIOTT, J.A.R. "National assistance and national decay". Fort.Rev. 112. (1922). pp.370-82.

788. MARRIOTT, J.A.R. "Poverty, pauperism and public assistance:. Fort.Rev. 113. (1923). pp.503-12.

789. MARSHALL, A. "The poor law in relation to state-aided pensions". Econ.J. II. (1892). pp.186-91.

790. MARSHALL, A. "Poor law reform". Econ.J. II. (1892). pp.371-9.

791. MARSHALL, D. The English poor in the 18th century: a study in social and administrative history. London: 1926. Reissued, 1969. pp.xvi + 292. LSE; CUL.

792. MARSHALL, D. "The old poor law (1662-1795)". Ec.H.R. (1st ser.). VIII. (1937-38). pp.38-47.

793. MARSHALL, H.J. On the tendency of the new poor law seriously to impair the morals and condition of the working classes. London: 1842. pp.48. G.

794. MARSHALL, H.J. Socialism and the poor law. London: 1927. pp.21. LSE.

795. MARSHALL, J.D. "The Nottinghamshire reformers and their contribution to the new poor law". Ec.H.R. (2nd ser.). 13. (1960-61). pp.382-396.

796. MARSHALL, J.D. The old poor law 1795-1834. London: 1968. pp.50. (Studies in Economic History). DHSS; LSE; CUL.

797. MARTINEAU, H. Poor law and paupers illustrated. London: 1833-4. 4 vols. in 2. G.

798. MARTINEAU, J. The English country labourer and the poor law

in the reign of Queen Victoria. London: 1901. pp.32. LSE.

799. MASERES, F.   A proposal for establishing life-annuities in
      parishes for the benefit of the industrial poor.   London:
      1772. pp.68. G.

800. [MASERES, F.] Consideration on the bill now depending... for
      enabling parishes to grant life annuities to poor person, etc.
      London: 1773. pp.60. G.

801. MASON, M.H.   Classification of girls and boys in workhouses,
      and the legal powers of boards of guardians for placing them
      beyond the workhouse. London: 1884. pp.32.

802. MAUDE, W.C. Poor law handbook. 1903. [Source: SM2].

803. McCASHIN, T. "Rural dole payments". Soc.Stud. 4. (1975).
      pp.366-79.

804. McCORD, N. "The implementation of the 1834 Poor Law Amendment
      Act on Tyneside".   Int.Rev.Soc.Hist.   XIV.   (1969).
      pp.90-108.

805. McDOUGALL, A.   "The English poor law, with special reference
      to progress in its administration during the Queen's reign".
      Manch.Statist.Soc.Trans. (1897-98). pp.9-31.

806. McVAIL, J.C.   Report on poor law medical relief in certain
      unions in England and Wales. London: 1909. pp.338.

807. MESS, H.A. "Modern alternatives to the poor law". Pol.Q. 2.
      (1936-37). pp.380-9.

808. MINISTRY OF HEALTH.   Annual local taxation returns.   England
      and Wales 1927-34.   Part 1.   Expenditure on poor relief.
      London: [1927-34]. 1 vol. DHSS.

809. MINISTRY OF HEALTH.   Poor law: report of a special inquiry
      into various forms of test work.   London: 1930.   pp.44.
      (Cmd. 3585).

810. MINISTRY OF HEALTH.   Persons in receipt of poor relief.
      London: 1930-48 (annual). unpag. DHSS.

811. MINISTRY OF HEALTH.   Local government financial statistics.
      Part 1. Poor relief. England and Wales 1934-1936. London:
      1936, 1938. 1 vol. DHSS.

812. MINISTRY OF HEALTH.   The poor law. (Lecture by Sir Arthur
      Lowry). London: 1930. (unpub). pp.11. DHSS.

813. MINISTRY OF RECONSTRUCTION. Report by the Local Government
      Committee on the transfer of functions of poor law authorities
      in England and Wales. (MacLean Report). London: 1918.
      pp.26. (Cd. 8917). DHSS.

814. MINISTRY OF HEALTH.   Local government financial statistics.
      Part 1. Poor relief. England and Wales 1934-1936. London:
      1936, 1938. 1 vol. DHSS.

815. MINISTRY OF RECONSTRUCTION. Reconstruction problems. No.32. Poor law reform. London: 1919. pp.24. DHSS.

816. MISHRA, R.C. A history of the relieving officer in England and Wales from 1834 to 1948. [Ph.D. (London) thesis]. Unpublished: 1969. pp.508. Typescript. LSE.

817. MOLYNEUX, J.W.H. Correspondence between the Poor Law Board and J.W.H.M. London: 1862. pp.27. LSE.

818. MONCK, J.B. General reflections on the system of the poor law, with a short view of Mr. Whitbread's Bill. London: 1807. pp.48. G.

819. MONTAGUE, F.C. The old poor law and the new socialism; or pauperism and taxation. London: 1866. pp.66. (Cobden Club pamphlet). LSE.

820. MORGAN, J.S. "The break-up of the poor law in Britain, 1907-47: an historical footnote". Can.J.Econ.Polit.Sci. XIV. (1948). pp.209-19.

821. MORRISON, R.J. Proposals to abolish all poor laws, except for the old and infirm; and to establish asylum farms, on which to locate the destitute and able-bodied poor; who might thereon maintain themselves, and benefit the country £18,600,000 annually. London: [1842]. pp.18. LSE.

822. MOSS, J. Poor Law Act, 1927, with an introduction and annotated index. London: 1927. pp.xxx + 304. LSE.

823. MOSS, J. The Relieving Officers' handbook, being a complete and practical guide to the law relating to the powers, duties and liabilities of Relieving Officers. 7th ed. London: 1938. pp.xxx + 447. DHSS; Sq.

824. MOWATT, W.M. "The poor law authorities' part in local government". Pub.Admin. VII. (1929). p.387.

825. MUIRHEAD, J.H. By what authority? The principles in common and at issue in the Reports of the Poor Law Commission. 2nd ed. London: 1909. pp.102. CUL. (Reprinted 1910 [entitled The starting point of poor law reform. Being articles upon the principles in common and at issue in the reports of the Poor Law Commission with a plea for agreement as to first steps.].) CUL; LSE.

826. MURRAY, H. Poor law administration and proposed legislative amendments. Edinburgh: 1881. pp.24. TCD.

827. NASMITH, J. The duties of overseers of the poor and the present system of poor law. London: [1799]. pp.72. G.

828. NATIONAL ASSOCIATION FOR THE PROMOTION OF SOCIAL SCIENCE. Workhouses and women's work. London: 1858. pp.53. LSE.

829. NATIONAL COMMITTEE FOR THE PREVENTION OF DESTITUTION. Index to the minority report of the Poor Law Commission. London: 1911. pp.89. LSE.

830. NATIONAL COMMITTEE FOR THE PREVENTION OF DESTITUTION. An outline of the proposals to break up the poor law; on the lines of the minority report of the poor law commission. London: 1911. pp.14. LSE; U.

831. NATIONAL COMMITTEE FOR THE PREVENTION OF DESTITUTION. The charter of the poor. London: [1911]. pp.24. U.

832. NATIONAL COMMITTEE TO PROMOTE THE BREAK-UP OF THE POOR LAW. Minority report of the poor law commission. Volume 1. Break-up of the poor law. London: 1909. pp.ix + 601. LSE; U.

833. NATIONAL COMMITTEE TO PROMOTE THE BREAK-UP OF THE POOR LAW. How the minority report deals with children. London: 1909. pp.15. U.

834. NATIONAL COMMITTEE TO PROMOTE THE BREAK-UP OF THE POOR LAW. How the Minority report deals with the sick, the infirm, and the infants. London: 1909. pp.15. U.

835. NATIONAL COMMITTEE TO PROMOTE THE BREAK-UP OF THE POOR LAW. How the minority report deals with unemployment. London: 1909. pp.15. LSE; U.

836. NATIONAL COMMITTEE TO PROMOTE THE BREAK-UP OF THE POOR LAW. The failure of the poor law. London: 1909. pp.11. U.

837. NATIONAL COMMITTEE TO PROMOTE THE BREAK-UP OF THE POOR LAW. The new charter of the poor: what is meant by the break-up of the poor law. London: 1909. pp.7. U.

838. NATIONAL CONFERENCE ON THE PREVENTION OF DESTITUTION. Report of the proceedings... London: 1911. pp.xxvi + 766. CUL.

839. NATIONAL UNION OF CONSERVATIVE AND UNIONIST ASSOCIATIONS. A public scandal: glaring cases of abuses under the administration of socialist poor law guardians. London: 1928. pp.16. (Leaflets, 1928, No.2823). LSE.

840. [NELSON, W.] The duty of overseers of the poor. To be delivered to them at their appointment, being first signed and sealed, by the justices, in their petty sessions... By a country magistrate. London: 1802. pp.27. G.

841. NEVILLE, C. The new poor law justified: with suggestions for the establishment of insurance offices for the poor. London: 1838. pp.30. G.

842. NICHOL, W. Proposal for the development of the principle of assurance as an instrument for the gradual extinction of pauperism. Edinburgh: 1847. pp.(2) + 25. G.

843. NICHOLL, S.W. A summary view of the report and evidence relative to the poor laws, published by order of the House of Commons, with observations and suggestions. York: 1818. pp.112. TCD; G.

844. [NICHOLLS, G.] Eight letters on the management of our poor, and the general administration of the poor law. By an

overseer. Newark: 1822. pp.xii + 70. RIA.

845. NICHOLLS, G. A history of the English poor law in connection
with the state of the country and the condition of the people
(from 924 to 1843). London: 1854. 2 vols. pp.xxix + 408
and pp.vi + 467. CUL. Rev. ed. 1898-99. [ed. by H.G.
Willink]. 2 vols. Vol.1 924-1714. pp.lxxviii + 384. LSE;
DHSS; CUL. Vol.2. 1714-1853. pp.viii + 460. LSE; CUL. 3rd
vol. by Mackay. Reprint of Rev. ed. London: 1967. 3 vols.
(inc. Mackay). CUL; LSE.

846. NICHOLLS, R.H. Practical remarks on the severities of the new
poor law. London: 1837. pp.34. G.

847. NICOLL, D. An essay on outdoor poor relief. London: [1880].
pp.xxx + 79. LSE.

848. NOLAN, A.M. A treatise of the law for the relief and
settlement of the poor. London: 1805. 2 vols. Vol.3. 1825.
pp.xx + 467. LSE; G.

849. NOORDIN, R.M. Through a workhouse window: being a brief
summary of three years spent by the youngest member of a Board
of Guardians in the course of his duties. London: 1929.
pp.vii + 216. LSE.

850. NORRIS, W. A letter on the new poor law, its origin and
intended effect. London: 1836. pp.36. LSE.

851. NOTTINGHAM WORKING MEN'S ASSOCIATION. Address to the people
of England on the new poor law. London: [1838]. pp.18. G.

852. NUNN, T.H. A Council of Social Welfare: a note and
memorandum in the report of the Royal Commission on the Poor
Law. London: [1909]. pp.115. LSE.

853. O'CONOR, W.A. "Poor Laws". Manch.Statist.Soc.Trans.
(1880-81). pp.97-122.

854. OAKESHOTT, J.F. The humanizing of the poor law. London:
1894. pp.40. (Humanitarian League. Publications 13).
Another ed. London: 1894. pp.23. (Fabian Tract 54). New
and revised ed. 1905. pp.23. LSE.

855. OASTLER, R. Damnation, eternal damnation, to the
field-begotten coarser food, new poor law: a speech. London:
1837. pp.24. LSE; G.

856. OASTLER, R. Brougham versus Brougham on the new poor law.
London: 1847. pp.xxxviii + 44. G.

857. OWEN, H. A manual for overseers, collectors of poor rates,
and vestry clerks as to their poweers, duties and
responsibilities. 3rd ed. London: 1875. pp.viii + 236.
CUL. 4th ed. 1878. pp.viii + 248. CUL. 5th ed. 1880.
pp.viii + 280. CUL. 6th ed. 1882. pp.viii + 286. CUL.
7th ed. 1884. pp.viii + 293. CUL. 8th ed. 1887. pp.viii
+ 316. LSE.

858. OWEN, H. The Poor Rate Assessment and Collection Act, 1869.

6th ed. London: 1871. pp.84. CUL.

859. OWEN, H. The Pauper Inmates Discharge and Regulations Act, 1871... and Casual Poor Act, 1882... 3rd ed. London: 1882. 4th ed. London: 1884. pp.60. CUL.

860. OXLEY, G.W. Poor relief in England and Wales 1601-1834. Newton Abbott: 1974. pp.159. CUL; LSE.

861. PAGE, F. The principle of the English poor laws illustrated and defended, by an historical view of indigence in civil society. London and Bath: 1822. pp.108. G; TCD. 2nd ed. with additions. London and Dublin: 1829. pp.130. G; RIA. 3rd ed. with additions. London and Dublin: 1830. pp.130 + 72. G; TCD; NLI; RIA.

862. PALMER, W. Principles of the legal provision for the relief of the poor. Four lectures, partly read at Gresham College, in Hilary Term, 1844. London: 1844. pp.120. G.

863. PARKER, H.W. A digest of the law relating to the relief of the poor containing the statutes with the adjuged cases under titles alphabetically arranged. London: 1849. pp.viii + 715. CUL.

864. PARKINSON, H. The problem of poor law reform. London: [1910]. pp.18. U.

865. PARKINSON, H. La loi des pauvres anglaise: (supplement au mouvement social, mai 1911). n.p. n.d. pp.16. LSE.

866. [PARR, S.?] Considerations on the poor law and the treatment of the poor. London: 1817. pp.64. G.

867. PARRY, E.A. "The insolvent poor". Fort.Rev. 63. (1898). pp.797-804.

868. PASHLEY, R. Pauperism and poor law. London: 1852. pp.viii + 428. LSE; G; S.

869. PASHLEY, R. Observations on the Government Bill for abolishing the removal of the poor and redistributing the burden of the poor rate. London: 1854. pp.31. LSE.

870. PASQUET, D. Londres et les ouvriers de Londres. Paris: 1913. pp.762. CUL.

871. PATERSON, J.(ed.). An abridgement of cases upon Poor Law (1857-1863). (In continuation of Archbold's Poor Law cases, originally Mr. Lumley's Poor Law cases, Vol.4). London: 1864. pp.xxv + 83 + 26. Sq.

872. PEASE, E.R. The abolition of poor law guardians. London: 1906. pp.24. (Fabian Tract 126). LSE.

873. PEEK, F. Social wreckage: a review of the laws of England as they affect the poor. London: 1883. pp.ix + 279. LSE; G; S.

874. PEEK, F. The uncharitableness of inadequate relief.

London: [1879]. pp.67. LSE.

875. PEEK, F.   Our laws and our poor. London: 1875. pp.vii +
      190. LSE.

876. PERCEVAL, J.T.   Observations on the new poor law: its
      injustice. London: 1838. pp.38. G.

877. PERRY, S.   The powers under the new poor law of the vestry
      meetings, the boards of guardians, justices of the peace, and
      the Poor Law Commissioners, considered in a letter to Lord
      John Russell, Secretary of State for the Home Department.
      London and Brentwood: 1838. pp.20. G. 3rd ed. London and
      Brentwood: 1839. pp.38. G.

878. PETERKEN, W.B.   Practical procedure in reference to the
      administration of poor law relief. London: 1930. pp.47.
      BL.

879. PHELPS, L.R.   The majority report and the unemployed.
      London: [1910]. pp.15. LSE.

880. PHELPS, L.R.   "Modern criticisms of the poor law". Econ.Rev.
      VII. (1897). pp.374-84.

881. PHILLIPS, R.   The four letters of Sir R. Phillips to Lord
      Viscount Melbourne on the new Poor Law Amendment Act;
      addressed to the understandings of the just. By John Bull.
      Southampton: [1841]. pp.36. C.

882. PLUM, T.W.   Remarks on the operation of the parochial
      settlement laws. London: 1845. pp.30. C.

883. POOCK, A.   "English poor law: its history and modern
      developments". Manch.Statist.Soc.Trans. (1910-20). pp.1-33

884. POOR LAW.   Report of a special inquiry into various forms of
      test work. London: 1929. pp.44. (B.P.P. 1929-30, XVII).
      LSE.

885. POOR LAW ANNUAL.   The guardians' and officers' companion for
      1907-8 (and 1911-12). London: 1907-11. 2 vols. LSE.

886. POOR LAW BOARD.   General regulations of the Poor Law Board
      relating to the classification of the inmates of
      workhouses...:   and return of the number in classes, in each
      workhouse, etc. London: 1854. pp.19. (B.P.P. 1854, LV).
      LSE.

887. POOR LAW BOARD.   Circular letter of the Poor Law Board as to
      irremovable poor and common fund chargeability, 24 & 25
      Vict.c.55. London: 1862. pp.12. TCD.

888. POOR LAW BOARD.   Circular letter of the Poor Law Board to
      boards of guardians, as to the Union Assessment Committee Act,
      1862. London: 1862. pp.18. TCD.

889. POOR LAW BOARD.   Circular letter of the Poor Law Board as to
      the rating of tithes. London: 1863. pp.12. TCD.

890.   POOR LAW BOARD. Orders of the Poor Law Board and of the Local Government Board relating to the Board of Management of the Metropolitan Asylum District and the several institutions under their control;... revised to 31st January, 1891. London: 1891. pp.vii + 318 + liv. LSE.

891.   POOR LAW COMMISSIONERS. Extracts from the information received by His Majesty's commissioners as to the administration and operation of the poor law. London: 1833. pp.xxii + 432. LSE.

892.   POOR LAW COMMISSIONERS. Orders regulating the meetings of the boards of guardians, and their proceedings thereat, and defining the duties of some of the officers appointed by the guardians; with some instructions relative to valuation and rating. Dublin: 1839. pp.46. RIA.

893.   POOR LAW COMMISSIONERS. Official circulars of public documents and information, directed by the poor law commissioners to be printed. London: 1840. 9 Vols. NLS.

894.   POOR LAW COMMISSIONERS. Official circulars of public documents and information; directed by the Poor Law Commissioners to be printed chiefly for the use of the members and permanent officers of Boards of Guardians, under the Poor Law Amendment Act. Vol.1. Numbers 1-10. London: 1840. pp.144. DHSS.

895.   POOR LAW COMMISSIONERS. Report on an inquiry into the sanitary conditions of the labouring population of Great Britain, with appendices. London: 1842. pp.xxxi + 457. LSE.

896.   POOR LAW COMMISSIONERS. Copy of articles 9,10,11 and 12 of the general work-house rules issued by the Poor Law Commissioners etc. London: 1844. (B.P.P. 1844. XL). LSE.

897.   POOR LAW COMMISSIONERS. Copy of any letter and general rule issued by the Poor Law Commissioners relating to the employment of paupers in pounding... bones, etc. London: 1846. pp.50. (B.P.P. 1846, XXXVI). LSE.

898.   POOR LAW COMMISSIONERS. Copy of minute of the dissention of one of the Poor Law Commissioners, on the subject of bone-crushing by paupers in workhouses etc. London: 1846. pp.10. (B.P.P. 1846, XXXVI). LSE.

899.   POOR LAW COMMISSIONERS. General order of the poor law commissioners for regulating the administration of out-door relief, &c. &c. Dublin: 1847. pp.24.

900.   POOR LAW COMMISSONERS. Copy of a report made in 1834 inquiring into the administration and practical operation of the poor laws. London: 1905. pp.378. DHSS; LSE.

901.   POOR LAW CONFERENCES. Reports (for the years 1875, 1877-1930). London: 1876-1930. 43 vols. LSE; CUL.

902.   [POOR LAW INSPECTORS.] Reports of poor law inspectors. London: 1867-68. pp.691. (B.P.P. 1867-68, LXI). LSE.

903. [POOR LAW INSPECTORS.] Copies of reports of poor law inspectors... on the boundaries of unions in their respective districts etc. London: 1870. pp.48. (B.P.P. 1870, LVIII). LSE.

904. POOR LAW OFFICERS JOURNAL. Poor law administation: aged deserving poor. Manchester: [1900]. pp.16. LSE.

905. POOR LAW OFFICERS JOURNAL. The poor law and the coal strike together with an appendix containing the local government board's circular letter 19th March, 1912, on exceptional unemployment. London: 1912. pp.15. LSE.

906. POOR LAW OFFICERS JOURNAL. The law relating to the relief of the poor. 2nd ed. London: 1923. 2nd imp. 2nd ed. 1924. pp.277. CUL.

907. POOR LAW OFFICERS JOURNAL. The Government Bill to consolidate the enactments relating to the relief of the poor in England and Wales. London: [1926?]. pp.viii + 152. LSE.

908. POOR LAW OFFICERS JOURNAL. Board of Guardians (Default) Act in operation. London: 1927. pp.17. LSE.

909. POOR MAN'S GUARDIAN SOCIETY. The first annual report. London: 1834. pp.100. G.

910. POTTER, R. Observations on the poor laws, on the present state of the poor, and on houses of industry. London: 1775. pp.72. CUL.

911. POYNTER, J.R. Society and pauperism: English ideas on poor relief, 1795-1834. London: 1969. pp.xxv + 367. DHSS; LSE; CUL.

912. PRATT, J.T. The act for the amendment and better administration of the laws relating to the poor, in England and Wales. With explanatory notes and a copious index. London: [1834]. pp.140. G. 2nd ed. with a preface containing a popular outline of the Act. London: 1834. pp.xxviii + 140. G.

913. PRATT, J.T. A collection of the statutes in force for the relief and regulation of the poor. London: 1834. G. 4th ed. 1847. pp.xxii + 738. CUL.

914. [PRESTON, W.C.] The bitter cry of outcast London: an inquiry into the condition of the abject poor. London: 1885. pp.32. LSE.

915. PRETYMAN, J.R. Dispauperization: a popular treatise on poor law evils. London: 1878. pp.293. LSE; G.

916. PRICHARD, D. Digest; or, an entire new and complete body of the law concerning the poor, from the earliest period to the present time, arranged under proper heads, comprising a great number of reported cases not to be found in any other work of this kind; together with many other determined cases never before printed, taken from the notes of Henry Dealtry, Esq.,

Clerk of the rules of the Court of King's Bench. Pt. 1.
1791. 4to. BL.

917. RICHARDS, J.   A letter to the Earl of Liverpool on the
agricultural distress of the country; its cause demonstrated
in the unequal system of taxation, and a just system
suggested. 2nd ed. London: 1822. pp.66 LSE.

918. RICHARDSON, W. Observations on the occasional scarcities and
poor law in England. London: 1811. pp.64. LSE.

919. RICHARDSON, J. A letter on an alteration in the poor law, the
employment of the people, and a reduction in the poor rate.
London: 1831. pp.90. C; G.

920. RICHARDSON, J. A proposal for a change in the poor law and
the reduction of the poor's rate by the beneficial employment
of the labourers. London: [1831]. pp.47. LSE.

921. RIGBY, E.A. The powers and duties of guardians of the poor.
London: [1899?]. pp.20. LSE.

922. ROBERTS, D. "How cruel was the Victorian poor law?". Hist.J.
VI. (1963). pp.97-107.

923. ROBERTS, G.J. A practical guide to poor law prosecutions,
together with full police court procedure and the necessary
forms and documents. London: 1912. pp.xix + 168. BL.

924. ROBERTS, S. England's glory; or, the good old poor law.
London: 1836. pp.56. C; G.

925. ROBERTS, S. Lord Brougham and the new poor law. London:
1838. pp.72. LSE; G.

926. ROBERTS, S. A defence of the poor law with a plan for the
suppression of mendicity and for the establishment of
universal parochial benefit societies. Sheffield: 1819.
pp.52. LSE.

927. ROBERTS, S. The pauper's advocate: a cry from the brink of
the grave against the new poor law. London: 1841. pp.112.
G.

928. ROBINSON, M.F. The poor law enigma. London: 1911. pp.x +
189. LSE; S.

929. ROBINSON, W. A breviary of the poor laws... London: 1827.
2 parts. BL.

930. ROBINSON, W. Lex parochialis: or, a compendium of the laws
relating to the poor with the adjudged cases on parochial
settlements, to the 7th year of King George the fourth. (An
appendix of precedents to Lex parochialis...). London: 1827.
2 parts. BL.

931. RODWELL, W. An analytical index to the Act for the Amendment
of the Poor Law, etc. Ipswich: 1834. pp.35. G.

932. ROGERS, A.G.L. (ed.). The state of the poor. A history of

the labouring classes in England, with parochial reports. London: 1929. pp.li + 383. BL. (An abridged edition of the work by Sir Frederick Morton Eden first published in 1797.)

933. ROSE, M.E.   "The anti-poor law movement in the north of England". Nth.Hist. I. (1966). pp.60-91.

934. ROSE, M.E.   "The allowance system under the new poor law". Ec.H.R. (2nd ser.). 19. (1966). pp.607-620.

935. ROSE, M.E.   "The anti-poor law agitation". In J.T. Ward (ed). Popular movements c.1830-1850. London: 1970. pp.78-94.

936. ROSE, M.E.   The English poor law 1780-1930.   Newton Abbott: 1971. pp.335. DHSS; LSE; CUL; Sq.

937. ROSE, M.E.   The relief of poverty 1834-1914.   London: 1972. pp.64. DHSS; LSE; CUL.

938. ROSS, E.M.   Woman and poor law administration 1857-1909. 1956. Fo. iii + 305. (Typescript). LSE.

939. ROYAL COMMISSION ON THE POOR LAWS AND RELIEF OF DISTRESS. Report of the Royal Commission on the Poor Laws and the Relief of Distress.   Vol.1.   (Parts I-VI of the majority report). (Hamilton Report). London: 1909. pp.565. (Cd. 4499). DHSS.

940. ROYAL COMMISSION ON THE POOR LAWS AND RELIEF OF DISTRESS. Report of the Royal Commission on the Poor Laws and the Relief of Distress. (Minority Report). (Wakefield Report). London: 1909. pp.716. (Cd. 4499). DHSS.

941. ROYAL COMMISSION ON THE POOR LAWS AND RELIEF OF DISTRESS. Appendix Vol.XX. Report by Mr. Cyril Jackson on boy labour together with a memorandum from the General Post Office on the conditions of boy messengers.   London: 1909.   pp.230. (Cd.4632). DHSS.

942. ROYAL COMMISSION ON THE POOR LAWS AND RELIEF OF DISTRESS. Appendix Vol.XXV. Statistics relating to England and Wales. London: 1911. pp.902. (Cd. 5077). DHSS.

943. [RUFFHEAD, O.] A digest of the poor laws, in order to their being reduced into one Act. With references to the statutes, and marginal observations. London: 1768. pp.xxvii + 74. G.

944. RUGGLES, T.   The history of the poor;   their rights, duties and the laws respecting them. London: 1793. 2 vols. G. A new edition corrected, and continued to the present time. London: 1797. pp.423. G.

945. RUSSELL, C.   The Catholic in the workhouse. Popular statement of the law as it affects him, the religious grievances it raises, with practical suggestions for reform. London: 1859. pp.47. BL.

946. RYAN, P.   "The poor law in 1926".   in Margaret Morris (ed.). The general strike. Harmondsworth: 1976. pp.358-78. Sq.

63

947.   SALISBURY, W.   A treatise on the practical means of employing the poor in manufacturing articles of British growth.   London: 1820.   pp.46.   G.

948.   SALTER, F.R.   Some early tracts on poor relief.   1926.   pp.xx + 128.   CUL.

949.   SAUNDERS, R.   Observations on the present state and influence of the poor laws, founded on experience, and a plan proposed for the consideration of parliament.   1799.   pp.xv + 173.   MT.

950.   SAUNDERS, R.   An abstract of observations on the poor law. London: 1802.   pp.viii + 44.   G.

951.   SAUNDERS, W.H.   An address upon the practical means of gradually abolishing the poor laws.   London: 1821.   pp.125. G.   3rd ed.   London: 1821.   BL.

952.   [SAVAGE, W.]   Case on the 43rd Elizabeth for the relief of the poor.   London: 1837.   pp.26.   LSE.

953.   SCOTT, J.   Observations on the present state of the parochial and vagrant poor.   London: 1773.   pp.136.   G.

954.   SCOTT, S.   Digest of the poor laws.   1773.

955.   SCROPE, G.P.   Plea for the abolition of slavery in England as produced by an illegal abuse of the poor law, common in the southern counties.   London: 1829.   pp,.vi + 44.   LSE.

956.   SCROPE, G.J.   A letter to the magistrates of the South of England, on the urgent necessity of putting a stop to the illegal practice of making up wages out of rates, to which alone is owing the misery and revolt of the agricultural peasantry.   London: 1830.   pp.26.   NLI.

957.   SCROPE, G.P.   A second letter to the magistrates of the South of England, on the propriety of discontinuing the allowance system, the means for employing or disposing of the excess of labour, and for diminishing the unequal pressure of the poor rate.   London: 1831.   pp.54.   LSE; G.

958.   SCURFIELD, H.   Royal Commission on the Poor Laws and Relief of Distress: a course of nine lectures delivered on the report of the above-named Commission in Sheffield, during the winter of 1909-10.   Sheffield: 1912.   pp.56.   (Sheffield Weekly News reprints).   BL.

959.   SCURR, J.   The reform(!) of the poor law.   London: 1927. pp.16.   LSE.

960.   SEARBY, P.   "The relief of the poor in Coventry".   Hist.J. 20.   (1977).   pp.345-61.

961.   SEDGWICK, J.   A letter to the rate-payers of Great Britain on the repeal of the poor-laws;   to which is subjoined the outline of a plan for the abolition of the poor-rates at the end of three years.   London: 1833.   pp.172.   TCD.

962.   SELECT COMMITTEE ON POOR LAW RELIEF.   Report.   London: 1888.

(H.C. 363).

963. SELLERS, E. "Foreign remedies for English poor law defects".
      Nineteenth Century. LXII. (1907). pp.770-96.

964. [SENIOR, N.W.]   Outline of the Poor Law Amendment Act.
      London: 1834. pp.26. G.

965. SENIOR, N.W. Statement of the provision for the poor, and of
      the condition of the labouring classes, in a considerable
      portion of America and Europe... Being the preface to the
      foreign communications contained in the Appendix to the Poor
      Law Report. London: 1835. pp.vii + 238. G; CUL; LSE.

966. SENIOR, N.W. Remarks on the opposition to the Poor Law
      Amendment Bill. London: 1841. pp.117. LSE.

967. SHAW & SONS.   Shaw's annotated edition of the Poor Law
      Institutions Order, 1913. London: 1914. pp.116. LSE.

968. SHAW, J. Parish Law: or a guide to Justices of the Peace,
      ministers, churchwardens, overseers of the poor, constables,
      surveyors of the highways, vestry-clerks and all others
      concerned in parish business: compiled from the common,
      statute, and other authentic books;   as also from some
      adjudged cases never before published: together with correct
      forms of warrants, commitments, indictments, presentments,
      convictions, etc... 5th ed. ("with many new cases, and the
      Acts of Parliament continued to the present time: with
      observations on the last Vagabond Act").   In the Savoy
      [London?]: 1743. pp.374 + (12). CUL. 9th ed.
      (similarly endorsed). 1755. pp.402 + (20). CUL.

969. SINGLE, T. Hints to Parliament for a general act to prevent
      parochial squabbles for a reduction of one half of the poors'
      sick rate, and to better the condition of the poor. London:
      1824. pp.(2) + 50. TCD.

970. SLATER, G. "The relief of the poor". In H.J. Laski et al.
      (eds.), A century of municipal progress, 1835-1935. London:
      1935. pp.332-69.

971. SLESSER, H.H. (ed.). A Bill to provide for the more effectual
      prevention of destitution and the better organisation of
      public assistance (with explanatory notes).   London: 1910.
      pp.19. 2nd ed. London: 1910. pp.46. Sq.

972. SMITH, J.T. The parish; its powers and obligations at law,
      as regards the welfare of every neighbourhood, and in relation
      to the state. London: 1854. pp.xi + 611. BL; CUL. 2nd ed.
      (with additions). 1957. BL.

973. SMITH, P.G. Hints and suggestions as to the planning of poor
      law buildings. London: 1901. pp.viii + 151. BL.

974. SMITH, T. The old poor law and the new poor law contrasted.
      London: 1840. pp.34. LSE.

975. SOCIETY FOR BETTERING THE CONDITION AND INCREASING THE
      COMFORTS OF THE POOR.   Reports, 1797-8, 1811-15.   London:

1798-1815. 8vols. LSE; G.

976. SOCIETY FOR PROMOTING THE RETURN OF WOMEN AS POOR LAW
GUARDIANS. Annual Report. London: 1889/90-1899/1900.
[Incomplete]. LSE.

977. SOPHIAN, T.J. The Poor Law Act, 1927. With full notes,
introduction... London: 1927. pp.xix + 134. Sq.

978. SOUTHERN, J.W. The unemployed: an examination of some of the
causes and remedies of poverty. Manchester: 1888. pp.24.
LSE.

979. SPEDDING, T.S. Letters on the poor laws. London: 1847.
pp.viii + 87. LI.

980. SPENCER, T. Observations on the state of the poor and the
practical tendencies of the new poor law. London: 1835.
pp.56. C.

981. SPENS, W.C. Protest against the abrogation of the laws of
removal and settlement, with suggestions as to their
modification and alteration. Edinburgh: 1881. pp.47. CUL.

982. SPENS, W.C. Should the poor law in all cases deny relief to
the able-bodied poor? Edinburgh: 1879. pp.47. CUL.

983. SPRIGGE, J.J. Shortcomings of the machinery for pauper
litigation. London: 1893. pp.89. LSE.

984. STANLEY-MORGAN, R. "The poor law unions and their records".
Amat.Hist. II. (1954). pp.11-15.

985. STEER, J. Parish law: being a digest of the law relating to
the civil and ecclesiastical government of parish and the
relief of the poor. London: 1881. pp.xxi + 458. LSE.

986. STEVENS, J. The poor law an interference with the divine law
by which welfare of society are maintained. London: 1831.
pp.104. G.

987. STIRLING, T.H. The question propounded; or, how will Great
Britain ameliorate and remedy the distresses of its workmen
and others out of employment? London: 1849. pp.25. LSE.

988. STRATTON, J.Y. Method of improving the labouring classes by
altering the conditions of poor relief and providing them with
a system of insurance through the Post Office. London: 1872.
pp.29. G.

989. STRICKLAND, G. A Discourse on the poor laws of England and
Scotland, on the state of the poor in Ireland and on
emigration. 2nd ed. 1830. pp.viii + 139. LSE.

990. SWABEY, M.C.M. A practical explanation of the duties of
parish officers in electing guardians under the Poor Law
Amendment Act, 1837. BL.

991. SYMONDS, J.F. The relieving officer. London: 1886. pp.123.
4th ed. 1896. pp.120 + 6. 5th ed. 1904. pp.xxiv + 149.

LSE.

992.   SYNNOTT, N.J.   "The Labourers' Acts and the poor law".   N.I.R.
       22.   (1904-5).   pp.129-39.

993.   SYNNOTT, N.J.   "The Labourers' Bill".   N.I.R.   25.   (1906).
       pp.321-30.

994.   TALLACK, W.   Poor relief and the diminution of pauperism: a
       British desideratum.   London, January 125th 1895:   The problem
       of poor relief.   London: 1895.   pp.4.   NLI.

995.   TAYLOR, J.S.   "The mythology of the old poor law".
       J.Econ.Hist.   29.   (1969).   p.292.

996.   TEIGNMOUTH, LORD.   "The 'dole' system a century ago".
       Engl.Rev.   XXXIX.   5.   (1924).   pp.630-8.

997.   THE PAMPHLETEER.   On the means of benefiting the poor.
       London: 1820.   pp.12.   G.

998.   THE TIMES.   The report of the Poor Law Commission.   London:
       [1909].   pp.48.   CUL.

999.   THEOBALD, W.   The Poor Law Amendment Act;   with a commentary
       on the powers of the commissioners...   London: 1834.   BL.
       1835.   [Source: SM2].

1,000. THEOBALD, W.   Collection of all the statutes relative to
       parochial settlements and the government and maintenance of
       the poor.   1836.   [Source: SM2].

1,001. THEOBALD, W.   A practical treatise on the poor laws as altered
       by the Poor Law Amendment Act and other statutes...   and an
       appendix of the statutes.   London: 1836.   pp.xxviii + 902 +
       47.   CUL.   New ed.   1837...   containing a supplement.   pp.47.
       CUL; BL; TCD.

1,002. THEOBALD, W.   A supplement to Theobald's practical treatise on
       the poor laws;   containing an expository and critical
       statement of all the poor law cases reported since that
       publication, together with the poor law statutes, 7 Wm. IV & 1
       Vict. and notes upon them.   London: 1837.   pp.52.   TCD.

1,003. TIERNEY, B.   Medieval poor law: a sketch of canonical theory
       and its application in England.   London: 1959.   pp.xi + 169.
       DHSS; LSE; Sq.

1,004. TOONE, W.   A practical guide to the duty and authority of the
       overseers of the poor;   with full and plain directions to them
       in the execution of their office.   Interspersed with numerous
       precedents of summonses, warrants, orders, etc. relating to
       the poors' law and parish matters in general.   London: 1815.
       pp.viii + 191.   2nd ed. with additions.   1822.   pp.iv + 242 +
       (6).   CUL.

1,005. [TOWNSEND, J.]   A dissertation on the poor laws.   London:
       1917.   pp.108.   G; TCD.

1,006. TOWNSEND, J.   A dissertation on the poor laws.   With a foreword by Ashley Montague and afterword by Mark Neumann. [Originally published London: 1817]. Berkeley and London: 1971. pp.86. CUL.

1,007. TOYNBEE, C.M. "Poverty and the poor law". Econ.Rev. X. (1900). pp.316-22.

1,008. TURNER, C.J.R. Suggestions for systematic inquiry into the case of applicants for relief. With an appendix... London: n.l. 2nd ed. n.l. 3rd ed. revised and enlarged. 1872. BL.

1,009. TWINING, L. Recollections of workhouse visiting and management during 25 years. London: 1880. pp.xx + 217.

1,010. TWINING, L. "Workhouse cruelties". Nineteenth Century. XX. 117. (1886). pp.709-14.

1,011. TWINING, L. A letter on some matters of poor law administration. London: 1887. pp.70. BL.

1,012. TWINING, L. Poor relief in foreign countries, and out-door relief in England. London: 1889. pp.63. LSE.

1,013. TWINING, L. Workhouses and pauperism; and women's work in the administration of the poor law. London: 1898. pp.xi + 276. LSE.

1,014. UDALL, H. Practical compendium of the poor laws, and the evidence required in an appeal to the Quarter Sessions. 1836. [Source: SM2].

1,015. UNITED KINGDOM. A proclamation for the due observation of certain statutes made for the suppressing of rogues, etc. London: 1661. pp.(6). G.

1,016. UNITED KINGDOM. The law concerning the poor...; adding several forms of orders of sessions, warrants, etc. London: 1705. pp.240.

1,017. UNITED KINGDOM. Poor-law; or, The law... relating to the settling, maintenance, and employment of the poor, etc. London: 1724. pp.144. G.

1,018. UNITED KINGDOM Report from the committee appointed to make enquiries relating to the employment, relief, and maintenance of the poor, etc. n.p.: 1776. pp.iv + 78. LSE.

1,019. [UNITED KINGDOM.] Substance of a bill for promoting industry amongst the labouring classes of the community, and for the relief of the criminal poor. London: 1807. pp.44. G.

1,020. UNITED KINGDOM. An Act... for the better relief... of the poor, etc. London: 1813. pp.144. LSE.

1,021. UNITED KINGDOM. Report from the commission on poor houses and poor rates. London: 1813-14. pp.16. (B.P.P. IV). LSE.

1,022. UNITED KINGDOM. Report from commission on the state of mendicity in the metropolis. London: 1814-15. pp.100. (B.P.P. III). LSE.

1,023. UNITED KINGDOM. Report from the select committee on the poor laws. London: 1817. pp.169. (B.P.P. VI). LSE.

1,024. UNITED KINGDOM. Report from the select committee on the poor laws (1818). London: 1818. pp.85. (B.P.P. V.). LSE.

1,025. UNITED KINGDOM. Report of the Lords committee on the poor laws. 1817. London: 1818. pp.208. (B.P.P. V). LSE.

1,026. UNITED KINGDOM. Report (1817) from the select committee on the poor laws. London: 1819. pp.29. (B.P.P. II). LSE.

1,027. UNITED KINGDOM. Report from the committee on the poor laws. London: 1819. pp.37. (B.P.P. II). LSE.

1,028. UNITED KINGDOM. Report from the select committee on that part of the poor laws relating to the employment or relief of able-bodied persons from the poor rate. London: 1828. pp.62. (B.P.P. IV). LSE.

1,029. UNITED KINGDOM. Report from the select committee of the House of Lords appointed to consider the poor laws. London: 1831. pp.421. (B.P.P. VIII). LSE.

1,030. UNITED KINGDOM., Act for the amendment... of the law relating to the poor, etc. London: 1834. pp.(60) + 104. LSE.

1,031. UNITED KINGDOM. Report from Her Majesty's Commissioners for inquiring into the administration and practical operation of the poor laws. London: 1834. 13v. (B.P.P. XXVII-XXXIX). LSE.

1,032. UNITED KINGDOM. Annotated reports of the poor law commissioners for England and Wales. London: 1835-1848. (B.P.P.). LSE.

1,033. UNITED KINGDOM. Act for the amendment... of the law relating to the poor, etc. London: 1836. pp.xxiv + 104. LSE.

1,034. UNITED KINGDOM. First (-22nd) report from select committee on the Poor Law Amendment Act. London: 1837. (B.P.P. XVII). LSE.

1,035. UNITED KINGDOM. First (-49th) report from select committee on the Poor Law Amendment Act, etc. London: 1837-8. (B.P.P. XVIII). LSE.

1,036. UNITED KINGDOM. Report of the poor law commissioners... on the continuance of the poor law commission, and on some further amendments of the law relating to the relief of the poor. London: 1840. pp.xii + 190. (B.P.P. XVII). LSE.

1,037. UNITED KINGDOM. Poor Law Board: official circulars of public documents and information. London: 1840-6. vols.1-6 (in 1). LSE.

1,038. UNITED KINGDOM. Copies of orders, etc. issued by the poor law commissioners relating to the Poor Law Amendment Act; with an account of money expended for the relief and maintenance of the poor, etc. in England and Wales, from 1834 to 1840 inclusive. London: 1841. pp.37. (B.P.P. XXI). LSE.

1,039. UNITED KINGDOM. Copies of general orders issued by the poor law commissioners. London: 1841. pp.74. (B.P.P. XXI). LSE.

1,040. [UNITED KINGDOM.] Poor Law Commissioners report on an inquiry into the sanitary conditions of the labouring population of Great Britain, with appendices. London: 1842. pp.xxi + 457. LSE.

1,041. UNITED KINGDOM. First (-third) report from the select committee on medical poor relief, etc. London: 1844. (B.P.P. IX). LSE.

1,042. UNITED KINGDOM. Report from the select committee on poor relief (Gilbert Unions) etc. London: 1844. pp.xiv + 484. (B.P.P. X). LSE.

1,043. UNITED KINGDOM. Copy of articles 9, 10, 11 and 12, of the general workhouse rules issued by the Poor Law Commissioners, etc. London: 1844. (B.P.P. XL). LSE.

1,044. UNITED KINGDOM. Report from the select committee on Medical Poor Relief Commission, 1844, etc. London: 1845. pp.viii + 108. (B.P.P. XII). LSE.

1,045. UNITED KINGDOM. Report of the commissioners for administering the law for relief of the poor in England, 1848. London: 1849. pp.83. (B.P.P. XXV). LSE.

1,046. UNITED KINGDOM. Annual reports of the Poor Law Board, 1850-64, 1866-71. London. (B.P.P.). LSE.

1,047. UNITED KINGDOM. Poor relief: return... as respects the unions, parishes under Boards of Guardians, incorporations and parishes under local Acts and Gilbert's Act, etc. London: 1857-8. (B.P.P. XLIV). pp.xi + 181. LSE.

1,048. UNITED KINGDOM Minutes of evidence taken before the Select Committee on Irremovable Poor, etc. London: 1859. (B.P.P., sess.2, VII). pp.vii + 196. LSE.

1,049. UNITED KINGDOM. Copies of letters of instruction to poor law inspectors, of orders issued, and of inquiries... instituted with reference to the cases of defalcation and embezzlement by poor law officers in the metropolis. London: 1860. pp.73. (B.P.P. LVIII). LSE.

1,050. UNITED KINGDOM. First (-third) report from the select committee on poor relief, etc. London: 1862. (B.P.P. X). LSE.

1,051. UNITED KINGDOM. Report from the Select Committee on Poor Relief, etc. London: 1864. (B.P.P. IX). pp.143. LSE.

1,052. UNITED KINGDOM. Report on the poor laws of certain of the United States, and on the combination there of private charity with official relief. London: 1877. pp.91. (B.P.P.

XXXVII). LSE.

1,053. [UNITED KINGDOM.] A statement of the names of the several unions and poor law parishes in England and Wales; and of the population area, and rateable value thereof in 1881, etc. London: 1887. pp.iv + 428. (B.P.P. 1887, LXX). LSE.

1,054. UNITED KINGDOM. Report from the select committee of the House of Lords on poor law relief, etc. London: 1888. pp.xxix + 871. (B.P.P. XV). LSE.

1,055. UNITED KINGDOM. First Report of the commissioners for inquiring into the administration and operation of the poor law in 1834. London: 1894. pp.v + 301. LSE.

1,056. UNITED KINGDOM. The first report of the commissioners for inquiring into the administration and operation of the poor laws in 1834. London: 1894. pp.v + 301. LSE.

1,057. UNITED KINGDOM. Copy of the report made in 1834 by the commissioners for inquiring into the administration and practical operation of the poor laws. London: 1905. pp.viii + 378. LSE.

1,058. UNITED KINGDOM. Poor law commissioners: report of 1834. London: 1906. pp.vii + 378. (B.P.P. CII). LSE.

1,059. UNITED KINGDOM. Report of the Royal Commission on the poor laws and relief of distress (with minutes of evidence). London: 1909. (B.P.P. XXXVII-XLIV). LSE.

1,060. UNITED KINGDOM. Report... on the effects of employment or assistance given to the "unemployed" since 1886 as a means of relieving distress outside the poor law. London: 1909. pp.xxvi + 757. (B.P.P. XLIV). LSE.

1,061. UNITED KINGDOM. Royal commission on the poor laws and relief of distress: apps. London: 1910. (B.P.P. XLVI-LV). LSE.

1,062. [UNITED KINGDOM.] Out-door relief orders: report of the departmental committee on the administration of out-door relief. London: 1911. pp.62. (Cd. 5525). LSE.

1,063. [UNITED KINGDOM.] First report of departmental committee with respect to the poor law orders. London: 1913. pp.xiii + 271. (Cd. 6968). LSE.

1,064. [UNITED KINGDOM.] Poor law reform. London: 1919. pp.23. LSE.

1,065. UNITED KINGDOM. Provisional proposals for poor law reform prepared in the Ministry of Health, etc. London: 1925. pp.6. LSE.

1,066. UNITED KINGDOM Report of committee on schemes of assistance to necessitating areas. London: 1926. (B.P.P. XIV). pp.37. LSE.

1,067. UNITED KINGDOM. Report... upon the Poor Law Bill [House of Lords], etc. London: 1926. pp.x + 59. (B.P.P. VI). LSE.

1,068. UNITED KINGDOM. Consolidated Bills, 1927...: report upon the Poor Law Bill [House of Lords], etc. London: 1927. pp.xcii + 82. (B.P.P. V). LSE.

1,069. UNITED KINGDOM. Administration of the poor law: extract from the annual report of the Ministry of Health for 1927-28, etc. London: 1928. pp.138. LSE.

1,070. [UNITED KINGDOM.] Poor law. Report of a special inquiry into various forms of test work. London: 1929. pp.44. (Cmd. 3585). (B.P.P. 1929-30, XVII). LSE.

1,071. UNUS PUPULI. (Pseud). A letter to Mr. Scarlet on the poor law. London: 1822. pp.88. G.

1,072. VANE, C.W. Substance of the speech delivered in the House of Commons on the subject of the agricultural distress of the country, and the financial measures proposed for its relief. 3rd ed. London: 1822. pp.103. LSE.

1,073. VANE, C.W. Substance of a second speech delivered in the House of Commons on the subject of the agricultural distress of the country and the financial and other measures proposed for its relief. London: 1822. pp.78. LSE.

1,074. VINCENT, G.G. Letter to Mr. J. Bower exposing the unprincipled nature of the new poor law. London: 1838. pp.27. G.

1,075. VINOGRADOFF, P. (ed.). Oxford studies in social and legal history. Vol.3. Part 2. One hundred years of poor law administration in a Warwickshire village, by A.W. Ashby. Oxford: 1912. CUL.

1,076. VIVIAN, R. Thoughts on the causes and cure of excessive poor rates. Injustice of rating the funds in aid of the land. London: 1817. pp.(iv) + 32. G.

1,077. VULLIAMY, A.F. The duties of relieving officers and the administration of out-relief. London: 1904. pp.xvi + 195 + xxxix. (Local government library 3).

1,078. WADDINGTON, W.H. "The absorption of the work of the poor law authorities in London by the London County Council". Pub.Admin. IX. (1931). p.49.

1,079. WAKEFIELD, H.R. & OTHERS. Nine lectures on the report of the Royal Commission on the Poor Law and relief of distress. Sheffield: 1910. pp.56. LSE.

1,080. WALKER, G. The poor law - indispensable. London: 1914. pp.26. LSE.

1,081. WALKER, G. The evolution of the English poor law. London: 1917. pp.8. LSE.

1,082. WALKER, G. Poor law reform. London: 1927. pp.16. LSE.

1,083. WALKER, G.P. Our poor law system: the "workhouse". London:

1868. pp.8. LSE.

1,084. WALLAS, G. "The history of the poor law". Co-operative Wholesale Societies. <u>Annual for 1894</u>. pp.262-85.

1,085. WALSH, HON. G. Dock labour in relation to poor law relief. London: 1906. pp.46. (Cd.4391). LSE.

1,086. WALTHEW, R. A moral and political essay on the English poor law. London: 1814. pp.144. G.

1,087. WATKINSON, W.R. The relieving officer looks back; the last years of poor law in Holderness. Withernsea: 1955. pp.38. DHSS; LSE.

1,088. WEBB, B. The poor law medical officer and his future. London: 1909. pp.7. LSE; U.

1,089. WEBB, B. The abolition of the poor law. London: 1918. pp.11. (Fabian Tracts No.185). LSE.

1,090. WEBB, B. The English poor law: will it endure? London: 1928. pp.32. LSE.

1,091. WEBB, S. The reform of the poor law. [London]: 1890. pp.4. (Extracts from the Political World, February 8th, 13th, 20th, 1890). LSE (xerox copy). And in Fabian Tract No.17. London: 1891. CUL.

1,092. WEBB, S. "The reform of the poor law". <u>Contemp.Rev.</u> LVIII. (1890). pp.95-120.

1,093. WEBB, S. The reform of the poor law. London: 1890. pp.20. (Fabian Tract 17). LSE.

1,094. WEBB, S. Le probleme de l'assistance publique en Angleterre. Paris: 1912. pp.80. LSE.

1,095. WEBB, S. & B. (eds.). The public organisation of the labour market: being part two of the minority report of the Poor Law Commission. I. The able-bodied under the poor law. II. The able-bodied and voluntary agencies. III. The able-bodied under the Unemployed Workmen Act. IV. Distress from unemployment as it exists today. V. Proposals for reform. London: 1909. pp.xiii + 345. CUL.

1,096. WEBB, S. & B. (eds.). The break-up of the poor law: being part one of the minority report of the Poor Law Commision. London: 1909. pp.xvii + 601. CUL.

1,097. WEBB, S. & B. (eds.). The public organisation of the labour market: being part two of the minority report of the Poor Law Commission. London: 1909. pp.xiii + 345. CUL; LSE.

1,098. WEBB, S. & B. English poor law policy. London: 1910. pp.xv + 379. (English Local Government Vol.10). DHSS; CUL. Reprinted, with a new introduction by W.A. Robson. 1963. Sq.

1,099. WEBB, S. & B. The prevention of destitution. London: 1911. pp.vi + 348. CUL. Reissued. 1920. pp.xvi + 348. CUL.

1,100. WEBB, S. & WEBB, B. Le probleme de l'assistance publique en Angleterre. London: 1912. pp.80. LSE.

1,101. [WEBB, S. & WEBB, B.] Reports and papers on the relief of distress, 1914-15. n.p. 1914-15. 5 vols. (MS, mimeographed, printed and typescript). LSE.

1,102. WEBB, S. & B. English local government: statutory authorities for special purposes. London: 1922. pp.521. CUL.

1,103. WEBB, S. & B. English poor law history. Part 1. The old poor law. London: 1927. pp.xxvi + 447. CUL.

1,104. WEBB, S. & B. English poor law history. Part 2. For the last 100 years. London: 1927. 2 vols. Sq. Reprinted. 1963. DHSS.

1,105. WESTON, C. Remarks on the poor law and on the state of the poor. Brentford: 1802. pp.166. G; CUL.

1,106. WETHERELL, C. The present state of the poor law question. London: 1833. G.

1,107. WEYLAND, J. A short inquiry into the policy, humanity and past effects of the poor law. London: 1807. pp.xliv + 382. LSE; G.

1,108. WEYLAND, J. The principle of the English poor law illustrated from the evidence given by the Scottish proprietors (before the Corn Committee) on the connexion observed in Scotland between the price of grain and the wages of labour. London: 1815. pp.82. KI;TCD; LSE.

1,109. WEYLAND, J. Observations on Mr. Whitbread's poor bill, and on the population of England. London: 1807. pp.65. LSE; G.

1,110. WHITBREAD, S. Substance of a speech on the poor law. London: 1807. pp.107. LSE; G.

1,111. WHITE, J.M. Some remarks on the statute law affecting parish apprentices, with regulations applicable to local districts and parishes, for allotting and placing out poor children, in conformity to the 43 Eliz.c.2, and subsequent statutes. London: 1829. pp.108. TCD.

1,112. WHITE, J.M. Remarks on the Poor Law Amendment Act, as it affects unions, or parishes, under the government of guardians, or select vestries. London: 1834. pp.52. LSE; C; TCD.

1,113. WILKINS, H. Memorandum on the administration of the poor law. London: 1895. pp.32.

1,114. WILLCOCK, J.W. Law relating to the ordering and settlement of the parish poor. 1829. [Source: SM2].

1,115. WILLINK, H.G. The principles of the English poor law. London: 1896. pp.27.

1,116.   WILLIS, J.   On the poor laws of England.   The various plans
         and opinions of Judge Blackstone [and others] stated
         and considered, with proposed amendments of easy execution to
         give effect to the present laws and to the views of the
         government.   London: 1808.   pp.78.   G.

1,117.   WILSON, H.B.   The poor law crisis: reform or revolution?
         Birmingham:' 1910.   pp.95.   LSE.

1,118.   WILSON, W.C.   Remarks on certain operations of the new poor
         law.   Kirkby Lonsdale: 1838.   pp.31.   LSE; C; G.

1,119.   [WILMOT, R.]   Disinherited;   or, principle and expediency
         explained as affecting public welfare and private happiness;
         in answer to Poor Law and Paupers by Harriet Martineau.
         London: 1835.   2 vols. in 1.   G.

1,120.   WODEHOUSE, E.H.   Report on out-door relief administration in
         seventy unions.   London: 1872.   pp.129.   DHSS.

1,121.   WOHL,   A.S.   "The   bitter   cry   of   outcast   London".
         Int.Rev.Soc.Hist.   XII.   (1968).   pp.189-245.

1,122.   WOODROOFE,   K.   "The   Royal   Commission   on   the   Poor   Laws,
         1905-09".   Int.Rev.Soc.Hist.   XXII.   (1977).   pp.137-164.

1,123.   WOODWARD, E.G. & WOODWARD, E.R.   The Poor Law Act, 1927, with
         introduction,   notes   and   cross   references.   London: 1927.
         pp.xiv + 167.

1,124.   WOODWARD, G.   Archbold's poor law.   16th ed.   London: 1930.
         pp.xliii + 490 + 65.   CUL.

1,125.   WYNNE, E.   Analysis of the law concerning parochial provision
         for the poor, with an appendix.   1767.

1,126.   YOUNG, A.A.   The poor law: is any alteration of it necessary
         or tolerably practicable?   London: 1839.   pp.24.   LSE.

1,127.   YOUNG, SIR W.   Considerations on the subject of poor-houses
         and   work-houses,   their   pernicious   tendency,   and   their
         obstruction to the proposed plan for amendment of the poor
         laws;   in a letter to the Rt. Hon. W. Pitt, from Sir William
         Young.   London: 1796.   pp.53.   CUL.

1,128.   ZAGDAY, M.I.   "Bentham and the poor law".   In G.W. Keeton & G.
         Schwarzenberger (eds.).   Jeremy Bentham and the law.   London:
         1948.   pp.58-67.

(b) Poor Law, Scotland

1,129.   ANON.   Committee appointed by the Commissioners of Police, to
         inquire into the practicability of suppressing the practice of
         common begging etc.   Report.   Edinburgh: 1812.   pp.19.   G.

1,130.   ANON.   Committee to suggest a plan for affording relief to the
         labouring classes in the city and suburbs.   Edinburgh: 1816.
         pp.16.   G.

1,131. ANON. "The Scottish system of poor law". DUM. 3. (1834).
        pp.508-22.

1,132. ANON. Poor laws and pauperism in Scotland. [By
        J.H.B.]. Edinburgh: [1841?]. pp.24. C.

1,133. ANON. Amendment of the poor law of Scotland. Edinburgh:
        1867. NLS.

1,134. ANON. "The Scottish poor law". Westm.Rev. 94. (1870).
        pp.340-67.

1,135. ANON. Report by Distress Committee for the city of Edinburgh
        for the year ending 15 May 1908. Edinburgh: 1908. pp.44.
        DHSS.

1,136. ALISON, W.P. Remarks on the report of Her Majesty's
        commissioners on the poor laws of Scotland, presented to
        parliament in 1844, and on the dissent of Mr. Twisleton from
        that report. Edinburgh: 1844. pp.312. TCD; G.

1,137. ALISON, W.P. Observations on the management of the poor in
        Scotland, and its effects on the health of the great towns.
        Edinburgh and London: 1840. pp.198. G; NLI; RIA; TCD. 2nd
        ed. Edinburgh and London: 1840. pp.123. G.

1,138. ALISON, W.P. Reply to the pamphlet entitled "Proposed
        alteration of the Scottish Poor Law considered and commented
        on by David Monypenny, Esq. of Pitmilly". Edinburgh and
        London: 1840. pp.75. G; TCD.

1,139. ALISON, W.P. Further illustrations of the practical operation
        of the Scottish system of management of the poor. London:
        1841. pp.32. G.

1,140. ALISON, W.P. Reply to Dr. Chalmers' objections to the
        improvement of the legal provision for the poor in Scotland.
        Edinburgh and London: 1841. pp.62. TCD.

1,141. ALISON, W.P. On the present state of the law of settlement
        and removal of paupers in Scotland. Read at the statistical
        section of the British Association at Belfast, on Monday 6th
        September, 1852. Dublin: 1852. pp.16. NLI; RIA; TCD.

1,142. ASSOCIATION FOR OBTAINING AN OFFICIAL INQUIRY INTO THE
        PAUPERISM OF SCOTLAND. Second report of the Committee, etc.
        Edinburgh: 1841. pp.57. LSE.

1,143. BEGG, J. Pauperism and the poor law. Edinburgh: 1849.
        pp.96. LSE.

1,144. BURN, W.L. "The Scottish poor law and the Poor Law Act 1834".
        Pub.Admin. X. (1932). p.388.

1,145. BURNS, R. A plea for the poor of Scotland and for an enquiry
        into their condition. Paisley: 1841. pp.36. LSE.

1,146. CAGE, R.A. "The making of the old Scottish poor law". P.& P.
        69. (1975). pp.113-18.

1,147.   CAGE, R.A.   The Scottish poor law, 1745-1845.   Edinburgh: 1981. pp.175. LSE.

1,148.   CENTRAL BOARD FOR THE RELIEF OF DESTITUTION IN THE HIGHLANDS AND ISLANDS OF SCOTLAND, EDINBURGH SECTION.   Reports... for 1848-(1850). Edinburgh: [1848]-1851. 3 vols. LSE.

1,149.   CENTRAL BOARD FOR THE RELIEF OF DESTITUTION IN THE HIGHLANDS AND ISLANDS OF SCOTLAND, GLASGOW SECTION.   Report on the islands of Mull, Ulva, Iona, Tiree and Coll, and on part of the parish of Morven... October, 1849. Glasgow: [1849]. pp.36 LSE.

1,150.   CENTRAL BOARD FOR THE RELIEF OF DESTITUTION IN THE HIGHLANDS AND ISLANDS OF SCOTLAND, GLASGOW SECTION.   Commitee of management report... 24th December, 1849. Glasgow: [1850]. pp.36. LSE.

1,151.   CHALMERS, T. Doctor Chalmers and the poor laws: a comparison of Scotch and English pauperism, and evidence before the Committee of the House of Commons. Edinburgh: 1911. pp.xii + 235.

1,152.   COOK, J. A brief view of the Scottish system for the relief of the poor, and of some proposed changes in it. Edinburgh: 1841. pp.80. G.

1,153.   CORMACK, A.A. Poor relief in Scotland: an outline of the growth and administration of the poor law in Scotland from the middle ages to the present day. Aberdeen: 1923. pp.xi + 215. LSE; CUL.

1,154.   CORMACK, A.A. Poor relief in Scotland: The old and the new. Glasgow: 1926. pp.24. LSE.

1,155.   CRAIG, A. Memoir regarding the law of settlement of paupers in Scotland, etc. Edinburgh: 1841. pp.31. LSE.

1,156.   CURROR, D. The Scottish poor law and some contrasts between its principle and the practices. Edinburgh: 1870. pp.30. G.

1,157.   DEPARTMENT OF HEALTH FOR SCOTLAND. Report of Departmental Committee on Poor Law in Scotland. Edinburgh: 1938. pp.40. (Cmd. 5803). LSE.

1,158.   DUNLOP, A. A treatise on the laws of Scotland relating to the poor. Edinburgh: 1825. pp.(iv) + 152. BL; LSE; G. New ed. 1854. n.l.

1,159.   DUNLOP, C.S.M. A treatise on the law of Scotland, relative to the poor. Edinburgh and London: 1825. pp.152. G.

1,160.   FERGUSON, T. The dawn of Scottish social welfare. A survey from medieval times to 1863. [Edinburgh]: 1948. pp.ix + 321. CUL.

1,161.   FERGUSON, T. Scottish social welfare 1864-1914. Edinburgh: 1958. pp.xi + 609. DHSS; CUL.

1,162. GLADSTONE, D.E. "The new poor law in Scotland: the administrative reorganisation of the first quinquennium". Soc. & Econ.Ad. 9. (1975). pp.115-127.

1,163. GLASGOW UNEMPLOYED RELIEF FUND. Report of the administration of the Glasgow Unemployed Relief Fund during the winter of 1878-9, drawn up, under the direction of the Acting Committee, by Kenneth M. MacLeod. Glasgow: 1879. pp.48. LSE.

1,164. GRAHAM, J.E. & FORBES, J.W. Digest of arbitration decisions by the Local Government Board, 1898 to 1914, under the powers conferred by the Poor Law, Scotland, Act, 1898. Paisley: 1915. pp.xxxix + 104. Bod.

1,165. HANCOCK, W.N. What are the causes of the distressed state of the Highlands of Scotland? Belfast: 1852. pp.16. BL.

1,166. HANCOCK, W.N. "On the Scotch branch of the poor removal question". J.S.S.I.S.I. 8. (1879-85). pp.178-81.

1,167. HAY, W. Decisions on the poor law of Scotland in the Court of Session and awards by arbitration, condensed. Edinburgh: 1859. pp.x + 192. LSE.

1,168. HENDERSON, W.O. "The cotton famine in Scotland and the relief of distress". S.H.R. 30. (1951). pp.154-64.

1,169. HORSFALL TURNER, S. "Ability as the measure of taxation for poor relief in Scotland". E.J. XVI. (1906). pp.337ff.

1,170. IVORY, T. (ed.). Pauperism and the poor law. Edinburgh: 1870. pp. irreg. G.

1,171. KING, G. Modern pauperism and the Scottish poor laws, including hints for the amendment of the Poor Law Act 1845. Aberdeen: 1871. pp.76. TCD.

1,172. KIRKWOOD, J.D. (ed.) Poor law magazine for Scotland. First series, 1858-76. Glasgow: 1859-67. 9 vols. Second series. Glasgow: 1868-72. 5 vols. Third series (ed. W.A. Brown & J.A. Reid). Glasgow: 1873-90. 18 vols. Fourth series. (ed. J.A. Reid & A.O. Deas). Glasgow: 1891-1902. 12 vols.

1,173. LAMOND, R.P. The Scottish poor laws: their history, policy, and operation. Edinburgh: 1870. New ed. Glasgow: 1872. pp.xvi + 400. G.

1,174. LEES, J.J. Poor laws of Scotland as regulated by Poor Law Amendment Act, and instructions of the Board of Supervision. Edinburgh: 1847. NLS.

1,175. LINDSAY, J. The Scottish poor law. Its operation in the north-east from 1745-1845. Ilfracombe: 1975. pp.168. CUL.

1,176. LOCAL GOVERNMENT BOARD FOR SCOTLAND. Departmental Committee to inquire into the system of poor law medical relief... report and minutes. Edinburgh: 1904. (Cd. 2008, 2022). LSE.

1,177. LOCH, C.S. Poor relief in Scotland: its statistics and development, 1791-1891. New York: 1976. pp.271-370. (Facsimile reprint of a paper read before the Royal Statistical Scoiety in 1898). LSE.

1,178. MACKAY, G.A. Practice of the Scottish poor law. Edinburgh: 1907. pp.xii + 242. LSE.

1,179. MACMORRAN, A. & MACMORRAN, M.S.J. The Poor Law Statutes, comprising the statutes in force relating to the poor; and to guardians... from 1879 to 1889 inclusive... with notes and index. London: 1890. A continuation of The statutes in force relating to the poor laws... by W.C. Glen, 1873-79.

1,180. MARSHALL, H.J. "The poor law in necessitous areas". Edin.Rev. 250. (1929). pp.65-81.

1,181. McNEEL-CAIRD, A.M. (ed.). Decisions under the new Poor Law Act, in the sheriff courts, etc. Edinburgh: 1847. pp.48. LSE.

1,182. McNEEL-CAIRD, A. The poor law manual for Scotland: principles of the poor laws and decisions in sheriff courts. [Source: SM5]. 5th ed. 1848. pp.xiv + 328. CUL. An. ed. 1848. 6th ed. ...to present time. Edinburgh: 1851. pp.xviii + 481. BL.

1,183. METCALFE, W. The principle and law of assessing property to the poor's rate, under the 43rd of Elizabeth, cap.2, stated and illustrated by numerous adjudged cases, and the method of assessment practised in Glasgow and Paisley, with remarks on the "parochial assessment act", Mr. Shaw Lefevre's declaratory bill, and the means for obtaining an equitable settlement of the rating question. In a letter addressed (by permission), to the Right Honourable the Earl of Hardwicke. London: 1839. pp.46. TCD.

1,184. MITCHISON, R. "The making of the old Scottish poor law". P.& P. 63. (1974). pp.58-93. "A Rejoinder?". P.& P. 69. (1975). pp.119-21.

1,185. M'NEEL-CAIRD, A. The Poor Law Manual for Scotland: containing the principles of the poor laws; and decisions in sheriff courts... 5th ed. Edinburgh: 1848. pp.xiv + 328. CUL.

1,186. MONILAWS, G.H. A catechism on pauperism and the poor law in Scotland. Edinburgh: 1845. pp.50. C.

1,187. MONYPENNY, D. Remarks on the poor law. Edinburgh: 1834. pp.250. G. 2nd ed. 1836. pp.xxiii + 389. S.

1,188. MONYPENNY, D. Proposed alteration of the Scottish poor laws, and of the administration thereof, as stated by Dr. Alison, in his "Observations on the management of the poor in Scotland", considered and commented on. Edinburgh: 1840. pp.119. G; TCD.

1,189. MONYPENNY, D. Additional remarks on the proposed alteration of the Scottish poor laws, and the administration thereof.

Edinburgh: 1841. pp.176. TCD.

1,190. MUIR, G.W. Suggestions for the improvement of the Scotch poor
        laws. Glasgow: 1848. pp.19. C.

1,191. NICHOLLS, G. A history of the Scotch poor law, in connection
        with the condition of the people. London: 1856. pp.x + 288.
        LSE; CUL; G.

1,192. ORR DEAS, A. Digest of decisions in the Supreme Courts
        relating to the poor law and local government in Scotland
        (being a continuation of Reid's Digest). Glasgow: 1897.
        NLS.

1,193. REID, J.A. Digest of Supreme Court decisions relating to the
        poor law of Scotland. 2 vols. 1880-85. Continuation by
        A.Orr Deas, 1885-97. 1897. (q.v.) (Source: SM5).

1,194. SCOTLAND, LOCAL GOVERNMENT BOARD. Rules and regulations for
        the management of poorhouses. Glasgow: 1908. pp.36. LSE.

1,195. SCOTLAND. Rules, instructions, and recommendations to
        parochial authorities issued by the Board of Supervision for
        the Relief of the Poor in Scotland. Edinburgh: 1854. irreg.
        LSE.

1,196. SCOTLAND. Removal of poor persons: memorandum by the
        Department of Health for Scotland with respect to the removal
        of poor persons within Scotland and from Scotland to England,
        etc. Edinburgh: 1932. pp.18. LSE.

1,197. SCOTTISH NATIONAL COMMITTEE TO PROMOTE THE BREAK-UP OF THE
        POOR LAW. The minority report for Scotland. London: 1909.
        pp.vii + 79. G.

1,198. SCOTUS (Pseud.). The Scottish poor laws: examination of
        their policy, history and practical action... Edinburgh:
        1870. pp.xii + 227. BL.

1,199. SINCLAIR, SIR G. Observations on the new Scottish poor law.
        Edinburgh: 1849. pp.92. TCD.

1,200. SMITH, J.G. Digest of the law of Scotland relating to the
        poor. Edinburgh: 1859. pp.viii + 280. G. 2nd ed.
        Edinburgh: 1867. 3rd ed. Edinburgh: 1878.

1,201. STALLARD, J.H. The Scottish poor law examined in its relation
        to vagrancy. Edinburgh: 1870. pp.20. G.

1,202. TAYLOR, J. Remarks on pauperism, its prevention and its
        relief. Edinburgh: 1843. pp.174. LSE.

1,203. THOMSON, J. Letter on the impolicy of the law of parochial
        settlement. Edinburgh: 1845. pp.22. G.

1,204. UNITED KINGDOM. Report from Her Majesty's Commissioners for
        inquiring into the administration and practical operation of
        the poor laws in Scotland. Edinburgh: 1844. 7v. (B.P.P.
        XX-XXVI). LSE.

1,205.   UNITED KINGDOM. Report from the select committee on poor law
         (Scotland);... with the... minutes of evidence. London:
         1868-9. (B.P.P. XI). LSE.

1,206.   UNITED KINGDOM. Report from the select committee on poor law,
         Scotland, etc. London: 1870. pp.xxvi + 527. (B.P.P. XI).
         LSE.

1,207.   UNITED KINGDOM. Report from the select committee on poor law
         (Scotland), with procedure. London: 1871. pp.xli. (B.P.P.
         XI). LSE.

1,208.   UNITED KINGDOM. Report from the departmental committee on
         habitual offenders, vagrants, beggars, inebriates, and
         juvenile delinquents (Scotland), etc. London: 1895. 2v.
         (B.P.P. XXXVII). LSE.

1,209.   UNITED KINGDOM. Royal Commission on the poor laws and relief
         of distress: report on Scotland. London: 1909. pp.ix +
         314. (B.P.P. XXXVIII). LSE.

1,210.   WALKER, W.S. A practical analysis of the Act 8 & 9 Victoriae
         cap. 83, for the amendment and better administration of the
         laws relating to the relief of the poor in Scotland. 3rd ed.
         Edinburgh and London: 1845. pp.44. G. 4th ed. Edinburgh
         and London: 1845. pp.48. G.

1,211.   WATSON, W. The poor law from the poor man's standpoint.
         Edinburgh: 1870. pp.22. G.

(c) Poor Law, Ireland

1,212.   ANON. The office and duty of high and petty constables,
         church-wardens, overseers of the poor, parish-watches,
         surveyors of high-ways; bridges and causeys... and masters of
         houses of correction in Ireland. Dublin: 1720. pp.(4) +
         247. NLI.

1,213.   ANON. Enquiries into the principal causes of the general
         poverty of the common people of Ireland. With remedies
         propos'd for removing of them. Dublin: 1724. pp.25. CUL.

1,214.   ANON. A scheme for establishing poor-houses, in the Kingdom
         of Ireland, published by order of the Dublin Society. Dublin:
         1768. pp.15. NLI; 2nd ed. Dublin: 1768. pp.15. CUL.

1,215.   ANON. Account of the procedure and state of the fund...
         instituted for the relief of the poor and for punishing
         vagabonds and sturdy beggars in the county of the city of
         Dublin, etc. [Dublin]: 1774. pp.24. LSE.

1,216.   ANON. A scheme for erecting county poor-houses, in the
         Kingdom of Ireland. 2nd ed. Dublin: 1798. pp.15. CUL.

1,217.   ANON. A method of improving the condition of the Irish poor.
         Suggested in a letter to Samuel Whitbread, Esq. M.P. Dublin:
         1810. pp.26. CUL; NLI.

1,218.   ANON. A method of improving the condition of the Irish poor.

Suggested in a letter to Samuel Whitbread, Esq. M.P. Dublin: 1810. pp.26. CUL.

1,219. ANON. "Ought Ireland to have poor laws?". <u>D.& L.Mag.</u> 2. (1826). pp.495-504.

1,220. ANON. Remarks on 'Observations on the necessity of a legal provision for the Irish poor... by John Douglas, Esq.', with an epitome of the poor laws of England and proving their superiority over those of Scotland. Illustrated by contrasted cases in both countries, by T.B. Edinburgh: 1828. pp.40. RIA.

1,221. ANON. Instructions given by the commissioners appointed to enquire into the state of the poor of Ireland to the assistant commissioners. Dublin: 1834. pp.56. RIA.

1,222. ANON. Instructions given by the Commissioners appointed to enquire into the state of the poor of Ireland to the assistant commissioners. Dublin: 1834. pp.56. RIA.

1,223. ANON. "Irish labourers: Poor Law Commission, appendix to report (A)". <u>Westm.Rev.</u> 27. (1835). pp.65-91.

1,224. ANON. "Poor laws in Ireland". <u>Westm.Rev.</u> 27. (1836). pp.332-65.

1,225. ANON. (Chairman of an English Poor Law Union). A letter to the Right Hon. Lord J. Russell, on the principles of the Irish Poor Law Bill. London: 1836. pp.27. LI.

1,226. ANON. Abstract of the final report of the Commissioners of Irish poor inquiry; and also letters written to ministers by Messrs. N.W. Senior, and G.C. Lewis, in consequence of applications from government for their opinions on that report. With remarks upon the measures now before Parliament for the relief of the destitute in Ireland. 2nd ed. London: 1837. pp.66. BCL; NLI; RIA.

1,227. ANON. Strictures on the proposed poor law for Ireland, as recommended in the report of George Nicholls, Esq. London: 1837. pp.2 + 90. BCL; CUL; TCD. 2nd ed. London: 1838. pp.108. RIA.

1,228. ANON. Thoughts on the proposed introduction of the poor laws into Ireland. London: 1837. pp.32. BL; C.

1,229. ANON. Abstract of the final report of the Commissioners of Irish Poor Inquiry; with remarks thereon, and upon the measure now before Parliament for the relief of the destitute in Ireland. London: 1837. pp.36. LI.

1,230. ANON. "The Poor Law Board for Ireland". <u>DUM.</u> 10. (1837). pp.69-78.

1,231. ANON. Remarks on the Bill for the more effectual relief of the destitute poor in Ireland. By Philo-Hibernus. 2nd ed. revised and enlarged. London: 1837. pp.45. CUL.

1,232. ANON. Observations explanatory of the orders of the Poor Law

Commissioners regulating the first election of guardians; and of some of the provisions of the Irish poor law. Dublin: 1838. pp.32. RIA.

1,233. ANON. Digest of the Act of Parliament for the relief of the poor in Ireland, 1 & 2 Vict. c.56; with an index, and the Act. 2nd ed. Dublin: 1838. pp.120. RIA; TCD.

1,234. ANON. A few cursory observations n the proposed Bill for establishing poor laws in Ireland. By an Irish M.P. for a western county. London: 1838. pp.20. CUL; LI. [By A.H. Lynch?].

1,235. ANON. An Act (1 & 2 Victoriae, c.56) for the more effectual relief of the destitute poor in Ireland; with notes, forms and an index. London: 1839. pp.203 + (40). G.

1,236. ANON. The Acts (1 & 2 Vict.c.56 and 2 Vict.c.1) for the more effectual relief of the destitute poor in Ireland; with notes, forms and an index. London: 1839. pp.228. Z.

1,237. ANON. A report of the case of Mary Kelly, against Morgan Langan, Thomas Holden, and Richard Murphy, overseers of the parish of St. Nicholas without, in the City of Dublin, for refusing to receive and provide for an infant under the age of twelve months, deserted by its parents, and exposed within their said parish, on the night of Wednesday, the 11th of March, 1840, before Alderman Darley, Chief Magistrate of Police, and Arthur Hamilton, Esq., barrister magistrate, head office of police, Dublin, heard on the 10th day of March, 1840. Dublin: 1840. pp.40. NLI.

1,238. ANON. Important suggestions in relation to the Irish poor laws to ameliorate the condition of the labouring class by a gentleman of Lincoln's Inn. Dublin: [1842]. pp.xxxii + 532. LSE.

1,239. ANON. Measures which can alone ameliorate effectually the condition of the Irish people. London: 1847. pp.68. CUL.

1,240. ANON. The Irish Poor Relief and Vagrants Acts, 1847. Dublin: 1847. pp.36. Z.

1,241. ANON. Irish poor law question. A letter to the Rt. Hon. Lord John Russell. From an Irish landlord. London: 1847. pp.(2) + 8. CUL.

1,242. ANON. The measures which can alone ameliorate effectually the condition of the Irish people. London: 1847. pp.68. CUL.

1,243. ANON. The settlement and removal of the poor considered. London: 1847. pp.58. G; TCD.

1,244. ANON. General order of the Poor Law Commissioners for regulating the administration of out-door relief, &c.&c. By authority. Dublin: 1847. pp.24. Z.

1,245. ANON. "The Irish crisis - the poor law". DUM. 31. (1848). pp.537-52.

1,246. ANON.   Irish poor law: past, present, and future. London:
        1849. pp.(ii) + 59. BL.

1,247. ANON. "The poor law versus the poor - our rate in aid". <u>DUM</u>.
        33. (1849). pp.656-66.

1,248. ANON.   Observations on the Board of Works, the new poor law
        and other topics of present interest and importance in
        Ireland. London: 1849. pp.38. NLI.

1,249. ANON.   "The Times and the new Irish poor law". <u>DUM</u>.   33.
        (1849). pp.221-7.

1,250. ANON.   "The Times, the poor law and the Poor Law Committee".
        <u>DUM</u>. 33. (1849). pp.401-10.

1,251. ANON.   "Ireland under the poor law". <u>DUM</u>.   35.   (1850).
        pp.137-50.

1,252. ANON.   "Free trade and the poor law's incompletion". <u>DUM</u>.
        35. (1850). pp.270-6.

1,253. ANON. Ireland. Its landlords: its poor law: and its system
        of national education. Dublin: 1851. pp.48. UCD.

1,254. ANON.   The collectors' manual, containing an explanation of
        the mode of appointment, duties, powers, and liabilities of
        collectors of poor rate: with a selection of official and
        legal opinions, and instructions to collectors in cases of
        difficulty, together with an abstract of the duties of poor
        rate collectors under the Parliamentary Voters Act, prepared
        from official documents under the authority and with the
        sanction of the Poor Law Commissioners. Dublin: 1851. pp.x
        + 72. n.l.

1,255. ANON.   "The Irish poor law inquiry". <u>DUM</u>.   58.   (1861).
        pp.60-70.

1,256. ANON. "The Irish poor laws". <u>DUM</u>. 57. (1861). pp.709-20.

1,257. ANON.   The Irish poor in English prisons and workhouses. A
        letter to a Member of Parliament.   London: 1866.   pp.14.
        CUL.

1,258. ANON. "Royal Commission on the Poor Laws - Ireland". <u>Lab.G</u>.
        XVII. (1909). pp.152-154.

1,259. A BARRISTER.   Thoughts on the poor of Ireland and means of
        their amelioration. Dublin: 1831. pp.100. NLI.

1,260. ALCOCK, T. ST. L.   Observations on the Poor Relief Bill for
        Ireland, and its bearing on the important subject of
        emigration, etc. London: 1847. pp.30. BL; CUL; TCD.

1,261. ARCHBOLD, J.F.   The statutes 24 & 25 Vict. cc.55, 76, 59,
        relating to the irremoveability of paupers from unions;   to
        the passing of paupers to Ireland;   and to vaccination: with
        notes. London: 1861. pp.54. TCD.

1,262. ARNOTT, SIR J.   The investigation into the conditions of the children in the Cork workhouse: with an analysis of the evidence. Cork: 1859. pp.(2) + xii + 54 + 12. NLI.

1,263. BANKS, B. Compendium of the Irish poor law: containing the acts for the relief of the destitute poor in Ireland and various statutes connected therewith... Dublin: 1872. pp.16 + 1132. NLI.

1,264. BARON, F. The mirror of the poor laws. Enniskillen: 1841. pp.19. C.

1,265. BARROW, H. The relief of the poore, and advancement of learning: proposed. Dublin: 1656. pp.9. CUL.

1,266. BERMINGHAM, T. Remarks on the proposed Poor Law Bill for Ireland, addressed to George Poulett Scrope. London: 1838. pp.14. LSE.

1,267. BEW,P. & NORTON,C. "The Unionist state and the outdoor relief riots of 1932". Ec.& Soc.Rev. 10. (1978-79). pp.255-65.

1,268. BINDON, D. A scheme for supplying industrious men with money to carry on their trades, and for better providing for the poor of Ireland. Dublin: 1729. pp.22 + (2). Bod; RIA. 2nd ed. Dublin: 1729. RIA; TCD. 3rd ed. Dublin: 1750. p.28. NLI; RIA.

1,269. BORRETT, W.P. Three letters upon a poor law and public medical relief for Ireland, to Daniel O'Connell, Esq., M.P. London and Dublin: 1838. pp.24. G; NLI.

1,270. BOSWORTH, J. The contrast; or, the operation of the old poor laws contrasted with the recent Poor Law Amendment Act, and the necessity of a legal provision for the poor generally, but especially for Ireland. London: 1838. pp.42. G; TCD.

1,271. BRITISH MEDICAL ASSOCIATION. Reports on the poor law medical system in Ireland. London: 1904. pp.63. (See Evatt, Sir G.H.J.).

1,272. BUTT, I. The Poor Law Bill for Ireland examined, its provisions and the report of Mr. Nicholls contrasted with the facts proved by the poor inquiry commission in a letter to Lord Viscount Morpeth M.P., His Majesty's principal Secretary of State for Ireland. Dublin: 1837. pp.44. CUL; NLI; RIA; TCD.

1,273. C. "Poor laws for Ireland". DUM. 6. (1835). pp.24-31.

1,274. [CARMALT, W.] A defence of the English poor laws, with remarks on the applicability of the system to Ireland. By a select vestryman of the parish of Putney. London: 1831. pp.102. G.

1,275. CHALMERS, DR. "Evidence before the committee of the House of Commons on the subject of a poor law for Ireland [1830]". In: Dr. Chalmers and the poor laws. [Preface by Mrs. George Kerr and Introduction by Miss Grace Chalmers Wood]. Edinburgh: 1911. pp.66-235. CUL.

1,276. CLEMENTS, R.B. The present poverty of Ireland convertible into the means of her improvement, under a well-administered poor law; with a preliminary view of the state of agriculture in Ireland. London: 1838. pp.viii + 178. CUL; LSE.

1,277. COLLISON BLACK, R.D. Economic thought and the Irish question 1817-1870. Cambridge: 1960. pp.xiv + 299. CUL.

1,278. COMMITTEE FOR ENQUIRING INTO THE CONDITION OF THE POORER CLASSES IN IRELAND. Selections of parochial examinations relating to the destitute classes in Ireland, etc. Dublin: 1835. pp.430. LSE.

1,279. CONNERY, J. The reformer, or, an infallible remedy to prevent pauperism and periodical returns of famine, with other salutary measures... and establishing the futility of the plan of William Smith O'Brien Esq., M.P. Cork: 1831. pp.16. NLI. 5th ed. Limerick: 1833. pp.61. G; NLI. 6th ed. Limerick: 1833. RIA. 6th [sic] ed. London and Dublin: 1836. pp.72. G; RIA. 5th [sic] ed. Limerick: 1837. pp.62. NLI.

1,280. CONWAY, J.G. "The approach to an Irish poor law, 1829-33". Eire. 6. (1). (1971). pp.65-81.

1,281. COOLOCK COMMUNITY LAW CENTRE (IRELAND). Social welfare appeals. Dublin: 1980. pp.[1] + 49. DHSS.

1,282. [CORRIE, J.] Remarks on the poor law for Ireland. By Philo-Hibernus. London: 1837. pp.26. NLI.

1,283. [CORRIE, J.] Remarks on the bill for the more effectual relief of the destitute poor in Ireland. By Philo-Hibernus. 2nd ed. revised and enlarged. London: 1837. pp.48. NLI.

1,284. CULLEN, M. A letter to James Grattan... in which the subject of poor laws being introduced into Ireland is considered. Dublin: 1824. pp.35. NLI.

1,285. CURRAN, H. "The workhouse child". New Ire.Rev. 6. (1896-7). pp.137-41.

1,286. DALY, R. A letter to the editor of the Church Examiner on the subject of a legal provision for the poor of Ireland. Dublin: 1829. pp.20. G; NLI; RIA; TCD.

1,287. DAWSON, C. "Suggested substitutes for the present poor law system". J.S.S.I.S.I. 11. (1906). pp.428-38.

1,288. DAY, S.R. "The crime called out-door relief". Ir.Rev. 2. (1912-13). pp.72-80.

1,289. DEVLIN, P. Yes we have no bananas: outdoor relief in Belfast 1920-39. Belfast: 1981. pp.ix + 195. DHSS.

1,290. DODD, W.H. "A common poor fund for the metropolis". J.S.S.I.S.I. VIII. (1881). pp.159-64.

1,291. DOLAN, J. "Reform of the workhouse". New Ire.Rev. 18. (1902-3). pp.322-9.

1,292. DOUGLAS, J. Observations on the necessity of a legal provision for the Irish poor, as the means of improving the condition of the Irish people, and protecting the British landlord, farmer and labourer. London and Dublin: 1828. pp.40. CUL; G; NLI; RIA.

1,293. DOYLE, J. Letter on the establishment of a legal provision for the Irish poor, and on the nature and destiny of church property. London: 1831. pp.133. LSE.

1,294. DOYLE, J.W. Letter to Thomas Spring Rice, Esq., M.P. on the establishment of a legal provision for the Irish poor, and on the nature and destination of church property. Dublin and London: 1831. pp.133. G; NLI; RIA; TCD.

1,295. DUNNE, J.P. Waiting the Verdict. Pensions or pauperism. Necessitous widows and orphans in the Free State. Dublin: 1928. pp.8. NLI.

1,296. EASON, C. Review of the report of the Commission on the Relief of the Sick and Destitute Poor, including the Insane Poor, appointed by the Government of the Irish Free State. Dublin: 1928. pp.29. LSE.

1,297. EASON, C. "Report of the Irish Poor Law Commission". J.S.S.I.S.I. XVI. (1928). pp.17-32. Discussion. pp.33-43.

1,298. EIRE, SEANAD EIREANN. Report of the Special Committee on poor law relief. 1929. (R.48).

1,299. EVATT, SIR G.J.H. A report on the poor law medical system in Ireland, with special reference to the dispensary medical service. London: 1904. (Supplement to the British Medical Journal).

1,300. FARLEY, D. Social insurance and social assistance in Ireland. Dublin: 1964. pp.182. DHSS; LSE; CUL.

1,301. FIELD, W. Suggestions for the improvement of the Irish poor law. Dublin: 1883. pp.25. NLI; BCL.

1,302. FLOOD, H. Poor laws. Arguments against a provision for paupers if it be parochial or perpetual. Dublin: 1830. pp.16. RIA.

1,303. GODLEY, J.R. Observations on an Irish poor law... Dublin: 1847. pp.32. NLI.

1,304. GRIERSON, G.A. The circumstances of Ireland considered with reference to the question of poor laws. London and Dublin: 1830. pp.64. G; NLI; RIA.

1,305. HACKETT, E.A. The Irish grand jury system with a note on the Irish poor law system, 1898. London: 1898. pp.39. LSE.

1,306. [HALIDAY, C.] Necessity of combining a law of settlement with local assessment in the proposed bill for the relief of the poor of Ireland. Dublin: 1838. pp.60. TCD.

1,307. HAMILTON, J. On poor law and labour rate: a letter from a resident Irish landowner. Dublin: 1847. pp.16. C.

1,308. HANCOCK, W.N. A history of the Irish poor laws, and the differences between the administration of the English and Irish systems: being a lecture delivered in the Mechanics' Institute, Lurgan... 12th May 1862. Lurgan: 1862. pp.16. NLI.

1,309. HANCOCK, W.N. The law of poor removals and chargeability, etc. Dublin: 1871. pp.23. G.

1,310. HANCOCK, W.N. On the anomolous differences in the poor laws in Ireland and England: being an address to the Trades Union Congress... 1880. Dublin: 1880. pp.21. NLI; LSE.

1,311. HANCOCK, W.N. "On the anomalous differences in the poor laws of Ireland and of England: an address to the Trades Union Congress". J.S.S.I.S.I. VIII. (1881). pp.123-42.

1,312. HINCHY, J. A plan for a modified system of poor laws, and employment for the people of Ireland. Dublin: 1834. pp.8. G; NLI; RIA.

1,313. HINCKS, T.D. A short account of the different charitable institutions of the City of Cork, with remarks. Cork: 1802. pp.62. NLI; RIA.

1,314. HOARE, H.N.H. On the development of the English poor law. London: 1893. pp.28. TCD.

1,315. [HUTCHINSON, F.] A letter to a Member of Parliament concerning the employing and providing for the poor. Dublin: 1723. pp.16. G.

1,316. IRISH WOMEN'S SUFFRAGE AND LOCAL GOVERNMENT ASSOCIATION. Papers read at a conference of women poor law guardians and others. Dublin: 1903. pp.52. LSE.

1,317. KENNEDY, J.P. Analysis of projects proposed for the relief of the poor of Ireland; more especially that of Mr. George Nicholls, embodied in a Bill now before Parliament; that of the Commissioners for inquiring into the condition of the poorer classes in Ireland and that which has been brought into partial operation by the author. London and Dublin: 1837. pp.54. CUL; G; NLI; RIA; TCD.

1,318. KIDD, J. 1 & 2 Victoriae I, chap.56. An Act for the more effectual relief of the destitute poor in Ireland, with prefatory remarks and a copious index. Dublin: 1838. pp.xxxvii + 143. G; RIA; LI.

1,319. KINAHAN, D. An outline of a plan for relieving the poor of Ireland, by an assessment on property. Dublin: 1829. pp.32. CUL; NLI; RIA.

1,320. KINAHAN, D. Outline of a plan for employing the poor of Ireland. London: 1831. pp.36. NLI.

1,321. KINAHAN, D. The system of relief for the poor as used in the

Dublin Mendicity Institution, adapted to general use, considered in a letter. Dublin: 1847. pp.10. NLI; RIA.

1,322. LANCASTER, J. A letter to John Foster, Esq., Chancellor of the Exchequer for Ireland, on the best means of educating and employing the poor, in that country. London: 1805. pp.40. QUB; RIA; TCD.

1,323. LEWIS, SIR G.C. Report on the state of the Irish poor in Great Britain. London: 1836. pp.104. KI. (Reprint of Appendix G to the Report of the Royal Commission on condition of poorer classes in Ireland.)

1,324. LEWIS, SIR G.C. Remarks on the third report of the Irish poor inquiry commissioners; drawn up by the desire of the Chancellor of the Exchequer, for the purpose of being submitted to his Majesty's Government. London: 1837. pp.58. TCD; G.

1,325. LYNCH, A.H. Measures to be adopted for the employment of the labouring classes in Ireland; detailed in an address to the electors of Galway; ith an appendix containing abstracts of the reports of some of the provincial associations in Belgium. London: 1837. pp.252. CUL.

1,326. LYNCH, A.H. An address to the electors of Galway, on the Poor Law Bill for Ireland. With an appendix, containing extracts from the evidence taken before the Commissioners of Poor Inquiry, Ireland. London: 1838. pp.142. G; NLI; RIA; TCD; LI.

1,327. MacCORMACK, H. A plan for the relief of the unemployed poor. Belfast: 1830. pp.32. C; G.

1,328. MACDONAGH, O. "The poor law system and the Irish question, 1830-55". Chr.R. 12. (1958). pp.26-37.

1,329. MACNAGHTEN, SIR F.W. Poor laws – Ireland. Observations upon the report of George Nicholls, Esq. London: 1838. pp.58. G; NLI; RIA; TCD.

1,330. MAGUIRE, J.F. Removal of Irish poor from England and Scotland; showing the nature of the law of removal, the mode in which it is administered, the hardships which it inflicts, and the necessity for its absolute and unconditional repeal. London: 1854. pp.134. RIA; CUL.

1,331. [MAQUIRE, S.J.] "The early workhouses in Galway". Galway Reader. 4. (Nos.2 & 3). (1954). pp.71-9.

1,332. MARTIN, J. Observations on the evils and difficulties of the present system of poor laws in Ireland; with suggestions for removing or obviating them considered. Dublin: 1848. pp.30. UCD; BL. Dublin: 1849. pp.29. LSE.

1,333. MARTIN, R.M. Poor laws for Ireland: a measure of justice to England; of humanity to the people of both islands; and of self-preservation for the Empire. With a practical development of an improved system of settlement, assessment, and relief. London: 1833. pp.(4) + 49. CUL; KI; NLI; RIA;

TCD; G.

1,334. MAUNSELL, H. The only safe poor law experiment for Ireland.
        Dublin: 1838. pp.15. C.

1,335. MCCULLAGH, W.T. Letter to the presentative peers of Ireland,
        on the ministerial measure of the Irish poor laws. Dublin and
        London: 1838. pp.12. CUL.

1,336. McDOWELL, R.B. The Irish administration 1801-1914. London:
        1964. pp.xi + 238.

1,337. MEEKINS, R. Plan for the removal of pauperism, agrarian
        disturbances and the poor rate in Ireland. Dublin: 1847.
        BL.

1,338. MERIVALE, H. Five lectures on the principles of a legislative
        provision for the poor in Ireland. Delivered in 1837 and
        1838. London: 1838. pp.118. TCD.

1,339. MONTEAGLE, LORD. "The Irish workhouse system". New Ire.Rev.
        6. (1896-7). pp.129-32.

1,340. MOONEY, T.A. Compendium of the Irish poor Law. Dublin:
        1888. Supplement to the compendium of the Irish poor law, and
        general manual for poor law guardians, containing statutes or
        portions of statutes which impose duties on, or otherwise
        affect, boards of guardians in Ireland; together with the
        regulations and principal orders and instructional circulars
        issued by the Local Government Board for Ireland during the
        period from the 1st of January, 1888, to the passing of the
        Local Government (Ireland) Act, 1898. Compiled as a
        continuation of the compendium of the Irish poor law. Dublin:
        1898. pp.xii + 504. QUB.

1,341. MOORE, A. Compendium of the Irish poor law: containing the
        statutes for the relief of the destitute poor in Ireland, and
        the general orders issued by the Poor Law Commissioners to
        unions in Ireland... 2nd ed. Dublin: 1846. Sq. Another
        ed. 1850. p.xxi + 992. LSE.

1,342. MORRIS, J. A complete abstract of the new Irish Poor Law Act
        with all its clauses disencumbered of legal technicality and
        repetition and the entire rendered familiar and instructive to
        every class of reader. Dublin: 1838. pp.40. RIA. 2nd ed.
        Dublin: 1839. pp.52. RIA.

1,343. MORRIS, J. Tables compiled for the use of valuators,
        guardians, rate payers, etc., under the Irish Poor Relief Act;
        also supplying a mode of distributing the annual value of a
        holding or tenement let in parts, after being valued as a
        whole, without requiring a new valuation. Dublin: 1840.
        pp.32. NLI.

1,344. MOYLAN, T.K. "Vagabonds and sturdy beggars". Dub.Hist.Rec.
        1. (1939). pp.11-18, 41-9, 65-74.

1,345. MULHALL, M. "Boarding out workhouse children". New Ire.Rev.
        6. (1896-7). pp.133-7.

1,346. NAPER, J.L.W. An address to the landlords and landholders of the County of Meath in particular, and to those of Ireland in general, on the new Poor Law Bill. Dublin: 1837. pp.36. CUL. 2nd ed. Dublin: 1837. pp.36. NLI; RIA; CUL.

1,347. NAPER, J.L.W. The present circumstances of the Union of Oldcastle submitted to the consideration of the Parliamentary committee now sitting for the reconstruction of the Irish poor laws; with some propositions for their amendment. Dublin: 1849. pp.26. RIA.

1,348. NICHOLLS, Sir G. Report of G. Nicholls to... Secretary of State... on poor law, Ireland (Holland and Belgium). London: 1837. 3 vols. (in 1). G.

1,349. NICHOLLS, SIR G. Poor laws, Ireland: report... to Her Majesty's principal Secretary of State for the Home Department. London: 1837. pp.67. LSE.

1,350. NICHOLLS, G. Poor laws - Ireland. Third report to H.M. Secretary of State for the Home Department containing the result of an inquiry into the condition of the labouring classes and the provision for the relief of the poor, in Holland and Belgium. London: 1838. pp.24. NLI.

1,351. NICHOLLS, G. Poor laws - Ireland. Three reports to Her Majesty's principal Secretary of State for the Home Department. London: 1838. pp.viii + 172. BL; CUL; NLI; RIA; TCD; LSE.

1,352. NICHOLLS, SIR G. A history of the Irish poor law, in connexion with the condition of the Irish people. London: 1856. pp.x + 424. RDS; LSE; CUL.

1,353. NOLAN, T.P. A practical treatise on the law relating to the poor rate in Ireland. Dublin: 1900. pp.xii + 282. NLI.

1,354. O'BRIEN, G. "The establishment of poor-law unions in Ireland, 1838-43". I.H.S. 23. (1982). pp.97-120.

1,355. O'BRIEN, L. Ireland in 1848: the late famine and the poor laws. London: [1848]. pp.45. LSE.

1,356. O'BRIEN, W.S. Plan for the relief of the poor in Ireland; with observations on the English and Scotch poor laws. London: 1830. pp.60. G; NLI; RIA; TCD. Dublin: 1831. pp.63. CUL; LSE; G; NLI.

1,357. O'CONNOR, D.C. Seventeen years' experience of workhouse life: with suggestions for reforming the poor law and its administration. Dublin: 1861. pp.82. TCD.

1,358. O'MALLEY, T. A word or two on the Irish Poor Relief Bill, and Mr. Nicholls' Report. London: 1837. pp.24. C.

1,359. O'MALLEY, T. Poor laws - Ireland. An idea of a poor law for Ireland. 2nd ed. London: 1837. pp.86. NLI; RIA.

1,360. O'NEILL, T.P. "The Irish workhouse during the great famine". Chr.R. 12. (1958). pp.15-25.

1,361. O'NEILL, T.P. "Poverty in Ireland, 1815-45". <u>Flklfe.</u> 11. (1973). pp.22-33.

1,362. O'NEILL, T.P. "The Catholic Church and the relief of the poor". <u>Arch.Hib.</u> 31. (1973). pp.132-45.

1,363. PAGE, F. Observations on the state of the indigent poor in Ireland, and the existing institutions for their relief: being a sequel to "The principle of the English poor laws illustrated and defended". London and Dublin: 1830. pp.(2) + 72. CUL; TCD.

1,364. PARKER, W. Observations on the intended amendment of the Irish Grand Jury law, now under consideration... with... hints relative... to the distressed state of the poor. Cork: 1816. pp.xxiv + 184. RIA.

1,365. PARKER, W. A plan for the general improvement of the poor of Ireland. [Cork?]: 1816. pp.x + 158. NLI; RIA.

1,366. PARKER, W. A plea for the poor and industrious. Part the first. The necessity of a national provision for the poor in Ireland; deduced from the argument of the Rt. Rev. R. Woodward, late Lord Bishop of Cloyne. Cork: 1819. pp.xxxvi + 159 + (6). RIA.

1,367. PARKER, W. An essay on the employment which bridges, roads, and other public works may afford to the labouring classes, by the general and effectual amendment of the Grand Jury laws: with observation on the Act of the 58th Geo.3, chapter 57. Cork: 1819. pp.viii + 49. RIA.

1,368. PETRIE, F.W.H. The Irish poor law rating as it affects tithe rent-charge property. London: 1866. pp.8. NLI; TCD. 2nd ed. London and Dublin: 1867. pp.8. TCD. 3rd ed. London and Dublin: 1870. pp.8. NLI.

1,369. PHELAN, D. Reform of the poor law system in Ireland; or facts and observations on the inadequacy of the existing system of poor relief. Dublin: 1859. pp.72. NCI; RIA; G; LSE.

1,370. PHILO-HIBERNUS. Remarks on the poor law for Ireland. London: 1837. pp.26. NLI.

1,371. PHILO-HIBERNUS. Remarks on the bill for the more effectual relief of the destitute poor in Ireland. 2nd ed. London: 1845. pp.48. BCL; NLI; RIA; LSE.

1,372. POOR LAW COMMISSIONERS. Guardians manual of the law of chargeability under the Irish Poor Relief Acts. Dublin: 1864. pp.39. NLI.

1,373. POWELL, M. "The workhouses of Ireland". <u>Univ.Rev.</u> 3. (7). (1963). pp.3-16.

1,374. PURDON, F. Suggestions on the best mode of relieving the present prevailing distress in the south of Ireland, for the consideration of Mr. Grant and Sir John Newport, and the members for Ireland. Dublin: 1818. pp.22. NLI; RIA.

1,375. QUINN, M. "Enniskillen Poor Law Union (1840-9)". Clogh.Rec. (1969-72). pp.498-513.

1,376. REVANS, J. Evils of the state of Ireland: their causes and their remedy - a poor law. London: [1835]. pp.152. G; UCD. 2nd ed. revised and corrected. London: [1837]. pp.161. G; NLI; RIA.

1,377. RICHARDS, J. Speech in the House of Commons, May 2, 1833, on a motion for the introduction of poor laws into Ireland; with historical notes &c. London: 1833. pp.35 + (4). CUL.

1,378. RICKMAN, J. Poor laws in Ireland. London: 1833. pp.16. NLI; RIA.

1,379. ROBINS, J.A. "Charter schools and poor law records". Ir.Archiv.Bull. 3(1). (1973). pp.2-6.

1,380. [ROWAN, A.B.] What's to be done? Or a collection of the various suggestions for amending the poor law, with observations. Tralee: 1849. pp.28. RIA.

1,381. SADLER, M.T. The speech of Michael Thomas Sadler, M.P. for Newark, in the House of Commons, on... the third of June, on proposing poor laws for Ireland, preparatory to a general measure in behalf of the labouring classes of England. London: 1830. pp.51. G.

1,382. SANDIFORD, T. Permanent reduction of the poor rates in Ireland, by three pence in the pound. To be effected by the formation of a new public health service. Dublin: 1884. pp.12. QUB.

1,383. SANDYS, M. A letter to the Right Honourable Henry Grattan, on the state of the labouring poor in Ireland. Dublin: 1796. pp.39. CUL; NLI; RIA; TCD.

1,384. [SCROPE, G.P.] A letter to the agriculturists of England, on the expediency of extending the poor law to Ireland, by a landowner. London: 1830. pp.24. G; NLI.

1,385. SCROPE, G.P. Plan of a poor-law for Ireland, with a review of the arguments for and against it. London: 1833. pp.94. NLI; RIA. 2nd ed. 1834. pp.24. KI; NLI; RIA; LSE.

1,386. SCROPE, G.P. Remarks on the Government Irish Poor-Law Bill, in a letter to Lord John Russell. London: 1837. pp.24. CUL; NLI.

1,387. SCROPE, G.P. Letters to the Right Hon. Lord John Russell, on the expediency of enlarging the Irish poor law to the full extent of the poor law in England. London: 1846. pp.91. G; NLI; RIA; TCD; LSE.

1,388. SCROPE, G.P. Remarks on the Irish Poor Relief Bill. London: 1847. pp.32. CUL; G; NLI; TCD.

1,389. SCROPE, G.P. Reply to the speech of the Archbishop of Dublin delivered in the House of Lords... March 26th, 1847, and the protest, signed R. Dublin, Monteagle, Radnor, Mountcashel, against the Poor Relief (Ireland) Bill. London: 1847. pp.41. G; NLI; RIA; TCD; CUL.

1,390. SCROPE, G.P. The Irish relief measures past and present. London: 1848. pp.(2) + v + 96. G.

1,391. SCROPE, G.P. The Irish poor law. How far has it failed? A question addressed to the common sense of his countrymen. (With extracts from and references to the evidence given before the Committee of the two Houses of Parliament now sitting on the subject). London: 1849. pp.60. G; TCD.

1,392. SCROPE, G.P. Draft report... on the Irish poor law. London: [1849]. pp.7. G.

1,393. SCULLY, V. Poor rate (Ireland). Present system of collection: its evils, and the remedy. Dublin: 1850. pp.46. BL; NLI; RIA; TCD.

1,394. SENIOR, N.W. A letter to Lord Howick, on a legal provision for the Irish poor; commutation of tithes, and a provision for the Irish Roman Catholic clergy. London: 1831. pp.104. G. 2nd ed. London: 1831. pp.104. LSE; BCL; KI; RIA; G; NLI; TCD. 3rd ed. With a preface, containing suggestions as to the measures to be adopted in the present emergency. London: 1831. pp.xvii + 104. G; RIA.

1,395. SHACKLETON, A. "On the anomalous differences in the poor laws of Ireland and England with reference to outdoor relief, area of taxation, etc." J.S.S.I.S.I. 8. (1879-85). pp.282-8.

1,396. SHACKLETON, E. Proposal of a public provision for the poor of Ireland, on a principle conducive at once to the interests of all classes. Dublin: 1824. ppp.20. RIA; TCD.

1,397. SHACKLETON, E. Poor laws the safest, cheapest and surest cure for boyism of every kind in Ireland. Dublin: 1832. pp.8. NLI.

1,398. SHARKEY, R.F. A proposal for the more speedy relief of the poor of Ireland, in seasons of scarcity. Dublin: 1806. pp.v, (1), 6-32. QUB.

1,399. SHREWSBURY, EARL OF Thoughts on the Poor Relief Bill for Ireland: together with reflections on her miseries, their causes, and their remedies. London: 1847. pp.(2) + 84. CUL.

1,400. SMYTH, J. Observation on the poor laws, as regards their introduction into Ireland, the mendicity institutions established in that country, and the drainage of the wet lands and bogs. Dublin: 1830. pp.19. CUL.

1,401. STANLEY, J. Ireland and her evils. Poor laws fully considered - their introduction into Ireland destructive of all landed interest. Dublin: 1836. pp.116. RIA; TCD.

1,402. STANLEY, W. The policy of a poor law for Ireland,

analytically examined. Dublin: 1835. pp.29. NLI.

1,403. STANLEY, W. Remarks on the government measure for establising
a poor law in Ireland; chiefly with reference to the existing
amount of pauperism, as stated in the report of the Irish Poor
Inquiry Commissioners; and necessary extent and character of
the means for its relief. 2nd ed. London: 1837. pp.41. G;
NLI; RIA; TCD.

1,404. STEWART, J.V. A letter to the Earl of Clarendon, on the
subject of poor laws. Letterkenny: 1849. pp.20. WELB.

1,405. SWIFT, J. A proposal for giving badges to the beggars in all
the parishes of Dublin. Dublin: 1737. pp.25 + (3). CUL;
RIA; TCD. London: 1737. pp.16. BL; CUL.

1,406. T.B. Remarks on 'Observations on the necessity of a legal
provision for the Irish poor, etc., by John Douglas, Esq.',
with an epitome of the poor laws of England, and proving their
superiority over those of Scotland. Illustrated by contrasted
cases in both countries. Edinburgh: 1828. pp.40. G; RIA.

1,407. THE COURIER. The Irish Poor Law Bill: two letters to Daniel
O'Connell in reply to his letters to his constituents.
London: 1838. pp.20. C.

1,408. TORRENS, R. A letter to the Right Honourable Lord John
Russell, on the ministerial measure for establishing poor laws
in Ireland, and on the auxiliary measures which it will be
necessary to employ in carrying that measure into effect.
London: 1837. pp.149. G; RIA; TCD. Another ed. London:
1838. pp.97. G; NLI.

1,409. TREVOR, J. The poor removal law. An alien act against the
Irish. Chester: 1855. pp.23. LSE.

1,410. TYLDEN, SIR J. On Irish poor laws. Addressed to Lord
Viscount Morpeth. Sittingbourne: 1837. pp.30. NLI.

1,411. "UNION CLERK". Philanthropy versus Phelanthropy; or, a short
reply to the observations of Denis Phelan, M.D., on reform of
the poor laws in Ireland. Dublin: 1859. pp.14. RIA.

1,412. UNITED KINGDOM. Report from committee respecting the poor of
Ireland. London: 1803-4. (B.P.P. V). pp.3. LSE.

1,413. UNITED KINGDOM. Report from the Select Committee on the
Employment of the Poor in Ireland. London: 1823. (B.P.P.
VI). pp.201. LSE.

1,414. UNITED KINGDOM. Report of the Select Committee on the State
of the Poor in Ireland: being a summary of the first, second
and third reports of evidence taken before that Commission.
London: 1830. (B.P.P. VII). pp.171. LSE.

1,415. UNITED KINGDOM. First (-third) report of evidence from the
Select Committee on the State of the Poor in Ireland. London:
1830. (B.P.P. VII). pp.854. LSE.

1,416. UNITED KINGDOM. Report of G. Nicholls... on poor laws,

Ireland. London: 1837. pp.37. (B.P.P. LI). LSE.

1,417. UNITED KINGDOM. Second (and third) report of G. Nicholls... on poor laws, Ireland. London: 1837-8. (B.P.P. XXXVIII). LSE.

1,418. UNITED KINGDOM. Indexes to reports of Irish poor law commissioners, 1835-1839. London: 1845. pp.631. (B.P.P. XLIII. LSE.

1,419. UNITED KINGDOM. Report from the select committee of the House of Lords on the laws relating to the relief of the destitute poor... in Ireland, etc. London: 1846. 2v. (B.P.P. XI pt. 1 and 2). LSE.

1,420. UNITED KINGDOM. First (-6th) report from the select committee of the House of Lords appointed to inquire into the operation of the Irish poor law, and the expediency of making any amendment;... with the minutes of evidence. London: 1849. (B.P.P. XVI). LSE.

1,421. UNITED KINGDOM. First (-14th) report from the select committee [House of Commons] on poor laws (Ireland). London: 1849. (B.P.P. XV, pt. 1 and 2). LSE.

1,422. UNITED KINGDOM. Report from the select committee on poor relief, Ireland, etc. London: 1861. pp.xxii + 624 + (95). (B.P.P. X). LSE.

1,423. UNITED KINDOM. Report from the select committee of the House of Lords on the Poor Law Guardians (Ireland) Bill, etc. London: 1884-5. pp.ix + 271. (B.P.P. X). LSE.

1,424. UNITED KINGDOM. Report... on the effects of employment or assistance given to the "unemployed" since 1886 as a means of relieving distress outside the poor law in Ireland. London: 1909. pp.vii + 30. (B.P.P. XLIV). LSE.

1,425. UNITED KINGDOM. Royal Commission on the poor law and relief of distress: report on Ireland. London: 1909. pp.v + 88. (B.P.P. XXXVIII). LSE.

1,426. UNITED KINGDOM. Annual report of the commissioners for administering the laws for relief of the poor in Ireland. 1848-1864, 1866-1872. London. (B.P.P.). LSE.

1,427. VICE-REGAL COMMISSION ON POOR LAW REFORM IN IRELAND. Report, minutes and appendices. Dublin: 1906. (Cd.3202, 3203, 3204). LSE.

1,428. WALSH, J.B., BARON ORMATHWAITE. Poor laws in Ireland, considered in their probable effects upon the capital, the prosperity and the progressive improvement of that country. London: 1830. pp.(4) + 124. CUL 2nd ed. 1830. pp.124. G. 3rd ed. London: 1831. pp.124. G; TCD.

1,429. WARD, H.G. The first step to a poor law for Ireland. London: 1837. pp.(2) + 48. CUL.

1,430. WHATELEY, R. Substance of a speech delivered in the House of

Lords 26th of March, 1847, on the motion for a commission on Irish poor laws. London: 1847. pp.35. BL.

1,431. WHATELY, T. The evidence of the Rev. Thomas Whately before the committee of the House of Lords on the state of the poor in the years 1830, 1831; with introductory remarks on poor laws in Ireland and on an article in Quarterly Review, No.97. London: 1833. pp.56. NLI; RIA.

1,432. WOODWARD, R. A scheme for establishing county poor-houses, in the Kingdom of Ireland. Published by order of the Dublin Society. Dublin: 1766. pp.15. NLI; QUB; TCD. 2nd ed. Dublin: 1768. pp.15. BL; NLI.

1,433. WOODWARD, R. An argument in support of the right of the poor in the Kingdom of Ireland, to a national provision; in the appendix to which an attempt is made to settle a measure of the contribution due from each man to the poor, on the footing of justice. Dublin: 1768. pp.55. BL; CUL; G; LI; NLI. [without date or imprint]. pp.(2) + viii + 9-75. CUL; QUB. [Anr.ed.]. Dublin: 1772. pp.55. CUL; G; NLI; RIA; QUB; RDS. 3rd ed. Dublin: 1775. pp.xii + 68. CUL; NLI.[Anr.ed.]. Dublin: 1788. LI.

1,434. WOODWARD, R. An address to the public, on the expediency of a regular plan for the maintenance and government of the poor. With some general observations on the English system of poor laws... To which is added an argument in support of the right of the poor in the Kingdom of Ireland to a national provision. Dublin: 1775. pp.(4) + 91. CUL; KI; NLI; RIA; TCD. Reprinted. London: 1775. pp.vi + (2) + 93. CUL; NLI; QUB.

1,435. WOODWARD, R. Observations on the state and condition of the poor, under the institution, for their relief, in the city of Dublin. Dublin: 1775. pp.(2) + 5-20. LI.

1,436. WORSLEY, F.C. Ireland, Irish poor laws and the permanent causes of Irish poverty... London: 1842. pp.(2) + 26. CUL.

(d) Poor Law, Settlement and Removal

1,437. ANON. Compendium of the laws. I. Concerning lawful settlements. II. Laws for the preservation of game. III. Concerning the laws against highwaymen, gamesters, etc., by O.T. 1712. 1715. 6 fol. + pp.299. n.l.

1,438. ANON. The settlement and removal of the poor considered. London: 1847. pp.60. TCD; CUL.

1,439. ANON. The report of the committee relating to the apprehending and conveying of vagabonds. London: 1759. pp.(2) + 28. CUL.

1,440. ANON. "Vexatious legislation on parish settlements". L.M. 36. (1846). pp.160-4.

1,441. ANON. Parish settlements and pauperism. London: 1828. pp.62. TCD. [By Edward Mangin]. BL; LSE.

1,442.   ANON.   Cases and resolutions of cases, adjudg'd in the Court
of King's Bench [1685-1727] , concerning settlements and
removals. 2nd ed. 1729. pp.(4) + 160 + (20). LSE. 3rd ed.
(1685-1732). 1732. pp.(24) + 326 + (30). LI. 4th ed.
(1685-1733). 1742. pp.(24) + 417 + (30). CUL.

1,443.   ANON.   Memorandum on the law of settlement and removal.
London: [1879]. pp.14. LSE.

1,444.   ANON.   Some observations relating to the jurisdiction of
justices of peace, particularly with regard to the removing
poor persons. London: 1743. pp.8. G.

1,445.   ARCHBOLD, J.F.   The law relative to examinations and grounds
of appeal in cases of orders of removal; with forms in all
cases which occur in practice. London: 1847. pp.xvi + 178.
CUL; G.

1,446.   ARCHBOLD, J.F.   The new Poor Law Amendment Act, 11 & 12 Vict.
c.31, relating to the removal, grounds of removal, and
appeals, with a practical introduction and notes. London:
1848. pp.42. TCD.

1,447.   ARCHBOLD, J.F.   The act to amend the laws relating to the
removal of the poor, 19 Vict. cap.66; with notes and
observations. 4th ed. London: 1846. pp.28. TCD.

1,448.   ARCHBOLD, J.F.   The whole of the new practice in poor law
removals and appeals. 2nd ed. London: 1849. pp.46. TCD.

1,449.   BRADY, C.   The practricability of improving the dwellings of
the labouring classes, with remarks on the law of settlement
and removal of the poor. London: 1854. pp.60. NLI; RIA.

1,450.   BURROW, SIR J. (ed.).   Decisions, King's Bench, upon
Settlement Cases from 1732. London: 1768. pp.xv + 625 +
(44) + pp.629-653. 4to. Continuation. [1768]-72. pp.(2) +
pp.627-718 + 10. 1771. 4to. Second Continuation. [1772]-76.
pp.(8) + pp.719-864. 4to. 1776. Sq. 2nd ed. 1732-76.
pp.(8) + 846 + (18). 4to. 1786. Dublin: 1790.

1,451.   CALDECOTT, T.   Reports of cases relative to the duty and
office of a Justice of the Peace, from Michaelmas term 1776,
inclusive to Michaelmas term 1785, inclusive. [Sometimes
referred to as Caldecott, settlement cases.] Dublin: 1790.
Z. Another ed. London: 1776-1785. BL. In 3 parts. Other
eds. London: 1786; 1789. Sq. 1797. pp.389. [Sometimes
with pp.389-593 (containing later material) added]. Another
ed. 1800. pp.593. LI; Sq.

1,452.   COURT OF KING'S BENCH.   Sessions cases adjudged in the Court
of King's Bench, chiefly touching settlements... (1710-1748).
London: 1750. 2 vols. pp.vi + (10) + 432 + (40); (16) +
395 + (20). Sq; LSE; CUL.

1,453.   COURT OF KING'S BENCH.   Cases of settlement, King's Bench.
Cases and resolutions of cases, adjudg'd in the Court of
King's Bench, concerning settlements and removals (1685-1733).
4th ed. London: 1742. pp.24 + 417 + 30. Sq.

1,454.   COX, E.W.   The practice of poor removals, as regulated by the
         recent statutes... with observations, forms, and all the
         cases...   London: 1848.   pp.60.   CUL.   Another ed.   1849.
         [Cases decided to the end of Trinity Term, 1849].   pp.85.
         BL; G.

1,455.   CROSS, R.A.   The Acts relating to the settlement and removal
         of the poor, with notes of cases...   London: 1853.   pp.xvi+
         293.   BL; CUL; TCD.

1,456.   DAVEY, H.   Poor law settlement and removal.   London: 1908.
         pp.xxix + 364.   2nd ed.   1913.   pp.xxxvi + 449.   3rd ed.
         1925.   pp.xxxvi + 376.   CUL; LSE.

1,457.   GAMBIER, E.J.   Treatise on parochial settlement.   1828.   2nd
         ed. 1835.   [Source: SM 2].

1,458.   LEWIN, SIR G.A.   Summary of the law of settlement.   London:
         1827.   pp.xx + 498.   LSE.

1,459.   LIDBETTER, E.J.   Settlement and removal.   London: 1922.
         pp.xii + 164.   DHSS; Sq.

1,460.   LUMLEY, W.G.   A popular treatise on the Law of Settlement and
         Removals.   2nd ed.   London: 1842.   pp.200.   CUL.

1,461.   LUMLEY, W.G.   The Act to amend the laws relating to the
         removal of the poor, 9 & 10 Vict. c.66;   with a practical
         commentary and index.   2nd ed.   with additional observations,
         and the Poor Law Commissioner's circular letter (dated 17th
         September 1846).   London: 1846.   pp.48.   TCD.

1,462.   LUMLEY, W.G.   The Act to amend the laws relating to the
         removal of the poor, 9 & 10 Vict. c.66;   with a practical
         commentary and index.   2 ed.   London: 1846.   pp.48.   TCD.

1,463.   LUMLEY, W.G.   The Act to amend the procedure in respect of
         orders for the removal of the poor in England and Wales, and
         appeals thereform (11 & 12 Vict. c.31);   with a commentary and
         notes.   London: 1848.   pp.30.   TCD.

1,464.   LUMLEY, W.G.   The Poor Removal and Union Chargeability Acts:
         with introductory essays and commentaries.   2nd ed. (with an
         appendix containing the act relating to the removal of Scotch
         and Irish Poor and the Metropolitan Houseless Poor Acts).
         London: 1865.   pp.200.   CUL.

1,465.   MAUDE, W.C.   The principles of the law relating to the relief,
         irremoveability and settlement of the poor.   Manchester:
         1899.   pp.52.   BL.   4th ed.   London: 1927.   pp.xxv + 234.   BL

1,466.   MONTAGUE, F.C.   "The law of settlement and removal".   L.Q.R.
         4.   (1888).   pp.40-50.

1,467.   NOLAN, M.   A treatise on the laws for the relief and
         settlement of the poor.   London: 1805.   2 vols.   G.   4th ed.
         London: 1825.   3 vols.   G.

1,468.   NORTH, R.   A discourse of the poor.   Shewing the pernicious
         tendency of the laws now in force for their maintenance and

settlement: containing likewise some considerations relating to national improvement in general. London: 1753. pp.viii + 89. BL.

1,469. P.S.C. "On the law of settlement under 59 Geo. 3, c.50, and 6 Geo.4, cl.57". L.M. 9. (1833). pp.96-109.

1,470. PIGOTT, G. The laws of settlement and removal; their evils and remedy. London: 1862. pp.50. CUL; TCD.

1,471. S. "Parochial settlements". L.M. 32. (1844). pp.166-73.

1,472. SCULTHORPE, J. A compendium of the laws relating to the removal and settlement of the poor... 1st ed. London. n.1. 2nd ed. (including the latest statutes). 1827. BL.

1,473. STYLES, P. "The evolution of the law of settlement". University of Birmingham Historical Journal. 9. (1963). pp.33-63.

1,474. SYMONDS, J.F. A handbook on the laws of settlement and removal of union poor as amended by the 39 and 40 Vic. c.61, with a collection of statutes. London: 1882. pp.xii + 182. CUL. 2nd ed. 1887. pp.xxvii + 222. CUL. 3rd ed. 1891. pp.xxii + 256. CUL. 4th ed. by J. Scolefield and G.R. Hill, entitled The law of settlement and removal... 1903. pp.xxiv + 226 + 18. CUL.

1,475. SYMONDS, J.F. The law of settlement and removal of union poor. London: 1887. LSE.

1,476. SYMONS, J.C. Parish settlements and the practice of appeals. With the law and evidence of each class and the grounds of objection. London: 1844. pp.xxi + v + 243. 2nd ed. 1846. pp.xlv + 326 + 64. CUL; BL; LSE.

1,477. UNION CLERKS' SOCIETY. Report of the committee appointed to consider the Bill to consolidate and amend the laws relating to parochial settlement. London: 1845. pp.8. C.

1,478. UNITED KINGDOM. Cases and resolution of cases... concerning settlements and removals, etc. London: 1729. pp.160. LSE.

1,479. UNITED KINGDOM. Reports from comms. on the laws which concern the relief and settlement of the poor, etc. London. (H.C.C. IX. 1775-1788). pp.239-735. LSE.

1,480. UNITED KINGDOM. First (-eighth) report from the select committee on settlement and poor removal, etc. London: 1847. (B.P.P. XI). LSE.

1,481. UNITED KINGDOM. Reports to the Poor Law Board on the law of settlement, and removal of the poor. London: 1850. pp.viii + 211. (B.P.P. XXVII). LSE.

1,482. UNITED KINGDOM. Report... on the law of settlement and removal of the poor, etc. London: 1851. pp.xxiii + 352. (B.P.P. XXVI). LSE.

1,483. UNITED KINGDOM. Report from the select committee on poor removal, etc. London: 1854. pp.xii + 783. (B.P.P. XVII). LSE.

1,484. UNITED KINGDOM. Report from the select committee on poor removal, etc. London: 1854-5. pp.xvi + 395. (B.P.P. XIII). LSE.

1,485. UNITED KINGDOM. Report from the select committee on irremovable poor, etc. London: 1857-8. pp.vi + 28. (B.P.P. XIII). LSE.

1,486. UNITED KINGDOM. Report from the select committee on the irremovable poor, etc. London: 1860. pp.xviii + 549. (B.P.P. XVII). LSE.

1,487. UNITED KINGDOM. Return of destitute poor removed from England and Scotland to Ireland, from 1st December 1860 to 1st December 1862...; and the cause or authority for... removal. London: 1863. (B.P.P. LII). pp.53. LSE.

1,488. UNITED KINGDOM. Report from the Select Committee on Poor Removal, etc. London: 1878-9. (B.P.P. XII). pp.xiv + 225. LSE.

1,489. VULLIAMY, A.F. The law of settlement and removal of paupers... London: 1895. pp.xii + 274. Sq. 2nd ed. 1906. pp.xvi + 336. CUL.

1,490. WHITE, J.M. Parochial settlements an obstacle to poor law reform. London: 1835. pp.30. G; TCD.

(e) Poor Law, Children

1,491. ANON. The physical and moral condition of the children and young persons employed in mines and manufactures. Illustrated by extracts from the reports of the commissioners for inquiring into the employment of children and young persons in mines and collieries, and in the trades and manufactures in which numbers of them work together, not being included under the terms of the Factories Regulation Act. London: 1843. pp.280. TCD.

1,492. ANON. "Children under the poor law". Lab.G. XVI. (1908). p.38.

1,493. CARPENTER, M. What shall we do with our pauper children? London: [1861]. pp.23. LSE.

1,494. CHANCE, W. Children under the poor law. London: 1897. pp.xii + 443. LSE; S.

1,495. DAVENPORT-HILL, F. Children of the state: the training of juvenile paupers. London: 1889. pp.vii + 370. LSE.

1,496. DAVENPORT-HILL, F. "The system of boarding out pauper children". E.J. III. (1893). p.62ff.

1,497. EDWARDS, A.D. Children of the poor. London: 1909. pp.74. LSE.

1,498. HANWAY, J. An earnest appeal for mercy to the children of the poor... London: 1756. pp.141. CUL.

1,499. HILL, J.M. The Poor Law Act of 1889, as affecting deserted children, etc. London: 1890. pp.15. LSE.

1,500. INGRAM, J.K. Additional facts and arguments on the boarding-out of pauper children, etc. 1876. pp.23. LSE.

1,501. LEACH, R.A. Pauper children: their education and training. A complete handbook to the law relating to pauper children, etc. London: 1916. BL.

1,502. MACDOUGALL, J.P. The boarding-out of pauper children in Scotland. n.p.: [1904?]. pp.33. LSE.

1,503. MACNAMARA, T.J. Children under the poor law: a report to the President of the Local Government Board. London: 1908. pp.25. BL.

1,504. MASON, M.H. Classification of girls and boys in workhouses, and the legal powers of boards of guardians for placing them beyond the workhouse. London: 1884. pp.32.

1,505. 'MELANTIUS'. Letters addressed to Mrs. Peter La Touche... containing a state of the orphan-houses of England, Ireland, Zealand and Holland. Dublin: 1793. pp.37. QUB.

1,506. PERCIVAL, T. Poor law children. London: [1912]. pp.xv + 409. LSE; CUL.

1,507. PETTIGREW, T.J. The pauper farming system, etc. London: 1836. pp. v + 131. LSE.

1,508. PINCHBECK, I. & HEWITT, M. Children in English society. Volume II, from the eighteenth century to the Children Act, 1948. London: 1973. pp.354. CUL.

1,509. RIIS, J.A. The children of the poor. London: 1892. pp.xii + 300. G.

1,510. SKELTON, J. Pauperism and the boarding-out of pauper children in Scotland. London: 1877. pp.xvi + 145. LSE.

1,511. SPARGO, J. The bitter cry of the children. New York: 1906. pp.xxiii + 237. U.

1,512. UNITED KINGDOM. Copies of report... on the boarding out of pauper children in Scotland and... in England. London: 1870. (B.P.P., LVIII). pp.189. LSE.

1,513. UNITED KINGDOM. Report to the Board of Supervisors on the system in Scotland of boarding pauper children in private dwellings. London: 1893. (B.P.P., XLIV). pp.46. LSE.

1,514. UNITED KINGDOM Children under the poor law. London: 1908. (B.P.P., XCII). pp.25. LSE.

1,515. WILLIAMS, E.M.N. Report on the condition of the children who are in receipt of the various forms of poor law relief in England and Wales. London: 1910. pp.285. LSE.

(f) Vagrancy

1,516. ANON. Observations upon the vagrant laws; proving that the statutes in Queen Elizabeth's time are the most proper foundation for a law of that nature: and that all alterations that have been made since, have been for the worse. London: 1742. pp.13. G.

1,517. ANON. A letter to a member of parliament, on the impropriety of classing players with rogues and vagabonds in the Vagrancy Act. London: 1824. pp.22. TCD.

1,518. ANON. Protest against the spirit and practice of modern legislation, as exhibited in the new Vagrant Act. London: 1824. pp.44. LSE.

1,519. ANON. The Vagrant Act, in relation to the liberty of the subject. By a Barrister. pp.55. TCD. Postscript to the Vagrant Act, etc. London: 1824. pp.(2), 57-89. TCD. 2nd ed. with postscript. London: 1824. pp.89. BL; G.

1,520. ANON. "The relief of vagrants and of the unemployed in Germany and England". Char.Org.Rev. 4. (1888). pp.81-92.

1,521. ANON. "Persons found in suspicious circumstances". J.Cr.L. 11. (1947). pp.430-8; 12. (1948). pp.103-11.

1,522. ADOLPHUS, J. Observations on the Vagrant Act, and some other statutes, and on the powers and duties of justices of the peace. London: 1824. pp.112. G; TCD.

1,523. BAKER, T.B. Vagrancy. To be read at the Social Science meeting, at Belfast, September 19th, 1867. Gloucester: 1867. pp.12. NLI.

1,524. BEIER, A. "Vagrants and the social order in Elizabethan England". P.& P. 64. (1974). pp.3-29.

1,525. CURRY, G. "A bundle of vague diverse offences; the vagrancy laws with special reference to the New Zealand experience". A-A.L.R. 1. (1972). pp.523-36.

1,526. DAVEY, S. The law relating to casual paupers. London: 1899. p.91. LSE; CUL.

1,527. DAVIES, C.S.L. "Slavery and Protector Somerset: the Vagrancy Act of 1547". Ec.H.R. (2nd ser.). XIX. (1966). pp.533-49.

1,528. DAWSON, W.H. The vagrancy problem: the case for measures of restraint for tramps...; with a study of continental detention colonies and labour houses. London: 1910. pp.xv + 270. LSE.

1,529. DELANEY, K. "A future for 'sus'". K.C. 31. (1979). pp.47-51.

1,530. DEPARTMENTAL COMMITTEE ON VAGRANCY. Report, minutes and appendices. London: 1906. (Cd. 2852, 2891, 2892). LSE.

1,531. DEUTSCH, F. "'Sus' - developments in 1980". New Community. 8. (1980). pp.175-6.

1,532. DOOLAN, B. "Some aspects of the Vagrancy Act, 1824, section 4". I.L.T.S.J. 107. (1973). pp.203-4, 213-4, 219-20.

1,533. DOUGLAS, W.O. "Vagrancy and arrest on suspicion". Yale L.J. (1960-61). pp.1-14.

1,534. EUROPEAN COMMISSION OF HUMAN RIGHTS. Publications. Series A: Judgment and Decisions [A] 14. De Wilde, Ooms and Versyp Cases: "Vagrancy" Cases; judgment of 10 March 1972; question of the application of Article 50 of the Convention. Strasbourg: Council of Europe, 1972, pp.22. (in English). LSE.

1,535. EUROPEAN COMMISSION OF HUMAN RIGHTS. Publications. Series B: Pleadings, Oral Arguments and Documents [B12]. De Wilde, Ooms and Versyp Cases: "Vagrancy" Cases; question of the application of Article 50 of the Convention (1971-1972). Strasbourg: Council of Europe, 1973. pp.97, 99-126. (in English and French). LSE.

1,536. FERGUSSON, R.M. The vagrant: what to do with him. London: 1911. pp.x + 62. LSE.

1,537. GILBERT, T. Plan for the better relief and employment of the poor; for enforcing and amending the law respecting... vagrants; and for improving the police. London: 1781. pp.(iv) + 136. LSE.

1,538. GLEN, W.C. The Pauper Inmates Discharge and Regulation Act, 1871, and the Casual Poor Act, 1882, together with the Metropolitan Houseless Poor Acts, 1864 and 1865, with notes and official documents on vagrancy. 2nd ed. London: 1882. pp.58. LSE.

1,539. GRAHAM, R. "The prostitute and the beggar". Court. 2(3). (1977). pp.16-20.

1,540. HACKETT, W. "The Irish bacach, or professional beggar reviewed archeologically". Ulster J. Arch. 9. (1861-2). pp.256-71.

1,541. HONEYMAN, J.H. "The inadequacies of penal enactments as a means of eradicating vagrancy". Westm.Rev. 162. (1904). pp.41-6.

1,542. JONES, D.J.V. "'A dead loss to the country'; the criminal vagrant in mid-nineteenth century Wales". Welsh Hist.Rev. 8. (1976-7). pp.312-44.

1,543. LAMBERT, J. Vagrancy laws and vagrants: a lecture delivered to members of the Salisbury Literary and Institution... March 23 1868. Salisbury: [1868]. pp.48. LSE.

1,544. LEIGH, L.H. "Powers of arrest in relation to vagrancy and related offences". _Crim.L.R._ (1974). pp.157-65.

1,545. LEIGH, L.H. "Vagrancy, morality and decency". _Crim.L.R._ (1975). pp.381-90.

1,546. LUMLEY, W.G. The minute of the Poor Law Board for the repression of vagrancy: with introductory observations, and a statement of the penal provisions now in force for this object. London: [1848]. pp.56. TCD.

1,547. MARTIN, M. An appeal to public benevolence, for the relief of beggars; with a view to a plan for suppression of beggary. London: 1812. pp.18. G.

1,548. MOSLEY, J.V. Poor law administration in England and Wales, 1834 to 1850 with special reference to the problem of able-bodied pauperism. 1975. Fo.335. Typescript Ph.D. (London) thesis: unpublished. UCL.

1,549. NATIONAL COUNCIL FOR CIVIL LIBERTIES. Vagrancy: an archaic law. London: 1975. pp.16. LSE.

1,550. O'CONNOR, P. Britain in the sixties: vagrancy. London: 1963. pp.186. DHSS.

1,551. POUND, J.F. Poverty and vagrancy in Tudor England. London: 1971. pp.120. LSE; CUL.

1,552. RACKSTRAW, J.W. "Vagrancy and petty crime". _Howard J._ (1926-29). pp.352-5.

1,553. RADEVSKY, T. "Suspected persons and intent". _L.S.G._ 76. (1979). p.522.

1,554. REPUBLIC OF IRELAND. Report of the commission on itinerancy. Dublin: 1963. pp.166. DHSS.

1,555. RIBTON-TURNER, C.J. A history of vagrants and vagrancy and beggars and begging [illustrated]. London: 1887. pp.xxii + 720. CUL; U; LSE.

1,556. SELECT COMMITTEE ON THE STATE OF MENDICITY. Report from the Select Committee on the State of Mendicity in the Metropolis. London: 1816. pp.21. (B.P.P. 1816, V). LSE.

1,557. SHERRY, A.H. "Vagrants, rogues and vagabonds". _Cal.L.R._ 48. (1960). pp.557-73.

1,558. SLACK, P.A. "Vagrants and vagrancy in England, 1598-1664". _Ec.H.R._ (2nd ser.). 27. (1974). pp.360-379.

1,559. SOCIETY FOR THE SUPPRESSION OF BEGGARS. The first report of the society, instituted in Edinburgh on 25th January, 1813, for the suppression of beggars, for the relief of occasional distress, and for the encouragement of industry among the poor, etc. Edinburgh: 1814. pp.39 + 43. LSE.

1,560. STEWART, J. Of no fixed abode: vagrancy and the welfare state. Manchester: 1975. pp.viii + 200. DHSS.

1,561. UNITED KINGDOM. An ordinance... for the... relief... of the poore, and the punishment of vagrants, etc. London: 1647. pp.8. G.

1,562. UNITED KINGDOM. An Act... for the relief... of the poor, and the punishing of vagrants... of London, etc. London: 1649. pp.20. LSE.

1,563. UNITED KINGDOM. Report from the Select Committee on the Laws relating to the Irish and Scotch Vagrants.   London: 1828. (B.P.P. IV). pp.18. LSE.

1,564. UNITED KINGDOM. Report from the Select Committee on Irish Vagrants. London: 1833. (B.P.P. XVI). pp.43. LSE.

1,565. UNITED KINGDOM. Resolutions passed by the boards of guardians in Ireland, relative to the suppression of mendicancy and vagrancy. London: 1840. (B.P.P., XLVIII.) pp.12. LSE.

1,566. UNITED KINGDOM.   Reports and communications on vagrancy. London: 1847-8. pp.iv + 108. (B.P.P. LIII). LSE.

1,567. UNITED KINGDOM.   Report on vagrancy made... by poor law inspectors. London: 1866. pp.210. (B.P.P. XXXV). LSE.

1,568. UNITED KINGDOM.   Report of the Departmental Committee on Vagrancy, with evidence.   London: 1906.   (B.P.P. CIII). pp.123 + 503 +208. LSE.

1,569. UNITED KINGDOM.   Report of the Departmental Committee on Vagrancy in Scotland.   London: 1935-36.   pp.92.   (B.P.P. 1935-36, XIV). LSE.

1,570. VORSPAN, R. "Vagrancy and the new poor law in late Victorian and Edwardian England". E.H.R. 92. (1977). pp.59-81.

Section 3   Charities and Friendly Societies

1,571.   ANON.   Instructions for the establishment of friendly societies, with a form of rules and tables applicable thereto. London: 1835. RIA.

1,572.   ANON.   "Proceedings of council.   National insurance. Char.Org.Rep. 7. (1878). pp.223-224.

1,573.   ACLAND, J.   A plan for rendering the poor independent on public contributions, founded on the basis of the friendly society, etc. London: 1786. pp.viii + 62. G. A plan for rendering the poor independent on public contributions. Exeter: 1786. pp.vi + 59. BL.

1,574.   ACTUARY.   Considerations on the necessity of appointing a board of commissioners for the protection and encouragement of friendly societies. London: 1824. pp.16. U.

1,575.   ASSOCIATION OF INDUSTRIAL ASSURANCE COMPANIES AND COLLECTING FRIENDLY SOCIETIES.   Short story of industrial insurance. London: [1922?]. pp.57. DHSS.

1,576.   BELL, L.H.   The respective spheres of the state and of voluntary organisation in the prevention and relief of poverty in London at the present day. London: 1935. pp.270. LSE.

1,577.   BOSANQUET, C.B.P.   The organisation of charity: the history and mode of operation of the Charity Organisation Society. London: 1875. pp.15. LSE.

1,578.   BOSANQUET, H.   The administration of charitable relief. London: 1898. pp.27. LSE.

1,579.   BOURNE, H.C.   "Pride and prejudice".   Char.Org.Rev.   6. (1890). pp.19-24.

1,580.   BOURNE, J.   A short history of friendly societies in general and of the Birmingham Ebenezer Provident Sick Society in particular.   [Birmingham?]: 1913. pp.14. LSE.

1,581.   BRABROOK, E.W.   Provident societies and industrial welfare. London: 1898. pp.224. DHSS.

1,582.   BROWN, C.H.L. & TAYLOR, J.A.G.   Friendly societies. London: 1933. pp.xii + 95. (reprint 1944). DHSS; CUL.

1,583.   CASTRES, A.   Ways and means for suppressing beggary and relieving the poor by erecting general hospitals and charitable corporations, etc. London: 1726. pp.128. G.

1,584.   [CHARITY COMMISSIONERS.] Public charities: analytical digest of the commissioners' reports, ec. London: 1835. pp.453. (B.P.P. 1835, XL). LSE.

1,585.   [CHARITY COMMISSIONERS.] Public charities: analytical digest of the reports made by the commissioners...; digest of schools and charities for education; return of charities to be distributed to the poor. London: 1843. 3v. (B.P.P. 1843, XVI-XVIII). LSE.

1,586. [CHARITY COMMISSIONERS.] Reports of the Charity Commissioners for England and Wales, etc. London: 1854 to date. (BPP). LSE (incomplete).

1,587. CHARITY ORGANISATION SOCIETY. [Reports, leaflets and press-cuttings relating to the Association for the Prevention of Pauperism and Crime in the Metropolis, later the Society for Organising Charitable Relief and Repressing Mendicity. Afterwards the Charity Organisation Society.] London: 1868-70. LSE.

1,588. CHARITY ORGANISATION SOCIETY. Manual of the Society for Organising Charitable Relief and Repressing Mendicity: objects and mode of operation of the society, etc. London: 1870-1881. 4 vols. LSE.

1,589. CHARITY ORGANISATION SOCIETY. Annual charities register and digest. London: 1890, 1895, 1898, 1901, 1905-13, 1926 onwards. LSE.

1,590. CHARITY ORGANIZATION SOCIETY. The prevention and relief of distress: a handbook of information respecting the statutory and voluntary means available, etc. London: 1922. pp.viii + 140. RSS.

1,591. CHARITY ORGANISATION SOCIETY. The prevention and relief of distress: a handbook of information respecting the statutory and voluntary means available etc. London: 1931. pp.vii + 185. LSE; CUL.

1,592. CHESTERMAN, M. Charities, trusts and social welfare. London: 1982. pp. LSE; CUL; Sq.

1,593. CLEGG, C. Friend in deed. The history of a life assurance office. London: 1958. pp.xxxviii + 160. DHSS; CUL.

1,594. CLEGHORN, J. Thoughts on the expediency of a general providence institution, for the benefit of the working classes, etc. Edinburgh: 1824. pp.43. U.

1,595. COMMITTEE ON THE LAW AND PRACTICE RELATING TO CHARITABLE TRUSTS. Report. London: 1952. pp.iv + 251. (B.P.P. 1952-43, VIII). LSE.

1,596. COOPER, S. Definitions and axioms relating to charity, charitable institutions and the poor's laws. London: 1764. pp.x + 170. LSE.

1,597. CRACKNELL, D.G. Law relating to charities. London: 1973. pp.xlviii + 256. CUL.

1,598. CUNNINGHAM, J.W. A few observations on friendly societies and their influence on public morals. London: 1817. pp.32. G.

1,599. DAVIS, W. Hints to the philanthropists; or, a collective view of practical means for improving the condition of the poor and labouring class. Bath: 1821. pp.viii + 160. G.

1,600. DIPROSE, J. & GAMMON, J. Reports of law cases affecting friendly societies. Manchester: 1897. pp.xx + 669. DHSS.

1,601. DUNCAN, J.S. Collections related to the systematic relief of the poor at different periods, and in different countries with observations on charity, etc. London: 1815. pp.220. LSE.

1,602. EDEN, SIR F.M. Observations on friendly societies, etc. London: 1801. pp.32. G.

1,603. EQUITABLE LABOUR EXCHANGE ASSOCIATION. Rules and regulations of the Equitable Labour Exchange, Gray's Inn Road, London. For the purpose of relieving the productive classes from poverty, by their own industry, and for the mutual exchange of labour for equal value of labour. London: 1832. pp.14. NLI.

1,604. FOWKE, V. DE S. Industrial and Provident Societies Act, 1893. London: 1894. pp.188. DHSS.

1,605. FOWLE, T.W. The poor law, friendly societies and old age destitution. Oxford: 1892. pp.23.

1,606. FRIENDLY SOCIETIES. British labour struggles: contemporary pamphlets 1727-1850. Friendly societies 1798-1839. New York: 1972. (7 pamphlets, reprinted with original pagination: pp.,65, 12, 15, 10, 31, 15, 14). CUL.

1,607. FULLER, F.B. The law relating to friendly societies and industrial and provident societies. London: 1926. pp.xlviii + 684. LSE. 2nd ed. 1898. pp.xxix + 282. CUL.

1,608. GOSDEN, D.H.J.H. The friendly societies in England, 1815-1875. Manchester: 1961. pp.viii + 262. DHSS.

1,609. GRAY, B.K. A history of English philanthropy: from the dissolutin of the monasteries to the taking of the first census. London: 1967. pp.xv + 302. DHSS; CUL.

1,610. GRAY, B.K. & HUTCHINS, B.L. (eds.). Philanthropy and the state or social politics. London: 1908. pp.339. CUL.

1,611. HARDWICK, C. The history, present position and social importance of friendly societies. 3rd ed. Manchester: [1893]. pp.xiv + 170. LSE.

1,612. HENDERSON, C.R. (ed.). Modern methods of charity: an account of the systems of relief, public and private, in the principal countries having modern methods. New York: 1904. pp.xiv + 715. S.

1,613. HINE, J. Observations on the necessity of a legislative measure for the protection and support of endowed public charities. London: 1842. pp.87. LSE.

1,614. HOBHOUSE, A. A lecture on the characteristics of charitable foundations in England, delivered... 1868. London: 1868. pp.viii + 40. LSE.

1,615. HUTT, R.   "Trade unions as friendly societies, 1912-1952".
        Yorkshire Bull. of Econ. and Soc.Res.   7.   (1).   (1955).
        pp.69-85.

1,616. JAMES, J.H.   A practical application of the Joint Stock
        Companies and Friendly Societies Acts, to the registration and
        government of assurance societies, etc.   London: 1851.
        pp.xvi + 570. CUL.

1,617. JONES, G. History of the law of charity: 1532-1827. London:
        1969. pp.270. DHSS; LSE. CUL.

1,618. JORDAN, W.K.   Philanthropy in England, 1480-1660.   London:
        1959. pp.410. DHSS; LSE; CUL.

1,619. JORDAN, W.K.   The charities of London, 1480-1660.   The
        aspirations and the achievements of the urban society.
        London: 1960. pp.461. DHSS; CUL.

1,620. JORDAN, W.K.   The charities of rural England, 1480-1660.
        London: 1961. pp.484. LSE; CUL.

1,621. KEETON, G.W.   Modern law of charities.   London: 1962.
        pp.xxxv + 345. DHSS; LSE; CUL.

1,622. KEETON, G.W. & SHERIDAN, L.A.   Modern law of charities.
        Belfast: 1971. pp.404. LSE.

1,623. LAMB, A.   The statutes relating to friendly, industrial and
        provident societies; with an introduction and notes. London:
        [1867]. pp.128. TCD.

1,624. LEWIS, W.A. & OTHERS. Private charity in England, 1747-1757.
        New Haven: 1938. pp.xv + 132. LSE.

1,625. LINCOLN, J.A. (ed.). The way ahead: the strange case of the
        friendly societies. [Manchester]: 1946. pp.68. LSE; DHSS.

1,626. MACKAY, T. On the cooperation of charitable agencies with the
        poor law, etc. London: 1895. pp.12. LSE.

1,627. MACKAY, T. The state and charity.   London: 1898. pp.viii
        + 201. Sq.

1,628. MACKAY, T. "The theory, necessity and limits of state action
        in respect of the relief of the poor". Char.Org.Rev. (n.s.).
        XXVI.   156.   (December 1909).   pp.379-86.   XXVII.   157.
        (January 1910). pp.6-16.

1,629. MOFFREY, R.W. A century of oddfellowship. Manchester: 1910.
        pp.214. DHSS.

1,630. MORGAN, H.D.   The expedience and method of providing
        assurances for the poor, and of adopting the improved
        constitution of friendly societies, constructed upon
        principles calculated to ensure their stability and prevent
        their insolvency and governed by regulations in conformity
        with the Act 10 Geo.Geo.IV.c.56. Oxford: 1830. pp.58. KI;
        TCD.

1,631. MOWAT, C.L. The Charity Organization Society, 1869-1913: its ideas and work. London: 1961. pp.xii + 188.

1,632. NATIONAL CONFERENCE OF FRIENDLY SOCIETIES. Report of the special meeting July 28th and 29th, 1911. [Manchester: 1911]. pp.150. LSE.

1,633. NATIONAL COUNCIL FOR SOCIAL SERVICE. Charity law and voluntary organisations: report of the Goodman Committee. London: 1976. pp.ix + 150. CUL; LSE; DHSS.

1,634. NEISSON, F.G.P. Legislation on friendly societies, the principles on which it should be based, also a review of the chief features of the legislative enactments hitherto. London: 1870. pp.77. LSE.

1,635. NEWMAN, T.S. History of the Hearts of Oak Benefit Society, 1842-1942. London: 1942. pp.204. DHSS.

1,636. NEWMAN, T.S. The story of friendly societies and social security. London: 1945. pp.40. DHSS.

1,637. NIGHTINGALE, B. Charities. London: 1973. pp.xii + 372. DHSS; LSE; CUL.

1,638. OBLER, J. "Private giving in the welfare state". Brit.Jo.Pol.Sci. 11. (1981). pp.17-48.

1,639. OWEN, D. English philanthropy, 1660-1960. London: 1965. pp.xiii + 610. DHSS; LSE. CUL.

1,640. PRATT, J.T. The laws relating to friendly societies, etc. London: 1846. pp.x + 180. S.

1,641. PROCHASKA, F.K. "Women in English philanthropy, 1790-1830". Int.Rev.Soc.Hist. XIX. (1974). pp.426-445.

1,642. REGISTRY OF FRIENDLY SOCIETIES. Memorandum of instructions, Trade Union Act, 1913. London: [1913?]. pp.15. LSE.

1,643. REGISTRY OF FRIENDLY SOCIETIES AND OFFICE OF THE INDUSTRIAL ASSURANCE COMMISSIONER. Guide to the Friendly Society Acts and the Industrial Assurance Acts. London: 1962. pp.ix + 192. LSE; Sq.

1,644. ROBERTSON, A. Periodical savings applied to provident purposes; with remarks on the constitution and practice of friendly, odd-fellows', building... societies etc. London: 1852. pp.66. G.

1,645. RODGERS, B. Cloak of charity: studies in 18th century philanthropy. London: 1949. pp.185. DHSS; LSE; CUL.

1,646. ROOFF, M. Voluntary societies and social policy. London: 1957. pp.iv + 320. LSE.

1,647. ROOFF, M. A hundred years of family welfare: a study of the Family Welfare Association (formerly Charity Organisation Society) 1869-1969. London: 1972. pp.400. DHSS.

1,648. ROSE, G.   Observations on the Act for the Relief and
        Encouragement of Friendly Societies...; forms of the several
        instruments necessary...; with an abstract of the Act; by
        the gentleman who framed the Bill. London: 1794. pp.ii +
        34. G.

1,649. ROYAL LIVER FRIENDLY SOCIETY.   Royal Liver Friendly Society
        1850-1950. Liverpool: 1950. pp.54. DHSS.

1,650. SCRATCHLEY, A.   Treatise on friendly societies, containing an
        exposition of the true law of sickness with rules and tables,
        etc. 10th ed. London: 1859. pp.xliv + 160 + 70. LSE.

1,651. SIM, J.D.S.   Pratts friendly societies.   14th ed.   London:
        1909. pp.lxxv + 280. DHSS; CUL.

1,652. SIMEY, M.B.   Charitable effort in Liverpool in the nineteenth
        century. Liverpool: 1951. pp.150. CUL.

1,653. SOUTHERN, R. & ROSE, P.P.   Handbook to the Industrial and
        Provident Societies Acts, 1893 to 1961. 2nd ed. Manchester:
        1961. pp.228. LSE.

1,654. TAMLYN, J.   A digest of the laws of friendly societies and
        savings banks, etc. London: 1827. pp.xiv + 138. G.

1,655. THE CO-OPERATIVE UNION.   The Industrial and Provident
        Societies Act, 1893. Manchester: 1894. pp.170. DHSS.

1,656. TOWNSHEND, MRS.   The case against the Charity Organisation
        Society. London: 1911. pp.19. (Fabian Tract No.158). LSE;
        CUL.

1,657. TREBLE, J.H.   "The attitudes of friendly societies towards the
        movement in Great Britain for state pensions, 1878-1908".
        Int.Rev.Soc.Hist. XV. (1970). pp.266-299.

1,658. UNITED KINGDOM.   Report from the Select Committee on Friendly
        Societies. London: 1852. pp.x + 132. (B.P.P. 1852, V).
        LSE.

1,659. UNITED KINGDOM.   Report of the Registrar of Friendly Societies
        in England. London: 1856-70, 1873, 1875. LSE.

1,660. WATSON, A.W.   Some points of interest in the operations of
        friendly societies, railway benefit societies and collecting
        societies. London: 1910. pp.97. DHSS.

1,661. WATSON, A.W.   Memorandum with regard to friendly societies and
        old age pensions schemes. Unpub.: 1897. pp.5. DHSS (RCAP
        COLL).

1,662. WEBB, S. & B.   The sphere of voluntary agencies in the
        prevention of destitution. London: 1911. pp.46. UL.

1,663. WHITE, N.   A handy book on the law of friendly, industrial and
        provident, building and loan societies.   London: 1865.
        pp.viii + 85. U.

Section 4   Specific Benefits

(a) <u>Workmen's Compensation</u> (including Employers' Liability)

See also, Part II, Section 6 (Industrial Injury and Disease)

1,664.   ANON.   Digest of cases and decisions under the Employers' Liability Act, 1880.   London: 1893.   pp.xxvi + 291.   LSE.

1,665.   ANON   Workmen's Compensation Act, 1897, with full extracts from the statutes therein referred to.   London: [1897].   pp. iv + 26 + 14.   LSE.

1,666.   ANON.   "The Workmen's Compensation Act, 1897".   <u>S.J.</u>   42. (1897-8).   pp.606-7.

1,667.   ANON.   "Principles established by a year's appeals under the Workmen's Compensation Act, 1897".   <u>S.J.</u>   43.   (1898-9). pp.583-4.

1,668.   ANON.   "Workmen's compensation schemes".   <u>Lab.G.</u>   7.   (1899). pp.260-261.

1,669.   ANON.   "Appeals under the Workmen's Compensation Act".   <u>S.L.T.</u> 7.   (1899-1900).   pp.146-7.

1,670.   ANON.   "The second year's appeals under the Workmen's Compensation Act, 1897".   <u>S.J.</u>   44.   (1899-1900).   pp.587-9.

1,671.   ANON.   "The Workmen's Compensation Act in the House of Lords". <u>S.J.</u>   45.   (1900-1).   pp.323-4.

1,672.   ANON.   "Recent workmen's compensation cases".   <u>S.J.</u>   46. (1901-2).   pp.98-9.

1,673.   ANON.   "The meaning of 'accident' in Workmen's Compensation Acts".   <u>N.I.J.</u>   4.   (1903-4).   pp.186-7, 191-2.

1,674.   ANON.   "Schemes under the Workmen's Compensation Act in relation to claims under the Employers' Liability Act".   <u>S.J.</u> 48.   (1903-4).   pp.188-9.

1,675.   ANON.   "Workmen's compensation".   <u>Lab.G.</u>   XII.   (1904). p.230.

1,676.   ANON.   "The Workmen's Compensation Bill".   <u>S.J.</u>   50. (1905-6).   pp.400-1.

1,677.   ANON.   "Workmen's insurance.   Accident insurance and employers' liability.   Great Britain and Ireland". <u>I.L.O.Bull.</u>   (1906).   pp.LXXV-LXXXII.

1,678.   ANON.   Householders and servants under the new Workmen's Compensation Act: a simple guide.   London: [1906?].   pp.12. LSE.

1,679.   ANON.   "Compensation for industrial diseases".   <u>Lab.G.</u>   XV.

(1907). pp.165-166.

1,680. ANON. "Compensation for industrial diseases". <u>Lab.G.</u> XVI.
(1908). pp.369-370.

1,681. ANON. "A view of the Workmen's Compensation Act, 1897, 1906".
<u>J. Comp.Leg.</u> 9. (1908-9). pp.572-573.

1,682. ANON.   "Workmen's   insurance: accident   insurance".
<u>I.L.O.Bull.</u> (2nd ser.). VI. (1911). pp.CXIX-CXXII.

1,683. ANON.   "Recent cases on workmen's compensation".   <u>S.J.</u>
(1912-13). pp.698-9, 714-5.

1,684. ANON.   "Suspension of weekly payments under the Workmen's
Compensation Act". <u>S.L.T.</u> 2. (1913). pp.34-6.

1,685. ANON.   "The new workmen's compensation rules".   <u>S.J.</u>   58.
(1913-14). pp.806-7.

1,686. ANON.   "Practice points in workmen's compensation".   <u>S.J.</u> 58.
(1913-14). pp.683-4.

1,687. ANON. "Workmen's accidents and wilful misconduct". <u>S.J.</u> 60.
(1915-16). pp.234-5.

1,688. ANON.   "Some recent decisions on workmen's compensation".
<u>S.J.</u> 62. (1917-18). p.738.

1,689. ANON.   "Workmen's compensation and contractor's repudiation".
<u>S.J.</u> 66. (1921-2). pp.293-4.

1,690. ANON.   "The Workmen's Compensation Acts, 1906 and 1923.
Accident directly caused by disobedience to orders".   <u>S.J.</u>
68. (1923-4). pp.159-60.

1,691. ANON.   "The new Workmen's Compensation Act"   <u>S.J.</u>   68.
(1923-4). pp.296, 221.

1,692. ANON. "Alien workers under workmen's compensation legislation
in the British Empire". <u>I.Lab.R.</u> IX. (1924). pp.708ff.

1,693. ANON. "Workmen's compensation legislation in Great Britain in
1922". <u>I.Lab.R.</u> IX. (1924). pp.954.

1,694. ANON.   "An epitome of recent decisions on the Workmen's
Compensation Act, 1906".   <u>S.J.</u>   69.   (1924-5).   pp.157-8,
174-5, 190-2.

1,695. ANON.   "A summary of recent workmen's compensation cases".
<u>S.J.</u> 70. (1925-6). pp.295-6, 316.

1,696. ANON. "Service of notice and medical certificate, for purpose
of diminution of compensation payable to workmen". <u>S.J.</u> 70.
(1926). p.923.

1,697. ANON.   "Workmen's compensation: procedure for ending or
diminishing weekly payments". <u>S.J.</u> 70. (1926). pp.788-9.

1,698. ANON.   "Two recent workmen's compensation decisions on dependency". <u>S.J.</u> 71. (1927). pp.71-2.

1,699. ANON. "Workmen's compensation: the Acts of 1923 and 1925".
        <u>S.J.</u> 71. (1927). pp.809.

1,700. ANON. "Workmen's compensation and the League of Nations".
        <u>S.L.T.</u> [1928]. pp.133-4.

1,701. ANON. "Workmen's compensation for silicosis". <u>Lab.G.</u> 36.
        (1928). pp.320-1.

1,702. ANON. "Workmen's compensation: employers' grievance". <u>S.J.</u>
        73. (1929). p.120.

1,703. ANON. "Workmen's compensation. A simplified exposition".
        <u>S.J.</u> 75. (1931). pp.319-20, 338-9, 352.

1,704. ANON. "Workmen's Compensation Act. Declaration of liability
        or award for a nominal sum". <u>S.J.</u> 76. (1932). pp.104-5.

1,705. ANON. "Silicosis and compensation". <u>L.R.</u> 25. (1936).
        pp.125-6.

1,706. ANON. "Workmen's compensation: disablement from industrial
        disease". <u>L.J.</u> LXXXIV. (1937). pp.253, 272.

1,707. ANON. "Workmen's compensation in fatal cases". <u>L.J.</u>
        LXXXIII. (1937). p.6

1,708. ANON. "New Workmen's Compensation Bill". <u>L.R.</u> 32. (1943).
        p.133.

1,709. ANON. "Workmen's Compensation Act. Notes on the Act of
        1943". <u>S.L.T.</u> [1943]. pp.17-18.

1,710. ANON. "National insurance". <u>Ind.L.R.</u> 1. (1946-47).
        pp.59-62.

1,711. ANON. "Monthly review of current events. <u>Porter v. Princess
        Royal Colliery Co. Ltd.</u>". <u>Ind.L.R.</u> 1. (1946-47).
        pp.197-198.

1,712. ANON. "Monthly review of current events. <u>Sharpen v. W.B.
        Bawn & Co. Ltd.</u>". <u>Ind.L.R.</u> 1. (1946-47). pp.303-306.

1,713. ANON. "Review of current events. Some recent workmen's
        compensation cases". <u>Ind.L.R.</u> 3. (1948-49). pp.9-11.

1,714. ANON. "Review of current events. Some recent workmen's
        compensation cases". <u>Ind.L.R.</u> 4. (1949-50). pp.66-68,
        125-127, 181-183.

1,715. ANON. (and SAMUELS, H.) "Workmen's compensation" [Regular
        notes of cases]. <u>Ind.Welfare.</u> 11. (1929) and subsequent
        years.

1,716. ACKERMAN, S.B. Practice of workmen's compensation insurance.
        Chicago: 1925. pp.vii + 196. LSE.

1,717. AGGS, W.H. "Employers' liability and workmen's compensation".

L.M.R. (5th ser.). 24. (1898-9). pp.462-74.

1,718. AMERICAN MEDICAL ASSOCIATION. Workmen's compensation laws,
etc. Chicago: [1915]. pp.71. LSE; P.

1,719. ARONSON, V.R. The Workmen's Compensation Act, 1906. London:
1909. pp.xi + 559. Sq; DHSS; CUL.

1,720. BALL, F.N. "Elementary law of industry. (1) The workmen's
compensation system". Ind.L.R. 1. (1946-47). pp.59-62.

1,721. BARBER, W. Notes and explanations of the Workmen's
Compensation Act, 1906. Bradford: [1906]. pp.16. LSE.

1,722. BARLOW, M. "The insurance of industrial risks". E.J. VII.
(1897). pp.354-67.

1,723. BARLOW, M. "The insurance of industrial risks, 1897-1901".
E.J. 11. (1901). pp.345-53.

1,724. BARNETT, H.N. Accidental injuries to workmen with reference
to Workmen's Compensation Act, 1906... with article on
injuries to the organs of special sense by Cecil E. Shaw...
and legal introduction by Thomas J. Campbell. London: 1909.
pp.vii + 376. CUL.

1,725. BARTH, P.S. & HUNT, H. Workers' compensation and work-related
illnesses and diseases. Cambridge, Mass.: 1980. pp.xi +
391. DHSS.

1,726. BARTRIP, P.W.J. & BURMAN, S.B. The wounded soldiers of
industry: industrial compensation policy 1833-1897. Oxford:
1983. pp.xi + 253. Sq.

1,727. BAYLEE, J.T. "The Workmen's Compensation Act: what it is and
what it might be". Westm.Rev. 156. (1901). pp.68-72.

1,728. BEAUMONT, W.M. Injuries of the eyes of the employed and the
Workmen's Compensation Act: problems in prognosis. London:
1907. pp.viii + 160.

1,729. BELLAMY, B.W. Special supplement of workmen's compensation
tables. London: 1944. [Butterworths Emergency Legislation
Service (annotated). Statutes Supplement No.6a]. LSE.

1,730. BENSON, A. "English coal miners' trade union accident funds,
1850-1900". Ec.H.R. (2nd ser.). 28. (1975). pp.401-412.

1,731. BENTHALL, A. Precis of the Workmen's Compensation Act, 1906.
London: 1907? pp.10. LSE.

1,732. BEVEN, T. Law of employer's liability and workmen's
compensation. 1st ed. London: 1898. pp.xxxvi + 326 + xxx.
CUL. 2nd ed. 1899. pp.xlv + 424 + xxxix. CUL. 3rd ed.
1902. pp.lxv + 570 + lviii. CUL. 4th ed. 1909. pp.lxxxiii
+ 953. DHSS.

1,733. BEVEN, T. "'Volenti non fit injuria' in the light of recent
labour legislation". J.Comp.Leg. 8. (1907). pp.185-195.

1,734. BEVERLEY, F. A digest of cases decided under the Workmen's Compensation Acts 1897-1906 in the House of Lords, Court of Appeal in England and Ireland, Divisional and High Courts in England and Court of Session in Scotland... London: 1910. pp. xx + 152. CUL.

1,735. BEVERLEY, F. (ed.). A digest of cases decided under the Workmen's Compensation Act 1897-1909. 2nd ed. London: 1912. pp.xxviii + 219. Sq.

1,736. BIRRELL, A. Law of employers' liability at home and abroad. London: 1897. pp.123. LSE; C; G.

1,737. BLECKLY, H. Employers' liability for workmen. Warrington: 1878. pp.19. LSE.

1,738. BOWSTEAD, W. The law relating to the Workmen's Compensation Acts, 1897 and 1900. With an appendix by W. Bowstead. London: 1901. pp.xviii + 313. Sq; CUL.

1,739. BOWSTEAD, W. Outline of the law relating to workmen's compensation under the Workmen's Compensation Acts, 1897 and 1900. London: 1902. pp.64. LSE.

1,740. BROWN, S.S. On compensation for accidents to workmen in the United Kingdom. n.p.: [1897]. pp.15. LSE.

1,741. BROWNE, E. Employers' liability; past and prospective legislation, with special reference to "contracting out". London: 1896. pp.32. LSE.

1,742. BROWNE, E. Workmen's compensation: the Act explained. London: 1898. pp.32. LSE.

1,743. BUREAU OF LABOR STATISTICS OF THE U.S. DEPARTMENT OF LABOR. Workmen's insurance and compensation series: laws of United States and other countries including Great Britain. 1914-1918. Washington D.C.: 1914-18. 3 vols. DHSS.

1,744. BUTTERWORTH, RUEGG, A.H. & KNOCKER, D. (eds.). Workmen's compensation cases. London: 1911-. LSE.

1,745. BUTTERWORTH & CO. LTD. Digest of leading cases on workmen's compensation. London: 1933. pp.lxxxvi + 479 + 31. LSE.

1,746. CAMPBELL, G.L. Industrial accidents and their compensation. London: 1911. pp.xii + 105. LSE.

1,747. CANADA. Final report on laws relating to the liability of employers to make compensation to their employees for injuries received in the course of their employment which are in force in other countries. Toronto: 1913. pp.xx + 733. LSE.

1,748. CHAMBERS, R.C. "Workmen's compensation". In W.A. Robson (ed.). Social Security. London: 1943. pp.55-74. LSE. 2nd ed. 1945. pp.63-83. LSE.

1,749. CHARTRES, J. Judicial interpretation of the law relating to workmen's compensation. London: 1915. pp.1 + 753. Ll; Sq.

1,750. CHURCH OF ENGLAND. HOUSE OF LAYMEN FOR THE PROVINCE OF CANTERBURY. Report of the committee on the Workmen's Compensation Act, 1906, June 1907. London: 1907. pp.10. LSE.

1,751. CLAY, W.G. "The law of employers' liability and insurance against accidents". J.Comp.Leg. 2. (1897). pp.1-111.

1,752. CLEGG, A.T. "Workmen's Compensation Act 1897". Jur.Rev. XI. (1899). p.137.

1,753. COHEN, J.L. Workmen's compensation in Great Britain. 1923. pp.232. LSE; DHSS.

1,754. COLLIE, J. Medico-legal examinations and the Workmen's Compensation Act, 1906. London: 1912. pp.128. 2nd ed. as amended by subsequent Acts. 1922. pp.157. CUL; DHSS.

1,755. COLLIE, J. Malingering and feigned sickness. With notes on the Workmen's Compensation Acts, assisted by A.H. Spicer. London: 1913. pp.xii + 340. 2nd ed., revised and enlarged. 1917. pp.xvi + 664. CUL; DHSS.

1,756. COLLIE, J. Workmen's compensation, its medical aspect. London: 1933. pp.vii + 160. LSE; CUL.

1,757. COLLIE, R.J. Medical evidence and the laws relating to compensation for injury. London: 1909. pp.ii + 38. LSE.

1,758. COLLIE, R.J. Medico-legal aspect of the British Workmen's Compensation Act, 1906. A paper read at Brussels, Sept. 10th-14th, 1910. London: 1911. pp.41. [IIIieme Congres internationale des maladies professionelles.]. CUL; LSE.

1,759. CONNOLLY, T.J.D. Handbook on Workmen's Compensation Acts, 1906-23. Edinburgh and London: 1925. pp.xlii + 752. Sq.

1,760. CONNOLLY, T.J.D. Workmen's compensation... Edinburgh: 1929. pp.viii + 176. BL. (Popular Law Series No.4, by A. McNeill). Supplement, 1932. n.l.

1,761. CONSERVATIVE CENTRAL OFFICE. [Workmen's Compensation Acts]. London: [1905?]. In two parts. [Leaflets, Nos. 342, 343.] LSE.

1,762. CRAIG, W.T. Case law of workmen's compensation, collected from the decisions of the House of Lords and the courts of the United Kingdom. Edinburgh: 1913. 12 parts. BL.

1,763. DAVIE, P.C. Silicosis and asbestosis compensation schemes. London: 1932. pp.176. Sq.

1,764. DAWBARN, C.Y.C. Employers' liability re their servants at common law and under the Employers' Liability Act, 1880 and the Workmen's Compensation Acts, 1897 and 1900. 2nd ed. London: 1903. pp.xxxii + 299. CUL. 3rd ed. London: 1907. pp.xi + 564 + 31. CUL.

1,765. DAWBARN, C.Y.C. Workmen's compensation appeals. The case law for the legal years 1910-11; 1911-12; 1912-13. London: 1912; 1913. pp.xiii + 128; xv + 199; xvi + 131. BL.

1,766. DAWBARN, C.Y.C. Workmen's compensation practice. London: 1914. pp.xv + 1448 + 11. DHSS.

1,767. [DEPARTMENTAL COMMITTEE ON COMPENSATION FOR INDUSTRIAL DISEASES.] Second report of the Departmental Committee on Compensation for Industrial Diseases. London: 1908. 2 vols. (B.P.P. 1908, XXXV). LSE.

1,768. [DEPARTMENTAL COMMITTEE ON COMPENSATION FOR INJURIES TO WORKMEN.] Minutes of evidence taken before the Departmental Committee on Compensation for Injuries to Workmen. London: 1905. pp.404. (B.P.P. 1905, LXXV). LSE.

1,769. [DEPARTMENTAL COMMITTEE ON WORKMEN'S COMPENSATION.] Report of the Departmental Committee on Workmen's Compensation. Volume I. Report and appendices. London: 1904. pp.236. (B.P.P. 1904, LXXXVIII). LSE.

1,770. DODD, W.F. Administration of workmen's compensation. New York and London: 1936. pp.xviii + 845. CUL.

1,771. DODS, M. "A chapter of accidents: an essay on the history of disease in workmen's compensation". L.Q.R. 39. (1923). pp.60-88.

1,772. DOWNEY, E.H. Workmen's compensation. New York: 1924. pp.xxv + 223. LSE; U.

1,773. EDWARDS, A.G. The Workmen's Compensation Acts: an outline of certain anomalies which appear to exist in the position of workmen, when the provisions of the 1925 Act are compared with those of the 1906 Act. London: 1928. pp.12. LSE. (Pamphlet Collection).

1,774. EDWARDS, C. The Compensation Act, 1906. London: 1907. pp.vi + 126. LSE.

1,775. ELLIOTT, A. The Workmen's Compensation Acts: being an annotated study of the Workmen's Compensation Act, 1897, with an introduction by... Judge Parry. 2nd ed. London: 1901. pp.xxxii + 378. 3rd ed., revised. 1903. pp.xxxi + 444. 4th ed. entitled The Workmen's Compensation Act, 1906... 1907. pp.xxxi + 582. 5th ed. 1909. pp.xxix + 728. 6th ed. 1912. pp.xxxviii + 862. 7th ed. 1915. pp.xlviii + 804. 8th ed. by Montague Berryman, entitled Elliott on the Workmen's Compensation Acts. 1925. pp.xxxiv + 775. BL. 9th ed. 1926. pp.xxxviii + 792. Sq.

1,776. FABIAN SOCIETY. The Workmen's Compensation Act: what it means, and how to make use of it; with text of the Act. London: 1901. pp.19. (Fabian Tracts No.82). LSE.

1,777. [FARRER COMMITTEE.] Report of the committee appointed to consider whether the Post Office should provide facilities for workmen's compensation insurance. (Farrer report). London: 1907. pp.11. (Cd. 3568). DHSS.

1,778. FINCH, H.J. Guide to Workmen's Compensation Act, 1925-1943. Cardiff: 1944. pp.63. DHSS.

1,779. FIRMINGER, F.L. The Workmen's Compensation Acts, 1906, and the County Court rules relating thereto: with notes. London: [1907]. pp.xxiv + 386. CUL. 2nd ed. [including the 1909 Act]. 1910. pp.xv + 575. Sq.

1,780. FLUX, A.W. "Compensation Acts in Europe". E.J. VIII. (1898). pp.559ff.

1,781. FLUX, A.W. Compensation for industrial accidents. Manchester: [1898]. pp.40. G.

1,782. FOOT, A. The practice of insurance against accidents and employers' liability. London: 1907. pp.206. CUL. 2nd ed. 1908. pp.215. CUL. 3rd ed. 1909. pp.215 + (25). CUL.

1,783. GAVAN-DUFFY, T. Liberalism plus capitalism: the right for the Compensation Act in committee; with complete division lists. London: I.L.P. [1907?]. pp.16. LSE.

1,784. GLEGG, A.T. Commentary on the Workmen's Compensation Act, 1897. Edinburgh: 1898. pp.vii + 152. BL. 2nd ed. 1899. pp.x + 172. CUL; DHSS.

1,785. GLEGG, A.T. "The Workmen's Compensation Act, 1897". S.L.T. 10. (1902-3). pp.22-4, 36-7.

1,786. GLEGG, A.T. & ROBERSON, M.A. Digest of cases decided under the Workmen's Compensation Acts 1897 and 1900... down to the end of August 1902. With the Acts annotated and indexed. Edinburgh: 1902. pp.xvi + 244. CUL; BL.

1,787. GOLDING, C.E. Workmen's Compensation Insurance. With a summary of the statutory law relating thereto. London: 1922. pp.104. LSE; (2nd ed.). 1929. pp.108. CUL.

1,788. GORDON, W.E. (ed.). Reports of cases under the Workmen's Compensation Acts... also cases on insurance law. London: 1912-1918. 7v. LSE.

1,789. GRANT, I.F. "Drunkenness in workmen's compensation". S.L.T. 2. (1914). pp.79-80.

1,790. GRANT, I.F. "Workmen's compensation: 'added peril'". Jur.Rev. XXX. (1918). p.162.

1,791. GREENWOOD, J.H. Amount of compensation and review of weekly payments under the Workmen's Compensation Act, 1906. London: 1909. pp.ix + 72. BL.

1,792. GRIFFITHS, H.E. Injury and incapacity, with special reference to industrial insurance. London: 1935. pp.viii + 270. CUL.

1,793. GRIFFITHS, H.E. "Workmen's compensation as it affects rehabilitation". Ind.Welfare. XXIV. (1942). pp.107-109.

1,794. HANES, D.G. The first British Workmen's Compensation Act, 1897. London: 1968. pp.ix + 124. (Yale College Series 8). DHSS; LSE; Sq.

1,795. HENDERSON, A. "Workmen's compensation". Nineteenth Century.
        120. (July-Dec. 1936). pp.728-35.

1,796. HILL, SIR J.G.   "Employers, employees and accidents".
        J.Comp.Leg. 11. (1910-11). pp.55-67.

1,797. HILL, W.E. The law and practice relating to Workmen's
        Compensation and Employers' Liability, being a practical guide
        to the Employers' Liability Act, 1880;   the Workmen's
        Compensation Act, 1897; the material sections of the Factory
        and Workshop Acts, 1878 to 1895; and Lord Campbell's Act.
        London: 1898. pp.xvi + 255 + 116 (Supp.). CUL.

1,798. HILL, W.E.   The Workmen's Compensation Act, 1906... with
        explanatory notes, list of employers and servants within the
        Act, and index. 2nd ed. London: 1907. pp.xi + 74. BL;
        CUL; DHSS.

1,799. HILL, W.E. The Law of Workman's Compensation and Employers'
        Liability... London: 1907. pp.xxiii + 483. CUL.

1,800. HIRSCHFIELD, J. "A few observations on workmen's compensation
        in Germany and here".   J.Comp.Leg.   13.   (1912-13).
        pp.119-122.

1,801. [HOME OFFICE.] Statistics of proceedings under the Workmen's
        Compensation Acts, 1897 and 1900, and the Employers' Liability
        Act, 1880. London: 1899- . (B.P.P.) LSE (incomplete).
        (And see other entries below).

1,802. HOME OFFICE.   Statistics of proceedings under the Workmen's
        Compensation Act, 1906 during the years 1915 to 1918. London:
        1919. pp.10. LSE.

1,803. HOME OFFICE. Memorandum on the Workmen's Compensation Acts,
        1906 and 1923. London: 1924. pp.20. LSE; DHSS.

1,804. HOME OFFICE. 1st, 2nd and 3rd Reports by the Departmental
        Committee appointed to inquire and report as to certain
        proposed extensions of the schedule of industrial diseases to
        which section 43 of the Workmen's Compensation Act, 1925
        applies. (Rolleston Report). London: 1923, 1933 and 1936.
        unpag. DHSS.

1,805. HOME OFFICE. First report of the Departmental Committee on
        compensation for silicosis dealing with the Refractories
        Industries (Silicosis) Scheme, 1919. (Locker-Lampson Report).
        London: 1924. pp.91. DHSS.

1,806. HOME OFFICE. Memorandum on the Workmen's Compensation Act,
        1925. London: 1929. pp.22. LSE; DHSS.

1,807. HOME OFFICE. Memorandum on the Workmen's Compensation Acts,
        1925-1931. London: 1932. pp.23. LSE; DHSS.

1,808. HOME OFFICE.   Workmen's compensation: Statistics of
        compensation and proceedings under the Workmen's Compensation
        Acts and the Employers' Liability Act 1880 in Great Britain
        for the year 1934. London: 1936. unpag. (Cmd. 5077).
        DHSS.

1,809.   HOME OFFICE.   Workmen's compensation: Statistics of compensation and proceedings under the Workmen's Compensation Acts and the Employers' Liability Act 1880 in Great Britain for the year 1936.   London: 1936.   unpag.   (Cmd. 5722). DHSS.

1,810.   HOME OFFICE.   Workmen's compensation: Statistics of compensation and proceedings under the Workmen's Compensation Acts and the Employers' Liability Act 1880 in Great Britain for the year 1935.   London: 1937.   unpag.   (Cmd. 5557). DHSS.

1,811.   HOME OFFICE.   Memorandum on the Workmen's Compensation Acts, 1925-1938.   London 1938.   pp.23.   LSE; DHSS.

1,812.   HOME OFFICE.   [Report of]   the Departmental Committee on compensation for card room workers.   London: 1939.   pp.32. LSE.

1,813.   HOME OFFICE.   Workmen's compensation: Statistics of compensation and proceedings under the Workmen's Compensation Acts and the Employers' Liability Act 1880 in Great Britain for the year 1937.   London: 1939.   unpag.   (Cmd. 5955). DHSS.

1,814.   HOME OFFICE.   Workmen's compensation: Statistics of compensation and proceedings under the Workmen's Compensation Acts and the Employers' Liability Act 1880 in Great Britain for the year 1938.   London: 1940.   unpag.   (Cmd. 6203). DHSS.

1,815.   HOME OFFICE.   Memorandum on the Workmen's Compensation Acts, 1925-1943.   London: 1944.   pp.18.   LSE; DHSS.

1,816.   HOWELL, G.   National industrial insurance and employers' liability.   London: 1880.   pp.32.   LSE.

1,817.   HOWELL, G.   Employers' Liability Act (1880)..., with introduction and notes.   London: [1881?].   pp.16.   LSE.

1,818.   INGLIS, J.   On the Workmen's Compensation Act of 1897.   Paper read before the Civic Society of Glasgow.   n.p.:   1897. pp.16.   TCD.

1,819.   INTERNATIONAL LABOUR CONFERENCE.   Report on equality of treatment for national and foreign workers as regarding workmen's compensation for accidents.   [With supplement report and final vote].   Geneva: 1924-25.   3 vols.   LSE; P.

1,820.   INTERNATIONAL LABOUR CONFERENCE.   Workmen's compensation for occupational diseases: partial revision of the Convention. Geneva: 1933.   pp.xi + 328.   LSE.

1,821.   INTERNATIONAL LABOUR CONFERENCE.   Workmen's compensation for occupational diseases: supplementary report.   Geneva: 1934. pp.22.   LSE (Pamphlet Coll.).

1,822.   INTERNATIONAL LABOUR CONFERENCE.   Report on equality of treatment for national and foreign workers as regarding workmen's compensation for accidents (with supplement report and final vote). Geneva: 1924-25. 3 vols. LSE.

1,823. INTERNATIONAL LABOUR OFFICE. Report on workmen's compensation. Geneva: 1915, p.199. LSE.

1,824. JACKSON, T.C. The law of master and servant (including apprenticeship) and the Employers and Workmen Act, 1875, the Employers Liability Act 1880, and the Workmen's Compensation Act 1906. London: 1907. pp.viii + 180. CUL; IALS.

1,825. JASTROW, H. "Workmen's insurance legislation in Germany". Fort.Rev. 61. (1897). pp.379-86.

1,826. JORDAN, H.H. Workmen's compensation and the physician. London: 1941. pp.xi + 180. LSE.

1,827. KELLY, R.J. The Workmen's Compensation Act (1906). The new law of master and servant. A popular handbook on the rights and liabilities of employment, with the final rules, forms... and a chapter on the relation of the Act to seamen by W.H. Boyd. 2nd ed. Dublin: 1908. pp.xv + 369. BL; Sq.

1,828. KNOCKER, D. Accidents in their medico-legal aspect; by leading medical and surgical authorities. London: 1901. pp.xxviii + 1254. BL.

1,829. KNOCKER, D. Workmen's compensation digest, containing reported decisions of present authorities... under the Workmn's Compensation Acts, 1897, 1900 and 1906. London: 1912. pp.xxviii + 455 + 38. 2nd ed. by S.H. Noakes. 1933. pp.lxxxvi + 479 + 30. 2nd cumulative supplement by R. Marven Everett. 1942. pp.vii + 18. Sq; LSE

1,830. KNOWLES, C.M. The law relating to compensation for injuries to workmen being an exposition of the Workmen's Compensation Act, 1906, and of the case law relevant thereto. London: 1907. pp.xxxv + 278. CUL. 2nd ed. 1907. pp.xliii +460. 3rd ed. 1912. pp.lxi + 590. BL; CUL. 4th ed. 1924. pp.lxxii + 502. BL; Sq; DHSS.

1,831. KNOWLES, C.M. "State control of industrial accident insurance". J.Comp.Leg. 2. (1920). pp.29-50.

1,832. LAWES, E.T.H. The law of compensation for industrial diseases being an annotation of section 8 of the Workmen's Compensation Act, 1906, with chapters upon the powers and duties of certifying surgeons and medical referees... and including a special treatise upon every disease to which the Act now applies, etc. London: 1909. pp.xii + 288 + 18. Sq.

1,833. LAWSON, J.J. Labour rights for workmen's compensation. London: 1939. pp.8. LSE.

1,834. LEVY, H. "Workmen's compensation reform". Ind.Welfare. XXVI. (1944). pp.171-173.

1,835. LONDONDERRY, THE MARCHIONESS OF. "The 'Conservative' Compensation (Workmen's) Bill of 1897". Nineteenth Century. 42. (July-Dec. 1897). pp.349-52.

1,836. LORD, J.W.   Employers' liability and workmen's compensation laws. n.p.: 1912. pp.22. LSE.

1,837. LYNN, H.   The Workmen's Compensation Act, 1906, with explanatory notes and decided cases. London: 1907. pp.xvi + 194. 2nd ed. 1907. pp.xvi + 210. BL; CUL. 3rd ed. 1909. pp.xx + 282. Sq.

1,838. MALLALIEU, W.C.   "Joseph Chamberlain and workmen's compensation". J.Econ.Hist. 10. (1950). pp.45-57.

1,839. MINING ASSOCIATION OF GREAT BRITAIN. Workmen (Compensation for Accidents) Bill: deputation to the Foreign Office. London: 1897. pp.40. LSE.

1,840. MINISTRY OF NATIONAL INSURANCE. Memorandum on the Workmen's Compensation Acts, 1925-1945. London: 1946. pp.19. DHSS; LSE.

1,841. MINISTRY OF NATIONAL INSURANCE.   Workmen's Compensation (Supplementation) Bill: explanatory memorandum by the Ministry of National Insurance.   London: 1951.   pp.4. (B.P.P. 1950-51, XXVII). LSE.

1,842. MINISTRY OF PENSIONS AND NATIONAL INSURANCE.   Workmen's Compensation and Benefit (Amendment) Act, 1965.   London: 1965. pp.9. DHSS.

1,843. MINTON-SENHOUSE, R.M.   The Employers' Liability Act, 1880... London: 1892. pp.xx + 115. CUL.

1,844. MINTON-SENHOUSE, R.M. & EMERY, G.F.   Accidents to workmen, etc. London: 1898. pp.lii + 378. LSE; CUL.

1,845. MINTON-SENHOUSE, R.M.   The case law of the Workmen's Compensaton Act, 1897, intended to supplement part III of accidents to workmen. London: 1899. pp.xii + 44. BM. 2nd ed. 1900. pp.xxvi + 100. CUL.

1,846. MINTON-SENHOUSE, R.M.   Accidents to workmen. London: 1902. pp.lxviii + 492. DHSS.

1,847. MINTON-SENHOUSE, R.M.   Workmen's compensation cases. London: 1902-8. 9 vols. LSE.

1,848. MINTON-SENHOUSE, R.M.   Digest of workmen's compensation cases: being a digest of the reports of cases known as 'workmen's compensation cases'.   London: 1903.   pp.xii + 57.   4 vols. Sq.

1,849. MINTON-SENHOUSE, R.M.   Workmen's Compensation Act, with explanatory notes. London: 1907. pp.xii + 61. LSE.

1,850. MINTON-SENHOUSE, R.M.   Workmen's compensation cases, continued as Butterworths' compensation cases.   London: 1909-1950. Vols. 10-41.   (With Scottish and Irish supplements to Vols. 24-40). Sq.

1,851. MOONEY, F.M.   Workmen's Compensation Acts, 1897 and 1900.

[Dublin?]: 1904. n.l. [Source: SM3].

1,852. MOZLEY-STARK, A. The duties of an arbitrator under Workmen's Compensation Act, 1897, with notes on the Act and rules... London: 1898. pp.viii + 136. CUL; DHSS.

1,853. NASH, R. The Accidents Compensation Act, 1897. Leicester: 1897. pp.13. LSE.

1,854. NASH, V. "The Employers' Liability Bill". Fort.Rev. 55. (1894). pp.244-54.

1,855. NEAL, J. "Workmen's compensation reform". L.Q.R. 37. (1921). pp.85-94.

1,856. NEWMAN, T.S. Handbook to the Workmen's Compensation Acts, 1906-1923. London: 1959. pp.50. DHSS.

1,857. NOAKES, S.H. Butterworth's digest of leading cases on workmen's compensation. London: 1933. pp.lxxxvi + 479. Sq.

1,858. O'SHEA, A.F. Workmen's compensation insurance. London: 1943. pp.vi + 174. CUL; DHSS.

1,859. OMEGA. "Workmen's compensation proceedings. The new fees". S.L.T. [1929]. pp.97-8.

1,860. ONTARIO. Report on workmen's compensation for injuries. Toronto: 1900. pp.47. LSE.

1,861. PACKER, L. History and operation of workmen's compensation in Great Britain. Washington: 1912. pp.71. LSE.

1,862. PARRY, E.A. "The Workmen's Compensation Act: what it was to be and what it is". Fort.Rev. 68. (1900). pp.67-73.

1,863. PARSONS, A. & BERTRAM, T.A. The Workmen's Compensation Acts, 1897 and 1900. pp.xviii + 156. 2nd ed. 1902. pp.xxvii + 215. 3rd ed. by A. Parsons and Raymund Allen, entitled The Workmen's Compensation Act 1906. 1907. pp.xxxiv + 366. 4th ed. 1910. pp.xliv + 471. BL; CUL. 5th ed. by A. Parsons. 1914. pp.xlvii + 449 + 29. Sq.

1,864. PHILLIPS, P.D. "Workers' compensation law and the future". A.L.J. 17. (1943). pp.110-114, 141-145.

1,865. PHILLIPS, P.D. "Recasting workers' compensation". A.L.J. 19. (1945-46). pp.62-66.

1,866. PRINGLE, A.S. "The new Workmen's Compensation Bill and jury trials". S.L.T. 14. (1906-7). pp.3-4.

1,867. ROBERT-JONES, M. Handbook to the Workmen's Compensation Act, 1897. Cardiff: 1897. pp.80. LSE.

1,868. ROBERTS, W.H. & WALLACE, G. The common law and statutory duty and liability of employers, etc. London: 1908. pp.lxxxiv + 1014 + 120. LSE.

1,869. ROBINSON, A. Employers' liability under the Workmen's

Compensation Act, 1897, and the Employers' Liability Act, 1880. London: 1898. pp.xii + 125. CUL. 2nd ed. by the author and J.D. Stuart Sim... with rules under the Workmen's Compensation Act, 1897... including precedents of schemes of compensation under the... Act, 1897. 1898. pp.xii + 248. Sq.

1,870. ROBSON, W.A. "Industrial relations and the state: a reform of workmen's compensation". Pol.Q. I. (1930). p.511.

1,871. ROBSON, W.A. "Industrial law". L.Q.R. 51. (1935). pp.195-210.

1,872. ROBSON, W.A. "Workmen's compensation. McLaughlin v. Caledonia Stevedoring Company Ltd. 54 T.L.R. 910". M.L.R. 2. (1938-9). pp.168-9.

1,873. ROYAL COMMISSION ON WORKMEN'S COMPENSATION. Minutes of evidence. London: 1939. pp.752. LSE.

1,874. ROYAL COMMISSION ON WORKMEN'S COMPENSATION. Report. London: 1945. pp.7. (Cmd. 6588). (B.P.P. 1944-45, VI). DHSS; LSE.

1,875. RUEGG, A.H. The Employers' Liability Act, 1880, etc. A tratise upon the Employers' Liability Act, 1880. London: 1882. pp.xii + 131. CUL. 2nd ed. 1892. pp.xii + 255. CUL. 3rd ed. 1898. pp.xx + 388. CUL; S. 4th ed., [entitled: The Employers' Liability Act, 1880 and the Workmen's Compensation Act, 1897]. 1899. pp.xii + 412 + 27. CUL. 5th ed. 1901. pp.xxxvi + 462 + 27. CUL. 6th ed. [entitled: The Employers' Liability Act, 1880, and the Workmen's Compensation Acts, 1897 and 1900]. 1903. pp.xxxii + 558 + 32. LSE; CUL.

1,876. RUEGG, A.H. & KNOCKER, D. Workmen's compensation cases. London: 1911-. LSE.

1,877. RUEGG, A.H. & STANES, H.P. The Workmen's Compensation Act, 1906, etc. London: 1922. pp.liv + 526 + 30. LSE; CUL.

1,878. SAMUELS, H. "Workmen's compensation as it concerns the works doctor". Ind.Welfare. XXIII. (1941). pp.152-153, 173-175.

1,879. SCANLAN, J.J. & EDIN, P. The mutilated hand and the Workmen's Compensation Act, 1906. London: 1913. pp.90. CUL; DHSS.

1,880. SECRETARY OF STATE FOR THE HOME DEPARTMENT. Statistics of compensation and of proceedings under the Workmen's Compensation Acts and the Employers' Liability Act 1880, during the years 1921 to 1930. London: 1923-32. 1 vol. DHSS.

1,881. SECRETARY OF STATE FOR THE HOME DEPARTMENT. The Byssinosis (Workmen's Compensation) Scheme, 1941 and the Byssinosis (Benefit) Scheme, 1941. London: 1941. pp.9. DHSS.

1,882. SELECT COMMITTEE ON EMPLOYERS' LIABILITY FOR INJURIES TO THEIR SERVANTS. Report. London: 1876. pp.101. (B.P.P. 1876, IX). LSE.

1,883. SELECT COMMITTEE ON EMPLOYERS' LIABILITY FOR INJURIES TO THEIR
SERVANTS. Report. London: 1877. pp.xx + 162. (B.P.P.
1877, X). LSE.

1,884. SELECT COMMITTEE ON THE EMPLOYERS' LIABILITY ACT... Report
from the Select Committee on the Employers' Liability Act
(1880) Amendment Bill, etc. London: 1886. pp.xviii + 648.
(B.P.P. 1886, VIII). LSE.

1,885. SEXTON, J. A criticism of the Workmen's Compensation Act,
1906... perilous judicial decisions: workmen's rights
endangered. Liverpool: 1906. pp.15. LSE.

1,886. SHAND, A.B. The law of employment: a system of insurance by
the mutual contributions of masters and workmen the best
provision for accidents, etc. Edinburgh: 1879. pp.44. LSE.

1,887. SHERMAN, P.T. Notes on malingering under workmen's
compensation laws. [[New York]: 1913. pp.16. LSE.

1,888. SNOWDEN, P. The new Workmen's Compensation Act made plain:
the workman's guide. London: 1907. pp.15. LSE.

1,889. SOPHIAN, T. "Some aspects of workmen's compensation law".
S.L.T. [1926]. pp.59-60, 74-6, 95-7, 108-9, 122-3.

1,890. SOPHIAN, T. "Right of employer to cease weekly payments under
section 12 of the Workmen's Compensation Act, 1925". S.L.T.
[1928]. pp.96-8.

1,891. SPAFFORD, C.H. The legal aspect of industrial diseases
(sections 43 and 44 of the Workmen's Compensation Act, 1925).
London: 1934. pp.xxxiv + 236 + [9]. Sq.

1,892. STONE, G. & GROVES, K.G. Stone's insurance cases, including
all English, Scotch, Irish, Canadian and Indian, and many
Australian and New Zealand decisions relating to all insurance
risks other than marine; together with all cases upon
workmen's compensation and employers' liability. London:
1914. pp.xxxii + 726. CUL; BL; Sq.

1,893. SYM, J.D. "Workmen's Compensation Act 1897". Jur.Rev. IX.
(1897). p.415.

1,894. TAYLOR, A. The Workmen's Compensation Act, 1897... with
introduction and notes. Glasgow and Edinburgh: 1898.
pp.xxiii + 105. CUL.

1,895. TAYLOR, B. "The casualties of industry". Fort.Rev. 92.
(1912). pp.1104-18).

1,896. TAYLOR, J.O. "A workmen's compensation point. What are
'children'?". S.L.T. [1927]. pp.57-9.

1,897. THOMAS, G.N.W. Leading cases in workmen's compensation.
London: 1913. pp.xvii + 122 + 21. Sq; CUL; DHSS.

1,898. THOMPSON, R.T. "The Workmen's Compensation Act, 1897".
Nineteenth Century. 43. (Jan.-June 1898). pp.899-914.

1,899.   THOMPSON, R.T.   The Workmen's Compensation Act, 1897: a plea
         for revision. London: 1901. pp.v + 96. LSE.

1,900.   THOMPSON, W.H. "The Workmen's Compensation Bill". L.R. XII.
         (1923). pp.85ff.

1,901.   THOMPSON, W.H. "The Workmen's Compensation Bill". M.C.L.R.D.
         12. (1923). pp.85-6.

1,902.   THOMPSON, W.H. Workmen's compensation, 1924: an outline of
         the Acts. London: 1924. pp.96. BL. 2nd ed. 1924.
         pp.110. LSE; BL.

1,903.   THOMPSON, W.H. Workmen's compensation: the new Act
         explained. London: [1940]. pp.48. LSE; BL.

1,904.   THOMPSON, W.H. Workmen's compensation up-to-date... London:
         1944. pp.72. [LRD]; BL; LSE.

1,905.   TILLYARD, F.   "Fifty years of workmen's compensation".
         Ind.L.R. 2. (1947-48). pp.250-260.

1,906.   TRADES UNION CONGRESS.   GENERAL COUNCIL AND LABOUR PARTY,
         NATIONAL   EXECUTIVE   COMMITTEE.   Workmen's   compensation.
         London: [1927]. pp.11. LSE.

1,907.   TRADES UNION CONGRESS. The revised new Bill for workmen's
         compensation, etc. London: n.d. pp.32. LSE.

1,908.   TRADES UNION COUNCIL. GENERAL COUNCIL & OTHERS.   Joint
         committee on workmen's compensation.   The new bill for
         workmen's compensation...;   with foreword and explanatory
         memorandum. London: 1928. pp.32. LSE.

1,909.   TRADES UNION CONGRESS. GENERAL COUNCIL. The trade unions and
         workmen's compensation: the case for reform. London: 1939.
         pp.6. LSE.

1,910.   TRADES UNION CONGRESS. John Smith has an accident: a case
         for workmen's compensation. London: [1933]. pp.8. LSE.

1,911.   TURNER, E.R. A treatise on the Employer's Liability Act,
         1880,... to which is added a chapter on Lord Campbell's
         Act,... London: 1882. pp.xvi + 182. CUL.

1,912.   TURNER-SAMUELS, M. & GEDDES, D. The Workmen's Compensation
         Act, 1925 and the workmen's compensation rules, 1926. London:
         1927. pp.iii + 282. DHSS.

1,913.   UMPHERSTON, F.A. A commentary on the Workmen's Compensation
         Act, 1906... With comparative tables of the Workmen's
         Compensation Acts, 1897, 1900 and 1906, and acts of sederunt
         arranged by J. Hossell Henderson. Edinburgh: 1907. pp.xxi +
         369. BL.

1,914.   UMPHERSTON, F.A.   Workmen's Compensation Act, 1925 and
         relative act of sederunt. With comparative tables and notes.
         Edinburgh and Glasgow: [1926]. pp.97. Sq.

1,915.   UNITED KINGDOM. Workmen's Compensation Act, 1897, with full

extracts from the statutes therein referred to. London:
[1897]. pp.iv + 26 + 14. LSE.

1,916. UNITED KINGDOM. Second report of the Departmental Committee
on Compensation for Industrial Diseases. London: 1908.
(B.P.P. XXXV). 2 vols. LSE.

1,917. UNITED KINGDOM. Convention between the United Kingdom and
France in regard to workmen's compensation for accidents.
London: 1910. (B.P.P., CXII). pp.385-390. LSE.

1,918. UNITED KINGDOM. Report of the departmental committee
appointed to inquire and report whether the following diseases
can properly be added to those enumerated in the third
schedule of the Workmen's Compensation Act, 1906, namely:
cowpox; Dupuytran's contract.; clonic spasm of the
eyelids... writers' cramp. London. 1913. (B.P.P. XVII).
2v. LSE.

1,919. UNITED KINGDOM. Workmen's compensation rules and orders.
London: 1914. pp.iv + 202. LSE.

1,920. UNITED KINGDOM. Report of the Industrial Commissioner etc.
London: 1925 to date. LSE.

1,921. UNITED KINGDOM. Convention between the United Kingdom and
Denmark respecting compensation to workmen for accidents
arising out of their employment. London: 1927. (B.P.P.
XXVI). pp.7. LSE.

1,922. UNITED KINGDOM. Workmen's Compensation Acts, 1925 to 1930:
the silicosis and asbestosis (medical arrangements) scheme,
1931: refractories industries: worker's register. London:
1931. pp.24. LSE.

1,923. UNITED KINGDOM. Memorandum on the Workmen's Compensation
Acts, 1925-1931. London: 1932. pp.23. LSE.

1,924. UNITED KINGDOM. Report (and second report) by the
departmental committee appointed to inquire and report as to
certain proposed extensions of the schedule of industrial
diseases to which section 43 of the Workmen's Compensation
Act, 1925, applies. London: 1932-3. 2 vols. LSE.

1,925. UNITED KINGDOM. Report by the departmental committee on
certain questions arising under the Workmen's Compensation
Acts. London: 1937. pp.iv + 115. (B.P.P. 1937-38, XV).
LSE.

1,926. UNITED KINGDOM. Workmen's compensation: interim (and second
interim) report of the departmental committee on Alternative
Remedies (Contributory Negligence). London:
[1944-45. 2 vols. (B.P.P. 1944-45, VI). LSE.

1,927. UNITED KINGDOM. Report of the Royal Commission on Workmen's
Compensation. London: 1945. pp.7. (Cmd. 6588). (B.P.P.
1944-45, VI). DHSS; LSE.

1,928. UNITED STATES. BUREAU OF LABOR STATISTICS; DEPARTMENT OF
LABOR. Workmen's insurance and compensation series: laws of

United States and other countries including Great Britain, 1914-1918. Washington: 1914-18. 3 vols. DHSS.

1,929. UNITED STATES. UNEMPLOYMENT COMPENSATION BUREAU. UNEMPLOYMENT COMPENSATION INTERPRETATION SERVICE. Benefit decisions of the British umpire: a codification and text of selected decisions. Washington: 1938. pp.ix + 867. (Benefit Series. General Supplements, No.1). LSE.

1,930. VALENTINE, G.D. "Workmen's compensation: accidents to minor workmen". Jur.Rev. XXIV. (1912). p.1.

1,931. WAMSLEY, A.W. The Workmen's Compensation Act. Manchester: 1900. pp.129. S.

1,932. WEIR, J. Workmen's compensation: digest of cases decided in England, Scotland and Ireland. London: 1902. pp.vii + 120. MT.

1,933. WELSON, J.B. & BRYANT, F.W. Workmen's compensation insurance: its principles and practice. London: 1923. pp.176. 2nd ed. 1930. pp.iii + 212. BL; LSE.

1,934. WILLES, R.A. The judicial development of the Workmen's Compensation Act. Birmingham: 1910. pp.41. LSE.

1,935. WILLIS, W.A. The Workmen's Compensation Act, 1906, with notes etc. London: 1920. pp.lxxvi + 636 + 61. LSE.

1,936. WILLIS, W.A. The Workmen's Compensation Acts, 1906 to 1924, with notes etc. London: 1925. pp.xcviii + 656 + 69. LSE.

1,937. WILLIS, W.A. The Workmen's Compensation Act, 1925, with notes, rules, orders, and regulations. London: 1926. pp.c + 725. LSE.

1,938. WILLOUGHBY, W.F. Workingmen's insurance. London: 1898. pp.xii + 386. S.

1,939. WILSON, SIR A. & LEVY, H. Industrial assurance. London: 1937. pp.519. DHSS.

1,940. WILSON, SIR A.T. & LEVY, H. Workmen's compensation. Vol.1. Social and political development. London: 1939. pp.xxi + 328. DHSS; LSE; CUL.

1,941. WILSON, SIR A.T. & LEVY, H. Workmen's compensation. Vol.2. The need for reform. London: 1941. pp.xii + 383. DHSS; LSE; CUL.

1,942. WILSON, SIR A. "Workmen's compensation". Pol.Q. X. (1939). p.232.

1,943. WILSON, M. "Contracting-out of the Workmen's Compensation Act". E.J. 11. (1901). pp.23-30.

1,944. WILSON, R. A manual of the Workmen's Compensation Act, 1897. Glasgow: 1897, 1898, 1899. pp.85. DHSS.

1,945. WOLFF, H.W. "Working men's insurance". E.J. V. (1895).

pp.612ff.

1,946. WORKMEN'S COMPENSATION SUPPLEMENTATION BOARD. Workmen's
        compensation supplementation scheme 1951. London: 1951.
        pp.7. (Leaflet W.S.1). LSE.

Workmen's Compensation, Scotland

1,947. ANON. "Workmen's compensation. Sheriff's power to deal with
        questions of status". S.L.T. [1935]. pp.106-7.

1,948. ANON.   "Workmen's compensation: quarterly review of
        decisions". S.L.T. [1938]. pp.13-6, 121-4, 161-4. [1939].
        pp.2-5, 105-9, 177-80.   [1940].   pp.3-5, 37-40, 81-4, 97-8,
        117-19.   [1941].   pp.11-13, 81-3, 145-8. [1942]. pp.35-7,
        59-61. [1943]. pp.25-6, 29-30. [1944]. pp.2-4, 19, 46-7.
        [1945]. pp.28-9. [1946]. pp.1-2, 45-6. [1947]. pp.10-12,
        65-8. [1948]. pp.1, 10-11, 123-6.

1,949. CONNOLLY, T.J.D. "Workmen's Compensation Bill". S.L.T.
        [1925]. pp.89-90.

1,950. CONNOLLY, T.J.D.   "Workmen's compensation legislation".
        S.L.T.   [1926]. pp.115-17.

1,951. CONNOLLY, T.J.D.   "Non-attachability of workmen's
        compensation". S.L.T. [1927]. pp.165-8.

1,952. CONNOLLY, T.J.D. "Court fees in workmen's compensation cases.
        Workmen litigants put in favoured position". S.L.T.
        [1928]. pp.49-50.

1,953. CONNOLLY, T.J.D. "Misrepresentation as to industrial disease.
        Notes on some workmen's compensation decisions". S.L.T.
        [1929]. pp.146-7.

1,954. CONNOLLY, T.J.D.   "Workmen's compensation: new act of
        sederunt". S.L.T. [1933]. pp.91-2.

1,955. CONNOLLY, T.J.D.   "Workmen's compensation. Questions which
        may be determined by compensation".   S.L.T.   [1934] .
        pp.141-3.

1,956. CONNOLLY, T.J.D. Workmen's compensation. Contravention of
        statutory prohibitions". S.L.T. [1934]. pp.210-11.

1,957. CONNOLLY, T.J.D. "Workmen's compensation. Two House of Lords
        decisions". S.L.T. [1934]. pp.121-3.

1,958. CONNOLLY, T.J.D. "The last employer. 'Pay first - then seek
        relief'". S.L.T. [1934]. pp.133-4.

1,959. CONNOLLY, T.J.D. "Workmen's compensation. The position of
        the adopted child". S.L.T. [1935]. pp.145-6.

1,960. CONNOLLY, T.J.D. "Workmen's Compensation Act, 1925. Some
        recent decisions". S.L.T. [1935]. pp.201-3, 226-9.

1,961. CONNOLLY, T.J.D.   "Workmen's compensation: Richards v.

Goskar". S.L.T. [1936]. pp.237-8.

1,962. CONNOLLY, T.J.D. "Workmen's Compensation Act, 1925. Some recent decisions". S.L.T. [1936]. pp.197-202.

1,963. CONNOLLY, T.J.D. "Workmen's Compensation Acts. Some recent decisions". S.L.T. [1937]. pp.197-203.

1,964. SPENS, W.C. & YOUNGER, R.T. Employers and employed:... exposition of the law of reparation for physical injury. Glasgow: 1887. pp.xxiv + 612. G.

1,965. T.S. "Workmen's compensation". S.L.T. (1923). pp.97-8.

Workmen's Compensation, Ireland

1,966. ANON. "Official action on the decisions of the International Labour Conference. Irish Free State. Formal ratification of the convention concerning workmen's compensation for occupational diseases (1925)". I.L.O.Bull. (3rd ser.). XIII. (1928). pp.48-49.

1,967. ANON. "An enquiry into workmen's compensation reform in the Irish Free State". I.Lab.R. XVI. (1927). pp.93ff.

1,968. ANON. "Workmen's compensation - the complaints and the remedy". I.L.T.S.J. 100. (1966). pp.15-17.

1,969. BLAKE, B.ST.J. The working of the Social Welfare (Occupational Injuries) Act 1966. Dublin: 1969. pp.29. (Society of Young Solicitors, Lecture 42). Sq.

1,970. CAMPBELL, T.J. Workmen's compensation: a popular synopsis of the acts and cases... 1st ed. n.l. 2nd ed. Dublin: 1901. pp.viii + 128. BL. 3rd ed. London: 1902. pp.viii + 150. 4th ed. 1906(?). n.l. 5th ed. Dublin: 1908. QUB.

1,971. COMMISSION ON WORKMEN'S COMPENSATION. (CHAIRMAN: JUSTICE SHANNON). Report. Dublin: 1962. pp.358. CUL.

1,972. HANNA, H. The Workmen's Compensation Act, 1897, as applied to Ireland, with full explanation, notes, forms... Dublin: 1897. pp.viii + 166. 2nd ed. By H.Hanna and T.D. Kingan, entitled The law of workmen's compensation, with the Irish rules and forms. 1907. pp.xix + 393. QUB.

1,973. IRELAND. DEPARTMENT OF FINANCE. Report of the comptroller and auditor general [of his examination of] the accounts of the Occupational Injuries Fund for the year ended 31 March 1972. Dublin: 1974. pp.5. (Prl. 3865). DHSS.

1,974. IRISH FREE STATE. Report (with appendices) of the Departmental Commission on Workmen's Compensation. Dublin: 1925. pp.84. LSE.

1,975. IRISH FREE STATE Statistics of workmen's compensation. Dublin: 1928- LSE.

1,976. IRISH FREE STATE Report of the Special Commission on the

Workmen's Compensation (Increase of Compensation) Bill, 1929. Dublin: 1929. pp.vii. LSE.

1,977. IRISH FREE STATE Second report of the Departmental Committee on Workmen's Compensation. Dublin: [1930]. pp.15. LSE.

1,978. J.S. "Workmen's compensation. The progress of the Act in Ireland". N.I.J. 2. (1901-2). pp.9-10, 22.3

1,979. KAIM-CAUDLE, P.R. Compensation for occupational injuries. Dublin: Institute of Public Administration. 1966. unpag. Administration. Vol.14. No.1. DHSS.

1,980. NORTHERN IRELAND. Workmen's Compensation Act (N.I.), 1927: summary with regard to the giving of notices of accidents. Belfast: 1932. p.1. LSE.

1,981. O'MAHONEY, U. "Workmen's compensation in Ireland and the House of Lords. Does an appeal lie?". N.I.J. 2 (1901-2). p.141.

1,982. PORTER, S.C. The law relating to employers' liability and workmen's compensation with the Irish rules and forms. Dublin: 1908. pp.xiv + 275. QUB.

1,983. REPUBLIC OF IRELAND. Social Welfare (Occupational Injuries) Act 1966: disablement benefit for accidents at work. Dublin: Department of Social Welfare. 1967. pp.12. DHSS.

1,984. REPUBLIC OF IRELAND. Social Welfare (Occupational Injuries) Act 1966: injury benefit for accidents at work. Dublin: Department of Social Welfare. 1967. pp.8. DHSS.

1,985. SHILLMAN, B. Law relating to employer's liability and workmen's compensation in Ireland... Dublin: 1934. n.1. 2nd ed. 1943. pp.xxxvi + 502. Sq; BL.

1,986. SHILLMAN, B.(ed.). Irish workmen's compensation cases, vol.1, 1934-8. Dublin: 1939-. [Private publication]. Sq.

(b) Old Age Pensions

See also Part II, Section 9 (Old age)

1,987. [ANON] Pensions for all at sixty, and an eight hours day; by the chairman of a Yorkshire school board. London: 1892. pp.ix + 45. LSE.

1,988. ANON. Elveden voluntary scheme for sick pay and old age pensions to the working classes. Suffolk: 1896. pp.11. DHSS (RCAP COLL).

1,989. ANON. "Old age pension schemes". Lab.G. VI. (1898). p.195.

1,990. ANON. "Report from the select committee on aged deserving poor". Lab.G. VII. (1899). pp.227-228.

1,991. ANON. "Old age pensions". Lab.G. XV. (1907). p.229.

1,992. ANON. Law of old age pensions. London: [1908?]. pp.16. LSE.

1,993. ANON. "Old age pensioners and aged pauperism". Lab.G. XXI. (1913). pp.369.

1,994. ANON. "The new British Pensions Act". I.Lab.R. XIII. (1926). pp.361, 506.

1,995. ANON. Operation of laws providing benefits in case of injury, sickness, old age, and death in Great Britain". Int.Lab.Rev. XXIX. (1934). ppp.108ff.

1,996. ANON. "Social services II: pensions". L.R. XXV. (1936). pp.127ff.

1,997. BAILEY, F. Pensions at 60. London: 1924. pp.16. LSE.

1,998. BAILWARD, W.A. A reply to Mr. Charles Booth's latest proposal concerning old-age pensions and the aged poor. London: [1899] . pp.8. LSE.

1,999. BARLOW, C.A.M. & GOMME, G.L. The Old Age Pensions Act, 1908. London: 1908. pp.180. CUL.

2,000. BARTLEY, M. & SEAGER-HUNT, F. Old Age Provident Pensions Bill. (House of Commons Bill 87). London: 1897. pp.4. DHSS (RCAP COLL). 2nd ed. (H.C. Bill 25). 1989. pp.4. DHSS (RCAP COLL).

2,001. BAYLEE, J.T. "Voluntary versus state pensions". Westm.Rev. 151. (1899). pp.620-3.

2,002. BEMAN, L.T. (ed.). Selected articles on old age pensions. New York: 1927. pp.lxxii + 359. LSE.

2,003. BESANT, L.C. National old age pension scheme. Unpub.: 1894. pp.29. DHSS (RCAP COLL).

2,004. BIRDSALL, E.J. Old age pensions: ways and means: a new proposal. [Scarborough]: 1908. pp.7. LSE.

2,005. BIRKMYRE, W. Old age pensions. 3rd ed. Glasgow: [1890?]. pp.44. TCD.

2,006. BOARD OF CUSTOMS AND EXCISE. Old age pensions. Instructions to pension officers. London: 1929. pp.iv + 140. DHSS.

2,007. BOARD OF CUSTOMS AND EXCISE. Instructions relating to old age pensions. London: 1937. pp.214. DHSS.

2,008. BOGGIS-ROLFE, D.H. A handbook to the Old Age Pensions Act, 1908. London: 1908. pp.130 + xv. CUL.

2,009. BOOTH, C. Enumeration and classification of paupers, and state pensions for the aged. London: 1890. pp.44. n.1.

2,010. BOOTH, C. Pauperism: a picture; and, The endowment of old age: an argument. London: 1892. pp.xiii + 355. LSE.

2,011. BOOTH, C. The aged poor in England and Wales: conditions. London: 1894. pp.vii + 527. LSE.

2,012. BOOTH, C. Reply to old age pensions and the aged poor: a proposal. London: 1899. pp.7. LSE.

2,013. BOOTH, C. Old age pensions and the aged poor. London: 1899. pp.xi + 75. LSE; U.

2,014. BOOTH, C. "Poor law statistics as used in connection with the old age pension question". E.J. IX. (1899). pp.212ff.

2,015. BOWACK, W.M. Poverty and old age in relation to the state. A practical solution to the problem. Edinburgh: 1896. pp.56. DHSS (RCAP COLL). 1895. pp.32. LSE.

2,016. BRITISH CONSTITUTION ASSOCIATION. Summary of the case against old age pensions. London: [1907]. pp.15. (Leaflets No.14). LSE.

2,017. BURDETT, H.C. A practical scheme for old age pensions. Unpub.: 1896. pp.16. DHSS (RCAP COLL).

2,018. BURDETT, H. "The friendly societies and old age pensions". To-morrow. 3. (1897). pp.68-82.

2,019. CASSON, W.A. Old Age Pensions Act, 1908... annotated and explained, etc. London: 1908. pp.xxviii + 171. LSE.

2,020. CHAMBERLAIN, N. Widows, orphans and old age pensions. London: 1925. pp.4. DHSS.

2,021. CHANCE, SIR W. Old age pensions and the poor law. London: 1908. pp.14. LSE; P.

2,022. CHESTER FRIENDLY SOCIETIES. Old age pension scheme. Chester: unpub. 1896. unpag. DHSS (RCAP COLL).

2,023. CHIEF REGISTRAR OF FRIENDLY SOCIETIES. Old age pensions (non-contributory scheme). (Correspondence). London: 1908. pp.23. (House of Commons Paper No.177). DHSS.

2,024. COMMITTEE ON OLD AGE PENSIONS. Old-age pensions: objections to a Bill... to provide for the granting by county councils of pensions in old age, etc. London: [1899]. pp.5 LSE.

2,025. COMMITTEE ON OLD AGE PENSIONS. Old-age pensions and poor relief. London: [1899]. pp.6. (Papers No.8). LSE.

2,026. COMMITTEE ON OLD-AGE PENSIONS. Old age pensions: a collection of short papers. London: 1903. pp.247. LSE; DHSS.

2,027. COSBY, D.S.A. "The old age pensions bill". Westm.Rev. 170. (1908). pp.333-7.

2,028. DAVISON, R.C. & OTHERS. Proposals for the extension of old age pensions and national health insurance. London: 1938. pp.19. DHSS.

2,029. DEPARTMENTAL COMMITTEE ON THE AGED DESERVING POOR. Financial aspects of proposals made by the Select Committee of 1899: report. London: 1900. pp.1 + 93. (Cd.67). LSE.

2,030. DRAGE, G. The problem of the aged poor. London: 1895. pp.xvii + 375. LSE; S; CUL.

2,031. ELLIS, C.C. The Old Age Pension Acts... 1908 and 1911, and regulations made thereunder, with notes and index. Edinburgh: 1911. CUL.

2,032. EVANS, D.O. Old Age Pensions Act 1908, with notes together with regulations and official circulars issued by the local government boards. London: 1908. pp.x + 224. CUL; DHSS; LSE.

2,033. FABIAN SOCIETY. Old age pensions at work. London: 1899. pp.4. (Fabian Tracts, No.89). LSE; CUL.

2,034. GILBERT, B.B. "The decay of nineteenth century provident institutions and the coming of old age pensions in Great Britain". Ec.H.R. (2nd ser.). 17. (1964-65). pp.551-563.

2,035. HOARE, H.J. Old age pensions. London: 1915. pp.xi + 196. DHSS; CUL.

2,036. HOLLAND, B. "Old age pensions". E.J. VIII. (1898). pp.333ff.

2,037. HOLLAND, L. Suggestions for a scheme of old age pensions. Unpub: [1897]. pp.33. DHSS.

2,038. LABOUR PARTY. Special conferences on unemployment and old age pensions. London: [1907?]. pp.7. LSE.

2,039. LEACH, R.A. The Old Age Pensions Act, 1908, etc. London: 1908. pp.viii + 84. S.

2,040. LEACH, R.W. Widows', Orphans' and Old Age Contributory Pensions Act, 1925 with regulations thereunder and Old Age Pension Acts, 1908-24, and relevant provisions of the National Health Insurance Act, 1924. London: 1925. pp.198. DHSS.

2,041. LOCAL GOVERNMENT BOARD. Tables which have been prepared in connection with the question of old age pensions with a preliminary memorandum. London: 1907. pp.54. (Cd. 3618). DHSS.

2,042. LOCH, C.S. Old age pensions and pauperism. London: 1892. pp.59. LSE.

2,043. MacDONALD, J.M. Old age pensions. A practical scheme. London: 1895. pp.7. DHSS. (RCAP COLL).

2,044. MacDONALD, T.P. & DAVIE, G. Handbook of widows, orphans and old age contributory pensions. London: 1930. pp.104. BL; DHSS.

2,045. MACKAY, C.S. & WILSON, A. Old age pensions. London: 1941. pp.138. DHSS.

2,046. METCALFE, J.   The case for universal old age pensions.
        London: 1899. p.viii + 220. LSE; U.

2,047. MILLAR, F. & ROGERS, F.   [MURRAY, H. (ed.)].   Old age
        pensions. London: 1903. pp.226. DHSS.

2,048. MINISTRY OF HEALTH. Husband or parent dying on or after 4th
        January, 1926. (Widows', Orphans' and Old Age Contributory
        Pensions Act, 1925). Instructions to inspectors. (O.S. 42C
        revised). London: 1926. pp.32. DHSS.

2,049. MINISTRY OF HEALTH. Widows' and orphans' pensions. (Widows',
        Orphans' and Old Age Contributory Pensions Act, 1925).
        Instructions to inspectors. (O.S. 42C (1927)). London:
        1927. pp.75. DHSS.

2,050. MINISTRY OF HEALTH.   Widows', Orphans' and Old Age
        Contributory Pensions Act, 1929. Instructions to inspectors.
        O.S.42D. (1929). London: 1929. pp.34. DHSS.

2,051. MINISTRY OF HEALTH.   Widows', Orphans' and Old Age
        Contributory Pensions Act, 1929. Instructions to Inspectors.
        O.S. 42E (1929). London: 1930. pp.12. DHSS.

2,052. MINISTRY OF HEALTH.   Widows', Orphans' and Old Age
        Contributory Pensions Acts. Instructions to inspectors. O.S.
        42C. London: 1934. pp.134. DHSS.

2,053. MINISTRY OF HEALTH.   Contributory Pensions (Voluntary
        Contributors) Act, 1937. The new pensions scheme. London:
        1937. pp.7. DHSS.

2,054. MINISTRY OF HEALTH. The new pensions scheme. London:
        [1937]. pp.8. LSE.

2,055. MINISTER OF PENSIONS. Memorandum by the Minister of Pensions
        on certain points arising in connection with the
        administration of pensions. London: 1933. pp.6. (Cmd.
        1748). DHSS.

2,056. MINISTRY OF PENSIONS. Report of the departmental committee of
        inquiry into the machinery of administration of the Ministry
        of Pensions (Tryon Report). London: 1921. pp.156 + iv.
        DHSS.

2,057. MORRISON, J. Notes of a scheme for the payment of old age
        pensions. Unpub.: [1897]. pp.8. DHSS (RCAP COLL).

2,058. NATIONAL CONFERENCE ON OLD AGE PENSIONS. Review of ten years'
        progress, 1916 to 1926, etc. Newcastle-upon-Tyne:
        [1927]. pp.28. LSE.

2,059. NATIONAL OLD AGE PENSIONERS' ASSOCIATION. The origin and
        development of the NOAPA. London: 1940. pp.24. DHSS.

2,060. NATIONAL OLD AGE PENSIONS LEAGUE. Report of inauguration,
        October 24th, 1894. Birmingham: [1894]. pp.39. LSE.

2,061. NATIONAL UNION OF CONSERVATIVE AND UNIONIST ASSOCIATIONS.

Leaflets (1895) No.294; (1906) No.436; (1909) Nos. 789, 807, 864, 915. Old age pensions. London: 1895-1909. 7 parts. LSE.

2,062. NEWMAN, T.S. & LEE, A.G. Guide to widows', orphans' and old age pensions. London: 1928. pp.46. DHSS. Rev. ed. 1929. pp.64. DHSS. Rev. ed. 1936. pp.64. DHSS.

2,063. OLD AGE PENSIONS COMMITTEE. Minutes of evidence. London: 1897. pp.147. DHSS (RCAP COLL).

2,064. OLD AGE PENSIONS COMMITTEE. Memorandum and summary of schemes submitted to Royal Commission on the Aged Poor, and of other proposals. List of books and papers and index of principal press notices. Unpub.: [1897]. pp.43 + 10 + 14. DHSS (RCAP COLL).

2,065. OLD AGE PENSIONS COMMITTEE. Questions to friendly societies and replies sent in by them. Unpub.: [1897]. pp.18. DHSS (RCAP COLL).

2,066. OLD AGE PENSIONS COMMITTEE. Report of the committee on old age pensions. (Chairman: Lord Rothschild). London: 1898. pp.210. (C.8911). DHSS (RCAP COLL).

2,067. OLD AGE PENSIONS COMMITTEE. Old age pensions. London: 1903. pp.247. DHSS.

2,068. ORGANISED LABOUR FOR PROMOTING OLD AGE PENSIONS FOR ALL. Annual Report. London: [1900] - ser. n.l.

2,069. PAULIN, D. Old age pensions and pauperism. A present-day problem. Edinburgh: 1896. pp.32. DHSS (RCAP COLL).

2,070. PHELPS, L.R. "Old age pensions". Econ.Rev. 3. (1893). pp.475-85.

2,071. PILLING, W. Old age pensions: scheme for the establishment of a government superannuation fund. London: 1898. pp.viii + 50. LSE; P.

2,072. PILTER, J. Contributory scheme for old age pensions. Beccles: [1911]. pp.12. LSE.

2,073. PILTER, J. A scheme for old age pensions, age 55-65. Paris: n.d. 4 vols. LSE.

2,074. POST OFFICE SAVINGS BANK. Old age pensions. Unpub. 1896. unpag. DHSS. [RCAP Coll].

2,075. PRESIDENT OF THE LOCAL GOVERNMENT BOARD. Report of the Departmental Committee on the financial aspects of the proposals made by the Select Committee of the House of Commons of 1899 about the aged deserving poor. London: 1900. pp. i + 93. (Cd. 67). DHSS.

2,076. PUBLISHERS' SYNDICATE AMALGAMATED. Old age pensions: an appeal on behalf of the aged poor. Coventry: [1907?]. pp.33. LSE.

2,077.   ROBERTS, A.C.   A comparison of national pension schemes and a proposed scheme for amending the Act of 1908.   London: 1910. pp.73.   LSE; DHSS.

2,078.   ROGERS, F.   The care of the aged in other countries and in England.   London: 1905.   pp.24.   LSE; P.

2,079.   ROGERS, F. & MILLAR, F.   Old age pensions: are they desirable and practical?   London: 1903.   pp.xiii + 226.   LSE.

2,080.   ROSE, G.   Observations on the poor law and on the management of the poor in Great Britain.   London: 1805.   pp.48.   LSE; G.

2,081.   ROYAL COMMISSION ON THE AGED POOR.   Old age pensions.   A miscellaneous collection of papers and pamphlets written in the late nineteenth century... submitted to the Royal Commission on the Aged Poor.   Various published and unpublished works.   1880-.   55 items.   DHSS.

2,082.   ROYAL COMMISSION ON THE AGED POOR.   Royal Commission on the Aged Poor appointed to consider whether any alterations in the system of poor law relief are desirable in the case of persons whose destitution is occasioned by incapacity for work resulting from old age, or whether assistance could otherwise be afforded in those cases.   Vol.I.   Report.   London: 1895. (C.7684).   Vol.II.   Minutes   of   evidence.   (C.7684-I). Vol.III. Minutes of evidence.   (C.7684-II).   (Chairman: C.T. Ritchie).   (Fascimile reprint published Shannon: 1970).   In 2 vols.   (B.P.P., poor law, 28, 29).

2,083.   SCANLAN, T.   "Mr. Chamberlain's pension scheme: a friendly society view of it".   Westm.Rev.   137.   (1892).   pp.357-63.

2,084.   SCANLON, T.   "The   report   of   the   committee   on   old   age pensions".   Fort.Rev.   64.   (1898).   pp.575-80.

2,085.   SELLERS, E.   "The working of the old age relief law in Copenhagen".   National Review.   (November 1896).   pp.390-400. DHSS. [RCAP COLL].

2,086.   SHACKLETON, J.   Social alemioration: a treatise upon Mr. Alexander Atkinson's national pension scheme.   Bradford: 1897.   pp.266.   Sq.

2,087.   SHARP, D.   A scheme for a national system of rest-funds (or pensions) for working people.   London: 1892.   pp.8.   DHSS. [RCAP COLL].

2,088.   SIMON, E.M.   "The new Old Age Pensions Act and some undecided points".   Fort.Rev.   107.   (1920).   pp.560-67.

2,089.   SIRES, R.V.   "The   beginnings   of   British   legislation   for old-age pensions".   J.Econ.Hist.   XIV.   (1954).   p.229.

2,090.   SPENDER, J.A.   State and pensions in old age.   London: 1892. pp.165.   DHSS.

2,091.   STEAD, F.H.   How old age pensions began to be.   London: 1909. pp.328.   CUL.

2 History of Social Security to 1946

2,092. SUTHERLAND, W. Old age pensions: in theory and practice with some foreign examples. London: 1907. pp.x + 227 + 40. DHSS; CUL.

2,093. TAYLOR, W. State pensions. A paper read before the Bath Liberal Association, on March 12th, 1892. Bristol: 1892. pp.10. TCD.

2,094. TOWNSEND, M.E. Suggestions submitted to the committee [on old age pensions]. Unpub. [1896]. pp.1. DHSS.

2,095. TULLIS, J. Old age pensions: a scheme for the formation of a citizens national union. A contribution towards the solution of the problem of pauperism. London: 1892. pp.40. TCD.

2,096. TURNER, G. The case for state pensions in old age. London: 1899. pp.15. (Fabian Tracts No.73). LSE; CUL.

2,097. TYLOR, L. Old age allowances. Cardiff: 1895. pp.18. LSE.

2,098. UNITED KINGDOM. Report of the Royal Commission on the aged poor appointed to consider whether any alterations in the system of poor law relief are desirable, in the case of persons whose destitution is occasioned by incapacity for work resulting from old age, etc. London: 1895. 3v. (B.P.P. XIV-XV). LSE.

2,099. UNITED KINGDOM. Report of the Committee on Old Age Pensions. London: 1898. pp.iv + 210. (B.P.P. XLV). LSE.

2,100. UNITED KINGDOM. Provision for old age by government action in certain European countries. London: 1899. pp.59. (B.P.P. XCII). LSE.

2,101. UNITED KINGDOM. Report from the Select Committee on Aged Deserving Poor, etc. London: 1899. pp.xlvi + 259. (B.P.P. VIII). LSE.

2,102. UNITED KINGDOM. Report on the financial aspects of the proposals made about the aged deserving poor. London: 1900. p.1 + 93. (B.P.P. X). LSE.

2,103. UNITED KINGDOM. Reports from Select Committee on the Aged Pensioners Bill; with proc., etc. London: 1903. pp.xvi + 163. (B.P.P. V). LSE.

2,104. UNITED KINGDOM. Report of the Departmental Committee on Old Age Pensions. London: 1919. 2v. (B.P.P. XXVII). LSE.

2,105. UNITED KINGDOM. Widows', Orphans', and Old Age Contributory Pensions Act, 1925: precis of decisions on appeals made under section 29(2) of the Act. London: 1927. pp.60. LSE.

2,106. UNITED KINGDOM. Widows', Orphans', and Old Age Contributory Pensions Act, 1925: precis of decision on appeals made under section 29(2) of the Act. London: 1927. pp.60. LSE.

2,107. UNITED KINGDOM. Consolidated Bills, 1936: report upon the Old Age Pensions Bill [H.L.], the National Health Insurance

Bill [H.L.], etc. London: 1935-6. pp.71. (B.P.P. XXXVIII). LSE.

2,108. UNITED KINGDOM. Old Age Pensions Act, 1936: financial instructions for pension committees and sub-committees. London: 1946-47. (1). (B.P.P. 1946-47, XV). LSE.

2,109. [UNITED KINGDOM STATUTES.] 1908. 8 Edw.7.ch.40. The Old Age Pensions Act, 1908, together with the official regulations. 2nd ed. London: 1908. pp.ie + 84. LSE.

2,110. WARDE, W.A. Proposed scheme for provisions of old age and pauper relief. Unpub: [1897]. pp.9. DHSS (RCAP COLL).

2,111. WEBB, S. Paupers and old age pensions. London: 1907. pp.15. (Fabian Tracts No.135). LSE; CUL.

2,112. WILKINSON, J.F. Pensions and pauperism. London: 1892. pp.127. S.

2,113. WILKINSON, J.F. "The English poor law and old age". Contemp.Rev. LXIV. (1893). pp.670-80.

2,114. WILLIAMS, P.M. The development of old age pensions policy in Great Britain, 1878-1925. Ph.D. (London) thesis: 1970. Unpublished. pp.484. LSE.

2,115. WILLIAMS, J.A. "Old age pensions". Westm.Rev. 144. (1895). pp.193-202.

2,116. WILSON, A. & MACKAY, G.S. Old age pensions. An historical and critical study. London: 1941. pp.xx + 238. CUL.

2,117. WRIGHT, W.C. "The landlords to pay old age pensions". Westm.Rev. 151. (1899). pp.501-8.

Old Age Pensions, Ireland

2,118. EIRE. Old age pensions, instructions to pension officers. Dublin: 1925. unpag. DHSS.

2,119. IRISH FREE STATE. Report of the Old Age Pensions Committee of Enquiry. Dublin: 1926. pp.24 + xvii. LSE.

2,120. JOHNSTON, W.J. & MULDOON, J. Old age pensions in Ireland. Dublin: 1908. pp.96.

2,121. KELLY, R.J. Old Age Pensions Act, 1908. Dublin: 1908. pp.viii + 103.

2,122. MACDERMOTT, W.R. "The basis for old age pensions in Ireland". N.I.R. 10. (1898-9). pp.371-8.

(c)   Widows' Benefits

2,123. MINISTRY OF HEALTH. Husband or parent dying on or after 4th January, 1926. (Widows', Orphans' and Old Age Contributory Pensions Act, 1925). Instructions to inspectors. (O.S. 42C revised). London: 1926. pp.32. DHSS.

2,124. MINISTRY OF HEALTH. Widows' and orphans' pensions. (Widows',
Orphans' and Old Age Contributory Pensions Act, 1925).
Instructions to inspectors.   (O.S. 42C (1927)).   London:
1927. pp.75. DHSS.

2,125. MINISTRY OF HEALTH.   Widows', Orphans' and Old Age
Contributory Pensions Act, 1919. Instructions to Inspectors.
(O.S. 42D (1929)). London: 1929. pp.34. DHSS.

2,126. MINISTRY OF HEALTH.   Widows', Orphans' and Old Age
Contributory Pensins Act, 1919. Instructions to inspectors.
(O.S. 42E (1929)). London: 1930. pp.12. DHSS.

2,127. MINISTRY OF HEALTH.   Widows', Orphans' and Old Age
Contributory Pensions Acts.   Instructions to inspectors.
(O.S. 42C). London: 1934. pp.134. DHSS.

(d)   Health Insurance

Because the National Insurance Act 1911 dealt both with health
insurance and unemployment insurance, it is not always easy to classify
items as being exclusively about one benefit or the other. In general,
where a work covers both benefits it is cited in this section.

See also, Unemployment Insurance.

2,128. ANON. Facts and observations relating to the administration
of medical relief to the sick poor in England and Wales.
London: 1843. pp.32. R150.

2,129. ANON. "National insurance and national character". Edin.Rev.
CCXVIII. (1913). pp.22-41.

2,130. ANON. "Health insurance. Report on first year's working".
Lab.G. XXI. (1913). pp.286-287.

2,131. ANON. "National health insurance. Report of second year's
working". Lab.G. XIII. (1914). pp.242-243.

2,132. ANON. "National health insurance in England from 1918 to
1923". I.Lab.R. IX. (1924). pp.587ff.

2,133. ANON. "Proposed reform of national health insurance in Great
Britain". I.Lab.R. XIV. (1926). pp.72.

2,134. ANON. "Disablement benefit under the British health insurance
system". I.Lab.R. XXVIII. (1933). pp.192ff.

2,135. ANON. Approved societies handbook; being a revised handbook
for the guidance of approved societies in their administration
of benefits under the National Health Insurance Acts, 1924 to
1932. London: 1933. pp.67. LSE.

2,136. ANON. "Social services 6: national health insurance". L.R.
XXV. (1936). pp.223ff.

2,137. AGGS, W.H. The National Health Insurance Act, 1924. London:

1924. pp.xxii + 175. TCD.

2,138. ALDEN, P. Sickness and invalidity pensions. London: 1911. pp.12. LSE.

2,139. ANCIENT ORDER OF FORESTERS' FRIENDLY SOCIETY. Report of official valuer: National Insurance Bill. n.p.: 1911. LSE.

2,140. ASSOCIATIONS OF INSURANCE COMMITTEES IN ENGLAND, SCOTLAND AND WALES, FEDERATION COMMITTEE. National health insurance: administration of grants in aid; Report [of] deputation at the Treasury, on Friday, 3rd July, 1914. [Durham?: 1914]. pp.13. LSE.

2,141. ATONE, SIR G. Questions and answers on national insurance: a practical and clear handbook for all. London: 1912. pp.xxi + 224. n.l.

2,142. BEADLES, H.S. A review of the National Health Insurance system of England. n.p. [1924]. pp.4. LSE.

2,143. BOARD OF TRADE. Commission on Compulsory Insurance. Minutes of evidence taken before the departmental committee appointed... to consider and report whether any... changes in the existing law... of insurance are desirable in the light of statutory provisions relating to compulsory insurance, etc. London: 1936. pp.326. LSE.

2,144. BRABROOK, SIR E. "State invalidity insurance". E.J. XXI. (1911). pp.1ff.

2,145. BRABROOK, E. "National contributory insurance". Fort.Rev. 93. (1913). pp.371-8.

2,146. BREND, W.A. An examination of the medical provision of the National Insurance Act. London: 1912. pp.42. LSE.

2,147. BROWNE, SIR E. & WOOD, SIR H.K. The law of national insurance. London: 1912. pp.xlvii + 444. 2nd ed. 1912. pp.xlviii + 436 + 42. CUL; BL; DHSS.

2,148. BROWNE, E. & WOOD, H.K. The law of national health insurance. The National Insurance (Health) Acts, 1911 to 1918. London: 1919. pp.415. BL.

2,149. BULL, S.L. An historical and critical analysis of British health insurance. [1938]. fo. v + 282. LSE.

2,150. CANADA, DEPARTMENT OF NATIONAL HEALTH AND WELFARE, RESEARCH DIVISION. Health insurance in Great Britain, 1911-1948. Ottawa: 1952. pp.viii + 163. (Social security series, memoranda, No.11). LSE.

2,151. CARR, A.S.C., GARNETT, W.H.S. & TAYLOR, J.H. (eds.). National insurance. London: 1912. pp.xxx + 504. DHSS. 2nd ed. 1912. pp.xxxii + 587. Sq. 3rd ed. 1912. pp.xxxii + 748. 4th ed. 1913. pp.xliii + 1284. DHSS.

2,152. CASSWELL, J.D. The law of domestic servants; with a chapter on the National Insurance Act, 1911. London: 1913. pp.xix +

126. 2nd ed. London: 1914. pp.xix + 126. BL.

2,153. [CHANCELLOR OF THE EXCHEQUER.] Report of the Departmental Committee on sickness benefit claims under the National
Insurance Act 1911. (Schuster Report). Cd. 7687. London:
1914. pp.87. DHSS.

2,154. CLARKE, O. The National Insurance Act, 1911: being a
treatise on the scheme of national health insurance and
insurance against unemployment created by that Act, with the
incorporated enactments, full introduction by Sir John Simon.
London: 1912. pp.c + 338 + 52. Sq. 2nd ed. 1913. pp.civ
+ 467 + 65. BL; CUL; Sq.

2,155. COLLIE, J. The effects of recent legislation upon sickness
and accident claims. London: 1916. pp.23. LSE; P.

2,156. CONFERENCE BETWEEN REPRESENTATIVES OF THE FEDERATION OF MASTER
COTTON SPINNERS' ASSOCIATIONS THE NORTH AND NORTH-EAST
LANCASHIRE COTTON SPINNERS' AND MANUFACTURERS' ASSOCIATION AND
MEMBERS OF PARLIAMENT, LONDON, 1911 Cotton employers and the
National Insurance Bill. Manchester: 1911. pp.34. LSE.

2,157. COOKE, O.H. The National Insurance Act explained. Chester:
1911. pp.48. 2nd ed. 1912. pp.52. 3rd ed. London: 1912.
pp.52.

2,158. CROASDELL, W.C. The National Insurance Act: how it works and
what it secures. London: 1913. pp.99. BL.

2,159. DALTON, J.P.   An introduction to sickness insurance.
Johannesburg: 1934. pp.viii + 116. LSE.

2,160. DAWES, J.A. National health insurance: part I of the
National Insurance Act, 1911, indexed and summarised. London:
1912. pp.81. LSE.

2,161. DEPARTMENTAL COMMITTEE ON APPROVED SOCIETIES' ADMINISTRATION
ALLOWANCE Report. London: 1921. pp.iii + 20. (Cmd. 1291).

2,162. EVANS, D.O. The Insurance Bill made clear: a guide for the
million. London: 1911. pp.94. LSE; R.

2,163. EVANS, SIR L.W. The National Insurance Bill: summary. 4th
ed. with notes. London: 1911. pp.88.

2,164. EVANS, SIR L.W.   The National Insurance Act, 1911:
summary... with explanatory chapters and full index. London:
1912. pp.152. LSE.

2,165. FACULTY OF INSURANCE.   Report of the Commission of
Investigation into National Health Insurance. London: 1917.
pp.iv + 31. DHSS; LSE.

2,166. FAMILY WELFARE ASSOCIATION. Approved societies under the
National Insurance Act, 1911. [London]: 1912. pp.6. LSE.

2,167. FORRESTER, G.P. "A national insurance scheme in practice".
Fort.Rev. 89. (1911). pp.995-1006.

2,168. FOSTER, W.J. & TAYLOR, F.G. National health insurance. London: 1934. [1933]. pp.xi + 263. 2nd ed. 1935. pp.xv + 278. DHSS; CUL. 3rd ed. 1937. pp.xv + 288. Sq; LSE.

2,169. FOTHERGILL, E.R. State sickness and invalidity insurance. London: 1911. pp.12. LSE; P.

2,170. FRASER, J.A.L. The National Insurance Act, 1911. London: 1912. pp.xii + 216. Bod.

2,171. GARLAND, C.H. Insurance against consumption. London: 1912. pp.120. DHSS.

2,172. GILBERT, B.B. "The British National Insurance Act of 1911 and the commercial insurance lobby". J.Brit.Stud. 4. (1965). pp.127-48.

2,173. GOWERS, E.A. Report by the Chief Inspector to the National Insurance Commission (England) on an inquiry into the reasons why certain insured pesons became deposit contributors. London: 1913. pp.9. (Cd.7034). LSE.

2,174. GRAY, A. Some aspects of national health insurance. London: 1923. pp.29. LSE; DHSS; S.

2,175. HARRIS, H.J. National health insurance in Great Britain. 1911 to 1921. Washington, D.C.: 1923. pp.iv + 103. (U.S. Bureau of Labour Statistics Bulletin 312). BL; DHSS.

2,176. HARRIS, R.W. National health insurance in Great Britain 1911-1946. London: 1946. pp.224. Sq; DHSS; LSE.

2,177. HARRIS, R.W. & SACK, L.S. Medical insurance practice: a work of reference to the medical benefit provisions of the National Health Insurance Acts. London: 1922. pp.xvi + 327. Bod. 2nd and rev. ed. 1924. pp.xii + 347. Bod. 4th ed. London: 1937. pp.xv + 383. BL.

2,178. HASBACH, W. Die Englische Arbeiterversicherungswesen. Leipzig: 1883. pp.xvi + 447. LSE.

2,179. HOFFMAN, F.L. Poor law aspects of national [health] insurance. Nevada, N.J.: 1920. pp.46. LSE.

2,180. HOFFMAN, F.L. National health insurance and the medical profession. Newark, N.J.: 1920. pp.122. DHSS.

2,181. HOFFMAN, F.L. Address on the methods and results of national health insurance. New York: 1920. pp.72. DHSS.

2,182. HOFFMAN, F.L. National health insurance and the friendly societies. Newark, N.J.: 1921. pp.101. DHSS; LSE.

2,183. HONIGSBAUM, F. The struggle for a Ministry of Health, 1914-1919. London: 1970. pp.80. DHSS; LSE.

2,184. HUNTINGTON, E.H. "British health and unemployment insurance and standards of living". In: Essays in social economics in honor of Jessica Blanche Peixotto. London: 1935. pp.165-190. LSE.

2,185. INDEPENDENT ORDER OF ODD FELLOWS, MANCHESTER UNITY, FRIENDLY SOCIETY. National Insurance Bill: amendments drafted and passed by the committee appointed to carry out the resolutions of the Brighton A.M.C. London: 1911. Fo.11. LSE.

2,186. INGRAM, T.A. "The National Insurance Act". Fort.Rev. 91. (1912). pp.40-51.

2,187. INSURANCE COMMITTEE FOR THE COUNTY OF LONDON. Administration of medical benefit under the National Insurance Act, 1911 to 1913. London: 1914. pp.174. LSE.

2,188. INTERDEPARTMENTAL COMMITTEE APPOINTED TO CONSIDER PROPOSALS FOR FACILITATING THE PAYMENT THROUGH THE POST OF BENEFITS UNDER THE NATIONAL INSURANCE ACT. Report. London: 1914. pp.11. (Cd. 7245). LSE.

2,189. KNIGHTS' Handbook for the use of health insurance committees. London: 1913. pp.xii + 377. DHSS.

2,190. LABOUR PARTY. Reports on building for peace and national health insurance to be presented by the Standing Joint Committee of Industrial Women's Organisations to the National Confederation of Labour Women... 1934. London: 1934. pp.32. LSE.

2,191. LAING, J.M. A few notes on the National Insurance Act, 1911. Birmingham: 1913. pp.29. DHSS.

2,192. LAWRENCE. Report of the Royal Commission on National Health Insurance (Lawrence Report). London: 1926. pp.394. (Cmd. 2596). DHSS.

2,193. LEE, A.G. & NEWMAN, T.S. National health insurance manual. London: 1929. pp.245. DHSS. 1934. pp.358. DHSS.

2,194. LEES-SMITH, H. Memorandum on the position of women under the Insurance Bill: (and revised memorandum). London: 1911. 2 parts. LSE.

2,195. LEMBERGER, J. "National Health Insurance Commission". E.J. XXXVI. (1926). pp.680ff.

2,196. LESSER, H. "Common problems in health insurance administration". Ind.Welfare. XVII. (1935). (March). pp.16-19.

2,197. LESSER, H. The National Health Insurance Acts, 1936-1938; with explanatory notes, reported cases, decisions of the Minister of Health, etc. London: 1939. pp.lxiv + 1281. LSE.

2,198. LEVY, H. "The economic history of sickness and medical benefit before the Puritan revolution". Ec.H.R. (1st ser.). XIII. (1943). pp.42-57.

2,199. LEVY, H. "The economic history of sickness and medical benefit since the Puritan revolution". Ec.H.R. (1st ser.). XIV. (1944-45). pp.135-160.

2,200.   LEVY, H.   National health insurance: a critical study.
         Cambridge: 1944. pp.365. DHSS; CUL.

2,201.   LIBERAL PUBLICATION DEPARTMENT. The National Insurance Bill:
         its proposals summarised and explained. London: 1911.
         pp.32.

2,202.   LLOYD GEORGE, D. The people's insurance. London: 1911.
         pp.161.   3rd ed. "containing the text of the National
         Insurance Act, 1911, together with explanations of the
         Insurance Commissioners". 1912. pp.vii + 303. DHSS; CUL.

2,203.   LLOYD, J.H. (ed.).   National Insurance Acts, 1911 and 1913:
         medical and sanatorium benefit regulations. London: 1914.
         pp.232. BL.

2,204.   LOCAL GOVERNMENT PRESS CO.   National Insurance Act 1911
         together with official explanatory memoranda, model rules for
         approved societies, and official replies to points relating to
         the administration. 4th imp. London: 1912. pp.xix + 382.
         DHSS.

2,205.   LOCH, C.S. The National Insurance Bill, etc. London: 1911.
         pp.48. LSE.

2,206.   LONDON CHAMBER OF COMMERCE. National Insurance Bill. London:
         1911. pp.16. LSE.

2,207.   LOVAT-FRASER, J.A.   The National Insurance Act, 1911...
         London: 1912. pp.xii + 216. CUL.

2,208.   LOWRY, E.W. Can the doctors work the Insurance Act? London:
         1912. pp.64. LSE.

2,209.   McCLEARY, G.F.   The British scheme of national health
         insurance. Baltimore: 1930. pp.11. LSE.

2,210.   McCLEARY, G.F. National health insurance. London: 1932.
         pp.x + 185. DHSS.

2,211.   McCURDY, C.A. & LEES-SMITH, H.B.   The people's guide to the
         Insurance Act: the Act complete with introduction and full
         explanatory notes. 2nd and rev.ed. London: 1912. pp.175.
         DHSS; LSE.

2,212.   McNAMARA, W.H.   "The medical profession and the Insurance
         Act". Westm.Rev. 180. (1913). pp.477-84.

2,213.   MINISTRY OF HEALTH. Report of the departmental committee on
         approved societies' administration allowance.   (Kinnear
         Report). London: 1921. pp.iii + 20. (Cmd. 1291). DHSS.

2,214.   MINISTRY OF HEALTH. Report of the National Health Insurance
         (International Arrangements) Board to the National Health
         Insurance Joint Committee and to the Irish insurance
         commissioners. London: 1927. pp.27. (Cmd. 2965). DHSS.

2,215.   MINISTRY OF HEALTH.   National health insurance:
         administration of additional benefits. London: [1930] .

pp.8. LSE.

2,216. MINISTRY OF HEALTH. National health insurance: control of expenditure on sickness and disablement benefits. London: [1931]. pp.13. LSE.

2,217. MINISTRY OF HEALTH. National health and pensions insurance: voluntary insurance. London: 1933. pp.8. [Memoranda 243/X]. LSE.

2,218. MINISTRY OF HEALTH. Outline of national health insurance. London: 1935. pp.20. DHSS.

2,219. MINISTRY OF HEALTH. Receipt and disposal of health, pensions and unemployment insurance contributions. London: 1936. pp.20. DHSS.

2,220. MINISTRY OF HEALTH. Receipt and disposal of health, pensions and unemployment insurance contributions. London: 1936. pp.20. DHSS.

2,221. MINISTRY OF HEALTH. National health insurance and contributory pensions insurance. London: 1939. pp.34. LSE; DHSS.

2,222. MINISTRY OF HEALTH. National health insurance. London: 1939. pp.58. DHSS.

2,223. MINISTRY OF HEALTH AND SECRETARY OF STATE FOR SCOTLAND. Report of the interdepartmental committee on insurance medical records. (Rolleston Report). London: 1920. pp.28. DHSS.

2,224. MINISTRY OF LABOUR. EMPLOYMENT AND INSURANCE DEPARTMENT. Local employment committee: Advice as to earning capacity of disabled sailors and soldiers. London: 1920. pp.4. LSE.

2,225. MINISTRY OF NATIONAL INSURANCE AND OTHERS. National Health Insurance Joint Committee. Minutes of meetings Nos.1-177, December 1911 to June 1948. London: 1948. 13 vols. DHSS.

2,226. MONEY, SIR L.G.C. A nation insured: the National Insurance Act explained. London: 1911. pp.68. BL. 2nd ed. 1911. pp.78. BL. 3rd ed. 1912. pp.78.

2,227. MORAN, C.G. The alphabet of the National Insurance Act, 1911. London: 1912. pp.vi + 164. LSE.

2,228. MORGAN, G. Public relief of sickness. London: 1923. pp.195. DHSS.

2,229. NATIONAL ASSOCIATION OF TRADE UNION APPROVED SOCIETIES. National health insurance. London: [1934]. pp.34. LSE.

2,230. NATIONAL CONSERVATIVE UNION. National Insurance Act, 1911. (Summary by L. Worthington Evans). London: 1912. pp.156. DHSS.

2,231. NATIONAL HEALTH INSURANCE COMMISSION. National Insurance Act, 1911: model rules for administration of medical benefit; (with model rules A-F). London: 1912. 9 pts. LSE.

2,232. NATIONAL HEALTH INSURANCE COMMISSION. Constitution of
        insurance commissions, 1913; appointment by approved
        societies... of the representatives of insured persons;
        statement... of the numbers of insured persons, the membership
        of approved societies, etc. London: 1913. (B.P.P., LVI).
        pp.7. LSE.

2,233. NATIONAL HEALTH INSURANCE COMMISSION. New system of medical
        certification of incapacity of insured persons for work.
        London: 1914. pp.23. LSE.

2,234. NATIONAL HEALTH INSURANCE COMMISSION. Memoranda of decisions
        under s.66 of the National Insurance Act 1911, and s.27(2) of
        the National Insurance Act 1913. 2nd ed. London: 1914-25.
        3 vols. LSE.

2,235. NATIONAL HEALTH INSURANCE COMMISSION. Reports of inquiries
        and appeals under the National Health Insurance (Medical
        Benefit) Regulations (England) 1913. London: 1917-1924. 1
        vol. unpag. DHSS.

2,236. NATIONAL HEALTH INSURANCE COMMISSION. National Health
        Insurance Act, 1918: summary of principal provisions.
        London: 1918. pp.23. LSE.

2,237. NATIONAL HEALTH INSURANCE COMMISSION Model rules for an
        approved society... which also carries on private business.
        London: 1919. pp.24. LSE.

2,238. NATIONAL HEALTH INSURANCE COMMISSION. National Health
        Insurance Acts, 1911-1920. Summary of the... provisions of
        the N.H.I. Acts, 1911-1920, for the information of members of
        approved societies. London: 1920. pp.20. LSE.

2,239. NATIONAL HEALTH INSURANCE COMMISSION. National Health
        Insurance Act, 1924. [Summary of provisions] for the
        information of members of approved societies. London: 1925.
        pp.20. LSE.

2,240. NATIONAL HEALTH INSURANCE COMMISSION. National Health
        Insurance Act, 1928: supplement to the approved societies'
        handbook (1925 ed.). London: 1928. pp.52. LSE.

2,241. NATIONAL HEALTH INSURANCE COMMISSION. Memoranda of decisions
        as to liability or title to insurance, 1912-31. London:
        1931. pp.228. LSE.

2,242. NATIONAL HEALTH INSURANCE JOINT COMMITTEE. The Statutes,
        Regulations and Orders relating to National Health
        Insurance... London: 1916. pp.xii + 679. CUL.

2,243. NATIONAL INSURANCE WEEKLY. The National Insurance Weekly,
        Vol.1, Nos.1-9. London: 1912. pp.280. DHSS.

2,244. NATIONAL UNION OF CONSERVATIVE AND UNIONIST ASSOCIATIONS. The
        National Insurance Act, 1911; actuaries' reports. London:
        [1912?]. pp.16. LSE.

2,245. NATIONAL UNION OF WOMEN WORKERS. COMMITTEE TO FURTHER WOMEN'S

INTEREST UNDER THE NATIONAL INSURANCE ACT. Women and local insurance commissions. London: [1912]. pp.4. LSE.

2,246. NEWMAN, T.S. & LEE, A.G. Guide to national health insurance. 1st ed. London: 1925. pp.48. DHSS. Rev. ed. 1929. pp.48. DHSS. Rev. ed. 1933. pp.55. DHSS. 4th ed. 1936. pp.63. DHSS.

2,247. ORRISS, W.G. The National Health Insurance Act: an alternative scheme. London: 1913. pp.20. LSE.

2,248. PARKER, H.A. National health insurance. London: 1933. pp.15. DHSS.

2,249. PITHER, P.J. "Additional benefits under national insurance". Ind.Welfare. XIV. (1932). pp.370, 372.

2,250. PRINGLE, A.S. The National Insurance Act, 1911, explained, annotated, and indexed. Edinburgh, London: 1912. pp.xx + 544. Sq.

2,251. REES, J.A. The ABC of the national insurance scheme. London: 1911. pp.64. BL. 2nd ed. 1911. pp.63. BL. 4th ed. The ABC of the National Insurance Act. 1912. pp.71. BL.

2,252. ROBERTS, H. "The Insurance Bill, the doctors, and national policy". Nineteenth Century. LXX. (1911). pp.152-62.

2,253. SALE, C.V. National health insurance: the parliamentary Bill examined and compared with the German scheme. London: 1911. pp.26. LSE; P.

2,254. [SALE, C.V.] National health insurance. Proposals for an alternative to the government bill. London: 1911. pp.26. LSE.

2,255. SAMUEL, H.B. The Insurance Act and yourself. London: 1912. pp.112.

2,256. SCHUSTER, E.J. "National health insurance in England and Wales". J.Comp.Leg. 12. (1911-12). pp.11-32.

2,257. SCHUSTER, E.J. National health insurance. 2nd ed. London: 1911. pp.32. LSE.

2,258. SHEPAR, W.J. "The British National Insurance Act". Am.Pol.Sc.Rev. 6. (1912). pp.229-34.

2,259. SMITH, T. Everybody's guide to the Insurance Act. London: 1912. pp.vii + 304. 2nd ed. 1912. pp.viii + 357. BL. 3rd ed. entitled Everybody's guide to the Insurance Acts, 1911-1913... 1914. pp.xii + 506. CUL; DHSS.

2,260. TRADES UNION CONGRESS & LABOUR PARTY. National health insurance medical benefit. London: [1923]. pp.15. LSE.

2,261. TRADES UNION CONGRESS. Insurance for health; pensions for age: (an analysis and criticism on National Health Insurance and Contributory Pensions Act, 1932). London: [1933]. pp.8. LSE.

2,262.   UNITED KINGDOM.   Copy of memorandum explanatory of the principal amendments which it is proposed to incorporate in the National Insurance Bill.   London: 1911.   (B.P.P., LXXIII).   2 vols.   LSE.

2,263.   UNITED KINGDOM.   Report of the actuaries in relation to... the National Insurance Bill, 1911.   London: 1911.   (B.P.P., LXXIII).   7 vols.   LSE.

2,264.   UNITED KINGDOM.   The National Insurance Act, 1911, together with official explanatory memoranda.   London: 1911.   pp.xi + 180.   LSE.

2,265.   UNITED KINGDOM   Return containing explanatory memorandum with regard to... the National Insurance Bill.   London: 1911. (B.P.P. LXXIII).   4 vols.   LSE.

2,266.   UNITED KINGDOM.   National health insurance: statutory, rules and orders.   London: 1913.   pp.430.   LSE.

2,267.   UNITED KINGDOM.   Memoranda of decisions under section 66 of the National Insurance Act, 1911, and section 27(2) of the National Insurance Act, 1913.   London: 1914-1926.   3 vols (in 1).   LSE.

2,268.   UNITED KINGDOM.   Report of the departmental committee on sickness benefit claims under the National Insurance Act. London: 1916.   (B.P.P., 1914-16, XXX-XXXI).   5 vols.   LSE.

2,269.   UNITED KINGDOM.   Report... on the administration of the National Insurance Act, part 1 (health insurance).   London: 1917.   (B.P.P., 1913-17).   LSE.

2,270.   UNITED KINGDOM.   The statutes relating to national health insurance and regulations affecting the administration of approved societies.   London: 1918.   pp.iv + 306.   LSE.

2,271.   UNITED KINGDOM.   Memoranda of decisions as to liability to insurance under the National Health Insurance Acts.   London: 1928-29.   7 vols.   LSE.

2,272.   UNITED KINGDOM.   The statutes, regulations and orders relating to national health insurance.   Part I.   Statutes.   London: 1929.   pp.ix + 207.   LSE.

2,273.   UNITED KINGDOM.   Approved societies handbook: being a revised handbook for the guidance of approved societies in their administration of benefits under the National Health Insurance Acts, 1924 to 1932.   London: 1933.   pp.367.   LSE.

2,274.   UNITED KINGDOM.   Report of the Commission on Compulsory Insurance.   London: 1934-35.   pp.82.   (B.P.P. XII).   LSE.

2,275.   UNITED STATES.   National health insurance in Great Britain, 1911-21.   Washington: 1923.   pp.103.   LSE.

2,276.   UNITED STATES.   BUREAU OF RESEARCH AND STATISTICS. Unemployment insurance and health insurance in Great Britain, 1911-1937.   Washington: [1938].   pp.v + 44.   [Reports, 3].

LSE.

2,277. VANN, J.C. "What lies behind the new Social Security Act?".
S.J. 117. (1973). pp.754-5.

2,278. WALLIS, G. Free medical aid to the poor without pauperism, in
lieu of the present method of poor law medical relief. 2nd
ed. Bristol: 1856. pp.10, 3-34. LSE.

2,279. WATSON, SIR A.K The analysis of a sickness experience.
Cambridge: 1930. pp.32. DHSS.

2,280. WATSON, A.W. National health insurance (a statistical
review). London: 1927. pp.434-486. DHSS.

2,281. WATSON, SIR A.W. "National health insurance: a statistical
review". R.Statist.Soc.J. XC. (1927). pp.433-73.
Discussion. pp.473-86.

2,282. WATTS, J.H. The National Insurance Bill. London: 1911.
pp.286. CUL.

2,283. WATTS, J.H. Law relating to national insurance. With an
explanatory introduction, the text of the National Insurance
Act, 1911, annotated and appendices containing regulations...
London: 1913. pp.vii + 664. CUL; DHSS.

2,284. WEBB, B. Complete national provision for sickness: how to
amend the Insurance Act. London: 1912. pp.16. LSE.

2,285. WEBB, S. & WEBB, B. The state and the doctor. London: 1910.
pp.xii + 276. LSE.

2,286. WILLIS, W.A. National health insurance through approved
societies: being a practical legal treatise incorporating the
operative orders and regulations. London: 1914. pp.xxx +
494. DHSS; LSE; Sq; CUL.

2,287. WILSON, H.B. Suggestions as to the medical assistance of the
poor... prepared for the Royal Commission on the Poor Laws,
etc. Birmingham: 1907. pp.31. LSE.

2,288. WOOD, K. & NEWMAN, T.S. National health insurance manual.
London: 1925. pp.200. DHSS.

2,289. WOOD, SIR H.K. & NEWMAN, T.S. National health insurance
manual. 4th ed. London: 1924. pp.206. Rev.ed. by T.S.
Newman and A.G. Lee. London: 1930. pp.245. Another rev.ed.
1934. pp.358.

Health Insurance, Scotland

2,290. GIBSON, R. & HARAH, T.S. Scottish national insurance.
Edinburgh: 1912. pp.689. DHSS.

2,291. GREEN & SONS. National health insurance. Edinburgh: 1930.
pp.230. DHSS.

2,292. HOGGE, J.M. Scotland insured. London: 1913. pp.104. LSE.

2,293. LITTLE, E.G. "National health insurance". <u>Edin.Rev.</u> 249. (1929). pp.129-44.

2,294. SCOTTISH BOARD OF HEALTH. Report on the administration of national health insurance in Scotland during the years 1917-1919. London: 1920. pp.86. (Cmd. 827). DHSS.

2,295. UNITED KINGDOM. National health insurance: handbook for the use of insurance committees in Scotland. Edinburgh: 1915. pp.viii + 256. LSE.

Health Insurance, Ireland

2,296. DIGNAN, REV. J. Social security: outlines of a scheme of national health insurance. Sligo: 1945. pp.40. Sq.

2,297. DUFFY, L.J. "National health insurance from the workers' standpoint". <u>J.S.S.I.S.I.</u> XVI. (1928). pp.49-59.

2,298. EASON, J.C.M. "Statement of the view of employers in the Irish Free State on the system of national health insurance". <u>J.S.S.I.S.I.</u> XVI. (1928). pp.60-7.

2,299. IRELAND [EIRE]. SEANAD EIREANN. Select Committee on the National Health Insurance Bill... Report. Dublin: 1933. pp.x + 69. LSE.

2,300. IRELAND. VOLUNTARY HEALTH INSURANCE BOARD. Voluntary health insurance. Dublin: 1957. pp.14. DHSS.

2,301. IRISH FREE STATE. National health insurance: valuation regulations, 1925. Dublin: 1925. pp.11. LSE.

2,302. IRISH FREE STATE Appendices to the interim report of the Committee on Health Insurance and Medical Services. Dublin: [1925]. pp.158. LSE.

2,303. IRISH FREE STATE. Report of the Committee on the Relief of the Sick and Destitute Poor, including the insane poor. Dublin: 1927. pp.xv + 163. LSE.

2,304. IRISH FREE STATE. Final Report of the Committee on Health Insurance and Medical Services. Dublin: 1927. pp.56. LSE.

2,305. IRISH FREE STATE Report on the administration of national health insurance in all Ireland from 1st April 1921, to 31st March 1922, [Saorstat] Eirrean f. 1st April 1922, to 31st March 1928. Dublin: 1928. pp.80. LSE.

2,306. NORTHERN IRELAND. MINISTRY OF LABOUR AND NATIONAL INSURANCE. Annual report. Belfast: 1922. LSE.

2,307. RIORDAN, R.G. "National health insurance". <u>J.S.S.I.S.I.</u> XVI. (1928). pp.44-8.

(e)   Unemployment Insurance

          See also, Health Insurance, above; and Part II, Section 8
          (Unemployment)

2,308.   ANON.   "The relief of vagrants and of the unemployed in
          Germany and England". Char.Org.Rev. IV. (1888). pp.81-92.

2,309.   ANON. "Unemployed Workmen Act, 1905". Lab.G. XIII. (1905).
          p.293.

2,310.   ANON. "Assistance of unemployment benefit funds out of public
          money". Lab.G. XIV. (1906). pp.227-228.

2,311.   ANON. "Foreign and colonial systems of poor relief". Lab.G.
          XIX. (1911). pp.202-203.

2,312.   ANON. "Unemployed benefits of trade unions". Lab.G. XIX.
          (1911). pp.202-203.

2,313.   ANON. "National workmen's insurance. Great Britain and
          Ireland: National Insurance Act of 16th December, 1911".
          I.L.O. Bull. (2nd ser.). VII. (1912). pp.CIX-CXXX.

2,314.   ANON.   "Unemployment insurance". Lab.G. XXI. (1913).
          pp.42-43.

2,315.   ANON. "Unemployment insurance. Courts of referees". Lab.G.
          XXI. (1913). pp.247-248.

2,316.   ANON.   "Unemployment insurance". Lab.G. XXI. (1913).
          pp.283-284.

2,317.   ANON.   "Government assistance to trade unions for
          unemployment". Lab.G. XXII. (1914). pp.358-359.

2,318.   ANON. "The Unemployment Insurance Act, 1920". Lab.G. 28.
          (1920).

2,319.   ANON. "Unemployment: remedial measures". Lab.G. 29.
          (1921). pp.60-1.

2,320.   ANON. "Unemployment insurance: an international survey".
          I.Lab.R. VI. (1922). pp.365ff.

2,321.   ANON. "The government and unemployment". L.R. XI. (1922).
          pp.11ff.

2,322.   ANON. "Notes on unemployment problems: payments to the
          unemployed". I.Lab.R. VII. (1923). pp.302ff.

2,323.   ANON. "Notes on unemployment problems: payments to the
          unemployed". I.Lab.R. VII. (1923). pp.898ff.

2,324.   ANON.   "The Ministry of Labour of Great Britain. II.
          Employment and Insurance Department". J.Comp.Leg. 5.
          (1923). pp.189-205.

2,325.   ANON. "Government measures to relieve unemployment". Lab.G.
          31. (1923). pp.316-17.

2,326.   ANON. "Report on the unemployment insurance scheme". Lab.G.

31. (1923). pp.394-5.

2,327. ANON. "Analysis of claims to unemployment insurance benefit". Lab.G. 31. (1923). pp.395-6.

2,328. ANON. "Unemployment insurance: revised statistics". Lab.G. 31. (1923). pp.397-8.

2,329. ANON. "Unemployment insurance. Report by National Confederation of Employers' Organisations". Lab.G. 32. (1924). pp.40-41.

2,330. ANON. "Report on an investigation into claims to unemployment benefit". Lab.G. 32. (1924). pp.79-80.

2,331. ANON. "Unemployment insurance: analysis of claims to benefit during the 'fourth special period'". Lab.G. 32. (1924). pp.234-6.

2,332. ANON. "Unemployment benefit in Great Britain". I.Lab.R. X. (1924). pp.296ff.

2,333. ANON. "Unemployment benefit. Government Bills - cost and statistics - legal cases". M.C.L.R.D. 13. (1924). p.108.

2,334. ANON. Unemployment insurance in Great Britain: a critical examination. By the authors of "The third winter of unemployment" and "Is unemployment inevitable?" London: 1925. pp.68. CUL.

2,335. ANON. Unemployment insurance in Great Britain: a critical examination. London: 1925. pp.68. LSE.

2,336. ANON. Unemployment Insurance in Great Britain. London: 1925. pp.68. DHSS.

2,337. ANON. "Claimants to unemployment benefit in Britain". I.Lab.R. XII. (1925). pp.685ff.

2,338. ANON. "Report on an investigation into claims to unemployment benefit: November, 1924". Lab.G. 33. (1925). pp.190-1.

2,339. ANON. "An inquiry into unemployment insurance for agricultural workers in Great Britain". I.Lab.R. XV. (1927). pp.272.

2,340. ANON. "The Unemployment Bill". M.C.L.R.D. 16. (1927). pp.176-7.

2,341. ANON. Unemployment insurance by the editors of "Poor Law Officers Journal". London: 1928. pp.18. DHSS.

2,342. ANON. "Unemployment and poor relief". L.R. XVII. (1928). pp.32ff.

2,343. ANON. "Unemployed benefit claimants. Report of an investigation of April, 1927". Lab.G. 36. (1928). pp.118-19.

2,344. ANON. "Relief of unemployment: action taken or proposed by

H.M. Government.   Migration;   training schemes;   juvenile
unemployment centres;   forest holdings; Canadian harvesters'
schemes". Lab.G. 36. (1928). pp.276-7.

2,345. ANON. "Unemployment Insurance Acts: report of committee of
enquiry". Lab.G. 37. (1929). p.398.

2,346. ANON.   "Poor law and unemployment relief".   L.R.   XIX.
(1930). pp.63ff.

2,347. ANON.   "Unemployment insurance revision".   M.C.L.R.D. 20.
(1931). 274-5. 21. (1932). 13-14, 70, 92.

2,348. ANON. "Royal Commission on unemployment insurance". Lab.G.
39. (1931). pp.210-11.

2,349. ANON.   "Changes in the estimated numbers insured against
unemployment, 1923-1931", Lab.G. 39. (1931). pp.414-17.
[1923-32].   40.   (1932).   pp.406-10.   [1923-33].   41.   (1933).
pp.396-400.

2,350. ANON. "Numbers on employment exchange registers. Effect of
recent changes in the unemployment scheme".   Lab.G.   39.
(1931). p.457.

2,351. ANON. "Unemployment insurance revision". L.R. 20. (1931).
pp.174-5. 21. (1932). pp.13-14, 70, 92.

2,352. ANON.   "Unemployment insurance".   L.R.   20.   (1931).
pp.259-60.

2,353. ANON. "Unemployment insurance revision". M.C.L.R.D. 20.
(1931). pp.274-5. 21. (1932). pp.13-14, 70, 92.

2,354. ANON.   "Royal Commission on unemployment insurance: final
report". Lab.G. 40. (1932). pp.402-5.

2,355. ANON.   "Unemployment Insurance Acts.   Occupation during
unemployment. Effect on claims for benefit or transitional
payments". Lab.G. 41. (1933). pp.202.

2,356. ANON. "Persons insured against unemployment in Great Britain
at July, 1932. Analysis by sample". Lab.G. 41. (1933).
pp.314-18, 356-60.

2,357. ANON.   "The Unemployment Bill".   L.R.   XXII.   (1933).
pp.276ff.

2,358. ANON.   "Unemployment insurance and libel".   L.J.   LXXX.
(1935). p.90.

2,359. ANON.   "Unemployment insurance in agriculture.   Report of
unemployment insurance statutory committee".   Lab.G.   43.
(1935). pp.47-8.

2,360. ANON. "Unemployment insurance: exclusion of inconsiderable
employments". Lab.G. 43. (1935). p.91.

2,361. ANON.   "Seasonal workers: conditions for receipt of
unemployment benefit. Report of the unemployment insurance

statutory committee". <u>Lab.G.</u> 43. (1935). pp.188-9.

2,362. ANON.   "Unemployment insurance in employments of
inconsiderable extent". <u>Lab.G.</u> 43. (1935). p.212.

2,363. ANON.   "Remuneration limit for unemployment insurance of
non-manual workes.   Report of the unemployment insurance
statutory committee". <u>Lab.G.</u> 44. (1936). pp.120-1.

2,364. ANON. "Share fishermen in relation to unemployment insurance.
Report of the unemployment insurance statutory committee".
<u>Lab.G.</u> 44. (1936). p.441.

2,365. ANON. "Social services III; unemployment insurance". <u>L.R.</u>
XXV. (1936). pp.151ff.

2,366. ANON. "Unemployment insurance statutory committee. Report as
to the extension of unemployment insurance to outdoor private
domestic servants". <u>Lab.G.</u> 45. (1937). pp.469-70.

2,367. ANON. "Report on the Draft Unemployment Insurance (Insurable
Employments) Regulations, 1937". <u>Lab.G.</u> 45. (1937). p.470.

2,368. ANON.   "Holidays in relation to unemployment insurance.
Report by the unemployment insurance statutory committee".
<u>Lab.G.</u> 46. (1938). p.426.

2,369. ANON.   "Unemployment fund surplus". <u>L.R.</u> 27. (1938).
pp.78-9.

2,370. ANON.   "Unemployment insurance and assistance.   Emergency
regulations". <u>Lab.G.</u> 47. (1939). p.360.

2,371. ANON. "Holiday credit and unemployment insurance". <u>Ind.L.R.</u>
1. (1946-47). pp.171-172.

2,372. ANON.   "Social security and unemployment in Lancashire".
<u>Political and Economic Planning.</u> XIX. (1952).

2,373. APPLETON, W.A. Unemployment: a study of causes, palliatives
and remedies. London: [1923?]. pp.157. LSE.

2,374. APPLETON, W.A. National Insurance Act: the critical position
of trade unions. An appeal to organized workers. London:
1912. pp.4.

2,375. ASBURY, W. & RACKLAM, C.D. Royal Commission on Unemployment
Insurance, December 1930 - November 1932: an abridgement of
the minority report signed by the Labour members of the
Commission. London: 1933. pp.73. LSE.

2,376. ASHLEY, W.J.   "The National Insurance Bill.   Part II.
Unemployment." <u>E.J.</u> XXI. 82. (1911). pp.266-74.

2,377. BAILWARD, W.A. Some impressions of the first six months'
working of compulsory insurance against unemployment in
England. London: 1913. pp.16. LSE.

2,378. BAKKE, E.W. "Basic realities in a system of unemployment
benefit". In Murdock, G.P. (ed), <u>Studies in the science of</u>

society. New Haven, Conn.: 1937. pp.29-41.

2,379. BAKKE, E.W.   Insurance   or   dole?   The   adjustment   of
        unemployment insurance to economic and social facts in Great
        Britain. New Haven: 1935. pp.xiii + 280. LSE; CUL.

2,380. BANKING UNEMPLOYMENT INSURANCE BOARD, THE. Special scheme for
        "contracting out" under the Unemployment Insurance Act, 1920:
        rules, annual reports, specimen forms and final statement.
        London: 1922-1948. Var.pag. DHSS.

2,381. BEAUCHAMP, W.   "Insurance against unemployment".   Westm.Rev.
        175. (1911). pp.604-12.

2,382. BECKER, J.M. Experience rating in unemployment insurance: an
        experiment in competitive socialism.   Baltimore, London:
        1973. pp.403. CUL.

2,383. BELL, J.G., BLUNDUN, B.Y. & DREYER, E.   "Administrative
        aspects of social insurance".   Pub.Admin.   V.   (1927).
        pp.344, 358, 373.

2,384. BETTERTON (INTERDEPARTMENTAL) COMMITTEE.   Report on the
        co-ordination of administrative and executive arrangements for
        the grant of assistance from public funds on account of
        sickness, destitution and unemployment. (Betterton Report).
        London: 1925. pp.167. Cmd.2011. DHSS.

2,385. BEVERIDGE, W.H. The problem of the unemployed. London:
        [1906]. pp.323-41. LSE.

2,386. BEVERIDGE, W.H.   "The Unemployed Workmen Act, in 1906-7".
        Sociol.Rev. I. (1908). pp.79-83.

2,387. BEVERIDGE, W.H.   Unemployment.   A problem of industry.
        London: 1909. pp.317. CUL. 1917. pp.xvi + 405. LSE. New
        ed. 1930. pp.xxxvii + 514. CUL.

2,388. BEVERIDGE, W.H. Unemployment insurance. Proceedings of the
        Board of Trade under Part II of the National Insurance Act,
        1911. First report, appendices. London: 1913. pp.viii +
        82. (Cd.6965). LSE.

2,389. BEVERIDGE, W.H.   Unemployment insurance: Committee on
        Centralisation, 1915: Typescript, Memoranda and Minutes.
        London: 1915. 26 parts in 1. LSE.

2,390. BEVERIDGE, W.H. A new proposal for unemployment insurance.
        Manchester: 1923. pp.1. LSE.

2,391. BEVERIDGE, SIR W.   "Unemployment".   Pol.Q.   I.   (1930).
        p.326.

2,392. BEVERIDGE, SIR W.H. The past and present of unemployment
        insurance. London: 1930. pp.47. LSE; DHSS.

2,393. BEVERIDGE, SIR W.H.   Causes and cures of unemployment.
        London: 1931. pp.70. LSE.

2,394. BEVERIDGE, SIR W.H.   The unemployment insurance statutory committee. London: 1937. pp.55. [University of London, LSEPS. Political pamphlets No.1]. LSE; DHSS; CUL.

2,395. BOARD OF TRADE. National Insurance Bill (Pt.2. Unemployment): tables showing the rules and expenditure of trade unions in respect of unemployment benefits, and also showing earnings in the insured trades. London: 1911. pp.iv + 327. LSE.

2,396. BOURNVILLE WORKS. An unemployment relief scheme: notes on an experiment made by the Bournville Village Trust, 1932-33. Birmingham: 1933. pp.14. LSE.

2,397. BRADSHAW, L. How to avoid the peril of the unemployed; the Unemployed Act and its failure; the Labour Party and their new Bill; criticism and an alternative. Kettering: 1907. pp.32. BL.

2,398. BROWN, K.D. Labour and unemployment 1900-1914. Newton Abbott: 1971. pp.219. DHSS; LSE; CUL.

2,399. BROWN, K.D. "The Labour party and the unemployed question 1906-1910". Hist.J. 14. (1971). pp.599-616.

2,400. BULL, SIR W. "Unionism and state insurance". O.& C.Rev. 15. (1911). p.172-85.

2,401. BURNS, E.M. British unemployment programs 1920-1938. Washington: 1941. pp.385. DHSS; LSE.

2,402. CARLILE, W. "The problem of the unemployed and suggestions for its solution". Fort.Rev. 78. (1905). pp.1965-73.

2,403. CARR, A.S.C. Escape from the "dole": unemployment insurance or employment assurance? London: 1930. pp.38. LSE.

2,404. CARTER, H.P. The problem of the unemployed miner and its solution. London: 1928. pp.16. LSE.

2,405. CASSON, W.A. Unemployed Workmen Act 1905. London: 1905. pp.129. DHSS.

2,406. CENTRAL (UNEMPLOYED) BODY FOR LONDON. Preliminary report upon the work of the Central (Unemployed) Body for London (Unemployed Workmen Act, 1905) to 12th May, 1906. London: 1906. pp.84. DHSS.

2,407. [CHANCELLOR OF THE EXCHEQUER]. Report of the committee appointed to consider and advise with regard to the application of the National Insurance Act to outworkers. Vol.I. (Hatch Report). Cd. 6178. London: 1912. pp.20. DHSS.

2,408. CHIOZZA MONEY, L.G. "National insurance and labour unrest". Fort.Rev. 94. (1913). pp.763-74

2,409. CLAY, SIR A.T.F. The unemployed and legislation. London: [190-]. pp.13.

2,410. CLAY, SIR A.T.F. "The unemployed and the Unemployed Workmen Act". Mon.Rev. XXI (1905). pp.78-102.

2,411. CLAY, H.   London: 1929. pp.x + 208. DHSS.

2,412. CLEE, C.R.   Explanatory notes on the Unemployment Insurance
        Act, 1920.   Sections 1-4, persons insured.   Manchester:
        Prev.Publ. 1920. unpaged. DHSS.

2,413. COHEN, J.L.   Insurance against unemployment with special
        reference to Britain and American conditions. London: 1921.
        pp.536. LSE; DHSS; CUL.

2,414. COHEN, J.L. Social insurance and the worker. London: [1924?].
        pp.23. LSE.

2,415. COHEN, J.W. Unemployment insurance and agricultural labor in
        Great Britain. Washington: 1940.   pp.viii + 32.   (Social
        Science Research Council.   Committee on Social Security.
        Pamphlet Series, No.2). LSE.

2,416. COHEN, P. Unemployment insurance and assistance in Britain.
        London: 1938. pp.272. Sq; LSE; DHSS; CUL.

2,417. COLE, G.D.H.   Unemployment and industrial maintenance.
        London: 1921. pp.16. LSE.

2,418. COMMITTEE APPOINTED TO CONSIDER AND ADVISE WITH REGARD TO THE
        APPLICATION OF THE NATIONAL INSURANCE ACT TO OUTWORKERS.
        Report and minutes. London: 1912. (Cd. 6178, 6179).

2,419. CREW, A.   The Unemployment Insurance Acts, 1920-1927...
        assisted by R.J. Blackham. London: 1928. p.xvi + 195. CUL;
        LSE.   Another ed.   1920-1930, (with A. Forman)   1930.
        pp.xviii + 220. Sq.

2,420. CUNNISON, J.   "Some factors affecting the incidence of the
        national insurance contributions". E.J.   XXIII.   (1913).
        pp.367-78.

2,421. DAILY NEWS.   The Unemployment Insurance Act, 1920:
        explanation and summary. London: 1920. pp.16. LSE.

2,422. DAVISON, R.C. The unemployed: old policies and new. London:
        1929. pp.xii + 292. CUL; DHSS.

2,423. DAVISON, R.C.   What's wrong with unemployment insurance?
        London: 1930. pp.73. LSE.

2,424. DAVISON, R.C. Unemployment insurance in Great Britain. Rome:
        1930. pp.8. LSE. (Pamphlet Collection).

2,425. DAVISON, R.C. The new Unemployment Act popularly explained.
        London: 1934. pp.32. LSE.

2,426. DAVISON, R.C. British unemployment policy: the modern phase
        since 1930. London: 1938. pp.x + 136. LSE; DHSS.

2,427. DAWES, J.A. Unemployment insurance. London: 1912. pp.18.
        DHSS.

2,428. DEACON, A.   "Concession and coercion: the politics of unemployment insurance in the twenties". In Asa Briggs and John Saville. <u>Essays in Labour History 1918-1939.</u> London: 1977. pp.9-35.

2,429. DEARNLEY, I.H. The "needs test" for unemployment insurance, transitional payments and public assistance. London: 1931. pp.6 + 62. Harvard Law School.

2,430. DRAGE, G. The unemployed. London: 1894. pp.xiv + 277. BL; CUL.

2,431. ELIAS, S. Our reply to the Royal Commission on unemployment. London: [1931]. pp.15. LSE.

2,432. EMMERSON, H.C. & LASCELLES, E.C.P. Guide to the Unemployment Insurance Acts. London: 1926. pp.vii + 172. Revised and enlarged ed. 1928. pp.x + 244. 3rd ed. 1930. pp.vii + 262. BL. 4th ed. 1935. pp.vi + 280. BL. CUL. 5th ed. 1939. pp.vii + 292. Sq; LSE; DHSS.

2,433. ENGINEERING AND ALLIED EMPLOYERS' NATIONAL FEDERATION. Unemployment: its realities and problems. London: 1933. pp.vi + 94. LSE.

2,434. EVENING STANDARD. Is the dole abused? A series of 8 articles. London: January 21st-30th, 1925. LSE.

2,435. EXLEY, C.H. The guide to the law and administration of the needs test. Liverpool: 1933. pp.86. DHSS.

2,436. FABIAN SOCIETY. The Insurance Bill and the workers: criticisms and amendments of the National Insurance Bill, prepared by the Executive Committee. London: 1911. pp.19.

2,437. FABIAN SOCIETY. FABIAN WOMEN'S GROUP. How the National Insurance Bill affects women. London: [1911?]. pp.20.

2,438. FABIAN SOCIETY. RESEARCH DEPARTMENT COMMITTEE OF ENQUIRY INTO INSURANCE. Preliminary memorandum submitted by Sidney Webb. London: [c.1913?]. Fo. 18. LSE.

2,439. FABIAN SOCIETY. The working of the Insurance Act. London: 1914. pp.31. U.

2,440. FABIAN SOCIETY. Royal Commission on Unemployment Insurance, December 1930 - November 1932. London: 1933. pp.73. LSE. (Pamphlet Collection).

2,441. FAMILY WELFARE ASSOCIATION. The Unemployed Workmen Bill. [London: 1905?]. pp.8. LSE.

2,442. FEDERATION OF MASTER PROCESS ENGRAVERS. UNEMPLOYMENT COMMITTEE. Unemployment insurance scheme: report to the joint industrial council, 14th November, 1921. London: 1921. pp.7. LSE.

2,443. FOLEY, F.S. The National Insurance Act, 1911, as it affects employers and workmen. London, Manchester: 1911. pp.61. Bod.

2,444. FORESTER, R.F.   "The British National Insurance Act".
        Q.J.Econ. XXVI. (1912). pp.275-312.

2,445. FUSS, H. & CHRISTIE TAIT, D.   "Unemployment benefits and
        measures for occupying the unemployed in Great Britain".
        I.Lab.R. XXVII. (1933). pp.595ff.

2,446. GENERAL FEDERATION OF TRADE UNIONS.   Report of the special
        general   council   meeting,   to   consider   apprenticeships
        interrupted by the war, state unemployment insurance. London:
        1919. pp.23. LSE.

2,447. GIBBON, I.C.   Unemployment insurance: a study of schemes of
        assisted insurance.   London: 1911. pp.xvii + 354.   DHSS;
        CUL.

2,448. GIBBON, I.G.   "Compulsory insurance against unemployment".
        E.J. 20. (1910). pp.172-81.

2,449. GIBSON, R.S.   "The incentive to work as affected by
        unemployment insurance and the poor law respectively".
        Manch.Sch. 1. (1930). pp.21-7.

2,450. GILSON, M.B.   Unemployment insurance in Great Britain: the
        national system and additional benefit plans.   New York:
        1931. pp.xii + 560. DHSS.

2,451. GILSON, M.B. & RICHIES, E.J.   "Employers' additional
        unemployment benefit schemes in Great Britain".   I.Lab.R.
        XXI. (1930). pp.348ff.

2,452. GOUGH, G.W. "The economics of the Insurance Act". Engl.Rev.
        XI. (1912). pp.634-44.

2,453. GSELL, E.   D. Arbeitslosenverisicherung in Grossbritannien.
        Zurich: 1927. pp.xv + 156. LSE.

2,454. HALL, R.L.   "Unemployment".   In Barnett House Survey
        Commission, A survey of the social services in the Oxford
        district, 1, London: 1938. pp.99-109. LSE.

2,455. HANNINGTON, W.   The meaning of the Blanesburgh report.
        London: 1927. pp.15. LSE.

2,456. HANNINGTON, W.   A short history of the unemployed.   London:
        1938. pp.96. LSE.

2,457. HARDIE, J.K.   The Unemployment Bill.   London: 1905. pp.16.
        LSE.

2,458. HARRIS, J.   Unemployment and politics.   A study in English
        social policy 1886-1914. Oxford: 1972. pp.411. CUL.

2,459. HIGGS, M.   How to deal with the unemployed.   London: 1904.
        pp.xii + 202. LSE.

2,460. HILTON, J.   "The state and the unemployed: the report of the
        Royal Commission on Unemployment Insurance".   Pol.Q.   IV.
        (1933). p.16.

2,461. HILTON, J. "The public services in relation to the problem of unemployment". Pub.Admin. XV. (1937). p.3.

2,462. HOHMAN, H.F. "The status of unemployment insurance in Great Britain". J.Polit.Econ. XLII. (1934). pp.721-52.

2,463. [HUMPHRY, A.M.] The Unemployed Workmen Act as administered during the winter of 1905-1906; a paper read at a meeting of the Poor Law Workers Society June 25 1906. [London: 1906]. pp.24. LSE.

2,464. INDEPENDENT LABOUR PARTY. The abolition of destitution and unemployment. Manchester: 1910. pp.33. LSE.

2,465. INTERNATIONAL ASSOCIATION FOR SOCIAL PROGRESS. BRITISH SECTION. Memorandum on unemployment insurance in Great Britain. London: 1927. pp.14. LSE.

2,466. INTERNATIONAL ASSOCIATION FOR SOCIAL PROGRESS. Report of the British section on unemployment insurance and public assistance. London: 1932. pp.40. LSE.

2,467. INTERNATIONAL LABOUR OFFICE. British legislation on unemployment insurance. Geneva: 1920. pp.16. LSE.

2,468. JACKSON, C. "Insurance against unemployment". Fort.Rev. 107. (1920). pp.306-15; 478-87.

2,469. JENNINGS, W.I. "Poor relief in industrial disputes". L.Q.R. 46. (1930). pp.225-234.

2,470. KENNEDY, J.M. "National insurance and industrial unrest". Fort.Rev. 93. (1913). pp.465-77.

2,471. KERR, K. Royal Commission on unemployment insurance: evidence of the railway companies: statement of evidence on behalf of the railway companies. London: 1921. pp.34. LSE.

2,472. LABOUR RESEARCH DEPARTMENT. Standards of starvation: five years of government policy towards the unemployed. London: 1936. pp.15. LSE.

2,473. LEES-SMITH, H.B. "The Unemployed Workmen Bill". E.J. XV. (1905). pp.248-54.

2,474. LENNARD, R. "The government's scheme for insurance against unemployment". E.J. XXI. 83. (1911). pp.335-45.

2,475. LESSER, H. Unemployment insurance, with special reference to individual firms and industries. London: [1921]. pp.31. LSE.

2,476. LOCH, C.S. The state and the unemployed. [London: 1893]. pp.19. (Family Welfare Association Occasional Papers. Second Series No.21). LSE.

2,477. LOCH, C.S. La lutte pour le travail et les inemployes. Paris: 1906. pp.27. LSE.

2,478. LONDON AND DISTRICT RIGHT TO WORK COUNCIL. Lloyd George and unemployment insurance: an exposure of the unemployment proposals of the National Insurance Bill, and how it will affect the workers. London: n.d. pp.8. LSE.

2,479. LONDON TRADES COUNCIL. The unemployed regulations must go. London: [1936]. pp.7. LSE.

2,480. LOW, S.P. & COULES, ST. V.F. Unemployment insurance. London: 1933. pp.xi + 123. DHSS; LSE; CUL.

2,481. MACDONALD, J.R. The new unemployed Bill of the Labour Party. London: 1907. pp.15. BL.

2,482. MACMILLAN & CO. Unemployment insurance in Great Britain. London: 1925. pp.68. DHSS.

2,483. MACNAMARA, T.J. The great Insurance Act: addresses to working men. London: 1912. pp.xiv + 54. DHSS.

2,484. MARLIN, E. Le chomage involontaire et la legislation anglaise. Paris: 1924. pp.221. LSE.

2,485. MARRIOTT, J.A.R. "The problem of unemployment". Fort.Rev. 109. (1921)., pp.362-73.

2,486. MARRIOTT, J.A.R. "Labour unrest and insurance by industries". Fort.Rev. 112. (1922). pp.823-36.

2,487. MARRIOTT, J.A.R. "Comprehensive national insurance". Fort.Rev. 115. (1924). pp.697-707.

2,488. McVIE, A. Seamen and the National Insurance Act: a short practical guide to the position of seafarers and the special provisions that have been made for all classes serving in the British Mercantile Marine. Glasgow: 1912. pp.27. BL.

2,489. METROPOLITAN LIFE INSURANCE COMPANY. SOCIAL INSURANCE SECTION. British experience with unemployment insurance. [New York: 1832-33]. 6 parts. (Monographs, Nos.7-12). LSE.

2,490. METROPOLITAN LIFE INSURANCE COMPANY. SOCIAL INSURANCE SECTION. rev. ed. [New York]: [1935]. pp.83. LSE.

2,491. MILLER, F.M. "The unemployment policy of the National Government, 1931-1936". Hist.J. 19. (1976). pp.453-76.

2,492. MILLIS, H.A. & MONTGOMERY, R.E. Labor's risk and social insurance. London and New York: 1938. pp.453. CUL.

2,493. MILLS, H.V. Poverty and the state; or, work for the unemployed. An enquiry into the causes... of enfored idleness... London: 1886. pp.382. BL. Later ed. 1889. pp.193. LSE.

2,494. MINISTRY OF AGRICULTURE AND FISHERIES AND SCOTTISH OFFICE. Report of the Inter-Departmental Committee on Agricultural Unemployment Insurance. London: 1926. pp.107. DHSS.

2,495. MINISTRY OF HEALTH, INSURANCE DEPARTMENT. Instructions to inspectors. London: [1921]. pp.191 + xxviii. LSE. 1925. pp.200. DHSS.

2,496. MINISTRY OF HEALTH, INSURANCE DEPARTMENT. Supplement to the instructions to inspectors, unemployment insurance. London: [1923]. pp.60. LSE. DHSS.

2,497. MINISTRY OF HEALTH. INSURANCE DEPARTMENT. Unemployment insurance instructions. London: 1929. pp.88. DHSS.

2,498. MINISTRY OF LABOUR. National Insurance (Unemployment) Acts, Unemployment Insurance Acts and Out-of-Work Donations Scheme. Selected decisions given by the Umpire prior to 19th April 1928. London: series 1914-1928. 3 vols. DHSS.

2,499. MINISTRY OF LABOUR. Unemployment insurance. Decisions given by the Umpire respecting claims to benefit, 1914-1921. London: series 1914-. 4 vols. DHSS.

2,500. MINISTRY OF LABOUR. Unemployment insurance. Decisions given by the umpire respecting claims to benefit, 1922-1948, Vols.I - XVIII. London: series. 1922- . 18 vols. DHSS.

2,501. MINISTRY OF LABOUR. Instructions to employment exchanges and branch employment offices as to the issue of out-of-work donation policies and payment of out-of-work donation. London: 1919. pp.140. DHSS. ("Confidential" - librarian suggests application to Dept. of Employment.)

2,502. MINISTRY OF LABOUR. Interim report of committee of inquiry into the scheme of out-of-work donation. London: 1919. pp.6. (Cmd. 196). Final Report. pp.18. (Cmd. 305). Evidence (Cmd. 407). LSE.

2,503. MINISTRY OF LABOUR. EMPLOYMENT AND INSURANCE DEPARTMENT. Unemployment insurance. Arrangements with associations under section 17 of the Unemployment Insurance Act, 1920. London: 1920. pp.130. DHSS. 2nd ed. 1924. pp.78. DHSS. 3rd ed. 1927. pp.94. DHSS.

2,504. MINISTRY OF LABOUR. EMPLOYMENT AND INSURANCE DEPARTMENT. Circulars and Memoranda on the Unemployment Insurance Acts, 1920-1922. London: [1921-23]. 8 parts. LSE.

2,505. MINISTRY OF LABOUR. Report of the committee appointed to consider the position of out-workers in relation to unemployment insurance. London: 1923. pp.14. DHSS.

2,506. MINISTRY OF LABOUR. Report on national unemployment insurance to July 1923, with a short account of the out-of-work donation scheme (Nov. 1918 to March 1921) and appendices. London: 1923. pp.231. DHSS; Sq.

2,507. MINISTRY OF LABOUR. EMPLOYMENT AND INSURANCE DEPARTMENT. Code of general instructions to divisional and local staff regarding indirect claims to unemployment benefit. London: 1923. pp.53. DHSS.

2,508. MINISTRY OF LABOUR. EMPLOYMENT AND INSURANCE DEPARTMENT. Unemployment insurance appeals work. Code of general instructions to divisional controllers and appeals officers. London: 1923. pp.49. DHSS.

2,509. MINISTRY OF LABOUR. Report on an investigation into the personal circumstances and industrial history of claimants to unemployment benefit, November 5th-10th, 1923. London: 1924. pp.90. DHSS.

2,510. MINISTRY OF LABOUR. EMPLOYMENT AND INSURANCE DEPARTMENT. Unemployment insurance. Supplement for use of local education authorities in England and Wales administering unemployment insurance at juvenile employment bureaux, under section 6 of the Unemployment Act, 1923. London: 1924. pp.28. DHSS.

2,511. MINISTRY OF LABOUR. Unemployment insurance. Code of general instructions to divisional and local office staff. London: 1924. pp.544. DHSS.

2,512. MINISTRY OF LABOUR. Unemployment Insurance Acts, 1920-1924: extended benefit and dependants' benefit: codified directions for the guidance of local commissions and officers of the Ministry of Labour. London: 1925. pp.55. LSE.

2,513. MINISTRY OF LABOUR. Unemployment Insurance Acts. Selected decisions given by the Umpire... respecting claims for benefit and transitional payments, 1925-38, Vols.IV-XVII. London: series 1925-. 13 vols. DHSS.

2,514. MINISTRY OF LABOUR. EMPLOYMENT AND INSURANCE DEPARTMENT. Unemployment Insurance Acts, 1920-1925. Scope and insurability. Instructions for the guidance of divisional and local office staff and local education authorities. London: 1926. pp.59. DHSS; LSE.

2,515. MINISTRY OF LABOUR. EMPLOYMENT AND INSURANCE DEPARTMENT. Unemployment insurance. Unemployment book and contributions. Instructions to divisional and local staff and local education authorities. London: 1926. pp.113. DHSS.

2,516. MINISTRY OF LABOUR. Report of the Committee on Unemployment Insurance. (Blanesburgh Report). London: 1927. 2 vols. DHSS; LSE.

2,517. MINISTRY OF LABOUR, EMPLOYMENT AND INSURANCE DEPARTMENT. Unemployment insurance. Claims for benefit. Including the matter of claims for ordinary and dependants' benefit; claims register; proof of unemployment; continuity rule; computation and payment; closing of claims etc. Instructions to divisional and local staff and local education authorities. London: 1928. pp.191. DHSS.

2,518. MINISTRY OF LABOUR. EMPLOYMENT AND INSURANCE DEPARTMENT. Unemployment Insurance Acts 1920-1927. Analytical guide to decisions given by the Umpire respecting claims for benefit and out-of-work donation prior to 19th April 1928. London: 1928. pp.167. DHSS.

2,519. MINISTRY OF LABOUR. Unemployment insurance. Circulars, 1928-1943, numbers 129 to 581. London: 1928- . 2 vols. DHSS.

2,520. MINISTRY OF LABOUR. Report on an investigation into the personal circumstances and industrial history of 9,748 claimants to unemployment benefit, April 4th-9th, 1927. London: 1928. pp.93. DHSS.

2,521. MINISTRY OF LABOUR. NATIONAL ADVISORY COUNCILS FOR JUVENILE EMPLOYMENT (ENGLAND AND WALES, AND SCOTLAND). Second reports. Age of entry into unemployment insurance as affected by the school-leaving age. London: 1929. pp.23. (Cmd.3427).

2,522. MINISTRY OF LABOUR. EMPLOYMENT AND INSURANCE DEPARTMENT. Unemployment insurance. Consideration and rating of claims and benefit. Instructions to divisional and local staff and local education authorities. London: 1929. pp.147. DHSS.

2,523. MINISTRY OF LABOUR. Report of the Committee on procedure and evidence for the determination of claims for unemployment insurance benefit, (Morris Report), and minutes of evidence. London: 1929. pp.301. DHSS.

2,524. MINISTRY OF LABOUR. Unemployment Insurance Acts 1920-1929. Analytical guide to decisions given by the umpire rspecting claims for benefit before 13th March 1930. London: 1930. pp.230. DHSS.

2,525. MINISTRY OF LABOUR. Unemployment Insurance Acts 1920-1931. Supplement to the analytical guide to decisions given by the umpire respecting claims for benefit. London: 1932. pp.66. DHSS; LSE.

2,526. MINISTRY OF LABOUR. Local office code. London: 1933-1950. var.pag. DHSS.

2,527. MINISTRY OF LABOUR. Report of Departmental Committee on the operation of the anomalies regulations. London: 1933. pp.18. (Cmd. 4346). LSE.

2,528. MINISTRY OF LABOUR. Summary of Unemployment Insurance Acts, 1920-1934. London: 1934. pp.28. DHSS; LSE.

2,529. MINISTRY OF LABOUR. Choice of employment and administration of unemployment insurance, and assistance with respect to boys and girls under the age of 18. London: 1934. pp.12. LSE.

2,530. MINISTRY OF LABOUR. Memorandum on the establishment and conduct of courses of instruction for unemployed boys and girls, England and Wales. London: 1934. pp.38. LSE.

2,531. MINISTRY OF LABOUR. Memorandum on the institution of legal proceedings for the enforcement of attendance at authorised courses of instruction for unemployed boys and girls; England and Wales. London: 1934. pp.6. LSE.

2,532. MINISTRY OF LABOUR. Unemployment Insurance Acts: analytical guide to decisions by the umpire respecting claims for benefit. Unemployment Insurance Code 7, pt.1. Introduction and statutory conditions. London: 1936. pp.134. LSE.

2,533. MINISTRY OF LABOUR. Instructions regarding proposals for establishment, estimates of expenditure and other matters incidental to the provision of courses of instructions for unemployed juveniles. London: 1937. unpag. DHSS.

2,534. MINISTRY OF LABOUR. Instructions regarding registration and placing, labour clearing, recovery of advance of fares and local committees. London: 1937. unpag. DHSS.

2,535. MINISTRY OF LABOUR. Instructions regarding unemployment insurance. London: 1937. unpag. DHSS.

2,536. MINISTRY OF LABOUR. Divisional Office Code. Instructions regarding divisional office routine, local office arrangements, inspection, staff, premises etc., branch managers, local agents, and divisional cash discrepancies committees. London: 1938. unpag. DHSS.

2,537. MINISTRY OF LABOUR. Tables relating to employment and unemployment in Great Britain: regulations and industrial analysis for persons insured against unemployment. London: 1939-. LSE.

2,538. MINISTRY OF LABOUR AND MINISTRY OF NATIONAL INSURANCE. Analytical guide to decisions by the umpire respecting claims for benefit. Part 4. Anomalies regulations. London: 1935. pp.32. DHSS.

2,539. MINISTRY OF LABOUR AND MINISTRY OF NATIONAL INSURANCE. Analytical guide to decisions by the umpire respecting claims for benefit. Part 1. Introduction and statutory conditions. London: 1936. pp.134. DHSS.

2,540. MINISTRY OF LABOUR AND MINISTRY OF NATIONAL INSURANCE. Analytical guide to decisions by the umpire respecting claims for benefit. Part 2. Disqualification for receipt of benefit (excluding trade disputes). Recovery of benefit and travelling expenses. Special arrangements with associations. London: 1938. pp.110. DHSS.

2,541. MINISTRY OF LABOUR AND MINISTRY OF NATIONAL INSURANCE. (Unemployment Insurance Acts). Analytical guide to decisions by the Umpire respecting claims for benefit. Part 3. Disqualification for receipt of benefit: employment lost through trade disputes. London: 1938. pp.110. DHSS.

2,542. MINISTRY OF LABOUR AND MINISTRY OF NATIONAL INSURANCE. Analytical guide to decisions by the umpire respecting claims for benefit. Part 5. Dependants' benefits. London: 1946. pp.54. DHSS.

2,543. MOORHOUSE, E.G. & WOODHOUSE, J.R. National Insurance Act 1911. A handbook for employers. 2nd ed. Liverpool: 1912. pp.65. CUL.

2,544. MORLEY, F. Unemployment relief in Great Britain: a study in state socialism. London: 1924. pp.xix + 203. LSE; CUL; DHSS.

2,545. MORTON, C.A. The unemployed: a short play descriptive of their hardships and experience of poor law relief. Bristol: [1927]. pp.23. LSE.

2,546. NATIONAL ADVISORY COUNCILS FOR JUVENILE EMPLOYMENT. Second report: age of entry into unemployment insurance. London: 1929-30. pp.23. (B.P.P. 1929-30, XV). LSE.

2,547. NATIONAL CITIZENS' UNION. EDINBURGH BRANCH. The maintenance of strikers or persons locked out and their dependants. Edinburgh: 1927. pp.8. LSE.

2,548. NATIONAL CONFEDERATION OF EMPLOYERS' ORGANISATIONS. Report on unemployment insurance. London: 1924. pp.30. LSE.

2,549. NATIONAL CONFEDERATION OF EMPLOYERS' ORGANISATIONS. Unemployment Insurance (No.2) Bill, 1924. Memorandum. London: 1924. pp.8. LSE.

2,550. NATIONAL CONFEDERATION OF EMPLOYERS' ORGANISATIONS. Unemployment insurance: confederation's evidence to Royal Commission on unemployment insurance. London: 1931. pp.22. LSE.

2,551. NATIONAL CONGRESS AND MARCH COUNCIL. Next steps in the fight against the new Unemployment Act. London: [1934]. pp.8. LSE.

2,552. NATIONAL COUNCIL OF WOMEN OF GREAT BRITAIN. Domestic service under the National Insurance Bill. London: [1911]. pp.4. LSE.

2,553. NATIONAL INDUSTRIAL CONFERENCE BOARD. New York: 1922. pp.vi + 127. (Research Reports No.51). LSE; CUL.

2,554. NATIONAL JOINT COUNCIL REPRESENTING THE TRADES UNION CONGRESS, THE LABOUR PARTY AND THE PARLIAMENTARY LABOUR PARTY. Memorandum on unemployment insurance by industry. London: [1923?]. pp.32. LSE.

2,555. NATIONAL JOINT COUNCIL REPRESENTING THE TRADES UNION CONGRESS, THE LABOUR PARTY AND THE PARLIAMENTARY LABOUR PARTY. Special national conference on unemployment insurance and the report of the Blanesburgh Committee, etc. London: 1927. pp.14. LSE.

2,556. NATIONAL LIBERAL FEDERATION. Report of the National Liberal Federation committee on unemployment insurance and the report of the Liberal Women's unemployment enquiry group. London: 1933. pp.20. LSE.

2,557. NATIONAL UNEMPLOYED WORKERS' MOVEMENT. The Royal Commission's final attack on the unemployed: to action against more starvation; an examination of the late Labour government's Royal Commission on Unemployment's final proposals. London: [1933]. pp.16. LSE.

2,558. NEWMAN, T.S. Unemployment insurance. Summary of provisions of the "special scheme" applicable to the insurance industry. London: 1921. pp.23. DHSS.

2,559. NEWMAN, T.S. & LEE, A.G. Guide to unemployment insurance. London: 1925. pp.47. DHSS; LSE. Rev. ed. 1928. pp.47. DHSS.

2,560. NEWMAN, T.S. The insurance of women under the National Health Insurance Act. London: 1933. pp.83. DHSS.

2,561. NEWS CHRONICLE. Summary of the final report of the Royal Commission on unemployment insurance. London: 1932. pp.72. LSE.

2,562. NORTHCOTT, C.H. "Unemployment relief measures in Great Britain". Polit.Sci.Q. XXXVI. (1921). pp.420-32.

2,563. PETCH, A.W. (comp.). Unemployment Insurance Acts, 1920-25: an explanatory memorandum. Manchester: [1926]. pp.23. LSE.

2,564. PFISTER, B. Die entwicklung der arbeitslosenversicherung und der arbeitslosigkeit in England. Stuttgart: 1936. pp.viii + 196. LSE.

2,565. PORRITT, E. "The British National Insurance Act". Polit.Sci.Q. XXVII. (1912). pp.260-80.

2,566. PRICE, J.F.C. "Unemployment insurance". Pub.Admin. V. (1927). pp.160-75.

2,567. RADFORD, E.A. Unemployment: a suggested remedy. London: 1925. pp.12. LSE.

2,568. 'REGIONALITER'. "Administrative justice: a study of unemployment insurance courts and military service hardship committees". Pol.Q. XIII. (1941). pp.442-54.

2,569. REID, J. The economics of the Insurance Act. Middlesbrough: [1911?]. pp.8.

2,570. ROBERTS, A.C. "The government scheme of national insurance". Nineteenth Century. LXIX. (1911). pp.1141-56.

2,571. ROWNTREE & CO. LTD. Unemployment benefits: regulations. York: 1922. pp.16.

2,572. ROWNTREE, B.S. "Prevention and compensaation for unemployment". I.Lab.R. IV. (1921). pp.455ff.

2,573. ROWNTREE, B.S. & LASKER, B. Unemployment. A social study. London: 1911. pp.xx + 317. BL; LSE; C; S; CUL.

2,574. ROYAL COMMISSION ON UNEMPLOYMENT INSURANCE. First Report of the Royal Commission on Unemployment Insurance. London: 1931. pp.74. (Cmd. 3872). DHSS; LSE.

2,575. ROYAL COMMISSION ON UNEMPLOYMENT INSURANCE. Final report of the Royal Commission on Unemployment Insurance. London: 1932. pp.vii + 529. (Cmd. 4185). DHSS; LSE.

2,576. ROYAL COMMISSION ON UNEMPLOYMENT INSURANCE. Appendices to the minutes of evidence. London: 1931-2. pp.669. LSE.

2,577. SCHLOSS, D.F. Insurance against unemployment. London: 1909. pp.x + 132. CUL.

2,578. SELECT COMMITTEE ON DISTRESS AND WANT OF EMPLOYMENT. First report. London: 1895. (H.C. 111). LSE.

2,579. SELECT COMMITTEE ON DISTRESS AND WANT OF EMPLOYMENT. Second report. London: 1895. (H.C. 253). LSE.

2,580. SELECT COMMITTEE ON DISTRESS AND WANT OF EMPLOYMENT. Third report. London: 1895. (H.C. 365). LSE.

2,581. SELECT COMMITTEE ON DISTRESS AND WANT OF EMPLOYMENT. Final report. London: 1896. (H.C. 321). LSE.

2,582. SJOEBERG, F. & SIMON, H. Arbeitsvermittlung und Arbeitslosenversicherung in England: ein Vergleich mit Deutschland. Stuttgart: 1930. pp.63. LSE.

2,583. SMITH, SIR L. "Economic security and unemployment". E.J. XX. (1910). pp.513ff.

2,584. SMITH, T. Knight's guide to the Insurance Act for employers and cashiers. London: 1912. pp.11.

2,585. SMYTH, J.L. Unemployment insurance. London: [1930]. pp.7. LSE.

2,586. SNELL, J.S. & OTHERS. Statement prepared by the mayors of East Lancashire 1930, containing their suggestion that existing contributions made by employers in respect of national health and unemployment insurance should be made a national charge. Darwen: 1930. pp.13. [Typescript]. LSE.

2,587. SPENDER, H. "Unemployment insurance". Contemp.Rev. XCV. (1909). pp.24-36.

2,588. STEVENSON, E.F. Unemployment relief: the basic problem. London: 1934. pp.284. LSE; DHSS; CUL.

2,589. SWANISH, P.T. Trade disputes disqualification clause under the British Unemployment Insurance Acts. Chicago, Ill.: 1937. pp.ix + 73. (Studies in Business Administration, Vol.VIII, No.1). BL.

2,590. TAWNEY, R.H. The school-leaving age and juvenile unemployment. London: [1934]. pp.31. LSE.

2,591. TAYLOR, W. Social insurance and state provision for the unemployed. London: 1936. pp.13. DHSS.

2,592. TEELING, W. "Unemployment policy - lessons from abroad". Fort.Rev. 135. (1934). pp.167-76.

2,593. TILLYARD, F. (Assisted by F.N. Ball). Unemployment insurance in Great Britain, 1911-48. Leigh-on-Sea: 1949. pp.ix + 233. CUL; LSE.

2,594. TOYNBEE, H.V. "The problem of the unemployed". Econ.Rev. XV. (1905). pp.291-305.

2,595. TRADES UNION CONGRESS. Unemployment relief: the government's record and labour policy. London: [1923?]. pp.16. LSE.

2,596. TRADES UNION CONGRESS.   The administration of Unemployment Insurance Acts. London: 1923. pp.24. DHSS; LSE.

2,597. TRADES UNION CONGRESS & LABOUR PARTY. Unemployment insurance: principles of labour policy. London: [1926]. pp.20. LSE.

2,598. TRADES UNION CONGRESS.   GENERAL COUNCIL.   Administering unemployment insurance. London: 1929. pp.23. LSE.

2,599. TRADES UNION CONGRESS. GENERAL COUNCIL. Royal Commission on unemployment insurance: the Trades Union Congress scheme for state provision for unemployment benefit. London: 1931. pp.22. LSE.

2,600. TRADES UNION CONGRESS. GENERAL COUNCIL. Fair play for the unemployed. London: [1931]. pp.23. LSE.

2,601. TRADES UNION CONGRESS. The government evades its national responsibility: TUC criticism of the Unemployment Bill, 1933. London: [1933]. pp.12. LSE.

2,602. TRIBE, SIR F.N.   The educational provisions of the Unemployment Bill. Loughborough: 1934. pp.11. BL.

2,603. TRIER, S. "Insurance against want of employment: a short report on a Norwegian law and a Danish bill". E.J. XVII. (1907). pp.138ff.

2,604. UNEMPLOYED RESEARCH AND ADVICE BUREAU. Guide to unemployment insurance. London: [1939]. Part 1. pp.16. (National Unemployed Workers' Movement). LSE.

2,605. UNEMPLOYMENT GRANTS (VISCOUNT ST. DAVIDS') COMMITTEE. Report of proceedings. London: 1924-. LSE.

2,606. UNEMPLOYMENT INSURANCE ADVISORY COMMITTEE.   Unemployment Insurance (No.3) Act, 1931:   second report on draft regulations. London: [1932]. pp.10. (B.P.P. 1932-3, XV). LSE.

2,607. UNEMPLOYMENT INSURANCE BOARD.   Final report 1921-1948. London: 1948. pp.22. DHSS.

2,608. UNEMPLOYMENT INSURANCE STATUTORY COMMITTEE. Report on Draft Unemployment (Inconsiderable Employments) (Persons under Sixteen) Regulations. London: 1935. pp.19. LSE.

2,609. UNEMPLOYMENT INSURANCE STATUTORY COMMITTEE. Report on the remuneration limit for insurance on non-manual workers. London: 1936. LSE.

2,610. UNEMPLOYMENT INSURANCE STATUTORY COMMITTEE.   Unemployment Insurance Act, on remuneration limit for insurance of non-manual workers. London: 1936. pp.36. LSE.

2,611. UNEMPLOYMENT INSURANCE STATUTORY COMMITTEE. Report on the Draft Unemployment Insurance (1. Employments) Regulations, 1937. London: 1937. pp.14. LSE.

2,612.   UNEMPLOYMENT INSURANCE STATUTORY COMMITTEE. Report as to the extension of unemployment insurance to outdoor private domestic servants. London: 1937. pp.10. LSE.

2,613.   UNEMPLOYMENT INSURANCE STATUTORY COMMITTEE. Report as to holidays and suspensions in relation to unemployment insurance. London: 1938. pp.21. LSE.

2,614.   UNITED KINGDOM. Report on agencies and methods for dealing with the unemployed. London: 1893. pp.ii + 438. LSE.

2,615.   UNITED KINGDOM.   London Unemployed Fund: preliminary statement, etc. London: 1905.   pp.56.   (B.P.P. LXXIII). LSE.

2,616.   UNITED KINGDOM.   Report of the Queen's unemployed fund, 1905-6. London: 1906. pp.131. LSE.

2,617.   UNITED KINGDOM.   Return as to the procedure of distress commissions in England and Wales, and of the Central (Unemployed) Body for London under the Unemployed workmen Act, 1905, etc. London: 1907-14. (B.P.P.) LSE.

2,618.   UNITED KINGDOM.   Insurance against unemployment in foreign countries. n.p.: [1908?]. pp.30. LSE.

2,619.   UNITED KINGDOM.   Replies by distress committees to questions circulated on the subject of the Unemployed Workmen Act, 1905. London: 1909. pp.v + 81. (B.P.P. XLV). LSE.

2,620.   UNITED KINGDOM.   National Insurance Bill (Part 2. Unemployment): tables showing the rules and expenditure of trade unions in respect of unemployment benefits, and also showing earnings in the insured trades. London: 1911. pp.iv + 327. LSE.

2,621.   UNITED KINGDOM. Report of committee appointed to consider and advise with regard to the application of the National Insurance Act to Outworkers (Chair: E.F.G. Hatch). London: 1912.   Vol.1.   pp.21.   (Cd. 6178).   Vol.2.   Minutes of evidence etc. (Cd. 6179). LSE.

2,622.   UNITED KINGDOM. National unemployment insurance. Decisions of the umpire respecting claims to benefit. London: 1912-21. 4 vols. 1921-29. 8 vols. LSE; DHSS.

2,623.   UNITED KINGDOM.   Unemployment insurance...:   copy of regulations... under... the National Insurance Act, 1911. London: 1913. (B.P.P. 1912-13. LXXVIII). LSE.

2,624.   UNITED KINGDOM. National Insurance Act, 1911: Part 2 - Unemployment Insurance: Parts 2 and 3 of the Act with Schedules. London: 1913. pp.68. LSE.

2,625.   UNITED KINGDOM. Unemployment insurance: decisions given by the umpire respecting demarcation of trades, etc. London: 1913.   pp.viii + 309.   LSE; DHSS.   Another vol.   1914. Another vol. 1918.

2,626.   UNITED KINGDOM.   National Insurance Act, 1911:   pt. 2:

Unemployment insurance: instructions respecting the applications for and payment of benefit. London: 1914. pp.xiv + 222. LSE.

2,627. UNITED KINGDOM. Report of interdepartmental committee to consider proposals for facilitating the payment through the post of benefits under the National Insurance Act. London: 1914. pp.11. (Cd. 7245). LSE.

2,628. UNITED KINGDOM. Unemployment Insurance Bill, 1929: explanatory memorandum on clauses. London: 1919. pp.17. (B.P.P. 1929-30, XXV). LSE.

2,629. UNITED KINGDOM. Out-of-work donation: decisions given by the umpire respecting claims to out-of-work donations. Nos. 1-4270. London: 1919-1920. 3v. LSE; DHSS.

2,630. UNITED KINGDOM. Report on national unemployment insurance to July 1923, with a short account of the out-of-work donation scheme (November 1918 to March 1921). London: 1923. pp.231. LSE.

2,631. UNITED KINGDOM. Report on an investigation into the personal circumstances and industrial history of 10,000 claimants to unemployment benefit. London: 1924. pp.90. P.

2,632. UNITED KINGDOM. Report on an investigation into the personal circumsances and industrial history of 10,903 claimants to unemployment benefits... 1924. London: 1925. pp.127. LSE.

2,633. UNITED KINGDOM. Report of the interdepartmental committee on agricultural unemployment insurance. London: 1926. pp.107. LSE.

2,634. UNITED KINGDOM. Report of interdepartmental committee on migration and social insurance. (Maclean Report). London: 1926. pp.32. (Cmd. 2608). LSE.

2,635. UNITED KINGDOM. Report on an investigation into the employment and insurance history of a sample of persons insured against unemployment in Great Britain. London: 1927. pp.108. LSE.

2,636. UNITED KINGDOM. Report on an investigation into the personal circumstances and industrial history of 9,748 claimants to unemployment benefit, April 4th to 9th, 1927. London: 1928. pp.93. LSE.

2,637. UNITED KINGDOM. Report of the committee on procedure and evidence for the determination of claims for unemployment insurance benefit. London: 1929. pp.60. (B.P.P. 1929-30, ZXVII). LSE.

2,638. UNITED KINGDOM. Unemployment Insurance Bill, 1919: explanatory memorandum on clauses. London: 1929. pp.17. (B.P.P. 1929-30, XXV). LSE.

2,639. UNITED KINGDOM. Report of the committee on procedure and evidence for the determination of claims for unemployment insurance benefit and minutes of evidence. (Moon's Report).

London: 1929. pp.iii + 301. LSE.

2,640. UNITED KINGDOM. Extracts from the rules of registered trade unions in respect of the seeking of work as a condition for the receipt of unemployment benefit. London: 1929-30. (B.P.P. XXV). pp.20. LSE.

2,641. UNITED KINGDOM. National unemployment insurance. Specially selected decisions on benefit and donation, 1912-28. London: 1929. April 1928-March 1930. DHSS.

2,642. UNITED KINGDOM. Summary of Unemployment Insurance Acts, 1920-1930. London: 1930. pp.20. LSE.

2,643. UNITED KINGDOM. Unemployment Insurance (National Economy) (No.2) Order, 1931. London: 1931. pp.8. LSE.

2,644. UNITED KINGDOM. Appendices to the minutes of evidence taken before the Royal Commission on Unemployment Insurance. London: 1931-2. pp.669. LSE.

2,645. UNITED KINGDOM. Report by the commissioners appointed to administer transitional payments in the county of Durham. London: [1932]. pp.24. (B.P.P. 1932-33, XV). LSE.

2,646. UNITED KINGDOM. Report on the operation of the anomalies regulations. London: [1932]. pp.18. (B.P.P. 1932-3, XV). LSE.

2,647. UNITED KINGDOM. Report of the Government actuary on the financial provisions of part 1 of the bill relating to unemployment insurance. London: [1932]. pp.6. (B.P.P. 1932-3, XV). LSE.

2,648. UNITED KINGDOM. Final report of the Unemployment Grants Commission, 20th December, 1920, to 31st August, 1932. London: 1932-33. pp.35. (B.P.P. XV). LSE.

2,649. UNITED KINGDOM. Summary of Unemployment Insurance Acts, 1920-1934. London: 1934. pp.28. LSE.

2,650. WEBB, S. The war and the workers: handbook of some immediate measures to prevent unemployment and relieve distress. London: 1914. pp.23. (Fabian Tract No.176). LSE; CUL.

2,651. WEBB, S. & GARDNER, R. "The Insurance Act at work". Contemp.Rev. CVI. (1914). pp.41-51.

2,652. WHITESIDE, N. "Unemployment policy and the public record". B.S.S.L.H. 38. (1979). pp.58-9.

2,653. WHITESOLE, N. "Welfare insurance and casual labour: a study of administative intervention in industrial labour 1906-26". Ec.H.R. 32. (1979). p.507.

2,654. WILSON, E.C. "Unemployment insurance and the stability of wages in Great Britain". I.Lab.R. XXX. (1934). pp.767ff.

2,655. WITMER, H.L. "Some effects of the English Unemployment Insurance Acts on the number of unemployed relieved under the

175

poor law". Q.J.Econ. LXV. pp.262-88.

2,656. WOLMAN, L. English experience with unemployment insurance. New York: 1925. pp.15. LSE.

2,657. WOLMAN, L. "Some observations on unemployment insurance". Am.Econ.Rev. XIX. (1929). Supp. pp.23.

2,658. ZEFFERTT, C. Procedure in disputes, complaints, inquiries under parts I and III of the National Insurance Act 1911. London: 1913. pp.117. DHSS.

Unemployment Insurance, Ireland

2,659. GEARY, R.C. & DEMPSEY, M. A study of schemes for the relief of unemployment in Ireland. Dublin: 1977. pp.vi + 50. (Broadsheet No.14). DHSS.

2,660. IRISH FREE STATE. Commission on the Relief of Unemployment, 1927: First interim report. Dublin: 1927. pp.5. LSE.

2,661. [IRISH FREE STATE]. Exchange of notes between the government of the Irish Free State and the Swiss government respecting unemployment insurance. Dublin: 1930. pp.4. LSE.

2,662. MINISTRY OF NATIONAL INSURANCE. Unemployment Insurance (Eire Volunteers) Act, 1946: Report on the operation and completion of the Eire volunteer scheme. London: 1950. pp.3. DHSS.

2,663. NORTHERN IRELAND. Interim (and final) report of the Committee of enquiry on unemployment insurance and employment exchanges. Belfast: 1922. 2 vols. (Cmd. 2 and 11). LSE.

2,664. NORTHERN IRELAND. Industrial insurance: report of the Industrial Assurance Commissioner for Northern Ireland for the period ended 31st December 1925 (and 1926). Belfast: 1926-27. 2v. LSE.

2,665. NORTHERN IRELAND. Unemployment insurance: memorandum on financial resolution. Belfast: 1929. pp.7. (Cmd. 102).

2,666. NORTHERN IRELAND. Unemployment Insurance Act: selected decisions given by the umpire for Northern Ireland respecting claims to benefit. Belfast: 1931. pp.91. LSE.

2,667. O'SULLIVAN, J.J. "Unemployment insurance", in F.C. King (ed.), Public administation in Ireland. London: 1949. Vol.2. pp.225-35. LSE.

(f)   Unemployment Assistance

2,668. ANON. "The Unemployment Bill". L.R. 32. (1933). pp.276-8.

2,669. ANON. "The Unemployment Bill in committee". L.R. 23. (1934). pp.60-1.

2,670. ANON. "Unemployment Bill progress". L.R. 23. (1934). pp.78-9.

2,671. ANON.   "The Unemployment Act 1934". L.R.   23.   (1934).
        pp.124-6.

2,672. ANON.   "The administration of the Unemployment Act". L.R.
        23. (1934). pp.184.

2,673. ANON.   "The Unemployment Act, 1934". S.J.   78.   (1934).
        pp.907-8.

2,674. ANON.   "The Unemployment Assistance Act, 1934". S.J.   79.
        (1935). pp.223-4.

2,675. ANON.   "Social services 4:   Unemployment Assistance Board".
        L.R.   25. (1936). pp.179ff.

2,676. ANON.   "Social services 5:   public assistance". L.R.   25.
        (1936). pp.198ff.

2,677. ANON.   "Labour and public assistance". L.R.   26.   (1937).
        pp.40ff.

2,678. ANON.   "Unemployment assistance". L.R.   26.   (1937).
        pp.211-12.

2,679. ANON.   "New means test bill". L.R. 30. (1941). pp.42-3.

2,680. ANON.   "Unemployment assistance and supplementary pensions.
        New code of regulations". Lab.G. 52. (1944). pp.2-3.

2,681. ASHFORD, E.B. & GLEN,   A.P.   Glen's law relating to
        unemployment assistance. London: 1934. pp.xii + 176. Sq;
        DHSS; CUL; LSE.

2,682. BURRUP, MATHIESON & CO. LTD.   A great social reform.   The
        regulations of the Unemployment Assistance Board popularly
        explained. London: 1934. pp.20. DHSS.

2,683. CARR-SAUNDERS, A.M. "Current social statistics: unemployment
        and poor relief". Pol.Q. VII. (1935). p.111.

2,684. CARR-SAUNDERS, A.M.   "The Unemployment Assistance Board".
        Pol.Q. VII. (1935). p.538.

2,685. CLARKE, J.J.   Public assistance being the relevant sections
        from social administration including the poor laws. London:
        1934. pp.viii + 264 + xxix. DHSS.

2,686. CLARKE, J.J.   Public assistance and unemployment assistance.
        London: 1934. n.1. 2nd ed. 1937. pp.x + 342. BL; Sq.

2,687. CLARKE, J.S.   The Assistance Board. London: 1941. pp.28.
        LSE.

2,688. CLARKE, J.S. "The assistance board".   In W.A. Robson (ed.).
        Social security.   London: 1943.   pp.126-55.   2nd ed.
        pp.135-64. LSE.

2,689. CONNOLLY, J.   An easy guide to the new Unemployment Act.
        London: National Unemployed Workers' Movement.   [1934] .

pp.19. LSE.

2,690. DAVISON, R.C.   "The new scheme of unemployment relief".
        Pol.Q. V. (1934). p.376.

2,691. DAVISON, SIR R.C.   The new Unemployment Act popularly
        explained: a simple description of insurance benefit, the new
        unemployment assistance scheme, training and voluntary
        occupation. London: 1934. pp.32. BL.

2,692. DEACON, A.   "Thank you God, for the means-test man."   N.S.
        56. (1981). pp.519-20.

2,693. ELIAS, S.   Mass murder: an exposure of the new unemployment
        assistance scales. London: [1932]. pp.14. LSE.

2,694. ELIAS, S.   A simple explanation of the new unemployment
        assistance scales. London: [1935]. pp.15. LSE.

2,695. FORD, P.   Incomes, means-tests and personal responsibility.
        London: 1939. pp.ix + 86.

2,696. HANNINGTON, W.   The new Unemployment Bill: what it means.
        London: [1933]. pp.16. [National Unemployed Workers
        Movement]. LSE.

2,697. HANNINGTON, W.   An exposure of the unemployment social service
        schemes. London: [1934?]. pp.16. LSE.

2,698. HANNINGTON, W.   Why do they march?   Explaining what the new
        unemployment assistance scales and regulations will mean.
        London: [1936]. pp.12. LSE.

2,699. HANNINGTON, W.   Government's new attack upon unemployed
        workers: what the poor law "reform" proposals mean. London:
        n.d. pp.8. LSE.

2,700. HARRIS, C.   "The Unemployment Bill".   Nineteenth Century.
        CXV. (1934). pp.38-49.

2,701. HETHERINGTON, H.J.W.   "Public assistance".   Sociol.Rev. XXVI.
        (1934). pp.1-21.

2,702. INTERNATIONAL ASSOCIATION FOR SOCIAL PROGRESS.   Report of the
        British section on unemployment insurance and public
        assistance. London: 1932. pp.40.

2,703. KING, J.W.   To hell with the dole!   How to abolish
        unemployment! Scarborough: 1936. pp.19. LSE.

2,704. KUENZEL, I. Wachsender Staatsinterventionismus in England als
        Folge des Arbeitelosenpromlems. Heidelberg: 1936. pp.135.
        LSE.

2,705. LABOUR PARTY.   The iniquitous means test. London: [1933].
        pp.12. LSE.

2,706. LYNES, T.   "The politics of need".   N.S. 42. (1977).
        pp.513-514.

2,707. McKENZIE, G. Unemployment assistance guide. London: 1936. pp.55. LSE.

2,708. MILLER, F.M. "National assistance or unemployment assistance? The British cabinet and relief policy, 1932-33". J.Contemp.Hist. 9. (1974). (2). pp.163-184.

2,709. MILLER, F. "The British unemployment assistance crisis of 1935". J.Contemp.Hist. 14. (1974).

2,710. MILLETT, J.D. The unemployment assistance board: a case study in administrative autonomy. London: 1940. pp.300. LSE; Sq; CUL; DHSS.

2,711. [NATIONAL LABOUR COMMITTEE.] Unemployment assistance: the new regulations. London: [1936]. pp.8. LSE.

2,712. POLITICAL AND ECONOMIC PLANNING. "Unemployment assistance reviewed". Planning. IV, 75. (May, 1936). pp.1-10.

2,713. SMYTH, J.L. Notes on the unemployment assistance regulations, 1936. London: [1936]. pp.4. LSE.

2,714. STANFORD, P.T. "Unemployment assistance in Great Britain". Am.Pol.Sci.Rev. XXXI. (1937). pp.433-54.

2,715. THE ASSISTANCE BOARD DEPARTMENTAL WHITLEY COUNCIL (Staff Side). Social security. London: [1942]. pp.28. LSE.

2,716. UNEMPLOYMENT ASSISTANCE BOARD. Annual Report. London: 1935. (Cmd. 5177). 1936. (Cmd. 5526). 1937. (Cmd. 5752). 1938. (Cmd. 6021). 1939. (Cmd. 6700). 1944. (Cmd. 6700). 1945. (Cmd. 6883). 1946. (Cmd. 7184). 1947. (Cmd. 7502). DHSS; LSE.

2,717. UNEMPLOYMENT ASSISTANCE BOARD. Inquiry into the work of outdoor investigation (Organisation report No.2). London: 1936. var.pag. DHSS.

2,718. UNITED KINGDOM. Unemployment Bill, 1933: explanatory memorandum on clauses. London: 1933-34. 2 pts. (B.P.P. XXI). LSE.

2,719. UNIVERSITY OF LIVERPOOL. Report on co-operation between the unemployment assistance board, the local authority and voluntary associations in Liverpool. Liverpool: 1938. pp.64. LSE.

2,720. WARBURTON, E. & BUTLER, C. "Disallowed". The tragedy of the means test. London: 1935. p.vii + 160. LSE.

(g)   Employment Exchanges

2,721. ANON. "Labour Exchanges Act, 1909. General regulations made by the Board of Trade in pursuance of section (2) of the Labour Exchanges Act, 1909". Lab.G. 18. (1910). pp.39-41.

2,722. ANON. "Work of the Board of Trade labour exchanges in 1912". Lab.G. 21. (1913). pp.43-6. "...in 1913", 22. (1914).

pp.43-6. "...in 1914", 23. (1915). pp.43-6. "...in 1915",
24. (1916). pp.48-50. "...in 1916", 25. (1917). pp.54-7.
"...in 1917", 26. (1918). pp.53-5. "...in 1919", 28.
(1920). pp.61-2. "...in 1920", 29. (1921). pp.66-7.
"...in 1921", 30. (1922). pp.55-6.

2,723. ANON. "The migration of women's labour through the employment
exchanges". Lab.G. 25. (1917). pp.92-3.

2,724. ANON. "The committee of enquiry into the work of the
employment exchanges". Lab.G. 28. (1920). pp.665-6.

2,725. ANON. "Fifty years of the employment exchanges (1910-1960)".
Lab.G. 68. (1960). pp.1-3.

2,726. ANON. "The unemployed register". Lab.G. 68. (1960).
pp.423-4.

2,727. BERGSTROM, O. "Employment services in Britain: a Swedish
view". D.E.G. 76. (1968). pp.544-6.

2,728. BEVERIDGE, W.H. Labour exchanges in the U.K. n.p.: 1910.
pp.37. LSE.

2,729. BEVERIDGE, W.H. "Labour exchanges and the unemployed". E.J.
XVII. (1907). pp.66ff.

2,730. BOARD OF TRADE. Labour exchanges. London: 1914. pp.4.
LSE.

2,731. BOARD OF TRADE. Labour exchanges and unemployment insurance.
London: 1914-15. vols.16-21. LSE.

2,732. BOARD OF TRADE. Report on the proceedings of the Board of
Trade under the Labour Exchanges Act, 1909. London: 1915.
pp.244. LSE.

2,733. CHEGWIDDEN, T.S. & MYRDDIN-EVANS, G. The employment exchange
service of Great Britain. London: 1934. pp.xv + 310. LSE.

2,734. GERARD, C. Le chomage en Angleterre et le fonctionnement des
'labour-exchanges'. London: 1911. pp.138 + 154. LSE.

2,735. GIDE, P. Les bourses du travail en Angleterre. Paris: 1913.
pp.xvi + 123. LSE.

2,736. GOOD, T. Unemployment insurance and labour exchanges".
Westm.Rev. 171. (1909). pp.544-51.

2,737. HILL, P. The unemployment services. London: 1940. pp.116.
DHSS; CUL.

2,738. KEELING, F. The labour exchange in relation to boy and girl
labour. London: 1910. pp.vi + 76. LSE; U.

2,739. KNOWLES, G.W. Junior labour exchanges: a plea for closer
co-operation between labour exchanges and educational
authorities. London: 1910. | pp.32. LSE.

2,740. MACGREGOR, D.H. "Labour exchanges and unemployment". E.J.

XVII.   (1907).   pp.585ff.

2,741.   MINISTRY OF LABOUR.   Report of the Committee of Enquiry into the work of the employment exchanges, November 1920.   (Barnes Report).   London: 1920. pp.32. (Cmd. 1054). DHSS.

2,742.   MINISTRY OF LABOUR, EMPLOYMENT AND INSURANCE DEPARTMENT. Unemployment insurance.   Supplement for use of local education authorities in England and Wales administering unemployment insurance at juvenile employment bureaux, under section 6 of the Unemployment Act, 1923. London: 1924. pp.28. DHSS.

2,743.   MINISTRY OF LABOUR.   Instructions to employment exchanges and branch employment offices as to the issue of out-of-work donation policies and payment of out-of-work donation. London: 1919. pp.140. DHSS.

2,744.   SCAMMELL, E.T.   A national labour bureau with affiliated labour registries. Exeter: 1893. pp.16. LSE.

2,745.   SCHLOSS, D.F.   Report to the Board of Trade on agencies and methods for dealing with the unemployed in certain foreign countries. London: 1904. pp.xi + 236. LSE.

2,746.   SEYMOUR, J.B.   The British employment exchanges.   London: 1928. pp.x + 292. LSE; S.

2,747.   [UNITED KINGDOM.]   Report on agencies and methods for dealing with the unemployed. London: 1893. pp.ii + 438. LSE.

(h)   Family Allowances

2,748.   ANON.   "Family allowances.   A note on some industrial schemes". Ind.Welfare. XX. (1938). pp.359-360.

2,749.   ARTHUR, R.   State endowment for families, and the fallacy of the existing basic wage system. Sydney: 1919. pp.15. LSE; P.

2,750.   BEDWELL, C.E.A.   "Family allowances".   J.Comp.Leg.   22. (1940). pp.199-202.

2,751.   BEVERIDGE, SIR W.H.   Family allowances.   (MS., typescript, printed): 1921-1933. in 1. LSE.

2,752.   BEVERIDGE, SIR W.H. & OTHERS.   Six aspects of family allowances. London: 1927. pp.23. LSE; P.

2,753.   BLACKMORE, J.S. & MELLONIE, F.C.   "Family endowment and the birth-rate in the early nineteenth century". Ec.H.R.   1. (1926-1929). pp.204-213, 412-418.

2,754.   BONVOISIN, G. & MAIGNEN, G.   Allocations familiales et caisses de compensation. Paris: 1930. pp.vii + 352. LSE; CUL.

2,755.   BRAILSFORD, H.N.   Families and incomes: the case for children's allowances. London: [1926]. pp.16. LSE.

2,756.   BURNS, E.M. (ed.).   Children's allowances and the economic welfare of children. New York: Citizens Committee for Children. 1968. pp.200. DHSS.

2,757. CADBURY, L.J. A population policy and family allowances. n.p.: 1939. pp.8. LSE.

2,758. [CHANCELLOR OF THE EXCHEQUER]. Family allowances: memorandum by the Chancellor of the Exchequer. London: 1941-42. pp.11. (B.P.P. 1941-42, IX). LSE.

2,759. COHEN, J.L. Family income insurance: a scheme of family endowment by the method of insurance. London: 1926. pp.47. LSE.

2,760. FAMILY ENDOWMENT SOCIETY. Observations explanatory of the principle and practical results of the system of assurance proposed by the Family Endowment Society. London: 1836. pp.16. LSE.

2,761. FAMILY ENDOWMENT SOCIETY. The Family Endowment Society. [London: 1930?]. pp.4. LSE.

2,762. FAMILY ENDOWMENT SOCIETY. Family allowances today. London: 1941. pp.(4). LSE.

2,763. FARRELL, R.H. The origin and development of family allowances. London: 1961. pp.62. DHSS. ("Confidential - restricted to government service").

2,764. GRAY, A. Family endowment. London: 1927. pp.136. DHSS; CUL.

2,765. HALL, P. & OTHERS. Chance, choice and conflict in social policy. London: 1975. pp.555. DHSS; LSE.

2,766. HARBEN, H.D. The endowment of motherhood. London: 1910. pp.23. (Fabian Tract No.149). LSE; CUL.

2,767. HENDERSON, A. The cost of a family. Manchester: 1949. pp.33. DHSS.

2,768. HOFFNER, C. "Recent developments in compulsory systems of family allowances". I.Lab.R. XLI. (1940). pp.337ff.

2,769. HUBBACK, E.M. A new plea for family allowances. London: 1943. pp.8. LSE.

2,770. HUNTER, E.E. Wages and families: why workers should support children's allowances. London: [1929]. pp.8. LSE.

2,771. INTERNATIONAL CONGRESS ON FAMILY AND POPULATION, 1946. Allocations familiales: la mere au foyer; rapports, etc. Brussels: [1946]. pp.75. LSE.

2,772. JEWSON, D. Socialists and the family: a plea for family endowment. London: [1926]. pp.7. LSE.

2,773. KING, P. "Family allowances". Cath. Bull. 28. (1938). pp.310-2.

2,774. LABOUR PARTY. Motherhood and child allowances. London: [1922]. pp.16. LSE.

2,775. LAFITTE, F. "The history of family help". N.S. 25. (1973). pp.206-208.

2,776. LANCET, THE. Family allowances. Aylesbury: [1940]. pp.32. LSE.

2,777. LAND, H. "It all began with Pitt...". Poverty. (1967). (2). pp.13-14.

2,778. LAND, H. Large families in London. London: 1970. pp.154. (Occasional Papers on Social Administration No.32). DHSS; CUL.

2,779. LAND, H. "The family wage". Fem.Rev. 6. (1980). pp.55-77.

2,780. LAND, H. "The mantle of manhood". New Statesman. 102. (1981). pp.16-18.

2,781. MACNICOL, J. The movement for family allowances 1918-45: a study in social policy development. London: 1980. pp.xiii + 243 + bibliog. DHSS; CUL.

2,782. MARONEY, R.M. The family and the state: considerations for social policy. London: 1976. pp.142. LSE.

2,783. MELAS, R. "Consideration of the family factor in determining social insurance benefits". Bull. I.S.S.A. VI. (1953). pp.261-278.

2,784. NATIONAL INDUSTRIAL ALLIANCE. The case for and against family allowances. London: [1939]. pp.25. LSE.

2,785. NATIONAL UNION OF SOCIETIES FOR EQUAL CITIZENSHIP. National family endowment. Birmingham: 1920. pp.6. LSE.

2,786. NISSEL, M. "The family and the welfare state". N.S. 53. (1980). pp.259-62.

2,787. PICKARD-CAMBRIDGE, F.O. State maintenance. London: [1897]. pp.16. LSE.

2,788. PIDDINGTON, A.B. The next step: a family basic income. Melbourne: 1925. pp.iv + 68. LSE.

2,789. POLITICAL AND ECONOMIC PLANNING. POPULATION POLICIES COMMITTEE. Family allowances as a population policy. [Unpublished]: [1938]. pp.14. LSE.

2,790. POSADA, C.G. La prevision familiar. [Madrid]: 1929. p.16. LSE.

2,791. PRENGOWSKI, P. Workers' family allowances. London: 1831. pp.96. LSE; CUL.

2,792. RATHBONE, E.F. Wages plus family allowances. London: [1924]. pp.8. LSE. Rev.ed. 1925. pp.8. LSE.

2,793. RATHBONE, E.F.   The disinherited family: a plea for the endowment of the family. London: 1927. pp.xii + 345. Royal Statistical Society; DHSS; LSE.

2,794. RATHBONE, E.F.   The case for the immediate introduction of a system of family allowances, and alternative proposals for such a system. London: 1940. pp.16. LSE.

2,795. RATHBONE, E.   The case for family allowances. Harmondsworth: 1940. pp.118. DHSS; LSE.

2,796. RATHBONE, E.   Family allowances. London: 1949.   pp.293. LSE; DHSS.

2,797. RHYS-WILLIAMS, LADY.   Something to look forward to.   London: 1943. pp.232. DHSS.

2,798. RHYS-WILLIAMS, LADY.   Family allowances and social security. London: 1944. pp.24. DHSS.

2,799. RICHARDSON, J.H. "The family allowance system". E.J. XXXIV. (1924). pp.373ff.

2,800. SOCIALIST PARTY OF GREAT BRITAIN.   Family allowances: a socialist analysis. London: [1943]. pp.16. LSE.

2,801. STOCKS, M.D. The case for family endowment. London: 1927. pp.96. LSE; CUL.

2,802. TOUT, H. "A statistical note on family allowances". E.J. L. (1940). pp.51ff.

2,803. TRADES UNION CONGRESS AND LABOUR PARTY.   Joint Commission on the Living Wage etc. Interim report on family allowances and child welfare. London: 1928. pp.41. LSE.

2,804. TRADES UNION CONGRESS GENERAL COUNCIL.   Family allowances: text of the minority and majority reports issued by the T.U.C., and Labour Party Joint Commitee. London: 1930. pp.36. LSE.

2,805. UNITED KINGDOM.   Mothers' pension in the U.S.A.   London: 1918. pp.iv + 19. LSE.

2,806. UNITED STATES.   Laws relating to mothers' pensions in the U.S., Canada, Denmark and New Zealand. Washington: 1919. pp.316. (Children's Bureau 63). LSE.

2,807. VIBART, H.H.R. Family allowances in practice: an examination of the development of the family wage system and of the compensation fund principally in Belgium, France, Germany, and Holland. London: 1926. pp. x + 237. LSE; CUL.

2,808. VLASTO, O.   Foreign and colonial experiments in family allowances. London: 1924. pp.9. LSE.

2,809. WILLIAMS, J.E.R.   Proposals for simplifying and reducing income tax; also making provision for family allowances and social security in a draft post-war budget. London: [1946]. pp.19. LSE.

2,810. WOMEN'S COOPERATIVE GUILD. Notes for the study of family allowances. London: [1925]. pp.8. LSE.

(i)   War Pensions

2,811. HOGGE, J.M. & GARSIDE, T.H. War pensions and allowances. London: 1918. pp.463. DHSS; CUL.

2,812. KNAPMAN, H.J. The origin and history of war pensions appeal tribunals. London: 1953. pp.66. DHSS.

2,813. LABOUR PARTY. War pensions. London: [1950]. pp.22. LSE.

2,814. MINISTRY OF PENSIONS. The local war pensions committees' handbook, 1920. London: 1920. pp.164 + vii. DHSS.

2,815. MINISTRY OF PENSIONS. Report on the provision made for the care, maintenance, education and employment of children of officers and men killed or disabled in the Great War. London: 1935. pp.24. DHSS; LSE.

2,816. MINISTRY OF PENSIONS. Guide to voluntary organisations and funds assisting officers, men and women who served in His Majesty's Forces and their dependants. London: 1937. pp.111. DHSS.

2,817. MINISTRY OF PENSIONS. Compensation for civilians injured or killed in air raids. London: 1941. pp.16. LSE.

2,818. MINISTRY OF PENSIONS. War pension for civilians and members of the civil defence services. London: 1944. pp.32. DHSS.

2,819. MINISTRY OF PENSIONS AND MINISTRY OF PENSIONS AND NATIONAL INSURANCE. War pension appeals. High Court and Court of Sesson judgments 1944-1957. London: 1944-1957. 6 vols. DHSS.

2,820. MINISTRY OF PENSIONS. (CHAPMAN, S. & PRENDERGAST, R.H.). Report of selected war pensions appeals under section 6(2) of the Pensions Appeal Tribunals Act, 1943. Vols.1-5. London: 1945. 5 vols. DHSS.

2,821. MINISTRY OF PENSIONS. Retired, deceased or disabled members of the armed forces and dependants thereof. World War II. London: 1949. pp.44. (Cmd. 7699). DHSS.

2,822. MINISTRY OF PENSIONS AND NATONAL INSURANCE. Index to the reports of selected war pension appeals. Unpub: n.d. unpag. DHSS.

2,823. MINISTRY OF PENSIONS AND NATIONAL INSURANCE. War pensions. Memorandum for the guidance of the Ministry's overseas pensions agents in Australia. London: 1956. unpag. DHSS.

2,824. MINISTRY OF PENSIONS AND NATIONAL INSURANCE. Pensions for disablement or death due to service in the forces after 2nd September 1939. London: 1956. pp.51. DHSS. Rev. ed. 1958. pp.52. DHSS.

2,825. MINISTER OF PENSIONS AND NATIONAL INSURANCE. Report on war pensioners for the year 1957. London: 1958. pp.vi + 77. (HC 251). DHSS.

2,826. MINISTRY OF PENSIONS AND NATIONAL INSURANCE. War pensions: index to Treasury letters. Blackpool: 1959. pp.210. DHSS.

2,827. MINISTRY OF PENSIONS AND NATIONAL INSURANCE. War pensions arising from service in the forces after 2nd September 1939. London: 1965. pp.57. DHSS.

2,828. PARRY, E.A. & CODRINGTON, SIR A. War pensions: past and present. London: 1918. pp.x + 180. DHSS.

2,829. PENSIONS APPEAL TRIBUNALS. Entitlement appeals: notes for the guidance of appellants. London: 1973. pp.20. DHSS. Rev. ed. 1976. pp.10. DHSS.

2,830. RIORDAN, A. "The compelling presumption of attributability in British   war   pension   claims".   _A.L.J._   27.   (1953). pp.315-320.

2,831. ROBSON, W.A.   "Administrative Law. (Case Law)... Pensions Appeal Tribunal: views of the Minister are not medical evidence. Position of medical member". _Annual Survey of English Law._ (1945 - unpublished edition). pp.118-120. LSE.

2,832. TRADES UNION CONGRESS. War pension cases. London: 1946. pp.50. DHSS; LSE.

2,833. VETERANS ADMINISTRATION (U.S.). Medical care of veterans. Washington: 1967. pp.vii + 411. DHSS.

2,834. WAR OFFICE. Report of the Inter-departmental Committee on dependants' and disability pensions in a future Great War 1926-1930. (Paterson Report). London: 1930. pp.144. DHSS. (This is still classified as SECRET.)

2,835. WORLD VETERANS FEDERATION. Comparative study of legislation concerning veterans and war victims. Paris: 1962. 2 vols. DHSS.

Section 5 The Beveridge Report and Related Comment

2,836.   ANON.   "Social security: administrative   machinery and problems".   Pub.Admin.   XX.   (1942).   p.115.

2,837.   ANON.   "Social security plans in Great Britain".   I.Lab.R. LXVII.   (1943).   pp.46ff.

2,838.   ANON.   "The Beveridge report".   L.R.   32.   (1943).   pp.2-6.

2,839.   ANON.   "Anti-Beveridge".   L.R.   32.   (1943).   pp.18-19.

2,840.   ANON.   "Beveridge and the government".   L.R.   32.   (1943). pp.55ff.

2,841.   ANON.   "The new social insurance plan.   Proposals of H.M. government".   Lab.G.   52.   (1944).   pp.162-4.

2,842.   ABBOTT, E.   &   BOMPAS, K.   The woman citizen and social security: a criticism of the Beveridge report.   London: 1943.   pp.20.   LSE.

2,843.   ABEL-SMITH, B.   "Beveridge II: Another viewpoint".   N.S.   1. (1962-3).   (22).   pp.9-11.

2,844.   ASSISTANCE BOARD DEPARTMENTAL WHITLEY COUNCIL (STAFF SIDE). Social security.   London: [1942].   pp.20.   LSE.

2,845.   ASSOCIATION FOR PLANNING AND REGIONAL RECONSTRUCTION.   Maps for the national plan...:   a background to the Barlow report, and Scott report, the Beveridge report;   (with extracts). London: [1944].   pp.(iii) + 119.   LSE.

2,846.   BEVERIDGE, J.   Beveridge and his plan.   London: 1954. pp.239.   CUL.

2,847.   BEVERDIDGE, SIR W.H.   Insurance for all and everything. London: 1924.   pp.40.   DHSS.

2,848.   BEVERIDGE, W.H.   Social   insurance   and   allied   services: memoranda from organizations: appendix G to report by Sir William Beveridge.   London: 1942.   unpag.   (Cmd. 6405). DHSS.

2,849.   BEVERIDGE, W.H.   Social insurance and allied services: report by Sir William Beveridge.   London: 1942.   pp.244.   (Cmd. 6404).   DHSS.

2,850.   BEVERIDGE, SIR W.H.   The Beveridge Report in brief.   London: 1942.   pp.63.   DHSS.

2,851.   BEVERIDGE, SIR W.H.   Social insurance and allied services: Beveridge Report and Parliamentary Debate.   [A collection of papers]:   1942-1943.   var.pag.   DHSS.

2,852.   BEVERIDGE, SIR W.   Social security: some trans-Atlantic comparisons.   London: 1943.   pp.28.   DHSS.

2,853. BEVERIDGE, W. Power and influence. London: 1953. pp.448.
        CUL.

2,854. BUNBURY, SIR H. "Administration of the proposals in the
        Beveridge Report". Pub.Admin. XXI. (1943). pp.80-2.

2,855. BURNS, E.M. "Social security in Britain twenty years after
        Beveridge". Ind.Relations. (1963). pp.15-32.

2,856. BURNS, E.M. "The Beveridge report". Am.Econ.Rev. XXXIII.
        (1943). pp.512-33.

2,857. CALDER, A. The people's war. Britain 1939-45. London:
        1969. pp.656. DHSS.

2,858. CHAMBERS, SIR P. Forward from Beveridge. (The Beveridge
        Memorial Lecture 1969). London: 1967. pp.30. DHSS.

2,859. CLARKE, J.S. & COWARD, L.E. (eds.). Beveridge quiz. London:
        [1943]. pp.48. LSE.

2,860. CLARKE, R.W.B. "The Beveridge Report and after". In W.A.
        Robson (ed.). Social Security. London: 1943. pp.272-327.

2,861. COLE, G.D.H. Beveridge explained: what the Beveridge Report
        on social security means. London: 1942. pp.48. BL.

2,862. COLE, G.D.H. The Beveridge plan: where are we now? London:
        1943. pp.15.

2,863. COMMUNIST PARTY OF GREAT BRITAIN. Memorandum on the Beveridge
        Report and what must be done. London: 1943. pp.26. Sq.

2,864. COSTA, F.R. DA. O plano Beveridge criticado. [Madrid]: 1943.
        pp.79. LSE.

2,865. CURRAN, C. "Forward from Beveridge". Crossbow. 4. (1960).
        pp.25-26.

2,866. DAVISON, SIR R.C. Social security: the story of British
        social progress and the Beveridge plan. London: 1943.
        pp.62. LSE.

2,867. DAVISON, R.C. Insurance for all and everything. A plain
        account and discussion of the Beverdige plan. London: 1943.
        pp.32. DHSS.

2,868. FABIAN SOCIETY. SOCIAL SECURITY SUB-COMMITTEE. Social
        security: evidence submitted to the Interdepartmental
        Committee on Social Insurance and Allied Services. London:
        1942. pp.28. LSE.

2,869. GUEDES, M. O plano Beveridge. 2nd ed. Madrid: [c. 1950].
        pp.342. LSE.

2,870. HARRIS, J. William Beveridge: a biography. Oxford: 1977.
        pp.488. LSE.

2,871. HARRIS, J. "What happened after Beveridge?". N.S. 47.

(1979). pp.190-2.

2,872. INDUSTRIAL LIFE OFFICES. The Beveridge Report. Preliminary observations on the proposed changes. London: 1942. pp.16. DHSS.

2,873. INSTITUTE FOR STATISTICIANS. Forward from Beveridge. The Beveridge Memorial Lecture 1969 (Sir Paul Chambers). London: 1967. pp.30. DHSS.

2,874. KAIM-CAUDLE, P. "Moving on from Beveridge". Schriftenreihe fur Internationales und Vergleichende Sozialrecht. 3. (1979). pp.223-48.

2,875. KALDOR, N. "The Beveridge Report: the financial burden". E.J. LIII. (1943). pp.10ff.

2,876. KEITHLEY, J. "L'evolution de la securite sociale anglaise depuis le rapport Beverdige". Droit Social. (1978). pp.313-22.

2,877. LABOUR PARTY. Beveridge report: summary of principles and proposals. London: [1943]. pp.16. LSE.

2,878. LABOUR RESEARCH DEPARTMENT. Beveridge Report: industrial assurance. London: 1943. pp.32

2,879. LABOUR RESEARCH DEPARTMENT. Beveridge Report: what it means; a brief and clear analysis showing how if affects various sections, what changes it proposes, its financial basis, etc. etc. London: 1943. pp.16. LSE.

2,880. LABOUR RESEARCH DEPARTMENT. Social insurance: the government's plan explained; compared with "Beveridge" and with present practices; with a note on the price level and on the question "Can we afford it?". London: 1944. pp.19. Sq.

2,881. LYNES, T. "Beveridge and his blueprint". N.S. 63. (1983). pp.174-76.

2,882. MASS OBSERVATION. "Social security and parliament". Pol.Q. XIV. (1943). p.245.

2,883. MILHAUD, E. Le plan Beveridge. Geneva: 1943. pp.278. LSE; CUL.

2,884. MINISTRY OF RECONSTRUCTION. Social insurance, including industrial injury insurance. London: [1944]. p.31. LSE.

2,885. NATIONAL CONFERENCE OF FRIENDLY SOCIETIES. Social insurance and allied services. London: 1943. pp.35. DHSS.

2,886. NATIONAL COUNCIL FOR WOMEN OF GREAT BRITAIN. Memorandum for submission to the Interdepartmental Committee on Social Insurance and Allied Schemes. [London]: 1942. pp.9. LSE.

2,887. NATIONAL FEDERATION OF EMPLOYEES' APPROVED SOCIETIES. The Beveridge report on the social insurance and allied services. London: 1943. pp.23. LSE.

2,888. NEWMAN, T.S. Beveridge report: Lecture I. The object and basis of the scheme. Lecture II. Changes in existing schemes. Lecture III. Outline of the social security plan. London: 1943. unpag. (3 pamphlets). DHSS.

2,889. NEWS CHRONICLE AND THE STAR. Guide to the Beveridge Plan for social security. London: 1942. pp.64. DHSS.

2,890. OWEN, A.D.K. "The Beveridge Report: its proposals". E.J. LIII. (1943). pp.1ff.

2,891. OYLER-WATERHOUSE, W.A. Our fight for social security. London: [1943]. pp.41. LSE.

2,892. PAKENHAM, F. "The Beveridge Report: some reflections". Dub.Rev. CCXII. (1943). pp.21-31.

2,893. PETIT, C. La securite sociale en Grande Bretagne: le plan Beveridge. Paris: 1953. pp.71. LSE.

2,894. POLITICAL AND ECONOMIC PLANNING. Inter-departmental Committee on Social Insurance and Allied Services: memorandum of evidence by P.E.P. London: 1942. pp.(vi) + 45. (mimeographed). LSE.

2,895. POLITICAL AND ECONOMIC PLANNING. "Poverty ten years after Beveridge". Planning. XIX. (1952). pp.21-40.

2,896. RIDLEY, E. "The Beveridge report and public assistance". Pub.Admin. XXI. (1943). p.73.

2,897. ROBSON, W.A. Social security. London: 1943. pp.(ii) + 447. LSE. 2nd ed. 1945. pp.472. LSE. 3rd ed. 1948. pp.475. CUL.

2,898. ROBSON, W.A. "The Beveridge Report: an evaluation". Pol.Q. XIV. (1943). pp.150-63.

2,899. RUSSELL-JONES, A. "Workmen's compensation: common law remedies and the Beveridge Report". M.L.R. 7. (1943-44). pp.13-25.

2,900. SAXTON, C.C. Beveridge Report criticised. London: 1943. pp.32. DHSS.

2,901. SCHEU, F.J. El laborismo Britanico y el Plan Beveridge (Adonde va Inglaterra?). Buenos Aires: 1943. pp.179. LSE.

2,902. SELDON, A. "Beveridge: 20 years after". N.S. 1. (1962-63). (20). pp.9-12.

2,903. SERVOISE, R. Le 1er Plan Beveridge. [Paris]: n.d. [?1945]. pp.45. Le 2e Plan Beveridge. Paris: 1945. pp.35. LSE.

2,904. SOCIAL SECURITY LEAGUE. Beveridge strategy: report of the spearhead meeting held at the Livingstone Hall, London, on Oxtober 19th, 1943; principal speaker, Maurice Webb. London: 1943. pp.21. LSE.

2,905. WOOTTON, B. "Before and after Beveridge". Pol.Q. XIV.

(1943). p.357.

2,906. WOOTTON, B.F.   Social security and the Beveridge plan.
        London: [1944?].   pp.15.   LSE.

PART III   Social Security
Since 1946

Section 1   General Works

2,907.   ANON.   "National Insurance Bill".   Lab.G.   54.   (1946).
pp.40-2.

2,908.   ANON.   "National Insurance Act, 1946".   Lab.G.   54.   (1946).
p.214.

2,909.   ANON.   "National Insurance Act, 1946.   Draft regulations
submitted to national insurance advisory committee".   Lab.G.
56.   (1948).   pp.197-8.

2,910.   ANON.   "National insurance".   Lab.G.   56.   (1948).   pp.118-30;
pp.228-30;   pp.267-8.

2,911.   ANON.   "National insurance".   Lab.G.   57.   (1949).   pp.12,
43-4;   58.   (1950).   pp.196-8,   267.   59.   (1951).   pp.104-6,
190, 315, 427-8.   60 (1952).   pp.52-3, 93-4, 128-9, 239-40,
313-14.   61.   (1953).   pp.122-3, 201-2, 235-6, 272-5.   62.
(1954).   pp.121-3, 228-30, 412-14.   66.   (1958).   pp.12-13,
256-7, 295-7, 418.   67.   (1959).   pp.175-6, 252-3, 297-8, 336,
364-6.   68.   (1960).   pp.57, 104-5, 150-1, 191-3, 243-4,
282-3, 324, 361, 395, 428-9.   69.   (1961).   pp.11-12, 61, 106,
156-7, 199, 253, 288-9, 376-7, 450-1.   70.   (1962).   pp.10-11,
180, 226, 301-2, 420-1.   71.   (1963).   pp.59-60, 114, 315-6.
72.   (1964).   pp.105, 284-5, 330-1, 506.   73.   (1965).
pp.24-5, 219, 307-9.

2,912.   ANON.   "National Insurance Act 1946".   F.N.   (April 1952).
p.1.

2,913.   ANON.   "National insurance - teething troubles".   F.N.   (April
1953).   p.16.

2,914.   ANON.   "Notes on current events.   National insurance in the
welfare state".   Ind.L.R.   8.   (1953-54).   pp.2-7.

2,915.   ANON.   National insurance.   (Reprinted from volume 27 of
Halsbury's Laws of England, 3rd ed.).   London: 1959.
pp.649-918.   Sq.

2,916.   ANON.   "Social security.   Reasonable compromise".   N.S.   7.
(1966).   (192).   pp.21-22.

2,917.   ANON.   "National insurance.   Earnings-related short-term
benefits".   Lab.G.   74.   (1966).   pp.75, 129-30.

2,918.   ANON.   "A lawyer's guide to national insurance.   Part I - a
bird's eye view".   L.A.G.Bull.   (1974).   pp.216-223.

2,919.   ANON.   "Digest of recent social security legislation".
L.A.G.Bull.   (1975).   pp.122-123.

2,920.   ANON.   "Subordinate legislation under the Social Security Act
1975".   Welfare Rights Bulletin.   13.   (1976).   pp.9-12.

2,921. ANON. "Law and social work". Quest. 5. (1976). p.2.

2,922. ANON. "Social security under strain". N.S. 50. (1979).
p.194.

2,923. ANON. "Social insurance". T.U. Info. (Summer 1980).
pp.41-2.

2,924. ANON. "The Social Security (No.2) Act 1980". I.R.R.R.
(1980). pp.2-7.

2,925. ANON. "Developments and trends in social security 1978-1980".
Int.Soc.Sec.Rev. 33. (1980). pp.167-285.

2,926. ANON. "Summary of developments in the principal branches of
social security". Int.Soc.Sec.Rev. 33. (1980). pp.286-336.

2,927. ANON. "Benefits under attack". L.R. 69. (1980).
pp.258-59.

2,928. ANON. "State benefits: victim of Tory sabotage". L.R. 70.
(1981). pp.230-31.

2,929. ABEL-SMITH, B. The reform of social security. London: 1953.
pp.41. (Fabian Research Series No.161.). DHSS; LSE.

2,930. ABEL-SMITH, B. "National insurance and the national plan".
N.S. 7. (1966). (175). pp.17-18.

2,931. ABEL-SMITH, B. & TOWNSEND, P. The poor and the poorest.
London: 1965. pp.78. (Occasional papers on Social
Administration No.17). DHSS; LSE; CUL.

2,932. ALCOCK, P. "Social security under the Tories". Critical
Social Policy. 1(1). (1981). pp.102-106.

2,933. ALLBESON, J. (ed.). National welfare benefits handbook. 10th
ed. London: 1980. pp.168. DHSS. 11th ed. London:
[1981]. pp.ix + 149. DHSS.

2,934. ALLBESON, J. & DOUGLAS, J. National welfare benefits
handbook. 12th ed. London: 1982. pp.xii + 207. LSE.

2,935. BALL, F.N. National insurance and industrial injuries. Leigh
on Sea: 1948. pp.xvi + 508. DHSS; LSE; Sq.

2,936. BARR, N.A. & STEIN, B. Income support and the poverty trap:
revised September 1974. London: LSE and New York University.
1974. pp.15. DHSS.

2,937. BECKERMAN, W. & CLARK, S. Poverty and social security in
Britain since 1961. Oxford: 1982. pp.xi + 94. (Institute
for Fiscal Studies No.3). DHSS.

2,938. BOLDERSON, H. "Ambiguity and obscurity in policy-making for
social security". Policy and Politics. 10. (1982).
pp.189-301.

2,939. BOULTON, A.H. The law and practice of social security.

London: 1972. pp.xxv + 285. Sq; LSE; CUL; DHSS.

2,940. BOWRING, C.T. & LAYBORN LTD. National Insurance Act, 1959: a guide for employers. London: 1959. unpag. DHSS.

2,941. BOYSON, R. (ed.). Down with the poor; an analysis of the failure of the "welfare state" and a plan to end poverty. London: 1971. pp.130. LSE.

2,942. BRAND, G. "Les rapports du travail et la securite sociale dans les territoires non metropolitains... Grand-Bretagne. The law relating to labour conditions and social security in the United Kingdom dependencies." Congres Int. de dr.soc. (1958). pp.752-758

2,943. BRINKER, P.A. Economic insecurity and social security. New York: 1968. pp.x + 566. DHSS.

2,944. BROCKMAN, J. ST. L. (ed.). The law relating to national insurance (industrial injuries): the statutes, regulations and orders as now in force, annotated and indexed. London: 1961- Loose-leaf. Sq.

2,945. BROCKMAN, J.ST.L. The law relating to family allowances and national insurance. The statute, regulations and orders as now in force, annotated and indexed. Vols. I and II. London: 1961. pp.1208. DHSS; LSE; Sq. 2nd ed.rev. [edited by P.C. Nilsson]. 1973. 2 vols. LSE.

2,946. CAIRNS, M.B. "Some legal reflections upon the Gowers report 1949". Ind.L.R. 9. (1954-55). pp.116-125

2,947. CALVERT, H.G. "Parity in social security in Northern Ireland". Ir.Jur. 5. (1970). pp.70-88.

2,948. CALVERT, H.G. The welfare legal system: an inaugural lecture delivered before the University of Newcastle upon Tyne on 29 November 1971. Newcastle upon Tyne: 1971. pp.16. DHSS; LSE; CUL.

2,949. CALVERT, H. Social security law. London: 1974. pp.xxxviii + 318. DHSS; LSE; CUL; Sq. 2nd ed. [assisted by Susan V. Naylor]. 1978. pp. 1 + 549.

2,950. CALVERT, H. Cases and materials on social security law. London: 1979. pp.xxv + 376. DHSS.

2,951. CALVERT, H., GOODMAN, M. & PARTINGTON, M. (eds.). Encyclopedia of social security law. London: 1980. 2 vols. LSE.

2,952. CARR, C. "[Review of legislation]. United Kingdom: state insurance and health services". J.Comp.Leg. 30. (1948). pp.8-10.

2,953. CARSON, D. "Recent legislation: social security". J.S.W.L. (1979). pp.300-308.

2,954. CASEY, J.P. "National Insurance Act (N.I.) 1967". N.I.L.Q. 19. (1968). pp.83-5.

2,955. CASEY, J.P.   "Family Allowances & National Insurance Act (N.I.) 1968; Family Allowances & National Insurance (No.2) Act (N.I.) 1968". N.I.L.Q. 19. (1968). pp.477-8.

2,956. CASEY, J.P. "Damages and social security benefits - recent developments". Jur.Rev. 17. (1972). pp.22-31.

2,957. CENTRAL OFFICE OF INFORMATION. Social insurance in Britain. London: 1948. pp.31. DHSS.

2,958. CENTRAL OFFICE OF INFORMATION. REFERENCE DIVISION. Social security in Britain. 2nd ed. London: 1973. pp.47. LSE. 3rd ed. 1975. pp.iv + 37. DHSS. 4th ed. 1977. pp.iv + 44. DHSS.

2,959. CHESTER, T.E.   "Social security, work and poverty". Nat.West.B.Q.Rev. (Nov.) (1977). pp.38-46.

2,960. CHILD POVERTY ACTION GROUP. A policy to establish the legal rights of low income families: legal aid and advice. London: 1969. pp.8. (Poverty Pamphlet 1). DHSS; CUL.

2,961. CHILD POVERTY ACTION GROUP WELFARE RIGHTS WORKING PARTY. Which way welfare rights?   London: CPAG.   1975.   pp.38. DHSS.

2,962. CHILD POVERTY ACTION GROUP. Evidence to the Royal Commission on the Distribution of Income and Wealth. London: 1977. pp.60. DHSS.

2,963. CHILD POVERTY ACTION GROUP. Some notes for the second reading debate on the Social Security (No.2) Bill. [London: Child Poverty Action Group]. 1980. pp.27. DHSS.

2,964. CHILD POVERTY ACTION GROUP. Memorandum of evidence to the Social Security Advisory Committee from the Child Poverty Action Group. [London]: 1981. pp.10. DHSS.

2,965. CLAIMANTS UNIONS. Unsupported mothers' handbook. [Birmingham: 1974]. pp.17. LSE.

2,966. CLARKE, K. & MOCKLER, C.   An end to the earnings rule? London: 1976. pp.23. (CPC No.589). DHSS; LSE.

2,967. COETZEE, S. Flat broke: how the welfare state collapsed in Birmingham. [Birmingham]: Birmingham Welfare Rights Group. 1983. pp.51. DHSS.

2,968. COHEN, R. & RUSHTON, A.   Welfare rights.   London: 1982. pp.[viii] + 117. DHSS.

2,969. COLLEGE OF LAW LECTURES. Welfare law and practice. London: 1975. pp.80. Sq.

2,970. COMMUNIST PARTY OF GREAT BRITAIN. Memorandum on national insurance, presented to the Minister of National Insurance in connection with the five-yearly review of the national insurance benefits as provided in the National Insurance Act 1946. London: 1954. pp.20. Sq.

2,971.   CONSERVATIVE CENTRAL OFFICE.   What social security means to you. London: 1948.   pp.72.   LSE.

2,972.   CONSERVATIVE RESEARCH DEPARTMENT.   Social security and welfare: notes on current politics No.4.   London: 1969. pp.50-64.   DHSS.

2,973.   CONSERVATIVE RESEARCH DEPARTMENT.   Conservative Party conference debate on social security and health.   Third session.   8 October 1970.   London: 1970.   pp.48-55.   DHSS.

2,974.   COOPER, S.   Social security, welfare and benefit schemes: 1980-81.   London: 1980.   pp.[iii] + 63.   DHSS.

2,975.   CORDEN, J.   "Prisoners' rights and national insurance contributions".   <u>Howard J.</u>   15(2).   (1976).   pp.13-30.

2,976.   DELEECK, H.   "Efficacite et reforme de la securite sociale". [Effectiveness and reform of social security].   <u>Droit Social.</u> 9/10.   (1981).   pp.660-669.

2,977.   DEPARTMENT OF HEALTH AND SOCIAL SECURITY.   Reported decisions of the Commissioner under the National Insurance and Family Allowances Act.   London: HMSO.   serial pub'n.   var.pag. DHSS.

2,978.   DEPARTMENT OF HEALTH AND SOCIAL SECURITY;   CENTRAL OFFICE OF INFORMATION.   A guide to social security.   London: 1969. pp.60.   DHSS.

2,979.   DEPARTMENT OF HEALTH AND SOCIAL SECURITY.   "Social security in Great Britain".   <u>Int.Soc.Sec.Rev.</u>   XXV.   (1972).   pp.145-174.

2,980.   DEPARTMENT OF HEALTH AND SOCIAL SECURITY.   Explanatory memorandum on the Social Security Bill, 1972.   London: 1972. pp.25.   (Cmnd. 5142).   DHSS.

2,981.   DEPARTMENT OF HEALTH AND SOCIAL SECURITY.   Social Security Bill, 1972: report by the Government Actuary on the financial provisions of the bill relating to Great Britain.   London: 1972.   pp.30.   (Cmnd. 5143).   DHSS.

2,982.   DEPARTMENT OF HEALTH AND SOCIAL SECURITY.   Social Security Bill: regulation-making powers affecting occupational pension schemes and the way in which they might be used.   London: 1972.   pp.64.   DHSS; LSE.

2,983.   DEPARTMENT OF HEALTH AND SOCIAL SECURITY.   Social Security Act, 1973: notes on sections.   London: 1973.   pp.viii + 205. DHSS.

2,984.   DEPARTMENT OF HEALTH AND SOCIAL SECURITY.   "Social security research activities of the D.H.S.S."   <u>J.Soc.Pol.</u>   4.   (1975). pp.349-372.

2,985.   DEPARTMENT OF HEALTH AND SOCIAL SECURITY.   Seminar on social security research, Dormy House, Sunningdale, 7-9 April 1976. London: 1976.   unpaged.   DHSS.

2,986. DEPARTMENT OF HEALTH AND SOCIAL SECURITY. Social Security Bill: notes on clauses; House of Lords. [London]: 1980. pp.125. DHSS.

2,987. DEPARTMENT OF HEALTH AND SOCIAL SECURITY. The self-employed and National Insurance: a discussion document. London: 1980. pp.[26]. DHSS.

2,988. DEPARTMENT OF HEALTH AND SOCIAL SECURITY. Social Security Act 1980: notes on sections. [London]: 1980. pp.85. DHSS.

2,989. DEPARTMENT OF HEALTH AND SOCIAL SECURITY. Social Security (No.2) Bill: notes on clauses; House of Lords. London: 1980. pp.12. DHSS.

2,990. DEPARTMENT OF HEALTH AND SOCIAL SECURITY. Social security statistics 1981. London: 1981. pp.167. DHSS.

2,991. DEPARTMENT OF HEALTH AND SOCIAL SECURITY. Social security statistics 1982. London: 1982. pp.275. DHSS; LSE.

2,992. DEPARTMENT OF HEALTH AND SOCIAL SECURITY. Voluntary work and social security benefits. London: 1982. pp.8. DHSS.

2,993. DRABBLE, R. "A lawyer's guide to national insurance. Part IV - unemployment, sickness and retirement: some questions of law". L.A.G.Bull. (1974). pp.295-298.

2,994. DRABBLE, R. "Bars to benefit". Poverty. (1975). (32). pp.22-25.

2,995. DRABBLE, R. Contributory benefits: unemployment, sickness and death, maternity, pensions, child benefits. London: CPAG. 1977. pp.62. (CPAG Rights Guide 3). DHSS; LSE.

2,996. FABIAN SOCIETY. FABIAN WOMEN'S GROUP. The National Insurance Bill: a criticism. London: 1911. pp.28.

2,997. FERGUSON, T. "Poor, welfare and social services". In McLarty, M.R. and Paton, G.C.H. (eds.), A source book and history of administrative law in Scotland. [London]: 1956. LSE.

2,998. FIELD, F., MEACHER, M. & POND, C. To him who hath: a study of poverty and taxation. Harmondsworth: 1977. pp.254. DHSS; LSE.

2,999. FOSTER, G.H. Graduated national pensions as affecting local authorities. London: 1961. pp.xiii + 432. DHSS. (Supplement). 1961. pp.vi + [166]. Sq.

3,000. FULBROOK, J. Social security. London: 1980. pp.vii + 88 + bibliog. DHSS; LSE.

3,001. GAZDAR, J. National insurance. London: 1947. pp.ix + 74. 2nd ed. 1949. pp.vii + 96. DHSS; LSE.

3,002. GAZDAR, J. "National insurance. A survey". Ind.L.R. 6. (1951-52). pp.178-186.

3,003. GENERAL FEDERATION OF TRADE UNIONS. National Insurance Act, 1946. London: 1951. pp.27. LSE; DHSS.

3,004. GEORGE, V. Social security: Beveridge and after. London: 1968. pp.xiv + 258. Sq; DHSS; LSE; CUL.

3,005. GEORGE, V. Social security and society. London: 1973. pp.x + 154. DHSS; LSE; CUL.

3,006. GIBSON, G. "Wage relation in social security". N.S. 3. (1964). (84). pp.17-18.

3,007. GOLDING, P. & MIDDLETON, S. Images of welfare: press and public attitudes to poverty. Oxford: 1982. pp.vii + 283. LSE.

3,008. GORDON, A. Guide to the National Insurance Act, 1946. London: Labour Party. 1946. pp.36. DHSS; LSE.

3,009. GRIFFITH, J.A.G. "The place of parliament in the legislative process. Part II, 3. The National Insurance Act, 1946". M.L.R. 14. (1951). pp.433-436.

3,010. HARRIS, D.R. et al. Compensation and support for illness and injury. Oxford: 1984. pp.xix + 412. Sq.

3,011. HARVEY, A. & O'HIGGINS, P. "Rapport national... Grande-Bretagne. The role of fault in social security legislation". Actes du Septieme Congres International de Droit du Travail et de la Securite Sociale. (1970). pp.204-233.

3,012. HAUSER, M.M. "A survey of recent developments in social security in the United Kingdom". Soc.& Econ.Ad. 4. (1970). pp.115-36.

3,013. HILL, M. "Some implications of legal approaches to welfare rights". Brit.J.Soc.Wk. 4. (1974). pp.187-200.

3,014. HOUSE OF COMMONS LIBRARY, RESEARCH DIVISION. Social security benefits. London: 1972. fo.14. (Background Papers No.22). LSE.

3,015. HUDSON, A.H. "La securite sociale. Rapport national. Grande-Bretagne. Report on social security law". Congres Int. de dr.soc. (1958). pp.446-450.

3,016. HUNT, A. et al. Families and their needs, with particular reference to one-parent families... an enquiry carried out in 1970... on behalf of the DHSS. London: 1973. 2 vols. (Social Survey Reports (New Series) 466). LSE; DHSS.

3,017. IBBETT, J.P. Welfare law: refresher lecture. London: [Law Society]. 1976. pp.30. DHSS.

3,018. INDUSTRIAL LAW REVIEW. [Special issue on national insurance.] I,3. (August 1946).

3,019. INTERNATIONAL LABOUR OFFICE Systems of social security. Great Britain. Geneva: 1957. pp.xi + 73. LSE; DHSS.

3,020. INTERNATIONAL LABOUR OFFICE. Social security. A workers' educational manual. Geneva: 1958. pp.vi + 132. DHSS; LSE.

3,021. ISLINGTON FABIAN SOCIETY. About our welfare benefits. London: 1969. pp.22. DHSS; LSE.

3,022. ISTITUTO NAZIONALE DELLA PREVIDENZA SOCIALE. "Il plano del Partito Laburista Inglese per la riforma del regime di sicurezza sociale". Previdenza soc. 3. (1963). pp.809-825.

3,023. JORDAN, B. Paupers: the making of the new claiming class. London: 1973. pp.vi + 86. DHSS; LSE; CUL.

3,024. JORDAN, B. Poor parents: social policy and the "cycle of deprivation". London: 1974. pp.viii + 200. DHSS; LSE; CUL.

3,025. JORDAN, B. Freedom and the welfare state. London: 1976. pp.vi + 224. DHSS; LSE; CUL.

3,026. JOSEPH, SIR K. Social security: the new priorities. London: 1966. pp.36. DHSS; LSE.

3,027. JOSEPH, SIR K. A new strategy for social security. London: 1966. pp.10. DHSS.

3,028. KAIM-CAUDLE, P.R. "Selectivity and the social services". Lloyds B.R. 92 (April 1969). pp.26-45.

3,029. KAIM-CAUDLE, P.R. Comparative social policy and social security: a ten country study. London: 1973. pp.357. DHSS; LSE; CUL.

3,030. KEAST, H. Guide to national insurance. Leigh-on-Sea: 1949. pp.83. DHSS.

3,031. KEAST, H. Case law on national insurance and industrial injuries. Hadleigh, Essex: 1952. pp.xvi + 194 + [xi]. Sq; LSE.

3,032. KING, C.M. Advising the citizen: a handbook for workers in advice services. London: 1948. pp.xii + 121. LSE.

3,033. KINCAID, J.C. Poverty and equality in Britain: a study of social security and taxation. Harmondsworth: 1973. pp.278. DHSS; LSE; CUL. Rev. ed. 1975. pp.245. DHSS; LSE; CUL.

3,034. LABOUR PARTY. NATIONAL EXECUTIVE COMMITTEE. New frontiers for social security: a statement of comprehensive and radical proposals for the reform of our social security services. London: [1963]. pp.19. LSE; DHSS.

3,035. LABOUR PARTY. Social security. London: 1978. pp.[iii] + 38. (Labour Party Campaign Handbook). DHSS.

3,036. LABOUR PARTY. Social security: a Labour Party discussion document. London: 1981. pp.51. DHSS.

3,037. LABOUR RESEARCH DEPARTMENT. State benefits 1981; a guide for trade unionists. London: 1981. pp.32. Sq.

3,038.   LABOUR RESEARCH DEPARTMENT.   State benefits 1982:   a guide for
         trade unionists.   London: 1982.   pp.34.   DHSS.

3,039.   LAFITTE, F.   The future of social security.   Birmingham:
         University of Birmingham.   1966.   p.22.   (Discussion Papers,
         Series C. No.6).   DHSS.

3,040.   LAFITTE, F.   "The right means test".   N.S.   9.   (1967).
         pp.498-500.

3,041.   LAURIE, P.   Meet your friendly social security system.
         London: 1974.   pp.(8) + 190 + (7).   CUL.

3,042.   LEAPER, R.A.B.,   "New writing on social security".   Soc. &
         Econ.Ad.   7.   (1973).   pp.235-242.

3,043.   LESSER, H.   "Supplementary schemes under section 17 of the
         National Insurance Act".   Ind.L.R.   2.   (1947-48).   pp.64-70.

3,044.   LESSER, H.   "Some practical aspects of supplementary benefit
         schemes".   Ind.L.R.   2.   (1947-48).   pp.127-135.

3,045.   LISTER, R.   Social security: the case for reform.   London:
         1975.   pp.72.   (Poverty Pamphlet 22).   DHSS; LSE; CUL.

3,046.   LISTER, R.   Welfare benefits.   London: 1981.   p.xxvi + 284.
         DHSS.

3,047.   LOWE, R.   Welfare law - some paths through the jungle.
         London: 1974.   pp.23.   Sq.

3,048.   LYNES, T.   "The National Insurance Act, 1959".   M.L.R.   23.
         (1960).   pp.52-56.

3,049.   LYNES, T.   "Social security research".   In Michael Young
         (ed.).   Forecasting and the social sciences.   London: 1968.
         pp.ix + 166.   DHSS; LSE.

3,050.   LYNES, T.   "Social security".   N.S.   20.   (1972).   pp.183-184.

3,051.   LYNES, T.   "Muddling along on social security".   N.S.   49.
         (1979).   pp.78-9.

3,052.   MacDONALD, J.   Information and welfare benefits in Inverclyde:
         an evaluation.   Edinburgh: 1975.   pp.ii + 13.   DHSS.

3,053.   MANCHESTER AND SALFORD COUNCIL OF SOCIAL SERVICE.   Handbook of
         information for the use of social workers in the Manchester
         area.   Manchester: 1952.   pp.151.   DHSS.

3,054.   MANCHESTER AND SALFORD COUNCIL OF SOCIAL SERVICE.   Handbook of
         social services.   Manchester: 1966.   pp.156.   DHSS.

3,055.   MARSH, D.C.   National insurance and assistance in Great
         Britain.   London: 1950.   pp.xii + 187.   DHSS; CUL; LSE.

3,056.   MATTHEWMAN, J. & LAMBERT, N.   Tolley's social security and
         state benefits.   Croydon: 1982.   pp.xii + 433.   DHSS.

3,057. MAZZONI, G. "The relative character of the distinction between risk and need in social insurance". Bull. I.S.S.A. XII. (1959). pp.194-300.

3,058. McLAUGHLIN, R. "National Insurance (Old Persons' and Widows' Pensions and Attendance Allowance) Act (N.I.) 1970". N.I.L.Q. 21. (1971). pp.228-33.

3,059. METCALF, D. "Goodbye to national insurance". N.S. 52. (1980). pp.349-50.

3,060. MILLER, J.G. "Family law and the welfare state". Cambrian L.R. 6. (1975). pp.143-56.

3,061. MINISTRY OF NATIONAL INSURANCE. Working parties and committees digest 1946/47. Unpub. unpag. DHSS.

3,062. MINISTRY OF NATIONAL INSURANCE. National Insurance Act, 1946: preliminary draft of the National Insurance (Local Advisory Committees) Regulations, 1948, etc. London: 1947. pp.2. LSE.

3,063. MINISTRY OF NATIONAL INSURANCE. National Insurance Act, 1946: preliminary draft of the National Insurance (Claims and Payments) Regulations, 1948, properly to be made under sections 20(2)(b), 28, 46 and 52(2) of the... Act, etc. London: 1947. pp.11. LSE.

3,064. MINISTRY OF NATIONAL INSURANCE. Commonwealth Conference on national insurance held in London, 1947. London: 1947. pp.12. DHSS.

3,065. MINISTRY OF NATIONAL INSURANCE. Llawlyfr y teulu ynglyn ag yswiriant cenedlaethol. London: 1948. pp.35. DHSS.

3,066. MINISTRY OF NATIONAL INSURANCE. Family guide to the national insurance scheme. London: 1948. pp.31. DHSS.

3,067. MINISTRY OF NATIONAL INSURANCE. Domestic workers and national insurance. London: 1949. pp.6. DHSS.

3,068. MINISTRY OF NATIONAL INSURANCE. INFORMATION DIVISION. Background notes on the national insurance scheme. London: [1949]. LSE.

3,069. MINISTRY OF NATIONAL INSURANCE. National Insurance Acts: Selected decisions of the Minister on questions of classification and insurability. London: 1950- LSE.

3,070. MINISTRY OF NATIONAL INSURANCE. Index to decisions given by the commissioner on claims for benefit and other questions, etc. London: 1951. pp.ix + 208. LSE.

3,071. MINISTRY OF NATIONAL INSURANCE. INFORMATION DIVISION. Widows pensions. London: 1952. pp.3. (Pensions No.2). DHSS.

3,072. MINISTRY OF NATIONAL INSURANCE. INFORMATION DIVISION. Retirement pensions. 1. Major provisions. London: 1952. pp.7. (Pensions No.1). DHSS.

3,073. MINISTRY OF NATIONAL INSURANCE.   INFORMATION DIVISION.
Sickness benefit. London: 1952. pp.6. (Benefits No.1).
DHSS.

3,074. MINISTRY OF NATIONAL INSURANCE.   INFORMATION DIVISION.
Maternity benefit. London: 1952. pp.4. (Benefits No.2).
DHSS.

3,075. MINISTRY OF NATIONAL INSURANCE. INFORMATION DIVISION. Death
grant. London: 1952. pp.6. (Benefits No.3). DHSS.

3,076. MINISTRY OF NATIONAL INSURANCE. INFORMATION DIVISION. How,
when and where to claim benefit. London: 1952. pp.12.
(Benefits No.4). DHSS. Rev. ed. 1958. DHSS.

3,077. MINISTRY OF NATIONAL INSURANCE.   INFORMATION DIVISION.
Overlapping benefits, allowances and pensions. London: 1952.
pp.8. (Benefits No.5). DHSS. Rev. ed. 1958. DHSS.

3,078. MINISTRY OF NATIONAL INSURANCE.   INFORMATION DIVISION.
Benefits for dependants. London: 1952. pp.6. (Benefits
No.6). DHSS.

3,079. MINISTRY OF NATIONAL INSURANCE. National insurance scheme
review.   Departmental working group No.2: main report.
(Chairman: J.W. Dick). London: 1953. pp.vi + 180. (ES 68
61/1A). DHSS. ("Confidential").

3,080. MINISTRY OF PENSIONS AND NATIONAL INSURANCE. Social security
in Britain.   The scope and function of state insurance.
Background material No.2. London: 1954. pp.14. DHSS.

3,081. MINISTRY OF PENSIONS AND NATIONAL INSURANCE.   Reciprocal
arrangements with other countries as at 22.4.55.   London:
1955. unpag. (Circular 38/1955). DHSS.

3,082. MINISTRY OF PENSIONS AND NATIONAL INSURANCE, AND CENTRAL
OFFICE OF INFORMATION.   Everybody's guide to national
insurance. London: 1955. pp.32. LSE.

3,083. MINISTRY OF PENSIONS AND NATIONAL INSURANCE.   Reciprocal
arrangements with other countries as at 7.12.56.   London:
1956. unpag. (Circular 125/1956). DHSS.

3,084. MINISTRY OF PENSIONS AND NATIONAL INSURANCE.   Notes on
overlapping benefits, allowances and pensions. London: 1958.
pp.8. DHSS.

3,085. MINISTRY OF PENSIONS AND NATIONAL INSURANCE. WESTERN EUROPEAN
UNION SOCIAL SECURITY SUB-COMMITTEE. Social security for the
older worker, United Kingdom collective report.   London:
1958. pp.8 + 15. DHSS.

3,086. MINISTRY OF RECONSTRUCTION.   Social insurance.   Part I.
London: 1944. pp.64. (Cmd. 6550). DHSS.

3,087. MINISTRY OF SOCIAL SECURITY.   Everybody's guide to social
security. London: 1967. pp.60. DHSS.

3,088. MISHRA, R.   Society and social policy: theoretical perspectives on welfare. London: Macmillan, 1977. pp.188. CUL.

3,089. MOORE, P. "A lawyer's guide to national insurance. Part II - some overall legal concepts". L.A.G.Bull. (1974). pp.240-2.

3,090. MOORE, P. & DRABBLE, R. "A lawyer's guide to national insurance. Part III - the remaining overall legal concepts and family allowances". L.A.G.Bull. (1974). pp.268-271.

3,091. MOORE, P. Students' rights: social security, other benefits and housing. London: 1975. pp.61. (Rights Guide No.2). DHSS; LSE.

3,092. MORGAN, D. "Children in care and social security". J.S.W.L. (1981). pp.196-214.

3,093. MORRISON, A.C.L. & OTHERS. Outlines of law for social workers. London: 1948. pp.vii + 323 + 26. LSE; CUL.

3,094. MOSS, J. The health and welfare services handbook. 3rd ed. Ipswich: 1962. pp.397. DHSS.

3,095. MOSS, P. Welfare rights, project two: (a research report on public knowledge, misconceptions and attitudes about four welfare benefits). Liverpool: 1970. pp.17. LSE.

3,096. MOUNTNEY, G. "Welfare rites to realise rights". S.W.T. 9. (20). (1978). pp.20-21.

3,097. NATIONAL ASSOCIATION OF PENSION FUNDS. Memorandum to the Secretary of State for Social Services on the proposed earnings-related social security scheme. London: 1969. pp.14. DHSS.

3,098. NATIONAL CONSUMER COUNCIL. Social security: a consumer review: working papers of the joint Consumer Councils' social security committee. London: 1983. 1 portfolio. DHSS.

3,099. NATIONAL CONSUMER COUNCIL. Means tested benefits: a discussion paper. London: 1976. pp.111. (Discussion Paper 3). DHSS; LSE.

3,100. NATIONAL FEDERATION OF CLAIMANTS UNIONS. Claimants Union guidebook: a handbook from the Claimants Union movement. London: 1976. pp.46. DHSS.

3,101. NATIONAL INSURANCE FUND. Long-term financial estimates: report by the Government Actuary on the first quinquennial review under sectin 137 of the Social Security Act 1975. (H.C. 451, 1981/82). DHSS.

3,102. NELIGAN, D. "Some aspects of social security law". S.J. 113. (1969). p.883.

3,103. NEWMAN, D. Sampling techniques used in the collection of statistics of family allowances, national insurance and industrial injuries benefits in Great Britain. Rome: ISSA. 1956. pp.16. DHSS.

3,104. NEWMAN, T.S.   Guide to government's proposals for national insurance. London: 1945. pp.31. DHSS.

3,105. NEWMAN, T.S.   Digest of British social insurance... national insurance, family allowances... London: 1947. pp.xxx + 322. Supplement 1 [etc.]. London: 1947-. pp.xii + 123. CUL; DHSS.

3,106. NORTHERN IRELAND. National Insurance Bill (Northern Ireland): explanatory memorandum, etc. Belfast: 1946. pp.11. (Cmd. 237). LSE.

3,107. NORTHERN IRELAND. MINISTRY OF LABOUR AND NATIONAL INSURANCE. Family guide to the national insurance scheme. Belfast: 1948. pp.31. DHSS.

3,108. NORTHERN IRELAND. Family Allowances and National Insurance Acts (Northern Ireland), 1945 to 1964: Decisions by the commissioner (formerly by the umpire). Belfast: 1948-61. 1964-. pp. irreg. LSE; QUB.

3,109. NORTHERN IRELAND. National Insurance Act (N. Ireland), 1946: report by the Government Actuary on the first quinquennial review. Belfast: [1955]. (H.C. 1155). LSE.

3,110. NORTHERN IRELAND. MINISTRY OF LABOUR AND NATIONAL INSURANCE. Index to decisions given by the Commissioner/Umpire under the Family Allowances, National Insurance and Industrial Injuries Acts (Northern Ireland). Belfast: 1964. unpag. DHSS.

3,111. NORTHERN IRELAND. MINISTRY OF LABOUR AND NATIONAL INSURANCE. Index to decisions given by the commissioner/umpire under the Family Allowances, National Insurance and Industrial Injuries Acts (Northern Ireland). Belfast: 1974. unpag. DHSS.

3,112. NORTHERN IRELAND. DEPARTMENT OF HEALTH AND SOCIAL SERVICES. Family benefits and pensions in Northern Ireland. November 1976. Belfast: 1976., pp.48. DHSS. 2nd ed. 1975. pp.44. LSE.

3,113. NORTHERN IRELAND. DEPARTMENT OF HEALTH AND SOCIAL SERVICES. Family guide to the cash social security benefits and related services in Northern Ireland. Belfast: 1981. pp.62. DHSS.

3,114. NOTTING HILL SOCIAL COUNCIL.   "...A rambling Gothic pile..." the report of an independent enquiry into the functioning of the social security system. (Chairman: Elizabeth Winter). London: 1973. pp.30. DHSS.

3,115. OGUS, A.I. & BARENDT, E.M.   The law of social security. London: 1978. pp.lxxiii + 714. Sq. 2nd ed. 1982. pp.lxxvi + 664. LSE. Supplement. 1983. pp.xviii + 40. CUL; LSE; DHSS.

3,116. O'HIGGINS, P. "The efficacy of social security". In European Institute of Social Security, 1970 Year Book.   [Leuven] 1970. pp.63-75. Sq.

3,117. OUTER CIRCLE POLICY UNIT.   Beyond Beveridge: taxation, welfare and poverty. [London]: 1978. pp.iii + 84. DHSS.

3,118. OWEN, D. Guide to the National Insurance Act, 1946. London: 1948. pp.32. LSE.

3,119. PARROTT, A.L. Insurance principles and social security legislation. [1967]. unpub. pp.47. DHSS.

3,120. PARTINGTON, M. "Social Security Act 1979". I.L.J. 8. (1979). pp.186-7.

3,121. PARTINGTON, M. "Social Security Act 1980". I.L.J. 9. (1980). pp.197-9.

3,122. PARTINGTON, M. "Rules and Discretion in British social security law". In In Memoriam Sir Otto Kahn-Freund. (Gamillscheg, F. et al. (eds.)). Munich: 1980. pp.619-630.

3,123. PARTINGTON, M. & JOWELL, J. (eds.). Welfare law and policy. London: 1979. pp.xi + 266. LSE; CUL.

3,124. PEACOCK, A.T. "The national insurance funds". Economica. 16. (1949). pp.228-242.

3,125. PEARL, D. "Social security and the ethnic minorities". J.S.W.L. (1978). pp.24-35.

3,126. PEARL, D. & GRAY, K. Social welfare law. London: 1981. pp.[x] + 308 + bibliog. DHSS.

3,127. PERRIN, G. "The future of social security". Int.Soc.Sec.Rev. XXII. (1969). pp.3-27.

3,128. POLLARD, D. (gen.ed.). Social welfare law. London: 1977. Looseleaf, update by supplements and noter-up. Sq; DHSS; LSE.

3,129. POTTER, D.C.L. The National Insurance Act, 1946. With general introduction and annotations... London: 1946. pp.v + 269. BL. 2nd ed. by the author and D.H. Stansfield, entitled National insurance). 1949. pp.xix + 553. Sq; DHSS.

3,130. PRENTICE, R.E. "National insurance". In P. Archer (ed.). Social welfare and the citizen. Harmondsworth: 1957. pp.24-45.

3,131. PRESTATAIRE. "Social security - application of maxim ex turpi causa non oritur action". L.S.G. 76. (1979).

3,132. RAGG, N. "Benefits in Northern Ireland". S.W.T. 3. (13). (1972). p.13.

3,133. RAISBECK, B.L. Law and the social worker. London: 1977. pp.153. LSE; CUL.

3,134. REID, J. "National Insurance Act 1966". M.L.R. 29. (1966). pp.537-540.

3,135. REID, J. (ed.). "Social security. New legislation". I.L.J. 1. (1972). pp.49-53.

3,136. REID, J. (ed.). "Social security. National insurance".

I.L.J. 1. (1972). pp.176-180.

3,137. REID, J. "Social security. Department of Health and Social Security, Annual Report 1971". I.L.J. 1. (1972). pp.252-254.

3,138. REID, J. "Social security. Green paper: proposals for a tax credit system". I.L.J. 2. (1973). pp.52-56.

3,139. REID, J. "Social Security Act 1973". I.L.J. 2. (1973). pp.247-252.

3,140. REID, J. "New social security legislation". I.L.J. 5 (1976). PP.54-61.

3,141. ROBSON, W.A. "The National Insurance Act, 1946". M.L.R. 10. (1947). pp.171-179.

3,142. ROWLAND, M. (ed). Rights guide to non-means-tested social security benefits. 3rd ed. London: 1980. pp.[ii] + 137. DHSS. 4th ed. London: 1981. pp.160. DHSS.

3,143. ROWLAND, M. & SMITH, R. (eds.). Rights guide to non-means tested benefits. 5th ed. London: [1983]. pp.145. DHSS.

3,144. RUTHERFORD, M. & THOMAS, A.D. Welfare law and the divorce practitioner. London: College of Law, 1978. pp.28. CUL.

3,145. SAMUELS, A. Law for social workers. London: 1962. pp.viii + 292. DHSS; LSE; CUL; Sq.

3,146. SMITH, C. "Judicial attitudes to social security". B.J.L.S. 2. (1975). pp.217-221.

3,147. SMITH, C. & HOATH, D.C. Law and the underprivileged. London: 1975. pp.xxxx + 247. Sq; LSE.

3,148. SMITH, N.J. A brief guide to social legislation. London: 1972. pp.xxvi + 190. DHSS; LSE; CUL; Sq.

3,149. SMITH, P. "Welfare law in practice". N.L.J. 124. (1974). p.750.

3,150. SWAINSON, J.H. (comp., ed.). The law relating to social security and family allowances. The statutes, regulations and orders as now in force. London: HMSO, 1976. 3 vols. S; DHSS.

3,151. TITMUSS, R.M. "New guardians of the poor in Britain". In Shirley Jenkins (ed.). Social security in international perspective. New York: 1964. pp.xii + 255. DHSS.

3,152. TUNNARD, J. "Benefits for parents with children in care". L.A.G.Bull. (1980). pp.138-140.

3,153. UNITED KINGDOM. Social insurance. London: 1943-44. 2 pts. (B.P.P. VIII). LSE.

3,154. UNITED KINGDOM. National Insurance Bill, 1946: summary of main provisions of the national insurance scheme. London:

1946-46.   pp.11.   (B.P.P. XVI).   LSE.

3,155.   UNITED KINGDOM.   Proposed changes in the national insurance scheme.   London: 1951.   (B.P.P. 1950-51.   XXVII).   pp.4. LSE.

3,156.   UNITED NATIONS.   Organization and administration of social welfare programmes: A series of country studies: The United Kingdom of Great Britain and Northern Ireland.   New York: 1967.   pp.v + 48.   LSE; DHSS.

3,157.   UNIVERSITY OF BRISTOL.   DEPARTMENT OF ECONOMICS.   SOCIAL STUDIES SECTION.   A survey of families in which the breadwinner's earnings are interrupted by illness, injury or death.   Bristol: 1959.   pp.xxx + 124.   DHSS.

3,158.   UPTON, M.   "Reviving Rowntree: poverty lines and the levels of social security benefits for the unemployed: 1950-1978". Soc. Pol. & Admin.   14.   (1980).   pp.36-46.

3,159.   VANDYK, N.D.   "Medico-legal aspects of non-industrial national insurance claims".   Medico-Legal Jo.   XXII.   (1954).   p.66.

3,160.   WALKER, A. (ed.).   The poverty of taxation: reforming the social security and tax system.   London: 1982.   pp.63. (Poverty pamphlet; 56).   DHSS; LSE.

3,161.   WALLEY, SIR J.   Social security: another British failure? London: 1972.   pp.ix + 289.   DHSS; LSE.

3,162.   WARD, S.   The nonsense of earnings related supplement. London: 1975.   pp.9.   DHSS.

3,163.   WARD, S.   Social security at work.   London: 1982.   pp.201. DHSS.

3,164.   WEBB, P.R.H.   "Polygamy problems under the National Insurance Acts, 1946-1956".   M.L.R.   19.   (1956).   p.687-691.

3,165.   WHITE, R.   "Social security: a new field for lawyers".   S.J. 117.   (1973).   p.332.

3,166.   WHITEHEAD, F.   "Social Security statistics".   In Alderson, M. & Whitehead,   F.   Central government routine health statistics...   London: 1974.   pp.112.   DHSS.

3,167.   WICKS, M.   "One law for the poor".   N.S.   55.   (1981). pp.544-5.

3,168.   WILLMOTT, P.   "Kinship and social legislation".   Brit.Jo.Soc. IX.   (1958).   pp.126-142.

3,169.   ZANDER, M.   Social workers, their clients and the law. London: 1974.   pp.122.   CUL.   2nd ed.   1977.   3rd ed.   1981. LSE.

Section 2   Social Security Administration

(a) <u>General</u>

3,170. ANON. "Complaining to the ombudsman". <u>Welfare Rights Bull.</u>
10. (1976). pp.13-15.

3,171. ABELSON, I. "Getting written decisions from the SBC".
<u>L.A.G.Bull.</u> (1975). pp.213-214.

3,172. ADLER, M. & DU FEU, D. "Benefit from a computer". <u>N.S.</u> 27.
(1974). pp.67-68.

3,173. ADLER, M. & DU FEU, D. A computer based welfare benefits
information system: the Inverclyde project. Peterlee: 1975.
pp.iii + 56. DHSS.

3,174. ADLER, M. & DU FEU, D. "Technical solutions to social
problems?: some implications of a computer-based welfare
benefits information system". <u>J.Soc.Pol.</u> 6. (1977).
pp.431-447.

3,175. ARMAN, F.M. "National insurance and national assistance local
offices". <u>Pub.Admin.</u> XXIII. (1945). p.125.

3,176. ARMAN, F.M. National insurance and national assistance local
offices. London: Institute of Public Administration. 1946.
pp.12. DHSS.

3,177. ASSISTANCE BOARD, DEPARTMENTAL WHITLEY COUNCIL (STAFF SIDE).
Statement of case on grading, visiting and welfare work.
[Weston-super-Mare]: 1945. pp.14. LSE.

3,178. ATKINSON, A.B. & TRINDER, C. "Pride, charity and the history
of 'take-up'". <u>N.S.</u> 57. (1981). pp.262-3.

3,179. BENNETT, T. Making people better off: an action-research
study of rent/rate rebate claimants who were better off
claiming other benefits. Harlow District Council, Community
Services Department: 1981. pp.36. DHSS.

3,180. BRIGGS, E. & REES, M. Supplementary benefits and the
consumer. London: 1980. pp.[viii] + 172. (Occasional Papers
on Social Administration No.65). DHSS.

3,181. BURGESS, P. "Whose side is the Ombudsman really on?". <u>N.S.</u>
63. (1983). pp.55-56.

3,182. BURGESS, P.A. "Missed benefits". <u>N.S.</u> 26. (1973).
pp.534-536.

3,183. BURNS, E. "Suspension of benefit pending appeal". <u>Scolag.</u>
(1979). pp.94-5.

3,184. CLODE, D. "The changing map". <u>Health and Social Service
Journal</u>. 87. (4558). (1977). pp.1312-1314.

3,185.   COLEMAN, R.J.   Supplementary benefits and the administrative review of administrative action.   London: CPAG.   1971. pp.15. (Poverty Pamphlet No.7). DHSS; LSE; CUL.

3,186.   COMMITTEE OF PUBLIC ACCOUNTS. Session 1979-80. Twenty-sixth report. Social security benefits: costs of administration; estimated and statistical accounting. London: 1980. pp.x + 32. (HC 765). DHSS.

3,187.   COOPER, J.C., SKINNER, M.T. & WASHBROOK, F.E.   ADP resources for social security statistics. London: 1979. pp.[iii] + 36. DHSS.

3,188.   COWIE, W.B.   "The reorganisation of local offices: a case study in the Ministry of National Insurance".   Pub.Admin. XXVIII. (1950). p.319.

3,189.   COWIE, W.B.   "The re-organisation of local offices".   O.& M.Bull. 5. (1950). pp.3-13.

3,190.   COWIE, W.B.   "The re-organisation of local offices".   O.& M.Bull. 6. (1951). pp.19-35.

3,191.   DAVIES, M.   "A public service?".   N.S.   23.   (1973). pp.532-533.

3,192.   DEPARTMENT OF HEALTH AND SOCIAL SECURITY. Alphabetical list of places: list of places in Great Britain showing the names of the appropriate local office of the department dealing with supplementary benefits. London: 1971. pp.101. DHSS.

3,193.   DEPARTMENT OF HEALTH AND SOCIAL SECURITY. Social security statistics, 1972- London: HMSO. Annual. var.pag. DHSS.

3,194.   DEPARTMENT OF HEALTH AND SOCIAL SECURITY, REGIONAL DIRECTORATE.   Management in the regional organisation: an introductory handbook. London: 1975. pp.23. DHSS.

3,195.   DEPARTMENT OF HEALTH AND SOCIAL SECURITY. INTERNATIONAL RELATONS BRANCH LIBRARY.   Glossary of social security terms. English-French. London: 1977. var.pag. DHSS.

3,196.   DEPARTMENT OF HEALTH AND SOCIAL SECURITY. Committee on a Multi-purpose Claim Form (Means Tested Benefits) Report on the studies of claiming means-tested benefits. (Chairman: Frank Sutton). London: 1980. pp.[i] + 21. DHSS.

3,197.   DEPARTMENT OF HEALTH AND SOCIAL SECURITY. Reply to the first report from the Social Services Committee on arrangements for paying social security benefits. London: 1980. pp.[ii] + 61. (Cmnd.8106). DHSS.

3,198.   DEPARTMENT OF HEALTH AND SOCIAL SECURITY. A strategy for social security operations. London: 1980. pp.[ii] + 26. DHSS.

3,199.   DEPARTMENT OF HEALTH AND SOCIAL SECURITY & LOCAL AUTHORITY ASSOCIATIONS.   Joint Working Party on Relations with Social Services. Liaison in practice: guidance on liaison between local authority social services and social work departments and the supplementary benefit organisation of the Department of Health and Social Security. London: 1980. pp.[ii] + 26 + bibliog. DHSS.

3,200. DEPARTMENT OF HEALTH AND SOCIAL SECURITY. Review of government statistical services: report of the DHSS Study Team [by] Suzanne Reeve, David Clark and Peter Kendall. [London]: 1980. pp.[i] + 172. DHSS.

3,201. DEPARTMENT OF HEALTH AND SOCIAL SECURITY. Social security: operational strategy: report of a seminar. London: 1981. pp.[1] + 24. DHSS.

3,202. DEPARTMENT OF HEALTH AND SOCIAL SECURITY. Traffic in social security work between DHSS local and regional offices and headquarters: report of study carried out for Principal Establishments Officer. [London]: 1981. pp.[2] + 77. DHSS.

3,203. DEPARTMENT OF HEALTH AND SOCIAL SECURITY. Training in the eighties. London: 1981. pp.76. DHSS.

3,204. DEPARTMENT OF HEALTH AND SOCIAL SECURITY. Review of visiting procedures: report of a working party. London: 1981. pp.16. DHSS.

3,205. DEPARTMENT OF HEALTH AND SOCIAL SECURITY. Social security operational strategy: a framework for the future. London: 1982. pp.i + 62. DHSS.

3,206. DEPARTMENT OF HEALTH AND SOCIAL SECURITY. Social Security Operational Strategy Steering Group. Sub-Group on the Provision of Advice and Information. A strategy for social security operations. London: 1982. pp.[66]. DHSS.

3,207. DEPARTMENT OF HEALTH AND SOCIAL SECURITY. A guide to the DHSS local office complementing system. London: 1982. pp.10. DHSS.

3,208. DEPARTMENT OF HEALTH AND SOCIAL SECURITY. CENTRAL MANAGEMENT SERVICES. National introduction of postal claim form: monitoring and evaluation. London: 1983. pp.22. DHSS.

3,209. DEPARTMENT OF HEALTH AND SOCIAL SECURITY. Service to the public: a handbook of good practice. London: 1983. pp.101. DHSS.

3,210. DE SCHWEINITZ, E. & DE SCHWEINITZ, K. Interviewing on social security, as practised in the administration of retirement, survivors, disability and health insurance, and in the administration of supplemental security income. 2nd ed. Washington: 1977. pp.viii + 75. DHSS.

3,211. DE SMITH, S.A. "Les structures federales et supra-nationales et la legislation sociale. Rapport national. Grand-Bretagne". Congres Int.de dr.soc. (1958). pp.839-845.

3,212. FIRTH, D. An investigation of the success of redesigned supplementary benefit documents: a research study carried out by Research Institute for Consumer Affairs on behalf of the DHSS who funded the project. London: 1980. pp.28. DHSS.

3,213. FIRTH, D.   "An investigation of the success of redesigned supplementary benefit documents". Information Design Journal. (1981). pp.33-43.

3,214. FITZHERBERT, K.   "Groomed to give". N.S. 18. (1971). pp.141-143,

3,215. FORDE, M.   "Foreign social security institutions and the collateral benefits rules in Britain". M.L.R. 42. (1979). pp.389-408.

3,216. FRY, G.K.   "The establishment of the DHSS and of the Supplementary Benefits Commission". In The Administrative 'Revolution' in Whitehall. London: 1981. pp.113-115. DHSS.

3,217. GALLAS, J.   Workers' control and administration of social security. London: World Federation of Trade Unions. 1953. pp.19. DHSS; LSE.

3,218. GRAHAM, J.   Multi-purpose claim form trial in Northern Ireland: an evaluation. Belfast: 1980. pp.[v] + 108 + bibliog. DHSS.

3,219. GRAHAM, S. & BRASIER, F.   The multi-purpose claim form trial in Brighton. London: 1979. pp.89. DHSS.

3,220. GRANT, M.   "Recovery of overpaid benefit". L.A.G.Bull. (1975). pp.126-128, 157-158.

3,221. GUERRIER, D.H.   "Clerical training in the Department of Health and Social Security". In Programmed instructions in industry: a reference series of case histories. Vol.2. No.12. Oxford: 1968. pp.374-399. DHSS.

3,222. HARLOW, C.   "Discretion, social security and computers". M.L.R. 44. (1981). pp.546-555.

3,223. HARRIGAN, R.H., NEAL, D.G. & RACE, D.M.   A system for the calculation of apparent entitlement to a range of welfare benefits. Reading : University of Reading, Dept. of Applied Statistics. 1977. pp.ii + 19. DHSS.

3,224. HARRISON, P.   "Social security". N.S. 24. (1973). p.138.

3,225. INDUSTRIAL INJURIES ADVISORY COUNCIL. Time limits: report... on the time limits for claiming and obtaining... benefits, etc. London: 1952. pp.12. (B.P.P. 1951-52, XV). LSE.

3,226. INTERNATIONAL INSTITUTE OF PUBLIC FINANCE. The financial aspects of the administration of social insurance. Amsterdam: 1950. pp.496. DHSS.

3,227. KING, G.S.   The Ministry of Pensions and National Insurance. London: 1958. pp.162. LSE; DHSS; Sq.

3,228. LEWIS, L.   "Introducing change to the benefit services". D.E.G. 88. (1980). pp.464-467.

3,229. LISTER, R.   Take-up of means-tested benefits. London: 1974.

pp.24. (Poverty Pamphlet 18). DHSS; LSE; CUL.

3,230. LYNES, T.   "The multi-claim swap-form". N.S. 48. (1979).
        pp.577-8.

3,231. MILLAR, J.   Take up of means-tested benefits in work.
        Stanmore: 1982.   pp.iii + 31.   (DHSS cohort study of
        unemployed men working paper No.3). DHSS.

3,232. MINISTRY OF NATIONAL INSURANCE, STAFFING ADVISORY COMMITTEE.
        Absorption of staffs of approved societies. London: 1947.
        pp.30. DHSS; LSE.

3,233. MINISTRY OF NATIONAL INSURANCE. National Insurance Acts:
        selected   decisions   of   the   minister   on   questions   of
        classification and insurability. London: 1950. LSE.

3,234. MINISTRY OF PENSIONS. The Ministry of Pensions. Functions
        and organisation. London: 1950. pp.22. DHSS.

3,235. MINISTRY OF PENSIONS AND NATIONAL INSURANCE. Schedule of
        powers to determine claims and questions exercised by the
        Minister and the statutory authorities.   London: 1955.
        unpag. DHSS.

3,236. MINISTRY OF PENSIONS AND NATIONAL INSURANCE.   Selected
        decisions of the Minister on questions of classification and
        insurability under the National Insurance Acts.   London:
        1956. pp.14. DHSS. 1958. pp.21. DHSS.

3,237. MINISTRY OF PENSIONS AND NATIONAL INSURANCE. "XIVth general
        meeting [of the ISSA] , 1961.   Report X.   Registration and
        identification of insured persons and the collection of social
        insurance   contributions".   Bull.I.S.S.A.   XV.   (1962).
        (10-12). pp.121-169.

3,238. MINISTRY OF SOCIAL SECURITY. "The optimum size of an office".
        O. & M. Bull. 22. (1967). pp.61-69.

3,239. MOORE, P.   "Counter-culture in a social security office".
        N.S. 53. (1980). pp.68-69.

3,240. NAIRNE, P.   "Managing the DHSS elephant: reflections on a
        giant department". Pol.Q. 54. (1983). pp.243-256.

3,241. NIGHTINGALE, J.H.O.   "Direction par objectifs dans le service
        de la sante et de la securite sociale de Grande-Bretagne".
        Rev.Belge de Sec.Soc. IXI. (1977). pp.562-586.

3,242. OADES, B.C. & CARSWELL, J.P. Social security administration
        (Federal security agency) U.S.A.   London: 1947.   pp.48.
        DHSS.

3,243. O'HIGGINS, P.   "U.K. machinery for the maintenance of the
        value of social security benefits as affected by changes in
        the cost of living".   In Proceedings, International Society
        for Labour Law and Social Legislation, 6th Congress,
        Stockholm, August, 1966. n.l.

3,244. O'HIGGINS, P.   "Efficacy of administrative structures".   In

European Institute of Social Security, 1970 Year Book.
[Leuven]: 1970. pp.117-31. Sq.

3,245. O. & M. DIVISION, TREASURY. "Local office organisation III.
The work and layout of an area office of the National
Assistance Board". <u>O. & M. Bull</u>. 10. (1955). pp.26-47.

3,246. O. & M. DIVISION, TREASURY. "Local office organisation Part
IV.   Development in the Ministry of Pensions and National
Insurance". <u>O. & M. Bull</u>. 10. (1955). pp.8-18.

3,247. OFFICE OF POPULATION CENSUSES AND SURVEYS.   SOCIAL SURVEY
DIVISION.   Swansea social security office: survey of
customers. London: 1974. pp.177. DHSS.

3,248. PARTINGTON, M.   Claim in time: a study of the time limit
rules for claiming social security benefits.   London: 1978.
pp.xxv + 195. DHSS; Sq.

3,249. PICTON, C.   "Beyond the stereotype: another view of
supplementary benefits officers". <u>Brit.J.Soc.Wk.</u> 5. (1975).
pp.441-457.

3,250. PRIME MINISTER.   The Ministry of Pensions: proposed transfer
of functions. London: 1953. pp.10. (Cmd. 8842). DHSS.

3,251. REID, J. (ed.).   "Social security.   Problems of
classification". <u>I.L.J.</u> 1. (1972). pp.53-54.

3,252. RHODES, H.V.   Setting up a new government department.   An
account of the formation of the Ministry of National
Insurance. London: 1949. pp.48. DHSS.

3,253. RINGELING, A. "The passivity of the administration". <u>Policy
and Politics</u>. 9. (1981). pp.295-309.

3,254. SHERIDAN, L.A.   "Late national insurance claims: cause for
delay". <u>M.L.R.</u> 19. (1956). pp.341-364.

3,255. SOCIETY OF CIVIL AND PUBLIC SERVANTS. For whose benefit? The
case against cuts in home visiting in the Department of Health
and Social Security. London: 1977. pp.8. DHSS.

3,256. STREATHER, J.   "Clients v. claimants". <u>N.S</u> 44.   (1978).
pp.16-17.

3,257. TURNER, J.C.   Report on the study into payment of
supplementary benefit to residents of hostels and lodging
houses. London: 1982. pp.6. DHSS.

3,258. VANDYK, N.   The Minister of National Insurance as a judicial
authority. London: 1953. pp.14. DHSS.

3,259. WELFARE RIGHTS OFFICERS GROUP. A matter of form: a study of
the availability of social security leaflets at Department of
Health and Social Security local offices and at Post Offices
in 24 local authority areas in Great Britain.   London: 1976.
pp.ii + 18. DHSS.

3,260. WELSH CONSUMER COUNCIL.   One form for benefits?   A Welsh

Consumer Council study of multi-purpose claim forms in Merthyr Tydfil. Cardiff: 1977. pp.v + 67. DHSS.

3,261. WOOLSTON, H.T. "The joint local office experiment". Pub.Admin. XXXIII. (1955). pp.197-206.

(b) Advisory Committees (see also entries under specific benefits)

3,262. COUSSINS, J. (ed.). Dear SSAC. London: 1980. pp.71. DHSS.

3,263. DEPARTMENT OF HEALTH AND SOCIAL SECURITY. Social Security Advisory Committee. The Social Security Advisory Committee and the law. London: 1980. var. pag. DHSS.

3,264. DEPARTMENT OF HEALTH AND SOCIAL SECURITY. Social Security Advisory Committee. Non-contributory maternity grant: Social Security Advisory Committee to consider draft regulations. London: 1981. pp.[ii] + 6. DHSS.

3,265. HARRISON, E. "The work of the National Insurance Advisory Committee". Pub.Admin. XXX. (1952). p.149.

3,266. NATIONAL INSURANCE ADVISORY COMMITTEE. National Insurance Advisory Committee. National Insurance (Unemployment and Sickness Benefit) Amendment (No.2) Regulations, 1949. Report of the Committee. London: 1949. pp.5. (House of Commons Paper No.266). DHSS.

3,267. NATIONAL INSURANCE ADVISORY COMMITTEE. Report on the time limits for claiming benefit. London: 1952. (B.P.P. 1951-52. XV). pp.20. LSE.

3,268. NATIONAL INSURANCE ADVISORY COMMITTEE. Report on maternity benefits. London: 1952. pp.40. (B.P.P. 1951-52, XV). LSE.

3,269. NATIONAL INSURANCE ADVISORY COMMITTEE. Report on the availability question... in accordance with section 41(3) of the National Insurance Act, 1946, etc. London: 1953. pp.24. (B.P.P. 1952-53, XIV). LSE.

3,270. NATIONAL INSURANCE ADVISORY COMMITTEE. National Insurance (Unemployment and Sickness Benefit) Amendment Regulations, 1954: report of the N.I.A.C. London: 1954. pp.4. (B.P.P. 1953-54, XVI). LSE.

3,271. NATIONAL INSURANCE ADVISORY COMMITTEE. National Insurance (Maternity Benefit and Misc. Provisions) Regulations, 1954: report of the N.I.A.C., etc. London: 1954. pp.12. (B.P.P. 1953-54, XVI). LSE.

3,272. NATIONAL INSURANCE ADVISORY COMMITTEE. Draft of the National Insurance (Married Women) Amendment Regulation, 1954: report of the N.I.A.C., etc. London: 1954. (B.P.P. 1953-54, XVI). LSE.

3,273. NATIONAL INSURANCE ADVISORY COMMITTEE. National Insurance (Unemployment and Sickness Benefit) Amendment Regulations, 1954: report of the N.I.A.C. London: 1954. pp.4. (B.P.P. 1953-54, XVI). LSE.

3,274. NATIONAL INSURANCE ADVISORY COMMITTEE. Liability for
        contributions of persons with small incomes: report of the
        N.I.A.C. etc. London: 1955. pp.21. (B.P.P. 1954-55, VI).
        LSE.

3,275. NATIONAL INSURANCE ADVISORY COMMITTEE. National Insurance
        (Contributions) Amendment Regulations, 1955: report of the
        N.I.A.C. etc. London: 1955. pp.4. (B.P.P. 1955-56, XXII).
        LSE.

3,276. NATIONAL INSURANCE ADVISORY COMMITTEE. National Insurance
        (Determination of Claims and Questions) Amendment Regulations,
        1955: report of the N.I.A.C. etc. London:
[1955]. pp.5. (B.P.P. 1955-56, XXII). LSE.

3,277. NATIONAL INSURANCE ADVISORY COMMITTEE. National Insurance
        (Increase of Benefit and Misc. Provisions) Regulations, 1955:
        report of the N.I.A.C. etc. London: 1955. pp.5. (B.P.P.
        1953-55, VI). LSE.

3,278. NATIONAL INSURANCE ADVISORY COMMITTEE. National Insurance
        (Maternity Benefit and Misc. Provisions) Amendment
        Regulations, 1955: report of the N.I.A.C. etc. London:
        1955. pp.7. (B.P.P. 1954-55, VI). LSE.

3,279. NATIONAL INSURANCE ADVISORY COMMITTEE. National Insurance
        (Residence and Persons Abroad) Amendment Regulations, 1955:
        report of the N.I.A.C. etc. London: [1955]. pp.4. (B.P.P.
        1955-56, XXII). LSE.

3,280. NATIONAL INSURANCE ADVISORY COMMITTEE. National Insurance
        (Unemployment and Sickness Benefit) Amendment Regulations,
        1955: report of the N.I.A.C. London: 1955. PP.8. (B.P.P.
        1954-55, VI). LSE.

3,281. NATIONAL INSURANCE ADVISORY COMMITTEE. National Insurance
        (Residence and Persons Abroad) Amendment Regulations, 1955:
        report of the N.I.A.C., etc. London: [1955]. pp.4. (B.P.P.
        1955-56, XXII). LSE.

3,282. NATIONAL INSURANCE ADVISORY COMMITTEE. National Insurance
        (Maternity Benefit and Misc. Provisons) Amendment Regulations,
        1955: report of the N.I.A.C., etc. London: 1955. pp.7.
        (B.P.P. 1954-55, VI). LSE.

3,283. NATIONAL INSURANCE ADVISORY COMMITTEE. National Insurance
        (Increase of Benefit and Misc. Provisions) Regulations, 1955:
        report of the N.I.A.C. etc. London: 1955. pp.5. (B.P.P.
        1953-55, VI). LSE.

3,284. NATIONAL INSURANCE ADVISORY COMMITTEE. National Insurance
        (Determination of Claims and Questions) Amendment Regulations,
        1955: report of the N.I.A.C., etc. London:
[1955]. pp.5. (B.P.P. 1955-56, XXII). LSE.

3,285. NATIONAL INSURANCE ADVISORY COMMITTEE. National Insurance
        (Contributions) Amendment Regulations, 1955: report of the
        N.I.A.C., etc. London: 1955. pp.4. (B.P.P. 1955-56, XXII).
        LSE.

3,286.   NATIONAL   INSURANCE   ADVISORY   COMMITTEE.   Liability   for
contributions of persons with small incomes: report of the
N.I.A.C., etc.   London: 1955.   pp.21.   (B.P.P. 1954-55, VI).
LSE.

3,287.   NATIONAL INSURANCE ADVISORY COMMITTEE.   Benefit for very short
spells of unemployment or sickness: report of the N.I.A.C.
London: 1955.   pp.43.   (B.P.P. 1955-56, XXII).   LSE.

3,288.   NATIONAL   INSURANCE   ADVISORY   COMMITTEE.   National   Insurance
(Unemployment   and   Sickness   Benefit)   Amendment   Regulations,
1955:   report of the N.I.A.C.   London: 1955.   pp.8.   (B.P.P.
1954-55, VI).   LSE.

3,289.   NATIONAL   INSURANCE   ADVISORY   COMMITTEE.   Report...   on the
death grant question.   London: [1956].   pp.33.   (B.P.P.
1956-57, XV).   LSE.

3,290.   NATIONAL   INSURANCE   ADVISORY   COMMITTEE.   Report...   on the
question   of widows' benefit.   London: [1956].   pp.43.
(B.P.P. 1955-56, XXII).   LSE.

3,291.   NATIONAL   INSURANCE   ADVISORY   COMMITTEE.   Report...   on the
question of earnings limits for benefits.   London: [1956].
pp.54.   (B.P.P. 1955-56, XXII).   LSE.

3,292.   NATIONAL   INSURANCE   ADVISORY   COMMITTEE.   Report...   on the
question of dependency provisions.   London: [1956].   pp.39.
(B.P.P. 1955-56, XXII).   LSE.

3,293.   NATIONAL   INSURANCE   ADVISORY   COMMITTEE.   Report...   on the
question of contributions conditions and credits provisions.
London: 1956.   pp.62.   (B.P.P. 1955-56, XXII).   LSE.

3,294.   NATIONAL INSURANCE ADVISORY COMMITTEE.   National   Insurance
(Unemployment   and   Sickness   Benefit)   Amendment   Regulations,
1956:   report of the N.I.A.C.   London: [1956].   pp.6.
(B.P.P. 1955-56, XXII).   LSE.

3,295.   NATIONAL INSURANCE ADVISORY COMMITTEE.   National Insurance...
Regulations   (and   Amendment   Regulations)   1956   and   1957:
reports of the N.I.A.C. etc.   London: [1956-57].   10 parts.
(B.P.P. 1956-57, XV).   LSE.

3,296.   NATIONAL INSURANCE ADVISORY COMMITTEE.   National   Insurance
(Unemployment   and   Sickness   Benefit)   Amendment   Regulations,
1957:   report of the N.I.A.C.   London: [1957].   pp.4.
(B.P.P. 1956-57, XV).   LSE.

3,297.   NATIONAL INSURANCE ADVISORY COMMITTEE.   Report... on part-time
employment.   London: [1957].   pp.26.   (B.P.P. 1956-57, XV).
LSE.

3,298.   NATIONAL   INSURANCE   ADVISORY   COMMITTEE.   National   Insurance
(Widows'   Benefit   and   Retirement   Pensions)   Amendment
Regulations, 1957:   report of the N.I.A.C., etc.   London:
[1957].   pp.4.   (B.P.P. 1956-57, XV).   LSE.

3,299.   NATIONAL INSURANCE ADVISORY COMMITTEE.   National Insurance...

Amendment Regulations (and Regulations), 1957-58: reports of the N.I.A.C., etc. London: [1957]. 15 pts. (B.P.P. 1957-58, XV). LSE.

3,300. NATIONAL INSURANCE ADVISORY COMMITTEE. Report on National Insurance (New Entrants Transitional) Amendment Regulations, 1958... preceded by a statement by the Minister. London: 1958. pp.4. (HC 258). DHSS.

3,301. NATIONAL INSURANCE ADVISORY COMMITTEE. Report on National Insurance and Industrial Injuries (Collection of Contributions) Amendment Regulations, 1959... preceded by a statement by the Minister. London: 1959. pp.3. (HC 74). DHSS.

3,302. NATIONAL INSURANCE ADVISORY COMMITTEE. National Insurance (Unemployment and Sickness Benefit) Amendment Regulations, 1959 (and Amendment, No.2 Regulations, 1959): reports of the N.I.A.C., etc. London: [1959]. 2 vols. (B.P.P. 1958-59, XVI). LSE.

3,303. NATIONAL INSURANCE ADVISORY COMMITTEE. Regulations (and Amendment Regulations), 1959. Reports of the N.I.A.C., etc. London: [1959]. 7 parts. (B.P.P. 1958-59, XVI). LSE.

3,304. NATIONAL INSURANCE ADVISORY COMMITTEE. National Insurance... Regulations (and Amendment Regulations), 1959: reports of the N.I.A.C. etc. London: [1959]. 7 parts. (B.P.P. 1958-59, XVI). LSE.

3,305. NATIONAL INSURANCE ADVISORY COMMITTEE. Report on National Insurance (Graduated Retirement Benefit and Consequential Provisions) Regulations, 1961... preceded by a statement by the Minister. London: 1961. pp.3. (HC 156). DHSS.

3,306. NATIONAL INSURANCE ADVISORY COMMITTEE. Report on The National Insurance (Collection of Graduated Contributions) Amendment Regulations, 1961... preceded by a statement by the Minister. London: 1961. pp.3. (HC 157). DHSS.

3,307. NATIONAL INSURANCE ADVISORY COMMITTEE. Report on National Insurance (Classification) Amendment (No.2) Regulations 1970 (S.I. 1970 No.1704),... preceded by a statement made by the Secretary of State for Social Services in accordance with section 108(5) of that Act. (HC 163). London: 1970. pp.3. DHSS.

3,308. SOCIAL SECURITY ADVISORY COMMITTEE. Report on the Social Security (Claims and Payments) Amendment (No.2) Regulations 1982 (S.I. 1982 no.1344) and the Social Security (Unemployment, Sickness and Invalidity Benefit) Amendment (No.2) Regulations 1982 (S.I. 1982 no.1345). London: 1982. pp.11. (Cmnd. 8667). DHSS; LSE.

3,309. SOCIAL SECURITY ADVISORY COMMITTEE. Report on the Mobility Allowance (Motability Payment Arrangements) Amendment Regulations 1982 (S.I. 1982 no.1629). London: 1982. pp.7. (Cmnd. 8754). DHSS; LSE.

3,310. SOCIAL SECURITY ADVISORY COMMITTEE. Report on the Social

Security (Claims and Payments) Amendment Regulations 1982
(S.I. 1982 no.1241): the Child Benefit (Claims and Payments)
Amendment Regulations 1982 (S.I. 1982 no.1242). London:
1982. pp.9. (Cmnd.8656). DHSS; LSE.

3,311. SOCIAL SECURITY ADVISORY COMMITTEE. Report on the
Supplementary Benefit (Claims and Payments) Amendment
Regulatons 1982 (S.I. 1982 no.522). London: 1982. pp.10.
(Cmnd. 8772). DHSS; LSE.

3,312. SOCIAL SECURITY ADVISORY COMMITTEE. The Supplementary Benefit
(Requirements and Resources) Amendment Regulations 1982 and
The Supplementary Benefit (Miscellaneous Amendments)
Regulations 1982. London: 1982. pp.21. (Cmnd. 8598).
DHSS.

3,313. SOCIAL SECURITY ADVISORY COMMITTEE. Child Benefit (General)
Amendment Regulations 1982. London: 1982. pp.10. (Cmnd.
8586). DHSS.

3,314. SOCIAL SECURITY ADVISORY COMMITTEE. The Social Security
(Unemployment, Sickness and Invalidity Benefit and Credits)
Amendment Regulations 1982 (S.I. 1982 no.96): report of the
Social Security Advisory Committee. London: 1982. pp.11.
(Cmnd. 8486). DHSS.

3,315. SOCIAL SECURITY ADVISORY COMMITTEE. First report of the
Social Security Advisory Committee 1981. London: 1982.
pp.95. DHSS.

3,316. SOCIAL SECURITY ADVISORY COMMITTEE. The Social Security
(Contributions) (Mariners) Amendment Regulations 1982: report
of the Social Security Advisory Committee. London: 1982.
pp.9. (Cmnd. 8477). DHSS.

3,317. SOCIAL SECURITY ADVISORY COMMITTEE. Report on the Social
Security (Medical Evidence, Claims and Payments) Amendment
Regulations 1982. London: 1982. pp.8. (Cmnd. 8560). DHSS.

3,318. SOCIAL SECURITY ADVISORY COMMITTEE. Reports on the Social
Security Benefit (Dependency) Amendment Regulatons 1983 (S.I.
1983 no.1001) and the Family Income Supplements (Miscellaneous
Amendments) Regulations 1983 (S.I. 1983 no.1003) and the
Supplementary Benefit (Equal Treatment) Regulations 1983 (S.I.
1983 no.1004). London: 1983. pp.20. (Cmnd. 8993). DHSS;
LSE.

3,319. SOCIAL SECURITY ADVISORY COMMITTEE. Second annual report:
1982/83. London: 1983. pp.96. DHSS; LSE.

3,320. SOCIAL SECURITY ADVISORY COMMITTEE. Report on the
Supplementary Benefit (Resources) Amendment Regulations 1983.
London: 1983. pp.11. (Cmnd. 8824). DHSS; LSE.

3,321. UNITED KINGDOM. Seasonal workers: report of the National
Insurance Advisory Committee etc. London: 1952. (B.P.P.,
1951-52, XV). pp.25. LSE.

3,322. VANDYK, N.D. "The National Insurance Advisory Committee and
time limits for claims". Ind.L.R. 8. (1953-54).

pp.203-214.

3,323. VANDYK, N.D.   "The National Insurance Advisory Committee and national insurance regulations: a further note".   <u>Ind.L.R.</u> 9.   (1954-55).   pp.34-43.

Section 3   Social Security Adjudication

(a) <u>General</u>

3,324.   ANON.   "Decisions of the commissioner under the National
          Insurance Acts". <u>Lab.G.</u> 57. (1949). pp.119-20.

3,325.   ANON. "National insurance section". <u>Ind.L.R.</u> 5. (1950-51).
          pp.57-66, 131-136, 208-214, 292-295.

3,326.   ANON.   "Decisions of the commissioner under the National
          Insurance Acts". <u>Lab.G.</u> 60. (1952). pp.77-8.

3,327.   ANON.   "Decisions of the commissioner under the National
          Insurance Acts". <u>Lab.G.</u> 61. (1953). pp.110-1.

3,328.   ANON.   "Decisions of the commissioner under the National
          Insurance Acts". <u>Lab.G.</u> 63. (1955). pp.36-8.

3,329.   ANON.   Reported decisions of the commissioner under the
          National Insurance and Family Allowances Acts, 1948-64.
          London: 1955-66. Sq.

3,330.   ANON. "National insurance appeals". <u>L.J.</u>   CVIII.   (1958).
          p.487.

3,331.   ANON.   Index and digest of decisions given by the
          commissioners under the National Insurance (Industrial
          Injuries) Acts and the Family Allowances Acts. London: 1964.
          Vol.2. (Seventeenth supplement, 1971.) DHSS; LSE.

3,332.   ANON. "National insurance - recent commissioners' decisions".
          <u>L.A.G.Bull.</u> (1975). pp.96-97.

3,333.   ANON.   "Recent   cases   before   the   national   insurance
          commissioners". <u>L.A.G.Bull.</u> (1975). pp.321-322.

3,334.   ANON. "Appeals from the commissioners to the courts". <u>L.S.G.</u>
          77. (1980). p.1034.

3,335.   ANON.   "Social security law: a judicial function of the
          Secretary of State for Social Services". <u>L.S.G.</u> 80. (1983).
          pp.489-491.

3,336.   ALDER, J.E. "Representation before tribunals". <u>P.L.</u> (1972).
          pp.278ff.

3,337.   BASTOW, G. "National insurance notes". <u>L.A.G.Bull.</u> (1978).
          pp.40-41.

3,338.   BELL, K. Tribunals in the social services. London: 1968.
          pp.xiv + 98. DHSS; CUL; LSE; Sq.

3,339.   BELL, K. "Administrative tribunals since Franks". <u>Soc. &</u>
          <u>Econ.Ad.</u> 4. (1970). pp.279-305.

3,340.   BELL, K., COLLISON, P.,   TURNER, S. & WEBBER, S.   "National

insurance local tribunals". J.Soc.Pol. 3. (1974).
pp.289-315; 4. (1975). pp.1-24.

3,341. BELL, K. & OTHERS. Report of the research study on national
insurance local tribunals, 1970-73. Newcastle upon Tyne:
Department of Social Studies. [1974]. 2 vols. DHSS.

3,342. BIRMINGHAM UNIVERSITY. INSTITUTE OF JUDICIAL ADMINISTRATION.
The future of administrative tribunals: edited transcript of
the proceedings of a conference held at the University of
Birmingham in April 1971. Birmingham: 1971. pp.57. DHSS;
LSE.

3,343. BUTTON, W. "Pensions appeals tribunals". Medico-Legal Jo.
XVII. (1949). p.46.

3,344. CARSON, D.C. "National insurance tribunal decisions -
conflict between medical and lay authorities". N.I.L.Q. 24.
(1973). pp.147-51.

3,345. CHAPELTOWN CITIZENS ADVICE BUREAU. Tribunal Assistance Unit.
Social security appeals: a guide to National Insurance local
tribunals and medical appeal tribunals; also covers medical
boards, the Attendance Allowance Board, questions decided by
the Secretary of State, and appeals to the National Insurance
Commissioners. London: 1980. pp.xi + 226. DHSS.

3,346. CHILD POVERTY ACTION GROUP. Submission to the Justice - All
Souls Review Committee on Administrative Law. [London]:
[1981]. pp.33. DHSS.

3,347. COMMITTEE ON ADMINISTRATIVE TRIBUNALS AND ENQUIRIES. Report
and minutes of evidence. (Franks Committee). London:
1956-57. 2 vols. DHSS; LSE.

3,348. DE SMITH, S.A. "Administrative finality and judicial review".
M.L.R. 20. (1957). pp.394-397.

3,349. DEPARTMENT OF HEALTH AND SOCIAL SECURITY. Questionnaire on
administrative tribunals (issued by the Council on Tribunals)
and memoranda on health and social security administrative
tribunals. Unpublished: 1971. pp.83. DHSS.

3,350. DEPARTMENT OF HEALTH AND SOCIAL SECURITY. National Insurance
Acts: decisions of the Commissioners: application for leave
to appeal and appeal from decision. London: 1972- (irreg.).
LSE.

3,351. DIXON, R.G. Social security disability and mass justice; a
problem in welfare adjudication. New York: 1973. pp.190.
LSE.

3,352. ELCOCK, H.J. Administrative justice. London: 1969. pp.x +
111. DHSS; LSE.

3,353. FFOULKES, L. "Social security commissioners' decisions".
L.A.G.Bull. (1982). pp.102-4.

3,354. FITZGERALD, M. "National insurance section". Ind.L.R. 14.
(1959-60). pp.25-31, 145-151, 198-204.

3,355. FULBROOK, J., BROOKE, R. & ARCHER, P. Tribunals: a social court? London: 1973. pp.16. (Fabian Tract No.427). DHSS; LSE; CUL.

3,356. GAMBLE, A. "National insurance adjudication". <u>Scolag.</u> (1980). pp.33-8.

3,357. HARRISON, P. "The tribunals of the welfare state". <u>N.S.</u> 26. (1973). pp.462-465.

3,358. HERRON, S. "National insurance appeal tribunals". <u>Quest.</u> 5. (1976). pp.30-37.

3,359. HODGE, H. "Techniques for tribunals - I". <u>L.A.G.Bull.</u> (1973). pp.269-271.

3,360. HODGE, H. "Tribunal techniques - II". <u>L.A.G.Bull.</u> (1974). pp.13-14.

3,361. INTERNATIONAL SOCIAL SECURITY ASSOCIATION. XVth General Assembly, Washington, 1964. Appeals procedure in social security. Report II. Geneva: 1965. pp.155. DHSS.

3,362. JOWELL, J. "The legal control of administrative discretion". <u>P.L.</u> (1973). pp.178ff.

3,363. KAHN-FREUND, O. "Social security and the law courts". <u>F.N.</u> 9. (1959). p.5.

3,364. KEAST, H. "National insurance section". <u>Ind.L.R.</u> 6. (1951-52). pp.58-62, 130-138, 207-215, 299-304.

3,365. KEAST, H. "Administrative justice in the welfare state". <u>Ind.L.R.</u> 7. (1952-53). pp.24-31.

3,366. KEAST, H. "National insurance section". <u>Ind.L.R.</u> 7. (1952-53). pp.55-62, 131-138, 220-226, 298-303.

3,367. KEAST, H. "National insurance section". <u>Ind.L.R.</u> 8. (1953-54). pp.62-70, 219-228, 298-305.

3,368. KEAST, H. "National insurance section". <u>Ind.L.R.</u> 9. (1954-55). pp.60-67, 223-226.

3,369. KEAST, H. "National insurance section". <u>Ind.L.R.</u> 10. (1955-56). pp.151-153.

3,370. LACH, G. "Appeal tribunals and the national assistance scheme". <u>Pub.Admin.</u> XXVI. (1948). p.173.

3,371. LAMBETH. DIRECTORATE OF SOCIAL SERVICES. Hearing-aid: a proposal for three pilot projects to provide accessible representation for appellants before Supplementary Benefit Appeal Tribunals. London: 1976. var.pag. DHSS.

3,372. LAWRENCE, R. "Representation at national insurance tribunals". <u>B.J.L.S.</u> 5. (1978). pp.246-50.

3,373. LAWRENCE, R. Tribunal representation: the role of advice and advocacy services. London: 1980. pp.vii + 98. DHSS.

3,374. LAWRENCE, R. "Solicitors and tribunals". J.S.W.L. (1980). pp.13-25.

3,375. LORD CHANCELLOR'S DEPARTMENT. War Pensions (Special Review) Tribunal. Notes and digest of reports of war pensions appeal cases to 31st December 1946. London: 1947. pp.vi + 77. DHSS.

3,376. LORD CHANCELLOR'S DEPARTMENT. Pension appeal tribunals, assessment appeals: notes for the guidance of appellants. London: 1950. pp.6. LSE. Later ed. 1953. pp.5. DHSS.

3,377. McCORQUODALE, S. "The composition of administrative tribunals". P.L. (1962). pp.298ff.

3,378. MESHER, J. "Social security. Earnings related benefit". I.L.J. 3. (1974). pp.118-121.

3,379. MESHER, J. "Recent national insurance commissioners' decisions". J.S.W.L. (1978). pp.54-57.

3,380. MESHER, J. "Recent national insurance commissioners' decisions". J.S.W.L. (1979). pp.371-375.

3,381. MESHER, J. "Recent national insurance commissioners' decisions". J.S.W.L. (1980). pp.252-256.

3,382. MESHER, J. "Recent social security commissioners' decisions". J.S.W.L. (1981). pp.313-325.

3,383. MESHER, J. "Recent social security commissioners' decisions". J.S.W.L. (1982). pp.239-250.

3,384. MESHER, J. "Recent social security commissioners' decisions". J.S.W.L. (1982). pp.308-314.

3,385. MESHER, J. "The merging of social security tribunals". J.Law Soc. 10. (1983). pp.135-142.

3,386. MICKLETHWAIT, SIR R. Another experiment in legal procedure - national insurance. London: 1964. pp.10. DHSS.

3,387. MICKELTHWAIT, SIR R. The national insurance commissioners. London: 1976. pp.xxviii + 151. Sq.

3,388. MINISTRY OF NATIONAL INSURANCE. National Insurance Acts: selected decisions given by the commissioner on claims for retirement pension. London: 1948- . LSE.

3,389. MINISTRY OF NATIONAL INSURANCE. National Insurance Acts: selected decisions given by the commissioner on claims for guardian's allowance, maternity benefit and widow's benefit. London: 1948- . ser. LSE.

3,390. MINISTRY OF NATIONAL INSURANCE. Notes for chairmen and members of local tribunals appointed under the National Insurance Acts. London: 1948. pp.12. DHSS.

3,391. MINISTRY OF NATIONAL INSURANCE. National Insurance Acts: selected decisions given by the commissioner on claims for sickness benefit. London: 1948 to date. LSE.

3,392. MINISTRY OF NATIONAL INSURANCE. Index to decisions given by the commissioner on claims for benefit and other questions. London: 1951. pp.ix + 208. LSE.

3,393. MINISTRY OF PENSIONS AND NATIONAL INSURANCE. Reported decisions of the Commissioner under the National Insurance Acts. Vol.I 1948 to 1952. Vol.II 1953 to 1956. Vol.III 1957 to 1960. Vol.IV 1961 to 1964. London: var.dates. DHSS; LSE.

3,394. MINISTRY OF PENSIONS AND NATIONAL INSURANCE. Adjudication under the National Insurance and Industrial Injuries Acts, 1946 and its history. London: 1955. unpag. ("Restricted, for departmental use only").

3,395. MINISTRY OF PENSIONS AND NATIONAL INSURANCE. Schedule of powers to determine claims and questions exercised by the Minister and statutory authorities. London: 1955. unpag. DHSS.

3,396. MINISTRY OF PENSIONS AND NATIONAL INSURANCE. Selected decisions of the Minister on questions of classification and insurability under the National Insurance Acts. London: 1956. pp.14. DHSS. 1958. pp.21. DHSS.

3,397. MINISTRY OF PENSIONS AND NATIONAL INSURANCE. Index and digest of decisions given by the Commissioner under the National Insurance Act, 1946, as amended, the National Insurance (Industrial Injuries) Act, 1946, as amended, and the Family Allowances Act, 1945, as amended; by Edgar Jenkins. London: 1964-. 2 vols. LSE.

3,398. MINISTRY OF PENSIONS AND NATIONAL INSURANCE. Judgments of the High Court and Court of Session given in appeals brought against the Minister on matters relating to classification, insurability and contributions. London: 1965. unpag. DHSS.

3,399. MORRICK, C.   "Learning from the national insurance commissioners". L.A.G.Bull. (1976). pp.150-151.

3,400. NARAIN, J. "Social security appeal tribunals in Northern Ireland: a survey". N.I.L.Q. 30. (1979). pp.111-35.

3,401. NEWMAN, T.S. & DAVIES, W.T. The law affecting tribunals. London: 1950. pp.23. DHSS.

3,402. O'HIGGINS, P. "Adjudication of social security claims". Bull.I.L.S. 10. (1971). pp.16-17.

3,403. PARTINGTON, M. "National insurance benefits and industrial injuries: some problems". L.A.G.Bull. (1978). pp.113-5.

3,404. POLLARD, R.S.W.   Administrative tribunals at work.   A symposium. London: 1950. pp.xx + 154. (Studies in Public Administration No.3). DHSS; CUL; Sq.

3,405. ROBSON, W.A. "Administrative justice and injustice: a commentary on the Franks Report". P.L. (1958). pp.12ff.

3,406. SAFFORD, A. "The creation of case law under the National Insurance and National Insurance (Industrial Injuries) Acts". M.L.R. 17. (1954). pp.197-210.

3,407. SHERIDAN, L.A. "National insurance adjudication". J.S.S.I.S.I. (1955-56). pp.29-41.

3,408. SKOLER, D.L. & SEITZER, I.R. "Social security appeals systems: a nine-nation review. Int.Soc.Sec.Rev. 35. (1982). pp.57-77.

3,409. STOKES, D.S. "The administation in 1945 of some tribunals appointed by the Minister of Labour". In Pollard, R.S.W. (ed.). Administrative tribunals at work. London: 1950. pp.19-35. LSE.

3,410. STREET, H. Justice in the welfare state. London: 1968. pp.130. DHSS; LSE; CUL; Sq. 2nd ed. 1975. pp.130. (Hamlyn Lectures, 20th Series). DHSS; LSE; CUL; Sq.

3,411. SUMMERSKILL, E. "The functions of tribunals within the modern state". Brit.Jo.Admin.Law. I. (1954-55). pp.93-96.

3,412. TAYLOR-GOOBY, P. & LAKEMAN, S. Welfare benefits advocacy: official discretion and claimants' rights. York: 1977. pp.vi + 45. (Papers in Community Studies No.11). DHSS.

3,413. TURNER, S. "The trade union role in tribunals". Poverty. (1975). (32). pp.29-32.

3,414. VANDYK, N.D. "National insurance adjudication". Ind.L.R. 7. (1952-53). pp.176-185.

3,415. VANDYK, N.D. "The Minister of National Insurance as a judicial authority". Pub.Admin. XXXI. (1953). p.331-43.

3,416. [VANDYK] N.D. "Appeals from medical appeal tribunals". S.J. 106. (1962). pp.1020-3.

3,417. VANDYK, N.D. Tribunals and inquiries. London: 1965. pp.xxviii + 274. DHSS; LSE; Sq.

3,418. VANDYK, N.D. "Financing legal representation before tribunals: a proposal". S.J. 111. (1967). pp.642-643.

3,419. WADE, H.W.R. Towards administrative justice. London: 1963. pp.138. DHSS; LSE; Sq.

3,420. WRAITH, R.E. & HUTCHESSON, P.G. Administrative tribunals. London: 1973. pp.376. DHSS; LSE; CUL.

(b) Supplementary Benefit Appeals

3,421. ANON. "SBATs and the law". L.A.G.Bull. (1979). pp.106-108, 163-164.

3,422. ADLER, M. & BRADLEY, A. (eds.) Justice, discretion and poverty: supplementary benefit appeal tribunals in Britain. Abingdon: 1975. pp.vi + 229. DHSS. LSE. CUL. Sq.

3,423. BELL, K. "Supplementary benefit appeal tribunals". Case Con. No. 7. November 1968. pp.259-262.

3,424. BELL, K. Research study on supplementary benefit appeal tribunals, review of main findings: conclusions: recommendations. London: 1975. pp.vi + 25. DHSS.

3,425. BELL, K., TURNER, S. & WEBBER, S. Report of the research study on supplementary benefit appeal tribunals, 1973-75. Newcastle upon Tyne: Department of Social Studies. [1977]. 4 vols. DHSS.

3,426. BENSON, A. "SB appeals". N.S. 29. (1974). p.423.

3,427. BRADLEY, A.W. "Reform of supplementary benefit tribunals - the key issues". N.I.L.Q. 27. (1976). pp.96-119.

3,428. BROOKE, R. "Supplementary benefit appeals". N.L.J. 120. (1970). p.80.

3,429. BULL, D. "Supplementary benefit appeals: advocacy against policy decisions". L.A.G.Bull. (1975). pp.18-19.

3,430. CHAPELTOWN CITIZENS' ADVICE BUREAU. "I want to appeal": a guide to S.B. Appeal Tribunals. London: 1978. pp.130. 2nd ed. London: 1982. pp.(10) + 150. DHSS. 2nd ed. London: 1982. pp.150. DHSS.

3,431. CHAPELTOWN CITIZENS' ADVICE BUREAU. Tribunal Assistance Unit. Progress report: first two years (August 1976 - August 1978) by Clare Beckett and others. London: 1979. pp.[ii] + 35. (CAB Occasional Paper No.6). DHSS.

3,432. CHILD POVERTY ACTION GROUP. Guide to supplementary benefit appeals. London: CPAG. 1970. (Poverty Leaflet No.3). DHSS. Rev.ed. 1971. pp.7. CUL.

3,433. COLLINS, L. & EASTERBROOK, A. "Lay assistance to 'welfare' tribunal appellants". L.S.G. 73. (1976). p.819.

3,434. DAVIS, M. "R. v. Manchester Supplementary Benefit Appeals Tribunal, ex parte Riley [1979] 1 W.L.R. 426". L.T. 14. (1980). pp.63-5.

3,435. DEPARTMENT OF HEALTH AND SOCIAL SECURITY. Supplementary benefit appeal tribunals: a guide to procedure. London: 1977; pp.vi + 53. Rev.ed. London: 1982. pp.vi + 60. DHSS.

3,436. FULBROOK, J. The appellant and his case: the appellant's view of supplementary benefit appeal tribunals. London: 1975. pp.20. (Poverty Research Series 5). DHSS; LSE; CUL.

3,437. HARRIS, N. "The appointment of legally qualified chairmen for SBATs". N.L.J. 132. (1982). pp.495-496.

3,438. HARRIS, N. "Lawyers take over SBATs?". L.A.G. Bull. (1982).
        p.2.

3,439. HARRIS, N. "Solicitors, articled clerks and supplementary
        benefit - a survey". L.A.G. Bull. (1982). (Aug.).
        pp.11-12.

3,440. HARRIS, N. "The reform of the supplementary benefit appeals
        system". J.S.W.L. (1983). pp.212-227.

3,441. HERMAN, M. Administrative justice and supplementary benefits:
        a study of Supplementary Benefit Appeal Tribunals. London:
        1972. pp.68. (Occasional Papers on Social Administration
        No.47). DHSS; LSE; CUL.

3,442. HODGE, H. "Really: yet another tribunal?". L.A.G.Bull.
        (1975). pp.287-288.

3,443. KESSLER, E. & OTHERS. Combatting poverty: CABx, claimants
        and tribunals; a report of the NACAB/EEC Tribunal Project
        1976-1980. London: 1980. pp.[i] + 99. (CAB Occasional
        Paper No.11). DHSS.

3,444. LAWRENCE, R. Welfare advice and advocacy: a study of current
        provision in the N.W. Midlands. London: National Association
        of Citizens' Advice Bureaux. 1977. pp.37. (Occasional Paper
        No.1). DHSS.

3,445. LEGAL ACTION GROUP. Representation before tribunals:
        memorandum to the Lord Chancellor's Advisory Committee.
        London: 1974. pp.17. DHSS.

3,446. LEWIS, N. "Supplementary benefits appeal tribunals". P.L.
        (1973). pp.257-284.

3,447. LISTER, R. Justice for the claimant: a study of
        supplementary benefit appeal tribunals. London: 1974.
        pp.67. (Poverty Research Series No.4). DHSS; LSE; CUL.

3,448. LISTER, R. Council inaction: a report on the Council on
        Tribunals and its treatment of complaints about supplementary
        benefit appeal tribunals. London: 1975. pp.15. DHSS.

3,449. LISTER, R. "Supplementary Benefit Appeal Tribunals". S.W.T.
        6. (1975). p.516.

3,450. LISTER, R. "Bell ringing". N.S. 42. (1977). p.413.

3,451. PARTINGTON, M. "Comment: supplementary benefits appeals".
        P.L. (1979). pp.1-6.

3,452. PHILLIPS, R. "Supplementary benefit appeals tribunal: reform
        - a chairman's view". Fam.L. 10. (1980). pp.219-20

3,453. PRESTATAIRE. "The 'last resort' and the courts". L.S.G. 76.
        (1979). p.1156.

3,454. PROSSER, T. "Poverty, ideology and legality: supplementary
        benefit appeal tribunals and their predecessors". B.J.L.S.
        4. (1977). pp.39-60.

3,455. SAMUELS, A. "The solicitor and the supplementary benefit appeal tribunal". L.S.G. 73. (1978). p.578.

3,456. SAMUELS, A. "Supplementary benefit appeals tribunal: reform". Fam.L. 10. (1980). pp.74-7.

3,457. SAMUELS, A. "Supplementary benefit appeal tribunals". S.J. 124. (1980). pp.265-66.

3,458. SMITH, R. "Supplementary benefit appeals". L.A.G.Bull. (1981). pp.283-286.

3,459. WARREN, N. "Appeals from SBATs". L.A.G.Bull. (1978). pp.211-213.

3,460. WARREN, N. "Appealing from supplementary benefit tribunals". S.W.T. 9. (28). (1978). p.19.

3,461. WHITE, J.R.C. "Supplementary benefit - the new appellate arrangements". J.S.W.L. (1981). pp.185-188.

3,462. YATES, C. "Supplementary benefit appeals and the rules of evidence". J.S.W.L. (1980). pp.273-281.

Section 4   Social Security Benefits and Contributions

(a) <u>General</u>

3,463.   ANON.   "Wage-related benefits".   <u>L.R.</u>   LV.   (1966).   pp.51ff.

3,464.   ANON.   "Liabilities re the self-employed".   <u>P.H.</u>   LXXXV.   (1967).   pp.1227-1228.

3,465.   ANON.   "Insurance benefit - long term plans".   <u>L.R.</u>   LVIII.   (1969).   pp.156.

3,466.   ANON.   "Short term benefits axed".   <u>L.R.</u>   LX.   (1971).   pp.102ff.

3,467.   ANON.   "A lawyer's guide to national insurance.   Part VII - the new contribution rules".   <u>L.A.G.Bull.</u>   (1975).   p.96.

3,468.   ANON.   "State benefits".   <u>L.R.</u>   66.   (1977).   pp.174ff.

3,469.   ANON.   "Benefits under attack".   <u>L.R.</u>   69.   (1980).   pp.158-9.

3,470.   ANON.   "Liability for and recovery of contributions".   <u>L.S.G.</u>   77.   (1980).   pp.619-20.

3,471.   ADMIRALTY.   National Insurance Act, 1946.   Contributions and benefits for members of the armed forces.   London: 1950.   pp.22.   (Admiralty Fleet Order [AFO] No.3629/49).   DHSS.

3,472.   BOOTH, N.D.   Social security contributions.   London: 1982.   pp.xxviii + 204.   DHSS.

3,473.   BOOTH, N.D. (ed.).   DHSS official contributions guides.   London: 1983.   Looseleaf.   DHSS.

3,474.   CREEDY, J.   "Taxation and national insurance contributions in Britain".   <u>J.Pub.Econ.</u>   15.   (1981).   pp.379-388.

3,475.   DEPARTMENT OF HEALTH AND SOCIAL SECURITY.   "Proposals for an earnings-related social security system in Great Britain".   <u>Int.Soc.Sec.Rev.</u>   XXII.   (1969).   pp.174-189.

3,476.   DEPARTMENT OF HEALTH AND SOCIAL SECURITY.   Report by the Government Actuary on the draft of the Social Security Up-rating Order, 1975.   London: 1975.   pp.11.   (Cmnd. 6083).   DHSS.

3,477.   DEPARTMENT OF HEALTH AND SOCIAL SECURITY.   Report by the Government Actuary on the draft of the Social Security (Contributions, Re-rating) Order 1976.   London: 1976.   pp.8.   (Cmnd. 6688).   DHSS.

3,478.   DEPARTMENT OF HEALTH AND SOCIAL SECURITY   Social Security (Contributions) Bill 1980:   report by the Government Actuary on the financial provisions of the Bill.   London: 1980.   pp.11.   (Cmnd. 8091).   DHSS.

3,479. DEPARTMENT OF HEALTH AND SOCIAL SECURITY. Abstract of statistics for index of retail prices, average earnings, social security benefits and contributions. Newcastle upon Tyne: 1982. DHSS.

3,480. FIMISTER, G. & LISTER, R. Social Security the case against contribution tests: paper for submission to the Trades Union Congress Social Security Working Party. London: 1980. pp.15. DHSS.

3,481. GOODMAN, J.C. Social security in the United Kingdom: contracting out of the system. Washington; London: American Enterprise Institute for Public Policy Research. 1981. pp.72. DHSS.

3,482. GOVERNMENT ACTUARY'S DEPARTMENT. Report on the draft of the Social Security Benefits Up-rating Order 1980. London: 1980. pp.[ii] + 6. (Cmnd. 7971). DHSS.

3,483. HARDMAN, J.P. & ESSEX, P. A practical guide to the new social security contributions. London: 1975. pp.28. (Accountants Digest No.21). DHSS.

3,484. LUSTGARTEN, L.S. & ELLIOTT, M.J. "Benefits uprating: a problem in administrative law". N.L.J. 126. (1976). pp.756, 795.

3,485. MINISTRY OF NATIONAL INSURANCE. Notes on contributions and credits. London: 1953. pp.15. DHSS.

3,486. MINISTRY OF PENSIONS AND NATIONAL INSURANCE. Contributions reckoner. London: 1959. pp.129. DHSS.

3,487. MINISTRY OF PENSIONS AND NATIONAL INSURANCE. Abstract of statistics relating to level of benefits and contributions and other related matters. Second quinquennial report, 1960. London: 1960. unpag. DHSS.

3,488. MINISTRY OF PENSIONS AND NATIONAL INSURANCE. The National Insurance (Assessment of Graduated Contributions) Regulations, 1960. Explanatory memorandum. London: 1960. pp.7. DHSS.

3,489. MONTAGU, N. & OTHERS. Brought to account: report of the Rayner scrutiny team on the validation of national insurance contribution records. London: 1981. pp.[3] + 93. DHSS.

3,490. MUNRO, H. "Earnings-related short term benefit". N.L.J. CXVI. (1965-66). pp.1306, 1308-9.

3,491. O'HIGGINS, P. "Les problemes juridiques relatifs a la fixation des prestations de la securite sociale, notamment en fonction des modifications du cout de la vie et des salaires: rapport national". (Congres International de Droit du Travail et de la Securite Sociale, 6ieme, Stockholm, 1966. Actes.) Stockholm: 1968. Vol.I. pp.5. Text in English.

3,492. PRESTATAIRE. "Liability for and recovery of contributions". L.S.G. 77. (1980). pp.619-20.

3,493. ROHRLICH, G.F. "Les problemes juridiques relatifs a la fixation des prestations de la securite sociale, notamment en fonction des modifications du cout de la vie et des salaires. [Rapport general]. <u>Actes du Sixieme Congres International de Droit du Travail et de la Securite Sociale.</u> (1966). pp.19-67.

3,494.   WILLIAMS, D.W.   "Insurance as tax".   <u>N.S.</u>   34.   (1975). p.317.

3,495.   WILLIAMS, D.W.   "National insurance contributions - a second income tax". <u>Br.Tax Rev.</u> (1978). pp.84-98.

3,496.   WILLIAMS, D.W.   Social security taxation: a guide to contributions and contributory conditions under the Social Security Acts. London: 1982. pp.xxxiii + 536. LSE.

3,497.   WILLIAMS, D.W.   "Company directors and their social security contributions". <u>L.S.G.</u> 80. (1983). pp.838-39.

(b) Benefits and Damages

3,498.   ANON. "National insurance benefits and reduction of damages". <u>L.J.</u> CX. (1960). p.649.

3,499.   ATIYAH, P.S.   "Common law damages and social security: the need for integration". <u>Poverty.</u> (1970). (14). pp.17-18.

3,500.   COCKERELL, H.A.L.   "Accumulation of claims.   Payments, recourse and subrogation in private and social insurance". <u>J.B.L.</u> (1973). pp.214-225.

3,501.   DAVIES, P.J.   "Deducting benefits from damages: the only consistently logical conclusion". [<u>Nabi v. British Leyland (U.K.) Ltd</u>   [1980] 1 W.L.R. 529]. <u>M.L.R.</u>   44.   (1981). pp.222-6.

3,502.   EAGLESTONE, F.N.   "Damages and the disability pension". <u>P.H.</u> 87. (1969). pp.1866-1868.

3,503.   GANZ, G.   "Gourley's case and the unemployed". <u>M.L.R.</u>   28. (1965). pp.224-227.

3,504.   GILES, O.C. "Wages reqained and lost - Workmen's Compensation Act and National Health Insurance Act".   <u>M.L.R.</u>   3. (1939-40). pp.162-163.

3,505.   HODGE, H.   "Children's damages - effect on supplementary benefit". <u>L.A.G.Bull.</u> (1975). p.213.

3,506.   TRIMBLE, W.D.   "Unemployment benefit and damages". <u>N.I.L.Q.</u> 20. (1969). pp.65-71.

Section 5   Sickness and Disability

(a) Sickness Benefit

3,507.   ANON.   "Monthly review of current events.   The doctor as a judge".   Ind.L.R.   1.   (1946-47).   pp.232-233.

3,508.   ANON.   "Monthly review of current events.   Reinstatement and unemployment   insurance".   Ind.L.R.   1.   (1946-47). pp.365-367.

3,509.   ANON.   "The National Insurance Act.   Payment during sickness". Ind. Welfare   XXX.   (1948).   p.118.

3,510.   ANON.   "Das   system   der   sozialen   sicherheit   und   ihre Mittelaufbringung   in   den   Staaten   der   E.W.G.,   in Grossbritannien und in Danemark".   Recht der Arbeit.   (1963). pp.25-30.

3,511.   ANON.   "Sick pay survey".   L.R.   53.   (1964).   pp.165-6.

3,512.   ANON.   "Costing absenteeism: new controls at Alcan Foils". I.R.R.R.   (1982).   (Aug.).   pp.6-11.

3,513.   ANON.   "Sickness absence: self-certification round-up". I.R.R.R.   (1982).   pp.11-13.

3,514.   ANON.   "Self-certification: DHSS guidance",   I.R.R.R.   271. (1982).   pp.12-14.

3,515.   ANON.   "The vaccine damage payments scheme".   L.S.G.   80. (1983).   pp.1071-1073.

3,516.   BILSLAND, I.   Self certification: a guide.   London: 1982. pp.55.   DHSS.

3,517.   BROOKE, R.   "Social security and the sick".   N.L.J.   120. (1970).   p.999.

3,518.   BULL, D.   The new sickness certification: panacea or placebo? London: C.P.A.G.   1976.   pp.40.   DHSS.

3,519.   CHARTERIS, K.   "I hereby certify...".   D.E.G.   (1982). pp.149-151.

3,520.   CLARKE, J.S.   "National health insurance".   In W.E. Robson (ed.), Social security.   London: 1943.   pp.75-112.   2nd ed. London: 1945.   pp.84-121.   LSE.

3,521.   DEPARTMENT   OF   HEALTH   AND   SOCIAL   SECURITY.   Digest   of statistics analysing certificates of incapacity.   London: DHSS.   1961-64.   1 vol.   pp.223.   DHSS.   1964-67.   1 vol. pp.281.   DHSS.   1968-69.   1 vol.   pp.446.   DHSS.

3,522.   DEPARTMENT OF HEALTH AND SOCIAL SECURITY.   Patients' money in long-stay hospitals.   London: 1981.   pp.17.   DHSS.

3,523. FENN, P. "Sickness duration, residual disability and income replacement: an empirical study". E.J. 91. (1981). pp.158-78.

3,524. HOWARD, G. A guide to self-certification. London: Industrial Society. 1982. pp.47. DHSS.

3,525. INTERNATIONAL SOCIAL SECURITY ASSOCIATION. XIVth General Meeting, 1961. Report II. Volume and cost of sickness benefit in cash and kind. Geneva: 1961. 2 vols. DHSS.

3,526. JONES, G.M. "Incapacity for work among the insured population of Great Britain". Brit.Jo.Prev.Soc.Med. 13. (1959). pp.74-87.

3,527. KASTNER, F. "Soziale sicherheit in der Bundesrepublik und in Grossbritannien". O.krankenk. 19. (1963). pp.446-453.

3,528. KEAST, H. "Sick leave pay under national insurance". Ind.L.R. 3. (1948-49). pp.157-149.

3,529. LEE, K. "Assessment of the ability to work of the 'unfit'". Transactions of the Society of Occupational Medicine. 18. (1968). pp.61-66.

3,530. LEVY, H. "Sociology and health". Ind.L.R. 2. (1947-48). pp.140-157.

3,531. LEWIS, P. "Social security: the GP's role as watchdog". General Practitioner. (Nov. 1977). pp.14-16.

3,532. MARTIN, J. & MORGAN, M. Prolonged sickness and the return to work: a study for the Department of Health and Social Security of the circumstances of people who have received sickness benefits for between a month and a year, and the factors affecting their return to work: (draft report). London: [1975?]. pp.iii + 247. DHSS.

3,533. MINISTRY OF HEALTH. INSURANCE DEPARTMENT. The position of insurable persons in mental institutions. London: 1949. pp.3. (Circular 95/49). DHSS.

3,534. MINISTRY OF HEALTH. Report of the Inter-Departmental Committee on Medical Certificates. (Safford Report). London: 1949. pp.ii + 102. DHSS.

3,535. MINISTRY OF HEALTH. Medical certification for national insurance purposes. London: 1961. pp.9. DHSS.

3,536. MINISTRY OF PENSIONS AND NATIONAL INSURANCE. Digest of statistics analysing certificates of incapacity. London: 1950-. LSE.

3,537. MINISTRY OF PENSIONS AND NATIONAL INSURANCE. Report on an enquiry into the incidence of incapacity for work. Part I: Scope and characteristics of employers' sick pay schemes. Part II: Incidence of incapacity for work in different areas and occupations. London: 1964-1965. 2 vols. pp.87 + ccxxiv + 163. DHSS.

3,538.   NORTHERN IRELAND.   Prescribing and sickness benefit costs in
         Northern Ireland: report of the Health Advisory Committee.
         Belfast: 1969. pp.91. (Cmd. 528). LSE.

3,539.   OFFICE OF HEALTH ECONOMICS.   Work lost through sickness.
         London: 1965. pp.32. DHSS.

3,540.   OFFICE OF POPULATION CENSUSES AND SURVEYS.   SOCIAL SURVEY
         DIVISION.   Prolonged sickness and the return to work: an
         enquiry carried out in 1972/3 for the DHSS by Jean Martin and
         Margaret Morgan of the circumstances of people who hae
         received incapacity benefits for between a month and a year,
         and the factors affecting their return to work.   London:
         1975. pp.viii + 247. DHSS.

3,541.   RAI CHOUDHURI, S.   Sickness insurance in India and Britain.
         Calcutta: 1966. pp.xvi + 318.

3,542.   ROBB, D.F.   "Medical certification".   The Practitioner
         Supplement. (July, 1967). pp.3-8.

3,543.   SLEIGHT, R.L.   "Sickness and disability: the long-term
         problem". Policy Holder. 85. (1967). pp.1722-1726.

3,544.   STEELE, R.T.   "Sports injuries and sick pay".   S.J.   124.
         (1980). pp.354-55.

3,545.   THOMAS, R.B.   "Wages, sickness benefits and absenteeism".
         Int.J.Soc.Econ. 7. (1980). pp.51-61.

3,546.   TOMES, I. "Basic features of sickness insurance in European
         socialist countries". I.Lab.R. 95. (1967). pp.202-214.

3,547.   TREITEL, R.   "Demographic and invalidity characteristics of
         social security disability beneficiaries in the United
         States". Int.Soc.Sec.Rev. 34. (1981). pp.309-319.

3,548.   UNITED KINGDOM. Hospital in-patients: report of the National
         Insurance Advisory Committee... on the review of certain
         amounts payable to hospital in-patients.   London: 1952.
         (B.P.P. 1951-52. XV). PP.14. LSE.

3,549.   WHITEHEAD, F.E.   "Trends in certificated sickness absence".
         Social Trends. 2. (1971). pp.13-23.

3,550.   WHITEHEAD, F.E.   "Sickness and injury benefit".   Statistical
         News. May. (1969). pp.5.14-5.18.

3,551.   WILLMOTT, P. & WILLMOTT, P. "Off work through illness". N.S.
         1. (1962-63). (15). pp.16-18.

3,552.   WORTMANN, A.   "Zur sozialen Sicherheit in Grossbritanien".
         O.krankenk. 18. (1963). pp.417-424.

(b) Statutory Sick Pay

3,553.   ANON. "More overheads - going sick". L.S.G. 77. (1980). p.
         1201.

3,554. ANON. "The IRLIB guide to statutory sick pay - part 1. The general scheme of entitlement". I.R.R.R. (1982). Legal Information Bulletin. No.212. pp.2-12.

3,555. ANON. "Sick pay schemes - current practice and future change". I.R.R.R. 273. (1982). pp.2-10.

3,556. CHRISTIAN, C. "SSP: another twist in the tale". L.S.G. 80. (1983). pp.1598-1599.

3,557. CONFEDERATION OF BRITISH INDUSTRY. Why the Government needs to think again on sick pay. London: 1981. pp.[6]. DHSS.

3,558. COOPERS AND LYBRAND. Tolley's guide to statutory sick pay: implementing and operating SSP in practice. Croydon: 1983. pp.ix + 78. DHSS.

3,559. DEPARTMENT OF HEALTH AND SOCIAL SECURITY. Compensating employers for statutory sick pay: a consultative document. London: 1981. pp.[i] + 17. DHSS.

3,560. DEPARTMENT OF HEALTH AND SOCIAL SECURITY. Statutory sick pay: brief for employers' seminars. London: 1982. pp.35 + [17]. DHSS.

3,561. DEPARTMENT OF HEALTH AND SOCIAL SECURITY. Guidance on accountants' reports on employers' operation of statutory sick pay. London: 1982. pp.3. DHSS.

3,562. DISABILITY ALLIANCE. Compensating employers for statutory sick pay: the Disability Alliance's response to a DHSS consultative document. London: 1981. pp.[2] + 11. DHSS.

3,563. DUNN, A. "The statutory sick pay scheme - 2". L.A.G. Bull. (July, 1983), pp.81-84.

3,564. HOUSE OF COMMONS. Social Services Committee Session 1980-81. Second report: the government's proposals for income during initial sickness. (Chairman: Renee Short). London: 1981. pp.[26]. (HC 113). DHSS; LSE.

3,565. HOWARD, G. A guide to statutory sick pay. London: Industrial Society. 1982. pp.51. DHSS.

3,566. HOWARD, G.S. Statutory sick pay: a practical guide. London: 1983. pp.viii + 62. DHSS.

3,567. INCOMES DATA SERVICES. Sick pay. London: 1981. pp.24. (IDS Study, 236). DHSS.

3,568. INSTITUTE OF PERSONNEL MANAGEMENT. Sick pay schemes. London: 1971. pp.100. (IPM Information Report 7). DHSS.

3,569. KEARNS, J.L. Self-certification and employers' statutory sick pay. London: 1982. pp.16. DHSS.

3,570. KHAN, A.N. "Arrival of new sick pay". S.J. 127. (1983). pp.452-454.

3,571. LABOUR RESEARCH DEPARTMENT. Self-certification. London:

[1982]. pp.14. DHSS.

3,572. LEWIS, R. "The privatisation of sickness benefit". _I.L.J._
11. (1982). pp.245-254.

3,573. LONSDALE, S. Get well soon... or face poverty. London: Low
Pay Unit. 1981. pp.15. DHSS.

3,574. O'HIGGINS, M. "Income during initial sickness". _Policy and
Politics._ 9. (1981). pp.151-171.

3,575. PARTINGTON, M. "Income during initial sickness: a new
strategy (Cmnd. 7864)". _I.L.J._ 9. (1980). pp.193-7.

(c) Non-contributory Invalidity Pension

3,576. DEPARTMENT OF HEALTH AND SOCIAL SECURITY. Review of the
Household Duties test. London: 1983. pp.36. DHSS.

3,577. GLENDINNING, C. After working all these years: a response to
the report of the National Insurance Advisory Committee on the
"household duties" test for non-contributory invalidity
pension for married women. London: Disability Alliance.
1980. pp.[iii] + 64. DHSS.

3,578. HYMAN, M. "Housewives' non-contributory invalidity pension:
the case for abolition of the household duties test in the
United Kingdom". _Int.Soc.Sec.Rev._ 35. (1982). pp.319-332.

3,579. LARGE, P. "Disabled housewives". _Poverty._ (1974). (28).
pp.9-11.

3,580. LISTER, R. "Housewives' non-contributory invalidity pension".
L.A.G.Bull. (1979). pp.256-259.

3,581. LOACH, I. Disabled married women: a study of the problems of
introducing non-contributory pensions in November 1977.
London: Disability Alliance. 1977. pp.46. DHSS.

3,582. NATIONAL INSURANCE ADVISORY COMMITTEE. Report on a question
relating to the household duties test for a non-contributory
invalidity pension for married women. London: 1980. pp.24.
(Cmnd.7955). DHSS.

3,583. RICHARDS, M. "A study of the non-contributory invalidity
pension for married women". _J.S.W.L._ (1979). pp.66-75.

(d) Disability Benefits

3,584. ANON. "Monthly review of current events. Assessment of
disablement". _Ind.L.R._ 1. (1946-47). pp.371-374.

3,585. ANON. "Disablement pensions". _N.S._ 4. (1964). (92).
pp.20-22.

3,586. ANON. "New regulations affecting attendance allowance".
_L.S.G._ 77. (1980). p.548.

3,587.   ANON.   "Attendance   allowance - a take-up problem?".
Disability Rights Bulletin. (1981). pp.19-22.

3,588.   ABEL-SMITH, B. Social security provisions for the longer term
disabled in eight countries of the European Community (a case
study). [London]: [1981]. pp.[67]. DHSS.

3,589.   ABELSON,   I.   "The   lawyer   and   the   disabled   client".
L.A.G.Bull. (1976). pp.229-231.

3,590.   ANDERSON, J. A record of fifty years service to the disabled
from 1919 to 1969. London: 1970. pp.viii + 81. DHSS.

3,591.   AVERY, L. Disability: counting the costs: a study of the
take-up of supplementary benefit additional requirements.
[London]: 1983. pp.42. DHSS.

3,592.   BALDWIN, S. "Mobility allowance". N.S. 35. (1976). p.18.

3,593.   BALDWIN, S.   The financial consequences of disablement in
children. York: University of York, Social Policy Research
Unit. [1980]. 2 vols. DHSS.

3,594.   BOLDERSON, H. "Compensation for disability". J.Soc.Pol. 3.
(1974). pp.193-211.

3,595.   BRADSHAW, J.   The financial needs of disabled children.
London: 1975. pp.16. (Pamphlets on Disability No.2). DHSS.

3,596.   BRADSHAW, J. & BALDWIN, S. "Allowable attendance". N.S. 29.
(1974). p.292.

3,597.   BROOKE, R. "Social security and the disabled". N.L.J. 120.
(1970). p.952.

3,598.   CARSON, D. "Attendance allowances for the severely disabled".
N.L.J. 124. (1974). p.142.

3,599.   CARSON, D. "A lawyer's guide to national insurance. Part VI
- attendance allowances". L.A.G.Bull. (1975). pp.67-69.

3,600.   CENTRAL   COUNCIL   FOR   THE   DISABLED.   Mobility allowance.
London: 1975. pp.10. DHSS.

3,601.   CENTRAL COUNCIL FOR THE DISABLED. Report of the working party
on mobility allowance.   (Chairman: G. Wilson).   London:
1976. pp.64. DHSS.

3,602.   CHAPELTOWN CITIZENS ADVICE BUREAU. Disability project report:
September 1979 - August 1980. London: 1980. pp.[ii] + 35.
(CAB Occasional Paper No.12). DHSS.

3,603.   CHAPPELL, H. "Sex discrimination: invalids at home". N.S.
59. (1982). pp.58-59.

3,604.   CLARKE, G.A.   "Mobility allowance".   N.L.J.   133.   (1983).
pp.147-148.

3,605.   COOKE, K., BRADSHAW, J. & LAWTON, D. "Take-up of benefits by
families with disabled children". Child Care, Health and

Development. 9. (1983). pp.145-156.

3,606. COOKE, K.R. & STADEN, F.M. The impact of the mobility allowance: an evaluative study. London: 1981. pp.vii + 50. (Research Report No.7). DHSS.

3,607. COOPER, A. A guide to benefits for the handicapped children and their families. London: [1983]. pp.33. (Check Your Rights, 1). DHSS.

3,608. COOPER, A., TOWNSEND, P. & WALKER, A. Disability rights handbook for 1981: a guide to income benefits and services. London: [1981]. pp.83. DHSS.

3,609. DARNBOROUGH, A. (comp.). Directory for the disabled: a handbook of information and opportunities for disabled and handicapped people. Cambridge: 1981. pp.xiv + 242. DHSS.

3,610. DARNBROUGH, A. & KINRADE, D. Motoring and mobility for disabled people. London: Royal Association for Disability and Rehabilitation. [1981]. pp.352. DHSS.

3,611. DEPARTMENT OF HEALTH AND SOCIAL SECURITY. Cash benefits for the handicapped: a selective study of the schemes for some European countries in operation. London: 1972. pp.158. DHSS.

3,612. DEPARTMENT OF HEALTH AND SOCIAL SECURITY. Uprating of mobility allowance: statement prepared pursuant to section 37A(4) of the Social Security Act 1975 as amended by section 3(2) of the Social Security Act 1979. London: 1980. pp.3. (HC 596 1979-80). DHSS; LSE.

3,613. DILLEMANS, R. "Les handicapes et la securite sociale.
[Social security and the disabled.] ". Rev.Belge de Sec.Soc. 24. (1982). pp.18-30.

3,614. DISABILITY ALLIANCE. Poverty and disability: the case for a comprehensive income scheme for disabled people. London: 1975. pp.20. DHSS.

3,615. DISABILITY ALLIANCE. Disability rights handbook: a guide to income benefits and certain aids and services. London: 1976. pp.32. DHSS.

3,616. DISABILITY ALLIANCE. The government's record on behalf of people with disabilities. London: 1981. pp.[1] + 24. DHSS.

3,617. DISABILITY ALLIANCE. Disability rights handbook for 1982. 6th ed. London: 1981. pp.92. DHSS.

3,618. DISABLEMENT INCOME GROUP. DIG progress. Godalming: 1968- . (quarterly ser.). LSE.

3,619. DISABLEMENT INCOME GROUP CHARITABLE TRUST. Social security and disablement: a study of the financial provisions for disabled people in seven West European countries. Godalming: 1971. pp.vi + 61. DHSS.

3,620. DURWARD, L. That's the way the money goes: the extra cost of living with a disability. London: 1981. pp.[1] + 52. DHSS.

3,621. ELSON, J. "A national disability income". N.S. 10. (1967). pp.121-122.

3,622. GREGORY, P. Deafness and public responsibility. London. LSE.

3,623. HABER, L.D. "Disability, work and income maintenance: prevalence of disability, 1966". Social Security Bulletin. (1968). pp.14-23.

3,624. HOUSE OF COMMONS. LIBRARY. RESEARCH DIVISION. Invalid vehicle service and mobility allowance. London: 1976. pp.8. (Background Paper No.5). DHSS.

3,625. HOWE, SIR G. & RAISON, T. Disability policy: the next stage: a Conservative policy paper. London: 1974. pp.8. DHSS.

3,626. HUNT, P. Stigma: the experience of disability. London: 1966. pp.x + 176. DHSS.

3,627. HYMAN, M. The extra cost of disabled living: a case history study. London: National Fund for Research into Crippling Diseases. 1977. pp.196. DHSS.

3,628. INTERNATIONAL SOCIAL SECURITY ASSOCIATION. Social security and disability: issues in policy research. Geneva: 1981. pp.vii + 164. DHSS.

3,629. INTERNATIONAL SOCIETY FOR REHABILITATION OF THE DISABLED. Proceedings of the international seminar on rehabilitation programmes in workmen's compensation and related fields. New York: 1970. pp.vii + 142. DHSS.

3,630. JOHNSTONE, K. "How to help the disabled". N.S. 11. (1968). pp.601-602.

3,631. LOACH, I. The price of deafness: a review of the financial and employment problems of the deaf and hard of hearing. London: 1976. pp.34. DHSS.

3,632. LYNES, T. "Disabled income". N.S. 24. (1973). pp.244-246.

3,633. MACKENZIE, L. & AITKEN, C. "Elusive allowances". B.M.J. 283. (1981). pp.1587-1588.

3,634. McBRIDE, E.O. Disability evaluation and principles of treatment of compensable injuries. 6th ed. London: 1963. pp.xiv + 573. DHSS.

3,635. McGINNIS, E.B. "Mobility allowance: the other side of the trike". Social Work Service. 14. (1977). pp.50-51.

3,636. MESHER, J. "Recent national insurance commissioners' decisions: disability benefits". J.S.W.L. (1979). pp.442-448.

3,637. MESHER, J. "Recent social security commissioners' decisions: disability". J.S.W.L. (1981). pp.58-64.

3,638. MESHER, J. "Recent social security commissioners' decisions: disability benefits". J.S.W.L. (1982). pp.48-54.

3,639. MITCHELL, P. "Fostering a handicap". N.S. 37. (1976). p.500.

3,640. MORRIS, A. Needs before means: an exposition of the underlying purposes of the Chronically Sick and Disabled Persons Act 1970. London: [1971?]. pp.18. LSE.

3,641. OFFICE OF POPULATION CENSUSES AND SURVEYS. SOCIAL SURVEY DIVISION. Handicapped and impaired in Great Britain. An enquiry carried out on behalf of the Department of Health and Social Security, the Scottish Home and Health Department, the Welsh Office - in conjunction with other Government departments. London: 1971-72. DHSS. Part I. Handicapped and impaired in Great Britain by Amelia Harris, Elizabeth Cox and Christopher R.W. Smith. pp.330. Part II. Work and housing of impaired persons in Great Britain by Judith R. Buckle. pp.xxviii + 210. Part III. Income and entitlement to supplementary benefit in Great Britain, by Amelia I. Harris, Christopher R.W. Smith and Elizabeth Head. pp.vii + 74. LSE.

3,642. PETRE, P. "Essai de comparaison des prestations financieres accordees aux personnes handicappees en Belgique, France, Pays-Bas et Royaume-Uni". Rev.Belge de Sec.Soc. XIX. (1977). pp.808-833.

3,643. PHILLIPS, H. & GLENDINNING, C. Who benefits? Report of a welfare rights project with people with disabilities in North Yorkshire. London: 1981. pp.[ii] + 64 + bibliog. DHSS.

3,644. PIACHAUD, D., BRADSHAW, J. & WEALE, A. "The income effect of a disabled child". Epidemiology and Community Health. 35. (1981). pp.123-127.

3,645. PRESTATAIRE (pseud.). "Mobility allowance". L.S.G. 76. (1979). p.813.

3,646. PRESTATAIRE (pseud.). "New regulations affecting attendance allowance". L.S.G. 77. (1980). p.548.

3,647. REID, J. (ed.). "Social security. Disablement benefits". I.L.J. 1. (1972). pp.109-113.

3,648. REID, J. "Social security. Recent decisions on disablement benefit". I.L.J. 4. (1975). pp.122-126.

3,649. ROBERTS, G.S. "The mobility allowance - a review of the initial five years". Health Trends. 14. (1982). pp.13-15.

3,650. ROYAL ASSOCIATION FOR DISABILITY AND REHABILITATION. Mobility allowance. London: 1977. pp.12. DHSS.

3,651. SAINSBURY, S. "The drain on the disabled". N.S. 16. (1970). pp.1089-1092.

3,652. SAINSBURY, S. Registered as disabled. London: Bell, 1970.

pp.205. (Occasional Papers on Social Administration No.35). CUL.

3,653. SAINSBURY, S. Measuring disability. London: 1973. pp.125. (Occasional Papers on Social Administration No.54). CUL.

3,654. SHEPPERDSON, B. "Attending to need". N.S. 24. (1973). p.754.

3,655. SMITH, R. "Attendance allowance". Poverty. 48. (1981). pp.9-12.

3,656. TOPLISS, E. Provision for the disabled. Oxford, London: 1975. pp.ix + 153. CUL.

3,657. TOWNSEND, P. "The disabled need help". N.S. 10. (1967). pp.432-433.

3,658. TOWNSEND, P. "Help for the disabled". N.S. 33. (1975). pp.193-194.

3,659. TOWNSEND, P. The Government's failure to plan for disablement in old age: a commentary on the consultative document "A happier old age". Disability Alliance: 1979. pp.[ii] + 56. DHSS.

3,660. TUNNARD, J. "New benefits for the disabled". L.A.G.Bull. (1976). pp.33-34.

3,661. TUNNARD, J. Taken for a ride. London: 1976. pp.21. DHSS.

3,662. WALKER, A. Living standards in crisis: the combined impact of inflation and cuts in subsides and social services on the incomes of disabled people. London: Disability Alliance. 1977. pp.41. DHSS.

3,663. WALKER, A. "How to compensate the disabled". N.S. 46. (1978). pp.336-8.

3,664. WALKER, A. Poverty, disability and welfare rights: towards social justice for people with disabilities. Birmingham: British Association of Social Workers. 1980. pp.[2] + 19. DHSS.

3,665. WALKER, A. "Assessing the severity of disability for the allocation of benefits and services". Int.Soc.Sec.Rev. 34. (1981). pp.274-291.

3,666. WEIR, S. "Has International Year helped disabled people? N.S. 58. (1981). pp.540-541.

3,667. WILSON, J. "A comprehensive disability income scheme". Poverty. 48. (1981). pp.25-30.

Section 6   Industrial Injury and Disease

See also: Workmen's Compensation.

3,668. ANON.   "The National Insurance (Industrial Injuries) Bill".
        L.J. XCVI. (1946). p.169.

3,669. ANON.   "National Insurance (Industrial Injuries) Act, 1946".
        Lab.G. 54. (1946). pp.214-14.

3,670. ANON.   "The substitute for workmen's compensation". S.L.T.
        [1946]. pp.89-91.

3,671. ANON.   "Industrial Injuries Regulations". L.R. 37. (1948).
        pp.174, 183-4, 204-5.

3,672. ANON.   "Review of current events. The National Insurance
        (Industrial Injuries) Bill, 1948". Ind.L.R. 3. (1948-49).
        pp.3-5.

3,673. ANON.   "Workmen's compensation and national insurance". L.J.
        CII. (1952). p.129.

3,674. ANON.   "Notes on current events. Reform of the National
        Insurance (Industrial Injuries) Acts". Ind.L.R. 7.
        (1952-53). pp.243-244.

3,675. ANON.   "Industrial injury benefit: proving that incapacity is
        the result of an accident". S.J. 98. (1954). pp.657-8.

3,676. ANON.   "Industrial accidents and the law". F.N. 7. (1957).
        p.84.

3,677. ANON.   "Some financial aspects of employment injury
        insurance". Bull. I.S.S.A. XVIII. (1965). pp.331-402.

3,678. ANON.   "Those phoney accidents - what the men on the spot say
        about them". Safety & Rescue. (1969). 16.

3,679. ANON.   "Industrial injuries: accidents whilst travelling".
        L.S.G. 77. (1980). p.548.

3,680. ANON.   "They also serve who only stand and wait: accidents
        arising 'in the course of employment'". L.S.G. 77. (1980).
        p.812.

3,681. ANON.   "An individual proof system for compensating industrial
        diseases". I.R.R.R. 261. (1981). pp.6-9.

3,682. ANON.   "Industrial deafness litigation 1971-1981". I.R.R.R.
        261. (1981). pp.9-12.

3,683. BELL, J. How to get industrial injuries benefits. London:
        1966. pp.xv + 275. Sq.; DHSS.

3,684. BROWN, J.C.   "Is there still a place for the industrial
        injuries scheme?". Pol.Stu. 3. (1982). pp.121-138.

3,685. BURN, W.L. "Workmen's compensation: the new proposals".
        Nineteenth Century. 137. (Jan.-June 1945). pp.20-8.

3,686. CAREY, G.C.R. (etc.). Byssinosis in flax workers in Northern
        Ireland: a report to the Minister of Labour and National
        Insurance from the Department of Social and Preventive
        Medicine, the Queen's University of belfast. Belfast: 1965.
        pp.vii + 172. LSE.

3,687. CARMICHAEL, J.A.G. "Medical aspects of the Industrial
        Injuries Acts". Medico-Legal Jo. 42. (1974). p.44.

3,688. CARSON, D. "Reform of the industrial injuries scheme".
        J.S.W.L. (1982). pp.96-98.

3,689. CHEIT, E. & GORDON, M.S. (eds.). Occupational disability and
        public policy. London: 1963. pp.xii + 446. DHSS.

3,690. COMMISSION OF THE EUROPEAN COMMUNITIES. Recommended action of
        the Commission to Member States regarding the adoption of a
        European list of occupational disease. Explanatory statement.
        [Brussels]: 1962. pp.19. DHSS.

3,691. CURSON, C. "Accidents at work: the costs and advantages of a
        collective liability system". Soc. & Econ.Ad. 4. (1970).
        pp.108-114.

3,692. DENYER, R.L. "Special hardship allowance". N.L.J. 122.
        (1972). p.543.

3,693. DEPARTMENT OF HEALTH AND SOCIAL SECURITY. Reported decisions
        of the commissioner under the National Insurance (Industrial
        Injuries) Acts. London: HMSO. serial pub'n. var. pag.
        DHSS.

3,694. DEPARTMENT OF HEALTH AND SOCIAL SECURITY. Abstract of
        statistics of industrial disablement benefit, etc. London:
        DHSS. 1966-67, 1968, 1969. unpaged. DHSS.

3,695. DEPARTMENT OF HEALTH AND SOCIAL SECURITY. Handbook for
        industrial injuries medical boards. London: 1970. pp.vi +
        75. (Losseleaf). LSE; DHSS. 2nd ed. 1980. DHSS.

3,696. DEPARTMENT OF HEALTH AND SOCIAL SECURITY. Notes on the
        diagnosis of occupational diseases prescribed under the
        National Insurance (Industrial Injuries) Act 1965 (not
        including pneumoconiosis and allied occupational chest
        diseases). 5th ed. London: 1972. pp.65. DHSS.

3,697. DEPARTMENT OF HEALTH AND SOCIAL SECURITY. Reform of the
        industrial injuries scheme. London: 1981. pp.iv + 30.
        (Cmnd. 8402). DHSS.

3,698. DINSDALE, W.A. History of accident insurance in Great
        Britain. London: 1954. pp.xii + 362. DHSS.

3,699. DISABILITY ALLIANCE. Reforming the industrial injuries
        scheme: the wrong priorities. London: 1982. pp.16. DHSS.

3,700. DOHERTY, N.A. "Disincentives to work under the United Kingdom industrial injuries scheme". Int.J.Soc.Econ. 7. (1980). pp.341-52.

3,701. DRABBLE, R. "A lawyer's guide to national insurance. Part V - the industrial injuries scheme". L.A.G.Bull. (1975). pp.45-49.

3,702. FINCH, H.J. Industrial Injuries Act. London: 1948. pp.114. DHSS.

3,703. GHOSH, D. & LEES, D. Cost and compensation for personal injuries in industrial accidents: a case study. Nottingham: 1975. pp.ii + 19. (Discussion Papers in Industrial Economics No.18). DHSS.

3,704. HESMONDHALGH, S. "Painful pantomime". N.S. 22. (1972). p.33.

3,705. HIGUCHI, T. "The special treatment of employment injury in social security". I.Lab.R. 102. (1970). pp.109-26.

3,706. HILL, J.M. & TRIST, E.L. Industrial accidents, sickness and other absences. London: 1962. pp.58. (Tavistock Pamphlets No.4). LSE.

3,707. HOME OFFICE. Home Office consolidated circular to coroners on deaths from industrial accidents and diseases. (40/1956). London: 1956. pp.16. DHSS.

3,708. HOPKINS, R.R. A handbook of industrial welfare. London: 1955. pp.vi + 258. LSE.

3,709. INTERNATIONAL SOCIAL SECURITY ASSOCIATION. XIVth General Meeting, 1961. Employment accident insurance. Geneva: 1962. pp.658. DHSS.

3,710. INTERNATIONAL SOCIAL SECURITY ASSOCIATION. XIVth General Meeting, Istanbul, 1961. Organising and financing of insurance against employment accidents. Geneva: 1962. pp.147. DHSS.

3,711. INDUSTRIAL INJURIES ADVISORY COUNCIL. National Insurance (Industrial Injuries) Act, 1946: tuberculosis and other communicable diseases in relation to nurses and other health workers. London: 1950. pp.20. (B.P.P. 1950-51, XVI). LSE.

3,712. INDUSTRIAL INJURIES ADVISORY COUNCIL. Raynaud's phenomenon: report... on the question whether Raynaud's phenomenon should be prescribed under the Act. London: 1954. pp.16. (B.P.P. 1954-55, VI). LSE.

3,713. INDUSTRIAL INJURIES ADVISORY COUNCIL. Report... on the rules governing assessment of disablement in cases involving damage to an organ which, in a normal person, is one of a pair. London: [1956]. pp.10. (B.P.P. 1955-56, XXII). LSE.

3,714. INDUSTRIAL INJURIES ADVISORY COUNCIL. Byssinosis. London: [1956]. p.15. (B.P.P. 1955-56, XXII). LSE.

3,715. INDUSTRIAL INJURIES ADVISORY COUNCIL. Cadmium poisoning. London: [1956]. pp.11. (B.P.P. 1955-56, XXII). LSE.

3,716. INDUSTRIAL INJURIES ADVISORY COUNCIL. National Insurance (Industrial Injuries) Act, 1946: review of the prescribed diseases schedule. London: [1958]. pp.34. (B.P.P. 1957-58, XV). LSE.

3,717. INDUSTRIAL INJURIES ADVISORY COUNCIL. Vibration syndrome. Interim report on the question whether diseases of bones, joints, muscles, blood-vessels or nerves, of the hand, arm, or shoulder (including Raynaud's phenomenon) caused by vibrating machines should be prescribed under the Act. London: 1970. pp.13. (Cmnd. 4430). DHSS.

3,718. INDUSTRIAL INJURIES ADVISORY COUNCIL. Report on the question whether poisoning by acrylamide should be prescribed under the Act. London: 1972. pp.9. DHSS.

3,719. INDUSTRIAL INJURIES ADVISORY COUNCIL. Industrial diseases: a review of the Schedule and the question of individual proof. London: 1981. pp.76. (Cmnd. 8393). DHSS.

3,720. INDUSTRIAL INJURIES ADVISORY COUNCIL. Asbestos-related diseases without asbestosis. London: 1982. pp.17. (Cmnd. 8750). DHSS; LSE.

3,721. INDUSTRIAL INJURIES ADVISORY COUNCIL. Occupational deafness. London: 1982. pp.33. (Cmnd. 8749). DHSS; LSE.

3,722. INDUSTRIAL INJURIES ADVISORY COUNCIL. Neoplasm of the bladder. London: 1983. pp.13. (Cmnd. 8959). DHSS.

3,723. INGRAM, J.T. Industrial dermatoses and the Industrial Injuries Act. London: 1968. pp.v + 42. DHSS.

3,724. INTERNATIONAL LABOUR CONFERENCE. Proposed action by... the U.K... on the convention concerning workmen's compensation for accidents. London: 1949. pp.5. (B.P.P. 1948-49, XXXIV). LSE.

3,725. IRON TRADES EMPLOYERS INSURANCE ASSOCIATION LTD. Industrial injury claims. London: 1965. unpag. DHSS. 2nd ed. 1967. DHSS.

3,726. JENKINS, E. "Adjudication under the industrial injuries scheme with particular reference to the relationship between diseases and accidents". Journal of the Chartered Insurance Institute. 60. (1963).

3,727. KAIM-CAUDLE, P.R. "Compensation for occupational injuries". Admin 14. (1966). pp.24-37.

3,728. KING, SIR G. "Compensation for industrial injuries". Journal of the Chartered Insurance Institute. 47. (1950). pp.52-60.

3,729. LABOUR PARTY. A guide to the National Insurance (Industrial Injuries) Act, 1946. London: 1947. pp.19. DHSS; LSE.

3,730. LANE, R.E. "The prescription of industrial disease". F.N.

6. (October 1956). p.87.

3,731. LEES, D., GHOSH, D. & LAWSON, A. Economic aspects of industrial accidents in Great Britain. Stockport: 1976. pp.32. DHSS.

3,732. LEWIS, R. "Pneumonoconiosis and special hardship allowance". J.S.W.L. (1979). pp.114-118.

3,733. LEWIS, R. "Tort and social security: The importance attached to the cause of disability with special reference to the industrial injuries scheme". M.L.R 43 (1980). pp.514-31.

3,734. LEWIS, R. "Consultation and cuts. The review of industrial injuries benefit". J.S.W.L. (1980). pp.330-340.

3,735. LEWIS, R. "Compensation for occupational disease". J.S.W.L. (Jan. 1983). pp.10-21.

3,736. LEWIS, R. & LATTA, G. "Compensation for industrial injury and disease". J.Soc.Pol. 4. (1975). pp.25-55.

3,737. LYNES, T. "Industrial injuries scheme at the cross roads". N.S. 54. (1980). pp.323-4.

3,738. MARRIOTT, T.W. "Pneumoconiosis". Ind.L.R. 13. (1958-59). pp.2-11.

3,739. MESHER, J. "Recent social security commissioners' decisions: industrial injuries". J.S.W.L. (1982). pp.178-186.

3,740. MICKLETHWAIT, SIR R. "Industrial injuries benefits". Medico-Legal Jo. 37. (1969). pp.172-186.

3,741. MINISTRY OF NATIONAL INSURANCE. National Insurance (Industrial Injuries) Bill; explanatory memorandum by the Ministry of National Insurance. London: 1944-45. pp.12. (B.P.P. 1944-45, VII). LSE.

3,742. MINISTRY OF NATIONAL INSURANCE. National Insurance (Industrial Injuries) Bill: proposed changes in death benefits: explanatory memorandum, etc. London: 1945-46. pp.12. (B.P.P. 1945-46, XVI). LSE.

3,743. MINISTRY OF NATIONAL INSURANCE. National Insurance (Industrial Injuries) Bill. Index of subjects considered and debated during the passage of the Act. Unpub.: 1946. unpag. DHSS.

3,744. MINISTRY OF NATIONAL INSURANCE. Report of the Departmental Committee on Industrial Diseases. (Dale Report). London: 1948. pp.xvii + 97. (Cmd. 7557). DHSS; LSE.

3,745. MINISTRY OF PENSIONS AND NATIONAL INSURANCE. Reported decisions of the Commissioner under the National Insurance (Industrial Injuries) Acts. Vol.I. 1948-1952. Vol.II. 1953-1956. Vol.III. 1957-1960. Vol.IV. 1961-1964. London: HMSO. Var.pag. DHSS.

3,746. MINISTRY OF NATIONAL INSURANCE. Inter-departmental committee on the assessment of disablement due to specified injuries. (Hancock Report). London: 1949. pp.19. (Cmd. 7076). DHSS.

3,747. MINISTRY OF NATIONAL INSURANCE. INFORMATION DIVISION. Injury benefit (accidents at work). London: 1952. pp.5. (Industrial Injuries No.1). DHSS.

3,748. MINISTRY OF NATIONAL INSURANCE. INFORMATION DIVISION. Disablement benefit and supplementary benefits. London: 1952. pp.9. (Industrial Injuries No.2). DHSS.

3,749. MINISTRY OF NATIONAL INSURANCE. INFORMATION DIVISION. Industrial death benefit. London: [1952]. (Industrial Injuries No.3). DHSS.

3,750. MINISTRY OF NATIONAL INSURANCE. INFORMATION DIVISION. Prescribed industrial diseases including pneumoconiosis and byssinosis. London: 1952. pp.7. (Industrial Injuries No.4). DHSS.

3,751. MINISTRY OF NATIONAL INSURANCE. INFORMATION DIVISION. The industrial injuries insurance scheme and how it works. London: 1952. pp.4. DHSS.

3,752. MINISTRY OF PENSIONS AND NATIONAL INSURANCE. Pneumoconiosis (including silicosis and asbestosis). Procedure for claiming benefit. London: 1955. pp.9. DHSS.

3,753. MINISTRY OF PENSIONS AND NATIONAL INSURANCE. Notes for medical practitioners examining claimants for benefit in respect of prescribed diseases. London: 1958. pp.11. DHSS.

3,754. MINISTRY OF RECONSTRUCTION. 1943-1945. Social insurance. Part II. Workmen's compensation. London: 1944. pp.31. (Cmd.6551). DHSS.

3,755. MINISTRY OF SOCIAL SECURITY. Pneumoconiosis and allied occupational chest diseases. London: 1967. pp.iv + 23. DHSS; LSE.

3,756. MITCHELL, E. The employers' guide to the law on health, safety and welfare at work. London: 1975. pp.xviii + 394. DHSS.

3,757. NATIONAL COAL BOARD. National Insurance (Industrial Injuries) Colliery Workers Supplementary Scheme. Report by the Government Actuary. An interim review as at 31.12.1954. London: 1955. pp.11. DHSS. (Rev.ed. entitled: Coal industry. Supplementary benefit schemes). London: 1960. pp.23. DHSS.

3,758. NEWMAN, T.S. & PRIOR, T.W. Guide to Industrial Injuries Act. London: 1949. pp.32. DHSS.

3,759. NORTHERN IRELAND. National Insurance (Industrial Injuries) Bill (N.I.): explanatory memorandum etc. Belfast: 1946. pp.7. (Cmd. 235). LSE.

3,760. NORTHERN IRELAND. National Insurance Fund, National Insurance (Reserve) Fund, Industrial Injuries Fund. Accounts...

together with the report of the Comptroller and Auditor-General thereon. Belfast: annual, 1971-72. LSE.

3,761. OGUS, A.I. "Social security. Recent decisions on industrial injury benefit". I.L.J. 5. (1976). pp.188-191.

3,762. O'HIGGINS, P. "Labour law: 9. workers' compensation". A.S.C.L. (1965). pp.616-619.

3,763. O'HIGGINS, P. "Labour law: 9. workers' compensation". A.S.C.L. (1966). pp.639-641.

3,764. O'HIGGINS, P. "Labour law; 10. workers' compensation". A.S.C.L. (1967). ppp.639-640.

3,765. O'HIGGINS, P. & HEPPLE, B.A. "Labour law: 10. workers' compensation". A.S.C.L. (1968). pp.708-709.

3,766. PARKER, G.A. "National Insurance (Industrial Injuries) Act 1946". F.N. (April 1951). p.7.

3,767. PARKER, G.A. "Industrial injuries. Trade unions and legal assistance". F.N. 18. (1968). p.43.

3,768. PARKER, G.A. "Industrial diseases". F.N. 18. (1968). p.95.

3,769. PARKES, W.R. Occupational lung disorders. 2nd ed. London: 1982. pp.529. DHSS.

3,770. PARSONS, O.H. Workmen's compensation: accidents at work; a commentary on the government plan. London: [1945]. pp.24.[LRD]CUL.

3,771. PARSONS, O.H. Accidents at work: (a full analysis of the Industrial Injuries Act, 1946, and the Personal Injuries Bill, and how they will affect the worker). London: 1948. pp.48. LSE.

3,772. PARSONS, O.H. "Industrial Injuries Act. Possible amendments". L.R. 39. (1950). pp.189-93.

3,773. PARSONS, O.H. Guide to the Industrial Insurance Acts. London: 1961. pp.68. DHSS; Sq.

3,774. PARSONS, O.H. "Industrial injuries compensation". L.R. 69. (1980). pp.220-1.

3,775. PARTINGTON, M. "Pneumoconiosis etc. (Workmen's Compensation) Act 1979". I.L.J. 8. (1979). pp.187-8.

3,776. PARTINGTON, M. "Industrial injuries compensation - a discussion document". I.L.J. 9. (1980). pp.132-4.

3,777. PAYNE, D. "Compensation for industrial injuries". C.L.P. 10. (1957). pp.85-103.

3,778. PNEUMOCONIOSIS AND BYSSINOSIS BENEFIT BOARD. Leaflets. London: 1952-. LSE.

3,779.   POLLARD,   R.S.W.   Introducing   the   National   Insurance
         (Industrial Injuries) Acts, 1946 to 1948.   London: 1949.
         pp.42. DHSS. 2nd ed. 1954. pp.45. DHSS; LSE.

3,780.   POTTER, D. & STANSFIELD, D.H. National insurance (industrial
         injuries). London: 1950. pp.xix + 392. Sq; LSE; DHSS.

3,781.   POUPON, J.P.   "La protection de l'emploi des victimes
         d'accidents du travail ou de maladies professionnelles (loi du
         7 janvier 1981)". Droit Social. 12. (1981). pp.722-787.

3,782.   PRESTATAIRE.   "Industrial   accidents   and   the   continental
         shelf". L.S.G. 76. (1979). p.727.

3,783.   PRESTATAIRE.   "Occupational deafness".   L.S.G.   76.   (1979).
         p.900.

3,784.   PRESTATAIRE.   "Special hardship allowance under the Social
         Security Act 1975". L.S.G. 76. (1979). p.1045.

3,785.   PRESTATAIRE.   "Industrial   injuries: accidents   whilst
         travelling to work". L.S.G. 77. (1980). p.548.

3,786.   RAI CHOUDHURI, S. Social security in India and Britain: a
         study of the industrial injury schemes in the two countries.
         Calcutta: 1962. pp.xv + 328. LSE.

3,787.   REGAN, C.M. "Ascertaining entitlement to compensation for an
         industrial injury in the] U.K.". In Gunter Spielmeyer (ed.),
         Ascertaining entitlement to compensation for an industrial
         injury.   Brussels: 1965.   pp.149-64.   (Cases in Comparative
         Public   Administration,   International   Institute   of
         Administrative Sciences, Brussels). Sq.

3,788.   REID, J. "Industrial injuries and the teabreak". M.L.R. 29.
         (1966). p.389-396.

3,789.   ROBERTSON, B. & SAMUELS, H.   "National insurance and
         industrial pension and sickness schemes". Ind.Welfare. XXVI.
         (1944).

3,790.   ROOKE,   G.B.   "The   pneumoconiosis   medical   panels".
         Occupational Health. 35. (1983). pp.356-60.

3,791.   ROSE, P.B.   Comparative schemes for industrial injuries
         insurance in France and Britain". Ind.L.R. 14. (1959-60).
         [Part I] pp.66-79; [Part II] pp.118-133; [Part III]
         pp.181-197.

3,792.   ROSE, P.B. "Diseases under the National Insurance (Industrial
         Injuries) Act, 1946". Ind.L.R. 14. (1959-60). pp.10-14.

3,793.   ROWLAND, M. "Benefits for industrial injuries and diseases".
         L.A.G.Bull.   (1980).   pp.35-39, 87-89, 161-163, 262-4;
         (1981). pp.114-6.

3,794.   ROWLAND, M. The industrial injuries benefits scheme. London:
         1983. pp.xxvii + 122. DHSS.

3,795.   SCOBIE, W.E. A case study of the liability of a port employer to his employees. Cardiff: U.W.I.S.T. 1975. pp.198. DHSS.

3,796. SHANNON, N.P. & POTTER, D. The National Insurance (Industrial Injuries) Act, 1946. London: 1946. pp.238. (Butterworth's emergency legislation service (annotated). Statutes suppl. No.35). LSE; Sq. 2nd ed. by D.C.L. Potter and D.H. Stansfield. 1950. pp.xix + 392. Sq.

3,797. SINGLETON, W.T. & DEBNEY, L.M. (eds.). Occupational disability: the approaches of government, industry and the universities. Lancaster: 1982. pp.xi + 307. DHSS.

3,798. SMITH, P. Industrial injuries benefits. London: 1978. pp.xxv + 183. Sq.

3,799. SOCIETY OF LABOUR LAWYERS. Occupational accidents and the law. London: 1970. pp.16. (Fabian Research Series 280). LSE.

3,800. SOCRATES, G. "Review of industrial injuries scheme". Occupational Safety and Health. 10. (1980). p.36-37.

3,801. STEWART, E.G. "Social Welfare (Occupational Injuries) Act 1966". I.L.T.S.J. 108. (1974). pp.65-7.

3,802. THOMPSON, R. & THOMPSON, B. Accidents at work: a guide to your legal rights. London: 1963. pp.viii + 71. DHSS.

3,803. TRADES UNION CONGRESS. Industrial Injuries Acts: TUC guide. London: 1949. pp.166. DHSS.

3,804. TURNER, M.R. "Social security. Industrial injury benefit". I.L.J. 6. (1977). pp.123-124.

3,805. TURNER-SAMUELS, D.J. "Industrial Injuries Acts, 1946-1948". Ind.L.R. 6. (1951-52). pp.266-278.

3,806. UNITED KINGDOM. Minutes of proceedings on the National Insurance (Industrial Injuries) Bill. London: 1945-46. pp.25. (B.P.P. 1945-46, VIII). LSE.

3,807. UNITED KINGDOM. National Insurance (Industrial Injuries) Bill: proposed changes in death benefits: explanatory memorandum etc. London: 1945-46. pp.12. (B.P.P. 1945-46, XVI). LSE.

3,808. UNITED KINGDOM. National Insurance (Industrial Injuries) Act, 1946: tuberculosis and other communicable diseases in relation to nurses and other health workes. London: 1950. pp.20. (B.P.P. 1950-51, XVI). LSE.

3,809. UNITED KINGDOM. Report of the departmental committee appointed to review the diseases provisions of the National Insurance (Industrial Injuries) Act. London: 1955. pp.iii + 35. (B.P.P. 1955-56, XXII). LSE.

3,810. UNITED KINGDOM. National Insurance (Industrial Injuries) Act, 1946: review of the prescribed diseases schedule. London: [1958]. pp.34. (B.P.P. 1957-58, XV). LSE.

3,811.   UNITED KINGDOM.   National Insurance (Industrial Injuries) Acts
         and Regulations.   London: 1961. pp.637. Sq.

3,812.   VAINES, J.   "L'organisation de l'assurance en matiere
         d'accidents de travail.   Rapport national.   Grande-Bretagne.
         The national insurance (industrial injuries) scheme of Great
         Britain and Northern Ireland".   Congres Int. de dr.soc.
         (1958). pp.616-622.

3,813.   VANDYK, N.D.   "Decisions of the industrial injuries
         commissioner based on medical evidence".   Medico-Legal Jo.
         28. (1960). p.184.

3,814.   VANDYK, N.D.   "Decisions of the industrial injuries
         commissioner based on medical evidence".   S.J. 104. (1960).
         pp.1012-14, 1020-1.

3,815.   VESTER, H. & CARTWRIGHT, H.A.   Industrial injuries. London:
         1961. 2 vols. pp.xxi + 308 and pp.xiii + 173. (Vol.2 being
         a Digest of decisions). Sq; LSE.

3,816.   VOIRIN, M.   "What is the future of the employment accident
         branch in the light of the extension of compensation by social
         security for personal injury?".   Int.Soc.Sec.Rev.   33.
         (1980). pp.3-40.

3,817.   WALKER, A.   The industrial preference in state compensation
         for industrial injury and disease.   Soc.Pol and Admin.   15.
         (1981). pp.54-71.

3,818.   WALKER, A.   The case for reforming the industrial injuries
         scheme: the response of the Disability Alliance to the DHSS
         discussion document "Industrial injuries compensation".
         London: 1980. pp.34. DHSS.

3,819.   WARD, A.E.W.   "The Industrial Injuries Act".   Ind.L.R.   4.
         (1949-50). pp.224-241.

3,820.   WEAVER, H.   "Industrial Injuries Act".   L.R.   50. (1961).
         p.102.

3,821.   WEBB, E.A.   Industrial injuries: a new approach: the
         evidence of the Post Office Engineering Union to the Royal
         Commission on Civil Liability and Compensation for Personal
         Injury. London: 1974. pp.25. (Fabian Tract No.428). DHSS;
         LSE; CUL.

3,822.   WHITMORE, E.   Employers' liability insurance.   London: 1962.
         pp.xxiv + 231.   (Chartered Insurance Institute Insurance
         Handbook No.13). DHSS.

3,823.   WILSON, S.R.   "Occupational disease - the problems of a
         comprehensive system of coverage".   I.L.J.   1.   (1982).
         pp.141-155.

3,824.   YOUNG, A.F.   Industrial injuries insurance.   London: 1964.
         pp.192. DHSS; LSE; CUL; Sq.

Section 7   Birth and Death

(a) <u>Maternity Benefits</u>

3,825.   ANON.   "Maternity benefits - options for change".   <u>I.R.R.R.</u>
         238.   (1980).   pp.12-13.

3,826.   COUSSINS, J.   Maternity rights for working women.   London:
         NCCL.   1976.   pp.24.   DHSS; LSE.

3,827.   COUSSINS, J.   Swings and roundabouts: CPAG's response to "A
         fresh look at maternity benefits".   London: 1980.   pp.[i] +
         18.   DHSS.

3,828.   DALLEY, G.   "Maternity benefits: their present role and
         future development".   <u>J.S.W.L.</u>   (1981).   pp.329-334.

3,829.   DEPARTMENT OF HEALTH AND SOCIAL SECURITY.   A fresh look at
         maternity benefits: a consultative document inviting comments
         on   the   future   of   maternity   grant,   maternity   allowance,
         maternity pay.   London: 1980.   pp.12.   DHSS.

3,830.   MINISTRY OF NATIONAL INSURANCE.   National Insurance Act, 1946:
         preliminary   draft   of   the   National   Insurance   (Maternity
         Benefit) Regulations, 1948, proposed to be made under sections
         14, 15, and 16 of the... Act, etc.   London: 1947.   pp.4.
         LSE.

3,831.   MINISTRY OF NATIONAL INSURANCE.   Preliminary draft of the
         National   Insurance   (Married   Women)   Amendment   Regulations,
         1953.   London: 1953.   pp.6.   LSE.

3,832.   SAMUELS, A.   "Maternity benefits: the theory, the law, the
         practice, and proposals for change".   <u>Fam.L.</u>   12.   (1982).
         pp.64-66.

3,833.   SOCIAL   SECURITY   ADVISORY   COMMITTEE.   The   Social   Security
         (Maternity   Grant)   Regulations   1981   (SI.   1981,   No.1157):
         report of the Social Security Advisory Committee in accordance
         with Section 10(3) of the Social Security Act 1980.   London:
         1981.   pp.5.   (Cmnd. 8336).   DHSS.

(b) <u>Death Benefits</u>

3,834.   BRADSHAW, J.   "A guide to gracious dying".   <u>Funeral Services
         Journal</u>.   (1966).   pp.480-490.

3,835.   CALVERT, H.   "Funerals with death".   <u>N.I.L.Q.</u>   20.   (1969).
         p.52.

3,836.   DEPARTMENT OF HEALTH AND SOCIAL SECURITY.   The death grant: a
         consultative document.   London: 1982.   pp.5.   DHSS.

3,837.   DRABBLE, R.   "The death grant".   <u>Poverty</u>.   (1972).   (24).
         pp.24-25.

3,838. HENNESSY, P.J.   Families, funerals and finances: a study of
        funeral expenses and how they are paid.   London: 1980.
        pp.viii + 150.   (Department of Health and Social Security
        Research Report No.6).   DHSS.

3,839. HOFFMAN, F.L.   Pauper burials and the internment of the dead
        in large cities.   London: 1919. pp.123. LSE.

3,840. JOHNSTON, K.   "Widows' pensions".   N.S.   12.   (1968).
        pp.87-88.

3,841. KENDALL, I. Beyond our means: the rise and fall of the death
        grant. Mitcham: 1980. pp.28. DHSS.

3,842. LYNES, T. "Death grants". N.S. 22. (1972). p.336.

3,843. MARRIS, P. Widows and their children. London: 1958. pp.xi
        + 172. DHSS.

3,844. PRESTATAIRE.   "Social security provision for widows and
        divorcees". L.S.G. 77. (1980). pp.399-400.

3,845. ROBILLIARD, St.J.   "Public policy and the widow".   [R. v.
        National Insurance Commissioner, ex parte Connor [1981] 1
        All E.R. 769]. M.L.R. 44. (1981). pp.718-21.

3,846. TORY REFORM COMMITTEE.   Report on industrial assurance,
        approved societies and death grant. London: 1944. pp.16.
        LSE.

3,847. WILSON, SIR A. & LEVY, H.   Burial reform and funeral costs.
        London: 1938. pp.248. DHSS; CUL.

Section 8   Unemployment

(a) <u>General</u>

3,848.   ANON.   "Monthly review of current events.   <u>Staynings v.</u> <u>Ministry of Pensions</u>".   <u>Ind.L.R.</u>   1.   (1946-47).   pp.196-198.

3,849.   ANON.   "Short time and unemployment pay".   <u>L.R.</u>   45.   (1956). pp.92-3).

3,850.   ANON.   "Supplemental unemployment benefits in the United States".   <u>F.N.</u>   7.   (1957).   p.4.

3,851.   ANON.   "Unemployment benefit for short time".   <u>L.R.</u>   47. (1958).   pp.178-9.

3,852.   ANON.   "Unemployment benefit and the trade disputes disqualification".   <u>L.R.</u>   48.   (1959).   pp.17-20.

3,853.   ANON.   "Unemployment benefit: trade disputes disqualification".   <u>L.R.</u>   56.   (1967).   pp.122-4.

3,854.   ANON.   "Unemployment benefit and occupational pensions".   <u>L.R.</u> 57.   (1968).   pp.177-8.

3,855.   ANON.   "Payment of benefits to unemployed people".   <u>D.E.G.</u> 89.   (1981).   pp.197-203.

3,856.   ANON.   "Voluntary registration and the new availability for work test".   <u>Welfare Rights Bull.</u>   50.   (1982).   pp.15-16.

3,857.   ALTMAN, R.   Availability for work: a study in unemployment compensation.   Cambridge, Mass.:   1950.   pp.xv + 350.   LSE.

3,858.   A.M.G.R.   "Damages and unemployment benefit".   <u>S.L.T.</u>   [1965]. pp.217-8.

3,859.   ATKINSON, A.B.   Unemployment benefits and incentives.   [London: Social Science Research Council].   1980.   pp.[1] + 33 + bibliog. (Social Science Research Council Programme: Taxation, Incentives and the Distribution of Income No.11).   DHSS.

3,860.   ATKINSON, A.B. & MICKLEWRIGHT, J.   Unemployment benefit and the FES sample 1972-1977.   [London] :   1980.   pp.35. (Unemployment project working note No.2).   DHSS.

3,861.   BENJAMIN, D.K. & KOCHIN, L.A.   "Unemployment and unemployment benefits in twentieth-century Britain: a reply to our critics".   <u>J.Pol.Econ.</u>   (1982).   pp.410-36.

3,862.   BEST, F. & MATTESICH, J.   "Short-time compensation systems in California and Europe".   <u>F.N.</u>   [1980].   N152-172.

3,863.   BOLDERSON, H.   "Discriminating against the long term unemployed in the social security system".   <u>Unemployment Unit</u> <u>Bulletin</u>.   2.   (1982).   pp.3-4.

3,864. BOOTH, A.E. "The administrative experiment in unemployment policy". <u>P.A.</u> 56. (1978). pp.139-58.

3,865. BURDETT, K. & HOOL, B. "Layoffs, wages and unemployment insurance". <u>Jo.Pub.Econ.</u> 21. (1983). pp.325-357.

3,866. BURGHES, L. & LISTER, R. (eds.). Unemployment: who pays the price? London: 1981. pp.116. (Poverty Pamphlet 53). DHSS; LSE.

3,867. CALVERT, H. "Social security law and the three-day week". <u>C.L.P.</u> 27. (1974). pp.146-164.

3,868. CASEY, J.P. "Unemployment benefit and damages: the need for a new approach". <u>Jur.Rev.</u> 14. (1969). pp.206-17.

3,869. CHILD POVERTY ACTION GROUP. Bashing the unemployed. London: 1971. pp.4. DHSS.

3,870. CHILD POVERTY ACTION GROUP. A new strategy for the unemployed, by Adrian Sinfield. London: 1971. DHSS.

3,871. CHILD POVERTY ACTION GROUP. Response to the Rayner Report on Payment of Benefits to Unemployed People. London: 1981. pp.[i] + 16. DHSS.

3,872. CLAIMANTS UNION. Unemployed: the fight to live; a Claimants Union handbook. London: 1977. pp.17. DHSS.

3,873. CLARKE, C.E. Unemployment insurance: notes on some problems with special reference to the experience in Great Britain. Rome: ISSA. 1959. pp.11. DHSS.

3,874. COHEN, J.L. The Canadian Unemployment Insurance Act - its relation to social security. Toronto: 1935. pp.167. CUL.

3,875. COWLING, K. & METCALFE, D. "Wage-unemployment relationships: a regional analysis for the U.K., 1960-65". <u>Bulletin of the Oxford University Institute of Economic and Statistics</u>. (29). (1967).

3,876. CREEDY, J. & DISNEY, R. "Eligibility for unemployment benefits in Great Britain". <u>Oxford Economic Papers</u>. 33. (1981). pp.256-273.

3,877. DEPARTMENT OF EMPLOYMENT. Unemployment benefit: fortnightly attendance and payment - report by the joint working party. London: 1978. pp.55. Sq.

3,878. DEPARTMENT OF EMPLOYMENT & DEPARTMENT OF HEALTH AND SOCIAL SECURITY. Payment of benefits to unemployed people. London: 1981. pp.[iii] + 101. DHSS.

3,879. DISNEY, R. "Theorising the welfare state: the case of unemployment insurance in Britain". <u>Jo.Soc.Pol.</u> 11. (1982). pp.33-57.

3,880. FENN, P. "Sources of disqualification for unemployment benefit, 1960-76". <u>B.J.I.R.</u> 18. (1980). pp.240-53.

3,881. FISHE, R.P.H. "Unemployment insurance and the reservation wage of the unemployed". Review of Economics and Statistics. 64. (1982). pp.12-17.

3,882. FITZGERALD, M. "National insurance section. Availability for employment'. Ind.L.R. 14. (1959-60). pp.108-116.

3,883. FULBROOK, J. Administrative justice and the unemployed. London: 1978. pp.xvii + 338. Sq.

3,884. GILBERT, B.B. "Winston Churchill versus the Webbs: the origins of British unemployment insurance". American Historical Review. (1966). pp.846-862.

3,885. HAMMOND, C. Unemployment benefit recipients in Australia, 1970-1980: an analysis. [Woden, A.C.T.] : Department of Social Security. 1981. pp.lv. (var.pag.). (Research paper No.1 (revised)). DHSS.

3,886. HAUSER, M.M. & BURROWS, P. The economics of unemployment insurance. London: 1969. pp.xvii + 213. DHSS.

3,887. HEY, J.D. & MAVROMARAS, K.G. "The effect of unemployment insurance on the riskiness of occupational choice". J.Pub.Econ. 16. (1981). pp.317-341.

3,888. HILL, M. Policies for the unemployed: help or coercion? London: 1974. pp.16. (Poverty Pamphlet 15). DHSS; LSE; CUL.

3,889. HOLDER, K. & PEEL, D.A. "The benefit/income ratio for unemployed workers in the United Lingdom". I.Lab.R. 118. (1979). pp.607-16.

3,890. HORTON, K.C. & KNAPP, B. "Unemployment benefit in the United Kingdom and the Federal German Republic". I.C.L.Q. 27. (1978). pp.890-7.

3,891. HOUSE OF COMMONS. LIBRARY. RESEARCH DIVISION. Unemployment benefit for occupational pensioners. London: 1976. pp.7. (Background Paper No.51). DHSS; LSE.

3,892. JORDAN, A. Work test failure: a sample survey of terminations of unemployment benefit. [Woden, A.C.T.] : Department of Social Security. 1981. pp.i + 42. DHSS.

3,893. JORDAN, B. "The dole volunteers". N.S. 53. (1980). pp.311-312.

3,894. KEAST, H. "National insurance section. Unemployment benefit and guaranteed weekly wages". Ind.L.R. 11. (1956-57). pp.183-188.

3,895. KEAST, H. "National insurance section. Unemployment benefit during suspension from work". Ind.L.R. 11. (1956-57). pp.254-257.

3,896. KEAST, H. "National insurance section. Unemployment benefit - misconduct disqualification". Ind.L.R. 12. (1957-58). pp.104-111.

3,897. KHAN, A.N. "Unemployment benefits deductible from damages". S.J. 125. (1981). pp.330-332.

3,898. LABOUR RESEARCH DEPARTMENT. A guide to unemployment benefit. London: 1959. pp.20. Sq.

3,899. LAMBERT, C. Available for work? Cardiff: 1982. pp.33. (Welsh Women's Aid). DHSS.

3,900. LAURIE, P. On the dole; your guide to unemployment and other benefits. London: 1976. pp.96. DHSS; LSE.

3,901. LEWIS, D. "Social security. Unemployment insurance". I.L.J. 5. (1976). pp.119-122.

3,902. LOWE, R. "Employment protection and unemployment benefit". L.S.G. 74. (1977). p.612.

3,903. MESHER, J. Compensation for unemployment. London: 1976. pp.xvii + 138. DHSS; LSE; CUL; Sq.

3,904. MESHER, J. "Unemployment benefit - recent numbered decisions". I.L.J. 7. (1978). pp.56-60.

3,905. MESHER, J. "Unemployment benefit severance pay". J.S.W.L. (1979). pp.118-121.

3,906. MESHER, J. "Recent national insurance commissioners' decisions: unemployment". J.S.W.L. (1979). pp.182-185.

3,907. MESHER, J. "Unemployment benefit and severance payments - Part II". J.S.W.L. (1980). pp.117-120.

3,908. MESHER, J. "Recent national insurance commissioners' decisions: unemployment benefit". J.S.W.L. (1980). pp.121-126.

3,909. MESHER, J. "Losing a job - compensation and social security. 1. Statutory payments". L.A.G.Bull. (1980). pp.158-160.

3,910. MESHER, J. "Losing a job - compensation and social security. 2. Non-statutory payments". L.A.G.Bull. (1980). pp.214-217.

3,911. MESHER, J. "Recent social security commissioners' decisions: unemployment". J.S.W.L. (1981). pp.179-184.

3,912. MICKLEWRIGHT, J. Earnings related unemployment benefit in Great Britain 1966-1980. [London] : 1981. pp.37. (Unemployment project working note No.4). DHSS.

3,913. MICKLEWRIGHT, J. On earnings related unemployment benefits and their relation to earnings. [Redhill] : 1983. pp.31. (Taxation incentives and the distribution of income No.46). DHSS.

3,914. MILLS, F.C. Contemporary theories of unemployment relief. New York: 1917. pp.178. LSE; U.

3,915. MINISTRY OF NATIONAL INSURANCE. Extension of unemployment benefit: general directions for chairmen and members of local tribunals. London: 1948. pp.8. DHSS.

3,916. MINISTRY OF SOCIAL SECURITY. Preliminary draft of the National Insurance (Occupational Pensioners) (Unemployment Benefit) Regulations, 1968. London: 1968. pp.5. LSE.

3,917. MOFFITT, R. & NICHOLSON, W. "The effect of unemployment insurance on unemployment: the case of federal supplemental benefits". Review of Economics and Statistics. 64. (1982). Feb. pp.1-11.

3,918. NARENDRANATHAN, W., NICKEL, S. & STERN, J. Unemployment benefits revisited. [London]: Centre for Labour Economics. 1983. pp.71. DHSS; LSE.

3,919. NATIONAL FEDERATION OF CLAIMANTS UNIONS. The fight to live: the Claimants Union handbook for the unemployed. London: 1975. pp.57. DHSS.

3,920. OGUS, A.I. "Unemployment benefit for workers on short-time". I.L.J. 4. (1975). pp.12-23.

3,921. PARTINGTON, M. (et al.). "Social security. Recoupment of social security benefits". I.L.J. 6. (1977). pp.192-193.

3,922. PARTINGTON, M. "Compensation for short-time working: new government proposals". I.L.J. 7. (1978). pp.187-90.

3,923. PARTINGTON, M. "Unemployment benefit and redundancy compensation: R. v. National Insurance Commissioner ex p. Stratton, R(U)1/79; [1979] 1 All E.R. 1 (D.C.); [1979] 2 All E.R. 278 (C.A.)". I.L.J. 8. (1979). pp.248-51.

3,924. PIACHAUD, D. The dole. London: London School of Economics. 1981. pp.[i] + 33 + bibliog. (Centre for Labour Economics, Discussion Paper 89). DHSS; LSE.

3,925. PISSARIDES, A. Efficient financing of unemployment insurance. London: London School of Economics. 1981. pp.[i] + 25 + bibliog. DHSS; LSE.

3,926. RACKHAM, C.D. "Unemployed insurance". In W.A. Robson (ed.), Social security. London: 1943. pp.113-25. 2nd ed. 1945. pp.122-34. LSE.

3,927. REID, J. "Social security. Recent unemployment benefit cases". I.L.J. 4. (1975). pp.51-55.

3,928. REUBENS, B.G. The hard to employ. European programs. New York and London: 1970. pp.xxii + 420. DHSS.

3,929. RIMMER, A.M. & BAILEY, T.I. "Maternity leave and unemployment benefit". Scolag. (1981). pp.332-3.

3,930. SAFFER, H. "Layoffs and unemployment insurance". Jo.Pub.Econ. 19. (1982). pp.121-29.

3,931. SHORT, C. "The Chancellor of the Exchequer's new scheme for the long-term unemployed. Unemployment Unit Bulletin. 3.

(1982). p.3.

3,932. SHOWLER, B. "Incentives, social security payments and unemployment". Soc. & Ec.Admin. 9. (1975). pp.98-107.

3,933. SHOWLER, B. & SINFIELD, A. (eds.). Workless state: studies in unemployment. London: 1981.

3,934. SINFIELD, A. "Benefits and the unemployed". Poverty. (1975). (32). pp.10-15.

3,935. SOCIALIST LABOUR LEAGUE. Tories attack the unemployed: the social security swindle. London: 1972. pp.38. (SLL Pocket Library No.3). DHSS.

3,936. STEPHENSON, P. "State help for the urban unemployed". Stud. 55. (1966). pp.193-201.

3,937. THIRLWALL, A.P. "Unemployment compensation as an automatic stabiliser". Bulletin of the Oxford University Institute of Economics and Statistics. 31. (1969). pp.23-37.

3,938. WEIR, S. "Crisis benefit". N.S. 27. (1974). pp.17-18.

3,939. WORKING PARTY ON IMPLICATIONS FOR NORTHERN IRELAND. Payment of benefits to unemployed people. [Belfast]: Department of Health and Social Services, Northern Ireland Department of Manpower Services. 1981. pp.[2] + 51. DHSS.

(b) Redundancy

3,940. BOWERS, J. "Handling redundancies: the unanswered questions". S.J. 124. (1980). pp.369-71.

3,941. DANIEL, W.W. "In defence of job centres". N.S. 56. (1981). pp.96-7.

3,942. DEPARTMENT OF EMPLOYMENT AND PRODUCTIVITY. Dealing with redundancies. London: 1968. pp.16. DHSS.

3,943. DEPARTMENT OF EMPLOYMENT AND PRODUCTIVITY. The redundancy payments scheme: a revised guide to the Redundancy Payments Acts 1965 and 1969. 4th rev. London: 1969. pp.32. DHSS.

3,944. JONES, R.M. "The role of public employment agencies in the labour market". I.R.J. 3. (1972). pp.43-50.

3,945. KAHN, H.R. Repercussions of redundancy. A local survey. London: 1964. pp.267. Sq; DHSS; LSE.

3,946. MINISTRY OF LABOUR. Security and change. Progress in provision for redundancy. London: 1961. pp.38. DHSS; LSE.

3,947. MUKHERJEE, S. Through no fault of their own: systems for handling redundancy in Britain, France and Germany. London: 1973. pp.iv + 284. DHSS.

3,948. ROBERTS, K. "The changing functions of the Youth Employment Service". Soc.& Econ.Ad. 3. (1969). pp.167-77.

3,949.   WILLIAMS, K.   "Wrongful dismissal.   Damages for wrongful dismissal, redundancy payments and supplementary benefits". I.L.J.   5.   (1976).   pp.180-82.

Section 9   Old Age

(a) <u>State Pensions</u>

3,950.   ANON.   "Old age pensioners and national insurance costs". <u>L.R.</u> XXXX. (1951). pp.80ff.

3,951.   ANON.   "Labour and state pensions".   <u>P.H.</u>   (3 Sept. 1964). pp.1240-42.

3,952.   ANON.   "New Pensions Bill".   <u>L.R.</u>   59.   (1970).   pp.31-5.

3,953.   ABEL-SMITH, B. & TOWNSEND, P.   New pensions for the old. London: 1955.   pp.27.   (Fabian Research Series No.171.) DHSS.

3,954.   AGE CONCERN.   Your rights by Patricia Hewitt.   Mitcham: National Old People's Welfare Council. 1973.   pp.49.   DHSS. 2nd ed. [by Patricia Hewitt].   pp.48.   DHSS; CUL.   3rd ed. [by Patricia Hewitt and Paul Lewis].   1975.   pp.61.   DHSS.   4th ed. [by Age Concern, entitled <u>Your Rights: for pensioners</u>]. 1976. pp.60. DHSS. 5th ed. [by Pat Conroy]. 1977. pp.72.   DHSS.

3,955.   AGE CONCERN, NORTHAMPTONSHIRE.   Present anomalies in laws and regulations adversely affecting the retired and elderly, compiled by P. Mitford-Barberton.   Northampton: Northamptonshire Age Concern, 1976. pp.16.   DHSS.

3,956.   ALTMANN, R.M. & ATKINSON, A.B.   State pensions, taxation and retirement income 1981-2031. London: Social Science Research Council. 1981. pp.42. (Discussion paper 29).   DHSS.

3,957.   ATKINS, S.   "The home responsibilities provision in the new state pension scheme". <u>J.S.W.L.</u> (1980). pp.33-39.

3,958.   ATKINSON, A.B.   "National superannuation: redistribution and value for money". <u>Bulletin of the Oxford University Institute of Ecopnomics and Statistics.</u> XXXII. (1970).   pp.171-85.

3,959.   ATKINSON, A.B.   "Pensions leapfrog".   <u>N.S.</u>   30.   (1974). pp.485-486.

3,960.   ATKINSON, J.A.   "The developing relationship between the state pension scheme and occupational pension schemes".   <u>Soc. & Econ.Ad.</u> 11. (1977). pp.216-225.

3,961.   BELL, C.D.   "Social Security Pensions Act 1975". <u>N.L.J.</u> 128. (1978). pp.167-169.

3,962.   BELLAIRS, C.   Old people: cash and care.   London: Conservative Political Centre. 1968. pp.23.   DHSS.

3,963.   BRACEY, H.E.   In retirement: pensioners in Great Britain and the United States. London: 1966. pp.xvi + 295.   DHSS.

3,964.   CHANCE, W.   State-aided pensions for old age. London: [1894?]. pp.31. LSE; P.

3,965. CHANCELLOR OF THE EXCHEQUER. Report of the committee on the economic and financial problems of the provision for old age. (Phillips Report). London: 1954. pp.iii + 120. (Cmd. 9333). DHSS.

3,966. COLE, D. & UTTING, J. The economic circumstances of old people. Welwyn: 1962. pp.139. (Occasional Papers on Social Administration No.4). DHSS; LSE; CUL.

3,967. COMMITTEE ON THE ECONOMIC AND FINANCIAL PROBLEMS OF THE PROVISION FOR OLD AGE. Report. London: 1954. pp.iii + 120. (B.P.P. 1954-55, VI). LSE.

3,968. CREEDY, J. "The British state pension: contributions, benefits and indexation". Bulletin of Oxford University Institute of Economics and Statistics. 44 (1982). pp.97-112.

3,969. CREEDY, J. State pensions in Britain. Cambridge: 1982. pp.ix + 102. DHSS.

3,970. CROSSMAN, R. The politics of pensions. Liverpool: 1972. pp.26. (Eleanor Rathbone Memorial Lecture No.19). DHSS; LSE; CUL.

3,971. DAVISON, R.C. & OTHERS. Proposals for the extension of old age pensions and national health insurance. London: 1938. pp.19. DHSS.

3,972. DEPARTMENT OF HEALTH AND SOCIAL SECURITY. Pensions - the way forward: the new earnings related scheme. London: 1969. pp.22. DHSS.

3,973. DEPARTMENT OF HEALTH AND SOCIAL SECURITY. Pension age: memorandum of evidence to the Equal Opportunities Commission by the DHSS. London: 1976. pp.18. DHSS; LSE.

3,974. DEPARTMENT OF HEALTH AND SOCIAL SECURITY. The new pensions scheme. London: 1969. pp.30. DHSS.

3,975. FOGARTY, M. (ed.). Retirement policy: the next fifty years. London: 1982. pp.viii + 216. (National Institute of Economic and Social Research, Policy Studies Institute, Royal Institute of International Affairs, joint studies in public policy; 5). DHSS.

3,976. GASELEE, J. "Pension schemes and the state". Ind.Welfare. 47. (1965). pp.169-170.

3,977. GERIG, D.S. "Pensionable age under old-age pension schemes". I.Lab.R. LXXII. (1955). pp.262-282.

3,978. GUILLEMARD, A.-M. (ed.). Old age and the welfare state. London: 1983. pp.265. DHSS.

3,979. HEMMING, R. The effect of state and private pensions on retirement behaviour and personal capital accumulation. Reading: 1975. pp.ii + 11. (University of Reading Discussion Paper in Economics Series A No.71). DHSS.

3,980. HEMMING, R., & KAY, J.A.   "Contracting out of the state
        earnings related pension scheme". Fisc.Stud. 2. (3).
        (1981). pp.20-32.

3,981. HEMMING, R. & KAY, J.A. "The costs of the state earnings
        related pension scheme". E.J. 92. (1982). pp.300-319.

3,982. HEWITT, P. Age Concern on pensioner incomes: a report... on
        the financial position and prospects of the retired. Mitcham:
        National Old People's Welfare Council. 1974. pp.24. DHSS;
        LSE.

3,983. HOUSE OF COMMONS. LIBRARY. RESEARCH DIVISION. Earnings rule
        for retirement pensioners.   London: 1976.   pp.12.
        (Background Paper No.53). DHSS.

3,984. HOUSE OF COMMONS. SOCIAL SERVICES COMMITTEE. Third report.
        Session 1980-81: age of retirement: together with the
        proceedings, minutes and appendices. London: 1982. 2 vols.
        ([HC]. 26,I+II). LSE; DHSS.

3,985. INCOMES DATA SERVICES. Guide to early retirement. London:
        1981. pp.[iii] + 116 + bibliog. DHSS.

3,986. INDUSTRIAL WELFARE SOCIETY. Further papers on government
        pension proposals; the implications... of the National
        Insurance Bill, 1959. London: 1960. pp.28.

3,987. INTERNATIONAL LABOUR OFFICE. "The evolution of state pension
        schemes in Great Britain". I.Lab.R. LXXXI. (1960).
        pp.456-479.

3,988. JORDAN, D. "New laws for the old". Age Concern Today. 15.
        (1976). p.23

3,989. JUDGE, K. "State pensions and the growth of social welfare
        expenditure". Jo.Soc.Pol. 10. (1981). pp.503-530. DHSS.

3,990. KEMP, F. & BUTTLE, B. Looking ahead: a guide to retirement.
        2nd ed. Plymouth: 1980. pp.117. DHSS.

3,991. KERR, M.S. "Some thoughts on the future of state pensions in
        the United Kingdom". Benefits Int. 4. (1974). pp.8-15.

3,992. LABOUR PARTY. National superannuation: Labour's policy for
        security in old age. 1st ed. London: 1957. pp.123. Rev.
        2nd ed. 1958. pp.125. DHSS; LSE.

3,993. LABOUR PARTY. Two pension plans. Labour and Tory plans
        compared. London: 1959. pp.12. DHSS.

3,994. LABOUR PARTY. The pensions fraud: a guide to the Tory scheme
        for poverty in old age. London: 1961. p.23. DHSS; LSE.

3,995. LEWIS, P. "New laws for the old. The new social security
        system". Age Concern Today. 4. (1975). pp.14-15.

3,996. LYON, S. "Pensions - the problem of disability". Ind.Soc.
        49. (1967). August. pp.26-27, 42.

3 Social Security since 1946

3,997.   MINISTRY OF NATIONAL INSURANCE. Selected decisions given by
         the Umpire on claims for increased pension on retirement:
         Increase of Contributory Pension Regulations, 1946. London:
         1947-. LSE.

3,998.   MINISTRY OF NATIONAL INSURANCE. National Insurance Acts:
         selected decisions given by the Commissioner on claims for
         retirement pension. London: 1948-. LSE.

3,999.   MINISTRY OF PENSIONS AND NATIONAL INSURANCE. National
         insurance retirement pensions. Reasons given for retiring or
         continuing at work. London: 1954. pp.136. DHSS.

4,000.   MINISTRY OF PENSIONS AND NATIONAL INSURANCE. Retirement and
         contributory old age pension and widows benefits (excluding
         widows' allowances). Abstract of statistics for the years
         1956 and 1957. London: 1958. unpag. DHSS. (For the years
         1957 and 1958). 1960. unpag. DHSS. (for the years 1959 and
         1960). 1961. unpag. DHSS.

4,001.   MINISTRY OF PENSIONS AND NATIONAL INSURANCE. Financial and
         other circumstances of retirement pensioners. Report on an
         enquiry by the Ministry of Pensions and National Insurance
         with the cooperation of the National Assostance Board.
         London: 1966. pp.x + 210. DHSS; LSE.

4,002.   MINISTRY OF SOCIAL SECURITY. Retirement pensions and widows'
         benefits: abstract of statistics for 1965. London: 1967.
         unpag. DHSS.

4,003.   NATIONAL FEDERATION OF OLD AGE PENSIONS ASSOCIATIONS. Report
         of conference. Blackburn: 1949 to date (incomplete). LSE.

4,004.   NATIONAL FEDERATION OF OLD AGE PENSIONS ASSOCIATIONS. Your
         pension: information about retirement pensions, supplementary
         pensions and allowances, National Health Service Acts [etc.].
         16th ed. London: 1971. pp.43. DHSS.

4,005.   NATIONAL OLD PEOPLE'S WELFARE COUNCIL. Statutory provision
         for old people. London: 1957. pp.27. LSE.

4,006.   NATIONAL OLD PEOPLE'S WELFARE COUNCIL. Age concern on
         pensioner incomes. London: 1971. pp.43. DHSS.

4,007.   NORTHERN IRELAND. MINISTRY OF HEALTH AND SOCIAL SERVICES.
         Financial and other circumstances of retirement pensioners in
         Northern Ireland. Belfast: 1966. pp.ix + 107. DHSS.

4,008.   PIACHAUD, D. "Supertaxing retirement". N.S. 18. (1971).
         pp.110-111.

4,009.   PIACHAUD, D. "Condition of retirement". N.S. 29. (1974).
         pp.83-84.

4,010.   SHENFIELD, B.E. Social policies for old age; a review of
         social provision for old age in Great Britain. London: 1957.
         pp.236. DHSS; LSE; CUL.

4,011.   SOLICITORS CLERKS PENSION FUND. "The Social Security Pensions
         Act 1975 - a summary of the main features and the implications

264

for employers and their employees". L.S.G. 74. (1977). pp.69.

4,012. TOLLEY, G.S. & BURKHAUSER, V. (eds.). Income support policies for the aged. Cambridge, Mass.: 1977. pp.xii + 194. DHSS.

4,013. TOWNSEND, P. & WEDDERBURN, D. The aged in the welfare state. London: 1965. pp.150. CUL; DHSS; LSE.

4,014. UNITED KINGDOM. Provision for old age: the future development of the national insurance scheme. London: [1958]. pp.23. (B.P.P. 1957-58, XXIV). LSE.

4,015. UNITED STATES. DEPARTMENT OF HEALTH, EDUCATION AND WELFARE. Old-age, survivors and invalidity programs throughout the world, 1954. Washington: 1954. pp.xiii + 122. (Division of Research and Statistics Report No.19). DHSS; LSE.

4,016. UNIVERSITY OF CAMBRIDGE. DEPARTMENT OF APPLIED ECONOMICS. Report on a pilot survey of the economic circumstances of old people in Greenwich and Bedfordshire. Cambridge: 1959. pp.97. DHSS.

4,017. WALKER, A. "The social consequences of early retirement". Pol. Q. 53. (1982). pp.61-72.

4,018. WALLEY, J. "Pension reform". In William A. Robson and Bernard Crick (ed.). The future of the social services. Harmondsworth: 1970. pp.147-79. Sq; LSE.

4,019. WEDDERBURN, D. "The old and the poor". N.S. 6. (1965). (147). pp.7-8.

4,020. WEDDERBURN, D. "Circumstances of the old". N.S. 7. (1966). (194). pp.16-17.

4,021. WILSON, J.P. "Geriatrics and the law". Age Concern Today. 79. (1967). pp.3-9.

4,022. WILSON, T. (ed.). Pensions, inflation and growth: a comparative study of the elderly in the welfare state. London: 1974. pp.x + 422. DHSS; LSE.

4,023. ZABALZA, A. & OTHERS. Social security and the choice between full-time work, part-time work and retirement. London: London School of Economics. 1979. pp.[i] + 36. DHSS.

4,024. ZABALZA, A., PISSARIDES, C. & BARTON, M. "Social security and the choice between full-time work, part-time work and retirement". Jo.Pub.Econ. 14. (1980). pp.245-276.

(b) Occupational Pensions

4,025. ANON. "Schemes providing for pensions for employees on retirement from work". Lab.G. 46. (1938). pp.172-4.

4,026. ANON. "Pensions: should we contract out?". L.R. 48. (1959). pp.186-8.

4,027. ANON. "National Insurance Act, 1959. Contracting out". <u>P.H.</u> LXXVII. (1959). pp.1446-1449.

4,028. ANON. "Company pension schemes". <u>L.R.</u> 49. (1960). pp.190-1.

4,029. ANON. "The new pension scheme". <u>F.N.</u> 10. (1960). p.65.

4,030. ANON. "The evolution of state pension schemes in Great Britain". <u>I.Lab.R.</u> 81. (1960). pp.456ff.

4,031. ANON. "New pensions and contracting out". <u>L.R.</u> 52. (1963). pp.95-6.

4,032. ANON. "Contracting-out: 1963 and after". <u>P.H.</u> (Dec. 1963). pp.1739-40.

4,033. ANON. "Preservation of pension rights. Report of a committee of the National Joint Advisory Council". <u>Lab.G.</u> 74. (1966). pp.163-4.

4,034. ANON. "Private pensions: green light still showing?". <u>P.H.</u> LXXXV. (1967). pp.1544-1549.

4,035. ANON. "Social security, state and private". <u>P.H.</u> 85. (1967). pp.1810-1818.

4,036. ANON. "Occupational pensions. What will happen?". <u>L.R.</u> 58. (1969). pp.190-2.

4,037. ANON. "Working with the state". <u>P.H.</u> LXXXVII. (1969). pp.217-218. See also, pp.178, 224, 312, 446, 856.

4,038. ANON. "Occupational pension and sick pay schemes: some further results of the new earnings survey". <u>D.E.G.</u> 79. (1971). pp.690-1.

4,039. ANON. "Tory pension swindle". <u>L.R.</u> 62. (1973), pp.5-7.

4,040. ANON. "Occupational pension schemes". <u>L.R.</u> 62. (1973). pp.33-5.

4,041. ANON. "Government proposes 50% union participation in company pension schemes." <u>I.R.R.R.</u> No.132. (1976). pp.9-11.

4,042. ANON. "Government proposals for legislation to end discrimination in occupational pension schemes". <u>I.R.R.R.</u> No.137. (1976). pp.2-10.

4,043. ANON. "Contracting out pension schemes: a need for urgency". <u>I.R.R.R.</u> No.146. (1977). pp.13-15.

4,044. ANON. "11.5 million pension scheme members". <u>D.E.G.</u> 85. (1977). pp.474-5.

4,045. ANON. "Occupational pension schemes and consultation with the unions: the legal requirements". <u>I.R.R.R.</u> No.149. (1977). pp.5-9.

4,046. ANON. "Legislative proposals for equal treatment of men and women in occupational pension schemes". <u>I.R.R.R.</u>   No.150. (1977).   pp.13-17.

4,047.   ANON.   "The Social Security Pensions Act 1975 - a summary of the main features and the implications for employers and their employees". <u>L.S.G.</u>   74.   (1977).   p.69.

4,048.   ANON.   "Scott report recommends inflation-proofing for pensions". <u>I.R.R.R.</u>   242.   (1981).   pp.9-11.

4,049.   ANON.   "Member participation in pension schemes". <u>I.R.R.R.</u>   251.   (1981).   pp.2-7.

4,050.   ANON.   "Pension schemes - information to members". <u>I.R.R.R.</u>   254.   (1981).   pp.2-7.

4,051.   ANON.   "Occupational pension schemes - the trade union approach". <u>I.R.R.R.</u>   258.   (1981).   pp.9-10.

4,052.   ABBOTT, R.W.   "Developments in occupational pension schemes". <u>Ind.Soc.</u>   48.   (1966-7).   pp.241-4.

4,053.   ALLEN OF ABBEYDALE, LORD.   "Pensions: urgent need for action". <u>P.H.</u>   95.   (1977).   pp.2191-2194.

4,054.   ARTHUR, T.G.   "Pensions and the role of the state". <u>Nat.West Bk.Q.Rev.</u>   (August 1978).   pp.36-46.

4,055.   ASSOCIATION OF BRITISH CHAMBERS OF COMMERCE.   National superannuation: a critical review of the proposals of the Labour Party. London: 1958.   pp.74.   DHSS.

4,056.   BANDEY, D.C.   "The pension scheme trustee". <u>N.L.J.</u>   130. (1980).   962.

4,057.   BARR, N.   "Labour's pension plan - a lost opportunity". <u>Br.Tax Rev.</u>   (1975).   pp.107-13.

4,058.   BELL, C.D.   "Social Security Pensions Act 1975". <u>N.L.J.</u>   128. (1978).   pp.267-269.

4,059.   BRIMBLECOMBE, R.E.   "Occupational pensions - countdown to 1978". <u>P.H.</u>   94.   (1976).   pp.2194-2198.

4,060.   BRITISH INSTITUTE OF MANAGEMENT.   The new state pension scheme: a decision for management. London: 1969.   pp.64. DHSS.

4,061.   BRUNET, E.   "Pensions and social security". <u>P.H.</u>   93. (1975).   pp.2326-2329.

4,062.   CALLIND, D.   Employee benefits in Europe: an international survey of state and private schemes in 16 countries. Epping: 1975.   pp.260.   LSE.

4,063.   CHATAWAY, C.   "Pensions: a new approach". <u>Crossbow.</u>   4(14). (1961).   pp.9-19.

4,064.   CHESTER, T.E.   "Private pensions or state benefits". <u>Nat. West.Bk. Q.Rev.</u>   (August 1972).   pp.35-47.

4,065. CONFEDERATION OF BRITISH INDUSTRY. Earnings-related social security: the national superannuation and social insurance bill. London: 1970. pp.25. DHSS.

4,066. CONFEDERATION OF BRITISH INDUSTRY. Guidance on provision of information to members of occupational pension schemes. London: 1973. pp.10. CUL.

4,067. CONFEDERATION OF BRITISH INDUSTRY. Social Security Pensions Act 1975: guidance for employers. London: 1976. pp.19. CUL.

4,068. CONSERVATIVE AND UNIONIST PARTY. Pensions. The Conservative plan explained. London: 1958. pp.14. DHSS; LSE.

4,069. COUNTER, K.N.S. "Pension schemes and the law of trusts". J.B.L. (1964). pp.118-23.

4,070. COUNTER, K.N.S. "Preservation of pension benefits". J.B.L. (1964). pp.229-34.

4,071. CROSSMAN, R.H.S. "Social security for the 1970s: Labour's plan". F.N. 13. (1963). pp.58-66.

4,072. CROWTHER, F. Shaw's guide to superannuation for local authorities. London: 1951. pp.xii + 102. 2nd ed. 1955. pp.xxxii + 206. 3rd ed. by A.C. Robb. 1962. pp.xxiv + 433. First... supplement. 1964. BL. 4th ed. 1966. Supplementary issue No.2 to 31.3.1969. 1969. Sq.

4,073. DEPARTMENT OF HEALTH AND SOCIAL SECURITY. The new pensions scheme: latest facts and figures with examples. London: 1969. pp.28. LSE.

4,074. DEPARTMENT OF HEALTH AND SOCIAL SECURITY. Strategy for pensions. London: 1971. pp.40. (Cmnd. 4755). DHSS.

4,075. DEPARTMENT OF HEALTH AND SOCIAL SECURITY. Implications for occupational schemes of the proposals in the government's White Paper "Strategy for pensions". London: 1971. pp.22. (Cmnd. 4755). DHSS.

4,076. DEPARTMENT OF HEALTH AND SOCIAL SECURITY. Social Security Bill: regulation-making powers affecting occupational pension schemes and the way in which they might be used. London: 1972. pp.64. DHSS; LSE.

4,077. DEPARTMENT OF HEALTH AND SOCIAL SECURITY. Social Security Act, 1973: Occupational pensions schemes. London: 1973. pp.39. LSE.

4,078. DEPARTMENT OF HEALTH AND SOCIAL SECURITY. Partnership with occupational pension schemes: consultative document on the effect on occupational pension schemes of the proposals in the Government's White Paper 'Better Pensions' (Cmnd. 5713). London: 1974. pp.19. DHSS.

4,079. DEPARTMENT OF HEALTH AND SOCIAL SECURITY. Second consultative document on equal treatment for men and women in occupational pension schemes. London: 1977. pp.60. DHSS.

4,080. DEPARTMENT OF HEALTH AND SOCIAL SECURITY & OCCUPATIONAL
        PENSIONS BOARD. Report of the Occupational Pensions Board in
        accordance with section 66 of the Social Security Act 1973 on
        the questions of solvency, disclosure of information and
        member participation in occupational pension schemes. London:
        1975. 3 vols. (Cmnd. 5904). DHSS.

4,081. DURHAM, W. Industrial pension schemes. London: 1956. pp.vi
        + 55. LSE.

4,082. FIRTH, A. "Pensions - the scene changes". P.H. XCI.
        (1973). pp.1793-1796.

4,083. FRYD, J. "The government's pensions strategy". I.L.J. 1.
        (1972). pp.61-73.

4,084. GENERAL AND MUNICIPAL WORKERS UNION. Guide to the Social
        Security Pensions Act 1975: Part I. The Act. Part II.
        Contracting out. Esher: 1976. pp.28. DHSS.

4,085. GFTU RESEARCH SERVICE. "'Top up' pension scheme - a trade
        union approach". Research Note. 1/1979. (April 1979).
        unpaged.

4,086. GILLING-SMITH, G.D. "Occupational pensions and the Social
        Security Act 1973". I.L.J. 2. (1973). pp.197-212.

4,087. GILLING-SMITH, G.D. The manager's guide to pensions.
        London: 1974. pp.132. [Institute of Personnel Management].
        Sq.

4,088. GILLING-SMITH, G.D. The complete guide to pensions and
        superannuation. Harmondsworth: 1967. pp.480. DHSS; LSE;
        CUL. Rev.ed. [reprint]. 1968. LSE; CUL.

4,089. GOULDING, E.A. "Occupational pensions". T.U. Info.
        (January, 1969). p.7.

4,090. GRACEY, H. "Social Security Bill 1972 - the way forward".
        Benefits Int. 2. (1972). pp.3-9.

4,091. HAGENBUCH, W. "The welfare state and its finances. National
        superannuation and some alternative solutions". P.H. LXXVI.
        (1958). pp.1052-1053.

4,092. HARDY, R. "Pensions: living with Crossman". P.H. 87.
        (1969). pp.1592-1596; 1720-1723.

4,093. HARDY, R. "Pensions - now what?". P.H. 88. (1970).
        pp.982-984.

4,094. HARDY, R. "The interregnum". P.H. 89. (1971).
        pp.1281-1284.

4,095. HARDY, R. "Friend or foe?". P.H. XC. (1972). pp.208-214.

4,096. HARDY, R. "Pensions: the costs of contracting out". P.H.
        94. (1976). pp.16-19.

4,097. HASLAM, G. "The Social Security Act 1973. Some general comments". Benefits Int. 3. (1973). pp.3-7.

4,098. HAWKINS, A. "The Social Security Pensions Act 1975". L.S.G. 73. (1976). p.433.

4,099. HEMMING, R. "State pensions and personal savings". Scot.Jo.Pol.Econ. 25. (1978). pp.135-47.

4,100. HOSKING, G.A. Pension schemes and retirement benefits. London: 1956. pp.viii + 372. CUL. 2nd ed. 1960. pp.xv + 466. DHSS; CUL. (Supplements 1960, 1961). 3rd ed. 1968. pp.412. CUL.

4,101. HOSKING, G.A. Hosking's pension schemes and retirement benefits. 4th ed. by K.M. McKelvey, A.E.G. Pound and T.G. Arthur. London: 1977. pp.ix + 372. Sq.

4,102. HOSKING, G.A. & LANE, R.C.B. Superannuation schemes. London: 1948. pp.vii + 323. BL.

4,103. HOWELLS, M.K. "Keeping pensions up to date". P.H. (Dec. 1964). pp.1839-1844.

4,104. HYMAMS, C. Handbook on pension and employee benefits: their provision and administration. London: 1973. 1 vol. Loose leaf format. CUL.

4,105. INCOMES DATA SERVICES. Guide to pensions schemes. London: 1980.

4,106. INSURANCE INSTITUTE OF LONDON. The effect of occupational pension schemes of future increases in the benefits of the state scheme. London: 1965. pp.60. DHSS; LSE.

4,107. JACKSON, J. Occupational pensions - the new law. London: 1977. pp.268. CUL.

4,108. JOHNES, A.J. Are salaries and retiring pensions to be governed by favour or justice? And will the Bankruptcy Act work? London: 1869. pp.20. G.

4,109. JOYCE, J. "Income-related pensions". Admin. 26. (1978). pp.259-66.

4,110. KEAST, H. "Modern trends in pension schemes". Ind.L.R. 8. (1953-4). pp.115-22.

4,111. KITTON, J.H. "National pensions: contracting out and kindred problems". P.H. LXXVIII. 1960. pp.231-234.

4,112. LABOUR PARTY. National superannuation. 1st ed. London: 1957. pp.123. Rev. 2nd ed. 1958. pp.125. DHSS; LSE.

4,113. LABOUR RESEARCH DEPARTMENT. Guide to company pension schemes. London: 1966. pp.16. DHSS.

4,114. LABOUR RESEARCH DEPARTMENT. Workers' guide to company pension schemes. London: 1973. pp.23. LSE.

4,115.   LABOUR RESEARCH DEPARTMENT.   Guide to company pension schemes
         and the Social Security Pensions Act 1975.   London: 1977.
         pp.29. Sq; DHSS.

4,116.   LANDER, M.   Occupational schemes in the U.K.   Manchester
         Statistical Society: 1980.

4,117.   LAWTON, A.D.   "Taxation of occupational pension schemes".
         N.L.J.   120.   (1970).   pp.297-8.

4,118.   LIFE OFFICES ASSOCIATION.   Retirement pensions.   London:
         1957. pp.16.   DHSS.

4,119.   LIFE OFFICES ASSOCIATION.   Progress by partnership.   London:
         1968. pp.20.   DHSS.

4,120.   LLEWLLYN, L.F. & JONES, A.B.   Pensions and the principles of
         their evaluation.   London: 1919. pp.xxvii + 702. DHSS; CUL.

4,121.   LONDON INSURANCE INSTITUTE.   The effect on occupational
         pension schemes of future increases in the benefits of the
         state scheme.   London: 1965. pp.60. (Advanced Study Groups.
         Reports No.177). LSE.

4,122.   LUCAS, H.   Pensions and industrial relations: A practical
         guide for all involved in pensions.   Oxford: 1977. pp.xiv +
         191. Sq.

4,123.   LUCAS, H. & WARD, S.   "Pensions bargaining".   Studies for
         Trade Unionists.   3 (10) (1977). pp.1-19.

4,124.   LYNES, T.   "National superannuation - what next?"   F.N.   20.
         (1970).   p.132.

4,125.   LYNES, T.   "Realism on pensions".   N.S.   55.   (1981).   p.285.

4,126.   MACKAY, ST.C. T.D.   "Contracting-out: how the Registrar of
         non-participating employments operates".   P.H.   LXXXI.
         (1963).   pp.486-488.

4,127.   MERTENS, J.   "La reforme des pensions au Royaume-Uni".
         Rev.Belge de Sec.Soc.   XIV.   (1972).   pp.365-371.

4,128.   MESHER, J.   "The Social Security Pensions Act 1975".   M.L.R.
         39. (1976).   pp.321-326.

4,129.   METROPOLITAN PENSIONS ASSOCIATION.   The Castle scheme and its
         effect on the design of occupational pension schemes   London:
         1975. pp.52.   LSE.

4,130.   MINISTRY OF LABOUR.   Preservation of pension rights.   London:
         1966. pp.68.   DHSS.

4,131.   MITCHELL, J.K.   Pension schemes.   London: 1968.   pp.107.
         DHSS.

4,132.   MUNRO, H.   "Retirement pensions after divorce".   N.L.J.   121.
         (1971).   p.159.

4,133. MURRAY, L. "The future of occupational pension schemes".
        P.H. 94. (1976). pp.2198b-2202.

4,134. N.E.L. PENSIONS LTD. 1978; a review of the new state
        pensions scheme. Dorking: [1977]. pp.32. DHSS.

4,135. NATIONAL ASSOCIATION OF PENSION FUNDS. The profits of the
        pension scheme. London: 1965. pp.39. DHSS.

4,136. NATIONAL ASSOCIATION OF PENSION FUNDS. The future
        relationship of state and occupational pensions. London:
        1968. pp.62. DHSS.

4,137. NOBLE LOWNDES GROUP. Social security and pension practice in
        Western Europe. 3rd ed. London: 1966. pp.58.

4,138. OGLESBY, P.R. "The Occupational Pensions Board". Benefits
        Int. 3. (1974). pp.8-10.

4,139. PEACOCK, A.T. "The economics of national superannuation".
        Three Banks Review. 35. (1957). pp.3-22.

4,140. PHILLIPS, W. Pension scheme precedents. London: 1957. xx,
        4702 [paras.], [17]. First supplement, 1961. [52]. Sq.

4,141. PILCH, M. & WOOD, V. Pension schemes. London: 1960.
        pp.222. DHSS.

4,142. PILCH, M. & WOOD, V. New trends in pensions. London: 1964.
        pp.223. DHSS; LSE.

4,143. PILCH, M. & WOOD, V. Managing pension schemes: a guide to
        company pension plans and the Social Security Act. London:
        1974. pp.xiv + 240. DHSS.

4,144. PILCH, M. & WOOD, V. Company pensions and the new Act.
        Epping: 1975. pp.31. DHSS.

4,145. PINGSTONE, G.W. "State pensions and their impact on
        occupational pension schemes". P.H. LXXVIII. (1960).
        pp.75-79.

4,146. POLITICAL AND ECONOMIC PLANNING. "Providing for pensions".
        Planning. XX. (1954). pp.93-116.

4,147. PRICE FORBES (LIFE AND PENSIONS) LTD. "National Insurance
        Act, 1959, and the effect on private pension schemes". Conv.
        (n.s.) 24. (1960). pp.92-100.

4,148. RAPHAEL, M. The origins of public superannuation schemes in
        England, 1684-1859. 1957. Fo. (iv) + 272. LSE.

4,149. REDDINGTON, F.M. "Pension funds - state and private". P.H.
        LXXVI. (1958). pp.1475-1477.

4,150. RHODES, G. Public sector pensions. London: 1965. pp.320.
        LSE.

4,151. RIX, S.E. & FISHER, P. Retirement-age policy: an
        international perspective. New York and Oxford: 1982.

pp.xxvii + 144.   DHSS.

4,152.   ROGERS, E.   "The outlook for occupational pension plans in the United Kingdom".   Benefits Int.   1.   (1971).   pp.3-9.

4,153.   SAMUELS, H.   "Pension and superannuation funds for employees. Notes on their legal position".   S.J.   72.   (1928).   pp.834-5.

4,154.   SAMUELS, H. & ROBERTSON, B.   Pension and superannuation funds, their formation and administration explained... with foreword by Sir J. Burn.   London: 1928.   pp. x + 134.   2nd ed.   1930. pp.xii + 148.   CUL.

4,155.   SELDON, A.   Pensions in a free society.   London: 1957.   pp.vi + 42.   DHSS.

4,156.   SELDON, A.   Pensions for prosperity.   London: 1960.   pp.48. DHSS.

4,157.   SELDON, A.   "Policy for pensions".   Crossbow.   6(23).   (1963). pp.37-42.

4,158.   SELDON, A.   "The role of the state in pensions".   P.H. LXXXII.   (1964).   pp.508-513.

4,159.   SELDON, A.   The great pension swindle.   London: 1970. pp.176.   DHSS.

4,160.   SERES, J.S.D. & SELLEY, J.W.   Pensions - a practical guide. London: 1979.

4,161.   SLEIGHT, R.L.   "Social security, state and private".   P.H. LXXXV.   (1967).   pp.1930-1931.

4,162.   SLEIGHT, R.L.   "Pensions: all out for vested interests". P.H.   LXXXVI.   (1968).   pp.498-502.

4,163.   SLEIGHT, R.L.   "Pensions: from each according to his means?". P.H.   LXXXVI.   (1968).   pp.1787-1789.

4,164.   SPILL, R.B.   "Occupational pension schemes under the 1975 Act: the options for negotiators".   I.R.R.R.   No. 123.   (1976). pp.2-6.

4,165.   THANE, P.   "The muddled history of retiring at 60 and 65". N.S.   45.   (1978).   pp.234-6.

4,166.   TITMUSS, R.   "Superannuation for all: a broader view".   N.S. 13.   (1969).   pp.315-317.

4,167.   VAN GELDER, R.   "Employers take a hard look at a major fringe benefit".   Ind.Soc.   48.   (1966-7).   pp.254-8.

4,168.   VANDYK, N.D.   "The future of retirement pensions.   Part 1. The background".   Ind.L.R.   9.   (1954-55).   pp.281-296.

4,169.   VANDYK, N.D.   "The future of retirement pensions.   Part II. The future".   Ind.L.R.   10.   (1955-56).   pp.18-31.

4,170.   WALLEY, SIR J.   "Social security through occupational pensions

- the government's strategy". <u>Pol.Q.</u>   44.   (1973). pp.167-183.

4,171. WARD, S. "Pension scheme trustees - powers and duties". <u>L.R.</u> 70. (1981). pp.214-15.

4,172. WARD, S. Pensions. London: 1981. pp.267. LSE.

4,173. WEDDERBURN, D. "Comparing the financial position of the aged in Britain and the United States". <u>Soc.Sec.Bull.</u> July (1968). pp.3-8.

4,174. WISEMAN, J. "Pensions in Britain". <u>Finanzarchiv.</u> XIX. (1959). pp.427-40.

Section 10   Family Income Support

(a) Family Allowances/Child Benefit

4,175.   ANON.   "Social legislation in wartime. Allowances for families of mobilised men".   I.Lab.R.   40.   (1939). pp.677-87.

4,176.   ANON.   "XVth general assembly [of the ISSA], 1964. Report XVII.   Report on the general principles on which scales for family allowances are determined".   Bull. I.S.S.A.   18. (1964).   pp.409-441.

4,177.   [ANON.]   The law relating to family allowances and national insurance.   The statutes, regulations and orders as now in force.   Annotated and indexed.   London: 1961.   2 vols.   Sq; LSE.

4,178.   ANON.   "Family allowances. The Minister explains".   Poverty. (1968).   (7).   pp.19-21.

4,179.   ANON.   "Child Benefit Bill".   L.R.   64.   (1975).   pp.108ff.

4,180.   ANON.   "Killing a commitment: the Cabinet v. the children". N.S.   36.   (1976).   pp.630-632.

4,181.   ANON.   "A one-nation budget".   Poverty.   51.   (1982). pp.19-21.

4,182.   ATKINSON, A.B.   "Child benefit".   N.S.   36.   (1976).   p.530.

4,183.   AYDON, C.H.   "A new plan for child poverty".   N.S.   9. (1967).   pp.93-94.

4,184.   BAGLEY, C.   The cost of a child: problems in the relief and measurement of poverty.   London: 1969.   pp.27.   DHSS; LSE.

4,185.   BARDE, R.   "Study of some problems relating to the payment of family allowances".   Int.Soc.Sec.Rev.   XXIV.   (1971). pp.501-537.

4,186.   BARNES, J.   Family allowances.   London: Conservative Political Centre.   1958.   pp.35.   DHSS.

4,187.   BOYER, F.   Des essais d'application du sursalaire familial et des caisses de compensation.   Paris: 1925.   pp.122.   LSE.

4,188.   BRADSHAW, J.   "Child benefit - what now?".   N.S.   37.   (1976). p.76.

4,189.   BRADSHAW, J.   "Child support".   N.S.   58.   (1981).   p.413.

4,190.   BRADSHAW, J. & PIACHAUD, D.   Child support in the European Community.   London: 1980.   pp.144.   (Occasional Papers on Social Administration No.66).   DHSS; LSE.

4,191.   BRADSHAW, J. & PIACHAUD, D.   "Family allowances and child tax allowances in Europe". Poverty. 47. (1980). pp.21-26.

4,192.   CHILD BENEFITS NOW CAMPAIGN. The great child benefit robbery.
         London: 1977. pp.32. DHSS.

4,193.   CHILD POVERTY ACTION GROUP. "A plan to help the low-paid and
         overcome family poverty: earned income relief. A memorandum
         to the Chancellor of the Exchequer". Poverty. (1971). (18).
         pp.14-20.

4,194.   CHILD POVERTY ACTION GROUP. No allowances for the mother, by
         Virginia Bottomley. London: CPAG. 1972. PP.15. DHSS; LSE.

4,195.   CORDEN, A., PIACHAUD, D. & BRADSHAW, J. "How Europe meets
         family costs". N.S. 54. (1980). pp.159-161.

4,196.   COUNCIL OF EUROPE SOCIAL COMMITTEE. Social cooperation in
         Europe: family policy laws and regulations designed to
         compensate for family commitments. Strasbourg: 1967. pp.95.
         DHSS; LSE; Sq.

4,197.   CROSS, R. "The Family Allowances Act, 1945". M.L.R. 10.
         (1947). pp.171-179.

4,198.   DE LUIGI, M. "Il regime degli assegni familiari in Gran
         Bretagna". Previdenza soc. (1964). pp.653-660.

4,199.   DIEUDE, C. Les allocations familiales: historique, etat
         actuel en France et a l'etranger, resultats acquis, nature
         economique et juridique, avenir de cette institution.
         Louvain: 1929. pp.259. LSE.

4,200.   FIELD, F. "Child's pay". Poverty. (1975-76). (33).
         pp.2-4.

4,201.   FLEMING, S. The family allowance under attack. Bristol:
         1973. pp.14. DHSS.

4,202.   FOGARTY, M.P. Family allowances. Your questions answered.
         Oxford: 1956. pp.32. DHSS.

4,203.   GILLIM, M.H. "Family allowances in Great Britain". In L.T.
         Wessman (ed.). Those having torches. London: 1954. LSE.

4,204.   HARVEY, A. "Absent children and family allowances"., N.L.J.
         126. (1976). p.700.

4,205.   HOCHARD, J. & CAO, J. "Family benefits and individual
         incomes". Int.Soc.Sec.Rev. XXVII. (1974). pp.121-141.

4,206.   HORTON, K.C. "Family allowances and maternity leave for
         working mothers in West Germany". L.S.G. 77. (1980).
         pp.356, 359.

4,207.   HOUGHTON, D. "The government's choice". Poverty. (1967).
         (2). p.7.

4,208.   HOUSE OF COMMONS. LIBRARY. RESEARCH DIVISION. Child
         benefit. London: 1977. pp.14. (Background Paper No.59).
         DHSS.

4,209. HOUSE OF LORDS. SELECT COMMITTEE ON THE EUROPEAN COMMUNITIES. Sixth report, session 1981-82: family benefits: 11200/80 Commission communication concerning the standardization of the system for paying family benefits to workers (COM(80)703 final) with minutes of evidence. London: 1982. pp.xi + 50. DHSS.

4,210. INTERNATIONAL ASSOCIATION FOR SOCIAL PROGRESS. BRITISH SECTION. Report on family provision through social insurance and other services. London: 1928. pp.18. LSE.

4,211. INTERNATIONAL SOCIAL SECURITY ASSOCIATION. XIth General Assembly, 1953. Report II. Family allowances. Geneva: 1954. pp.viii + 312. DHSS; LSE.

4,212. INTERNATIONAL SOCIAL SECURITY ASSOCIATION. XIIIth General Meeting, London, 1958. Report No.VI. The role of the child in relation to entitlement to family allowances. Geneva: 1959. pp.99. DHSS; LSE.

4,213. INTERNATIONAL SOCIAL SECURITY ASSOCIATION. XIVth General Meeting, 1961. Report VIII. Methods of financing family allowances and the administrative problems arising therefrom. Geneva: 1962. pp.iii + 98. DHSS.

4,214. IYER, S.N. "Degree of protection under family allowances schemes: a statistical study of selected countries". I.Lab.R. (1966). pp.477-486.

4,215. JOURNEES INTERNATIONALES D'ETUDES SUR LES PRESTATIONS FAMILIALES, ROME, 1953. Compte rendu. Rome: [1955]. pp.viii + 447. LSE.

4,216. KAIM-CAUDLE, P. "Selectivity in family allowances". In Social Services for All? London: Fabian. 1968. pp.16-29. DHSS.

4,217. KAYSER, A. "Study on the application of international bilateral and multilateral instruments relating to legislation on family benefits". Int.Soc.Sec.Rev. XX. (1967). pp.289-312.

4,218. LAND, H. "Provision for large families". N.S. 8. (1966). pp.795-796.

4,219. LAND, H. "Family allowances and the trade unions". Poverty. (1969). (12/13). pp.8-9.

4,220. LEWIS, P. Child interim benefit: an interim guide. London: National Council for One Parent Families. 1976. pp.ii + 13. DHSS. 2nd ed. 1976. pp.20. LSE.

4,221. LIBERAL PUBLICATION DEPARTMENT. Family allowances and social security. London: [1944]. pp.24. LSE.

4,222. LISTER, R. "The child benefit saga". Poverty. (1977). (37). pp.16-17.

4,223. LISTER, R. The great child benefit U-turn? A memorandum to

the Chancellor of the Exchequer.   London: 1980.   pp.30.
(Poverty Pamphlet 45). DHSS.

4,224. LISTER, R. Actions not words: a pre-Budget memorandum to the
Chancellor of the Exchequer on child benefit. London: 1981.
pp.[ii] + 40. DHSS.

4,225. LISTER, R.   Whatever happened to freedom of choice?   A
response to the proposals in Command Paper 8106 to pay child
benefits monthly. London: 1981. pp.[i] + 15. DHSS.

4,226. LYNES, T. "Ending child poverty". Plebs. (1966). pp.2-7.

4,227. MALCOLM, C.B.   "'Parent' and the Family Allowance Act (N.I.)
1966". N.I.L.Q. 21. (1969). pp.59-64.

4,228. MARKS, A. "Mother's little helper: child benefit". N.L.J.
127. (1977). p.531.

4,229. McCARTHY, M.A.   "Trade unions, the family, lobby and the
Callaghan government - the case of child benefits". Policy
and Politics. 11. (1983). pp.461-485.

4,230. McCLELLAND, J. (ed).   A little pride and dignity: the
importance of child benefit. London: 1982. pp.24. (Poverty
Pamphlet 54). DHSS; LSE.

4,231. MINISTRY OF NATIONAL INSURANCE. Memorandum on the effect of
the Family Allowances Act, 1945 on the Workmen's Compensation
Acts, 1925 to 1945. London: 1946. pp.9. LSE.

4,232. MINISTRY OF NATIONAL INSURANCE.   Family allowances and
National Insurance Bill, 1952. Memorandum by the Minister of
National Insurance. London: 1952. pp.4. (B.P.P. 1951-52,
XXV). LSE.

4,233. MORONEY, R.M. The family and the state: considerations for
social policy. London: 1976. pp.xii + 142. DHSS; LSE.

4,234. NEWMAN, T.S. Guide to the payment of family allowances to
2,600,000 families. London: 1945. pp.23. DHSS.

4,235. PIACHAUD, D.   "A profile of family poverty".   Poverty.
(1971). (19). pp.9-11.

4,236. PIACHAUD, D. Children and poverty. London: 1981. pp.29.
(Poverty Research Series 9). DHSS; LSE.

4,237. PIKE, M. Needs must. London: 1967. pp.7. (C.P.C. Outline
Series No.2). DHSS; LSE.

4,238. RANIVO, R.A. "Study of some problems relating to persons
entitled to family allowances". Int.Soc.Sec.Rev.   XXIV.
(1971). pp.538-556.

4,239. SAMUELS, A.   "Child poverty and family allowances".
Soc.Serv.Q. (1968-69). pp.91-95,

4,240. SOCIAL SECURITY ADVISORY COMMITTEE. The Child Benefit (Claims
and Payments) Amendment Regulation 1981 (S.I. 1981; no.1772);

report of the Social Security Advisory Committee. London: 1981. pp.7. (Cmnd. 8453). DHSS.

4,241. SWITZERLAND; EIDGENOSSISCHEN DEPARTMENTS DES INNERN. Die familienzulagenordnungen der EWG-Staaten, Grossbritanniens, Oesterreichs und der Schweiz. Berne: 1968. pp.115. DHSS; LSE.

4,242. TOWNSEND, P. & ATKINSON, T. "The advantages of universal family allowances". Poverty. (1970). (16/17). pp.18-22.

4,243. UNITED NATIONS. "Taxes on wages or unemployment and family allowances in European countries". Economic Bulletin for Europe. 4. (1952). pp.25-55.

4,244. UNITED NATIONS. Economic measures in favour of the family. A survey of laws and administrative regulations providing for economic measures in favour of the family in various countries, March 1952. New York: 1952. pp.xx + 175. DHSS.

4,245. VADAKIN, J.C. Child poverty and family allowances. New York: 1968. pp.xxiii + 222. DHSS.

4,246. VANDYK, N.D. "Family allowances". Brit.Jo.Soc. 7. (1956). pp.34-45.

4,247. WALLEY, SIR J. "A new deal for the family". Poverty. (1969). (10). pp.9-12.

(b) Family Income Supplement

4,248. ANON. "Family income supplement - a benefit for breadwinner families". L.S.G. 77. (1980). pp.906-7.

4,249. ATKINSON, A.B. & CHAMPION, B. Family income supplement and two parent families 1971-1980. [London]: 1981. pp.30. DHSS.

4,250. BARKER, D. "The family income supplement". N.S. 18. (1971). pp.240-242.

4,251. BARRITT, D.P. "Family Income Supplements Act (N.I.) 1971". N.I.L.Q. 22. (1971). pp.527-30.

4,252. BROWN, J.C. Family income support part 1. Family income supplement. London: 1983. pp.141. (Studies of the social security system No.2). DHSS.

4,253. DAPRE, B. & STANTON, D. "United Kingdom - family income supplement". Social Security. (1981). June. pp.48-59.

4,254. DEPARTMENT OF HEALTH AND SOCIAL SECURITY. Two-parent famiies receiving Family Income Supplement in 1972: a follow-up survey a year later; a further study of the financial and material circumstances of two-parent families receiving Family Income Supplement. London: 1976. pp.118. (Statistical and Research Report Series, No.13). DHSS.

4,255. ELKS, L. "Can we have a simple means-test?". Poverty. (1975). (31). pp.23-15.

4,256. ELKS, L. "Family income supplement: some legal problems".
        L.A.G.Bull. (1975). pp.124-126.

4,257. FIELD, F. "A tight FISt". N.S. 32. (1975). p.142.

4,258. KNIGHT, I.B. & NIXON, J.M. Two-parent families in receipt of
        Family Income Supplement, 1972: a study enquiring into the
        financial and material circumstances of two-parent families
        receiving a Family Income Supplement. London: 1975. pp.193.
        (DHSS Statistical and Research Report Series, No.9). DHSS.

4,259. LYNES, T. "Family income supertax". N.S. 17. (1971).
        pp.770-771.

4,260. LYNES, T. "Welfare men". N.S. 21. (1972). pp.505-506.

4,261. MAKINSON, C. Family income supplement claimants:
        methodological report. London: 1981. var.pag. DHSS.

4,262. MURIE, A. "Family income supplement and low incomes in
        Northern Ireland". Soc. & Econ.Ad. 8. (1974). pp.22-42.

4,263. PACK, J. On top of your pay. London: 1977. pp.5. DHSS.

4,264. REID, J. "Social security. New legislation. National
        Insurance Act 1971. Family income supplements". I.L.J.
        (1972). pp.49-53.

4,265. SANCTUARY, C.J. & NURSE, K.R. "Evaluation of changes to
        Family Income Supplement". Omega. 9. (1981). pp.469-480.

4,266. STACPOOLE, J. "Running FIS". N.S. 19. (1972). pp.64-66.

4,267. WYNN, M. "FIS and fatherless families". Poverty. (1970).
        (16/17). pp.23-24.

(c) Housing Costs Assistance

4,268. ANON. "Unreasonably High Rents - More will be met in full".
        SBC Notes and News. 3. (1975). p.1.

4,269. ANON. "The new housing benefits scheme". Welfare Rights
        Bull. 50. (1982). pp.1-13.

4,270. ANON. "Housing benefits - the transmogrification of rent and
        rate rebates and allowances: Part II. L.S.G. 79. (1982).
        p.1315.

4,271. ADVISORY COMMITTEE ON RENT REBATES AND RENT ALLOWANCES.
        Report No.3 (final report), January 1977 to March, 1983.
        London: 1983. pp.60. DHSS.

4,272. BRADBURY, K. (ed.). Do housing allowances work? Washington,
        D.C.: Brookings Institution. 1981. pp.xiv + 419. DHSS.

4,273. DEPARTMENT OF THE ENVIRONMENT AND THE WELSH OFFICE. Rents of
        tenants in receipt of supplementary benefit. London: 1970.
        pp.10. (Circular 3/70 DOE: 112/70 WO). DHSS.

4,274. DEPARTMENT OF HEALTH AND SOCIAL SECURITY. Social Security and Housing Benefits Bill: notes on clauses. Stanmore: 1981. pp.iii + 103. DHSS.

4,275. DONNISON, D. "A rationalisation of housing benefits". Three Banks Review. 131. (1981). pp.3-13.

4,276. HARVEY, A. "What help for poor tenants?". In Social services for all? London: Fabian Society. 1968. pp.61-75. DHSS.

4,277. HARVEY, A. "The rent stop". N.S. 28. (1974). p.258.

4,278. LANSLEY, S. & FIEGEHEN, G. Housing allowances and inequality. London: 1973. pp.24. (Young Fabian Pamphlet 36). DHSS.

4,279. LEGG, C. & BRION, M. The administration of the rent rebate and rent allowance schemes. London: 1976. pp.vi + 198. DHSS.

4,280. MATTHEWS, A. The identification of entitlement to housing benefit supplement: report of a survey. London: Office of the Chief Scientist. 1983. pp.iv + 43. DHSS.

4,281. MCGURK, P. & RAYNSFORD, N. A guide to housing benefits. London: 1982. pp.vi + 66. DHSS.

4,282. MEANS, R. & HILL, M. "The administration of rent rebates". J.S.W.L. (1982). pp.193-208.

4,283. PLAYFORD, C. "Housing and the poverty trap". Low Pay Review. 5. (1981). pp.8-12.

4,284. RITCHIE, J. & MATTHEWS, A. Take up of rent allowances: an in depth study. London: Social and Community Planning Research. 1982. pp.iv + var.pag. DHSS.

(d) Heating Costs Assistance

4,285. BERTHOUD, R. Fuel debts and hardship. London: 1981. pp.viii + 174. LSE; DHSS.

4,286. BRADSHAW, J. & HARRIS, T. (eds.). Energy and social policy. London: 1983. pp.x + 189. DHSS.

4,287. BRITISH ASSOCIATION OF SETTLEMENTS. Right to fuel campaign. Supply and demand: the policies of the national Right to Fuel campaign. London: 1977. pp.21. DHSS.

4,288. CHILD POVERTY ACTION GROUP & RESEARCH INSTITUTE FOR CONSUMER AFFAIRS. Cold comfort: a survey of heating resources and requirements in 18 low-income London homes. London: [1974]. pp.23. DHSS; LSE.

4,289. DEPARTMENT OF ENERGY. Review of payment and collection methods for gas and electricity bills: report of an informal inquiry. (Chairman: Gordon Oakes). London: 1976. pp.33. DHSS.

4,290.   DEPARTMENT OF ENERGY. Energy tariffs and the poor. London: 1976. pp.ii + 31. DHSS.

4,291.   ELECTRICITY CONSUMERS' COUNCIL. Fuel allowance. London: 1979. pp.[1] + 21. DHSS.

4,292.   ELECTRICITY CONSUMER'S COUNCIL. Problems with paying for fuel: the policy options. London: 1982. pp.69. DHSS.

4,293.   GRAY, M. & OTHERS. A policy for warmth. London: 1977. pp.23. (Fabian Tract No.447). DHSS; LSE; CUL.

4,294.   GREATER LONDON CITIZENS ADVICE BUREAUX SERVICE. Fuel debts and L.E.B. policy. London: 1981. pp.20. DHSS.

4,295.   HARLOW COUNCIL OF SOCIAL SERVICE. Fuel needs of the elderly. Harlow: 1972. pp.17. DHSS.

4,296.   HEATING ACTION GROUP. A guide to allowances for families and old people. London: 1973. pp.22. DHSS; LSE.

4,297.   HELD THE AGED.   Death in winter: a special report on inadequate heating conditions amongst the old. London: 1975. pp.20. DHSS.

4,298.   HESKETH, J.L.   Fuel debts: social problems in centrally heated council housing.   Manchester: Family Welfare Association of Manchester and Salford. 1975. pp.viii + 112. DHSS.

4,299.   JOHNSON, M. & ROWLAND, M. Fuel debts and the poor. London: 1976. pp.iv + 36. (Poverty Pamphlet 24). DHSS; LSE; CUL.

4,300.   LEWIS, P. Fuel poverty can be stopped: a response to "Fuel debts and hardship".   London: National Right to Fuel Campaign. 1982. pp.20. DHSS.

4,301.   NATIONAL CONSUMER COUNCIL. Paying for fuel: interim report to the Secretary of State for Prices and Consumer Protection. London: 1976. pp.30. DHSS; LSE.

4,302.   NATIONAL CONSUMER COUNCIL. Paying for fuel: report by the National Consumer Council to the Secretary of State for Prices and Consumer Protection. London: 1976. pp.viii + 238. (NCC Report No.2). DHSS.

4,303.   NATIONAL COUNCIL FOR ONE PARENT FAMILIES AND GINGERBREAD. Extra money for heating: how to claim a heating allowance if you claim supplementary benefit. London: 1976. pp.4. DHSS.

4,304.   NATIONAL COUNCIL FOR SOCIAL SERVICE. Fuel debts: an action guide. London: 1974. pp.15. DHSS.

4,305.   NATIONAL OLD PEOPLE'S WELFARE COUNCIL. Evidence from Age Concern England to the National Consumer Council enquiry into the effect of energy prices on the budgets of low-income households, including those on social security benefits. Mitcham: 1976. pp.12. DHSS.

4,306.   NATIONAL OLD PEOPLE'S WELFARE COUNCIL. Memorandum to Lord

Lovell-Davis on methods of payment for gas and electricity, 7 April 1976. Mitcham: 1976. pp.12. DHSS.

4,307. NATIONAL OLD PEOPLE'S WELFARE COUNCIL. Fuel debts. Mitcham: 1976. pp.12.

4,308. PITKIN, J. "Paying for fuel". L.A.G.Bull. (1981). pp.8-11.

4,309. SOUTHWICK NEIGHBOURHOOD ACTION PROJECT. Fuel cut-offs: a report. Southwick, Sunderland: 1980. pp.15. DHSS.

4,310. SUPPLEMENTARY BENEFITS COMMISSION. Fuel debts among low-income groups: memorandum of guidance. London: 1972. pp.11. DHSS.

4,311. WANDSWORTH RIGHTS UMBRELLA GROUP. Fuel debts handbook. 2nd ed. compiled by P. Gagg and others. London: 1977. pp.[44]. DHSS.

Section 11 National Assistance and Supplementary Benefit

(a) <u>National Assistance</u>

4,312. ANON. "Wilful neglect to provide reasonable maintenance for children". <u>J.Cr.L.</u> 15. (1951). pp.213-9.

4,313. ASSISTANCE BOARD DEPARTMENTAL WHITLEY COUNCIL(STAFF SIDE). Welfare, 1947: an examination of the Assistance Board's position in retrospect and prospect. London: 1947. pp.126. LSE.

4,314. ATKINSON, A.B., MAYNARD, A.K. & TRINDER, C.G. "National assistance and low incomes in 1950". <u>Soc. Pol. & Admin.</u> 15. (1981). pp.19-31.

4,315. BROWN, L.N. "National assistance and the liability to maintain one's family". <u>M.L.R.</u> 18. (1955). pp.110-119.

4,316. BROWN, L.N. "Separation agreements and national assistance". <u>M.L.R.</u> 19. (1956). pp.623-637.

4,317. BROWN, L.N. "Bastardy and the National Assistance Board". <u>M.L.R.</u> 20. (1957). pp.401-405.

4,318. CHAMBERS, R. "The National Assistance Act, 1948". <u>M.L.R.</u> 12. (1949). pp.69-72.

4,319. CRAWLEY, E. "Rational assistance". <u>Crossbow.</u> 3. (1959). pp.25-29.

4,320. DEPARTMENT OF HEALTH FOR SCOTLAND. National Assistance Act 1948. Information to local authorities. Edinburgh: 1948. pp.19. (DHS Circular 51/48). DHSS.

4,321. DOW, H.P.B. Shaw's national assistance. [With the National Assistance Act, 1948]. London: 1948. pp.xv + 363. Sq; DHSS.

4,322. GLENNERSTER, H. National assistance service or charity. London: 1962. pp.34. (Young Fabian Group 4). DHSS; LSE.

4,323. HILL, M.J. "The exercise of discretion in the National Assistance Board". <u>Pub.Admin.</u> (1969). pp.75-90.

4,324. JACKSON, J.M. "Poverty, national assistance and the family". <u>Scot.Jo.of Polit.Econ.</u> No.2. (June 1966). pp.238-250.

4,325. JEWELL, R.E.C. "The report of the National Assistance Board for 1952". <u>Pub.Admin.</u> XXXI. (1953). p.417.

4,326. KLEIN, J.P. "The edge of poverty". <u>N.S.</u> 1. (1962-63). (4). pp.9-13.

4,327. LIDBETTER, E.J. Maintenance and desertion. London: 1934. pp.xi + 180. (Handbooks for Public Assistance Officers 3). DHSS.

4,328. LYNES, T. National assistance and national prosperity. Welwyn: 1962. pp.55. (Occasional Papers on Social Administration No.5). LSE; DHSS; CUL.

4,329. MINISTRY OF HEALTH. National Assistance Act, 1948; National Assistance (Adaptation of Enactments) Regulations, 1950. London: 1951. unpag. (Circular No.14/51). DHSS.

4,330. MINISTRY OF NATIONAL INSURANCE. NATIONAL ASSISTANCE BOARD. Reception centres for persons without a settled way of living. London: 1952. pp.22. DHSS; LSE.

4,331. MOSS, J. "The end of the poor law". Fort.Rev. 162. (1947). pp.423-8.

4,332. MOSS, J. (ed.). The duties of local authorities under the National Asistance Act, 1948. London: 1948. pp.xix + 120. Sq.

4,333. NATIONAL ASSISTANCE BOARD. N.A.B. handbook. London: 1942. pp.66. LSE.

4,334. NATIONAL ASSISTANCE BOARD. Handbook for newcomers. (Interim ed.) London: 1948. pp.iv + 52. LSE.

4,335. NORTHERN IRELAND. Labour and National Insurance Report of the National Assistance Board for Northern Ireland 1956. (H.C. 1245) (N.I.). Belfast: 1957. pp.22. DHSS.

4,336. NORTHERN IRELAND. MINISTRY OF LABOUR AND NATIONAL INSURANCE Report of the National Assistance Board for N.I. 1956. (H.C. 1245). (N.I.). Belfast: 1957. pp.22. DHSS.

4,337. NORTHERN IRELAND. Labour and National Insurance Report of the National Assistance Board for Northern Ireland 1957. (H.C. 1296) (N.I.). Belfast: 1958. pp.18. DHSS.

4,338. NORTHERN IRELAND. Report of the National Assistance Board for Northern Ireland for year ended 31.12.58. (H.C. 1347). Belfast: 1959. DHSS.

4,339. NORTHERN IRELAND. Report of the National Assistance Board for Northern Ireland for the year ended 31st December 1962. (H.C. 1549). Belfast: 1963. pp.38. DHSS.

4,340. NORTHERN IRELAND. Report of the National Assistance Board for Northern Ireland for the year ended 31st December 1964. (H.C. 1654). Belfast: 1965. pp.36. DHSS.

4,341. NORTHERN IRELAND. Reports of the National Assistance Board for Northern Ireland. (H.C. 1717). Belfast: 1966. pp.33. DHSS.

4,342. NOTTINGHAMSHIRE WELFARE DEPARTMENT. National Assistance Act, 1948. Nottingham: 1955. pp.19. LSE.

4,343. STEELE, R.D. The National Assistance Act, 1948. With a general introduction and annotations. London: 1949. pp.vi + 156. Sq; DHSS.

4,344. STOWE, K.G. "Staff training in the National Assistance Board: problems and policies". Pub.Admin. 39. (1961). pp.331-352.

4,345. TILLYARD, F. "'Out of work donation' - the true dole". Ind.L.R. 3. (1948-49). pp.12-19.

4,346. UNITED KINGDOM. Summary of the provisions of the National Assistance Bill. London: 1947-48. pp.12. LSE.

4,347. UNITED KINGDOM. National Assistance Act, 1948: explanatory memorandum on the draft National Assistance (Determination of Need) Regulations, 1948. London: 1948. pp.10. LSE.

4,348. UNITED KINGDOM. National Assistance Act, 1948: explanatory memorandum on the draft National Assistance (Determination of Need) Amendment Regulations, 1951. London: 1951. (B.P.P. 1950-51 XXVII). pp.3. LSE.

4,349. UNITED KINGDOM. Explanatory memorandum on the draft National Assistance (Determination of Need) Amendment Regulations, 1952. London: 1952. (B.P.P. 1951-52, XXV). pp.8. LSE.

4,350. UNITED KINGDOM. Explanatory memorandum on the Draft National Assistance (Determination of Need) Amendment Regulations, 1954. London: 1954. 4. (B.P.P. 1954-55, XIII). LSE.

4,351. UNITED KINGDOM. Explanatory memorandum on the Draft National Assistance (Determination of Need) Amendment Regulations, 1955. London: 1955. 4. (B.P.P. 1955-56, XXXVI). LSE.

4,352. UNITED KINGDOM. Explanatory memorandum on the Draft National Assistance (Determination of Need) Amendment Regulations, 1957. London: 1957. 3. (B.P.P. 1957-58, XXIV). LSE.

4,353. UNITED KINGDOM. Improvements in national assistance. London: [1959]. pp.7. (B.P.P. 1958-59, XXV). LSE.

(b) Supplementary Benefits

4,354. ANON. "A beginner's guide to supplementary benefit". L.A.G. Bull. (1973). pp.66-69.

4,355. ANON. "Supplementary benefit - offences depend on mens rea". Fam.L. 4. (1974). pp.97.

4,356. ANON. "Conversation with Lord Collison". S.B.C. Notes & News. 3. (1975).

4,357. ANON. "New moves on leaflet problem - increasing availability". S.B.C. Notes & News. 5. (1976).

4,358. ANON. "New SB Leaflets". S.B.C. Notes & News. 9. (1977).

4,359. ANON. "Maintenance orders and supplementary benefit". Fam.L. 7. (1977). p.100.

4,360. ANON. "Living below their means: supplementary benefits". L.R. 67. (1978). pp.42ff.

4,361. ANON. "Supplementary benefits reviewed". L.R. 67. (1978).
        pp.236.

4,362. ANON. "Supplementary benefit and direct payments for fuel".
        L.A.G.Bull. (1978). pp.236-7.

4,363. ANON. "Kicking them when they are down". L.R. 69. (1980).
        pp.236-7.

4,364. ANON. "The supplementary benefit scheme". N.S. 54. (1980).
        pp.375, 421, 469.

4,365. ANON. "Benefits: putting the facts across". S.W.T. 11.
        (1980). No.45. p.21.

4,366. ANON. "Poor law: modern style". L.R. 69. (1980).
        pp.18-19.

4,367. ANON. "The supplementary benefit liability to maintain - the
        historical dimension". L.S.G. 77. (1980). pp.176-77.

4,368. ANON. "The supplementary benefit liability to maintain - the
        private liabilities". L.S.G. 77. (1980). p.292.

4,369. ANON. "Child maintenance and supplementary benefit". L.S.G.
        77. (1980). pp.812-13.

4,370. ANON. "The new Jerusalem? The supplementary benefits scheme
        transmogrified". L.S.G. 77. (1980). pp.1151-52.

4,371. ANON. "Supplementary benefit". Welfare Rights Bull. 47.
        (1982). pp.1-5.

4,372. ALLBESON, J. Rent-stop. London: 1980. pp.39. (Poverty
        Pamphlet 46). DHSS.

4,373. ALLEN, B.K. "Administration of discretion: some first
        thoughts". Case Con. (June 1968). pp.43-48.

4,374. ALTMANN, R.M. Take-up of supplementary benefit by male
        pensioners. [London]: Social Science Research Council. 1981.
        pp.22. DHSS.

4,375. ASSOCIATION OF COUNTY COUNCILS, ASSOCIATION OF METROPOLITAN
        AUTHORITIES AND DEPARTMENT OF HEALTH AND SOCIAL SECURITY,
        SUPPLEMENTARY BENEFITS COMMISSION. Assistance in cash: the
        rules of the Supplementary Benefits Commission and local
        authority social services departments. London: Association
        of County Councils etc. 1976. pp.11. DHSS.

4,376. ATKINSON, A.B. & MICKLEWRIGHT, J. Supplementary benefit,
        housing benefits and unemployment: evidence from the Family
        Expenditure Survey sample 1972-77. [London]: 1981. pp.50.
        (Unemployment project working note No.3). DHSS.

4,377. BANDALI, S. "Maintenance orders and supplementary benefits".
        Fam.L. 3. (1973). pp.165-168.

4,378. BENNETT, F. Your social security: know your rights; the
        questions and answers. Harmondsworth: 1982. pp.363.

4,379. BEVAN, D.E. & HARDY, W.R. Report for the European Institute of Social Security on social security supplementary schemes in the United Kingdom. London: 1973. pp.i + 54. DHSS.

4,380. BOND, N. Knowledge of rights and extent of unmet need amongst recipients of supplementary benefit. Coventry: Home Office and City of Coventry Community Development Project, in association with the Institute of Local Government Studies: 1972. pp.vi + 23. (Community Development Project Occasional Paper No.4). DHSS; LSE.

4,381. BRADFORD RESOURCE CENTRE. Social security: the new legislation; changes in rights and benefits. Bradford Resource Centre: [1980]. pp.[i] + 23. DHSS.

4,382. BRIGGS, E. & REES. T. "Lost in the puzzle of social security". N.S. 51. (1980). pp.60-1.

4,383. BROOKE, R. "Supplementary benefits - discretion". N.L.J. 120. (1970). p.728.

4,384. BRYAN, M.W. "The 'liable relative' rule". Fam.L. 10. (1980). pp.25-8.

4,385. BULL, D. "Failures of the Supplementary Benefits Commission". S.W.T. 6. (1975). p.422.

4,386. BULL, D. (ed.). Dear David Donnison: a five-part open letter to the new Chairman of the Supplementary Benefits Commission. Birmingham: British Association of Social Workers. 1976. pp.15. DHSS; Sq.

4,387. BULL, D. & BRADSHAW, J. "The supplementary benefits review". S.W.T. 9. (45). (1978). p.7.

4,388. BULL, D. & IVESON, C. "The clothes line". N.S. 23. (1973). p.187.

4,389. BURGHES, L. Living from hand to mouth: a study of 65 families living on supplementary benefit. London: 1980. pp.80. DHSS.

4,390. BURNS, E. "'Reform' of the supplementary benefits scheme". Scolag. (1980). pp.10-3.

4,391. CAMPAIGN FOR SINGLE HOMELESS PEOPLE. Supplementary benefits for single homeless people: a CHAR guide. London: 1980. pp.27. DHSS.

4,392. CARSON, D. "Social assistance: a review of the supplementary benefit scheme". J.S.W.L. (1979). pp.101-103.

4,393. CARSON, D. "The new supplementary benefit regulations. II. Description". J.S.W.L. (1980). pp.343-350.

4,394. CARSON, D. "Recent legislation: supplementary benefits". J.S.W.L. (1981). pp.101-120.

4,395. CARSON, D. "Recent legislation: supplementary benefits".

J.S.W.L. (1981). pp.351-364.

4,396. CASEY, J.P.   "Supplementary Benefits Act: lawyers law
aspects". N.I.L.Q. 19. (1968). pp.1-13.

4,397. CASEY, J.P.   "Social assistance in Northern Ireland".
N.I.L.Q. 19. (1968). pp.178-98.

4,398. CHILD POVERTY ACTION GROUP.   "Anti-wage-stop campaign".
Poverty. (1967). (3). pp.i-iv, 12-13.

4,399. CHILD POVERTY ACTION GROUP. The wage-stop. London: 1971.
pp.5. (Poverty leaflet No.2). CUL.

4,400. CHILD POVERTY ACTION GROUP. The definition of a householder,
by Robin Simpson. London: CPAG. 1972. pp.2. (Welfare Law
Notes).

4,401. CHILD POVERTY ACTION GROUP. Survey of supplementary benefit
recipients. London: CPAG. 1973. pp.6. DHSS.

4,402. CHILD POVERTY ACTION GROUP.   Citizens Rights Office. Four
weeks past "A-day": the new supplementary benefits scheme in
practice. London: 1980. pp.[ii] + 10. DHSS.

4,403. CHILD POVERTY ACTION GROUP. Three months on: a report on the
new supplementary benefit scheme. London: 1981. pp.[iii]
+ 19. DHSS.

4,404. CHURCHILL, R.C.   "Expenditure patterns of retired persons at
or immediately above their supplementary benefit level in
October 1972". Econ.Trends. 254. (1974). pp.lxxx-xcv.

4,405. CIVIL SERVICE DEPARTMENT, MANAGEMENT SERVICES AND DEPARTMENT
OF HEALTH AND SOCIAL SECURITY.   Working Party on the
arrangements for uprating supplementary benefit. A study of
the arrangements for uprating supplementary benefit. London:
DHSS. 1971 and 1972. pp.43 + annexures. DHSS.

4,406. CLARK, B. "Single payments for clothing". LAG Bull. (1981).
pp.116-118.

4,407. CREIGHTON, W.B.   "Judicial review in Scotland: Watt v. Lord
Advocate, 1977 S.L.T. 130 and 1979 S.L.T. 137". I.L.J. 8.
(1979). pp.118-21.

4,408. DAVIES, P.J.   "Damages and supplementary benefit?". [Plummer
v. P.W. Williams [1981] 1 All E.R. 91]. L.Q.R. 97. (1981).
pp.369-71.

4,409. DAVIS, M. "R. v. S. London SBAT, ex p. Holland and Szcelkun
(C.A., The Times, 2 June 1978)". L.T. 13. (1979).
pp.123-5.

4,410. DAVIS, M. "R. v. Bolton SBAT, ex p. Fordham [1981] 1 W.L.R.
28 (C.A.)". L.T. 15. (1981). pp.66-7.

4,411. DEPARTMENT OF THE ENVIRONMENT AND THE WELSH OFFICE. Rents of
tenants in receipt of supplementary benefit. London: 1970.
pp.10. (Circular 3/70 DOE: 112/70 WO). DHSS.

4,412.   DEPARTMENT OF HEALTH AND SOCIAL SECURITY.   Survey into differences in supplementary benefits local office work between Scotland and the rest of Great Britain.   Unpublished: 1970.   pp.74.   DHSS.

4,413.   DEPARTMENT OF HEALTH AND SOCIAL SECURITY.   Social assistance: a review of the supplementary benefits scheme in Great Britain.   London: 1978.   pp.133.   Sq.

4,414.   DEPARTMENT OF HEALTH AND SOCIAL SECURITY.   Decisions of the courts relating to supplementary benefits and family income supplements legislation.   London: 1980.   Loose-leaf.   With supplements as issued.   DHSS.

4,415.   DEPARTMENT OF HEALTH AND SOCIAL SECURITY.   Supplementary benefits handbook: a guide to claimants' rights.   7th revised ed.   London: 1980.   pp.243.   DHSS.

4,416.   DEPARTMENT OF HEALTH AND SOCIAL SECURITY.   Guidance to supplementary benefit officers: claims for single payments; the Supplementary Benefit (Single Payments) Regulations 1980.   [London: 1981].   pp.[i] + 25.   DHSS.

4,417.   DEPARTMENT OF HEALTH AND SOCIAL SECURITY.   Guidance to supplementary benefit officers on the treatment of claims from people undertaking voluntary work.   Stanmore: 1981.   pp.3.   DHSS.

4,418.   DEPARTMENT OF HEALTH AND SOCIAL SECURITY.   Guidance to supplementary benefit officers on the treatment of resources: the Supplementary Benefit Resources Regulations 1980.   Stanmore: 1981.   pp.[2] + 51.   DHSS.

4,419.   DEPARTMENT OF HEALTH AND SOCIAL SECURITY.   Guidance on Supplementary Benefit (Urgent Cases) Regulations 1980.   Stanmore: 1981.   pp.28.   DHSS.

4,420.   DEPARTMENT OF HEALTH AND SOCIAL SECURITY   Guidance to supplementary benefit officers: claims for single payments.   Regulation 19 (Redecoration).   Stanmore: 1981.   pp.[4].   DHSS.

4,421.   DEPARTMENT OF HEALTH AND SOCIAL SECURITY.   Single payments for fuel costs.   Stanmore: 1982.   pp.[2].   (CSBO memo No.9).   DHSS.

4,422.   DEPARTMENT OF HEALTH AND SOCIAL SECURITY.   Guidance to supplementary benefit officers on the treatment of claims from persons attending courses of education or training for not more than 21 hours a week.   Stanmore: 1982.   pp.[7].   (CSBO memo 10).   DHSS.

4,423.   DEPARTMENT OF HEALTH AND SOCIAL SECURITY.   Supplementary Benefits Policy Inspectorate.   Report on the effects of the new capital rule.   [Stanmore]:   1982.   pp.iv + var.pag.   DHSS.

4,424.   DEPARTMENT OF HEALTH AND SOCIAL SECURITY.   Supplementary benefits handbook: a guide to claimants' rights.   8th rev.ed.   London: 1982.   pp.153.   DHSS.   9th rev.ed.   London: 1983.   pp.159.   DHSS.

4,425. DEPARTMENT OF HEALTH AND SOCIAL SECURITY. Supplementary benefit: guidance for supplementary benefit officers, and procedural instructions. [Stanmore] : 1983. 2 vols. (Looseleaf). DHSS.

4,426. DEPARTMENT OF HEALTH AND SOCIAL SECURITY AND THE SUPPLEMENTARY BENEFIT COMMISSION. The right to help. London: 1969. pp.20. DHSS.

4,427. DEPARTMENT OF HEALTH AND SOCIAL SECURITY: SUPPLEMENTARY BENEFITS COMMISSION. Supplementary benefits handbook: a guide to claimants' rights. 5th ed. London: 1977. pp.115. (Supplementary Benefits Administration Papers 2). DHSS.

4,428. DONNISON, D. "Supplementary benefits: dilemmas and priorities". J.Soc.Pol. 5. (1976). pp.337-358.

4,429. DONNISON, D. "Under the safety net". S.B.C. Notes & News. 6. (1976).

4,430. DONNISON, D. "Against discretion". N.S. 41. (1977). 534-536.

4,431. DONNISON, D. "How much discretion?". S.B.C. Notes & News. 7. (1977).

4,432. DONNISON, D.V. "The emergence of an issue". N.S. 55. (1981). pp.153-4.

4,433. DOUGLAS, J. "Supplementary benefit and race". Poverty. 51. (1982). pp.8-12.

4,434. DRABBLE, R. "Exceptional circumstances additions to S.B.". L.A.G.Bull. (1973). pp.200-202.

4,435. DRABBLE, R. "Exceptional needs payments". L.A.G.Bull. (1973). pp.246-247.

4,436. DUFTON, A.E. The supplementary benefits system in Northern Ireland 1980-1981. Newtownabbey: Ulster Polytechnic, for Northern Ireland Consumer Council. 1981. pp.v + 65. DHSS.

4,437. ELKS, L. The wage stop: poor by order. London: 1974. pp.78. (Poverty Pamphlet 17). DHSS; LSE; CUL.

4,438. ELKS, L. "Supplementary benefit and the rent stop". L.A.G.Bull. (1974). pp.134-136.

4,439. ELKS, L. "Supplementary benefit and the rent share". L.A.G.Bull. (1974). pp.164-165.

4,440. ELKS, L. "Exceptional needs". N.S. 33. (1975). p.23.

4,441. ELKS, L. "Mitigating supplementary benefit fraud". L.A.G.Bull. (1977). pp.135-136.

4,442. ESAM, P. "Supplementary benefits". L.M. 60. (1978). p.482-5.

4,443. EVASON, E. "Supplementary welfare in Northern Ireland". Soc.Stud. 2. (1973). pp.59-62.

4,444. FFOULKES, L. "Social security: removal and travel expenses". L.A.G. Bull. (1981). pp.213-214.

4,445. FFOULKES, L. "Supplementary benefit resources: a guide to CSBO guidance". L.A.G.Bull. (1982). pp.3-6.

4,446. FFOULKES, L. "Supplementary benefit additional requirements: a guide to CSBO guidance". L.A.G.Bull. (1982). pp.77-78.

4,447. FFOULKES, L. "The new supplementary benefit regulations". L.A.G. Bull. (Sept. 1983). pp.113-115.

4,448. FIELD, F. "Four week murder". N.S. 27. (1974). p.19.

4,449. FIMISTER, G. Exceptional needs payment or "section one" payment? The development of one city's policy. Newcastle upon Tyne: 1977. pp.17. (Newcastle Welfare Rights Report No. 1). DHSS.

4,450. FIMISTER, G. "Payment myths". S.W.T. 13. (1982). p.14.

4,451. FULBROOK, J. "Dismissals and the 40% rule: R. v. Greater Birmingham S.B.A.T., ex p. Khan [1979] 3 All E.R. 759 (D.C.)". I.L.J. 9. (1980). pp.129-31.

4,452. GEARING, B. & SHARP, G. Exceptional needs payments and the elderly. Coventry: 1973. pp.ii + 5. (CDP Occasional Paper No.10). DHSS; LSE.

4,453. HAND, C. "Family provisions: are the right people receiving it?". Fam.L. 10. (1980). pp.141-4.

4,454. HARVEY, A. "Supplementary benefits - assessment of capital". N.L.J. 125. (1975). p.202.

4,455. HARVEY, A. "The earnings disregard". N.L.J. 125. (1975). p.814.

4,456. HARVEY, A. "New mortgages on SB". N.L.J. 125. (1975). p.972.

4,457. HARVEY, A. "Giving with one hand". N.L.J. 129. (1979). p.970.

4,458. HAYES, M. "Supplementary benefit and financial provisions orders". J.S.W.L. (1979). pp.216-225.

4,459. HODGE, H. "Capital and supplementary benefit". L.A.G.Bull. (1975). pp.70-71.

4,460. JONES, D. & WELLBURN, B. Fairer and more easily understood?: nine months of the supplementary benefit scheme in Newcastle upon Tyne. Newcastle upon Tyne: Newcastle Welfare Rights Service. 1981. pp.42. DHSS.

4,461. JONES, S. & STOREY, H. "Immigrants and supplementary benefit". L.A.G.Bull. (1982). pp.44-46, 64-65.

4,462.   JORDAN, B.   "Urgent need payments".   L.A.G.Bull.   (1974).
         pp.300-301.

4,463.   KELLY, G.   "No funds - no food - no fuel".   Quest.   6.
         (1977).   pp.9-13.

4,464.   KERR, S.A.   "Deciding about supplementary pensions: a
         provisional model".   Jo.Soc.Pol.   11.   (1982).   pp.505-517.

4,465.   KERR, S.A.   Final report: differential take-up   of
         supplementary pensions.   Edinburgh University, Department of
         Psychology: 1982.   pp.x + 212.   DHSS.

4,466.   KERR, S.   Making ends meet: an investigation into the
         non-claiming of supplementary pensions.   London: 1983.   pp.iv
         + 141.   (Occasional Papers on Social Administration, 69).
         DHSS; LSE.

4,467.   KINCAID, J.   "Plea for S.B. control".   N.S.   45.   (1978).
         p.135.

4,468.   LAMBETH.   SOCIAL SERVICES DEPARTMENT.   How to apply for an
         exceptional needs payment for clothing and bedding.   London:
         1976.   pp.11.   DHSS.

4,469.   LEACH, S.N.   "Relationships between supplementary benefits
         offices and social services departments".   Policy and
         Politics.   9.   (1981).   pp.349-371.

4,470.   LEAPER, R.A.B.   "Social assistance: a watershed".   Soc.Pol. &
         Admin.   13.   (1979).   pp.3-22.

4,471.   LEAPER, R.A.B.   "Cash caring: Belgium, Britain and France".
         Soc.Pol. & Admin.   16.   (1982).   pp.187-212.

4,472.   LEGAL ACTION GROUP.   A lawyer's guide to supplementary
         benefit.   London: 1976.   pp.72.   (Social Law and Practice
         Guides No.3).   DHSS; CUL.   2nd ed.   A guide to supplementary
         benefit law.   London: 1978.   pp.72.   CUL.   3rd ed. (by J.
         Levin).   pp.136.   1981.   DHSS.

4,473.   LEVIN, J.   "Supplementary benefit - a new legal structure?".
         L.A.G.Bull.   (1978).   pp.202-5.

4,474.   LEVIN, J.   "Supplementary benefit and maintenance for
         children".   L.A.G.Bull.   (1979).   pp.188-189.

4,475.   LEVIN, J.   "Lump sums, capital and the new supplementary
         benefit regulations".   L.A.G.Bull.   (1980).   pp.285-7.

4,476.   LEVIN, J. & PITKIN, J.   "The new SB scheme".   L.A.G. Bull.
         (1980).   pp.259-262.

4,477.   LISTER, R.   The administration of the wage stop.   London:
         1972.   pp.29.   (Poverty Pamphlet 11).   DHSS; CUL.

4,478.   LISTER, R.   The earnings rule.   London: 1972.   pp.7.   DHSS.

4,479.   LISTER, R.   Supplementary benefit rights.   London: 1974.

pp.128. Sq; DHSS; LSE.

4,480. LISTER, R. Social security: the case for reform. London: 1975. pp.72. (Poverty Pamphlet 22). DHSS; LSE; CUL.

4,481. LISTER, R. (ed.). Patching up the safety net: evidence to the review of the supplementary benefits scheme. London: 1977. pp.85. (Poverty Pamphlet 31). DHSS; CUL.

4,482. LISTER, R. "Patching up the safety net? Evidence to the review of the supplementary benefits scheme". Poverty. (1977). (38). pp.9-17.

4,483. LISTER, R. "Holes in the safety net". N.S. 43. (1978). p.672.

4,484. LISTER, R. "Social assistance: a civil servant's review". J.S.W.L. (1979). pp.133-136.

4,485. LISTER, R. "Social security: discretion please". N.S. 53. (1980). pp.455-456.

4,486. LISTER, R. "The new supplementary benefit regulations". J.S.W.L. (1980). pp.341-343.

4,487. LISTER R. & CARSON, D. "The new supplementary benefit regulations: comment and description". J.S.W.L. (1980). pp.342-380.

4,488. LISTER, R. & EMMETT, T. Under the safety net. London: 1976. pp.39. (Poverty Pamphlet 25). DHSS; LSE; CUL.

4,489. LIVERPOOL WELFARE RIGHTS RESOURCE CENTRE. Tightening the screw: Social Security Acts 1 and 2 with accompanying regulations: a briefing document. Liverpool: 1980. pp.[2] + 31. DHSS.

4,490. LOOSEMORE, J. "Wages in arrears and in advance - supplementary benefit resources". L.A.G.Bull. (1979). pp.260-1.

4,491. LOOSEMORE, J. "Policy and discretion in supplementary benefit decisions". N.L.J. 130. (1980). pp.495-8.

4,492. LOOSEMOORE, J. "New supplementary benefit scheme". N.L.J. 132. (1982). pp.115-119.

4,493. LOOSEMOORE, J. "New supplementary benefit scheme". N.L.J. 132. (1982). pp.143-145.

4,494. LOOSEMORE, J. "New supplementary benefit scheme - III". N.L.J. 132. (1982). pp.165-167.

4,495. LOOSEMORE, J. "New supplementary benefit scheme - IV". N.L.J. 132. (1982). pp.199-201.

4,496. LOWE, N.V. "Divorce and supplementary benefits". Fam.L. 6. (1976). pp.24-31, 59-63.

4,497. LOWE, N.V. & SMITH, C. "Supplementary benefit and magistrates: isolation, interplay and reform". <u>Fam.L.</u> 6. (1976). pp.101-105, 132-136.

4,498. LUSTGARTEN, L. "Social security: the new legislation - I". <u>N.L.J.</u> 131. (1980). pp.71-73.

4,499. LUSTGARTEN, L. "The new legislation - II: re-organising supplementary benefit". <u>N.L.J.</u> 131. (1981). pp.95-97.

4,500. LUSTGARTEN, L. "The new legislation - III". <u>N.L.J.</u> 131. (1981). pp.119-121.

4,501. LYNES, T. "Administering the wage stop". <u>N.S.</u> 10. (1967). pp.861-62).

4,502. LYNES, T. "The wage stop". <u>Poverty</u>. (1967). (2). pp.4-6.

4,503. LYNES, T. "The secret rules which control the awards of supplementary benefits". <u>Poverty</u>. (1967). (4). pp.7-9.

4,504. LYNES, T. The Penguin guide to supplementary benefits: supplementary benefits, the family income supplement and the appeals tribunal. Harmondsworth: 1972. pp.233. DHSS; LSE. 2nd ed. 1974. pp.232. DHSS; LSE; CUL. 3rd ed. 1975. pp.219. LSE; CUL. 4th ed. 1981. DHSS; LSE; Sq.

4,505. LYNES, T. "Four weeks misrule". <u>N.S.</u> 19. (1972). pp.110-112.

4,506. LYNES, T. "Wage stop". <u>N.S.</u> 22. (1972). pp.402-403.

4,507. LYNES, T. "Unkind disregards", <u>N.S.</u> 19. (1972). p.648.

4,508. LYNES, T. "Housing reparations". <u>N.S.</u> 23. (1973). pp.360-361.

4,509. LYNES, T. "A watchdog for the poor". <u>N.S.</u> 49. (1979). pp.674-5.

4,510. LYNES, T. "Discretion rules". <u>N.S.</u> 53. (1980). p.174.

4,511. MACPHERSON, S. "Lawyers and supplementary benefits". <u>Fam.L.</u> 5. (1975). pp.168-170.

4,512. MARSHALL, R. Families receiving supplementary benefit: a study comparing the circumstances of some fatherless families and families of the long term sick and unemployed. London: 1972. pp.88. (Statistical and Research Series No.1). DHSS; LSE.

4,513. McBRIDE, J. "Supplementary benefits and judicial review". <u>C.L.J.</u> 35. (1976). pp.196-198.

4,514. MEACHER, M. Scrounging on the welfare: the scandal of the four week rule. London: 1974. pp.127. DHSS; LSE.

4,515. MESHER, J. "The 1980 social security legislation: the great welfare state chainsaw massacre?". <u>B.J.L.S.</u> 8. (1981). pp.119-127.

4,516. MESHER, J. "Recent social security commissioners' decisions: supplementary benefit". J.S.W.L. (1981). pp.376-382.

4,517. MESHER, J. "Recent social security commissioners' decisions: supplementary benefits". J.S.W.L. (1982). pp.115-128.

4,518. MESHER, J. "Recent social security commissioners' decisions: supplementary benefits and family income supplement". J.S.W.L. (1982). pp.375-384.

4,519. MIDDLETON, R. Benefits of discretion: CHAR report on exceptional needs payments for the single homeless. London: 1980. pp.[ii] + 33. DHSS.

4,520. MINISTRY OF SOCIAL SECURITY. Administration of the wage stop: report by the Supplementary Benefits Commission to the Minister of Social Security. London: 1967. pp.iv + 12. DHSS.

4,521. MOORE, P. "Students and supplementary benefit". L.A.G.Bull. (1973). pp.176-179.

4,522. MOORE, P. "Supplementary benefit: reviews and late claims". L.A.G.Bull. (1974). pp.165-166.

4,523. MOORE, P. "Voluntary unemployment and the SBC". L.A.G.Bull. (1974). pp.183-185.

4,524. NATIONAL FEDERATION OF CLAIMANTS UNIONS. A load of bullshit: a counter-report on the right to live. London: 1972. pp.34. DHSS.

4,525. NIXON, J. The review of the supplementary benefits scheme: a case study. Ascot: 1980. pp.[ii] + 17 + bibliog. (CSC Working Paper No.25). DHSS.

4,526. NORTHERN IRELAND. MINISTRY OF HEALTH AND SOCIAL SECURITY. Report of the Supplementary Benefits Commission. Belfast: annual, 1966 to 1979. LSE; DHSS.

4,527. NORTHERN IRELAND. DEPARTMENT OF HEALTH AND SOCIAL SERVICES. Supplementary benefits handbook. Belfast: 1970. 2nd ed. 1973. 3rd ed. 1975. pp.viii + 70. 4th ed. 1980. DHSS.

4,528. NORTHERN IRELAND. MINISTRY OF HEALTH & SOCIAL SERVICES. Everybody's guide to social security in Northern Ireland. (Rev.ed.). Belfast: 1973. pp.74. LSE.

4,529. NORTHERN IRELAND. DEPARTMENT OF HEALTH AND SOCIAL SERVICES. Supplementary Benefits Commission. Final Report. (Chairman: R.J. Higgins). Belfast: 1980. pp.xi + 82. DHSS.

4,530. NORTHERN IRELAND. DEPARTMENT OF HEALTH AND SOCIAL SERVICES. Supplementary benefits handbook: a guide to claimants' rights. Belfast: 1980. pp.xvi + 113.

4,531. PARTINGTON, M. "Students on vacation and the supplementary benefits commission". N.L.J. 123. (1973). p.449.

4,532. PARTINGTON, M. "Divorce, social security and legal

education". <u>N.L.J.</u> 124. (1974). p.467.

4,533. PARTINGTON, M. "Overpaid supplementary benefit and the ombudsman". <u>L.A.G.Bull.</u> (1975). pp.269-271.

4,534. PARTINGTON, M. "'Social Assistance' and the unemployed: DHSS review of supplementary benefit". <u>I.L.J.</u> 8. (1979). pp.60-4.

4,535. PARTINGTON, M. "Reform of the supplementary benefits scheme". <u>Court.</u> 5. (1980). pp.9-13.

4,536. PARTINGTON, M. "Supplementary benefits: interpretation and judgment". <u>N.L.J.</u> 131. (1981). pp.547-549.

4,537. PIACHAUD, D. "The price of thrift". <u>Poverty.</u> 49. (1981). pp.15-17.

4,538. PRESTATAIRE. "Damages and supplementary benefit". <u>L.S.G.</u> 76. (1979). p.496.

4,539. PRESTATAIRE. "Supplementary Benefits Commission: annual report for 1978". <u>L.S.G.</u> 76. (1979). p.1250.

4,540. PRESTATAIRE. "The supplementary benefit liability to maintain - the historical dimension". <u>L.S.G.</u> 77. (1980). pp.176-7.

4,541. PRESTATAIRE. "The supplementary benefit liability to maintain - the private liabilities". <u>L.S.G.</u> 77. (1980). pp.292-3.

4,542. PROSSER, T. "Politics and judicial review: the Atkinson case and its aftermath". <u>P.L.</u> (1979). pp.59-83.

4,543. RAINSFORD, T.J. "Supplementary benefits in Northern Ireland". <u>S.W.T.</u> 3. (23). (1973). p.9.

4,544. REID, J. "Social security. S.B.C. and judicial review". <u>I.L.J.</u> 4. (1975). pp.183-185.

4,545. ROBERTS, H.V. (ed.). Decisions of the courts relating to supplementary benefits and family income supplements legislation. London: 1980. (updated). Loose-leaf. LSE.

4,546. ROWELL, M.S. "A happy hunting ground for lawyers - aspects of supplementary benefit law (I)". <u>Fam.L.</u> 12. (1982). pp.164-167.

4,547. ROWELL, M.S. "A happy hunting ground for lawyers - aspects of supplementary benefit law. (II)". <u>Fam.L.</u> 12. (1982). pp.199-202.

4,548. ROWELL, M.S. "Erosion of discretion in supplementary benefits". <u>N.L.J.</u> 132. (1982). pp.1001-1003.

4,549. ROWELL, M.S. & WILTON, A.M. "Supplementary benefits - the new scheme (ii)". <u>Fam.L.</u> 11. (1981). pp.49-53.

4,550. ROWELL, M.S. & WILTON, A.M. The law of supplementary benefits. London: 1982. pp.xxxi + 239. LSE; CUL.

4,551. RUST, T.   "Supplementary benefit and part-time education". L.A.G.Bull. (1982). pp.53-6.

4,552. RUTHERFORD, M.   "Matrimonial orders and supplementary benefit". Fam.L. 7. (1977). pp.234-236.

4,553. SCHLACKMAN RESEARCH ORGANISATION.   Report on research on public attitudes towards the supplementary benefit system. London: 1978. pp.xxix + 89. DHSS.

4,554. SHARMA, V. "Second class claimants". Poverty. 51. (1982). p.13.

4,555. SHEARER, A. The poor in hospital: a study of the incomes of people living in long-stay hospitals and residential homes. London: 1976. pp.14. (Pamphlets on Disability No.4)., DHSS.

4,556. SMITH, C. "Discretion or rule of thumb?". N.L.J. 123. (1973). p.167.

4,557. SMITH, C. "Discretion or legislation". N.L.J. 124. (1974). p.219.

4,558. SMITH, C.   "Social security. Supplementary benefits; 'abolition' of the four-week rule". I.L.J. 3. (1974). pp.249-251.

4,559. SMITH, R. "Recent social security commissioners' decisions on supplementary benefit". L.A.G.Bull. (1982). pp.21-24.

4,560. SMITH, R. "Decisions of the social security commissioners on supplementary benefits in 1982". L.A.G.Bull. (1982). pp.142-144.

4,561. SMITH, R.   "Recent decisions of the social security commissioners on supplementary benefit - (1 Procedure)". L.A.G. Bull. (1983). pp.123-25.

4,562. SMITH, R.   "Recent decisions of the social security commissioners on supplementary benefit - (2 Substance)". L.A.G. Bull. (1983). pp.133-35.

4,563. SOCIAL SECURITY ADVISORY COMMITTEE.   Reports on the Supplementary Benefit (Requirements, Resources, and Single Payments) Amendment Regulations 1983 and the Supplementary Benefit (Miscellaneous Amendments) Regulation 1983. London: 1983. pp.62. (Cmnd. 8978). DHSS; LSE.

4,564. STEVENSON, O.   "The problems of individual need and fair shares for all: supplementary benefits: a social worker's view". S.W.T. 1. (1). (1970). p.15.

4,565. STEVENSON, O. Claimant or client? A social worker's view of the Supplementary Benefits Commission. London: 1973. pp.234. DHSS; LSE; CUL.

4,566. STOCKER, E.O.F. & NILSSON, P.G. (eds.). The law relating to supplementary benefits and family income supplements. London: 1972 in progress. Cumulative, loose-leaf. LSE.

4,567. STOWELL, R. Disabled people on supplementary benefit: interim report. Oxford: 1980. pp.[iii] + 145. (Research Study No.3). DHSS.

4,568. STREET, H. "Judicial review refused". L.A.G.Bull. (1975). pp.118-119.

4,569. SUPPLEMENTARY BENEFITS COMMISSION. Fuel debts among low-income groups: memorandum of guidance. London: 1972. 11. DHSS.

4,570. SUPPLEMENTARY BENEFITS COMMISSION. Exceptional needs payments: administration of Section 7 of the Ministry of Social Security Act, 1966. London: 1973. pp.vi + 32. (Supplementary Benefits Administration Paper No.4). DHSS; LSE.

4,571. SUPPLEMENTARY BENEFITS COMMISSION. Training of staff. London: 1973. pp.vi + 40. (Supplementary Benefits Administration Paper No.3). DHSS; LSE.

4,572. SUPPLEMENTARY BENEFITS COMMISSION. SBC Notes and News. London: 1974-. irreg. var.pag. DHSS.

4,573. SUPPLEMENTARY BENEFITS COMMISSION. Living together as husband and wife. London: 1976. pp.iv + 31. (Supplementary Benefits Administration Paper No.5). DHSS; LSE.

4,574. SUPPLEMENTARY BENEFITS COMMISSION. Low incomes: evidence to the Royal Commission on the Distribution of Income and Wealth. London: 1977. pp.vi + 100. (Supplementary Benefits Administration Paper No.6). DHSS.

4,575. TRADES UNION CONGRESS. TUC guide to supplementary benefits. London: 1981. pp.79. Sq.

4,576. TRINDER, C. "Benefits: near collapse". N.S. 60. (1982). pp.301-302.

4,577. TUNNARD, J. "Mortgages and supplementary benefit". L.A.G.Bull. (1975). pp.184-186.

4,578. TUNNARD, J. "Another look at mortgages and supplementary benefit". L.A.G.Bull. (1977). pp.36-38.

4,579. WALKER, C. Changing social policy: the case of the supplementary benefits review. London: 1983. pp.173. DHSS.

4,580. WEIR, S. "Raising the benefit of wage-stopped claimants". L.A.G.Bull. (1973). pp.19-20.

4,581. WEIR, S. "The wage stop". L.A.G.Bull. (1973). pp.145-148.

4,582. WEIR, S. "Householders, non-householders and boarders". L.A.G.Bull. (1974). pp.81-83.

4,583. WEIR, S. Supplementary benefits: a guide for social workers. London: Community Care. 1975. pp.24. DHSS; LSE. Rev. ed. 1976. pp.28. DHSS.

4,584. **WEST. W.T.** "Supplementary benefits and education". <u>S.J.</u>
124. (1980). pp.249-52.

4,585. **WHATELY, C.** "More on mortgages and supplementary benefit.
Raising a new mortgage". <u>L.A.G.Bull.</u> (1975). pp.237-238.

4,586. **WILDING, R.** "Discretionary benefits". <u>S.W.T.</u> 3. (13).
(1972). p.5

4,587. **WILKINS, G. & PLUMMER, J.** Strangled by the safety-net:
report on the supplementary benefit scheme in Birmingham.
Birmingham: 1974. pp.46. DHSS.

4,588. **WYTHES, D.** "A review of the Review". <u>L.T.</u> 13. (1979).
pp.97-103.

Section 12 General Issues in Social Security Law and Policy

(a) <u>Fraud and Abuse and Measures of Control</u>

4,589. ANON. "Where are the workshy?'. <u>Poverty</u>. 9. (1968). pp.1-4.

4,590. ANON. "Ministry fraud and the question of intent". <u>J.P.</u> 144. (1980). pp.748-749.

4,591. ANTEBI, R.N. "State benefits as a cause of unwillingness to work". <u>British Journal of Psychiatry</u>. 117. (1970). pp.205-206.

4,592. CHILD POVERTY ACTION GROUP. Abuse and the abused: supplementary evidence requested by the Committee of Enquiry into abuse of social security benefits. London: 1972. pp.32. DHSS.

4,593. COWELL, F.A. "Income incentives for the working poor". <u>Three Banks Rev.</u> 122. (June 1979). pp.32-48.

4,594. DEACON, A. "The abuse of social security". <u>Pol.Q.</u> 44. (1973). p.349.

4,595. DEACON, A. In search of the scrounger: the administration of unemployment insurance in Britain 1920-1931. London: 1976. pp.110. (Occasional Papers in Social Administration No.60). DHSS; CUL; LSE.

4,596. DEACON, A. "Scrounger bashing". <u>N.S.</u> 42. (1977). pp.355-356.

4,597. DEACON, A. "The scrounging controversy: public attitudes towards the unemployed in contemporary Britain". <u>Soc. & Ec. Admin.</u> 12. (1978). pp.120-35.

4,598. DEPARTMENT OF HEALTH AND SOCIAL SECURITY/DEPARTMENT OF EMPLOYMENT. Report of the Committee on Abuse of Social Security Benefits. (Chairman: Sir Henry Fisher). London: 1973. pp.xii + 298. (Cmnd. 5228). DHSS.

4,599. DOHERTY, N.A. "National insurance and absence from work". <u>E.J.</u> 89. (1979). pp.50-63.

4,600. FIELD, F. & GRIEVE, M. Abuse and the abused. London: CPAG. 1972. pp.26. (Poverty Pamphlet No.10). LSE; CUL; DHSS.

4,601. FRANEY, R. Poor law: the mass arrest of homeless claimants in Oxford. [London]: 1983. pp.93. DHSS.

4,602. GOLDING, P. & MIDDLETON, S. "Why is the press so obsessed with welfare scroungers?" <u>N.S.</u> 46. (1978). pp.195-7.

4,603. HANDY, L.J. & TURNER, H.A. "Society at work: absenteeism in the mines". <u>N.S.</u> 7. (1966). (184). pp.17-18.

4,604. HARRISON, J.   "Supplementary benefit fraud: 1. The legal background". L.A.G. Bull. (1983). pp.9-11.

4,605. HARRISON, J.   "Supplementary benefit fraud - 2. Individual cases". L.A.G. Bull. (1983). pp.47-50.

4,606. HOWELL, R. Why work? A challenge to the Chancellor. London: 1976. pp.40. (CCPC Publications No.582). DHSS; LSE.

4,607. HURLEY, J.   "The cost of sickness and malingering". Industry Week. 6. (1970). pp.14-15.

4,608. JENKINS, R. "Doing a double". N.S. 44. (1978). p.121.

4,609. LABOUR PARTY. Abuse of social security benefits. Talking Points No.5. London: 1970. pp.8. DHSS.

4,610. LANGE, G. Fraud and abuse in Government benefit programs. (ed. Robert A. Bowers). Washington, D.C.: 1979. pp.[v] + 251 + bibliogs. DHSS.

4,611. LISTER, R.   "Report of the Committee on Abuse of Social Security Benefits". Poverty. (1973). (26). pp.9-11.

4,612. MCKAY, J.   "Scroungers in a fuller picture". LAG Bull. (1981). pp.178-180.

4,613. MEACHER, M. "Promoting the welfare of scroungers". Poverty. (1970). (15). pp.8-10.

4,614. MOGRIDGE, C.   "Social security: offences and defences". Court. 5. (1980). pp.3-8.

4,615. MOORE, P.   "Scroungermania again at the DHSS". N.S. 55. (1981). pp.138-9.

4,616. MORRIS, C.N. & DILNOT, A.W. The effects of the tax benefit system on the employment decision. London: 1982. pp.30. DHSS.

4,617. NICKELL, S.J.   "The effect of unemployment and related benefits on the duration of unemplyment". E.J. 89. (1979). pp.34-49.

4,618. O'HIGGINS, P.   "Disqualification for social security benefits in the U.K." In Proceedings, International Society for Labour Law and Social Legislation, 7th Congress, Warsaw, September 1970. n.l.

4,619. PAGE, R. The benefits racket. London: 1971. pp.158. Sq; DHSS; LSE; CUL.

4,620. REID, J. "Report of the Committee on Abuse of Social Security Benefits". I.L.J. 2. (1973). pp.174-178.

4,621. SAMUELS, A.   "Social security fraud". J.P. 145. (1981). pp.156-161.

4,622. WILKINSON, R. "Claims, hysteria and malingering". Journal of the Chartered Insurance Institute.   58.   (1961).   pp.101-114.

4,623.   YOUNG, A.F.   "Malingering before and in the welfare state".
Social Service Quarterly.   XXXV.   (1961).   pp.65-59.

(b) Treatment of Strikers

4,624.   ANON.   "Trade disputes disqualification".   T.U.Info.   (August
1967).   p.9.

4,625.   ANON.   "Social security in strikes".   L.R.   68.   (1979).
p.82.

4,626.   ANON.   "Strikers' families attacked".   L.R.   69.   (1980).
pp.136-7.

4,627.   ANON.   "How long does a trade dispute last?".   L.A.G. Bull.
(1981).   pp.11-12.

4,628.   BRADLEY, A.W.   "Trade disputes and the Court of Session".
Scolag.   [1978].   pp.240-1.

4,629.   CLAIMANTS UNION.   Claimants handbook for strikers.   London:
n.d. [c.1972].   pp.50.   Sq.

4,630.   COLE, W.J.   "The financing of the individual striker: a case
study in the building industry".   B.J.I.R.   XIII.   (1975).
pp.94-97.

4,631.   DURCAN, J.W. & McCARTHY, W.E.J.   "The state subsidy theory of
strikes: an examination of statistical data for the period
1956-1970".   B.J.I.R.   XII.   (1974).   pp.26-47.

4,632.   EAST LONDON CLAIMANTS UNION.   Claimants handbook for strikers.
London: c.1973.   pp.47.   BL.

4,633.   FITZGERALD, M.   "National insurance section.   Unemployment
benefit and trade disputes".   Ind.L.R.   13.   (1958-59).
pp.121-128.

4,634.   GENNARD, J.   Financing strikers.   London: 1977.   pp.xi + 184.
CUL.

4,635.   GENNARD, J.   "The effects of strike activity on households".
B.J.I.R.   19.   (1981).   pp.327-44.

4,636.   GENNARD, J. & LASKO, R.   "Supplementary benefit and strikers".
B.J.I.R.   XII.   (1974).   pp.1-25.

4,637.   GENNARD, J. & LASKO, R.   "The individual and the strike".
B.J.I.R.   XIII.   (1975).   pp.346-370.

4,638.   GORDON, D.   "Social benefits through a cloud".   L.S.G.   76.
(1979).   p.1060.

4,639.   HICKLING, M.A.   Labour disputes and unemployment insurance
benefits in Canada and England.   Don Mills, Ontario: 1975.
pp.vii + 243.   Sq.

4,640. HUNTER, L.C. "The state subsidy theory of strikes: a reconsideration". B.J.I.R. XII. (1974). pp.438-444.

4,641. KEAST, H. "National insurance section. Unemployment benefit and trade disputes". Ind.L.R. 11. (1956-57). pp.67-74.

4,642. LASKO, R. "The payment of supplementary benefit for strikers' dependants - misconception and misrepresentation". M.L.R. 38. (1975). pp.31-38.

4,643. LYNES, T. "Taxing strikers' savings". N.S. 17. (1971). p.354.

4,644. MOORE, P. Unemployed workers and strikers' guide to social security. London: 1974. pp.74. [Child Poverty Action Group. CPAG Rights Guide. No.1]. LSE.

4,645. NATIONAL FEDERATION OF CLAIMANTS UNIONS. Claimants handbook for strikers. London: 1974. pp.49. DHSS. Birmingham: 1975. CUL. London: [1971]. pp.40. CUL.

4,646. O'HIGGINS, P. & HEPPLE, B.A. "Labour law: 5. industrial conflict. F. Social security and strikes". A.S.C.L. (1972). pp.394-395.

4,647. PARTINGTON, M. "Unemployment, industrial conflict and social security". I.L.J. 9. (1980). pp.243-53.

4,648. REID, J. (ed.). "Social security. Strikes and state benefit". I.L.J. 2. (1973). pp.111-115.

4,649. SOCIETY OF CONSERVATIVE LAWYERS. Financing strikes: by a sub-committee of the Society of Conservative Lawyers. London: 1974. pp.15. [Conservative Political Centre]. LSE; DHSS.

4,650. UNIVERSITY OF CHICAGO. SCHOOL OF BUSINESS. Trade disputes disqualification clause under the British Unemployment Insurance Acts. Chicago. pp.ix + 73. (Studies in Business Administration. Vol.8, No.1). LSE.

(c) Accident Compensation

4,651. ANON. "Review of current events. The Law Reform (Personal Injuries) Bill, 1948." Ind.L.R. 3. (1948-49). pp.5-9.

4,652. ANON. "Personal injuries and the state". P.H. 87. (1969). pp.1857-1858.

4,653. ANON. "Compensation for injuries". Which. (1970). pp.312-318.

4,654. ALLEN, K. BOURN, C.J. & HOLYOAK, J. (eds.). Accident compensation after Pearson. London: 1979. pp.x + 262. Sq.

4,655. ATIYAH, P.S. Accidents, compensation and the law. London: 1970. pp.xxviii + 633. DHSS; CUL; LSE; Sq. 2nd ed. 1975. pp.646. LSE; CUL. 3rd ed. 1980. LSE.

4,656. CAMPBELL, I.B. The Accident Compensation Act. Wellington:

1973. pp.36. (Occasional Papers in Industrial Relations No.7). LSE. 2nd ed. 1974. pp.35. (Incorporating the A.C. Amendment Act, 1973 and the A.C. Amendment Act (No.2), 1973). LSE.

4,657. DAVIES, P.J. "State benefits and accident compensation". J.S.W.L. (1982). pp.152-160.

4,658. DOUGLAS-MANN, B., WEITZMAN, P. & CASSON, T. Accidents at work: compensation for all. London: Society of Labour Lawyers. 1974. pp.16. LSE.

4,659. DWORKIN, G. "Compensation and payments for vaccine damage". J.S.W.L. (1979). pp.330-336.

4,660. FAHY, J.L. The administration of the Accident Compensation Act 1972. Wellington, N.Z.: Accident Compensation Commission. 1976. pp.40. DHSS.

4,661. FLEMING, J.G. Accident law and social insurance. Canberra: 1956. 22. (fo). LSE.

4,662. FLEMING, J.G. "The Pearson report: its 'strategy'". M.L.R. 42. (1979). pp.249-69.

4,663. HARRIS, D.R. "Accident compensation in New Zealand: a comprehensive insurance system". M.L.R. 37. (1974). pp.361-376.

4,664. HASSON, R.A. & MESHER, J. "No-fault - private or social insurance?". I.L.J. 4. (1975). pp.168-180.

4,665. INDUSTRIAL LAW SOCIETY. "Report of the I.L.S. conference on personal injuries - social insurance or tort liability?". I.L.S. Bulletin. 6. (1969). pp.7-11.

4,666. INDUSTRIAL LAW SOCIETY. "Compensation for industrial injury. Memorandum of evidence submitted to the Royal Commission on civil liability and compensation for personal injury by the Industrial Law Society". I.L.J. 4. (1975). pp.195-217.

4,667. ISON, T.G. Accident compensation: a commentary on the New Zealand scheme. London: 1980. pp.xii + 201. DHSS; CUL.

4,668. LEES, D. "Paying for injury". N.S. 24. (1973). pp.562-563.

4,669. LEWIS, R. "No-fault compensation for victims of road accidents: can it be justified?". Jo.Soc.Pol. 10. (1981). pp.161-178.

4,670. MARKS, K.H. "A first in national no-fault. The Accident Compensation Act 1972 of New Zealand". A.L.J. (1973). pp.516-525.

4,671. MINISTRY OF TRANSPORT AND MOTOR INSURERS' BUREAU. Compensation of victims of uninsured drivers. London: 1946. (Reprinted 1962). pp.8. DHSS.

4,672. MINISTRY OF TRANSPORT AND MOTOR INSURERS' BUREAU.

Compensation of victims of untraced drivers. London: 1969. pp.11. DHSS.

4,673. MORRISON, E.A. "Private injuries and public benefits". Ind.L.Rev. 8. (1953-54). pp.264-273.

4,674. O'CONNELL, J. "No-fault insurance for Great Britain". I.L.J. 2. (1973). pp.187-196.

4,675. OGUS, A.I., CORFIELD, P. & HARRIS, D.R. "Pearson: principled reform or political compromise?". I.L.J. 7. (1978). pp.143-159.

4,676. PALMER, G. Compensation for incapacity: a study of law and social change in New Zealand and Australia. Wellington: 1979. pp.460. DHSS.

4,677. PALMER, G.W.R. "Accident compensation in New Zealand: the first two years". Am.J.Comp.L. 15. (1977). pp.1-45.

4,678. PARSONS, O.H. "The Monckton Report on alternative remedies". Ind.L.Rev. 1. (1946-47). pp.131-135.

4,679. PAYNE, D. "Compensating the accident victim". C.L.P. 13. (1960). pp.85-111.

4,680. RIDEOUT, R.W. "Compensation for injury at work - the Pearson Commission". F.N. 28. (1978). p.97.

4,681. ROYAL COMMISSION ON CIVIL LIABILITY AND COMPENSATION FOR PERSONAL INJURIES. (LORD PEARSON). Report. London: 1978. LSE.

4,682. SZAKATS, A. Compensation for road accidents: a study on the question of absolute liability and social insurance. Wellington: Sweet & Maxwell, 1968. pp.ix + 173. Sq.

4,683. TUNC, A. "L'avenir de la securite sociale et de la responsibilite civile en Grande-Bretagne (le rapport Pearson)". Droit social. (1978). pp.247-57.

4,684. UNGER, J. "Final Report of the Departmental Committee on Alternative Remedies". M.L.R. 10. (1947). pp.179-184.

4,685. VENNELL, M.A. "The scope of national no-fault accident compensation in Australia and New Zealand". A.L.J. (1975). pp.22-29.

4,686. WILLIAMS, D.W. "State-financed benefits in personal injury cases". M.L.R. 37. (1974). pp.281-296.

4,687. YOUNG, A.F. "Damages for injuries". N.S. 5. (1965). (119). pp.15-16.

(d) Sex Equality

4,688. ANON. "Women and social security - study of the situation in five countries". Int.Soc.Sec.Rev. XXVI. (1973). pp.75-133.

4,689. ANON. Women and social security: a handbook from the Claimants Union movement. Manchester: 1976. pp.(2) + 34. Sq.

4,690. ANON. "Sex equality in social security". L.S.G. 77. (1980). p.68.

4,691. ANON. "Social security provision for widows and divorcees", L.S.G. 77. (1980). pp.399-400.

4,692. ATKINS, S. "The EEC Directive on equal treatment in social security benefits". J.S.W.L. (1979). pp.244-250.

4,693. ATKINS, S. "Social Security Act 1980 and the E.E.C. Directive on equal treatment in social security benefits". J.S.W.L. (1981). pp.16-20.

4,694. AVERY, L. "Women and social security". Topical Law. (April 1981). pp.1-9

4,695. BENN, M. "Women denied equal treatment under new social security legislation". Rights. 5(1). (1980). p.9.

4,696. BURKHAUSER, R.V. (ed.). A challenge to social security: the changing roles of women and men in American society. New York: 1982. pp.xii + 272. DHSS.

4,697. DAVID, M.E. & LAND, H. "Are the new social security provisions better for women?". Benefits Int. 6. (1976). pp.9-11.

4,698. DEPARTMENT OF HEALTH AND SOCIAL SECURITY. Second consultative document on equal treatment for men and women in occupational pension schemes. London: 1977. pp.60. DHSS.

4,699. EQUAL OPPORTUNITIES COMMISSION. Women and low incomes: a report based on evidence to the Royal Commission on income distribution and wealth. Manchester: 1977. pp.i + 39. DHSS.

4,700. EQUAL OPPORTUNITIES COMMISSION. Sex equality and pension age: a choice of routes. London: 1977. pp.22. DHSS.

4,701. FREUNDLICH, E. "Social security for housewives". I.Lab.R. 50. (1944). pp.160ff.

4,702. GELBER, S.M. "Social security and women: a partisan view". I.Lab.R. 112. (1975). pp.431-444.

4,703. HEWITT, P. Rights for women: a guide to the Sex Discrmination Act, the Equal Pay Act, paid maternity leave, pension schemes and unfair dismissal. London: 1975. pp.102. DHSS.

4,704. LABOUR PARTY. Towards equality: women and social security. London: 1969. pp.23. DHSS; LSE.

4,705. LABOUR PARTY RESEARCH DEPARTMENT. Participation '69. Women and social security report. London: 1970. pp.22. (Information paper No.43). DHSS.

4,706.   LABOUR PARTY.   Participation '69:   women and social security.
         London: 1969.   pp.6.   DHSS.

4,707.   LAND, H.   "Women, work and social security".   Soc. & Econ.Ad.
         5.   (1971).   pp.183-192.

4,708.   LAROQUE, P.   "Women's rights and widows' pensions".   I.Lab.R.
         106.   (1972).   pp.1-10.

4,709.   LISTER, R.   "Social security: the option for married women
         and widows".   L.A.G.Bull.   (1977).   pp.86-89.

4,710.   LISTER, R. & WILSON, L.   The unequal breadwinner: a new
         perspective on women and social security.   London: 1976.
         pp.24.   DHSS; LSE.

4,711.   MONELL, P. & ELLIS, E.   "Sex discrimination in pension
         schemes: has community law changed the rules".   I.L.J.   11.
         (1982).   pp.16-28.

4,712.   NATIONAL FEDERATION OF CLAIMANTS UNIONS.   Women and social
         security: a handbook from the Claimants Union movement.
         London: 1975.   pp.ii + 33.   DHSS.

4,713.   NATIONAL LABOUR WOMEN'S ADVISORY COMMITTEE.   Discrimination
         against women.   London: 1968.   pp.23.   (Labour Party Research
         Dept.).   DHSS.

4,714.   PRESTATAIRE.   "Sex equality in social security".   L.S.G.   77.
         (1980).   p.68.

4,715.   REID, J.   "Social security.   Equal pay and opportunity - the
         implications for social security".   I.L.J.   3.   (1974).
         pp.175-179.

4,716.   ROSE, J.   "Social welfare for the woman on her own".   In Eva
         Wilson, The woman's handbook.   London: 1975.   pp.50-88.   CUL.

4,717.   SELECT COMMITTEE ON THE EUROPEAN COMMUNITIES.   Session
         1977-78.   Social security: R/48/77;   draft directive on
         equality of treatment for men and women in matters of social
         security.   London: 1977.   pp.vi + 25.   DHSS.

4,718.   UNITED STATES.   DEPARTMENT OF HEALTH, EDUCATION AND WELFARE,
         SOCIAL SECURITY ADMINISTRATION.   Women and social security:
         law and policy in five countries, by Dalmer Hoskins and Lenore
         Bixby.   Washington: 1973.   pp.v + 95.   (Research Report 42,
         DHEW Publication SSA 73-11800).   DHSS.

4,719.   WILLETT, J.C.   Women and poverty.   London: [193-?].   pp.38.
         LSE.

4,720.   WILSON, E.   Women and the welfare state.   London: 1977.
         pp.208.   DHSS; LSE.

(e) Cohabitation

4,721.   ANON.   "'Living together'.   New approach in doubtful cases".

and "'Living together'. Two views on the new approach".
S.B.C. Notes & News. 4. (1976).

4,722.   ALLFREY, R. "Social security cases: cohabitation and common
sense". L.A.G.Bull. (1981). pp.164-165.

4,723.   ALLTIMES, G. & MOORE, B. "D.H.S.S. - cohabitation enquiry".
Case Con. 19. (1975). p.18.

4,724.   BOTTOMLEY, A. et al. The cohabitation handbook: a woman's
guide to the law. London: 1981. pp.[4] + 236. DHSS.

4,725.   BROWN, A. Cohabitation in Great Britain - evidence from the
general household survey. London: 1981. pp.8. DHSS.

4,726.   BROWN, A. & KIERMAN, K. "Cohabitation in Great Britain:
evidence from the General Household Survey". Population
Trends. 25. (1981). pp.4-10.

4,727.   CHILD POVERTY ACTION GROUP. The cohabitation rule: a guide
for single, separated, divorced or widowed women claiming
supplementary benefit or national insurance benefit. London:
CPAG. 1972. pp.6. (Poverty Leaflet No.4). DHSS.

4,728.   CLAYTON, P. The cohabitation guide. London: 1981. pp.[iv]
+ 161. DHSS.

4,729.   DEPARTMENT OF HEALTH AND SOCIAL SECURITY. Cohabitation:
Report of the Supplementary Benefit Commission to the
Secretary of State for Social Services. London: 1971.
pp.11. DHSS.

4,730.   DYER, C. & BERLINS, M. Living together. Feltham: 1982.
pp.208. DHSS.

4,731.   EEKELAAR, J.M. & KATZ, S.M. (eds.). Marriage and cohabitation
in contemporary societies: areas of legal, social and ethical
change; an international and interdisciplinary study.
Toronto and London: 1980. pp.xviii + 454 + bibliogs. DHSS.

4,732.   FAIRBAIRNS, Z. "The cohabitation rule - why it makes sense".
Women's Studies International Quarterly. 2. (1979).
pp.319-327.

4,733.   FAIRBAIRNS, Z. "The cohabitation rule: why it makes sense".
Spare Rib. 104. (1981). pp.24-26.

4,734.   FREEMAN, M.D.A. & LYON, C.M. Cohabitation without marriage:
an essay in law and social policy. Aldershot: 1983. pp.vii
+ 228. DHSS.

4,735.   HODGE, H. "Cohabitation and benefit". L.A.G.Bull. (1973).
pp.97-99.

4,736.   LISTER, R. As man and wife? A study of the cohabitation
rule. London: 1973. pp.56. (Poverty Research Series No.2).
DHSS; LSE; CUL.

4,737.   OLIVER, D. "Rationalising the cohabitation rule". Fam.L. 9.
(1979). pp.10-22.

4,738. PARKER, D. "The cohabitant father". <u>N.L.J.</u> 133. (1983).
        pp.423-426.

4,739. PARKER, S. Cohabitees. Chichester: 1981. pp.xxii + 230.
        DHSS.

4,740. PARRY, M.L. Cohabitation. London: 1981. pp.xxv + 162.
        DHSS.

4,741. SIMPSON, R. "The cohabitation rule". <u>Poverty</u>. (1972).
        (23). pp.15-20.

4,742. SIMPSON, R. "The cohabitation rule". <u>Poverty</u>. (1974).
        (28). pp.18-23.

(f) One-Parent Families

4,743. ANON. Unsupported mothers handbook. London: n.d. [c.1972].
        pp.32. Sq.

4,744. ATKINSON, A.B. An adequate income for one-parent families.
        London: National Council for One Parent Families. 1977.
        pp.5. (Forward from Finer Pamphlet No.2). DHSS.

4,745. BLAKE, P. The plight of one parent families: based on
        evidence submitted by the Council for Children's Welfare to
        the Committee on One-Parent Families. London: Council for
        Children's Welfare. 1972. pp.20. DHSS.

4,746. COUNCIL FOR CHILDREN'S WELFARE AND NATIONAL COUNCIL FOR THE
        UNMARRIED MOTHER AND HER CHILD. Fatherless families: report
        of a conference held on Tuesday 30th June, 1964. London:
        1965. pp.37. DHSS.

4,747. DEPARTMENT OF THE ENVIRONMENT. Inner area study: Liverpool.
        Single parent families. Report by the consultants Hugh Wilson
        and Lewis Womersley. London: 1977. pp.31. DHSS.

4,748. DEPARTMENT OF HEALTH AND SOCIAL SECURITY. Report of the
        Committee on One-Parent Families. (Finer Report). London:
        1974. 2 vols. (Cmnd. 5629). DHSS.

4,749. EVASON, E. Just me and the kids: a study of single parent
        families in Northern Ireland. Belfast: 1980. pp.vi + 88.
        DHSS.

4,750. FIELD, F. "How good a model is FIS for a means-tested GMA?".
        <u>Poverty.</u> (1975). (31). pp.17-22.

4,751. FINER JOINT ACTION COMMITTEE. The income needs of one parent
        families. London: 1975. pp.15. DHSS; LSE.

4,752. FINER JOINT ACTION COMMITTEE. A guide to the Finer Report.
        London: 1975. pp.26. DHSS.

4,753. GEORGE, V. "Social security and one-parent families".
        <u>Poverty.</u> (1974). (28). pp.2-5.

4,754. GEORGE, V. "Why one parent families remain poor". Poverty.
        (1975). (31). pp.6-12.

4,755. GEORGE, V. & WILDING, P. Motherless families. London: 1972.
        pp.xi + 229. CUL.

4,756. GINGERBREAD. Submission to the Finer Committee - July 1971.
        London: 1971. pp.21. DHSS.

4,757. GINGERBREAD. One parent families - a Finer future. London:
        1973. pp.36. DHSS.

4,758. HARVEY, A. "One-parent family concessions". N.L.J. 125.
        (1975). p.480.

4,759. HOLMAN, R. Unsupported mothers and the care of their
        children. 1st ed. London: 1970. pp.58. DHSS. 2nd ed.:
        1972. pp.60. DHSS.

4,760. HOPKINSON, A. Single mothers - the first year: a Scottish
        study of mothers bringing up their children on their own.
        Edinburgh: Scottish Council for Single Parents. 1976.
        pp.xvii + 256. DHSS; LSE.

4,761. INTERNATIONAL SOCIAL SECURITY ASSOCIATION. GENERAL
        SECRETARIAT. "Income maintenance for one-parent families".
        Int.Soc.Sec.Rev. XXVIII. (1975). pp.3-60.

4,762. JORDAN, A. Sole parents on pensions: a sample survey of class
        'A' widow pensioners and supporting parent beneficiaries.
        Australia: Department of Social Security. 1982. pp.ii +
        146. (Research paper no.18). DHSS.

4,763. LABOUR PARTY. NATIONAL EXECUTIVE COMMITTEE. Evidence and
        recommendations submitted by the National Executive Committee
        of the Labour Party to the Finer Committee on One-Parent
        Families. London: 1971. pp.17. DHSS.

4,764. MARSDEN, D. Mothers alone: poverty and the fatherless
        family. London: 1969. pp.xiv + 282. DHSS; LSE; CUL. Rev.
        ed. Harmondsworth: 1973. pp.xvi + 412. DHSS; LSE; CUL.

4,765. MARSDEN, D. "What action after Finer?". N.S. 30. (1974).
        pp.817-818.

4,766. MILSOM, P. Unsupported mothers on social security. London:
        1971. pp.17. (Study pamphlet No.2). DHSS.

4,767. MOTHERS IN ACTION. Single mothers: survival notes. London:
        1973. pp.iii + 9. DHSS.

4,768. MULLER-FEIMBECK, L. & OGUS, A.I. "Social welfare and the
        one-parent family in Germany and Britain". I.C.L.Q. 25.
        (1976). 3.

4,769. NATIONAL COUNCIL FOR ONE PARENT FAMILIES. The Finer report:
        recommendations and responses, proceedings of a conference
        held on 20th and 21st February 1975. London: 1975. pp.30.
        LSE; CUL.

4,770.   NATIONAL COUNCIL FOR ONE PARENT FAMILIES.   Information.
         Current information concerning one parent families.   London:
         1976- . Periodical/serial. CUL.

4,771.   NATIONAL COUNCIL FOR THE SINGLE WOMAN AND HER DEPENDANTS. The
         single woman with dependants. London: 1969. pp.12. DHSS.

4,772.   NATIONAL COUNCIL FOR THE SINGLE WOMAN AND HER DEPENDANTS.
         Financial hardship and the single woman.   London: 1973.
         pp.6. DHSS; LSE; CUL.

4,773.   NATIONAL COUNCIL FOR THE UNMARRIED MOTHER AND HER CHILD;
         MARSDEN, D.   State support for the unmarried mother and her
         child. London: 1968. pp.14. DHSS.

4,774.   NATIONAL COUNCIL FOR THE UNMARRIED MOTHER AND HER CHILD.
         Forward for the fatherless: memorandum of evidence to the
         Committee on One-Parent Families, May 1971;   additional
         evidence, June, 1972. London: 1972. pp.viii + 259. DHSS.

4,775.   NATIONAL FEDERATION OF CLAIMANTS UNIONS. Unsupported mothers
         handbook. Birmingham: 1974. pp.32. DHSS. [1977]. pp.32.
         DHSS.

4,776.   OFFICE OF POPULATION CENSUSES AND SURVEYS.   SOCIAL SURVEY
         DIVISION. Families and their needs, with particular reference
         to one parent families. An enquiry carried out in 1970 by the
         Social Survey Division of the Office of Population Censuses
         and Surveys on behalf of the Department of Health and Social
         Security. By Audrey Hunt;   Judith Fox;   Margaret Morgan.
         London: 1973. 2 vols. DHSS.

4,777.   OXFORDSHIRE COUNTY COUNCIL.   SOCIAL SERVICES COMMITTEE.
         Report of the working party on single parent families.
         Oxford: 1971. pp.47. DHSS.

4,778.   POPAY, J., RIMMER, L. & ROSSITER, C.   One parent families;
         parents, children and public policy. London: 1983. pp.103.
         DHSS.

4,779.   REID, J.   "In the G.M.A. world".   M.L.R.   38.   (1975).
         pp.52-59.

4,780.   STREATHER, J. & WEIR, S. Social insecurity: single mothers
         on benefit. London: 1974. pp.62. (Poverty Pamphlet 16).
         DHSS; LSE; CUL.

4,781.   STREATHER, J. & WEIR, S.   "Single mothers on benefit".
         Poverty. (1974). (28). PP.6-9.

4,782.   STREATHER, J.   "A Finer future for one parent families?".
         Poverty. (1975). (31). pp.2-6.

4,783.   TOWNSEND, P.   "Problems of introducing a guaranteed
         maintenance allowance for one parent families".   Poverty.
         (1975). (31). pp.29-39.

4,784.   TUNNARD, J. No father no home? A study of 30 fatherless
         families in mortgaged homes. London: 1976. pp.iv + 43.
         (Poverty Pamphlet 28). DHSS; LSE; CUL.

4,785.   WEBB, D. (ed.). Finer report: action and inaction: the
         Government's record on implementing the Finer Report. London:
         National Council for One Parent Families. 1976. pp.12.
         DHSS.

4,786.   WIMPERIS, V. The unmarried mother and her child. London:
         1960. pp.397. DHSS.

4,787.   WYNN, M. Fatherless families. London: 1964. pp.212. DHSS;
         LSE; CUL.

(g) Costs of Caring

4,788.   ARNOLD, R. "The inequitable treatment for those caring for
         elderly or infirm relatives". Poverty. (1974). (28).
         pp.12-13.

4,789.   COMMITTEE ON PENSIONS FOR UNMARRIED WOMEN. Report. London:
         1938-39. pp.iv + 78. (B.P.P. 1938-39, XIV). LSE.

4,790.   NATIONAL COUNCIL FOR THE SINGLE WOMAN AND HER DEPENDANTS. The
         cost to a single woman of caring for elderly dependants.
         London: 1970. pp.4. DHSS.

4,791.   NATIONAL COUNCIL FOR THE SINGLE WOMAN AND HER DEPENDANTS.
         Problems of the single woman with dependants. London: 1970.
         pp.9. DHSS.

4,792.   NATIONAL COUNCIL FOR THE SINGLE WOMAN AND HER DEPENDANTS.
         Single women talking. London: 1970. pp.12. DHSS.

4,793.   NATIONAL COUNCIL FOR THE SINGLE WOMAN AND HER DEPENDANTS.
         Single women with dependants and the attendance allowance.
         London: 1972. pp.15. DHSS.

4,794.   NATIONAL COUNCIL FOR THE SINGLE WOMAN AND HER DEPENDANTS.
         Financial hardship and the single woman. London: 1973.
         pp.6. DHSS; LSE.

4,795.   NATIONAL COUNCIL FOR THE SINGLE WOMAN AND HER DEPENDANTS.
         Single women with elderly dependants and the Social Security
         Bill. London: 1973. pp.4. DHSS.

4,796.   NATIONAL COUNCIL FOR THE SINGLE WOMAN AND HER DEPENDANTS. The
         wages of caring. London: 1974. pp.8. DHSS; LSE; CUL.

4,797.   TREASURY. Committee on pensions for unmarried women. Minutes
         of evidence... on the complaints which are made as to the
         position of unmarried women under the Contributory Pensions
         Acts, etc. London: 1938-39. pp.240. LSE.

(h) Welfare Rights

4,798.   BROOKE, R. "Civic rights and social services". Pol.Q. 40.
         (1969). p.90.

4,799.   BROOKE, R. "Solicitors and welfare rights". N.L.J. 123.

313

(1973). p.63.

4,800. BROOKE, R. (ed.). Advice services in welfare rights. London: 1976. pp.36. (Fabian Research Series No.329). Sq.

4,801. BULL, D. Action for welfare rights. London: Fabian. 1970. pp.24. DHSS.

4,802. BURKITT, B. & DAVEY, A.G. "Choice and markets; the 'new Right's' approach to welfare". Soc. Pol. & Admin. 14. (1980). pp.257-65.

4,803. CAMPBELL, T.D. "Counterproductive welfare law". Brit.Jo.Pol.Sci. 11. (1981). pp.331-50.

4,804. EVASON, E. "Welfare rights - what a social worker should know". Quest 7. (1977). pp.12-18.

4,805. MANNING, M. "Welfare rights: the one that got away". Community Care. 98. (1976). pp.12-14.

4,806. McGRATH, M. "For the people by the people - a resident run advice centre". Brit.J.Soc.Wk. 5. (1975). pp.255-281.

4,807. MORRIS, P. "Can poverty lawyers redress the balance". Community Care. 16. (1974). pp.16-17.

4,808. PARTINGTON, M. "Some thoughts on a 'test-case strategy'". N.L.J. 124. (1974). p.236.

4,809. ROSE, H. Rights, participation and conflict. London: 1971. pp.17. (Poverty Pamphlet 5). DHSS; LSE.

4,810. ROSE, H. & JAKUBOWICZ, A. "The rise and fall of welfare rights". N.S. 45. (1978). pp.55-60.

4,811. SPEKE WELFARE ACTION GROUP. The SWAG report: an experiment in welfare rights. London: 1974. pp.35. DHSS.

4,812. SPRINGBOARD LANARK. HAMILTON WELFARE RIGHTS TEAM. Regents Way stall project report. [Team leader: Patricia A. Dorris]. Motherwell: 1977. pp.ii + 22. DHSS.

4,813. TITMUSS, R.M. "Welfare 'rights', law and discretion". Pol.Q. 42. (1971). p.113.

4,814. WATSON, D. "Welfare rights and human rights". J.Soc.Pol. 6. (1977). pp.31-46,

4,815. WEST, G. The national welfare rights movement: the social protest of poor women. New York: 1981. pp.xxi + 451. DHSS.

(i) Low Pay

4,816. ANON. "Official action on the decisions of the International Labour Conference. Great Britain. Formal ratification of the convention concerning the creation of minimum wage fixing machinery (1928)". I.L.O.Bull. (3rd ser.). XIV. (1929). pp.75-76.

4,817. ANON.   A   national   minimum   wage: report   of   an
        interdepartmental working party. London: 1969. pp.vii + 89.
        LSE.

4,818. BANKS, R.F. "Wages councils and incomes policy". B.J.I.R.
        V. (1967). pp.338-351.

4,819. BAYLISS, F.J. British Wages Councils. Oxford: 1962. pp.x +
        177. DHSS.

4,820. BERCUSSON, B. "Proposal to rescind fair wages resolution".
        I.L.J. 11. (1982). pp.271-2.

4,821. BLACK, B. and others. Low pay in Northern Ireland. London:
        1980. pp.[ii] + 48. (Low Pay Pamphlet No.12). DHSS.

4,822. BROWN, M. Sweated labour: a study of homework. London:
        1974. pp.26. (Low Pay Pamphlet No.1). DHSS; CUL.

4,823. BROWN, M. & WINYARD, S. Low pay in hotels and catering.
        London: 1975. pp.iii + 37. (Low Pay Pamphlet No.2). DHSS;
        LSE; CUL.

4,824. BROWN, M. & WINYARD, S. Low pay on the farm. London: 1975.
        pp.ii + 39. (Low Pay Pamphlet No.3). DHSS; LSE; CUL.

4,825. BULKLEY, M.E. The establishment of legal minimum rates in the
        box-making industry under the Trade Boards Act of 1909.
        London: 1915. pp.xii + 95. LSE.

4,826. BURNS, E.M. Wages and the state. A comparative study of the
        problems of state wage regulation. London: 1926. pp.443.
        CUL.

4,827. CLARK, D. "Inspecting wages". N.S. 38. (1976). p.20.

4,828. CRINE, S. The great pay robbery. London: 1981. pp.[1] + 18.
        (Low Pay Report 8). DHSS.

4,829. CRINE, S. & PLAYFORD, C.   Low pay and unemployment in
        Cornwall. London: 1981. pp.[4] + 46. (Low Pay
        Pamphlet No.18). DHSS.

4,830. DEPARTMENT OF EMPLOYMENT AND PRODUCTIVITY. A national minimum
        wage. Report of an interdepartmental working party. London:
        1969. pp.vii + 189. DHSS; LSE.

4,831. DUNCAN, C. Low pay: its causes, and the post-war trade union
        response. Chichester: 1981. pp.xv + 159. DHSS.

4,832. ERLAM, A. & BROWN, M. Catering for homeless workers: a study
        of low pay and homelessness amongst casual catering workers.
        London: 1976. pp.13. DHSS.

4,833. FIELD, F.(ed).   Low pay: Action Society Trust Essays.
        London: 1973. pp.141. DHSS; LSE.

4,834. FIELD, F. The rights of lower paid workers: a reply to the
        Employment Protection Bill: consultative document. London:

1974. pp.13. (Low Pay Papers No.1). LSE; CUL.

4,835. FIELD, F. (ed.). Are low wages inevitable? Nottingham: 1976. pp.144. DHSS.

4,836. FIELD, F. Unfair shares: the disabled and unemployed. London: 1977. pp.5. (Low Pay Paper No.20). DHSS; CUL.

4,837. FIELD, F. & WINYARD, S. Low wages councils. Nottingham: 1975. pp.11. (Spokesman Pamphlet No.49). DHSS.

4,838. FISHER, A. & DIX, B. Low pay and how to end it: a union view. London: 1974. pp.117. DHSS; CUL.

4,839. FOGARTY, M.P. The just wage. London: 1961. pp.309. LSE.

4,840. FYFE, J. & PETTMAN, B.O. Equal pay and low pay. Bradford: 1974. pp.iv + 39. (Report and Survey No.9). DHSS.

4,841. HARRISON, A.J. Low pay and child poverty. London: CPAG. 1972. p.19. DHSS.

4,842. HOUSE OF LORDS AND HOUSE OF COMMONS JOINT COMMITTEE. Eleventh report by the Joint Committee of the House of Lords and of the House of Commons appointed to consider all Consolidated Bills...; being a report upon the Wages Councils Bill [H.L.]; together with the proceedings of the Committee, etc. London: [1959]. pp.v + 2. (B.P.P. 1958-59, IV). LSE.

4,843. HOWELL, R. Low pay and taxation. London: 1976. pp.9. (Low Pay Paper No.8). DHSS; CUL.

4,844. HUMPHREY, W.A. The workers' share: a study in wages and poverty. London: 1930. pp.93. LSE.

4,845. INDEPENDENT LABOUR PARTY. Socialism in our time. Labour's road to power: the policy of the living income. London: [1926]. pp.15. LSE.

4,846. INDEPENDENT LABOUR PARTY. Living income. The living wage. London: [1928]. pp.12. LSE.

4,847. INTERNATIONAL LABOUR CONFERENCE. Minimum wage-fixing machinery. Geneva: 1927. pp.159. LSE.

4,848. INTERNATIONAL LABOUR CONFERENCE. Minimum report on minimum wage fixing machinery. Geneva: 1928. pp.vii + 149. LSE.

4,849. INTERNATIONAL LABOUR CONFERENCE. Supplementary report on wage fixing machinery. Geneva: 1928. pp.35. LSE.

4,850. INTERNATIONAL LABOUR OFFICE. The minimum wage. Geneva: 1939. pp.viii + 257. (Studies and Reports Series D (Wages and Hours of Work), No.22). LSE.

4,851. JORDAN, D. Short measures for the poor: wages council increases under pay policy - 1975-77. London: 1977. pp.9. (Low Pay Paper No.17). DHSS; CUL.

4,852. LOW PAY UNIT. Low pay and wages councils: a memorandum to

the Secretary of State for Employment. London: 1974. pp.13.
DHSS; CUL.

4,853.   LOW PAY UNIT. Axing low pay: a call for a trade union plan
of action against low pay. London: 1976. pp.11. (Low Pay
Papers No.9). LSE; CUL.

4,854.   MARQUAND, J. "Which are the lower paid workers?". B.J.I.R.
V. (1967). pp.359-374.

4,855.   McCALE, H. The state regulation of wages. London: 1911.
pp.14. LSE.

4,856.   MILNER, E.M. & MILNER, D. Labour and a minimum income for
all. Darlington: 1920. pp.12. LSE.

4,857.   MINERS' FEDERATION OF GREAT BRITAIN. The claim for legal
minimum wages for mineworkers. London: 1931. pp.39. LSE.

4,858.   MINISTRY OF LABOUR Hat, cap and millinery trade (Scotland):
order... confirming variations of minimum rates of wages, etc.
London: 1932. pp.11. LSE.

4,859.   MINISTRY OF LABOUR. Wages Councils Act, 1945, Retail
furnishing. Report of a Committee of Inquiry on an
application for the establishment of a Wages Council for the
retail furnishing and allied trades. London: 1947. pp.19.
LSE.

4,860.   MINISTRY OF LABOUR. Commission of inquiry on an application
for the establishment of a Wages Council for the retail food
trades, Report. Belfast: 1947. pp.18. LSE.

4,861.   MINISTRY OF LABOUR. Wages Councils Act, 1945, retail food.
Report of a Committee of Inquiry on an application for the
establishment of a Wages Council for the retail food trades.
London: 1947. pp.39. LSE.

4,862.   MINISTRY OF LABOUR. Wages Councils Act, 1945, retail drapery.
Report of a Committee of Inquiry on an application for the
establishment of a Wages Council for the retail drapery,
out-fitting and footwear trades. London: 1947. pp.15. LSE.

4,863.   MINISTRY OF LABOUR. Wages Councils Act, 1945, retail
bookselling. Report of a Committee of Inquiry on the question
whether a Wages Council should be established with respect to
workers and their employers in the retail bookselling,
newsagency, stationery, tobacco and confectionary trades.
London: 1947. pp.27. LSE.

4,864.   MINISTRY OF LABOUR. Wages Councils Act, 1945, hairdressing.
Report of a Commission of Inquiry on an application for the
establishment of a Wages Council for the hairdressing trade.
London: 1947. pp.11. LSE.

4,865.   MINISTRY OF LABOUR. Bread and flour distributive trades.
Report of a Committee on the question of the establishment of
a Wages Council for the wholesale and retail bread and flour
confectionary distributive trades. London: 1950. pp.16.
LSE.

4,866.   MINISTRY OF LABOUR.   Wages Councils Acts, 1945 to 1948.
         Rubber proofed garment making.   Report of a Committee of
         Inquiry appointed in 1955 to consider an application for the
         establishment of a Wages Council for the rubber proofed
         garment making industry. London: 1956. pp.15. LSE.

4,867.   MINISTRY OF LABOUR. Wages Council Acts, 1945 to 1948. Rubber
         Proofed Garment Making.   Report of a Committee of Inquiry on
         an application for the establishment of a Wages Council for
         the rubber proofed garment making industry. London: 1959.
         pp.15. LSE.

4,868.   MINISTRY OF LABOUR.   Wages Councils Act, 1959.   Sugar
         confectionery.   Report of the committee of inquiry on the
         sugar confectionery and food preserving wages council (Great
         Britain). London: 1961. pp.10. LSE.

4,869.   MORRIS, A. A minimum wage: a socialistic novel.   London:
         [1891]. pp.(6) + 232. G.

4,870.   NATIONAL AMALGAMATED UNION OF SHOP ASSISTANTS, WAREHOUSEMEN
         AND CLERKS.   Report of the minimum wages committee to the
         Liverpool conference, Easter, March 27th and 28th, 1910.
         London: [1910]. pp.10. LSE.

4,871.   NATIONAL ANTI-SWEATING LEAGUE.   Living wage for sweated
         workers. London: [1908]. pp.20. LSE.

4,872.   NATIONAL BOARD FOR PRICES AND INCOMES.   General problems of
         low pay.   Report No.169.   London: 1971.   pp.viii + 193.
         (Cmnd. 4648). DHSS.

4,873.   NORTHERN IRELAND.   MINISTRY OF LABOUR.   Wages Council Act
         (Northern Ireland), 1945.   Road haulage.   Report of a
         Commission of Inquiry on the question whether a Wages Council
         should be established with respect to road haulage workers and
         their employers. Belfast: 1948. pp.19. LSE.

4,874.   NORTHERN IRELAND.   Trade Boards Act (N.I.), 1923:   order of
         the Ministry of Labour confirming minimum rates of wages, etc.
         Belfast: 1926 -. LSE.

4,875.   OFFICE OF WAGES COUNCILS.   Wages orders.   London: irreg.
         1976-. LSE.

4,876.   PICKARD, B.   A reasonable revolution: being a discussion of
         the state bonus scheme: a proposal for a national minimum
         income. London: [1919]. pp.78. LSE.

4,877.   POND, C.   Taxing the social contract: a memorandum to the
         Chancellor of the Exchequer from the Low Pay Unit.   London:
         1975. pp.7. (Low Pay Papers No.2). LSE; CUL.

4,878.   POND, C.   A jubilee year for the low paid?   London: 1977.
         pp.4. (Low Pay Paper No.18). DHSS; CUL.

4,879.   POND, C. & WINYARD, S. The case for a national minimum wage.
         London: [1983].   pp.64.   (Low Pay Unit pamphlet, no.23).
         DHSS.

4,880.   RADICE, G. Low pay. London: 1968. pp.20. Rev.ed. Radice,
         G. & Edmonds, J. London: 1969. pp.20. (Fabian Research
         Series 170). LSE.

4,881.   RICHARDSON, J.H. A study on the minimum wage. London: 1927.
         pp.198. CUL.

4,882.   ROBSON, W.A. "Industrial law: legislation. The Wages
         Councils Act, 1945". A.S.E.L. (1945). unpublished.
         pp.67-72. LSE.

4,883.   SELLS, D. The British trade board system. London: 1923.
         pp.vii + 293. LSE.

4,884.   SELLS, D. British Wages Boards. A study in industrial
         democracy. Washington: 1939. pp.389. CUL.

4,885.   SIMPLEX, E. (pseud.). The minimum wage stunt. Keighley:
         1918. pp.32. LSE.

4,886.   SMART, W. A living wage. [Glasgow: 1893] pp.19. G.

4,887.   SMITH, C. The case for wages boards. London: [1908].
         pp.viii + 94. LSE.

4,888.   TAWNEY, R.H. The establishment of minimum rates in the
         chain-making industry under the Trade Boards Act of 1909.
         London: 1914. pp.xiii + 157. LSE.

4,889.   TAWNEY, R.H. The establishment of minimum rates in the
         tailoring industry under the Trade Boards Act of 1909.
         London: 1915. pp.xiii + 274. LSE.

4,890.   THOMAS, C. Short back and sides for the poor: a memorandum
         to the Hairdressing Undertakings Wages Council. London:
         1977. pp.7. (Low Pay Paper No.19). DHSS; CUL.

4,891.   THOMAS, C. The charge of the wages brigade: an assessment of
         the enforcement of minimum wages. London: 1978. pp.15.
         (Low Pay Paper No.21). DHSS.

4,892.   TILLYARD, F. The worker and the state. London: 1923.
         pp.viii + 298. CUL. 2nd ed. 1936. pp.x + 308. CUL. 3rd
         ed. 1948. pp.xii + 302. LSE; CUL.

4,893.   TRADES UNION CONGRESS. GENERAL COUNCIL. Low pay: a T.U.C.
         General Council discussion document based on the report of a
         working party of T.U.C. staff and trades union research
         officers. [London]: 1970. pp.57. LSE.

4,894.   TRINDER, C. & WINYARD, S. A new deal for farmworkers: the
         case for an independent inquiry into the pay of farmworkers.
         London: 1975. pp.ii + 7. (Low Pay Paper No.5). DHSS; CUL.

4,895.   UNITED KINGDOM. Regulations made by the Board of Trade under
         section 18 of the Trade Boards Act, 1909. London: 1910-11.
         LSE.

4,896.   UNITED KINGDOM. Report and special report from the Select

Committee on Trade Boards Act Provisional Order Bill, etc. London: 1914. pp.vi + 205. (B.P.P. 1914, X). LSE.

4,897. UNITED KINGDOM. Special report from the Select Committee on the Trade Boards Act Provisional Orders Bill, etc. London: 1914. pp.vi + 61. (B.P.P. 1914, X). LSE.

4,898. UNITED KINGDOM. State regulation of wages. London: 1919. pp.16. LSE.

4,899. UNITED KINGDOM. Report... of the committee apointed to enquire into the working and effects of the Trade Boards Acts. London: 1922. pp.55. (B.P.. 1922, X). LSE.

4,900. UNITED KINGDOM. Trade Boards Acts, 1909 and 1918: order of the Minister of Labour confirming minimum rates of wages. London: 1926-. LSE.

4,901. UNITED KINGDOM. Trade Boards Acts, 1909 and 1918: Jute Trade (G.B.): order confirming minimum rates of wages fixed for certain classes of female workers, and varieties of rates made for male and female workers effective from 7th May 1928. London: 1928. pp.14. LSE.

4,902. VAIZEY, J. "A minimum wage policy". Poverty. (1969). (11). pp.5-7.

4,903. WARD, S. & POND, C. The £6 trap. London: 1975. pp.7. (Low Pay Paper No.6). DHSS; LSE; CUL.

4,904. WILLIS, W.A. Trade boards at work: a practical guide to the operation of the Trade Boards Act, etc. London: 1920. pp.xiv + 112. LSE.

4,905. WINYARD, S. Who will protect the low paid? A submission to the Commission of Inquiry on the proposed abolition of the Industrial and Staff Canteen Undertakings Wages Council. London: 1975. pp.8. (Low Pay Paper No.7). DHSS; CUL.

4,906. WINYARD, S. Policing low wages: a study of the wages inspectorate. London: 1976. pp.iv + 40. (Low Pay Pamphlet No.4). DHSS; LSE; CUL.

4,907. WINYARD, S. Nine into two equals progress: an examination of the merging of the retail wages councils. London: 1976. pp.14. (Low Pay Paper No.10). DHSS; CUL; LSE.

4,908. WINYARD, S. The weak arm of the law: an assessment of the new strategy of minimum wage enforcement. London: 1976. pp.16. (Low Pay Paper No.13). DHSS; CUL.

4,909. WOMEN'S INDUSTRIAL COUNCIL. The case for and against a legal minimum wage for sweated workers. London: 1909. pp.24. LSE.

4,910. WOOTTON, B.F. Remuneration in a welfare state. Liverpool: 1961. pp.17. LSE.

4,911. WROTTESLEY, A.J.F. "Wages Councils". Ind.L.R. 6. (1951-52). pp.43-48.

4,912. WROTTESLEY, A.J.F. "The Catering Wages Act". Ind.L.R. 6.
(1951-52). pp.187-192.

Section 13 Irish Social Security Law

4,913. ANON. "Reform of social security legislation in Ireland".
Bull. I.S.S.A. IV. (1951). pp.20-27.

4,914. ANON. "Ireland and abroad: family allowances". T.U.Info.
(October, 1967). pp.2-5.

4,915. ANON. "The Social Welfare (Occupational Injuries) Act 1967".
I.L.T.S.J. 101. (1967). pp.341-2.

4,916. ANON. "Social security: Republic of Ireland reciprocal
agreement". N.L.J. 118. (1968). pp.1025-6.

4,917. BOYD, A.W. "Principles of social insurance". In F.C. King
(ed.). Public Administration in Ireland. Dublin: 1949.
Vol.2. pp.235-46; London: 1954. pp.236-47. LSE.

4,918. CINNEIDE, S.O. "The extent of poverty in Ireland". Soc.Stud.
1. (1972). pp.381-400.

4,919. CLARK, R. "Kiely v. Minister for Social Welfare - the case of
the tenacious widow". G.I.L.S.I. 72. (1978). pp.79-80.

4,920. CLARK, R.W. "Social welfare appeals in the Republic of
Ireland". Ir.Jur. 13. (1978). pp.265-83.

4,921. CLARK, R.W. "The Social Welfare Act 1983 - a commentary".
Journal of the Irish Society for Labour Law. 2. (1983).
pp.22-36.

4,922. COLLINS, C., HONOHAN, W.A., McCARTHY, C. & McGRATH, P.M.
"Symposium on the Government Green Paper 'A national income
related pension scheme'". J.S.S.I.S.I. 23. (130th Sess.).
(1976-77). pp.77-112.

4,923. CONAGHAN, A. "Social security: a comparison with European
conditions". Chr.R. 21. (1967). pp.261-71.

4,924. COUGHLAN, A. Aims of social policy - reform in Ireland's
social security and health services. Dublin: 1966. pp.20.
(Tuairim Pamphlet No.14). TCD.

4,925. COUNCIL FOR SOCIAL WELFARE. Conference on poverty 1981.
Report of the Kilkenny Conference. Blackrock, Co.Dublin:
1982. pp.433.

4,926. DOYLE, D. "Home assistance and poverty". Soc.Stud. 1.
(1972). pp.433-40.

4,927. EIRE. DEPARTMENT OF SOCIAL WELFARE. Guide to the social
insurance regulations. Dublin: 1955. pp.36. LSE.

4,928. FORDE, M. "The applicable social security law in the European
Court". Ir.Jur. 14. (1979). pp.83-105.

4,929. GARVIN, J. "Public assistance". In F.C. King (ed.). Public

Administration in Ireland. Dublin: 1944. pp.161-72. TCD.

4,930. GEARY, R.C. "Are Ireland's social security payments too small?". Ec.& Soc.Rev. 4. (1972-73). pp.343-8.

4,931. GEARY, R.C. "Are Ireland's social security payments too small? A rejoinder". Ec.& Soc.Rev. 5. (1973-74). p.123.

4,932. GROGAN, V. Administrative tribunals in the public service. Dublin: 1964. pp.76. DHSS; LSE.

4,933. HEFFERMAN, E.P. "Employee benefits and social security in the Republic of Ireland". Benefits Int. 3. (1974). pp.5-9.

4,934. IRELAND, REPUBLIC OF. National Economic and Social Council. Alternative strategies for family income support. Dublin: [1979]. pp.137. DHSS.

4,935. IRELAND. DEPARTMENT OF SOCIAL WELFARE. Summary of social insurance and assistance services, 1965- Dublin: Department of Social Welfare. Annual. var.pag. DHSS.

4,936. IRELAND. DEPARTMENT OF SOCIAL WELFARE. White paper containing government proposals for social security in Ireland. Dublin: 1949. pp.6. DHSS.

4,937. IRELAND. DEPARTMENT OF SOCIAL WELFARE. A national income-related pension scheme - a discussion paper. Dublin: 1976. pp.viii + 195. DHSS.

4,938. IRISH FREE STATE. Report of the Registrar of Friendly Societies to the Minister of Finance. Dublin: 1923, 1924. LSE.

4,939. IRISH FREE STATE. Report of the Industrial Assurance Commission. Dublin: [1924?]. pp.24. LSE.

4,940. JOYCE, L. & McCASHIN, A. Poverty and social policy: the Irish National Report presented to the Commission of the European Communities. Dublin: Institute of Public Administration. 1982. pp.[5] + 156. DHSS.

4,941. KAIM-CAUDLE, P.R. Social security in Ireland and Western Europe. Paper No.20. Dublin: Economic Research Institute. 1964. pp.48. DHSS; LSE.

4,942. KAIM-CAUDLE, P. Social policy in the Irish Republic. London: 1967. pp.120. CUL; DHSS; LSE.

4,943. KAIM-CAUDLE, P.R. "The future of social services in Ireland".. Admin. 15. (1967). pp.340-54.

4,944. KAIM-CAUDLE, P.R. "Income maintenance service in Ireland". Int.Rev.Ad.Sc. 38. (1968). pp.53-61.

4,945. KAIM-CAUDLE, P. "Pensions for the old, north and south". Fortnight. 6. (Nov. 1970). pp.5-6.

4,946. KAVANAGH, J. "Social policy in modern Ireland". Admin. 26. (1978). pp.318-30.

4,947. KEADY, P.J.   "The new Social Welfare Act of Eire".   <u>Bull. I.S.S.A.</u> 1. (1948). (4). pp.2-7.

4,948. LYNCH, J.   "The social responsibilities of government". <u>Chr.R.</u> 21. (1967). pp.211-23.

4,949. NATIONAL SOCIAL SERVICE BOARD. Relate: information bulletin of the National Social Service Board. Dublin: 1973 onwards. In progress.

4,950. NEVIN, D. "Are the poor less poor in 1974 than in 1971?". <u>Soc.Stud.</u> 4. (1975). pp.26-33.

4,951. O'CINNEIDE, S.   A law for the poor: a study of home assistance in Ireland.   Dublin: 1970.   pp.xiii + 146. (Institute of Public Administation (Dublin) Research Series, No.3). DHSS; LSE.

4,952. O'HIGGINS, J. & O'HIGGINS, M. "Are Ireland's social security payments too small? A comment". <u>Ec.& Soc.Rev.</u> 5. (1973-74). pp.113, 199.

4,953. O'SULLIVAN, J.J. "The new social welfare scheme". In F.C. King (ed.). <u>Public Administration in Ireland</u>. Dublin: 1954. Vol.3. pp.129-47. TCD.

4,954. REDDIN, B.S. "Social welfare benefits and employee pension plans in the Republic of Ireland". <u>Benefits Int.</u> 6. (1976). pp.15-21.

4,955. REPUBLIC OF IRELAND. Guide to the social services (M52/9). Dublin: 1957. 9th ed. pp.viii + 64. DHSS.

4,956. ROCHE, J.D. Poverty and income maintenance policies in Ireland 1973-80. Dublin: 1984. pp.xvi + 293. TCD.

4,957. SHEEHAN, M. The meaning of poverty. Blackrock, Co. Dublin: Council for Social Welfare. 1974. pp.137. DHSS; LSE.

PART IV Social Security: International and European Influences

Section 1 International Labour Organization

4,958. ANON. "Great Britain and the Washington Maternity Convention". I.L.O.Bull. (3rd ser.). IV. (July-Dec. 1921). pp.220-223.

4,959. ANON. "The present tendencies of compulsory sickness insurance". I.Lab.R. XV. (1927). pp.842ff.

4,960. ANON. "Unemployment insurance: tabular analysis of the legislation in force". I.Lab.R. XXIII. (1931). pp.48ff.

4,961. ANON. "The cost of social security". I.Lab.R. 65. (1952). pp.726ff.

4,962. ANON. "A comparative analysis of the cost of social security". I.Lab.R. 67. (1953). pp.292ff.

4,963. ANON. "Economic stability and social security". I.Lab.R. 77. (1958). pp.434ff.

4,964. ANON. "Appraisal of the I.L.O. programme, 1959-1964... Social security". I.L.O.Bull. (3rd ser.). XLIII. (1960). pp.32-34.

4,965. ANON. "Interpretations of decisions of the International Labour Conference. Sickness Insurance (Industry) Convention, 1927 (No.24); Sickness Insurance (Agriculture) Convention, 1927 (No.25);... Social Security (Minimum Standards) Convention, 1052 (No.102) [and] Social Security (Minimum Standards) Convention, 1952 (No.102)". I.L.O.Bull. (3rd ser.). 45. (1962). pp.226-230, 235-242.

4,966. BIONDI, C. "Medical jurisprudence in social insurance and the problem of unification". I.Lab.R. XIII. (1926). pp.793ff.

4,967. BULFILL, C.M. "The social security conventions and standard-setting functions of the I.L.O.". Int.Soc.Sec.Rev. XXII. (1969). pp.492-504.

4,968. COHEN, J.L. "The incidence of the costs of social insurance". I.Lab.R. XX. (1929). pp.816ff.

4,969. COHEN, J.L. "Unemployment insurance and public assistance". I.Lab.R. XXVI. (1932). pp.777.

4,970. COMMITTEE OF SOCIAL SECURITY EXPERTS. THIRD SESSION. "[Report of] a meeting... held at Geneva from 26 November to 8 December 1962...". I.L.O.Bull. (3rd ser.). 46. (1963). pp.205-212.

4,971. DEJARDIN, J. "The medical profession and social security". I.Lab.R. 69. (1954). pp.1ff.

4,972. ECKLER, S. "Modern social security plans and unemployment".

I.Lab.R. 48. (1943). pp.555ff.

4,973. FERDINAND-DREYFUS, J.   "Financial systems in social insurance". I.Lab.R. X. (1924). pp.583.

4,974. FISHER, P. "Minimum old-age pensions". (Two-part article). I.Lab.R. CII. (1970). pp.51-78; 277-317.

4,975. FORCHHEIMER, K.   "The financial problems of unemployment insurance". I.Lab.R. XIX. (1929). pp.483.

4,976. GRIESER, A. "The place of prevention in social insurance". I.Lab.R. XV. (1927). pp.860ff.

4,977. INTERNATIONAL LABOUR CONFERENCE. "Second session... (1920). Recommendation concerning unemployment insurance for seamen". I.L.O. Bull. (3rd ser.). 1. (1919-1920). pp.553-554.

4,978. INTERNATIONAL LABOUR CONFERENCE.   Report on equality of treatment for national and foreign workers as regards workmen's compensation for accidents. Geneva: 1924-5. 3 vols. (With supplement, report and final vote). LSE.

4,979. INTERNATIONAL LABOUR CONFERENCE. "Seventh session... 1925. Draft convention concerning workmen's compensation for accidents".   I.L.O. Bull.   (3rd ser.).   X.   (1925). pp.103-107.

4,980. INTERNATIONAL LABOUR CONFERENCE. "Seventh session... 1925. Recommendation concerning the minimum scale of workmen's compensation".   I.L.O.Bull.   (3rd ser.).   X.   (1925). pp.107-109.

4,981. INTERNATIONAL LABOUR CONFERENCE. "Seventh session... 1925. Recommendation concerning jurisdiction in disputes on workmen's compensation".   I.L.O. Bull.   (3rd ser.).   X. (1925). pp.109-110.

4,982. INTERNATIONAL LABOUR CONFERENCE. "Seventh session... 1925. Draft convention concerning workmen's compensation for occupational diseases".   I.L.O. Bull.   (3rd ser.).   X. (1925). pp.110-111.

4,983. INTERNATIONAL LABOUR CONFERENCE.   "Tenth session... 1927. Text of draft convention concerning sickness insurance for workers in industry and commerce and domestic servants". I.L.O. Bull. (3rd ser.). XII. (1927). pp.125-130; see too XVI (1931). pp.42-43.

4,984. INTERNATIONAL LABOUR CONFERENCE.   "Tenth session... 1927. Text of draft convention concerning sickness insurance for agricultural workers".   I.L.O.Bull.   (3rd ser.).   XII. (1927). pp.131-135; see too XVI. (1931). pp.42-32.

4,985. INTERNATIONAL LABOUR CONFERENCE.   "Tenth session... 1927. Recommendation concerning the general principles of sickness insurance".   I.L.O. Bull.   (3rd ser.).   XII.   (1927). pp.136-140; see too XVI. (1931). pp.42-43.

4,986. INTERNATIONAL LABOUR CONFERENCE.   Invalidity, old-age and widows' and orphans' insurance. Geneva: 1932. pp.vii + 312. LSE.

4,987.   INTERNATIONAL LABOUR CONFERENCE.   Second discussion...: invalidity, old-age and widows' and orphans' insurance. Geneva: 1933. pp.viii + 533. LSE.

4,988.   INTERNATIONAL LABOUR CONFERENCE. "Seventeenth session... 1933. Draft conventions concerning compulsory invalidity insurance". I.L.O.Bull. (3rd ser.). XVIII. (1933). pp.306-325; and see XXI. (1936). pp.170-172.

4,989.   INTERNATIONAL LABOUR CONFERENCE. "Seventeenth session... 1933. Draft conventions concerning compulsory old age insurance". I.L.O. Bull. (3rd ser.). XVIII. (1933). pp.326-343; and see XXI. (1936). pp.170-172.

4,990.   INTERNATIONAL LABOUR CONFERENCE. "Seventeenth session... 1933. Draft convention concerning compulsory widows' and orphans' insurance". I.L.O.Bull. (3rd. ser.). XVIII. (1933). pp.344-365; and see XXI. (1936). pp.170-172.

4,991.   INTERNATIONAL LABOUR CONFERENCE. "Seventeenth session... 1933. Recommendation concerning the general principles of invalidity, old age and widows' and orphans' insurance". I.L.O.Bull. (3rd ser.). XVIII. (1933). pp.366-373; and see XII. (1936). p.169.

4,992.   INTERNATIONAL LABOUR CONFERENCE. Supplement to the blue report on invalidity, old-age and widows' and orphans' insurance. Geneva: 1933. pp.40. LSE (Pamphlet Coll.).

4,993.   INTERNATIONAL LABOUR CONFERENCE, 17TH SESSION. Report... upon the working of the convention concerning workmen's compensation in agriculture. Geneva: 1933. pp.16. LSE.

4,994.   INTERNATIONAL LABOUR CONFERENCE. "Eighteenth session... 1934. Draft Convention [No.44] ensuring benefit or allowances to the involuntarily unemployed". I.L.O.Bull. (3rd ser.). XIX. (1934). pp.42-48.

4,995.   INTERNATIONAL LABOUR CONFERENCE. "Eighteenth session... 1934. Recommendation [No.44] concerning unemployment insurance and various forms of relief for the unemployed". I.L.O.Bull. (3rd ser.). XIX. (1934). pp.49-52.

4,996.   INTERNATIONAL LABOUR CONFERENCE. 19th session. Unemployment insurance and various forms of relief for the unemployed. Geneva: 1934. pp.187. LSE.

4,997.   INTERNATIONAL LABOUR CONFERENCE. Maintenance of rights... under invalidity, old-age and widows' and orphans' insurance on behalf of workers who transfer their residence from one country to another. Geneva: 1935. pp.251. LSE.

4,998.   INTERNATIONAL LABOUR CONFERENCE. "Nineteenth session... 1935. Draft convention [No.48] concerning the establishment of an international scheme for the maintenance of rights under invalidity, old-age and widows' and orphans' insurance". I.L.O.Bull. (3rd ser.). XX. (1935). pp.74-83.

4,999.   INTERNATIONAL LABOUR CONFERENCE.   Proposed act by H.M.
         Government... regarding the... draft convention ensuring
         benefit or allowances to the involuntarily unemployed,...
         draft convention concerning workmen's compensation, etc.
         London: 1935-36. 2 vols. (B.P.P. 1935-36, XXVII). LSE.

5,000.   INTERNATIONAL LABOUR CONFERENCE. 20th session. Report upon
         the working of the Convention No.19, concerning equality of
         treatment for national and foreign workes as regards workmen's
         compensation for accidents. Geneva: 1936. pp.27. LSE.

5,001.   INTERNATIONAL LABOUR CONFERENCE, 23RD SESSION. Report... upon
         the working of the convention (no.17) concerning workmen's
         compensation for accidents. Geneva: 1937. pp.51. LSE.

5,002.   INTERNATIONAL LABOUR CONFERENCE, 23RD SESSION. Report... upon
         the working of the convention (no.18) concerning workmen's
         compensation for occupational diseases.   Geneva: 1937.
         pp.31. LSE.

5,003.   INTERNATIONAL LABOUR CONFERENCE.   Proposed act by... the
         U.K.... regarding the draft convention no.56 (sickness
         insurance (sea)), etc. London: 1942-43. pp.4. (B.P.P.
         1942-43, XI). LSE.

5,004.   INTERNATIONAL LABOUR CONFERENCE. "Twenty-sixth session...
         1944. Recommendation [No.67] concerning income security".
         I.L.O.Bull. (3rd ser.). XXVI. (1944). pp.4-25.

5,005.   INTERNATIONAL LABOUR CONFERENCE. "Twenth-sixth session.
         Recommendation [No.68] concerning income security and medical
         care for persons discharged from the armed forces and
         assimilated services and from war employment". I.L.O.Bull.
         (3rd ser.). XXVI. (1944). pp.26-28.

5,006.   INTERNATIONAL LABOUR CONFERENCE. "Twenty-sixth session.
         Resolution concerning international administrative cooperation
         to promote social security". I.L.O.Bull. (3rd ser.). XXVI.
         (1944). pp.11-112.

5,007.   INTERNATIONAL LABOUR CONFERENCE. "Twenty-sixth session.
         Resolution concerning the definition of terms used in
         international conventions and recommendations concerning
         social security". I.L.O.Bull. (3rd ser.). XXVI. (1944).
         pp.112-113.

5,008.   INTERNATIONAL LABOUR CONFERENCE, 26TH SESSION. Reports 4.
         Social security principles and problems arising out of the
         war. Montreal: 1944. 2 vols. LSE.

5,009.   INTERNATIONAL LABOUR CONFERENCE. "Thirtieth session... 1947.
         Resolution concerning maintenance of rights of migrant workers
         under the social insurance schemes". I.L.O.Bull. (3rd ser.).
         XXX. (1947). pp.75-76.

5,010.   INTERNATIONAL LABOUR CONFERENCE. 35th session. Reports 5(a).
         Minimum standards of social security. Geneva: 1951-52. 2
         vols. LSE.

5,011.   INTERNATIONAL LABOUR CONFERENCE. "Thirty-fifth session...
1952. Convention [No.102] concerning minimum standards of
social security". I.L.O. Bull. (3rd ser.). XXXV. (1952).
pp.45-71.

5,012.   INTERNATIONAL LABOUR CONFERENCE. "Thirty-fifth session...
1952. Convention [No.103] concerning maternity protection
(revised 1952)". I.L.O.Bull. (3rd ser.). XXXV. (1952).
pp.73-82.

5,013.   INTERNATIONAL LABOUR CONFERENCE. 35th session. Reports 5(b).
Objectives and advanced standards of social security. Geneva:
1952. pp.iv + 164. LSE.

5,014.   INTERNATIONAL LABOUR CONFERENCE, 35TH SESSION, 1952. Reports
7. Revision of the Maternity Protection Convention, 1919,
no.3. Geneva: 1952. pp.81. LSE.

5,015.   INTERNATIONAL LABOUR CONFERENCE, 45TH SESSION. Reports 8.
Eighth item on the agenda; equality of treatment of nationals
and non-nationals in social security. Geneva: 1960-61. 2
pts. LSE.

5,016.   INTERNATIONAL LABOUR CONFERENCE. 45TH SESSION, 1961. Minimum
standards of social security. Geneva: 1961. unpag. DHSS.

5,017.   INTERNATIONAL LABOUR CONFERENCE, 46TH SESSION. Reports 5.
Fifth item on the agenda: equality of treatment of nationals
and non-nationals in social security. Geneva: 1961-62. 2
vols. LSE.

5,018.   INTERNATIONAL LABOUR CONFERENCE. Forty-sixth session... 1962.
Convention concerning equality of treatment of nationals and
non-nationals in social security". I.L.O.Bull. (3rd ser.).
45. (1962). (Supplement 3,I). pp.36-42.

5,019.   INTERNATIONAL LABOUR CONFERENCE. "Forty-sixth session...
1962. Resolution concerning the expansion of the activities
of the International Labour Organisation for the advancement
of social security". I.L.O.Bull. (3rd ser.). 45. (1962).
(Supplement 3,I). pp.44-45.

5,020.   INTERNATIONAL LABOUR CONFERENCE. 47TH SESSION, 1963. Report
VII(1). Benefits in the case of industrial accidents and
occupational diseases. Geneva: 1962. pp.iv + 172. DHSS;
LSE.

5,021.   INTERNATIONAL LABOUR CONFERENCE. 48TH SESSION, 1964. Report
V(1). Benefits in the case of industrial accidents and
occupational diseases. Geneva: 1963. pp.58. DHSS; LSE.

5,022.   INTERNATIONAL LABOUR CONFERENCE. 48TH SESSION, 1964. Report
V(2). Benefits in the case of industrial accidents and
occupational diseases. Geneva: 1964. pp.135. DHSS.

5,023.   INTERNATIONAL LABOUR CONFERENCE. "Forty-eighth session...
1964. Convention (121) concerning benefits in the case of
employment injury". I.L.O.Bull. (3rd ser.). 47. (1964).
(Supplement 3,I). pp.31-46, 46-49.

5,024. INTERNATIONAL LABOUR CONFERENCE. "Fifty-first session... 1967. Convention concerning invalidity, old-age and survivors' benefits". I.L.O.Bull. (3rd ser.). 50. (1967). (Supplement 3,I). pp.4-25; 36,-40.

5,025. INTERNATIONAL LABOUR CONFERENCE. 52ND SESSION, 1968. Report VI(1). Revision of Conventions Nos.24 and 25 concerning sickness insurance. Geneva: 1967. pp.iv + 80. DHSS; LSE.

5,026. INTERNATIONAL LABOUR CONFERENCE. "Fifth-third session... 1969. Convention (130) concerning medical care and sickness benefits". (3rd ser.). 52. (1969). pp.234-248, and 251-254.

5,027. INTERNATIONAL LABOUR CONFERENCE, 53RD SESSION, 1969. Report V(2). Revision of Conventions Nos.24 and 25 concerning sickness insurance. Geneva: 1969. pp.113. DHSS; LSE.

5,028. INTERNATIONAL LABOUR CONFERENCE. "Fifty-sixth session... 1971. Resolution concerning future activities of the International Labour Organisation in the field of social security". I.L.O.Bull. (3rd ser.). 54. (1971). pp.167-268.

5,029. INTERNATIONAL LABOUR OFFICE. "Operation of laws providing benefits in case of injury, sickness, old age and death in Great Britain". I.Labour R. XXIX. (1934). pp.108-15.

5,030. INTERNATIONAL LABOUR OFFICE. The International Labour Office and social insurance. Geneva: 1936. pp.viii + 219. (I.L.O. Studies and Reports, Series M (Social Insurance) No.12). LSE.

5,031. INTERNATIONAL LABOUR OFFICE. Workmen's compensation for silicosis in the Union of South Africa, Great Britain and Germany (with Supplement). Geneva: 1937. pp.147 + 2. (Studies and Reports Series F. (Industrial Hygiene) No.16). LSE.

5,032. INTERNATIONAL LABOUR OFFICE. The compensation of war victims: medical aid, compensation and war pensions. London: 1940. pp.91. (Studies and Reports. Series E (The Disabled) No.6). LSE.

5,033. INTERNATIONAL LABOUR OFFICE. Post-war trends in social security. Geneva: 1949. pp.83. LSE.

5,034. INTERNATIONAL LABOUR OFFICE. Objectives and minimum standards of social security. Report IV(1). Geneva: 1950. pp.130. DHSS; LSE.

5,035. INTERNATIONAL LABOUR OFFICE. The cost of social security. Geneva: 1952. pp.67. DHSS.

5,036. INTERNATIONAL LABOUR OFFICE. European regional conference. Report III. The financing of social security. Geneva: 1954. pp.ii + 154. DHSS; LSE.

5,037. INTERNATIONAL LABOUR OFFICE. The organisation of medical care under social security. Geneva: 1969. pp.vii + 241. DHSS.

5,038.   INTERNATIONAL LABOUR OFFICE. Introduction to social security.
Geneva: 1970. pp.vii + 215. DHSS; LSE.

5,039.   INTERNATIONAL LABOUR OFFICE. Income security in Europe in the
light of structural changes. Geneva: 1973. pp.ii + 111.
(Second European Regional Conference, 1974, Report III).
DHSS.

5,040.   INTERNATIONAL LABOUR OFFICE.   Social security for the
unemployed. Geneva: 1976. pp.viii + 70. DHSS.

5,041.   INTERNATIONAL LABOUR OFFICE. The Portuguese social security
system. Geneva: 1981. pp.iii + 82. DHSS.

5,042.   INTERNATIONAL LABOUR OFFICE. The cost of social security:
tenth international inquiry, 1975-1977. Geneva: 1981. pp.ix
+ 115. DHSS.

5,043.   INTERNATIONAL LABOUR OFFICE. The evaluation of permanent
incapacity for work in sickness insurance. Geneva. pp.xvi +
375. LSE. (Studies and Reports Series M (Social Insurance)
No.14). LSE.

5,044.   INTERNATIONAL LABOUR ORGANISATION.   "Report for the
forthcoming conference. Report IV . On special measures for
the protection of agricultural workers.   Protection of
agricultural workers against accident, sickness, invalidity
and old age". I.L.O. Bull. (3rd ser.). IV. (July-Dec.
1921). pp.171-176.

5,045.   INTERNATIONAL LABOUR ORGANISATION. The International Labour
Organisation and social insurance. Geneva: 1925. pp.68.
LSE.

5,046.   INTERNATIONAL LABOUR ORGANISATION.   Social insurance in
1932-1925 and 1937-1938. Geneva: 1932-38. unpag. DHSS.

5,047.   INTERNATIONAL LABOUR ORGANISATION.   Compulsory pension
insurance.   Comparative analysis of national laws and
statistics. Geneva, London: 1933. pp.xii + 782. (I.L.O.
Studies and Report, Series M (Social Insurance), No.10). LSE.

5,048.   INTERNATIONAL LABOUR ORGANISATION. The International Labour
Office and social insurance. Geneva, London: 1936. pp.viii
+ 219.   (I.L.O. Studies and Reports, Series M (Social
Insurance) No.12). LSE.

5,049.   INTERNATIONAL LABOUR ORGANISATION.   The evaluation of
permanent incapacity for work in social insurance. Geneva:
1937. pp.375. DHSS.

5,050.   INTERNATIONAL LABOUR ORGANISATION.   Maritime preparatory
conference, 1945. Report 6. Social insurance. Montreal:
1945. pp.65. LSE.

5,051.   INTERNATIONAL LABOUR ORGANISATION, IRON AND STEEL COMMITTEE,
2ND SESSION. Minimum income security. Geneva: 1947. pp.iv
+ 96. (Report No.3). LSE.

5,052.   INTERNATIONAL LABOUR ORGANISATION.   Action against unemployment. Geneva: 1950. pp.260. (Studies and Reports. New Series No.20). DHSS.

5,053.   INTERNATIONAL LABOUR ORGANISATION. International survey of social security. Geneva: 1950. pp.v + 236. (Studies and Reports, N.S. No.23). LSE.

5,054.   INTERNATIONAL LABOUR ORGANISATION. The cost of social security. Geneva: 1952. pp.67. DHSS.

5,055.   INTERNATIONAL LABOUR ORGANISATION. European Regional Conference Report III. The financing of social security. Geneva: 1954. pp.ii + 154. DHSS; LSE.

5,056.   INTERNATIONAL LABOUR ORGANISATION. Administrative practice of social insurance. Geneva: 1955. pp.iv + 86. (Studies and Reports, New Series No.40). DHSS; LSE.

5,057.   INTERNATIONAL LABOUR ORGANISATION. Unemployment insurance schemes. Geneva: 1955. pp.iv + 254. (Studies and Reports. New Series No.42). DHSS.

5,058.   INTERNATIONAL LABOUR ORGANISATION. The I.L.O. and social security. Geneva: 1960. pp.48. DHSS; LSE. 2nd ed. 1967. pp.52. DHSS.

5,059.   INTERNATIONAL LABOUR ORGANISATION. The cost of social security, 1949-1957. Geneva: 1961. pp.vii + 238. DHSS.

5,060.   INTERNATIONAL LABOUR ORGANISATION. The cost of social security. Geneva: 1964. pp.viii + 296. DHSS.

5,061.   INTERNATIONAL LABOUR ORGANISATION. The cost of social security: sixth international inquiry, 1961-1963. Geneva: 1967. pp.viii + 353. DHSS.

5,062.   INTERNATIONAL LABOUR ORGANISATION. Income security in the light of structural changes. Second European Regional Conference, Geneva, 1968. Report III. Geneva: 1968. pp.ii + 102. DHSS.

5,063.   INTERNATIONAL LABOUR ORGANISATION. Liste des instruments internationaux de securite sociale adoptes depuis 1946. Geneva: 1974. pp.xi + 148. DHSS

5,064.   INTERNATIONAL LABOUR ORGANISATION. Social and labour bulletin. Geneva: 1974-. ser.var.pag. DHSS.

5,065.   INTERNATIONAL LABOUR ORGANISATION. SOCIAL SECURITY DIVISION Unemployment protection under social security: an appraisal of the present situation and the role of the I.L.O. Geneva: 1975. pp.ii + 65. DHSS.

5,066.   INTERNATIONAL LABOUR ORGANISATION. The cost of social security: eighth international inquiry, 1967-1971. Geneva: 1976. pp.ix + 189. DHSS.

5,067.   INTERNATIONAL LABOUR ORGANISATION. Social security for the unemployed. Geneva: 1976. pp.viii + 70. DHSS.

5,068. INTERNATIONAL LABOUR ORGANISATION. General survey of the reports relating to the Equality of Treatment (Social Security) Convention, 1962 (No.118). Report of the Committee of Experts on the application of conventions and recommendations (Articles 19, 22 and 35 of the constitution) - Volume B. Geneva: 1977. pp.v + 90. (International Labour Conference, 63rd Session, 1977, Report III (Part 4B)). DHSS.

5,069. KORKISCH, H. "The financial resources of social insurance". I.Lab.R. X. (1924). pp.909ff.

5,070. LAROQUE, P. "The International Labour Organisaton and social security". Int.Soc.Sec.Rev. XXII. (1969). pp.469-479.

5,071. LEIFMANN-KEIL, E. "Index-based adjustments for social security benefits". I.Lab.R. 79. (1959). pp.487ff.

5,072. LORIGA, G. "The place of sickness insurance in the national health system". I.Lab.R. XV. (1927). pp.651ff.

5,073. MAURETTE, F. "Is unemployment insurance a cause of permanent unemployment?". I.Lab.R. XXIV. (1931). pp.663-84.

5,074. MYERS, R.J. & YOFFEE, W.M. "Social security issues: fiftieth international labour conference". Social Security Bulletin. 29(11). (1966). pp.20-37.

5,075. ORGANISING COMMITTEE OF THE FIRST SESSION OF THE INTERNATIONAL LABOUR CONFERENCE. "Draft Convention on Unemployment; recommendations; resolutions". I.L.O. Bull. (3rd ser.). 1. (1919-1920). p.376.

5,076. PERRIN, G. "L'action de l'Organisation Internationale du Travail en faveur de la coordination et de l'harmonisation des legislations de securite sociale". Rev.Belge de Sec.Soc. IX. (1969). pp.1115-1179.

5,077. PERRIN, G. "Reflections on fifty years of social security". Int.Soc.Sec.Rev. XXII. (1969). pp.564-603.

5,078. ROBBINS, C. "The I.L.O. and social security". Ind.Welfare. XXV. (1943). p.4.

5,079. SAVY, R. Social security in agriculture and rural areas. Geneva: 1972. pp.xii + 268. (ILO Studies and Reports, New Series, No.78). DHSS; LSE.

5,080. SECRETARY OF STATE FOR EMPLOYMENT. International Labour Conference. Proposed action by Her Majesty's Government in the United Kingdom of Great Britain and Northern Ireland on two recommendations adopted at the 53rd (1969) session of the International Labour Conference. London: 1970. pp.v + 33. (Cmnd. 4526). DHSS.

5,081. STEIN, O. "Building social security". I.Lab.R. XLIV. (1941). pp.247ff.

5,082. TAMBURI, G. "The I.L.O. and social security: the challenge of technical cooperation". Int.Soc.Sec.Rev. XXII. (1969). pp.480-491.

5,083. THOMAS, A.   "The Brussels International Financial Conference
and Unemployment Subsidies".   I.L.O.Bull.   (3rd ser.).   2.
(1920). (X). p.4.

5,084. TIXIER, A.   "Sickness insurance at the International Labour
Conference". I.Lab.R. XVI. (1927). pp.773.

5,085. TIXIER, A.   "Social insurance medical services".   I.Lab.R.
XXIX. (1934). pp.181ff.

5,086. VELDKAMP, M.J.   "The coherence of social security policy".
I.Lab.R. 108. (1973). pp.357-369.

5,087. VILLARS, V.   "Social security standards in the Council of
Europe: the I.L.O. influence".   I.Lab.R.   118.   (1979).
pp.342-54.

Section 2   International Social Security
                Association

5,088.   ANON.   "Social security conventions between contracting parties to the Treaty of Brussels".   Bull.I.S.S.A.   III. (1950).   (4).   pp.35-37.

5,089.   ANON.   "Social security conventions concluded by France with the Netherlands, the United Kingdom and Yugoslavia". Bull.I.S.S.A.   III.   (1950).   (8-9).   pp.23-26.

5,090.   ANON.   "Towards a new international social security code". Bull.I.S.S.A.   IV.   (1951).   pp.199-200.

5,091.   ANON.   "The Xth general meeting of the International Social Security Associaton".   Bull. I.S.S.A.   IV.   (1951). pp.265-272.

5,092.   ANON.   "The objectives and minimum standards of social security".   Bull.I.S.S.A.   IV.   (1951).   pp.321-326.

5,093.   ANON.   "The new International Convention on Social Security". Bull. I.S.S.A.   V.   (1952).   pp.196-219.

5,094.   ANON.   "From social insurance to social security.   Some important dates".   Bull. I.S.S.A.   V.   (1952).   pp.353-364.

5,095.   ANON.   "Draft European interim agreements relating to social security".   Bull. I.S.S.A.   VI.   (1953).   pp.279-292.

5,096.   ANON.   "The XIth general meeting and other meetings of the ISSA in Paris".   Bull. I.S.S.A.   VI.   (1953).   pp.339-382.

5,097.   ANON.   "The XIIth general meeting and the other ISSA meetings in Mexico".   Bull. I.S.S.A.   IX.   (1956).   pp.3-83.

5,098.   ANON.   "Social security convention between Sweden and the United Kingdom".   Bull. I.S.S.A.   X.   (1957).   pp.518-523.

5,099.   ANON.   "The XIIIth general meeting and other ISSA meetings in London".   Bull. I.S.S.A.   XI.   (1958).   pp.277-394.

5,100.   ANON.   "The fourteenth general meeting of the International Social Security Association, 1961".   Bull. I.S.S.A.   XIV. (1961).   pp.629-750.

5,101.   ANON.   "XIVth general meeting [of the ISSA], 1961.   Report 1. Developments and trends in social security, 1958-1960".   Bull. I.S.S.A.   XV.   (1962).   (6-8).   pp.5-224.

5,102.   ANON.   "XIVth general meeting, 1961.   Report VII.   The financial systems of old age insurance as influenced by economic development".   Bull. I.S.S.A.   XV.   (1962). pp.68-111.

5,103.   ANON.   "XIVth general meeting, 1961.   Report II.   The volume and cost of sickness benefits in kind and cash".   Bull. I.S.S.A.   XVI.   (1963).   pp.3-120.

4 International and European Influences

5,104. ANON.   "Social security in the national economy".   Bull.
        I.S.S.A.   XVII.   (1964).

5,105. ANON.   "Fifteenth general assembly of the International Social
        Security Association".   Bull. I.S.S.A.   XVII.   (1964).
        pp.321-440.

5,106. ANON.   "ISSA conference on social security research".
        Int.Soc.Sec.Rev. XXIII. (1970). pp.219-356.

5,107. ANON.   "XVIIth general assembly of the International Social
        Security Association".   Int.Soc.Sec.Rev.   XXIII.   (1970).
        pp.499-606.

5,108. ANON.   "XVIIIth general assembly of the International Social
        Security Association".   Int.Soc.Sec.Rev.   XXVI.   (1973).
        pp.363-489.

5,109. ANON.   "The XIXth general assembly of the International Social
        Security Association".   Int.Soc.Sec.Rev.   XXX.   (1977).
        pp.401-532.

5,110. BUFILL, C.M.   "Legal aspects of the practical application of
        international social security conventions".   Int.Soc.Sec.Rev.
        XX. (1967). pp.313-359.

5,111. COCKBURN, C. & HOSKINS, D.   "Social security and divorced
        persons". Int.Soc.Sec.Rev. XXIX. (1976). pp.111-151.

5,112. DOLE, G. "The situation of ecclesiastical personnel in social
        security: a comparative law study".   Int.Soc.Sec.Rev. XXVII.
        (1974). pp.535-556.

5,113. DOUBLET, J.   "Human   rights   and   social   security".
        Int.Soc.Sec.Rev. XXI. (1968). pp.483-495.

5,114. FARMAN, C.H.   "World trends in social security benefits,
        1935-1955". Bull. I.S.S.A. IX. (1956). pp.444-454.

5,115. FISHER, P.   "Developments and trends in social security
        (1967-1969)". Int.Soc.Sec.Rev. XXIV. (1971). pp.3-34.

5,116. I.S.S.A.   General   meeting: record of proceedings,
        resolutions, conclusions and recommendations. Geneva: 1947
        to date. LSE.

5,117. I.S.S.A.   VIIIth General Meeting, Geneva 4-9 October, 1947:
        report of the proceedings. Montreal: 1948. pp.440. DHSS.

5,118. I.S.S.A. [Report prepared for the] Xth General Meeting,
        Vienna, 3-7 July 1951. [Report on] technical problems
        involved in the administration of social security schemes.
        Geneva: 1951. pp.30. DHSS; LSE.

5,119. I.S.S.A.   Xth General Meeting.   Report No.1:   Recent
        developments in the field of social security. Geneva: 1951.
        pp.88. DHSS; LSE.

5,120. I.S.S.A. Report prepared for the Xth General Meeting, Vienna,

3-7 July 1951. Rehabilitation and assessment of benefit. Geneva: 1951. pp.148. DHSS.

5,121. I.S.S.A. Technical problems involved in the administration of social security schemes: manual of methods of identification of insured persons and organisation of records. Geneva: 1951. pp.226. LSE; DHSS.

5,122. I.S.S.A. "Conspectus of social security in 1951". Bull.I.S.S.A. IV. No.12. (Dec.1951).

5,123. I.S.S.A. "The new international convention on social security". Bull.I.S.S.A. V. (1952). pp.196-219.

5,124. I.S.S.A. Xth General Meeting. Report No.2: social security of independent workers. Geneva: 1952. pp.367. DHSS; LSE.

5,125. I.S.S.A. Xth General Meeting. Record of proceedings, resolution, recommendations, constitution and standing orders. Geneva: 1952. pp.vii + 152. DHSS.

5,126. I.S.S.A. XIth General Meeting. Report IV. Relations between social security institutions and the medical profession. Geneva: 1953. pp.593. DHSS.

5,127. I.S.S.A. 11th General Meeting, 1953. Reports 1. Recent developments in the field of social security. Geneva: 1954. pp.106. LSE.

5,128. I.S.S.A. The cost of social security 1949-1951. Geneva: 1955. pp.108. DHSS.

5,129. I.S.S.A. XIIth General Meeting, 1955. Record of the proceedings, resolution, recommendations and conclusions. Geneva: 1956. pp.139. DHSS.

5,130. I.S.S.A. XIIth General Meeting, 1955. Report No.I. The influence of vocational rehabilitation on the evaluation of invalidity. Geneva: 1956. pp.6. DHSS.

5,131. I.S.S.A. XIIth General Meeting, 1955. Report II. Sickness insurance, national monographs. Geneva: 1956. pp.320. DHSS; LSE.

5,132. I.S.S.A. 12th General Meeting, 1955. Recent developments in the field of social security, 1953-5. Geneva: [1956]. pp.243. LSE.

5,133. I.S.S.A. 12th General Meeting, 1955. Reciprocity in social insurance. Geneva: 1956. pp.91. LSE.

5,134. I.S.S.A. 12th General Meeting, 1955. Reports of the I.S.S.A. Permanent Committee on Unemployment Insurance. Geneva: [1956]. pp.50. LSE.

5,135. I.S.S.A. 12th General Meeting, 1955. Reports 4. Administrative problems of schemes providing protection against unemployment. Geneva: 1956. pp.iii + 261. LSE.

5,136. I.S.S.A. International review on actuarial and statistical

problems of social security. No. 1 - 1958. No. 7 - 1961.
Nos. 13 & 14 - 1967/68. Geneva: 1958. pp.v + 245. DHSS.
1962. pp.175. DHSS. 1969. pp.1036. DHSS.

5,137. I.S.S.A.   In the service of social security 1927-1957.
Geneva: 1958. pp.vii + 142. DHSS.

5,138. I.S.S.A.   XIIIth General Meeting. Recent developments in
social security 1955-1957. Geneva: 1958. pp.168. DHSS;
LSE.

5,139. I.S.S.A. 13th General Meeting, 1958. Reports 2. 1. Sickness
insurance: comparative study; summary of replies to the
I.S.S.A. questionnaire. [Geneva] : [1958] . (164). (fo.).
LSE.

5,140. I.S.S.A.   13th General Meeting, 1958. Reports 2. Sickness
insurance. Geneva: 1958. pp.49. LSE.

5,141. I.S.S.A.   XIIIth General Meeting, London, 1958. Report I.
Recent developments in social security. Geneva: 1959.
pp.149. DHSS.

5,142. I.S.S.A.   XIIIth General Meeting, 1958. Report No.III.
Old-age insursance. Geneva: 1959. pp.165. DHSS; LSE.

5,143. I.S.S.A. XIIIth General Meeting, London, 1958. Report No.IV.
The unification of the basis for measuring incapacity to work.
Geneva: 1959. pp.27. DHSS; LSE.

5,144. I.S.S.A.   XIIIth General Meeting, London, 1958.   Report
No.VII.   Administrative problems of protection against
unemployment for agricultural workers. Geneva: 1959. pp.58.
DHSS.

5,145. I.S.S.A.   XIIIth General Meeting, London, 12-11 May 1958.
Record of proceedings, resolutions and conclusions. Geneva:
1961. pp.141. DHSS.

5,146. I.S.S.A.   XIVth General Meeting, 1961. Report VII. The
financial systems of old-age insurance as influenced by
economic development. Bull.I.S.S.A. (October, 1962).
pp.68-111.

5,147. I.S.S.A.   "Developments and trends in social security
1958-1960". Bull.I.S.S.A. (1962). pp.8-224.

5,148. I.S.S.A. VIIth General Meeting, 1963. Particular aspects of
unemployment insurance for seasonal workers. Geneva: 1963.
pp.31. DHSS.

5,149. I.S.S.A. XIVth General Meeting, 1961. Report II, part III.
Volume and cost of sickness benefits in kind and cash.
Geneva: 1963. pp.iii + 362. DHSS.

5,150. I.S.S.A. XIVth General Meeting, Istanbul, 1961. Report No.II
on the volume and cost of sickness benefits in kind and cash.
Bull.I.S.S.A. (1963). pp.3-120.

5,151. I.S.S.A.   "Social security in the national economy".

Bull.I.S.S.A.   (1964 May-July).

5,152.   I.S.S.A.   "Occupational diseases.   Report VII".   Bull.I.S.S.A.
(1965).   pp.247-330.

5,153.   I.S.S.A.   "Some financial aspects of employment injury
insurance".   Bull.I.S.S.A.   (1965).   pp.331-403.

5,154.   I.S.S.A.   "The general principles on which scales for family
allowances are determined.   Report XVII".   Bull.I.S.S.A.
(1965).   pp.405-437.

5,155.   I.S.S.A.   XVth General Assembly.   Legislative trends in social
security.   Geneva: 1965.   pp.24.   DHSS.

5,156.   I.S.S.A.   XVth General Assembly, Washington, 1964.
Conclusions, recommendations and resolutions adopted by the
Xth General Assembly. Washington: 1965.   pp.49.   DHSS.

5,157.   I.S.S.A.   XVth General Assembly.   Developments and trends in
social security (1961-1963).   Report I.   Geneva: 1965.   pp.iv
+ 625.   DHSS.

5,158.   I.S.S.A.   XVth General Assembly, 1964.   Report XVIII.   Volume
and cost of sickness benefits in cash and kind.   Geneva:
1965.   unpag.   DHSS.

5,159.   I.S.S.A.   XVth General Assembly, Washington, 1964.   Social
services provided by social security agencies members of the
I.S.S.A.   Geneva: 1965.   pp.iii + 123.   DHSS.

5,160.   I.S.S.A.   XVth General Assembly, Washington, 1964.
Administrative problems arising from the relationship between
unemployment insurance benefit and benefits granted under
other branches of social security.   Geneva: 1965.   pp.54.
DHSS.

5,161.   I.S.S.A.   Legal, financial and administrative aspects of
social security administered by mutual benefit societies.
Report XI.   Geneva: 1965.   pp.54.   DHSS.

5,162.   I.S.S.A.   XVIth General Assembly, Leningrad, 1967.   Report 8.
Statistical inquiry into certain occupational diseases.
Report 14.   Inventory of measures and services designed to
promote rehabilitation in social security institutions.
Report 15.   Relations between social security institutions and
the medical profession.   Geneva: 1968.   pp.273.   DHSS.

5,163.   I.S.S.A.   XVIth General Assembly, Leningrad, 1967.   Investment
of old age, invalidity and survivors' insurance funds.   Report
X.   Geneva: 1968.   pp.57.   DHSS.

5,164.   I.S.S.A.   XVth General Assembly, 1969.   Report XIII.
Actuarial and statistical studies within the framework of
sickness insurance. Geneva: 1968.   pp.27.   DHSS.

5,165.   I.S.S.A.   XVIIth General Assembly, 1967.   Report XVII.   Volume
and cost of sickness benefits in cash and kind.   Geneva:
1968.   pp.207.   DHSS.

5,166.   I.S.S.A.   International social security review.   Year XXII.
         No.4.   1969.   Geneva: 1969.   pp.441-628.   DHSS.

5,167.   I.S.S.A.   The planning of social security: papers presented
         at the meeting on the sociology of social security.   (7th
         World Congress of Sociology: Varna 1970).   Geneva: 1971.
         pp.iii + 189.   (Studies and Research No.2).   DHSS; LSE.

5,168.   I.S.S.A.   XVIIth General Assembly, 1970.   Statutory powers of
         social security institutions.   Geneva: 1971.   pp.iv + 44.

5,169.   I.S.S.A.   Women and social security: report of a research
         conference on women and social security.   (Vienna, 1972).
         Geneva: 1973.   pp.iv + 245.   (Studies and Research No.5).
         DHSS; LSE.

5,170.   I.S.S.A.   The role of the social services in social security;
         trends and perspectives.   Report of a Round Table meeting,
         1973.   Geneva: 1974.   pp.154.   (Studies and Research No.6).
         DHSS.

5,171.   I.S.S.A.   XVIIIth General Assembly, 1973.   Report IX.
         Statutory powers of social security institutions.   Geneva:
         1974.   pp.ii + 72.   DHSS.

5,172.   I.S.S.A.   XVIIIth General Assembly, 1973.   Report I.
         Developments and trends in social security (1970-1972).
         Geneva: 1974.   pp.31.   DHSS.

5,173.   I.S.S.A.   SECRETARY-GENERAL.   "Developments and trends in
         social security, 1974-1977".   Int.Soc.Sec.Rev.   XXX.   (1977).
         pp.271-313.

5,174.   I.S.S.A.   "Developments and trends in social security
         1978-1980".   Int.Soc.Sec.Rev.   33.   (1980).   pp.267-336.

5,175.   I.S.S.A.   Securite sociale et invalidite: perspectives
         actuelles de la recherche.   Geneva: 1981.   pp.vii + 185.
         (Etudes et recherches No.17).   DHSS.

5,176.   I.S.S.A.   The teaching of social security.   Geneva: 1983.
         pp.viii + 135.   DHSS.

5,177.   JUILHA, M.   "Social security and the public: organisation of
         services in contact with the public, introduction of
         appropriate facilities, effect of automation at this level".
         Int.Soc.Sec.Rev.   XXX.   (1977).   pp.314-377.

5,178.   LAROQUE, P.   "Tendencies of social security legislation in the
         countries which signed the Brussels pact".   Bull. I.S.S.A.
         VI.   (1953).   pp.3-25.

5,179.   MAGREZ, M.   "Legal bases of financial control of social
         security: legal status of social security institutions
         subject to control".   Int.Soc.Sec.Rev.   XXIV.   (1971).
         pp.213-273.

5,180.   MAGREZ, M.   "Legal bases of financial control of social
         security - legal status of controlling bodies".
         Int.Soc.Sec.Rev.   XXVI.   (1973).   pp.3-72.

5,181.   MAGREZ, M.   "Legal bases of financial control of social security.   Procedures and purposes of control". Int.Soc.Sec.Rev. XXVII. (1974). pp.159-240.

5,182.   MALLET, A.   "Social protection of the rural population". Int.Soc.Sec.Rev. 33. (1980). pp.359-393.

5,183.   MARZIALE, F.   "Resolution of the Council of Europe on social security measures to be taken in favour of pensioners and persons remaining in activity after pensionable age". Int.Soc.Sec.Rev. XXIX. (1976). pp.284-289.

5,184.   MYERS, R.J.   "International trends in social security". Bull. I.S.S.A. XI. (1958). pp.41-51.

5,185.   PETROVIC, Z.   "Coordination and cooperation between the different branches of social security" Bull. I.S.S.A.   IX. (1956). pp.411-443.

5,186.   RHEE, H.A.   "Social security for older people". Int.Soc.Sec.Rev. XXV. (1972). pp.42-70.

5,187.   ROHRLICH, G.F.   "Maintaining social security pension schemes adequate and solvent - a transnational synopsis of problems and policies". Int.Soc.Sec.Rev. 33. (1980). pp.199-54.

5,188.   RYS, V.   "Comparative studies of social security: problems and perspectives". Bull. I.S.S.A. IX. (1966). pp.242-268.

5,189.   STACK, M.   "Minimum standards of social security: the proposed international convention".   Bull.I.S.S.A.   V. (1952). pp.137-143.

5,190.   STEPHENS, T.C.   Reciprocity in social insurance.   Geneva: 1956. pp.91. DHSS.

5,191.   STOCKMAN, H.W.   "History and development of social security in Great Britain". Bull. I.S.S.A. Jan.-Feb. (1957). pp.3-71.

5,192.   TITMUSS, R.M.   "The relationship between income, maintenance and social service benefits - an overview". I.S.S.A. Review. Year XX. No. 1. (1967). pp.57-66.

5,193.   TITMUSS, R.   "Equity, adequacy and innovation in social security".   In I.S.S.A. Conference on Social Security Research, Vienna 1969.   Geneva: 1970.   Year XXIII.   No.2. pp.219-345.

5,194.   TRACY, M.B.   "Contributions under social security programmes: survey in some selected countries". Int.Soc.Sec.Rev. XXIX. (1976). pp.66-85.

5,195.   VOIRIN, M.   "The relation of the employer to social security in connection with industrial accidents and occupational diseases". Bull. I.S.S.A. XVI. (1963). pp.297-306.

5,196.   WANNAGAT, G.   "Social security in teaching and research". Int.Soc.Sec.Rev. XXV. (1972). pp.37-41.

Section 3 Europe and the European Economic Community

(a) <u>General</u>

5,197.   ANON. "Social security in the six: lessons for - and from - Britain?". <u>European Community</u>. (Sept. 1967). pp.10-11.

5,198.   ANON. "Regulation (EEC) No.1408/71 of the Council of 14 June 1971 on the application of social security schemes to employed persons and their families moving within the Community". <u>Official Journal of the European Communities: Legislation</u>. No.L149/2. (1971). pp.416-463.

5,199.   ANON. "Regulation (EEC) No.2864/72 of the Council of 19 December 1972 amending Regulation (EEC) No.1408/71 on the application of social security schemes to employed persons and their families moving within the Community". <u>Official Journal of the European Communities: Legislation</u>. No.L306/1. (1972). pp.15-19.

5,200.   ANON. "Regulation (EEC) No.574/72 of the Council of 21 March 1972 fixing the procedure for implementing Regulation (EEC) No.1408/71 on the application of social security schemes to employed persons and their families moving within the Community". <u>Official Journal of the European Communities: legislation</u>. No.L74/1. (1972). pp.159-233.

5,201.   ANON. "Regulation (EEC) No.878/73 of the Council of 26 March 1973 amending Regulation (EEC) No.574/72 fixing the procedure for implementing Regulation (EEC) No.1408/71 on the application of social security schemes to employed persons and their families moving within the Community". <u>Official Journal of the European Communities: Legislation</u>. 16. (1973). L86/1-25.

5,202.   ANON. "Declarations of the original member states provided for in article 5 of Regulation (EEC) No.1408/71 of the Council of 14 June 1971 on the application of social security schemes to employed persons and their families moving within the Community". <u>Official Journal of the European Communities: Information and Notices</u>. 16. (1973). C12/11-22.

5,203.   ANON. "Written question No.599/72 by Mr. Adams to the Commission of the European Communities. [Subject: Withholding unemployment benefit from workers affected by lock-outs] ". <u>Official Journal of the European Communities: Information and Notices</u>. 16. (1973). C29/18-19.

5,204.   ANON. "Declarations of the new member states provided for in article 5 of Regulation (EEC) No.1408/71 of the Council, of 14 June 1971, on the application of social security schemes to employed persons and their families moving within the Community". <u>Official Journal of the European Communities: Information and Notices</u>. 16. (1973). C43/1-7.

5,205.   ANON. "Written question No.529/72 by Mr. Oele to the Commission... [Subject: Infringements of social welfare legislation by labour contractors"]. Official Journal of the European Communities: Information and Notices. 16. (1973). C67/57-58.

5,206.   ANON.   "Rules of the Administrative Commission on social security for migrant workers attached to the Commission of the European Communities". Official Journal of the European Communities: Information and Notices. 16. (1973). C68/25-31.

5,207.   ANON.   "Social security in the member states of the Community in 1973". Int.Soc.Sec.Rev. XXVII. (1974). pp.415-426.

5,208.   ANON.   "Regulation (EEC) No.1392/74 of the Council of 4 June 1974 amending Regulation (EEC) Nos.1408/71 and 574/72 on the application of social security schemes to employed persons and their families moving within the Community". Official Journal of the European Communities: Legislation. 17. (1974). L152/1-9.

5,209.   ANON.   ""Regulation (EEC) No.1689/74 of the Council of 15 October 1974 amending Article 107 of Regulation (EEC) No.574/72 fixing the procedure for implementing Regulation (EEC) No.1408/71 on the application of social security schemes to employed persons and their families moving within the Community". Official Journal of the European Communities: Legislation. 17. (1974). L183/1-2.

5,210.   ANON.   "Consultation of the Economic and Social Committee on a proposal for a council regulation amending Regulations (EEC) No.1408/71 and (EEC) No.574/72 on the application of social security schemes to employed persons and their families moving within the Community and on a supplement to the proposal for a regulation". Official Journal of the European Communities: Information and Notices. 17. (1974). C88/1-4.

5,211.   ANON.   "Council Regulation (EEC) No.1209/76 of 30 April 1976 amending Regulations (EEC) No.1408/71 and (EEC) No.574/72 on the application of social security schemes to employed persons and their families moving within the Community". Official Journal of the European Communities: Legislation. 19. (1976). L138/1-13.

5,212.   ANON.   "Council Regulation (EEC) No.2595/77 of 21 November 1977 amending Regulations (EEC) No.1408/71 and (EEC) No.574/72 on the application of social security schemes to employed persons and their families moving within the Community". Official Journal of the European Communities: Legislation. 20. (1977). L302/1-12.

5,213.   ANON.   "Social security in member states of the European Community in 1980". Int.Soc.Sec.Rev. 34. (1981). pp.206-212.

5,214.   AMIEL, B.   "Les Francais de l'etranger et la legislation sociale". Questions de Securite Sociale. 29. (1977). pp.246-252.

5,215.   BAECK, S.   "Fringe benefits in the E.E.C.". F.N. 24. (1974). p.19.

5,216. BAILEY, R. "The Treaty of Rome: social provisions". F.B.I. Review. May 1962. pp.41-43.

5,217. BAROIN, D. & LOOS, J. "Protection juridique et couverture sociale du travail a temps partiel en Europe". Droit Social. (1982). pp.560-566.

5,218. BOLDT, G. & OTHERS. La jurisdiction du travail et la jurisdiction de la securite sociale dans les pays de la Communaute europeenne situation au ler janvier 1968. Luxembourg: Office des Publications Officielles des Communautes Europeenes. 1968. pp.615. DHSS.

5,219. BONNET, R. Practical handbook of social security for employed persons and their families moving within the community. Brussels: CEC. 1973. pp.xxxvi + 236. DHSS.

5,220. BRODERICK, J.B. "Social expenditure and the social accounts of the EEC". J.S.S.I.S.I. 23. (128th Sess.). (1974-75). pp.150-76.

5,221. BROWN, E.D. "Labour law and social security". In G.W. Keeton and G. Schwarzenberger (eds.). English law and the Common Market. London: 1963. pp.178-196. CUL.

5,222. BROWN, E.D. "Labour law and social security. Harmonisation or co-existence?". C.L.P. 16. (1963). pp.178-196.

5,223. CENTRAL OFFICE OF INFORMATION, REFERENCE DIVISION. Britain in the European Community: social policy. London: 1975. pp.iv + 24. (COI Pamphlet 136). LSE.

5,224. COEFFARD, A. "Regulations governing social security for persons moving within the European Community". I.Lab.R. 121. (1982). pp.243-258.

5,225. COGHLAN, A. "Social policy in the European community". Soc.Stud. 2. (1973). pp.223-34.

5,226. COLLINS, C.D.E. The European Communities: the social policy of the first phase. London: 1975. pp.viii + 128; ix + 286. BL; LSE.

5,227. COLLINS, D. "Towards a European social policy". Journal of Common Market Studies. Sept. (1966). pp.16-48.

5,228. COMMISSION DES COMMUNAUTES EUROPEENES. Les etudes economiques et financieres sur la securite sociale: rapport de synthese. Bruxelles: 1971. pp.vi + 81. DHSS.

5,229. COMMISSION DES COMMUNAUTES EUROPEENES. Indicateurs de securite sociale. Bruxelles: 1971. pp.122. DHSS.

5,230. COMMISSION OF THE EUROPEAN COMMUNITIES. Comparative tables of the social security systems relating to employees in the three new member states of the European Communities: Denmark - Ireland - United Kingdom; situation on 1 July 1972. Luxembourg: 1973. pp.59. DHSS.

5,231. COMMISSION OF THE EUROPEAN COMMUNITIES. The new European social fund (entered into force on the first of May 1972): official texts. Brussels: 1973. pp.19. DHSS.

5,232. COMMISSION OF THE EUROPEAN COMMUNITIES. Comparative tables of the social security systems in the member states of the European Communities. (Situation at 1 July 1974). General system. 8th ed. Luxembourg: 1974. pp.125. DHSS. 9th ed. (in French). 1976. pp.133. DHSS.

5,233. COMMISSION OF THE EUROPEAN COMMUNITIES. Communication from the Commission to the Council: programme of pilot schemes and studies to combat poverty drawn up on accordance with the resolution of the Council of 21 January 1974 concerning a social action programme. Brussels: 1975. pp.10 + 22. DHSS.

5,234. COMMISSION OF THE EUROPEAN COMMUNITIES, DIRECTORATE-GENERAL FOR ECONOMIC AND FINANCIAL AFFAIRS. The impact of rising prices on taxation and social security contributions in the European Community. Luxembourg: 1976. pp.73. (Economic and Financial Series No.12). DHSS.

5,235. COMMISSION OF THE EUROPEAN COMMUNITIES. The perception of poverty in Europe: a report on a public opinion survey carried out in the member countries of the European Community as part of the programme of pilot projects to combat poverty, by Helene Riffault and Jacques-Rene Rabier. Brussels: 1977. pp.120. (V/171/77-E). DHSS.

5,236. COMMISSION OF THE EUROPEAN COMMUNITIES. Recueil des dispositions communautaires sur la securite. Luxembourg: 1980. pp.395. DHSS.

5,237. COMMISSION OF THE EUROPEAN COMMUNITIES. Compendium of Community provisions on social security. Luxembourg: 1981. pp.389. DHSS.

5,238. COMMISSION OF THE EUROPEAN COMMUNITIES. Comparative tables of the social security systems in the Member States of the European Communicity: (situation at 1 July 1980): general system. 11th ed. Luxembourg: 1981. pp.119. DHSS.

5,239. CONSERVATIVE POLITICAL CENTRE. European series 4. Social security in the Common Market. London: 1962. pp.4. DHSS.

5,240. DEGIMBE, J. "Le budget social Europeen". Rev.Belge de Sec.Soc. XIX. (1977). pp.180-195.

5,241. DENNETT, J., JAMES, E., ROOM, G., WATSON, P. Europe against poverty: the European poverty programme 1975-80. London: 1982. pp.vi + 250. LSE.

5,242. DEPARTMENT OF EMPLOYMENT. The European Social Fund; what it does; who can apply; how to apply. [London]: 1981. pp.[i] + 28. DHSS.

5,243. DEPARTMENT OF HEALTH AND SOCIAL SECURITY. Social security in the E.E.C. (position at 1st August 1969). London: 1969. unpaged. DHSS.

5,244.   DEPARTMENT OF HEALTH AND SOCIAL SECURITY. Tables of social security benefit systems in the Member States of the European Communities (position at 1 January 1981). London: 1981. pp.[148]. DHSS.

5,245.   DOSSER, D. & HAN, S.S.   Taxes in the EEC and Britain: the problem of harmonization. London: 1968. pp.46. DHSS.

5,246.   EUROPEAN COAL AND STEEL COMMUNITY. Rapport sur la comparaison du systeme britannique de securite sociale avec les systemes des pays de la communaute;   (with covering letter). Luxembourg: 1962.   pp.76 + (3).   (Doc. No. 3792/3/62f. Direction Generale Problemes du Travail, Assainissement et Reconversion). LSE.

5,247.   EUROPEAN COAL AND STEEL COMMUNITY.   THE HIGH AUTHORITY. Development and trends in the social security systems of the member countries and Britain. Luxembourg: 1966.   pp.169. DHSS.

5,248.   EUROPEAN COAL AND STEEL COMMUNITY.   (COAL COMMITTEE). Comparison of the social security systems operating in Great Britain and the Community countries. London: 1968. pp.70. DHSS.

5,249.   EUROPEAN COAL AND STEEL COMMUNITY. Rapport sur la comparaison du systems Britannique de securite sociale avec les systems des pays de la communaute. Brussels: 1970. pp.88. DHSS.

5,250.   EUROPEAN COMMUNITIES COMMISSION. La jurisdiction du travail et la jurisdiction de la securite sociale dans les pays de la Communaute Europeene: situation au ler janvier 1968. Luxembourg, ECC: 1970.   pp.615.   (European Coal and Steel Community, Collection du Droit du Travail). LSE.

5,251.   EUROPEAN COMMISSION.   "Draft Council recommendation on the principles of a Community policy with regard to retirement age".   Official Journal of the European Communities.   25. (1982). pp.12-13.

5,252.   EUROPEAN ECONOMIC COMMUNITY.   Translation of an extract relating to old age insurance from the comparative tables on social security. Luxembourg: 1961. pp.6. DHSS.

5,253.   EUROPEAN ECONOMIC COMMUNITY.   Etude sur la physionomie actuelle de la securite sociale dans les pays de la CEE. Brussels: 1962. pp.130. DHSS; LSE.

5,254.   EUROPEAN ECONOMIC COMMUNITY. Etude comparee des prestations de securite sociale dans les pays de la CEE. Brussels: 1962. pp.145. DHSS; LSE.

5,255.   EUROPEAN ECONOMIC COMMUNITY.   Financement de la securite sociale dans les pays de la CEE. Brussels: 1962. pp.164. DHSS.

5,256.   EUROPEAN ECONOMIC COMMUNITY. European treaty series no.48. European code of social security and protocol to the European code of social security.   Strasbourg: 1964.   pp.43 + 22. DHSS.

5,257. EUROPEAN ECONOMIC COMMUNITY. Les regimes complementaires de securite sociale dans les pays de la CEE. Brussels: 1967. pp.100. DHSS; LSE. (entitled): Supplementary social security schemes in the EEC countries. Brussels: 1967. pp.177. LSE.

5,258. EUROPEAN ECONOMIC COMMUNITY. Secondary legislation: English text. Part 10 and regulation 574/72 of 21 March 1972, fixing the procedure for implementing EEC Regulation No. 1408/71 on the application of social security schemes to employed persons and their families moving within the community. London: 1972. pp.126. DHSS.

5,259. FORDE, M. "Social assistance and the EEC's regulations". Leg.Iss. (1978/1). pp.9-28.

5,260. FORDE, M. "The conflict of individual labour laws and the EEC's rules". Leg.Iss. (1979/1). pp.85-104.

5,261. FORDE, M. "The self-employed and the EEC social security rules". I.L.J. 8. (1979). pp.1-18.

5,262. FORDE, M. "The vertical conflict of social security laws in the European Court". Leg.Iss. (1980/1). pp.23-58.

5,263. FORMAN, J. "Case law. A. Court of Justice. 109 R.J. Brack v. Insurance Officer. Case 17/76. Preliminary ruling of September 29, 1976 on request of the National Insurance Commissioner". C.M.L.Rev. 14. (1977). pp.231-240.

5,264. HALLSTEIN, W. Address delivered at the opening of the European Conference on Social Security, 10th December, 1962. Brussels: 1962. pp.16. DHSS.

5,265. ILLUMINATI, F. "Social security problems in the countries of the European Economic Community". Bull.I.S.S.A. (May-June 1963). pp.81-91.

5,266. JAMES, E. & LAURENT, A. "Social security: the European experiment". Social Trends. 5. (1974). pp.26-34.

5,267. JAMES, E. & WATSON, P. "Europe: a policy on poverty or a poverty of philosophy". Soc. Pol. & Admin. 14. (1980). pp.47-53.

5,268. KNORPEL, H. "Social security cases in the Court of Justice of the European Communities 1978-1980, Part I". C.M.L.Rev. 18. (1981). pp.579-600.

5,269. KNORPEL, H. "Social security cases in the Court of Justice of the European Communities, 1978-1980, part II". C.M.L.Rev. 19. (1982). pp.105-152.

5,270. KNORPEL, H. "Social security cases in the Court of Justice of the European Communities, 1981". C.M.L.Rev. 20. (1983). pp.97-123.

5,271. LASOK, K.P.E. "Employed and self-employed persons in E.E.C. social security law". J.S.W.L. (1982). pp.323-336.

5,272. LAWSON, R. "EEC benefits". <u>N.S.</u> 23. (1973). pp.700-701.

5,273. LAWSON, R. & REED, B. Social security in the European Community. London: P.E.P. 1975. pp.75. (European Series, No.23). DHSS; LSE.

5,274. LIPSTEIN, K. "Conflicts of laws in matters of social security under the EEC treaty". in F.J. Jacobs (ed.). European law and the individual. Amsterdam: 1976. pp.55-77. LSE; CUL.

5,275. LYON-CAEN, G. Droit social europeen. Paris: 1969. pp.465. LSE. (See next entry)

5,276. LYON-CAEN, G. & LYON-CAEN, A. Droit social international et europeen. 5th ed. Paris: 1980. pp.423. LSE.

5,277. MANAGEMENT COUNSELLORS INTERNATIONAL. Social security in the EEC: legally required benefits. Brussels: 1971. pp.58. DHSS.

5,278. McCALLUM, I.M. & SNAITH, T. "EEC and UK occupational pension schemes". <u>Eur.L.R.</u> 2. (1977). pp.266-73.

5,279. MEGRET, J. & OTHERS. Le droit de la Communaute Economique Europeene. 7. Politique sociale. Bruxelles: 1973. pp.142-51. CUL.

5,280. MERTENS, J. "La securite sociale dans le programme d'action sociale des Communautes Europeennes". <u>Rev.Belge de Sec.Soc.</u> XV. (1973). pp.1043-1050.

5,281. MINISTRY OF SOCIAL SECURITY. Social security in the EEC (as at 1st January 1967). London: 1967. unpag. DHSS.

5,282. MINISTRY OF SOCIAL SECURITY. Social security in the EEC (as at 1st May 1968). London: 1968. unpag. DHSS.

5,283. O'DONOVAN, V. "The co-ordination of social security benefits within the EEC". <u>N.L.J.</u> 126. (1976). pp.913, 1017.

5,284. OGILVY-WEBB, M. "Social security in Europe and Britain". <u>Social Service Quarterly</u>. Winter. (1967-68). pp.111-113.

5,285. PAGE, A.C. "The scope of Community and national rules against the overlapping of social security benefits". <u>C.M.L.Rev.</u> 17. (1980). pp.211-28.

5,286. PRESTATAIRE. "Social security: overlapping of benefits in the EEC". <u>L.S.G.</u> 78. (1981). pp.211-2.

5,287. RATCLIFF, A.R.N. State and private pension schemes in the European Economic Community and the United Kingdom. London: 1963. pp.50. DHSS.

5,288. REID, G.L. "Social security in Britain and the Six". <u>Banker</u>. (1963). pp.409-416.

5,289. RIBAS, J.J. "Observations on the financing of social security in the common market countries". <u>I.Lab.R.</u> 84. (1961).

pp.26-49.

5,290. RIBAS, J.J. Social security in the European Community. Rev. ed. Luxembourg: 1965. [London: 1965]. pp.15. (Community Topics 18). [first published in Bull. I.S.S.A. Dec. 1963]. DHSS; LSE.

5,291. RIBAS, J.J., JONCZY, M.J. & SECHE, J.C. Droit social europeen. Paris: [1978]. pp.708. LSE.

5,292. RIDDLES, M. "EEC social security legislation". Benefits Int. 10. (1980). pp.7-11.

5,293. RODGERS, B.N. "Social policy implications of Britain's entry to the Common Market". J.Soc.Pol. 2. (1975). pp.55-62.

5,294. SCHNORR, G. "L'apport du droit communautaire au droit du travail et de la securite sociale". Cah.dr.europ. 6. (1970). pp.544-556.

5,295. SELECT COMMITTEE ON THE EUROPEAN COMMUNITIES. Session 1977-78. Social security: R/48/77; draft directive on equality of treatment for men and women in matters of social security. London: 1977. pp.vi + 25. (HL23). DHSS.

5,296. STATUTORY PUBLICATIONS OFFICE. Secondary legislation of the European Communities, subject edition; legislation in force on 31 December 1972. Volume 10. Social affairs. London: 1973. pp.x + 335. DHSS.

5,297. STEINER, J. "EEC nationals: are some more equal than others?" [R. v. National Insurance Commissioner, ex parte Warry [1981] I.C.R. 90]. L.Q.R. 97. (1981). pp.365-369.

5,298. SZYSZCZAK, E. "Occupational pension schemes and Article 119 EEC". N.L.J. 131. (1981). pp.527-9.

5,299. TITMUSS, R.M. "Social security and the six". N.S. 18. (1971). pp.927-929.

5,300. TRINE, A. (ed.). Employers' liabilities under social service legislation in the countries of the European Common Market. Brussels: 1970. pp.469. DHSS; LSE.

5,301. TROCLET, L.-E. Elements de droit social europeen. Brussels: 1963. pp.358. LSE.

5,302. VAN LANGENDONCK, J. "Social security legislation in the E.E.C.". I.L.J. 2. (1973). pp.17-27.

5,303. WATSON, P. "Harmonisation of social security within the European Community - the history of a changing concept". Soc. & Econ.Ad. 11. (1977). pp.21-37.

5,304. WATSON, P. Social security law of the European Communities. London: 1980. pp.xii + 277. DHSS.

(b) Social Security and Migrant Workers

5,305. ANON.   "La Communaute Europeenne et les travailleurs migrants". [The European Community and migrant workers]. Rev.Belge de Sec.Soc. 22. pp.744-752.

5,306. ADMINISTRATIVE COMMISSION OF THE EUROPEAN COMMUNITIES ON SOCIAL SECURITY FOR MIGRANT WORKERS. "Decision No.86 of 24 September 1973 concerning the methods of operation and the composition of the Audit Board of the Administrative Commission of the European Communities on social security for migrant workers". Official Journal of the European Communities: Information and Notices. 16. (1973). C96/2-4.

5,307. BENTIL, J.K.   "ECC migrant workers and social security benefits law". S.J. 124. (1980). pp.266-68.

5,308. CAMPOPIANO, R.   "A measure of social welfare on behalf of migrant workers". Bull.I.S.S.A. IV. (1951). pp.358-362.

5,309. CENTRAL OFFICE OF INFORMATION.   "National insurance for migrants".   Home Affairs Survey.   183.   (Nov. 1950). pp.27-29.

5,310. COUNCIL OF EUROPE. Social services for migrant workers. Strasbourg: 1968. pp.92. DHSS.

5,311. CREUTZ, H.   "The I.L.O. and social security for foreign and migrant workers". I.Lab.R. 97. (1968). pp.351-369.

5,312. DELANNOO, P.   "La securite sociale des travailleurs migrants dans les conventions bilaterales". Rev.Belge de Sec.Soc. XI. (1969). pp.979-1002.

5,313. DELLIVRENNE, M.   "Administrative problems of social security for migrant workes in countries of the Common Market". Bull. I.S.S.A. XVIII. (1965).

5,314. EUROPEAN COMMUNITIES, ADMINISTRATIVE COMMISSION ON SOCIAL SECURITY FOR MIGRANT WORKERS. Social security for migrant workers. Guide No.1. Concerning the rights and obligations with regard to social security of employed persons going to work in [a member state of the European Communities]. Luxembourg: 1975. 9 vols. DHSS.

5,315. EUROPEAN COMMUNITIES, ADMINISTRATIVE COMMISSION ON SOCIAL SECURITY FOR MIGRANT WORKERS. Social security for migrant workers. Guide No.2. For persons staying temporarily in another member state of the European Communities (on holiday, on business, or visiting relatives). Luxembourg: 1976. pp.40. DHSS.

5,316. EUROPEAN COMMUNITIES, ADMINISTRATIVE COMMISSION ON SOCIAL SECURITY FOR MIGRANT WORKERS. Social security for migrant workers. Guide No.3. For posted workers, international transport workers regularly employed in more than one member state of the European Communities... Luxembourg: 1976. pp.47. DHSS.

5,317. EUROPEAN COMMUNITIES, ADMINISTRATIVE COMMISSION ON SOCIAL SECURITY FOR MIGRANT WORKERS. Social security for migrant workers. Guide No.4. Guide for pensioners who were formerly employed persons and for persons claiming a pension who are residing or staying temporarily in a member state of the European Communities. Luxembourg: 1976. pp.6. DHSS.

5,318. EUROPEAN COMMUNITIES, ADMINISTRATIVE COMMISSION ON SOCIAL SECURITY FOR MIGRANT WORKERS. Implementation of decisions Nos.103 and 104 of the Administrative Commission on Social Security for Migrant Workers: implementation of decision No.103 using ADP techniques. Luxembourg: 1977. pp.[iii] + 45. DHSS.

5,319. EUROPEAN COMMUNITIES. ADMINISTRATIVE COMMISSION ON SOCIAL SECURITY FOR MIGRANT WORKERS. Social security for migrant workers: guide no.1: concerning the rights and obligations with regard to social security of employed persons going to work in Ireland. 2nd ed. Luxembourg: 1979. pp.63. DHSS.

5,320. EUROPEAN ECONOMIC COMMUNITY. Commission Administrative de la Communaute Economique Europeeene pour la Securite Sociale des Travailleurs Migrants. Rapport Annuel. [Brussels]: 1958/9 to date. LSE.

5,321. EUROPEAN ECONOMIC COMMUNITY. Regulation No. 80/65/EEC, To amend and supplement Regulations Nos. 3 and 4 concerning social security for migrant workers. London: 1965. pp.5. DHSS.

5,322. EUROPEAN ECONOMIC COMMUNITY. La securite sociale des pays membres de la Communaute et les travailleurs migrants des pays tiers. n.l.: 1967. pp.90. DHSS.

5,323. HANOTIAU, B. Les problemes de securite sociale des travailleurs migrants. Brussels: 1973. pp.178. LSE.

5,324. HOLROYD, J. "EEC migrant workers in the United Kingdom". L.A.G.Bull. (1976). pp.276-278.

5,325. INTERNATIONAL LABOUR ORGANISATION. Social security for migrant workers. Geneva: 1977. pp.vii + 154. DHSS.

5,326. INTERNATIONAL SOCIAL SECURITY ASSOCIATION. Benefits for migrant workers: faster services for claimants; report of a European Regional Meeting on the Speeding Up of the Settlement of Migrant Workers' Benefit Claims, London 10-12 October 1979. (Chairman: Mr. Ian G. Gilbert). Geneva: 1980. pp.[iii] + 103. (European Series No.4). DHSS.

5,327. INTERNATIONAL LABOUR CONFERENCE. Maintenance of migrant workers' rights in social security (revision of convention no.48): fourth item on the agenda. Geneva: 1981. pp.47. (Report; IV(1)). DHSS.

5,328. INTERNATIONAL LABOUR CONFERENCE. Maintenance of migrant workers' rights in social security (revision of convention no.48): fourth item on the agenda. Geneva: 1982. pp.54. (Report IV(2)). DHSS.

5,329. INTERNATIONAL LABOUR OFFICE. Maintenance of migrant workers' rights in social security (revision of Convention No.48) International Labour Conference, 67th Session, 1981. Seventh item on the agenda. Geneva: 1980. pp.[ii] + 82. (Report VII(1)). DHSS.

5,330. MAAS, H.H. "The administrative commission for the social security of migrant workers. An institutional curiosity". C.M.L.Rev. 4. (1966-67). pp.51-63.

5,331. MARZIALE, F. "La securite sociale, l'assistance sociale et medicale en faveur des travailleurs migrants dans les instruments du Conseil de l'Europe". Rev.Belge de Sec.Soc. XV. (1973). pp.37-76.

5,332. MASELLI, G. "Social protection of migrant workers". Bull.I.S.S.A. III. (1950). (6). pp.1-13.

5,333. MAYRAS, H. "La jurisprudence de la Cour de Justice des Communautes europeennes en matiere de securite sociale des travailleurs migrants". Rev.Belge de Sec.Soc. XVI. (1974). pp.223-237.

5,334. MERTENS, J. "La Cour de Justice et la securite sociale des travailleurs migrants". Rev.Belge de Sec.Soc. XV. (1973). pp.333-351.

5,335. MOLES, R.R. "Social security for migrant workers". Int.Migration. (1964). pp.47-53.

5,336. MORGAN, M. "EEC: social security for the migrant worker". N.L.J. 130. (1980). pp.731-732.

5,337. NETTER, F. "Social security for migrant workers". I.Lab.R. (1963). pp.31-50.

5,338. PANAYOTOPOULOS, M. La securite sociale des travailleurs migrants: etude sur les reglements de la CEE et la situation de la Suisse. Geneva: 1973. pp.518. (Centre d'Etudes Juridiques Europeenes and Institut fur Europaisches und Internationales Wirtschafts - und Socialrecht. Etudes Suisses de Droit Europeen. Vol.9). LSE.

5,339. PEARL, D. "Social security and the immigrant". New Community. 3 (1974-5). pp.272-9.

5,340. PERL, G. "Cour de Justice des Communautes europeenes". Rev.Belge de Sec.Soc. XVII. (1975). pp.759-769.

5,341. PERRIN, G. "La securite sociale des etrangers et des migrants selon les instrument de l'Organisation Internationale du Travail (OIT)". Revue Belge de Securite Sociale. 23. (1981). pp.315-333.

5,342. SECHE, J.O. "The revision of regulations nos. 3 and 4 (social security of migrant workers) in the light of their interpretation by the Court of Justice". C.M.L.R. 6. (1968-69). pp.170-192.

5,343. VOIRIN, M. "La securite sociale des migrants et des droits de l'homme". Rev. trim. dr. europ. 4. (1968). pp.720-746.

5,344. WATILLON, L. "The problem of granting social security

benefits to the dependants of migrant workers". <u>Bull.I.S.S.A.</u>
VI. (1953). pp.83-90.

5,345. WEIR, S. "Ugandan Asians - one year later: supplementary
benefits - discrimination by non-discrimination". <u>New Comm.</u>
2. (1972-3). pp.379-80.

5,346. WYATT, D. "The social security rights of migrant workers and
their families". <u>C.M.L.R.</u> 14. (1977). pp.411-433.

(c) Council of Europe

5,347. COUNCIL OF EUROPE. Documentation prepared by the Research
Directorate of the Secretariat-General concerning economic and
social rights contained in international instruments and
national constitutions. Strasbourg: 1955. p.57. LSE.

5,348. COUNCIL OF EUROPE. Settlement of disputes in social law:
report adopted by the Social Committee of Western European
Union in May 1960. Strasbourg: 1961. pp.60. LSE.

5,349. COUNCIL OF EUROPE. European convention on social and medical
assistance and protocol with annexes, 1963. Strasbourg:
1963. pp.33 + 7. DHSS.

5,350. COUNCIL OF EUROPE. European interim agreement on social
security schemes relating to old age, invalidity and
survivors. Strasbourg: 1972. pp.20. (European Treaty
Series No.12). DHSS.

5,351. COUNCIL OF EUROPE. European Convention on Social Security and
supplementary agreement for the application of the European
Convention on Social Security. Strasbourg: 1972. pp.ii +
175. (European Treaty Series No.78). DHSS.

5,352. COUNCIL OF EUROPE. Explanatory report on the European
Convention on Social Security and on the supplementary
agreement for the application of the European Convention on
Social Security. Strasbourg: 1973. pp.278. DHSS.

5,353. COUNCIL OF EUROPE. European code of social security and
protocol to the European code of social security. Strasbourg:
1974. var.pag. (European Treaty Series No.48). DHSS.

5,354. COUNCIL OF EUROPE. European convention on the social
protection of farmers. Strasbourg: 1974. pp.14. (European
Treaty Series No.83). DHSS.

PART V   Miscellaneous Works

5,355.   ANON.   "Reference under the Order of His Excellency the
Governor-General in Council re the Employment and Social
Insurance Act". <u>C.B.R.</u> XIV. (1936). pp.530-532.

5,356.   ANON.   "In the matter of a reference as to whether the
Parliament of Canada had legislative jurisdiction to enact the
Employment and Social Insurance Act, being chapter 36 of the
Statutes of Canada, 1935". <u>C.B.R.</u> XIV. (1936). pp.532-540.

5,357.   ANON.   "Notes on current events.   Poverty and the welfare
state". <u>Ind.L.R.</u> 7. (1952-53). pp.82-83.

5,358.   ANON.   Melanges offerts a Leon-Eli Troclet: theme, droit
social national et international. Bruxelles: [1967]. pp.344.
LSE.

5,359.   ABBOTT, J.F.   "Unemployment, incentives and the negative
income tax". <u>Soc.Pol. & Admin.</u> 13. (1979). pp.186-205.

5,360.   ABEL-SMITH, B. & BAGLEY, C.   "The problem of establishing
equivalent standards of living for families of different
composition". in P. TOWNSEND (ed.). <u>The concept of poverty</u>.
London: Heinemann. 1970. pp.86-99. LSE.

5,361.   ADLER, M. & ASQUITH, S. (eds.).   Discretion and welfare.
London: 1981. pp.vii + 296. LSE; CUL.

5,362.   AGARWALA, A.N.   "The social security movement in India". <u>E.J.</u>
LVI. (1946). pp.568ff.

5,363.   AMIEL, B.   "1982 - mesures et projects concernant la securite
sociale". <u>Questions de Securite Sociale</u>.   34.   (1982).
pp.16-22.

5,364.   ATKINSON, A.B.   "Policies for poverty". <u>Lloyds B.R.</u>   110.
(April 1971). pp.17-28.

5,365.   ATKINSON, A.B.   "Income maintenance and income taxation".
<u>J.Soc.Pol.</u> 1. (1972). pp.135-148.

5,366.   ATKINSON, A.B.   "Social security: poverty is the test of
policy". <u>N.S.</u> 31. (1975). pp.645-646.

5,367.   ATKINSON, A.B.   "Social security: the future". <u>N.S.</u>   37.
(1976). pp.279-280.

5,368.   ATKINSON, A.B.   "Inequality under Labour". <u>N.S.</u> 48. (1979).
pp.194-5.

5,369.   ATKINSON, A.B.   "A tax strategy for the 1980's". <u>N.S.</u>   48.
(1979). pp.765-6.

5,370.   ATKINSON, A.B. (ed.).   Wealth, income and inequality.
Harmondsworth: 1973. LSE. 2nd ed. Oxford: 1980. pp.ix +
412. LSE; BL.

5,371. ATKINSON, A.B. The economics of inequality. 2nd ed. Oxford: 1983. pp.xii + 330. DHSS.

5,372. ATKINSON, A.B. Social justice and public policy. Brighton: 1983. pp.444. DHSS.

5,373. AUSTRALIA. COMMONWEALTH DEPARTMENT OF SOCIAL SERVICES. Social services of the Commonwealth. [Canberra] : 1953. pp.30. LSE.

5,374. AUSTRALIA. DEPARTMENT OF SOCIAL SECURITY. Review of the characteristics of long term unemployment benefit recipients in Australia, 1970-1977. Woden, A.C.T.: 1978. pp.38. (Research paper No.2). DHSS.

5,375. BARRATT BROWN, M. "The welfare state in Britain". Soc. Reg. (1971). pp.185-224.

5,376. BECKERMAN, W. "The impact of income maintenance payments on poverty in Britain, 1975". E.J. 89. (1979). pp.261-79.

5,377. BEENSTOCK, M. "Poverty, taxation and the welfare state". Crossbow. 22. (August 1980). pp.24-34.

5,378. BERTHOUD, R. The disadvantages of inequality: a study of social deprivation. London: 1976. pp.207. DHSS; CUL.

5,379. BOWEN, I. Acceptable inequalities: an essay on the distribution of income. London: 1970. pp.148. DHSS.

5,380. BROWN, C.V. Taxation and the incentive to work. Oxford: 1980. pp.v + 122. LSE.

5,381. BROWN, J.C. "Revenue allocation and anti-poverty policy". Pol.Stu. 2. (1981-2). pp.96-106.

5,382. BROWN, W. The earnings conflict: proposals for tackling the emerging crisis of industrial relations, unemployment, and wage inflation. London: 1973. pp.128. DHSS.

5,383. CALIFICE, A. "Financing social security". Rev.Belge de Sec.Soc. 21. (1979). pp.510-534.

5,384. CANADA, DEPARTMENT OF NATIONAL HEALTH AND WELFARE. Comparisons of social security expenditures in Canada, Australia, New Zealand, the United Kingdom and the United States, fiscal years 1959-60 to 1964-65, inclusive. Ottawa: 1967. pp.25. DHSS.

5,385. CANADA. Royal Commission on the Status of Pensions in Ontario. Report. (Chairman: Donna J. Haley). [Toronto]: 1980. 10 vols. DHSS.

5,386. CANTOR, M.E.L. "National insurance in its constitutional aspects". A.L.J. 2. (1928-29). pp.219-220.

5,387. CARTER, SIR C. & WILSON, T. Discussing the welfare state. London: 1980. pp.iv + 48. DHSS.

5,388. CENTRAL STATISTICAL OFFICE (WITH DEPARTMENT OF HEALTH AND

SOCIAL SECURITY). "The impact of taxes and social security benefits on different groups of households". Annual statements in Econ.Trends. (1962 to date). LSE.

5,389. CENTRAL STATISTICAL OFFICE. "International comparison of taxes and social security contributions". Annual statements in Econ.Trends. (1969 to date). LSE.

5,390. CHRISTOPHER, A., POLANYI, G., SELDON, A. & SHENFIELD, B. Policy for poverty: a study of the urgency of reform in social benefits and of the advantages and limitations of a reverse income tax in replacement of the existing structure of state benefits. London: 1970. pp.95. (IEA Research Monographs 20). LSE.

5,391. CLARK, S. & HEMMING, R. "Aspects of household poverty in Britain". Soc.Pol.and Admin. 15. (1981). pp.260-267.

5,392. COCKBURN, C. "The role of social security in development". Int.Soc.Sec.Rev. 33. (1980). pp.337-357.

5,393. COLLIER, J. "Old age pensions in Australasia". Reformer. 5. (1903). pp.549-56.

5,394. COOPER, G. & COLE, S.J. "New federal fair hearing regulations". Clearing House Review. V. (1971). pp.4-5, 22-23.

5,395. COOPER, M.H. "Tax credits: problems and principles". Soc. & Ec. Admin. 7. (1973). pp.136-52.

5,396. COPPELMAN, P.D. "Legal challenges to relative responsibility in old age security programs". Clearing House Review. VI. (1972). pp.212-220.

5,397. CORMACK, U. "The Seebohm Committee Report - a great state paper". Soc. & Ec. Admin. 3. (1969). pp.52-61.

5,398. CORSON, W. & NICHOLSON, W. The Federal Supplemental Benefits program: an appraisal of emergency extended unemployment insurance benefits. Kalamazoo, Mich.: W.E. Upjohn Institute for Employment Research. 1982. pp.x + 117. DHSS.

5,399. CUTRIGHT, P. "Political structure, economic development and national social security programs". American Journal of Sociology. LXX. (1965). pp.537-550.

5,400. CUTT, J., DIXON, J. & NAGORCKA, B. Income support policy in Australia: a dynamic approach. Canberra: 1977. pp. x + 255. DHSS.

5,401. DAY, B.V. "The underwriting environment: legal and sociological developments". P.H. 94. (1976). pp.1635-1644.

5,402. DEPARTMENT OF HEALTH AND SOCIAL SECURITY. "The British proposals for a tax-credit system. Main features of reform proposals, present status, concurrent pension and tax developments". Int.Soc.Sec.Rev. XXVII. (1974). pp.280-300.

5,403. DEPARTMENT OF HEALTH AND SOCIAL SECURITY. Tax/benefit model tables: the financial position of hypothetical families where the head is working or unemployed at April 1981. [London]: 1981. pp.[iv] + 55. DHSS.

5,404. DISNEY, R. The distribution of unemployment and sickness among the United Kingdom population. Reading: [1977]. pp.36. (Paper No.87). DHSS.

5,405. DONNISON, D.V. & CHAPMAN, V. Social policy and administration: studies in the development of social services at the local level. London: 1965. pp.270. DHSS; CUL; Sq.

5,406. DOUBLET, J. Securite sociale. 1st ed. Paris: 1957. pp.651. DHSS; LSE. 4th ed. revised and augmented. 1967. pp.663. Sq. 5th ed. Paris: 1972. pp.816. LSE.

5,407. DOUGLAS, P. "The United States Social Security Act". E.J. LXVI. (1936). pp.1ff.

5,408. DOWNING, R.I. National superannuation. Adelaide: 1958. pp.23. LSE.

5,409. DUPEYROUX, J.-J. Securite sociale. Eds. 1, 2. n.l. 3rd ed. Paris: 1969. pp.952. Sq.

5,410. EASTON, B. Social policy and the welfare state in New Zealand. Auckland: 1980. pp.182 + bibliogs. DHSS.

5,411. EUROPEAN INSTITUTE FOR SOCIAL SECURITY. EISS yearbook 1978-1980. Deventer, London: 1980. 2 vols. DHSS.

5,412. EVASON, E. "Poverty and social security in Northern Ireland". Quest. 2. (1975). pp.4-9.

5,413. EVASON, E. Poverty: the facts in Northern Ireland. London: 1976. pp.48. (Poverty Pamphlet 27). DHSS; LSE; CUL.

5,414. EVASON, E. Family poverty in Northern Ireland. London: 1978. pp.36. (Poverty Research Series No.6). CUL.

5,415. EVASON, E. Ends that won't meet: a study of poverty in Belfast. London: 1980. pp.104. (Poverty Research Series 8). DHSS.

5,416. EVERSLEY, D. "How society sees poverty: some notes on changing concepts in three countries". Pol.Stu. 2. (1981-2). pp.62-73.

5,417. FERAUD, L. L'economie de la securite sociale. Apercu sans mathematiques des principes, des methodes et du role de l'actuariat de la securite sociale. Paris: 1970. pp.iv + 123. DHSS.

5,418. FIELD, F. Poverty: the facts. London: 1975. pp.46. (Poverty Pamphlet 21). DHSS; LSE; CUL.

5,419. FIELD, F. The new corporate interest. London: 1976. pp.iv + 28. (Poverty Pamphlet 23). DHSS; LSE.

5,420. FIELD, F. "Freedom, inequality and the five welfare states".

N.S. 55. (1981). pp.363-5.

5,421. FRANKLIN, N.N. "The concept and measurement of 'minimum living standards'". I.Lab.R. 95. (1967). pp.271-298.

5,422. FREYSSINET, J. "Securite sociale, crise economique et productivite du travail". Droit Social. 12. (1981). pp.794-798.

5,423. GETZ WOLD, K. "Can the modern state afford more welfare?". F.N. (October 1955). p.75.

5,424. GOURJA, K. "The contribution of social security to development objectives: the role of income support measures". Int.Soc.Sec.Rev. 34. (1981). pp.131-150.

5,425. GRAY, H. "Towards a new welfare strategy", N.S. 11. (1968). pp.159-160.

5,426. GRAY, V.E. "An evolutionary pattern in insurance legislation". C.B.R. XXVIII. (1950). pp.493-523.

5,427. GRAYCAR, A. Welfare politics in Australia. South Melbourne: 1979. pp.viii + 231. DHSS.

5,428. GRAYCAR, A. "Experimentation and the Welfare State". Soc. Pol. & Admin. 14. (1980). pp.233-48.

5,429. GRAYCAR, A. (ed.). Retreat from the welfare state: Australian social policy in the 1980s. Sydney: 1983. pp.206. DHSS.

5,430. GUEST, D. The emergence of social security in Canada. Vancouver: [1980]. pp.xi + 257. DHSS.

5,431. HARRIS, R. "A review of the effects of taxes and benefits on household incomes 1961-1975". Econ.Trends. 279. (1977). pp.97-110.

5,432. HAYES, L.F. "Non-economic aspects of poverty". Australian J. of Social. Issues. (1970). pp.41-53.

5,433. HEYWOOD, J.S. & ALLEN, B.K. Financial help in social work: a study of preventive work with families under the Children's and Young Persons Act, 1963. Manchester: 1971. pp.viii + 93. DHSS; CUL.

5,434. HICKS, J.R. & HICKS, U.K. Standards of local expenditure. A problem of the inequality of incomes. Cambridge: 1943. pp.61. (National Institute of Economic and Social Research. Occasional Papers III). CUL.

5,435. HIGGINS, J. "Public welfare: the road to freedom?" J.Soc.Pol. 11. (1982). pp.177-199.

5,436. HILDEBRAND, G.H. Poverty, income maintenance and the negative income tax. New York: 1967. pp.iii + 68. DHSS.

5,437. HILL, M. & LAING, P. "The use of section 1 of the 1968 Children and Young Persons Act". Health and Social Service J.

88. (1978). pp.D17-D24. (Centre Eight Papers).

5,438. HORLICK, M. "The earnings replacement rate of old-age benefits: an international comparison". Social Security Bulletin. 33(3). (1970). pp.3-16.

5,439. HOWARD, D.S. Social welfare: values, means and ends. New York: 1969. pp.xi + 467. DHSS.

5,440. HOWE, G. In place of Beveridge? London: 1965. pp.18. LSE; DHSS.

5,441. HOWE, G. & LAMONT, N. "What do we really mean by selectivity". Crossbow. 12(47). (1969). pp.30-33.

5,442. HOWE, J.R. Two parent families: a study of their resources and needs in 1968, 1969 and 1970: an analysis based on family expenditure survey data. London: 1971. pp.18. (DHSS Statistical Report Series No.14). LSE.

5,443. HOWE, J.R. & WHITEHEAD, F.E. "Politics and the statistics of poverty - a rejoinder". Pol.Q. 43. (1972). p.232.

5,444. INGLES, D. Financing social security: an analysis of the contributory 'social insurance' approach. [Woden, A.C.T.]. 1982. pp.94. (Research paper No.19). DHSS.

5,445. INSTITUTE OF ECONOMIC AFFAIRS. Towards a welfare society. London: 1967. pp.40. (Occasional Paper 13). DHSS; LSE; CUL.

5,446. INSTITUTE OF ECONOMIC AFFAIRS. Policy for poverty. London: 1970. pp.95. DHSS.

5,447. INSTITUTE OF MUNICIPAL TREASURERS AND ACCOUNTANTS. METROPOLITAN AND HOME COUNTIES BRANCH. ASSOCIATES' SECTION. An investigation into the problem of assessment scales. London: 1954. pp.98. LSE.

5,448. INTERNATIONAL LABOUR OFFICE. Unemployment schemes. Geneva: 1955. pp.254. Studies and Reports. (N.S.). No.42. LSE.

5,449. ISLE OF MAN. BOARD OF SOCIAL SERVICES. Reports by the Government Actuary on the first quinquennial actuarial reviews of the Manx National Insurance Scheme and the Manx Industrial Injuries Scheme covering the period from 5th July 1948 to 31st March 1954. Douglas: 1957. pp.27. DHSS.

5,450. ISLE OF MAN. The Family Allowances, National Insurance, Industrial Injuries and National Health Service Contributions (Decimalisation of the Currency) Order 1970. Douglas: 1970. pp.iv + 22. DHSS.

5,451. ISLE OF MAN. The Supplementary Benefit (Isle of Man) (Determination of Requirements) Regulations 1970. Douglas: 1970. pp.3. DHSS.

5,452. JENKINS, S. (ed.). Social security in international perspective. New York: 1969. pp.xii + 255. CUL; DHSS; LSE.

5,453. JENKINSON, K.J. "Notes on the Commonwealth Employees' Compensation Act 1930-1964". A.L.J. 41. (1967-68). pp.112-118, 159-167.

5,454. JENKS, W. Social security as a world problem. Wellington, New Zealand: 1972. fo.19. (Victoria University of Wellington. Industrial Relations Centre. Occasional Papers in Industrial Relations No.6). LSE.

5,455. JERSEY. Family Allowances (Jersey) Law, 1951. Jersey: 1951. pp.ii + 33. DHSS.

5,456. JERSEY. Insular insurance law. Jersey: 1957. pp.iii + 93. DHSS.

5,457. JERSEY. Insular Insurance (Jersey) Law, 1950. (As amended 19th May, 1965). (Regulations and Orders). Jersey: 1965. unpag. DHSS.

5,458. JERSEY, SOCIAL SECURITY DEPARTMENT. Act dated 13 October 1970 and report of the Social Security Committee regarding attendance allowance for severely disabled persons together with a proposition relative thereto. St. Helier: 1970. pp.7. DHSS.

5,459. JERSEY, SOCIAL SECURITY COMMITTEE. Act dated 13 October 1970 and report of the Social Security Committee regarding social security in Jersey and proposals for its modernisation together with a proposition relative thereto. St. Helier: 1970. pp.79. DHSS.

5,460. JERSEY, SOCIAL SECURITY DEPARTMENT. A brief guide to the proposed new social insurance scheme. St. Helier: 1970. pp.8. DHSS.

5,461. JERSEY, SOCIAL SECURITY COMMITTEE. Act, dated 27 October 1971, of the Social Security Committee, together with a supplementary report and proposition regarding the proposed family allowance scheme. St. Helier: 1971. pp.12. DHSS.

5,462. JERSEY, SOCIAL SECURITY DEPARTMENT. A guide to the proposed new family allowances structure. St. Helier: 1971. pp.6. DHSS.

5,463. JERSEY, SOCIAL SECURITY DEPARTMENT. Social security in Jersey. St. Helier: 1973. pp.v + 37. DHSS.

5,464. JONES, M.A. The Australian welfare state. Sydney, London: 1980. pp.viii + 244. DHSS.

5,465. KAIM-CAUDLE, P. "Social policy and social work". Soc.Stud. 3. (1974). pp.445-56.

5,466. KALDOR, N. & OTTAWAY, A.K.C. The cost of social security. London: 1944. pp.12. LSE.

5,467. KATES, D.B. "Creating civil causes of action for the enforcement of rights which a legislature has statutorily declared without providing a civil remedy". Clearing House Review. 3. (1969). pp.65-66.

5,468. KAY, J.A., MORRIS, C.N. & WARREN, N.A. "Tax benefits and the incentive to seek work". Fisc.Stud. 1. (4). (1980). pp.8-25.

5,469. KENNAN, J.H. "The possible constitutional powers of the Commonwealth as to national health insurance". A.L.J. (1975). pp.261-267.

5,470. KEWLEY, T.H. Social security in Australia. Sydney: 1965. pp.vii + 401. CUL. 2nd ed. [1975].

5,471. KIRKPATRICK. E.K. Protecting social security beneficiary earnings against inflation; the foreign experience. Washington: US Government Printing Office. 1976. pp.iv + 35. (Staff Paper No.25; HEW publication No. (SSA) 77-11850). DHSS.

5,472. KLEIN, R. "The welfare state: a self-inflicted crisis". Pol.Q. 51. (1980). pp.24-34.

5,473. KOPITS, G. & GOTUR, P. "The influence of social security on household savings: a cross-country investigation". International Monetary Fund Staff Papers. 27. (1980). pp.161-189.

5,474. LAFITTE, F. "The future of social security". Soc. & Econ.Ad. 1. (1967). (1). pp.3-15.

5,475. LAMONT, S. Social security in Canada, 1977. [Ottawa]: Office of the Special Adviser, Policy Development. 1977. pp.iv + 104. DHSS.

5,476. LANSLEY, S. "What hope for the poor?" Lloyds B.R. 132. (April 1979). pp.22-37.

5,477. LAYARD, R., PIACHAUD, D. & STEWART, M. "The causes of poverty". Nat. West. Bk. Q.Rev. (February 1979). pp.30-47.

5,478. LE GRAND, J. The strategy of equality: redistribution and the social services. London: 1982. pp.xii + 192. DHSS.

5,479. LEAPER, R.A.B. "Subsidiarity and the welfare state". Soc. & Econ. Ad. 9. (1975). pp.82-97.

5,480. LEES, D. "A social security system for today". Crossbow. 6(23). (1963). pp.21-28.

5,481. LEES, D. "Poor families and fiscal reform". Lloyds B.R. 86. (October 1967). pp.1-15.

5,482. LEMAN, C. The collapse of welfare reform: political institutions, policy and the poor in Canada and the United States. Cambridge, Mass.: 1980. pp.xix + 292. DHSS.

5,483. LHUGUENOT, M. "Un changement difficile et necessaire: la securite sociale a reinventer". Droit Social. 12. (1981). pp.788-793.

5,484. LISTER, R. Moving back to the means test: a memorandum to the Chancellor of the Exchequer from the Child Poverty Action Group. London: 1980. pp.32. (Poverty Pamphlet 47). DHSS.

5,485. LYNES, T. French pensions. London: 1967. pp.163. LSE.

5,486. LYON-CAEN, G. "Le role de la faure dans le droit de la securite sociale. Rapport generale". Actes du Septieme Congres International de Droit du Travail et de la Securite Sociale. (1970). pp.11-30.

5,487. MacGREGOR, J. "A new strategy for social security". Crossbow. 7. (28). (1964). pp.29-33.

5,488. MAILLET, V. "La reforme de l'assiette des cotisations sociales: mythes et realites". Droit Social. 3. (1982). pp.245-247.

5,489. MAY, C.N. "Administration unveils welfare reform package - recipients must work for increased benefits". Clearing House Review. 3. (1969). pp.89, 101-102.

5,490. McCLEMENTS, L. Equivalence scales for children. London: 1975. pp.26. DHSS.

5,491. McCLEMENTS, L. The economics of social security. London: 1978. pp.xv + 239.

5,492. MEACHER, M. "A national equities issue to defeat poverty". Poverty. (1970). (14). pp.13-16.

5,493. MENCHER, S. "The problem of measuring poverty". British Journal of Sociology. 18. (1967). pp.1-11.

5,494. MILLS, C. Traite de securite sociale. Tome II. L'economie de la securite sociale. Paris: 1981. pp.x + 510 + bibliog. DHSS.

5,495. MINISTRY OF LABOUR. Family expenditure survey: reports: 1957/59; 1960/61; 1960-date. London. DHSS.

5,496. MINISTRY OF LABOUR AND NATIONAL SERVICE. Report of an enquiry into household expenditure 1953-54. London: 1957. pp.iv + 304. DHSS.

5,497. MINISTRY OF SOCIAL SECURITY. Circumstances of families: report of an enquiry... London: 1967. pp.xv + 160. DHSS; LSE.

5,498. MYERS, R.J. Social security. 2nd ed. Homewood, Ill.: 1981. pp.xxiv + 925. DHSS.

5,499. NEWMAN, N.(ed.). In cash or kind: the place of financial assistance in social work. Edinburgh: 1974. pp.150. LSE. 3rd. ed. Edinburgh: University of Edinburgh, Department of Social Administration, 1976. pp.ii + 162. DHSS.

5,500. NEWTON, J. Population projections and social security. [Canberra]: Department of Social Security. 1981. pp.v + 83. DHSS.

5,501. NEW ZEALAND. GOVERNMENT INSURANCE DEPARTMENT. Annual report, 31st December 1927. Wellingont: 1928. pp.7. LSE.

5,502. NEW ZEALAND PLANNING COUNCIL. The welfare state? Social policy in the 1980's. Wellington: 1979. pp.113. DHSS.

5,503. NORTHERN IRELAND. National Insurance Fund, National Insurance Reserve Fund, Industrial Injuries Fund Accounts, 1962-63. (H.C. 1579). Belfast: 1964. pp.15. DHSS.

5,504. NORTHERN IRELAND. DEPARTMENT OF FINANCE. STATISTICS AND ECONOMICS UNIT. Family expenditure survey: report for 1972. Belfast: [1973]. n.p. DHSS.

5,505. OFFICE OF ECONOMIC COOPERATION AND DEVELOPMENT. Public expenditure on income maintenance programmes. Paris: 1976. pp.121. (OECD Studies in Resource Allocation No.3). DHSS.

5,506. O'NEILL, M. & CIFFIN, S. Case study on divorce and social security in Canada, prepared for the ISSA Round Table meeting 'Social security provisions in case of divorce', Geneva, Switzerland, 29 June - 1 july 1977. Ottawa: Dept. of National Health and Welfare. 1977. pp.iv + 63. DHSS.

5,507. ORGANISATION FOR ECONOMIC CO-OPERATION AND DEVELOPMENT. The welfare state in crisis: an account of the Conference on Social Policies in the 1980s. Paris: 1981. pp.274. DHSS.

5,508. PARKER, H. The moral hazard of social benefits: a study of the impact of social benefits and income tax on incentives to work. London: 1982. pp.115. (IEA Research monographs, 37). DHSS.

5,509. PARKER, H. "Social security foments the black economy". Jo.Econ.Affairs. 3. (1982). pp.32,33,35.

5,510. PARTINGTON, M. "The scope and teaching of welfare law: report of a symposium". L.T. 8. (1974). pp.135-141.

5,511. PAUKERT, F. "Social security and income distribution: a comparative study". I.Lab.R. 98. (1968). pp.425-450.

5,512. PEACOCK, A.T. The economics of national insurance. London: 1952. pp.126. DHSS; LSE.

5,513. PEACOCK, A. "Problems of national insurance finance". Economic Digest. VI. (1953). pp.231-232.

5,514. PEACOCK, A.T. (ed.). Income redistribution and social policy: a set of studies. London: 1954. pp.296. DHSS.

5,515. PERRIN, G. "Les nouvelles frontieres de la securite sociale". Rev.Belge de Sec.Soc. XIX. (1977). pp.214-231.

5,516. PERRIN, G. "A propos du financement de la securite sociale". [About financing social security]. Rev.Belge de Sec.Soc. 22. (1980). pp.769-791.

5,517. PIACHAUD, D. "Poverty and taxation". Pol.Q. (1971). pp.31-44.

5,518. PIACHAUD, D. "Who are the poor, and what is the best way to help them?". N.S. 47. (1979). pp.603-6.

5,519. PIACHAUD, D. "Inequality and social policy". N.S. 47. (1979). pp.670-2.

5,520. POLITICAL AND ECONOMIC PLANNING. "Social security lessons from America". Planning. XX. (1954). pp.217-231.

5,521. POLITICAL AND ECONOMIC PLANNING. "Free trade and social security". Planning. XXII. (1957). pp.143-155.

5,522. PREST, A.R. Social benefits and tax rate. London: 1970. pp.30. (IEA Research Monographs No.22). DHSS.

5,523. REDDIN, M.J. "Views of the social insurance of tomorrow". F.N. 16. (1966). p.31.

5,524. REDDIN, M. "Some relationships between income taxation and social security". Int.Soc.Sec.Rev. XXIII. (1970). pp.113-120.

5,525. REID, G.L. "Views on social insurance". F.N. 17. (1967). p.6.

5,526. REID, G.L. & ROBERTSON, D.J. (eds.). Fringe benefits, labour costs and social security. London: 1965. pp.336. DHSS.

5,527. RICHARDSON, J.H. Economic and financial aspects of social security. London: 1960. pp.270. DHSS.

5,528. ROBERTSON, A. "Everything but the Maori funeral". P.H. 95. (1977). pp.2249, 2252.

5,529. RODGERS, B. "A new plan for social security". N.S. 12. (1968). pp.560-562.

5,530. ROSE, H. "Up against the Welfare State: the claimants unions". Soc. Reg. (1973). pp.179-204.

5,531. ROSENBERRY, S.A. "Social insurance, distributive criteria and the welfare backlash: a comparative analysis". Brit.Jo.Pol.Sci. 12. (1982). pp.421-447.

5,532. ROSS, S.G. New directions in social security considerations for the 1980s. Washington, D.C.: [1979]. pp.xii + 87. (SSA publication No.13-11950). DHSS.

5,533. RYS, V. "The sociology of social security". Bull. I.S.S.A. XVII. (1964). pp.3-34.

5,534. SACKVILLE, R. Law and poverty in Australia, second main report of the Commission of Inquiry into poverty. Canberra: 1975. LSE.

5,535. SACKVILLE, R. "Social security and family law in Australia". I.C.L.Q. 27. (1978). pp.127-67.

5,536. SAINT-JOURS, Y. "Securite sociale: replatrage ou reforme profonde?" <u>Droit Social</u>. 3. (1982). pp.248-252.

5,537. SANDFORD, C., POND, C. & WALKER, R. (eds.).   Taxation and social policy. London: 1980. pp.xiii + 242. DHSS; CUL.

5,538. SCARMAN, SIR L.   English law: the new dimension. London: 1974.   pp.xii + 88.   (The Hamlyn Lectures, 26th Series). DHSS.

5,539. SCARMAN, LORD JUSTICE. "Lawyers and the welfare state". <u>L.T.</u> 10. (1976). pp.67-73.

5,540. SCITOVSKY, T. Welfare and competition. The economics of a fully employed economy. London: 1952. pp.xvi + 457. DHSS.

5,541. SELDON, A. "Which way to welfare?" <u>Lloyds B.R.</u> 82. (October 1966). pp.34-48.

5,542. SELDON, A.   "Thaw in the Welfare State".   <u>Lloyds B.R.</u>   105 (July 1972). pp.18-33.

5,543. SELDON, A. Taxation and welfare: a report on private opinion and public policy. London: 1967. pp.70. DHSS; LSE.

5,544. SELDON, A. & GREY, H.   Universal or selective benefits? London: 1967. pp.70. (IEA Research Monograph No.8). DHSS; LSE.

5,545. SELECT COMMITTEE ON TAX CREDIT. Report and evidence. London: 1973. 3 vols. DHSS.

5,546. SKIDMORE, F. (ed.). Social security financing. Cambridge, Mass: 1981. pp.xiii + 295. DHSS.

5,547. SOCIAL DEMOCRATIC PARTY. POLICY GROUP ON POVERTY TAXATION AND SOCIAL SECURITY.   Attacking poverty: a policy for social security and personal taxation.   London: 1982.   pp.21. (Green paper No.11). DHSS.

5,548. SOCIOLOGUS.   "Social security in Austria".   <u>Bell</u>.   10. (1945). pp.329-37.

5,549. SPENCER, C.   "Seebohm: organisational problems and policy proposals". <u>Soc.& Ec.Admin.</u> 4. (1970). pp.172-85; 306-21.

5,550. STEVENS, C. Public assistance in France. London. LSE.

5,551. SUGDEN, R.   The political economy of public choice: an introduction to welfare economics. Oxford: 1981. pp.xiii + 217 + bibliog. DHSS.

5,552. SUTCH, W.B.   The quest for security in New Zealand 1840 to 1966. Wellington: 1966. pp.xvi + 512. CUL.

5,553. TITMUSS, R.M.   "The relationship between income maintenance and social service benefits - an overview". <u>Int.Soc.Sec.Rev.</u> XX. (1967). pp.57-66.

5,554. TITMUSS, R.M.   Social policy: an introduction.   London: 1974. pp.160. DHSS; LSE; CUL.

5,555. TOWNSEND, P. "Poverty, socialism and Labour in power". In Abel-Smith, B. and others. Socialism and affluence. London: 1967. pp.39-70. DHSS.

5,556. TOWNSEND, P. The concept of poverty. Working papers on methods of investigation and life-styles of the poor in different countries. London: 1970. pp.260. LSE; CUL.

5,557. TOWNSEND, P. "Politics and the statistics of poverty". Pol.Q. 43. (1972). p.103.

5,558. TOWNSEND, P. The scope and limitations of means-tested social services in Britain.   Stockport: Manchester Statistical Society. 1973. pp.31. DHSS; LSE.

5,559. TOWNSEND, P. Sociology and social policy. London: 1975. pp.xii + 371. DHSS; CUL.

5,560. TOWNSEND, P. & BOSANQUET, N.   Labour and inequality: 16 Fabian essays. London: 1972. pp.304. DHSS; LSE; CUL.

5,561. TOWNSEND, P., REDDIN, M. & KAIM-CAUDLE, P.   Social Services for all? Part One. London: 1968. pp.28 (Fabian Tract 382). CUL.

5,562. TRATTNER, W.I. From poor law to welfare state: a history of social welfare in America. London, New York: 1974. pp.xii + 276. CUL.

5,563. TROFIMYUK, N.A.   "The role of preventive measures in the social insurance of workers in the USSR". Int.Soc.Sec.Rev. 34. (1981). pp.168-174.

5,564. UNITED NATIONS. Methods of administering assistance to the needy. Study by the Secretary-General of programmes in seven countries. New York: 1952. pp.47. DHSS; LSE.

5,565. UNITED NATIONS International survey of programmes of social development. New York: 1955. pp.iv + 219. DHSS.

5,566. UNITED NATIONS. Proceedings of the international conference of Ministers responsible for social welfare. New York: 1968. pp.146. DHSS.

5,567. UNITED STATES.   Social Security Administration.   Social security financing and benefits: Report of the 1979 Advisory Council. Washington, D.C.: 1979. pp.ix + 366. DHSS.

5,568. UNITED STATES.   National Commission on Social Security. Social security in America's future: Final report of the National Commission on Social Security, March 1981. Washington, D.C.: 1981. pp.414. DHSS.

5,569. UNITED STATES.   President's Commission on Pension Policy. Coming of age: toward a national retirement income policy. [Washington, D.C.]: 1981. pp.ii + 131. DHSS.

5,570. UNITED STATES. DEPARTMENT OF HEALTH, EDUCATION AND WELFARE. "United States social security programmes: their application to non-nationals and to beneficiaries living abroad". Social Security Bulletin. Sept. (1964). pp.27-37.

5,571. UNITED STATES. SOCIAL SECURITY ADMINISTRATION. Social security legislation throughout the world. Washington: 1949. pp.iv + 176. (Bureau Report No.16). LSE.

5,572. UNITED STATES. SOCIAL SECURITY ADMINISTRATION. Social security programs throughout the world. Washington: 1964. pp.xxvi + 223. LSE. Further ed. 1967. pp.299. LSE.

5,573. VAIZEY, J. The cost of the social services. London: 1954. pp.24. (Fabian Research Series No.166). DHSS.

5,574. WALLEY, SIR J. "Selectivity in the social services". Soc.Serv.Q. XLII. (1969). pp.42-45.

5,575. WALTON, R. "Need: a central concept". Soc.Serv.Q. Summer. (1969). pp.13-17.

5,576. WATTS, H.W. & REES, A. (eds.). The New Jersey income-maintenance experiment. Volume II. Labour supply responses. New York, London: 1977. pp.xxxvi + 422. (Institute for Research on Poverty Monograph Series). DHSS.

5,577. WAXMAN, C.I. The stigma of poverty: a critique of poverty theories and policies. New York, Oxford: 1977. pp.xii + 148. DHSS.

5,578. WEBB, A. & SEIVE, J.E.B. Income redistribution and the welfare state. London: 1971. pp.125. (Occasional Papers on Social Administration No.41). CUL; DHSS; LSE.

5,579. WEBB, P.R.H. "Conflict of laws and Italian social security legislation". M.L.R. 28. (1965). pp.591-5.

5,580. WEDDERBURN, D.C. "Poverty in Britain today - the evidence". Sociol.Rev. 10. (1962). pp.257-282.

5,581. WEDDERBURN, D. "How adequate are our cash benefits?". N.S. 10. (1967). pp.512-516.

5,582. WEDDERBURN, D. "A cross-national study of standards of living of the aged in three countries". In P. Townsend (ed.). The concept of poverty. London: 1970. pp.193-204. LSE.

5,583. WEDDERBURN, D. (ed.). Poverty, inequality and class structure. London: 1974. pp.247. DHSS; LSE; CUL.

5,584. WEDEL, J. "Social security and economic integration II: their interaction with special regard to social cost". I.Lab.R. 102. (1970). pp.591-614.

5,585. WHITELEY, P. "Public opinion and the demand for social welfare in Britain". Jo.Soc.Pol. 10. (1981). pp.453-475.

5,586. WILDING, P. Poverty: the facts in Wales. London: 1977. pp.61., (Poverty Pamphlet 29). LSE; DHSS; CUL.

5,587. WILLIAMS, G. The state and the standard of living. London:

1936. pp.354. DHSS; LSE; CUL.

5,588. WILLIAMS, G. The price of social security. London: 1944. pp.vii + 199. DHSS; LSE.

5,589. WILLIAMSON, A. & ROOM, G. (eds.). Health and welfare states of Britain; an inter-country comparison. London: 1983. pp.245. DHSS.

5,590. WILLMOTT, P. (ed.). Poverty report 1976. London: 1976. pp.197. LSE.

5,591. WODDIS, M. "Some problems of poverty in Britain today". Marxism Today. Dec. (1967). pp.357-363.

5,592. WOOTTON, B. "Is there a welfare state? A review of recent social change in Britain". Polit.Sci.Q. (1963). pp.179-197.

5,593. WYNNE, E.A. Social security: a reciprocity system under pressure. Boulder, Colo.: 1980. pp.vii + 220. (Westview Special Studies in Contemporary Social Issues). DHSS.

5,594. YOUNG CONSERVATIVE AND UNIONIST ORGANISATION. Social security in the 70s. A report on the future of the welfare state. London: 1966. pp.46. DHSS; LSE.

5,595. YOUNG, A.F. Social services in British industry. London: 1968. pp.xiv + 258. LSE; Sq.

5,596. YOUNG, M. (ed.). Poverty report 1974: a review of policies and problems in the last year; a report of the Institute of Community Studies. London: 1974. pp.vi + 266. DHSS; LSE.

5,597. YOUNG, M. (ed.). Poverty report, 1975: a review of policies and problems in the last year. London: 1975. pp.vi + 207. (Report of the Institute of Community Studies). DHSS.

Author Index

Where an item in the bibliography is by two or more authors, each author appears in the following alphabetical list in the appropriate place. Where names are in square brackets, this is because the identity of the author is clear, but the name does not appear on the title page.

375

Author Index

Author Index

COMFORTS OF THE POOR. 65
SOCIETY FOR PROMOTING THE RETURN OF WOMEN AS POOR LAW
    GUARDIANS. 66
SOCIETY FOR THE SUPPRESSION OF BEGGARS. 105
SOCIETY OF CIVIL AND PUBLIC SERVANTS. 213
SOCIETY OF CONSERVATIVE LAWYERS. 304
SOCIETY OF LABOUR LAWYERS. 250
SOCIOLOGUS. 365
SOCRATES, G. 250
SOLICITORS CLERKS PENSION FUND. 264
SOPHIAN, T.J. 66,127
SOUTHERN, J.W. 66
SOUTHERN, R. 112
SOUTHWICK NEIGHBOURHOOD ACTION PROJECT. 283
SPAFFORD, C.H. 127
SPARGO, J. 102
SPEDDING, T.S. 66
SPEKE WELFARE ACTION GROUP. 314
SPENCER, C. 365
SPENCER, T. 66
SPENDER, H. 171
SPENDER, J.A. 139
SPENS, W.C. 66,132
SPILL, R.B. 273
SPRIGGE, J.J. 66
SPRINGBOARD LANARK. HAMILTON WELFARE RIGHTS TEAM. 314
STACK, M. 17,341
STACPOOLE, J. 280
STADEN, .M. 238
STALLARD, J.H. 80
STANES, H.P. 126
STANFORD, P.T. 179
STANLEY, J. 94
STANLEY, W. 94,95
STANLEY-MORGAN, R. 66
STANSFIELD, D.H. 249
STANTON, O. 279
STATUTORY PUBLICATIONS OFFICE. 349
STEAD, F.H. 139
STEELE, R.D. 285
STEELE, R.T. 234
STEER, J. 66
STEER, W.S. 17
STEIN, B. 17,193
STEIN, O. 333
STEINER, J. 349
STEPHEN, L.R. 5
STEPHENS, T.C. 341
STEPHENSON, P. 259
STERN, J. 258
STEVENS, C. 365
STEVENS, J. 66
STEVENS, R.B. 17
STEVENSON, E.F. 171
STEVENSON, O. 298
STEWART, E.G. 250
STEWART, J. 105
STEWART, J.V. 95
STEWART, M. 361
STIRLING, T.H. 66

410

413